The Social Processes of Aging and Old Age

ARNOLD S. BROWN

Northern Arizona University

PRENTICE HALL, Upper Saddle River, New Jersey 07458

Library of Congress Cataloging in Publication Data

Brown, Arnold S.
    The social processes of aging and old age / by Arnold S. Brown. —
2nd ed.
        p.   cm.
    Includes index.
    ISBN 0-13-449604-3
    1. Gerontology.   2. Old age—Social aspects.   3. Aged—Social
conditions.   4. Aging—Psychological aspects.   I. Title.
HQ1061.B77   1996
305.26—dc20   95-19370

Acquisitions editor: *Nancy Roberts*
Editorial/production supervision
    and interior design   *Edie Riker*
Buyer: *Mary Ann Gloriande*
Cover design: *Tom Nery*
Editorial assistant: *Pat Naturale*

**To my wife, Harriet,
for her love and commitment**

 © 1996, 1990 by Prentice-Hall, Inc.
Simon & Schuster / A Viacom Company
Upper Saddle River, New Jersey 07458

Printed in the United States of America

10   9   8   7   6   5   4   3   2   1

ISBN 0-13-449604-3

Prentice-Hall International (UK) Limited, *London*
Prentice-Hall of Australia Pty. Limited, *Sydney*
Prentice-Hall Canada Inc., *Toronto*
Prentice-Hall Hispanoamericana, S.A., *Mexico*
Prentice-Hall of India Private Limited, *New Delhi*
Prentice-Hall of Japan, Inc., *Tokyo*
Simon & Schuster Asia Pte. Ltd., *Singapore*
Editora Prentice-Hall do Brasil, Ltda., *Rio de Janeiro*

Contents

Preface

The inspiration for this book has come from a variety of experiences related to gerontology that it has been my privilege to have had over the past 25 years. Studying aging and old age theoretically, teaching it academically, working with it practically in program and policy development, researching it with different methods, and observing it interculturally during those years has taught me that gerontology is a truly dynamic and exciting field of endeavor.

I have learned that what it means to age and become an old person is by no means a static entity, but is constantly changing in all parts of the world today. I have learned, too, that well-established policies on aging are continuously being challenged even in societies in which old age has long been a privileged stage of life. I learned, further, that theories, practices, and policies related to aging continue to influence each other and, therefore, can never be understood as separate entities. I have also discovered that we have much to learn about aging through intercultural comparisons.

In this book I have attempted to be comprehensive in the selection of age-related topics, and have tried to discuss each topic with special emphasis on social processes and social change. The history of how each subject became important to aging is given. How policy, practice, and theory interact is also analyzed. In addition, special attention has been paid to intercultural comparisons with each topic.

In this second edition I have changed some of the topical emphases to reflect new and growing perceptions of aging. Topics, such as "Old Age as a Social Problem," and "Advocacy by and in Behalf of the Age," that received special attention in the first edition have been given less emphasis in the second edition. Other topics that received only limited or no attention in the first edition, have been dealt with in a major way, because they have become much more vital to gerontologists today. These include such topics as: "The Elderly as a Privileged Class and a Societal Burden," "Alzheimer's Disease," "Social Security," "Productive Aging," "Long-Term Care," and "Religion and Aging." These topics have received increasing amounts of attention in the gerontological literature, at gerontological workshops, conferences and organizational meetings, as well as in the political arena and the media. I have also included many more illustrative tables and figures throughout the book to help make the material more understandable to readers.

I want to express my special appreciation to several important people for the help and support they have given me on this project. My thanks go to Kooros Mahmoudi and Richard Fernandez, Chairmen of the Department of Sociology and Social Work at Northern Arizona University, and others in the department for the encouragement and support they have given me. Kevin

Meek also provided me with valuable help as a graduate assistant. Thanks, too, for the enthusiastic encouragement given me by staff members of the Northern Arizona Regional Gerontology Institute: Carole Mandino and Bonnie Anderson.

I am especially appreciative of the opportunity I was given by People to People International to visit the People's Republic of China in 1984 and the former Soviet Union in 1991, with teams of gerontologists and health care specialists from the United States. I am also grateful to China Advocates and to Gloria Cavanaugh, Executive Director of the American Society on Aging, for the privilege of returning to the People's Republic of China in 1993 with another team of gerontologists, and learning about the many changes in policies on aging that are taking place in that country. I am also indebted to Xiao Caiwei, staff member at China National Committee on Aging, for his willingness to share all that he knows about aging in China and about the many activities of the National Committee in person and in correspondence.

The person to whom I am the most grateful is my loving and patient wife, Harriet. She not only believed in me, but spent endless hours helping me with library research, typing, and editing of both the first and second editions. I could not have done it all without her help. I am also grateful to my daughter, Rita, for her help with research in the library.

Finally, thanks to Nancy Roberts and Pat Naturale at Prentice Hall, who have been very helpful and supportive. Also, the professional reviewers of my manuscripts gave me excellent suggestions of how the second edition could be improved, and I am very grateful to them for their help: Melissa Hardy, Florida State University; Dale A. Lund, University of Utah; Craig Forsyth, University of Soutwestern Louisiana.

1

The Emergence of Aging: An Important Area of Study

INTRODUCTION

Aging, or becoming older, is something that inevitably concerns every one of us as human beings. When we are young, we envy those who are older because they seem to enjoy so many more of life's privileges than we. When we become adults, the burdens of society often become so heavy that we often wish we were younger again when life seems to have been so much more carefree and romantic. In old age we may long for the earlier days of adulthood when life was perhaps filled with more meaning and purpose, and we had more say about the events of life. Aging is a subject that obviously concerns all humans because of our unique ability to have an awareness of ourselves and others and to conceptualize the future as well as the past and present (Hewitt, 1989, pp. 152–53). Because we have that unique capacity, we are all aware that we are experiencing the processes of aging and that those processes profoundly affect how we experience life on a daily basis.

So, what does it mean to grow older? What happens to us physically as we age? How does aging change our relationships with others? How does aging affect how we feel about ourselves? What happens to us financially as a result of getting older? How are families and other social institutions affected by the aging processes? What happens to the political and economic priorities of nations as their populations become older? These kinds of questions are becoming increasingly important to us as humans. They are also the kinds of questions that are being studied in the rapidly expanding field of gerontology.

Awareness of aging as an important aspect of life has always been part of the human experience. It has only been in recent years that it has also emerged as a vital concern to us as individuals and a major area of academic and scientific study. That has happened in the modern industrialized nations throughout the twentieth century and it is rapidly becoming important throughout the rest of the world as well.

Two somewhat different but closely related concerns have come to orient the field of gerontology. The processes of aging constitute one area of gerontological interest. We are interested in studying these processes because of the many ways in which they affect our lives (physically, socially, psychologically, economically, philosophically, religiously, and so on). The other area of interest to gerontologists and others is old age. The study of what it is like to be old is becoming of interest to virtually everyone, especially in the present era, when most nations of the world are modernized or becoming modernized. A special interest in old age has thus far dominated the field of gerontology, but there has recently been a growing interest in the aging processes as well. As the likelihood that most of us will reach old age has increased (something that was not nearly as true in the past), an understanding of how we arrive at that position in life, and how we may be able to prepare for it by controlling some aspects of the aging processes becomes much more vital to us.

The subject of aging has become increasingly important at many levels of modern social life. Growing numbers of individuals, especially from middle age on, are asking what will happen to them as they age. The impact of aging and of dealing with the aging process has also become a major concern to families, to the economic structure, to communities, to the healthcare professionals, to welfare agencies, to religious institutions, to the scientific community, and to entire nations. One cannot help but wonder why so much of the attention of such a broad spectrum of the world has been drawn to the subject of aging in such a relatively short period of time.

WHAT MAKES AGING AN IMPORTANT ISSUE?

In attempting to determine why aging has rapidly become such an important concern, gerontologists have discovered a number of factors that seem to be taking place on quite a broad cross-cultural basis. Together these factors have begun and will probably continue to rapidly and drastically change the experience of being old.

Perhaps the most important reason that aging is receiving so much attention is the substantial shift in the composition of populations that is taking place in most parts of the world today. At a time when the general populations of the industrial nations of the world are growing at relatively slow rates, the aged populations of those nations are growing rapidly. The elderly populations of nations are growing not only in sheer numbers but also in the percentages that they represent of the total populations of those nations (Cowgill, 1986, pp. 21–22; Ahmed and Smith, 1992). This growth is beginning to take place even in many of the world's developing countries. These trends have been developing in the United States and in Europe since the turn of the century, but the rates of growth in numbers of elderly people have been increasing since World War II in other parts of the world as well and are expected to increase even more dramatically during the next 50 years (Hoover and Siegel, 1986; Cowgill, 1986, pp. 22–27; Garrett, 1993).

The elderly population is increasing at such a rapid rate partly because of increased life expectancy, due in large measure to improved health care and health maintenance processes. Improved health care practices and advances in lifesaving technology have made it possible for most people to avoid death from ailments that once took the lives of many (Hoover and Siegel, 1986; Ward, 1984, pp. 32–33; Butler, Lewis, and Sunderland, 1991, pp. 7–8; Cunningham and Brookbank, 1988, p. 25; Conner, 1992, pp. 14–16). Thus, many people are now living to advanced ages to which only a privileged few once lived. These developments are, in fact, now having even more impact on the growth of the aged population than was predicted even a decade or two ago (Manton, 1991). Although the life span of humans has not yet increased (there were always those few who lived to be over 100 years old), life expectancy has increased dramatically.

A growing consciousness of the aged as a distinct and definable group is another factor that has helped to make aging an important issue today. Bryan Green raises the question about "how it is that the old so recently became visible and how this new social category (old age) came to be formed (Green, 1993, pp. 41–42). It seems fair to conclude that the sheer numbers of old people have increased our awareness of them. Looking at the history of aging, for example, Grob surmised that "perhaps their relatively small numbers before the end of the nineteenth century caused them to be overlooked" (Grob, 1986, p. 42). With so many elderly people in our midst, we have not only become more cognizant of them but we have also been influenced to think of them as a special category of people and to interact with them less as individuals and more as members of the age group into which they fit. That grouping tendency itself has served to draw attention to the aged. As Green puts it, "old age became a markedly visible phenomenon through the growth of a dense, multi-stranded semantic network around the term and synonyms for it" (Green, 1993, p. 42).

Grouping people into age-related groups is, in fact, a growing tendency for entire populations. In modern societies, increasing emphasis is placed on stages of the life cycle, each stage representing an advancing age level (Erickson, 1966; Sheehy, 1976, pp. 20–32; Perlmutter and Hall, 1985, pp. 4–29), and as Hareven points out, that has helped to shape "old age as a distinct stage of life" (Hareven, 1986, p. 112). We not only tend to think about and discuss life in those terms, but we also tend to organize our lifestyles around those stages, so that it is necessary to make major social and psychological adjustments as we move from one to the next (Rosow, 1967, pp. 35–40; Barrow, 1986, pp. 59–63; Matras, 1990, pp. 115–21). All of this inevitably draws attention to and helps to define the aging processes throughout life. Aging has also become a sociological fact of life and a major social issue.

A third factor that has made aging an issue is the way in which the aged have become characterized today. We have become aware of the aged not only because of their numbers and our tendency to group them as aged, but also because of the tendency in the recent past to define them as a group with unmet needs which neither they nor their families could meet with their own resources alone. The aged were defined as needy, and it was assumed that the society as a whole should respond to their needs (Cox, 1988, pp. 18–20; Kuypers and Bengtson, 1973).

In addition, and in part as a consequence of the above factors, aging has become a personal concern to people of all ages. We are constantly reminded that we are personally aging, and that that fact makes a difference in how we act and even think and feel about ourselves. For increasing numbers of college students, aging also represents one of the most viable and exciting career opportunities available.

CHANGING CHARACTERIZATIONS OF OLD AGE

As attention has been drawn to aging and particularly to those labeled as aged, we have changed our conceptualization of what it means to be old and of what constitutes old age. It is important to understand these changes because, ironically, the way in which elderly people are characterized helps to a large extent to create the situation and social conditions in which elderly people live.

There are traditionally two opposite conceptualizations of old age. According to the positive conceptualization, to be old is to be wise, to have high social status, to be respected, and to be in a position to exert much family and community influence. Much has been made of the fact that conceptualization of old age is especially prevalent in Oriental cultures (Palmore, 1975a; Treas and Wei Wang, 1993, p. 87). In fact, this has tended to be the prevailing way of thinking about the aged in the traditions of most cultures in the times when extended families served as the basic social and economic structure of society (Keith, 1982, pp. 3–4; Baum and Baum, 1980, pp. 105–6).

The second, essentially negative view of old age, is that old age inherently involves major and irreversible losses. To be old is to be physically incapacitated, to suffer the loss of mental capabilities, to become economically dependent, to experience social isolation, and to lose social status. (Kuypers and Bengtson, 1973; Matras, 1990, pp. 171–72).

Both of these characterizations have always been experientially legitimated (Baum and Baum, 1980, pp. 106–10; Schweitzer, 1983). On the one hand, the survival of societies and the preservation of the cultural wisdom of those societies have depended upon the experiential wisdom of older members. Surviving into old age was itself seen as a sign of having special qualities of wisdom. It could be argued that not all old people had great wisdom and that not all experiences necessarily brought wisdom. Nevertheless, it was certainly true that cultural wisdom did not come without experience, and old age was therefore the most important sign of wisdom; being old was defined positively as a result (Taranto, 1989).

On the other hand, physical and mental losses have always been more prevalent among the elderly than among the young. Until recently, senility has been thought to be not only related to but caused by the aging process (Butler, Lewis, and Sunderland, 1991, pp. 73–74). Even though modern science has largely discounted that notion, it is still clear that such losses are related to age. The older one gets, the more apt one is to experience physical and mental losses.

Both characterizations of old age have thus been used in the past, depending upon the circumstances of those being defined as old. A positive definition was applied to those whose physical and especially mental capacities were intact. A negative definition was applied to those experiencing mental and physical losses. In more recent years, though, negative views of old age have increasingly prevailed at the expense of the traditionally positive views. When they become old, individuals—even those who are still physically and mentally capable and vigorous—tend not to be afforded high social status, nor are they considered wise. Instead, regardless of their capabilities, they are considered to be dependent. Even if they need no special care or assistance, they tend to be ignored and treated as irrelevant by the rest of society.

One has to wonder why such a drastic change as this has taken place at the very time when life expectancy is increasing and more people are living longer. Of primary importance in this regard are how the processes of industrialization, modernization, and the accompanying mobilization of society are affecting people as they become older.

Cowgill and Holmes have theorized, for example, that this change has come about across a number of cultures as a direct result of modernization (Cowgill and Holmes, 1972). They note that as societies modernize, regardless of their past cultural traditions, the elderly members of those societies tend to lose status and become defined as dependent. One important factor about modernization that they contend contributes to that kind of social loss is modern education (Cowgill, 1981). In part, then, it has to do with the source of cultural knowledge on which societies depend. In nonmodernized societies, tradition plays a vital role in supplying the necessary knowledge base for survival and advancement, and the experiences that come with age tend to be the best source of such knowledge. In today's modernized, mechanized, computerized, and scientifically oriented societies, the great amount of knowledge that is available in books and on microfilms and computer tapes surpasses the knowledge that individuals acquire through personal experience. Perhaps the dominant perception today is that the wisdom of old age is relevant only to the past. If so, one has to wonder whether it is possible to restore the positive social status of the aged, and about what place experience may still play in the learning and maintenance of cultural traditions, and whether or not wisdom, apart from sheer knowledge, is in any way related to experiences that come from aging.

A third, quite different characterization of old age has emerged in the United States largely during the decade of the 1980s. It is what I would call viewing the elderly as a privileged class. It recognizes that increasing numbers of elderly retired people are capable of engaging in whatever physical and mental activities or work they want to. It also views them as living off the fat of the land or some as arrogantly consuming more than their fair share of the goods and services being produced but making little or no economic or social contributions to society.

Somewhat ironically this image of older people was almost totally ignored in the gerontological literature until the very late 1980s. In a recent book of readings dedicated to intergenerational relations, Marshall and colleagues refer to this as a form of "general conflict," based on "the argument that the young are being deprived of opportunities for well-being because of excessive allocation of resources to the old" (Marshall, Cook, and Marshall, 1993, p. 119). In that same volume, Bengtson discusses this new phenomenon in writing about "The New Problem of Age Groups and 'Generations,'" in which he describes it as a new and serious generation gap and a form of serious conflict.

He says that " the rhetoric of this new confrontation between age groups has already become harsh" (Bengtson, 1993, p. 8). Indications are that intergenerational conflict within families is also increasing in Japan (Campbell and Brody, 1985; Palmore, 1993). As Hickey puts it, "aging is still viewed as a problem by some people, but for different reasons than it was a generation ago—i.e., old people who were once viewed as 'disenfranchised' from society are now seen as 'entitled' to a disproportionate share of society's resources" (Hickey, 1992).

There seem to be three basic sources from which this new image of old age is coming today. In Japan it is fed by the burdens of caring for elderly in three-generation households. In the United States, it is in part being generated by the observations of individual people who view the participation of retired people in some form or another of recreation or tourism. This is particularly true in those parts of the country where retired people tend to live, such as many of the small communities and the many designated retirement communities in Arizona where retired people tend to move. It is very common for people who live and work in those areas to meet and serve elderly patrons as they eat in the restaurants, go to the motels, and drive the highways in expensive motor homes.

This kind of image first came to my attention in a graduate class on the sociology of aging that I was teaching in the early 1980s. A number of students in the class had worked in one part or another of the tourist trade, either near Sun City located west of Phoenix or in the Verde Valley of Arizona where many retired people live. I was surprised that all of these students generally viewed elderly people as a somewhat demanding privileged class of people, instead of as a dependent and helpless part of the population, which up to then had been the more typical characterization of older people.

The second source of the image of the aged as a privileged class in the United States is the combination of politics and the mass media. The growing discussion among politicians and journalists today about how "entitlements" are an unfair financial drain on the society is a powerfully effective expression of that image. It is an image of the elderly that has prompted former Senators (Paul Tsongas and Warren Rudman) to form a political action organization to challenge the right of elderly people to enjoy such privileges at what they define as the expense of younger American citizens. It has been the subject of special attention on such television programs as "20/20" on ABC and "Washington Week in Review" on PBS. Ignored in all of this are the many ways that elderly people do in fact contribute to the economy both as volunteers in their communities and in the millions of dollars they contribute to capital investments, which are vital to the economy of the country. It is, nevertheless, a growing, real, and very potent characterization of the aged today that gerontologists can no longer afford to ignore.

THE DEVELOPMENT OF GERONTOLOGY AS A SCIENTIFIC DISCIPLINE AND A RESEARCH AREA

Aging in America became an important area of study in the mid-twentieth century. As most gerontological authors admit, it is a relatively new scientific discipline (Green, 1993, pp. 9–10). In fact, some contend that it cannot even be considered a discipline (Adelman, 1986). Green argues that it is and provides an explanation of why it developed as a discipline. He contends that it developed because of changes that were taking place in the meanings of the terms "aging" and "old age." As he puts it, gerontology as an area of study "was founded on a newly dense multiplication of meanings around 'aging' and 'old age,' relayed through diverse, but connected, institutional language practices." To further explain this point, he adds that "a familiar phenomenon— growing old—was rendered sufficiently opaque and complex to become a subject of inquiry" (Green, 1993, p. 40). On a practical level, his point is that when the meanings of subjects such as aging and old age change and are no longer adequately comprehended by ordinary members of society, then these subjects become "compelling" subjects for the social sciences to become involved with and about which to develop a whole new discipline (Green, 1993, p. 42). The question that raises, though, is why the meanings of those terms would change. Part of the reason for that, as discussed above, was not only because the aged emerged as an increasingly large and visible part of the population, but also because, as a highly visible group, their social problems seemed serious enough to require the attention of the whole society (Atchley, 1978, pp. 4–21; Estes, 1979, p. 4). Scientific studies on aging called for to help to answer the puzzling questions surrounding those problems.

First, in contrast to a time in the past when the aged were an integral part of family and community life, it appeared that a substantial pattern of social disengagement and isolation had emerged during the middle part of the twentieth century. This pattern was disturbing to people in societies oriented to high levels of social activity and involvement. It seemed to suggest either that many of the aged were suffering some kind of psychological pathology, or that they were experiencing some kind of social deprivation, or both. The question of why disengagement tended to correlate with age dominated the theoretical work among social and psychological gerontologists in the United States for a quarter of a century.

A second problem area that developed, seemingly very closely associated with the problem of isolation, was what appeared to be quite severe social-psychological losses among elderly people. They seemed to be losing their sense of independence, their social status, and their self-esteem, and they were even developing an increase in the incidence of mental disorders (Lowenthal, 1968, pp. 220–34; Kuypers and Bengtson, 1973). It seemed that as the respect accorded them by the rest of society declined, their own sense of their importance also declined and they tended to acquiesce to being placed into a dependent situation. There are clear indications that old age has been perceived in terms of these kinds of losses for almost two centuries (Fischer, 1978, pp. 77–99), but not until the middle of the twentieth century did those perceptions pose serious problems. Social scientists along with social workers and others became interested in finding out why these kinds of losses were becoming so common a part of the experiences of old age in modern societies.

A third problem area concerning the aged was the experience of major losses in physical and mental functioning. With changes in life expectancy and increasing percentages of the population being made up of the very old, more attention was drawn to the rather unique physical and mental problems of the aged. People were beginning to survive the acute health problems that once took the lives of many people at younger ages. Now, however, they faced other more chronic and debilitating health problems. These problems usually did not directly kill people, but they tended to impair their functioning capacities and to make health care a long-term issue (Hickey, 1980, pp. 33–37; Bould, Sanborn, and Reif, 1989, pp. 57–59). This became an area of concern that neither the aged themselves nor the rest of society could ignore. The development of geriatrics as an important field of medicine, however, seems to have been particularly slow in coming. As Haber explains this, aging has been portrayed in the field of medicine "in such a way as to all but eliminate the notion of a healthy old age," and that "the present-day reluctance to specialize in this field can be linked to the original model on which it was based" (Haber, 1986, p. 67). The view of the elderly in need of long-term care has greatly contributed to the perception that the aged are a dependent group of people and to the growing belief that they place an excessive burden of care on the rest of the population. Long-term care has become defined as one of the most serious social problems associated with aging (Eustis, Greenburg, and Patten, 1984, pp. 1–4). As Sabo explains, "Currently, the health care systems in many countries are facing excessive workloads and high administrative costs, especially in the developing countries (Sabo, 1992).

A fourth problem area related to aging has to do with the economic losses among the aged population. This began to emerge as a quite serious social problem in the United States in the early part of the twentieth century, concurrent with industrialization and urbanization (Fischer, 1978, pp. 157–81). More and more elderly workers became unemployed, with few, if any, prospects for reemployment and with virtually no source of income. Furthermore, from an economic perspective, this unemployment was seen as a waste of productive resources, and that perception led to a serious discourse about unemployment as an issue to be investigated (Green, 1993, p. 39). In more recent years, even after the establishment of the social security program, the development of other pension programs, and some general improvement in the income levels of elderly people (Schulz, 1988, p. 61), the financial situation of a fairly large percentage of the aged in the United States remains inadequate, especially among women, the very old, minorities, and those in nonurban areas (Weeks, 1984, pp. 150–59; Caro, Bass, and Chen, 1993; Hendricks and Hatch, 1993, p. 51; McLaughlin and Jensen, 1993; Angel and Hogan, 1992), and indications are that future cohorts of the aged will be even worse off financially (Holden, 1993). The lack of economic support and the amount of economic strain among the elderly is also now becoming a problem in the People's Republic of China (Krause and Liang, 1993). The continued existence of this problem also contributes to and helps define the persistent perception of old people as dependent. Also, the elimination of elderly people from the work force remains an issue of discussion and study (Atchley, 1987, pp. 105–07). The perceived seriousness of this problem has greatly increased in just the last few years in the United States with the belief of many that social security is too expensive and cannot and will not survive.

Another part of what characterized the emergence of gerontology as a special area of concern and professional interest in America was the way the field became organized. Organizationally it took on an almost entirely applied form and political orientation (Green, 1993, pp. 11–12). First, as long ago as the 1920s an attempt was made for elderly people themselves to organize and do something about the growing amount of poverty among them (Lowry, 1980, pp. 190–91). Although that was a relatively unsuccessful attempt, it set the stage for more successful organizational efforts of that kind that would follow later. The classic example of that is the American Association of Retired People (AARP) that has the reputation of doing one of the most successful lobbying jobs in Washington, D.C. That organization also uses its own resources to fund applied research projects and provide numerous kinds of benefits to its members. Its organizational structure includes chapters in local communities, making it possible for millions of elderly Americans to become active in the ongoing gerontological discourse.

The second important type of organizational effort in the field of aging was the establishment of White House Conferences on Aging every 10 years. This has been an ad hoc process, to be sure (no permanent agency was formed and no law mandated that one of these must be held every 10 years), but, nevertheless, a powerfully political tradition was created. Politically appointed delegates were invited to Washington, D.C. to discuss the special needs of the elderly and draw up an elaborate set of recommendations of what the government could and should do to help meet those special needs.

White House conferences were held for three consecutive decades (1961, 1971, and 1981). None was held in 1991 due to the cost involved in a time of severe recession, but another one was held in May of 1995. There is little doubt that the 1961 White House Conference had a direct influence on the passage of such legislation as the Older Americans Act in 1965 and the establishment of the Medicare and Medicaid programs in the 1965 revisions of the Social Security Act. The other two conferences have also influenced the revisions that have been made in those laws since them. The 1981 White House Conference was dominated for the first time by elderly people themselves, and they effectively demonstrated that they represent a powerful political force and have become part of the discourse about aging and old age that Green says makes gerontology a discipline.

The third important organizational aspect of the field of aging in the United States was the formation of a vast network of federal, state, regional, and local community agencies to deal with and study the many problems that elderly people faced. This network of agencies was mandated by the original 1965 Older Americans Act, the subsequent revisions of that act, and other administrative decisions of the federal government. The notion of unmet needs was the primary impetus that prompted politicians and governmental bureaucrats in the 1960s and 1970s to create this network of research, program planning, and service delivery agencies to study and serve that need-oriented population. That resulted in the allocation and expenditure of vast sums of money in order to meet the needs of the aged that were defined as unmet. The two main federal agencies involved here were the Administration on Aging, located in the Department of Health and Human Services, and the Institute on Aging, part of the research-oriented Institutes of Health. These agencies touched the lives of millions of older Americans by studying the many problems related to aging and planning and administering elaborate programs to meet what had been defined as their many unmet needs. Just since the early 1980s, similar organizational efforts have been made in behalf of the elderly in the People's Republic of China. Included are the China National Committee on Aging, the China Research Center on Aging, and commitees on aging at the provincial and metropolitan levels (Caiwei, 1993). These organizational activities have not only provided services that were vital to many older people, but the research, planning, and service delivery processes involved have also greatly influenced the discourse about the new meanings of "aging" and "old age."

In addition, the establishment of the network of agencies in the United States led to another organizational component of the field of aging that is important in understanding gerontology as a new discipline (Estes, 1979, pp. 72–75; Binstock, 1981). Thousands of workers from a great variety of occupational backgrounds (i.e., medicine, social work, administration, planning, law, housing, research) were hired as employees of those agencies and/or contracted to do research. In those processes, they were drawn into one common focus of interest—aging and old age. Consequently, there was a proliferation of autonomous, nationwide age-related groups and organizations that were formed in America during the 1960s and 1970s. These groups were made up of people with common vested interests to defend and promote. Included were such organizations as the National Center for Black Aged, the National Indian Council on Aging, the Association of National Pro Personae Mayores, the National Association of State Units on Aging, the National Association of Area Agency Directors, the National Association of Nutrition Directors, the American Association of Homes for the Aging, the National Institute of Senior Centers, the Gerontological Society of America, the American Society of Aging, and the Association for Gerontology in Higher Education. They all claimed to advocate for the elderly people they served and in so doing they contributed greatly to the changing meanings of aging and old age. Estes contends, however, that they often lobbied more for their own vested interests than the needs of the elderly, or at least as the elderly themselves might define their own needs (Estes, 1979, p. 74). One of the vested interests that they all had in common was to continue to define old age as a time of dependency.

A pervasive and complicating factor is that, because of the strong attention paid to the interrelated social problems and dependencies of the aged, it has come to be assumed that the aged as a group are dependent and have needs that neither they nor their families are able to meet, and/or that they represent an unfair burden on society. These assumptions themselves strongly influence society's treatment of the aged and to a large extent have even become self-fulfilling prophecies, perpetuating of the problems that created the assumptions.

As noted above, many elderly people are increasingly being recognized by the public and by those in the political arena as being relatively well off financially and physically and mentally capable of living relatively independent lives. Despite that fact, it is ironic that professional gerontologists (i.e., medical practitioners, social workers, recreational workers, researchers) by and large continue to view the elderly as dependent. In part, the rationale for this is probably the legitimate assumption that there are, and always will be, a fairly large component of the elderly population who are indeed physically, mentally, socially and economically dependent upon others for survival. Not all of these practicing gerontologists provide services merely for the impaired, however. The elderly recipients of recreation programs and senior citizen centers, and many of the recipients of meals programs, for example, have no such impairments. Still, the provision of even those kinds of services are provided largely on the basis of the assumption that the recipients are dependent. What is the explanation for this? Why, for example, do the many gerontological journals continue to focus almost exclusively on the problems related to old age? Green raises this same kind of question by asking about "how, in gerontological writing, care for the elderly is made legibly rational under the joint demands of scientific, instrumental, and value rationality" (Green, 1993, pp. 74– 75). The key to answering that question, he says, is "a circuit of discourse connecting the vocabulary of care to the vocabulary of dependence." Estes calls this the "social creation of dependency" and points out that "dependency is not a 'given' but is a product of both intrinsic and extrinsic aging" (Estes, 1993). The only way to scientifically, instrumentally and ethically legitimize the provision of care is to label and treat the recipients of that care (of whatever type) as dependent. To do otherwise would bring the legitimacy of the services into question.

In that regard, it is interesting to note the issues that are being researched today. To get at that, a survey was done of the topics that were studied and reported during 1992 and 1993 in what are probably the two leading gerontology journals—the *Journal of Gerontology* and the *Gerontologist*. In effect that constitutes five different journals since the *Journal of Gerontology* is now divided into four journals. They include journals on biology, medicine, psychology, and social. The *Gerontologist* emphasizes applied gerontology in all areas of the field.

In Table 1-1 the 10 most frequent research topics that are addressed in the articles in those journals during those two years are listed. As would be expected, more than one issue is dealt with in a major way in some of the articles, and the numbers in the table reflect that fact. It is obvious from these data that a preponderance of the research being done is focused on physical and mental age-related losses, health care, and the problems related to those issues. Only two of these top 10 topics are not directly related to those issues—research methods and family and social relationships. Some of the research of even those topics also deal with health care and aging losses, however. Research on

TABLE 1-1   Frequency of Topics Being Researched By Journal During 1992 and 1993

					TOPIC					
JOURNAL	I	II	III	IV	V	VI	VII	VIII	IX	X
Gerontologist	1	9	43	24	31	15	8	9	2	2
Journal of Gerontology: Social	10	5	10	4	7	0	7	11	0	3
Journal of Gerontology: Psychology	8	45	0	2	2	12	7	4	0	2
Journal of Gerontology: Medical	37	7	0	16	0	3	6	0	5	3
Journal of Gerontology: Biological	46	0	0	6	0	7	2	0	9	4
Totals	101	66	53	52	40	37	30	24	16	14

TITLES OF RESEARCH TOPICS

I - Physical Impairment and Functioning

II - Mental Impairment and Functioning

III - Caregiving

IV - Health, Health Care, and Treatments

V - Institutionalization

VI - Alzheimer's Disease and Dementia

VII - Research Methods

VIII - Family and Social Relationships

IX - Physical Diseases and Injuries

X - Frail Elderly

family relationships, for example, often focuses on the elderly becoming dependent upon their families in a variety of ways.

All of this research is important to the field of aging, to be sure. Without these kinds of studies much of the lifesaving technology that we take for granted today would not be available, and life expectancy would not be what it is. Furthermore, we still do not know enough about and what to do about such issues as Alzheimers disease and the many problems related to caregiving. These are issues that continue to consume our time and resources with very little apparent progress toward solving the problems related to them.

However, the fact is that only a minority of elderly people, at any point in time, face the kinds of problems on which the vast majority of the research activities are spent. It is as though researchers, along with other gerontological professionals, have some kind of vested interest in keeping the focus on what continues to define the elderly as dependent. This seems to be ironical, at a time when the elderly are increasingly being seen as representing an unfair financial and social burden especially by the public and the government. The irony of it is that the government funds much of the research that is being done. Government funding would seem to make sense if more research were dedicated to such topics as productive aging, which would have the potential of relieving some of that burden.

Productive aging is indeed becoming an emphasis that some in the field are beginning to make, and a substantial number of elderly have expressed interest in it (Caro, Bass, and Chen, 1993). It has been found that as many as 5.3 million elderly in the United States have an interest in engaging in some kinds of productive roles (Caro, Bass, and Chen, 1993, p. 4).

An experience of my own convinces me of the interest that elderly people have in this issue. While serving on the planning committee for the 1989 Arizona Governor's Conference on Aging, I commented that we in gerontology need to begin making the point that the elderly actually do make social and economic contributions to their communities, in an attempt to combat the growing perception that they constitute an unfair burden to society. I suggested, therefore, that we consider making what their contributions are the theme at the Governor's Conference. The committee agreed and put me in charge of a workshop on Productive Aging, to be offered as one of six simultaneous workshops. It turned out to be the best attended and highest rated of all of the workshops offered that year. It had never been emphasized before, nor has it been since at the Arizona Governor's Conferences on Aging, but it is something in which many elderly are keenly interested.

To understand why productive aging is an important area of concern for gerontologists, we need to define what is meant by it. Productive aging has been used by some synonymously with "successful" and "normative" aging, as just another general term to emphasize that there are positive aspects of aging. Caro, Bass, and Chen make the point that, while it is, indeed, part of the emphasis on the positive aspects of aging, the focus on productive aging has different implications. The difference is that, while successful and normative aging stress what is important to individual older persons, productive aging implies the existence of specific roles that "older people can play in society" (Caro, Bass, and Chen, 1993, p. 7). As they define it, productive aging means "any activity by an older individual that produces goods or services, or develops the capacity to produce them, whether they are to be paid for or not"

(Caro, Bass, and Chan, 1993, p. 6). As part of the case they make for productive aging they also argue especially for the right of the aged to remain in the work force as paid employees, and they express what seems to be some bias against retirement as a viable social institution.

Some elderly persons, indeed, need to continue to work for financial and other reasons, and they ought to be allowed to do so without being discriminated against for doing so. Given the continued competitiveness in the work place, however, it is difficult to see how paid work on their part contributes much more to the economy than if they do not work. From an employer's perspective, for example, older workers cost them more, not less, and make it more expensive to produce their products.

It does not seem wise, either, for the emphasis on productive aging to challenge the validity of retirement as a viable social institution. Another emphasis that would seem to be even more important in defining productive aging is to select productive aging roles that are vital to society and that elderly people are uniquely able to fulfill, instead of those in which they compete with younger people. Those are the kinds of volunteer roles that many elderly Chinese have (Lewis, 1982; Treas, 1979), and there are a growing number of specific roles available to people in retirement in the United States as well, regardless of whether they serve with pay or as volunteers. Examples include (1) those active in the Senior Corps of Retired Executives Program, (2) retired political figures serving as ambassadors and diplomats, (3) low-income retired elderly serving as Senior Companions, (4) elderly people serving in a variety of roles in the Retired Senior Volunteer Program, and (5) retired ministers serving as interim pastors in a number of denominations.

It is obvious that gerontology as a discipline is by no means neatly organized in the sense that all of parts of the organization are systematically interrelated. Instead, there is a great deal of autonomy and independence on the part of those organizations identified here. Many of them also have competitive and even conflicting interests and relationships with each other. Because of that, some would argue that gerontology is too disorganized even to be considered a discipline at all. We need to remember, though, that there is one very important factor that does, indeed, tie it all together—the continuing dialogue about the changing meanings of aging and old age. In that sense the messiness itself helps to make gerontology a discipline. Without the autonomy and the competitive interests there would be little if any discourse, and that is what makes the field continue to be a vital one. More, not less, discourse is needed today.

Discovering the effects of the emphases on unmet needs and the provision of care on the aged and how those emphases may be changing, for example, is becoming a major interest to many social scientists today. That constitutes one of the primary concerns to be addressed in this book. How do the typical intervention processes being used to serve the aged affect the elderly recipients? Do the intervention processes serve to make them more independent as they are expected to do, or do they, in fact, create new dependencies? How are these intervention processes perhaps changing the structures of the families and family relationships of elderly recipients? Do they help build or diminish family ties and interdependencies between the older persons and others within the families? Do they tend to create substitute nonfamily relationships that may provide more, or less, security? To what extent are they a source of intergenerational conflict? Discourse on these kinds of questions is badly needed today.

THE GROWING IMPORTANCE
OF CROSS-CULTURAL COMPARISONS

In the search for answers to these kinds of pressing and unanswered questions, gerontologists are beginning to look comparatively at aging in other cultures. Until recently the cross-cultural literature on aging has focused on somewhat utopian or idealistic cultural situations, especially those in which old people enjoy high social status and have exceptionally high rates of longevity, as illustrated by Benet's analysis of the Abkhasian people in the Soviet province of Georgia (Benet, 1974). This literature has not served as a very useful source of comparison, however. It generally represents societies in which the people do not face the problems that we in the United States do. More importantly, this kind of literature often does not include comprehensive data that can be used for point-by-point, issue-by-issue comparisons of societies.

There is a growing amount of excellent cross-cultural literature on aging that now makes comprehensive comparisons much more possible. Cross-cultural studies of aging were begun in the 1960's by an international group of researchers who simultaneously studied a number of western cultures (Shanas and others, 1968). The work done in recent years by Palmore and by others on aging in Japan expanded the cross-cultural literature to a very different part of the modern world (Palmore, 1975b; Plath, 1983; Maeda, 1983). The work of Davis-Friedmann on aging in the People's Republic of China has added still another important dimension to this literature (Davis-Friedmann, 1983). The work of Cowgill and Holmes on the relationship between modernization and loss of social status among the aged added an important theoretical component to the cross-cultural literature (Cowgill and Holmes, 1972; Cowgill, 1986; Holmes, 1983). In addition, Fry and Palmore have compiled valuable collections of articles on aging in a great variety of cultural settings (Palmore, 1980; Fry, 1980). Journals such as *The International Journal of Aging* and *Bold* are dedicated to cross-cultural gerontology and provide valuable material for that type of comparisons. More and more articles on gerontological studies in other parts of the world are also found in other gerontological journals. Gerontology with an international emphasis is also the basis of many conferences and workshops around the world today, and they typically produce excellent cross-cultural material. Utilizing these sources and others, cross-cultural comparisons will be a major theme of this book.

Intercultural exchanges on issues of aging, such as those provided by organizations including the Citizen Ambassador Program of People to People International, China Advocates, and a number of the American universities, provide excellent opportunities to view firsthand how similarly and differently cultures define and deal with the issues of aging. I have had the great privilege of making two such visits to the People's Republic of China (one in 1984 with People to People International and another in 1993 with China Advocates), and one to Russia in 1992 with People to People International. These visits provided me the opportunity to observe and visit with elderly people in a number of different situations (in their homes, on the street, in hospitals, functioning in given roles in the communities, in leisure activities, etc.). These exchanges have made it possible for me to do comparisons between those countries as well as to compare each of them with America with regard to age-related issues. Here are two culturally very different countries that have been under Communist rule for some time, both of which are now experiencing economic reforms. I was impressed by three things as a result of visiting those countries. First, the amount of attention being paid to the elderly in the midst of those reforms was drastically different from one country to the other. Second, the place of the elderly in Chinese society now, compared to a decade ago, has changed dramatically. Third, in both countries, where the elderly have been guaranteed the care they needed in the past, they are increasingly left to provide for themselves or depend upon their families for the care they now need. This is even more true there than is true in the United States today. These themes will be elaborated upon throughout the book.

CONTRASTING APPROACHES TO THE STUDY OF AGING

As social scientists become involved in the study of aging, it is important to pay close attention not just to the empirical data available but also to how we approach the subject of aging. The set of assumptions that we make in order to make sense of the data may determine more about our predictive conclusions than what the data themselves mean. Different approaches often begin with contrasting assumptions about the phenomena under study. These sets of assumptions, or *theories*, are descriptions of what societies are like. There are a number of possible theories to guide the study of a subject such as the sociology of aging. There are points in most of these theories that overlap, to be sure, but often the main orienting or definitive concepts of the theories not only differ but also contrast with each other. This is especially true of two particular approaches used by social gerontologists.

One sociological approach, which is quite widely applied to the study of aging, emphasizes *social structures* or *systems* including societal values and norms and such social institutions as the family, the economy, and government (Rosow, 1967, pp. 8–30). The basic assumption of this approach is that we are all born into already existing and well-established social structures or systems. It is further assumed that the social situations or conditions in which we find ourselves are and will continue to be largely determined by those structures or systems. The social systems, therefore, are the primary focus of any social phenonomena being studied from this approach.

In applying this approach to the study of aging, attention is given to such social systems as work, retirement, welfare, health care, and the nuclear family. Studies with that kind of focus typically indicate that the involvement of the aged in these kinds of social systems is statistically correlated with such things as social isolation, low social status, dependency, and low self-esteem. When this is compared to the past, when most societies were basically agrarian, there was no retirement, the extended family was emphasized, and the family was responsible for welfare, one readily draws the conclusion that such social systems cause the conditions found among the aged. It is quite apparent that such a conclusion is based not simply on the data but on the study's focus on social systems, as illustrated by Rosow's analysis of *The Social Integration of the Aged* (Rosow, 1967, pp. 8–30).

The other approach sometimes applied to aging is what we might call the *social-processes* approach. While not denying that social systems are realities for humans, those who advocate the social-processes approach choose another factor on which to focus their studies. They believe it is more appropriate to focus on the social processes that are related to the phenomena being studied, such as communicating through language, negotiating and performing social roles, and learning. Rose's projection of the emergence of a subculture of aging out of peer interactional processes illustrates this approach (Rose, 1962). The basic assumption underlying this approach is that social systems are never fixed or stationary. Rather, they are constantly changing and are themselves the products of something else. Social changes and the social processes that bring them about are much more important realities than social systems. If it is indeed found that elderly persons have low social status, are socially isolated, and have low self-esteem, then examining the social processes related to the development of those conditions would not only explain a lot more about why these conditions exist, but should also reveal trends for the future. Retirement, for example, is not a fixed social entity. It is itself a social and economic process and will continue to change and emerge as something quite different than it has been in the past.

A distinct advantage of the social-processes approach is that it does not confine us to the necessity of either returning the aged to an ideal past or locking them into a deterministic and unsatisfactory present. Instead, predictions for the future depend entirely on current social processes inevitably changing present conditions. Whether the future represents improvement or not depends upon what the processes are, who is manipulating them, toward what ends, and for whose benefits.

CONCLUSION

Social processes will be the main analytical focus throughout this book. It is hoped that the use of this approach will enable the reader to recognize that conditions of the aged are not pessimistically determined but are products of dynamic social processes that are subject to manipulation and change. They may indeed be manipulated to the detriment and deprivation of the aged population, but that is by no means a foregone conclusion. They may just as readily be manipulated in the best interests of that segment of the population. The result depends upon how well we understand the dynamics of those processes and the good will and intentions of those who are best able to manipulate them. It is important to understand, though, that most of these processes are not just natural occurrences over which we have no control. Instead, they are processes that are increasingly manipulated to the advantage of some individuals and groups, often other than the aged themselves. An understanding of how the processes are manipulated and to whose advantage, then, is as important as an understanding of the processes themselves. What is often overlooked in all of this is the fact that people of all ages, and not just those who are presently older, have personal stakes in the manipulation of these processes. Students considering one or another of the many career opportunities in gerontology also have a professional stake in them.

REFERENCES

Achenbaum, W. Andrew, "Public Pensions as Intergenerational Transfers in the United States," in *Workers Versus Pensioners: Intergenerational Justice in an Ageing World*, eds. P. Johnson, C. Conrad, and D. Thomson (Manchester, NY: Manchester University Press, 1989), pp. 113-35.

Achenbaum, W. Andrew, *Shades of Gray: Old Age, American Values, and Federal Policies Since 1920* (Boston: Little, Brown, 1983).

Adelman, R. C., "The Dilemma of Research Training in Gerontology," *Educational Gerontology*, 12 no. 6 (1986), 579-84.

Ahmed, Bashir, and Stanley K. Smith, "How Changes in the Components of Growth Affect the Population Aging of States," *The Journal of Gerontology*, 47, no. 1 (January 1992), S27-37.

Angel, Jacqueline L., and Dennis P. Hogan, "The Demography of Minority Aging Populations," *Journal of Family History*, 16 (1992), 95-114.

Atchley, Robert C., "Aging As a Social Problem: An Overview," in *Social Problems of the Aging: Readings*, eds. Robert C. Atchley, S. L. Corbett and Mildred M. Selzer (Belmont, Calif.: Wadsworth, 1978), pp. 4-21.

Atchley, Robert C., *Aging: Continuity and Change* (Belmont, Calif.: Wadsworth, 1987).

Barrow, Georgia M. *Aging, the Individual, and Society* (St. Paul, Minn.: West, l986).

Baum, Martha, and Rainer C. Baum, *Growing Old: A Societal Perspective* (Englewood Cliffs, N.J.: Prentice Hall, l980).

Benet, Sula, *Abkhasians: The Long-Living People of the Caucasus* (New York: Holt, Rinehart, and Winston, 1974).

Bengtson, Vern L. "Is the 'Contract Across Generations' Changing? Effects of Population Aging on Obligations and Expectations Across Age Groups," in *The Changing Contract Across Generations*, eds. Vern L. Bengtson and W. Andrew Achenbaum (New York: Aldine de Gruyter, 1993), pp. 1-23.

Binstock, Robert H., "The Politics of Aging Interest Groups," in *The Aging in Politics: Process and Policy*, ed. R. B. Hudson (Springfield, Ill.: Charles C. Thomas, l981), pp. 47-85.

Bould, Sally, Beverly Sanborn, and Laura Reif, *Eighty-Five Plus: The Oldest Old* (Belmont, Calif.: Wadsworth, 1989).

Butler, Robert N., Myrna I. Lewis, and Trey Sunderland, *Aging and Mental Health: Positive Psychosocial and Biomedical Approaches* (New York: Macmillan, 1991).

Caiwei, Xiao, China National Committee on Aging, Beijing, China, correspondence with Arnold Brown, December 19, 1993.

Campbell, Ruth, and Elaine M. Brody, "Women's Changing Roles and Help to the Elderly: Attitudes of Women in the United States and Japan," *The Gerontologist*, 25, no. 6 (December 1985), 584-92.

Caro, Francis G., Scott A. Bass, and Yung-Peng Chen, "Introduction: Achieving a Productive Aging Society," in *Achieving a Productive Aging Society*, eds. Scott A. Bass, Francis G. Caro, and Yung-Peng Chen (Westport, Conn.: Auburn House, 1993), pp. 3-25.

Conner, Karen A. *Aging America: Issues Facing an Aging Society* (Englewood Cliffs, N.J.: Prentice Hall, 1992).

Cowgill, Donald O. *Aging Around the World*, (Belmont, Calif.: Wadsworth, 1986).

Cowgill, Donald O., "Aging and Modernization: A Revision of the Theory" in *Aging in America: Readings in Social Gerontology*, eds. Cary S. Kart and Barbara B. Manard (Sherman Oaks, Calif.: Alfred, 1981), pp. 111-32.

Cowgill, Donald O., and Lowell D. Holmes, *Aging and Modernization* (New York: Appleton-Century-Crofts, l972).

Cox, Harold, *Later Life: The Realities of Aging* (Englewood Cliffs, N.J.: Prentice Hall, l988).

Cunningham, Walter R., and John W. Brookbank, *Gerontology: The Psychology, Biology, Sociology of Aging* (New York: Harper & Row, 1988).

Davis-Friedmann, Deborah, *Long Lives: Chinese Elderly and the Communist Revolution* (Cambridge, Mass.: Harvard University Press, 1983).

Erickson, E. H., "Eight Ages of Man," *International Journal of Psychiatry*, 2 (1966), 281-97.

Estes, Carroll L. *The Aging Enterprise* (San Francisco: Jossey-Bass, 1979).

Estes, Carroll L., "The Aging Enterprise Revisited," *The Gerontologist*, 33, no. 3 (June 1993), 292-98.

Eustis, Nancy, Jay Greenburg, and Sharon Patten, *Long-Term Care for Older Persons: A Policy Perspective* (Monterey, Calif.: Brooks/Cole, 1984).

Fischer, David Hackett, *Growing Old in America* (New York: Oxford University Press, 1978).

Fry, Christine, ed., *Aging in Culture and Society: Comparative Viewpoints and Strategies* (New York: J. F. Bergin, 1980).

Garrett, Mario "Ageing in the Developing World: Trends and Needs," *Bold*, 4, no. 1 (November 1993), 8-12.

Green, Bryan S. *Gerontology and the Construction of Old Age: A Study in Discourse Analysis* (New York: Aldine de Gruyter), 1993.

Grob, Gerald N., "Explaining Old Age History: The Need for Empiricism," in *The Elderly, The Experts, and the State in American History*, eds., David Van Tassel and Peter N. Stearns (New York: Greenwood, 1986), pp. 30-45.

Haber, Carole, "Geriatrics: A Specialty in Search of Specialties," in *The Elderly, the Experts, and the State in American History*, eds. David Van Tassel and Peter N. Stearns (New York: Greenwood, 1986), pp. 66-84.

Hareven, Tamara, "Life-Course Transitions and Kin Assistance in Old Age: A Cohort Comparison," in *The Elderly, The Experts, and the State in American History*, eds., David Van Tassel and Peter N. Stearns (New York: Greenwood, 1986), pp. 110-25.

Harper, Sara, "Caring for China's Ageing Population: The Residential Option—A Case Study of Shanghai," *Ageing and Society*, 12, no. 2 (June, 1992), 157-84.

Hendricks, Jon, and Laurie R. Hatch, "Federal Policy and Family Life of Older Americans," in *The Remainder of Their Days: Domestic Policy and Older Families in the United States and Canada*, eds. Jon Hendricks and Carolyn J. Rosenthal (New York: Garland Publishing Co., 1993), pp. 49-73.

Hewitt, John P., *Dilemmas of the American Self* (Philadelphia: Temple University Press, 1989).

Hickey, Tom, "The Continuity of Gerontological Themes," *International Journal of Aging and Human Development*, 35, no. 1 (1992), 7-17.

Hickey, Tom, *Health and Aging* (Monterey, Calif.: Brooks/Cole, 1980).

Holden, Karen C., "Continuing Limits on Productive Aging: The Lesser Rewards of Working Women," in *Achieving a Productive Aging Society*, eds. Scott A. Bass, Francis G. Caro, and Yung-Peng Chen (Westport, Conn.: Auburn House, 1993), pp. 235-48.

Holmes, Lowell D., *Other Cultures, Elder Years: An Introduction to Cultural Gerontology* (Minneapolis, Minn.: Burgess, 1983).

Hoover, Sally L., and Jacob S. Siegel, "International Demographic Trends and Perspectives on Aging," *Journal of Cross-Cultural Gerontology*, 1, no. 1 (1986), 5-30.

Keith, Jennie, *Old People as People: Social and Cultural Influences on Aging and Old Age* (Boston: Little, Brown, 1982).

Krause, Neal, and Jersey Liang, "Stess, Social Support, and Psychological Distress Among the Chinese Elderly," *Journal of Gerontology*, 48, no. 6 (November 1993), P282-91.

Kuypers, Joseph A., and Vern L. Bengtson, "Social Breakdown and Competence: A Model of Normal Aging," *Human Development*, 16, no. 2, (1973), 181-201.

Lewis, Myrna, "Aging in the People's Republic of China," *International Journal of Aging and Human Development*, 15, no. 2 (1982), 79-105.

Lowenthal, Marjorie Fiske, "Social Isolation and Mental Illness," in *Middle Age and Aging: A Reader in Social Psychology*, ed. B. L. Neugarten (Chicago: University of Chicago Press, 1968), pp. 220-34.

Lowy, Louis, *Social Policies and Programs on Aging* (Lexington, Mass.: Lexington Books, 1980).

Maeda, Daisaku, "Family Care in Japan," *The Gerontologist*, 23, no. 6 (December 1983), 579-83.

Manton, Kenneth G., "The Dynamics of Population Aging: Demography and Policy Analysis," *The Milbank Quarterly*, 69, no. 2 (1991), 309-38.

Marshall, Victor W., Fay L. Cook, and Joanne G. Marshall, "Conflict over Intergenerational Equity: Rhetoric and Reality in a Comparative Context," in *The Changing Contract Across Generations*, eds., Vern L. Bengtson and W. Andrew Achenbaum (New York: Aldine de Gruyter, 1993), pp. 119-40.

Matras, Judith, *Dependency, Obligations, and Entitlements: A New Sociology of Aging, the Life Course, and Aging* (Englewood Cliffs, N.J.: Prentice Hall, 1990).

McLaughlin, Diane K., and Leif Jensen, "Poverty Among Older Americans: The Plight of Nonmetropolitan Elders," *Journal of Gerontology*, 48 no. 2, (March 1993), S44-54.

Palmore, Erdman B., ed., *International Handbook on Aging: Contemporary Developments and Research* (Westport, Conn.: Greenwood, 1980).

Palmore, Erdman B., "Is Aging Really Better in Japan?" *The Gerontologist*, 33, no. 5 (October 1993), 697-99.

Palmore, Erdman B. *The Honorable Elders* (Durham, N.C.: Duke University Press, 1975).

Palmore, Erdman B., "The Status and Integration of the Aged in Japanese Society," *Journal of Gerontology*, 30, no. 2 (March 1975), 199-208.

Plath, David, "Ecstasy Years'—Old Age in Japan," in *Growing Old in Different Societies: Cross Cultural Perspectives*, ed. Jay Sokolovsky (Belmont, Calif.: Wadsworth, 1983) pp. 147-53.

Perlmutter, Marion, and Elizabeth Hall, *Adult Development and Aging* (New York: John Wiley, 1985).

Rose, Arnold M., "The Subculture of the Aging: A Topic for Sociological Research," *The Gerontologist*, 2, (1962), 123-27.

Rosow, Irving, *Social Integration of the Aged* (New York: The Free Press, 1967).

Sabo, Rebeca, "Health and The Elderly," in *Population Aging: International Perspectives*, eds. Tarek M. Shuman, E. Percil Stanford, Anita S. Harbert, Mary Gwyne Schmidt, and Joan L. Roberts. (San Diego, Calif.: San Diego State University, 1992), pp. 163-67.

Schulz, James, *The Economics of Aging* (Dover, Mass.: Auburn House, 1988).

Schweitzer, Marjorie M., "The Elders: Cultural Dimensions of Aging in Two American Indian Communities," in *Growing Old in Different Societies: Cross-Cultural Perspectives*, ed. Jay Sokolovsky (Belmont, Calif.: Wadsworth, 1983), pp. 168-78.

Shanas, Ethel, Peter Townsend, Dorothy Wedderbaum, Henning Friis, Paul Milhoj, and Jan Stehouwer, *Old People in Three Industrial Societies* (New York: Atherton Press, 1968).

Sheehy, Gail, *Passages: Predictable Crises of Adult Life* (New York: Dutton, 1976).

Taranto, Maria A., "Facets of Wisdom: A Theoretical Synthesis." *International Journal of Aging and Human Development*, 19, no. 1, (1989), 1-21.

Treas, Judith, and Wei Wang, "Of Deeds and Contracts: Filial Piety Perceived in Contemporary Shanghai," in *The Changing Contract Across Generations*, eds. Vern L. Bengtson and W. Andrew Achenbaum (New York: Aldine de Gruyter, 1993), pp. 87-98.

Treas, Judith, "Social Organization and Economic Development in China: Latent Consequences for the Aged," *The Gerontologist*, 19, no. 1 (February 1979), 34-43.

Ward, Russell A., *The Aging Experience: An Introduction to Social Gerontology* (New York: Harper & Row, 1984).

Weeks, John R., *Aging: Concepts and Social Issues* (Belmont, Calif.: Wadsworth, 1984).

2

Changing Demographics of Aging

INTRODUCTION

On a trip to the People's Republic of China in 1984, a group of U.S. gerontologists, of which this author was a member, was told by Chinese officials about their elderly population. They explained that life expectancy was increasing dramatically, that elderly people represented an ever-increasing part of the Chinese population, and that generous retirement policies were being implemented throughout the country. They also related that the rapid growth of their population was quickly being brought under control with their new one-child-per-couple policy. The officials expressed much pride as they spoke of these facts.

Members of the group asked the Chinese officials how the changes had become possible, why the policies had been set, and what some possible future implications (negative and positive) of these policies and population trends might be. The Chinese officials explained that the policy of restricting the number of children would help the country avoid the numerous problems related to uncontrolled population growth. They also explained that their elderly population had increased because of the success of a health care system that equally served the entire population. However, they expressed very limited understanding that those policies and population trends might bring about some undesirable changes as well as desirable ones. Some of the elderly people with whom the group visited expressed serious misgivings about how the one-child-per-couple policy might effect their great tradition of family solidarity upon which even the government depended. Officials did not appear to have considered that that might be a negative consequence of their present situation.

On a return trip that I made to the People's Republic of China in 1993 with another team of gerontologists, we interacted especially with members of the China National Committee on Ageing. This agency was relatively new and inactive in 1984, but subsequently became actively focused on aging concerns. Again, they told about how life expectancy was ever on the rise, with the same sense of pride. They also told us, however, about the many age-related studies they had done and were doing and the programs they had initiated to deal with some of the problems about which they had become concerned. Most of those concerns were related to the questions that the first gerontology group had raised. One issue, about which they had become particularly aware and concerned, was what the consequences might be of the relationship between increased life expectancy and the rapid rate of economic reform in their country. Part of their concern seemed to be that, in the pursuit of economic opportunities, families were increasingly losing sight of their responsibilities to their elderly members. Therefore, one of the programs the committee was developing was to remind families of their caregiving responsibilities and train them in how to provide the care their elderly members might need. They have only just begun to consider, though, how their one-child-per-couple population control policy will inevitably challenge how effective that kind of program will be. In visiting and corresponding with Xiao Caiwei, a member of the China National Committee on Ageing staff, I posed the question of whether they may be expecting more from today's small Chinese families than those family units will be able to handle. That is something that they will undoubtedly have to consider sometime in the future.

What is important to understand about all of this is that it has to do with demographics. The questions being raised were about (1) how given populations are changing and will probably change in the future; (2) what policies and programs were being implemented; (3) how the changes have come about and why the policies were set; (4) how policies and population trends might be interrelated and produce even further unanticipated changes in the future; and (5) how certain kinds of people might be effected by those changes, negatively as well as positively. Demographic analysis, then, is not just a matter of juggling statistics. It is a valuable way of making sense out of changes in given populations, the reason for those changes, and the potential implications. A thorough demographic study could help officials in China anticipate future problems with their elderly population, for example. Another example of the implications of age-related demographic changes is how they apply to today's students. As I have learned from my own experience, because of those changes the field of gerontology is one of very few career fields that is expanding in the types and numbers of professional jobs available.

A distinction has been made between "formal demography" and "population analysis." Formal demography is defined as "the gathering, collating, statistical analysis, and technical presentation of population data." Population analysis is defined as "the systematic study of population trends and phenomena in relation to their social setting" (Peterson, 1975, p. 3). Others have referred to this as "applied demography" (Bould, Sanborn, and Reif, 1989, p. 31; Rives and Serow, 1984, p. 10).

Formal demography population distributions and trends tend to be treated on a factual basis, as though they were due only to natural processes over which we humans have little or no control. As Davis puts it, "It has, so to speak, kept away from messy population-resource problems" (Davis, 1991, p. 2). Any study of human history clearly shows, however, that this is hardly ever the case. The situations in which we humans find ourselves are to a large extent the results of actions that we take, either individually or collectively, as we define our circumstances and make decisions about appropriate actions (Hewitt, 1991, pp. 89–100; Davis, 1991, pp. 3–4). Therefore, in order to understand a phenomenon such as a growing elderly population, we must examine its development and its consequences (intended or unintended). We will thus be better prepared to assess, in turn, the future implications of present population distributions and trends.

DEMOGRAPHIC TRANSITIONS
AND THE POPULATION CONTROL MOVEMENT

Why are the numbers of old people throughout the world growing? Why are elderly populations growing faster in proportion to the rest of the world's populations? Why are societies as a whole growing older as the years go by? Why are these trends more applicable in some countries and much less so in others? Statistically these conditions are true because of changes that have taken place concerning three demographic factors: (1) birth rates; (2) death rates; and (3) migration patterns (Serow, Sly, and Wrigley, 1990, pp. 11–14). The question of why they have changed, though, can best be answered by looking at two processes related to population changes that have been unfolding throughout the world in recent years: (1) demographic transition and (2) the population control movement.

Demographic transition is both an explanation of an historical process and a theory of population change (Farley, 1987, p. 330). As a historical process it involves three periods (see Figure 2–1). The first period represents a time of relative population stability when death rates were about equal to birth rates, and both were relatively high. Statistics show that this was the situation throughout the world for many centuries. As Figure 2–2 shows, the world population grew only slightly for thousands of years of human history. This was true because although the birth rate remained high, so did the death rate. In fact there were times in parts of the world when famine or the spread of infectious diseases sent the death rate soaring, populations declined, and the survival of some societies was threatened (Peterson, 1975, pp. 416–29). Livi-Bacci explains this period by likening it to a lot of energy being used (high birth rates) and wasted (high death rates). He says this time can be characterized "not only by inefficiency but also by disorder." What he means by this is that "high levels of mortality and frequent catastrophes" were very prevalent and made it impossible to predict who would or would not survive into old age (Livi-Bacci, 1992, pp. 100–1).

The second period of the demographic transition represents a time when death rates and birth rates became imbalanced. As Livi-Bacci explains, "the beginning of mortality decline precedes that of fertility" (p. 103). The death rate is lowered as a result of a number of economic, social, and technological changes, while the birth rate remains relatively high. The result is a rapid rate of popula-

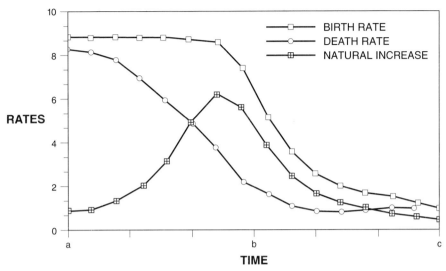

FIGURE 2–1   Demographic Transition Model (Source: Massimo Livi-Bacci, *A Concise History of World Population* (Cambridge, Mass.: Blackwell, 1992), p. 103.)

tion growth. This stage has largely taken place in the nineteenth and twentieth centuries and especially since World War II, when the growth of the population has become labeled "The Population Bomb" (Ehrlich, 1968, pp. 3–17), "The Population Explosion" (Cowgill, 1986, p. 22; Ehrlich and Ehrlich, 1990, pp. 9–23), or "The Demographic Crisis" (Ruffie, 1986, pp. 260–64).

This has been a phenomenon without historical precedence. It was clearly caused not so much by natural events, as some have contended, but rather by two sets of human actions. First, as societies became urbanized and industrialized, the quality of food, shelter, and clothing improved. Secondly, and

FIGURE 2–2   Historial Growth of the World's Population (Source: R. H. Wheeler and L. F. Bouvier, *Population: Demography and Policy* (New York: St. Martin's Press, 1981.)

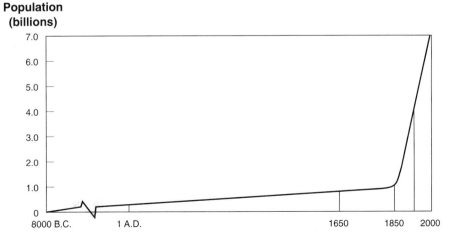

even more importantly, medical technology and public health were developed to save lives and to overcome the centuries-old problem of infant mortality. In effect, science solved one severe problem and created another. One of the results of this phenomenon was a dramatic increase in life expectancy at birth and in the number of people who lived to become part of the elderly population. Consequently, the aged population began to grow rapidly both in size and in proportion to the rest of the population (Schultz, 1981, pp. 39–43).

During this stage an intensive social movement began for the purpose of controlling population growth throughout the world. From the 1960s and into the 1990s, dire predictions have been made of mass starvation and deaths, economic depression, and worldwide poverty if growth of the world's populations is not controlled. Severe measures have been boldly suggested (Ehrlich, 1968, pp. 127–57; Ehrlich and Ehrlich, 1990, pp. 9–30). The early stages of this movement were initiated in the developed nations of the world, especially in the United States, with particular focus on third world countries, where populations were growing at the highest and most dangerous rates. The initial responses from third world countries were either indifferent or negative. Some national officials in Africa even accused those leading the movement of a conspiracy of racial genocide (Hartjen, 1977, pp. 188–91).

Demographic transition as a theory also emerged during this period and a heated dialogue on its validity took place (Hartjen, 1977, pp. 181–82; Davis, 1967, pp. 730–39). One expression of the theory relates particularly to the projected third stage of demographic transition. It states that the decline of death rates will always precede the decline of birth rates, resulting in rapid population growth for a time, but that nature itself will eventually control birth rates as the world becomes too crowded. This theory has both a biological base and a sociological base. Biologically it was based on a scientific experiment with fruit flies in a bottle that contained a given amount of food. The fruit flies' propagation increased until the food supply began to run out, when the growth essentially ceased. The assumption was that the human population would follow the same determined pattern (Peterson, 1975, p. 337). The counterargument by sociologists and demographers is that humans do not behave as fruit flies do. The human response to the environment is not a determined one that simply reflects the demands of the environment itself, but a cultural response, reflecting a whole array of concerns about their social lives (Davis, 1991, p. 3). As Peterson suggests, if human populations decline, they do so because parents decided for a variety of cultural reasons not to have children (Peterson, 1975, p. 338). Likewise, in answer to the question of why it is assumed that mortality declines first, Davis concludes that at the point in history when circumstances made it possible for people to live longer, "longevity was what people wanted, whereas small families were not" (Davis, 1991, p. 15). Presumably, decisions to have fewer children developed later. Davis raises the issue of why such decisions are made and concludes with what could be thought of as the sociological bases of the demographic transition. He says that the real basis of demographic transition theory is that it "is part of a general theory of economic change." Specifically what he means is that it is the product of the "industrial revolution" with its emphases on education, urbanization, economic development, and a better standard of living (Davis, 1991, p. 15). Apparently these are the cultural factors that eventually influence people to decide to have fewer children and smaller families.

Ronald Lee raises the question of whether or not fertility rates automatically respond to population density, as demographic transition theory assumes is true. He admits that there is some overall relationship between those two variables, but says that basically it depends upon economic responses to food shortages and how particular populations themselves respond to those shortages. From that perspective he reports recent evidence as showing that "third world economies are not currently sending clear signals of natural resource shortages or environmental problems induced by population growth" (Lee, 1991, p. 52). Consequently, populations continue to grow most rapidly in those parts of the world in which scarcity is the greatest. Thus, controlling population growth remains a vital issue because of the fairly widespread assumption that the earth has a limited "carrying capacity" that will soon be reached if the population of the world continues to grow at the present rate. Ironically, at the same time when many people are deeply concerned about population growth, Davis points out that others are just as concerned about "sustaining" some areas of population. Specifically, the populations of many small, rural communities in mid-west America are diminishing in size, aging, and facing the danger of no longer being able to produce the goods and services needed to sustain those populations. According to him, therefore, population itself is not the only vital issue. Just as important is finding and restoring a "balance between people and resources" (Davis, 1991, pp. 5–6).

Nevertheless, some have felt and still feel that, as a whole, controlling the population is a necessary part of what needs to be done, and that controlling the birth rates is the way to proceed. Many have also contended that immediate action must be taken to avoid the enormous problems that overwhelm the earth's environment. Whatever natural birth controls there might be would simply be too late. Human intervention is seen as absolutely vital (Hartjen, 1977, pp. 181–82; Ehrlich and Ehrlich, 1990).

As a direct result of the birth control movement, specific programs were initiated in many parts of the world. The major program emphasis has been on family planning. National governments have been urged to develop programs to make contraceptive methods available and to educate the public about birth control and family planning. In spite of substantial indifference and some opposition in developing countries, over 20 countries had implemented some form of family planning program by 1970 (Davis, 1971, pp. 363–405).

For some time, some analysts have doubted that the family planning approach would be effective enough to solve the population problem (Davis, 1971, pp. 730–39; Donaldson, 1990, p. 53–58). That skeptical attitude, coupled with the influence of such other factors as the women's movement, have made population control quite effective in the most industrialized nations. The birth rates have lowered substantially and the growth of those populations have been checked (Bogue and Tsui, 1981). In those parts of the world, there have thus been fewer babies being born while the number of elderly has continued to increase. The more the problem of population growth has been solved, the older the populations of those countries have become.

Some have even become concerned about what they see as the dire consequences of a population decline. As Teitelbaum and Winter explain, declining populations have more to do with lowering fertility rates than with lowering mortality rates, which inevitably leads to aging populations. The basic concern about this is the notion that as the populations of nations decline and age the vitality or dynamic of those nations will also decline (Teitelbaum and Winter, 1985). It is not very clear what kinds of vitality or dynamic tend to be missing from old and declining populations, but in all likelihood economics and politics are at least part of these people's concerns. If so, they ignore the fact that in today's world of huge multinational companies, thriving economic production can be taking place in struggling underdeveloped countries that have exploding and very young poverty-stricken populations without benefiting those populations or their political structures one iota (Ruffie, 1986, pp. 273–74). Neither has it had any influence on the control of the growth of those populations. Controlling populations is still seen by most analysts as a vital concern.

In recent years the great concern about the population control movement has, ironically but encouragingly, shifted location from the developed to the developing countries (Farley, 1987, p. 333). By the 1980s many of the developing countries had begun to become increasingly interested in economic development and increasingly aware that uncontrolled population growth was a major deterrent to economic prosperity. Consequently, some of these countries have also begun to cut their birth rates substantially (Schultz, 1980; Martin, 1988). Some have taken more drastic measures than would be acceptable in most industrialized countries. Problems related to extremely high worldwide population growth rates have by no means been solved (Brown, 1976; Farley, 1987, pp. 327–28). Some countries, particularly Asian (Davis, 1991, pp. 18–19), have nevertheless begun to join the developed countries in moving into the third period of the demographic transition through very deliberate means. Consequently, their populations are also getting older and the proportions of their populations who are old are rapidly increasing.

How demographic transition relates to population aging is what we are especially concerned about. Obviously one consequence of diminishing rates of both birth and death is that the population as a whole dramatically ages—the percentage of the population who are elderly increases while the percentage who are young decreases. Everyone agrees that this trend is primarily the result of lowering birth rates, but it must be remembered that there comes a time when the continuation of lowering death rates become an equally important factor. As recently explained in a report by the Population Division of the United Nations Department of Economic and Social Development, "When the magnitude of, and potential for, decline in fertility become limited and mortality concentrates at old age—practically when fertility is at the neighborhood of replacement level and life expectancy goes beyond the 70-year mark—mortality decline replaces fertility as the major driving force of population ageing" ("Demographic Transition and Ageing," 1993, p. 69). Practically, what that means is that populations continue to age, even after population growth is at replacement levels, and to a large extent that explains why the oldest of the old constitute the fastest growing part of the population in some parts of the world (Bould, Sanborn, and Reif, 1989, p. 32).

TRENDS AND DISTRIBUTIONS OF AGED POPULATIONS

In 1960 the total world population was about 3,037,020,000; by 1980 it had increased to 4,432,100,000, and by 1990 it had reached 5,292,200,000 (Weeks, 1993). Projections are that by the year 2000 the total population will be approximately 6,118,900,000 and in 2020 the world will have reached to a total population of 7,813,000,000 (see Table 2–1). The world population will have increased by 157.3 % in just 60 years, yet the rate of increase each 20 years continues to decline (45% from 1960 to 1980; 38.1% from 1980 to 2000; and 27.7% from 2000 to 2020). Progress is being made in controlling the growth of the population as a whole.

We see a different pattern, though, when we examine the world's elderly population, as shown in Table 2–1. In 1960, those 60 years old and over numbered 249,900,000 (8.2% of the total population) and by 1980, the number had increased to 375,800,000 (8.5% of the total). Projections indicate that those 60 and over will number about 590,400,000 (9.6% of the total) by the year 2000 and 975,600,000 by 2020, or 12.5% of the total population. Those 65 and over will have changed from 5.3% to 7.3% of the world population from 1960 to 2010 (Weeks, 1993). Instead of a declining rate of increase, as is the case with the population as a whole, those 60 and over are increasing at accelerated rates (50.4% from 1960 to 1980; 57.1% from 1980 to 2000; and 65.2% from 2000 to 2020) (Hoover and Siegel, 1986).

Of all the age groups, the percentages of increase over the 60-year period from 1960 to 2020 will have been far higher for the oldest of the old—those 80 years old or over. In 1960 they numbered 19,900,000 (less than 0.7% of the total population) and in 1980 there were 35,300,000 of them (0.8% of the total). The projections for years 2000 and 2020 put them at 59,600,000 (just under 1%) and 101,600,000 (1.3%) respectively. Those over 80 increased from 1960 to 1980 by as much as 77.6%. Between 1980 and 2000 they will have increased by 68.8% and between 2000 and 2020 by another 70.4%. Over the 60 years being analyzed

TABLE 2–1 Estimated and Projected Total and 60+ World Population Growth, 1960 to 2020

YEAR	NUMBER	PERCENT OF TOTAL	PERCENT INCREASE	CUMULATIVE PERCENT INCREASE
		World		
1960	3,037,020,000			
1980	4,432,100,000		45.0	45.0
2000	6,118,900,000		38.1	101.5
2020	7,813,000,000		27.7	157.3
		Sixty and Over		
1960	249,900,000	8.2		
1980	375,800,000	8.5	50.4	50.4
2000	590,400,000	9.6	57.1	136.3
2020	975,600,000	12.5	62.2	290.4
		Eighty and Over		
1960	19,900,000	.7		
1980	35,300,000	.8	77.6	77.6
2000	59,600,000	1.0	68.8	199.5
2020	101,600,000	1.3	70.4	410.6

SOURCE: Adapted from S. L. Hoover and J. S. Siegel, "International Demographic Trends and Perspectives on Aging," *Journal of Cross-Cultural Gerontology*, 1, no. 1 (1986), 5 30, Table I.

they will have increased by an astounding 410.6%, compared to only 157.3% for the total population (Hoover and Siegel, 1986). The population of the world as a whole is an aging population and the future of the world will depend upon how we cope with the changes implied by this fact.

It is noteworthy that in none of the regions of the world are the numbers of aged or their percentages relative to total populations decreasing. The extent of their increases do differ from one region of the world to another, however. There are two basic approaches used in dividing the world into regions and comparing them demographically. One approach is to classify the regions of the world according to their level of economic development. In this regard the "more-developed regions" (MDRs) of the world are compared to those classified as the "less-developed regions" (LDRs) of the world (Hoover and Siegel, 1986). The second approach is to classify the regions of the world according to the relative progress being made toward or through the third stage of the demographic transition—fertility decline. For these purposes, nations of the world are placed into one of three categories: (1) early-initiation countries, those whose total fertility rate (TFR) was below 5.0 in 1950–1955; (2) late-initiation countries, those whose TFR was above 5.0 in 1950–1955 and fell by more than 1.5 from 1950–1955 to 1985–1990; and (3) pre-initiation countries, those whose TFR remained above 5.0 during the entire 1950–1990 period ("Demographic Transition and Ageing," 1993).

In comparing the more-developed regions (MDRs) and the less-developed regions (LDRs) of the world, we note that more of the aged live in the LDRs than in MDRs (205.3 million versus 170.5 million in 1980). The opposite is true of those 70 and over and especially those 80 and over. As many as 6.5 million more of those 80 and over lived in MDRs than in LDRs in 1980. Projections for the year 2020, however, are that by then even more of those over 80 will live in LDRs than in MDRs (Hoover and Siegel, 1986). The population of the world, even elderly populations, tends to be concentrated in those countries of the world that are the least prepared to support their citizens, especially those who are old.

The MDRs have had, and will continue to have much higher proportions of elderly than the LDRs, however (see Figure 2–3). For example, those 60 and over in MDRs represented almost twice as high a percentage of the total populations as those in the LDRs in 1960 (12.5% vs. 6.3%). The percentage gap between LDRs and MDRs became even wider in 1980 (15.0% vs. 6.2%) and will continue to be wide in the year 2000 (18.1% vs. 7.4%) and in 2020 (21.8% vs. 10.5%). Those differences are even greater for those in the older age groups. Since 1960, those 80 years old and older in MDRs have represented percentages of the total populations about three times larger than those in the LDRs, and will continue to do so, at least until the year 2020. The region with the largest proportion of elderly is Europe and the region with the lowest proportion is Africa (Hoover and Siegel, 1986).

Obviously, the LDRs of the world continue to have younger populations even though the numbers of elderly are growing rapidly in those areas as well as in the MDRs. The regional differences in percentages of elderly people are due partly to the fact that the birth rates remain high in those areas. They are also due partly to differences in life expectancy. Life expectancy can be measured from birth or from any age after that. These two sets of figures are essentially the products of two kinds of mortalities. Infant or childhood mortality

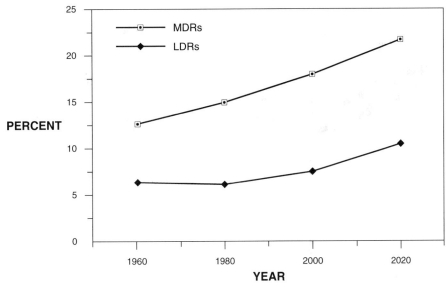

PERCENT

YEAR

FIGURE 2–3 Percentage of Those 60+ in More-Developed Regions and Less-Developed Regions by Year (SOURCE: Adapted from S. L. Hoover and J. S. Siegel, "International Demographic Trends and Perspectives on Aging," *Journal of Cross-Cultural Gerontology*, 1, no. 1 (1986), 5-30, Table III)

has the greatest influence on life expectancy at birth while adult mortality determines life expectancy at age 60. Obviously, the causes of those two types of mortality are quite different.

There are much greater differences between MDR and LDR in the at-birth life expectancy figures than in the at-age-60 life expectancy figures (see Table 2–2). On the one hand, the at-birth life expectancy for males living in MDRs is over 11 years more than those living in LDRs and over 16 years more for females. On the other hand, the at-age-60 life expectancy for males in MDRs is only 2.6 years more than for those in LDRs and 4.6 years more for females (Treas and Logue, 1986). As a whole, then, life expectancy and the bulging aged populations are more the results of saving children's lives than of elongating elderly people's lives.

Age and sex distributions of elderly populations are also important parts of demographic analysis. It is well known that the ratio of men to women (the number of males per 100 women) declines as people grow older. This is true in

TABLE 2–2   Life Expectancy at Birth and at Age 60 By Sex and Region, 1995–2000

	AT BIRTH		AT AGE 60	
REGION	MALE	FEMALE	MALE	FEMALE
World	61.9	65.1	15.4	17.1
More-developed regions	71.8	79.2	17.6	21.4
Less-developed regions	60.5	63.1	15.2	16.8

SOURCE: Adapted from J. Treas and B. Logue, "Economic Development and the Older Population," *Population and Development Review*, 12, no. 4 (December 1986), 648, Table 2.

all parts of the world regardless of cultural differences, economic conditions, or any other factors (Hoover and Siegel, 1986; Cowgill, 1986, pp. 27–28). It is true, however, that the sex ratios of the countries of the world vary greatly. Cowgill reports, for example, that they "vary from a high of 136 in Senegal to a low of 42 in Russia" (Cowgill, 1986, p. 28). As a whole they tend to be higher in LDRs than in MDRs of the world, but, with few exceptions, they tend to be dropping in both (Hoover and Siegel, 1986). The basic reason for these differences is that the LDRs have lower life expectancies, and, thus, much younger populations on the average than the MDRs. As life expectancy rises in the LDRs and their populations become older, the sex ratios will consequently also decline greatly. Hoover and Siegel explain that by the year 2000, "sharp declines are expected to occur in some less developed areas that now have relatively high sex ratios (e.g., South Asia, especially Pakistan, India, Bangladesh, and the Philippines)" (Hoover and Siegel, 1986). The older a given population is, the higher the percentage of women. Old age is primarily a woman's world.

When the sex ratios at birth and old age are compared in different regions, an interesting pattern develops, however. Statistics show that there are no differences between the MDRs and the LDRs in terms of the sex ratio at birth. In both areas the sex ratio at birth is slightly over 100 (more males than females). As Figure 2–4 shows, the sex ratio decreases with age in both areas but declines much more so in the MDRs than in the LDRs. For those 80 or older in 1990 the ratio among those in the LDRs was still nearly 70 compared to only about 40 in the MDRs ("Demographic Transition and Ageing," 1993, p. 83). Part of the reason for the sex ratio difference among the elderly in the LDRs

FIGURE 2–4 Sex Ratio by Age, 1990, in More- and Less-Developed Regions (Source: "Demographic Transition and Ageing," in *Population Aging: International Perspectives*, eds. T. M. Shuman, E. P. Stanford, A. S. Harbert, M. G. Schmidt, and J. L. Roberts (San Diego, Calif.: San Diego State University,1992), p. 83, Figure 3.)

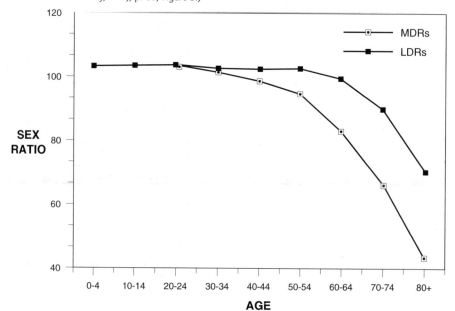

and the MDRs may well be because more of those in the LDRs than in the MDRs tend to live in rural areas. As Figure 2–5 shows, a similar pattern is found when the sex ratios in rural populations are compared to urban populations in the state of Arizona, using 1990 census data.

When regions of the world are compared according to their progress toward the completion of the third phase of the demographic transition, it is helpful to know which geographic areas of the world are included in each grouping. The United Nations Population Division article on the "Demographic Transition and Ageing" provides that kind of geographic description in the following quotation.

> All countries in the more developed regions are early-initiation countries except Albania, which is a late-initiation country. Most countries in Africa are pre-initiation countries. Only six African countries belong to the late-initiation group: Egypt, Morocco, Tunisia, Mauritius, South Africa and La Reunion. The majority of countries in Latin America are classified into the late-initiation group, but Latin America includes five pre-initiation countries (Bolivia, Guatemala, Haiti, Honduras and Nicaragua) and four early-initiation countries (Argentina, Barbados, Cuba and Uruguay) as well. Asia is mixed: Eastern Asia and Southeastern Asia are predominantly late-initiation; Southern Asia has six pre-initiation countries and only two late-initiation countries, but one of the two is India, which constitutes more than two-thirds of the population of Southern Asia; Western Asia is a mixture of eight pre-initiation countries, five late-initiation countries and two early-initiation countries. In Oceania, Fiji is late-initiation, and Papua New Guinea is pre-initiation. ("Demographic Transition and Ageing," 1993, p. 70)

Not surprisingly, the total world population is by no means evenly divided between these types of areas (see Figure 2–6). In 1990 a good-sized majority of the world population was found in the late-initiation countries (60%). This is

FIGURE 2–5 Sex Ratio by Age, 1990, in Urban and Rural Areas in Arizona (SOURCE: Adapted from "Age and Sex: 1990," in *1990 Census of Population: General Population Characteristics, Arizona* (1990 CP-1-4), 1992, pp. 41–42, Table 17.)

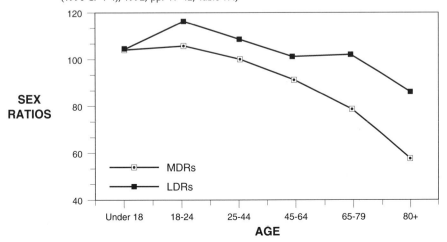

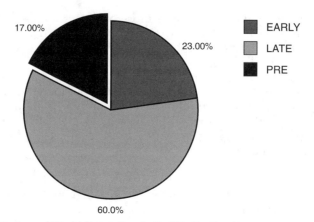

17.00%

23.00%

■ EARLY

☐ LATE

■ PRE

60.0%

FIGURE 2–6 Percentage of World Population By Fertility Decline (Source: "Demographic Transition and Ageing," in *Population Aging: International Perspectives*, eds. T. M. Shuman, E. P. Stanford, A. S. Harbert, M. G. Schmidt, and J. L. Roberts (San Diego, Calif.: San Diego State University, 1992.)

understandable when we learn that both China and India are included among those countries. Less than a fourth (23%) of the world population was found in the early-initiation countries. Even fewer (17%) were found in the pre-initiation countries, even though they now represent by far the most rapidly growing parts of the world.

When these regions are compared by age breakdown and over time, it becomes clearer how aging is related to declining fertility rates (see Table 2–3). The sizes of the under-15 part of the population, in both the early- and late-initiation countries, were proportionately lower in 1990 than they were in 1950.

TABLE 2–3   Estimates and Projections of Major Age Distribution by the Timing of the Initiation of Fertility Decline, Over Time

TIMING OF THE INITIATION OF FERTILITY DECLINE	1950	1970	1990	2025
	Percentage Aged under 15			
Pre-Initiation Countries	41.7	45.2	45.9	34.1
Late-Initiation Countries	37.1	41.2	32.8	22.1
Early-Initiation Countries	27.7	26.6	21.3	17.8
	Percentage Aged 15–64			
Pre-Initiation Countries	54.8	51.8	51.3	62.0
Late-Initiation Countries	59.0	54.9	62.3	68.1
Early-Initiation Countries	64.7	63.8	66.6	63.2
	Percentage Aged 65 and Over			
Pre-Initiation Countries	3.5	3.0	2.8	3.9
Late-Initiation Countries	3.9	3.9	4.9	9.8
Early-Initiation Countries	7.6	9.6	12.1	19.0

Source: Adapted from "Demographic Transition and Ageing," in *Population Aging: International Perspectives*, eds. T. M. Shuman, E. P. Stanford, A. S. Herbert, M. G. Schmidt, and J. L. Roberts. (San Diego, Calif.: San Diego State University, 1992), Table 1.

That is true even though those ages of people in the late-initiation countries had increased substantially between 1950 and 1970. The percentages of elderly people 65 and over, relative to the total populations, in those same countries continued to grow. This was especially true of those 75 and over. It is noteworthy that in the late-initiation countries the elderly portion of those populations was growing even while their fertility rates were also growing (had not yet begun to decline). That means that the percentages of those adults from age 15 to 64 in the late-initiation countries dropped substantially (from 59% to 54%) between 1950 to 1970. That by no means says that the actual numbers of that age group declined during that time. They just did not grow as rapidly as either those younger or older. It is important to realize, though, that those populations were beginning to age even before the beginning of declining birth rates, which is considered the primary force moving toward an aging population. Even in those countries in which fertility decline had not yet begun in 1990, the proportion of those 65 and over changed very little (less than one percentage point) during the period between 1950 and 1990.

According to the United Nations population projections to the year 2025, the process of fertility decline will also have begun in the pre-initiation countries and the populations worldwide will have already aged dramatically (see Table 2–3). In the pre-initiation countries the percentage of those 65 and older will have increased by only a little over 1 percentage point, but those 15–64 will have increased by more than 10 percentage points, and those under 15 will have decreased by more than 11 percentage points. Again, this does not mean that the number of children being born in those countries will even then be decreasing. It only means that the rate of increase will have lowered. According to these projections the number of children per woman in the pre-initiation countries will drop from about 6.5 in 1990 to about 3.0 in 2025 ("Demographic Transition and Ageing," 1993, p. 76). Nevertheless, the trend toward population aging will have begun even in the most rapidly growing populations of the world.

That trend will have become even more pronounced in the late-initiation countries. The percentage of the population in those countries who are 65 and older will have doubled between 1990 and 2025, increasing from 4.9% to 9.8%, and those in the 15–64 age bracket will have increased from 62.3% to 68.1%. At the same time those under 15 will have fallen by more than 10 percentage points (from 32.8% to 22.1%). By then those 65 and older will, for the first time in history, represent an even larger percentage (19.0%) than those under 15 (17.8%) of the populations of the early-initiation countries. In those countries the percentages of the total populations that even those in the 16 to 64 age bracket represent will have begun to drop during that time (from 66.6% in 1990 to 63.2% in 2025).

These kinds of statistics, showing the population aging process, raise questions about the issues of longevity and life expectancy. Much has been made of the claim that people in certain places in the world enjoy especially high longevity. Two specific areas have been particularly cited—the Caucasus nations of Georgia, Azerbaydzhan, and Armenia, that were once part of the Soviet Union (Benet, 1981), the village of Vilcabamba in southern Ecuador (Leaf, 1973), and the mountains of Guangxi Province in China (Kart, Metress, and Metress, 1992). Claims have been made in the Soviet press that several thousand centenarians live in the Caucasus areas. In Vilcabamba, Ecuador, the claim in the early 1970s was that as many as 16.4% of that population was made up of people over 60 years old. In China one lady was said to be 130 years old in 1990 (Ignatius, 1990).

The environments of these areas, the living conditions of the people, and their lifestyles have been analyzed for clues to the longevity they enjoy. It has been noted that all of the areas are rugged and mountainous, that the people are hard working and live simple, stress-free lives, and that their diets tend to be especially balanced and nutritious.

The claims of longevity in these areas have been severely challenged in recent years as having little or no factual basis (Freeman, 1982; Palmore, 1984; Bennet and Garson, 1986; Aiken, 1989, pp. 3–4). The challengers argue that the claims have been extremely exaggerated. Palmore concludes that the claims have been so exaggerated, in fact, that "gerontologists must look elsewhere to find the 'secret of longevity'" (Palmore, 1984). Even if there were some truth to the claims of greater longevity in some unique environments, giving them much analytical attention serves very limited purpose, simply because they are unique (not typical) environments. Most of the world's citizen do not and never will live in those kinds of environments, and there is good evidence that it would be fatal for many to try. Neither are most in the world today apt to live in socially simplistic communities. The much greater likelihood is that life for most of us, in old age as well as when we are younger, will become more, not less, complex.

Part of what the world's life expectancy statistics imply is how the various age levels balance out in given populations. One way of analyzing this is in terms of what is called "the old-age dependency ratio." It is based on the assumption that elderly people are economically dependent upon younger adults in any society. It is typically measured by comparing those in given populations who are 65 or older with those between the ages of 15 and 64.

Table 2–4 provides comparisons between the MDRs and the LDRs of the world on existing and projected old-age dependency ratios. As these figures show, projections are that the old-age dependency ratios will increase at least to the year 2025. Not surprisingly, the old-age dependency ratios are and will continue to be more than twice as high in the MDRs compared with the LDRs. The increase between 1950 and 2025 is also much greater in the MDRs than in the LDRs (154.2% compared to 86.2%), and that between 1990 and 2025 is expected to be about equal in both areas (65.7% vs. 63.2%), however.

TABLE 2–4   Old Age Dependency Ratios for the World, the More-Developed Regions, and the Less-Developed Regions Medium Variants, 1950–2025 (per 100 aged 15–64)

YEAR	WORLD	MORE-DEVELOPED REGIONS	LESS-DEVELOPED REGIONS
1950	8.4	11.8	6.5
1970	9.5	15.1	6.9
1990	10.1	18.1	7.4
2010	11.3	22.3	8.8
2025	14.8	30.0	12.1

SOURCE: Adapted from "Demographic Transition and Ageing," in *Population Aging: International Perspectives*, eds. T. M. Shuman, E. P. Stanford, A. S. Herbert, M. G. Schmidt, and J. L. Roberts. (San Diego, Calif.: San Diego State University, 1992), Table 3.

As shown in an analysis by Treas and Logue (see Table 2–5), projections on old age dependency ratios between 1985 and 2020 are expected to increase most markedly in Europe (193.3%). The next highest increase will be in East Asia (88.5%). Projections are that Africa will be the only part of the world where the old-age dependency ratio will decline during that 35-year period. The reason for that projected decline is primarily that the birth rate in African countries is expected to remain extremely high at least to the year 2020. China's concerted efforts to control its birth rate are undoubtedly the major reason for the projected increase of the old-age dependency ratio in East Asia.

The composition of the aged population is another significant demographic factor. The composition of a given population is determined by a number of factors. These include such things as (1) geographic distribution of the population, (2) the specific characteristics of the population, such as age and sex, and (3) the migration patterns in which the members of given populations have engaged which tend to change the distribution structures.

The geographical distribution of the elderly population in terms of residence in rural versus urban areas is important. While the general population of the world is becoming increasingly urbanized, that pattern does not necessarily characterize the older population. Hoover and Siegel report, for example, that during the years 1965–1975, 65% of the 25- to 29-year-old population in MDRs and 37% in LDRs were urbanized, compared with only 57% in MDRs and 30% in LDRs among those over 60 years of age (Hoover and Siegel, 1986). These differences were largely due to the greater tendency among younger adults to migrate from rural to urban areas. The tendency for proportionately more elderly people to remain in rural areas and younger adults to leave has serious implications for the social support needs of elderly populations. We will discuss these needs later. We should realize, however, that rural versus urban distributions in the future may well be determined as much by the migration patterns of the aged themselves as those of young adults. Future predictions must, therefore, consider both types of migration patterns since present migration patterns among the aged may well change. Frey makes the

TABLE 2–5   Estimated and Projected Old-Age Dependency Ratios (population aged 65+/population aged 15–64 x 100, 1985–2000)

REGION	1985	2000	2020	PERCENT INCREASE 1985–2000
World	9.5	10.5	12.8	34.7
More-developed regions	16.7	20.0	25.2	51.0
Less-developed regions	6.8	7.8	10.3	51.5
Africa	5.9	5.9	5.0	-15.3
East Asia	8.7	10.9	16.4	88.5
South Asia	6.0	7.0	9.3	55.0
Northern America	16.9	17.6	24.0	42.0
Latin America	7.7	8.4	11.0	42.9
Europe	19.4	48.8	56.9	193.3
Oceania	13.0	14.0	17.5	34.6

SOURCE: J. Treas and B. Logue, "Economic Development and the Older Population," *Population and Development Review*, 12, no. 4 (December 1986), 649, Table 3.

case, for example, that particular cohorts of elderly people can be expected to have different migration patterns than other cohorts (Frey, 1986). In addition, Fuguitt and Beale make the important point that the simple distinction between urban and rural areas fail to account for the present complexity involved in such categorizations today, at least in the United States. For example, not all nonmetropolitan areas any longer fit what was meant in the past by the term rural. Specifically, many such areas no longer have an agricultural base (Fuguitt and Beale, 1993).

One type of migration among the aged is related to retirement; this type is common in the United States. Flynn and colleagues studied this kind of migration from 1960 to 1980 (Flynn and others, 1985). Their findings revealed that, indeed, the migration of the aged may be radically changing from the pattern indicated by past analyses. For one thing, as shown in Table 2–6, it was discovered, that, overall, interstate migration of those 60 and over increased more during both decades (1960–1970 and 1970–1980) than migration of the population as a whole, and the increase in migration among the elderly from 1970 to 1980 was nearly twice the increase among the total population (50% vs. 26.6%). Greater percentages of the total population than of the population over 60 still migrate from state to state, but the present pattern indicates that the older adults are catching up. Much greater increases in rural or nonmetropolitan populations than in urban or metropolitan populations were also found during the 1970s, and these differences were much more pronounced then than they had been during any previous decade. This phenomenon became labeled "the nonmetropolitan turnaround of the 1970s," and was predicted by analysts as a pattern that would continue into the 1980s and beyond (Fuguitt and Beale, 1993). According to Fuguitt and Beale, these predictions have not been born out by the United States 1990 census, however. Instead, as they put it, "most observers were unprepared for yet another change, the 'turnaround reversal' of the 1980s." While the percentage of increase in the size of the aged population during the 1970s in nonmetropolitan areas (24.55%) was substantially greater than was true during the 1960s (13.32%), it decreased again during the 1980s to 17.33%. In contrast, there was very little change in the percentage increases of those found in metropolitan areas during any of the three decades between 1960 and 1990 (see Table 2–7).

The comparative net migration numbers between metropolitan and nonmetropolitan areas throughout the United States add another dimension to this reversal of tendencies described by Fuguitt and Beale. Net migration is determined by subtracting the amount of "natural increase" (that is, people becoming 65 years old who are living in the given area being studied) from the total amount of increase found. The results of these calculations show that the increases in metropolitan areas during all three decades were entirely due to natural increases. Statistically there were no immigration patterns in those areas. The only migration that took place from metropolitan areas was outmigration, particularly during the 1970s (over 3% vs. less than 1% during either the 1960s or the 1980s). In contrast, the percentage of inmigration to nonmetropolitan areas went from 2.11% in the 1960s to 7.3% in the 1970s and back to 4.84% during the 1980s. Statistically, there was no outmigration from nonmetropolitan areas during that 30-year period. The basic difference between the three decades was that a greater percent of elderly people migrated from

TABLE 2-6 Changes in the Numbers of Persons and Interstate Migrants Between 1960 and 1980 for the General Population and for the Population Age 60 Years and Over

	1960		1970		1980		% CHANGE IN VOLUME	
	n(000s)	RATE	n(000s)	RATE	n(000s)	RATE	1960–1970	1970–1980
Total U.S. Population	179,323		203,302		226,546		13.4	11.4
Age 60+ Population	22,820		27,538		35,637		20.7	29.4
Interstate Migrants:								
Age 5+	14,141	9.2	16,081	9.3	20,358	9.9	13.7	26.6
Age 60+	959	4.1	1,105	4.0	1,654	4.6	15.2	50.0

SOURCE: C. Flynn and others, "The Redistribution of America's Older Population: Major National Migration Patterns for Three Census Decades, 1960–1980," *Gerontologist*, 25, no. 3 (June 1985), 292–96, Table 1.

TABLE 2-7 Components of Change in the Population 65 and Over: United States Metro and Nonmetro, 1960–1990 (Numbers in Thousands)

	POPULATION		NATURAL INCREASE	NET MIGRATION	PERCENT CHANGE	COMPONENTS	
	INITIAL	FINAL				NI	MIG
1980–1990							
Metro	18,421	22,824	4,515	-112	23.90	24.51	-.61
Nonmetro	7,091	8,320	885	344	17.33	12.49	4.84
Total	25,511	31,144	5,400	232	22.08	21.17	.91
1970–1980							
Metro	14,774	18,435	4,108	-447	24.78	27.81	-3.03
Nonmetro	5,710	7,111	985	417	24.55	17.26	7.30
Total	20,484	25,547	5,093	-30	24.71	24.85	-.14
1960–1970							
Metro	11,616	14,365	2,778	-30	23.65	23.91	-.26
Nonmetro	4,908	5,562	551	102	13.32	11.21	2.11
Total	16,525	19,926	3,329	72	20.58	20.14	.44

SOURCE: G. Fuguitt and C. Beale, "The Changing Concentration of the Older Nonmetropolitan Population, 1960–1990," *Journal of Gerontology*, 48, no. 6, (November, 1993), S278–88.

metropolitan to nonmetropolitan areas during the 1970s than either the 1960s or the 1980s. Apparently, more of them either stayed put or moved from one nonmetropolitan area to another during the 1980s, for a variety of reasons. Nevertheless, the pattern of increased numbers of older people moving to nonmetropolitan areas was still prevalent in the 1980s. The percent of increase was just smaller than in the 1970s. This could hardly be considered a "turnaround reversal."

Another finding by Flynn's group shows changes in where retirees tended to migrate. Florida has had, and continued to have, by far the greatest number of elderly retirees in-migrating than any other state. In 1980 more than one-fourth of all those over-60 who migrated from one state to another moved to Florida. Furthermore, the numbers of the over 60 group moving to Florida had more than doubled from 1960 to 1980, and the percentages of interstate migrants over 60 moving to Florida also increased. However, there was also an increasing tendency toward out-migration from Florida during that same period. In 1980 a total of 92,000 people aged 60 and over moved out of the state, representing as many as 21% of the number who moved to that state that year. The number moving out of Florida doubled between 1970 to 1980 (Flynn and others, 1985).

California is the state where the second-highest numbers of elderly Americans move. The popularity of California as a state in which to retire is also clearly declining, however. The percentages of all 60-and-over interstate migrants moving to California went from 13.6% in 1960 to 10% in 1970, and to 8.7% in 1980. In addition, there was also a sizable out-migration pattern from California among the aged. A total of 141,000 moved out in 1980. That was only 4,000 less than moved to the state that same year, and it represented a 62% increase in out-migration from 1970. Apparently many of these out-migrants returned to their states of origin, a growing tendency especially for those from southern states (Longino and Biggar, 1981).

Arizona and Texas are rapidly becoming the two most attractive states for retirees. Between 1960 and 1980, the numbers moving to Arizona more than tripled and those moving to Texas increased by 191%. Furthermore, both states had relatively few elderly who left the state in 1980 (Flynn and others, 1985). These Sun Belt states are clearly the ones attracting the greatest numbers of retirees in the United States. Within the pattern of migration to the Sun Belt, though, shifts are emerging in terms of which states are the most desirable, and those shifts merit explanation.

An analysis of the rural/urban migration patterns among aged Americans, discussed before, should help to explain the meaning of the shifts in selected states. After the 1980 census it was discovered that the U.S. population as a whole had begun to reverse the well-established pattern of migrating from rural areas and small towns to the cities. It was elderly interstate migrants who took the lead in that tendency. The pattern of elderly people moving from one state to another, some leaving metropolitan areas, and choosing to live in small rural communities, began in the 1960s and continued through the 1970s (Longino, 1982; Longino and others, 1984; Bryant and El-Attar, 1984). This pattern has been specifically noted in the state of Arizona. Although more elderly people migrating to Arizona tended to settle in Maricopa (the Phoenix area) and Pima (the Tucson area) counties, by far the most rapid growth in the state has been taking place in the rural areas of such counties as Yavapai and

Mohave. In some of the very small towns in those counties the aged populations now represent over 40% of the total town populations. Most of the elderly in these communities have moved there by choice, partly for economic reasons but also to avoid the congestion of metropolitan areas (Brown, 1981).

Both of the tendencies of the elderly to migrate to nonmetropolitan areas and to favor the Sun Belt states have clearly continued through the 1980s. As noted above, even though the number of those moving to nonmetropolitan areas between 1980 and 1990 did not increase as much as those doing so between 1970 and 1980, they still increased by as much as 17.33%. Fuguitt and Beale also report that the southwest region of the country continued through the 1980s to be second only to Florida in the percentage increase of the 65-and-over population, and that over 54% of that increase was due to migration of the elderly from elsewhere in the country (Fuguitt and Beale, 1993). In addition, in April 1994 the Census Bureau reported that, according to their projections, by 2030 19.6% of the Arizona population will be 65 and older, making it second only to Florida in the percentage of elderly living there (Schmid, 1994). It is also noteworthy that even among a group of North Carolina retired elderly, who had chosen to move to a retirement community within the state, one of the other migration options that they had most frequently considered was to move to Arizona (Haas and Serow, 1993).

SIGNIFICANCE OF DEMOGRAPHIC TRENDS IN AGING

Present trends in world population indicate that the explosive and potentially destructive growth patterns are beginning to be controlled, not only among the developed nations but also throughout much of the world. Birth rates as well as death rates are decreasing and the rates of population growth are declining. Although not all of the predicted social and economic disasters resulting from rapid population growth have been avoided, population as a future social problem is apparently on the way to resolution in many parts of the world (Bogue and Tsui, 1981), primarily because of deliberate and sometimes drastic measures being taken to reduce birth rates to match the already lowered death rates. In many parts of Africa it is still a serious problem, probably to a large extent because of the continuing political turmoil on that continent, an environment that disallows attention to such problems as population control and economic development.

It is good news indeed that a potentially very destructive problem is being brought under control. What we must also realize, however, is that, in so doing, we humans have created dynamic forces of social change, and that social change inevitably has negative consequences as well as desirable ones. Even as the problem of rapid population growth is beginning to be solved, new problems related to aging are already emerging. Furthermore, the more rapidly the overall population problem is solved, the more difficult it will be to deal with the age-related problems. On the one hand those kinds of problems are totally ignored by some people as though they don't exist. On the other hand, others exaggerate the problems and propose outrageous solutions to them.

Generally, the more rapidly both death and birth rates are reduced, the more rapidly life expectancies rise, and the more rapidly populations age. Consequently, the oldest segment of the population grows the most rapidly.

This is complicated even more for the LDR countries by the fact that the birth rate still remains high, and the population in those countries will still grow quite rapidly even as they age. There will be high numbers of children to raise at the same time that there are increasing numbers of elderly for whom a substantial amount of care will be needed. These dynamic processes are already in force. They raise serious questions about physical, mental, social, and economic dependencies related to old age that must be answered, and we need to be careful to neither ignore nor overstate that issue, both of which are being done today.

The dependency ratios, previously discussed, have the most to do with the question of economic dependency that is being raised by many analysts today. Many see it as a severe threat to modern economic systems (Treas and Logue, 1986; Weaver, 1986). An important question concerning the so-called dependency ratio is whether its basic assumption is valid. Is it fair to assume that, as a whole, those 65 and over are economically dependent upon those between the ages of 15–64? There are, in fact, good reasons to question this assumption. After analyzing the extent that old-age dependency ratios exist internationally, Treas and Logue concede that the ratios "are inadequate measures for gauging the true burden of old-age dependency." They reason that we don't yet know enough about the cost of supporting elderly people and that obviously not all elderly are dependent (Treas and Logue, 1986). Our lack of knowledge about economic dependency is not the best reason for challenging the validity of the old-age dependency ratio assumption, however.

Measures of dependency ratios often include children under age 15 as well as adults 65 and over. The implication here is that children and old people are equally dependent on the rest of the population for economic support. Cowgill reports on a study that compared the amount of dependency of children and elderly people in 87 nations and territories throughout the world. It was discovered that children were much more dependent than the aged. Cowgill concludes, therefore, that overall economic dependency does not increase as populations age, as some would contend, since caring for elderly people actually costs less than caring for children and many elderly are not dependent at all (Cowgill, 1986, p. 35). While this evidence is important to consider, it does not, as such, challenge the basic assumption of the old-age dependency ratio.

The key issue to consider in challenging the old-age dependency ratio assumption is whether the aged contribute to the economy, and the extent to which they do so. Contrary to the popular notion that old people represent only an economic burden, there are, in fact, three ways in which they contribute to the economy. First, millions of those in retirement take on productive volunteer roles within the family and community as well as the marketplace. This is a growing pattern in developing and developed countries alike (Treas and Logue, 1986), and the economic contribution is enormous. Second, some elderly continue their work careers beyond the time when they could retire, and many reenter the work force on a part-time basis even after retiring.

The third major economic contribution made by the aged, especially in modern industrial nations is in terms of capital investments. Private pension funds, into which more and more elderly people have paid as workers, have become one of the most vital sources of economic development (Atchley, 1991, p. 336). These funds typically remain as sources of capital even after retirees draw pensions from them. These issues will be more completely discussed in Chapter 11.

The use of the old-age dependency measure is simply based on false and misleading assumptions. That does not mean, of course, that old age carries no economic dependency. The very old, who now represent the most rapidly growing part of the population, typically have the highest rates of poverty of any age group (Bould, Sanborn, and Reif, 1989, p. 131). In addition, they are typically the least able to use their skills productively. The fact that the majority of them are women also contributes to their deprived economic condition. It is no secret that women enjoy far fewer financial resources than men, especially if those women are single, widowed, and old.

As Davis has indicated (1991) the demographic transition and the issue of population control are very much related to modern-day economic development. Controlling populations and dealing with the circumstances that tend to result from that process, then, depend upon the signals that emanate from given economic conditions. On the one hand, as Livi-Bacci explains (1992), inadequate or no economic signals are being issued in many countries with severe economic conditions. Thus all ages of their populations continue to explode, as they sink deeper into poverty and have little or no hope of solving any of the problems they face.

On the other hand, while the efforts toward economic development and prosperity undoubtedly is the major driving force that brings about control of populations, it has not yet either adequately identified or dealt with the concerns about aging populations. Neither does it adequately deal with the kinds of unemployment problems it tends to produce. For example, as I learned on my 1993 trip there, the People's Republic of China is rapidly becoming one of the most successful economies in the world. They are achieving that goal partly on the basis of the successful implementation of a one-child-per-couple population control policy and going to a free-market economy. At the same time, however, unemployment has become a serious problem and retirement at relatively young ages has become almost universally required. In addition, neither health care nor retirement income benefits are any longer universally guaranteed to the elderly in that country. Ironically, the retired elderly who no longer have those benefits are expected to rely upon their families for the support they need at the very time when small families are mandated for the sake of an expanding economy. While these are issues that are largely being dealt with in the older industrialized nations, even in China they continue to be points of economic controversy and conflict.

The migration patterns of today's elderly raise further questions about their social dependency. The aged have the same, and perhaps more, need for social support from others in their most intimate environments. Yet, at least part of the migration patterns in which the elderly are involved have a great potential to deny them the social supports they need. As we have seen, some are opting not to migrate but to remain in the communities in which they have lived for most of their lives. These are typically small, rural communities from which younger people tend to migrate. Many of these aged find themselves being left behind by their families in communities that are diminishing in size and support services. This pattern is found internationally (Hoover and Siegel, 1986), and continues to exist in America into the 1990s (Fuguitt and Beale, 1993).

Increasing numbers of elderly are now migrating, particularly those in the more developed regions of the world. The migration pattern tends to be associated with social support deficits. Many choose to move to nonmetropolitan, small, rural communities or suburbs where they join others of their age peers. In these cases they tend to leave behind their social support networks and move to communities or neighborhoods with few support services and limited potential for the development of new support networks (Bryant and El-Attar, 1984; Hoover and Siegel, 1986). In these situations, which have been labeled "gerontic enclaves," the support networks are increasingly needed but are less available with the passage of time. All of this raises a very important question about the effect of increased longevity on quality of life (Haug and Folmar, 1986).

CONCLUSION

The demographic trends of the aged present both hope and challenges for the future of the aged. Life expectancies are on the increase. The elderly are increasingly free to make choices about where they want to live. If they are fairly well-to-do, they readily migrate from colder areas to warmer climates in retirement communities where they can interact with their age peers, and enjoy age-related activities and cultural amenities (Haas and Serow, 1993). Even those with limited financial resources are finding it increasingly possible to choose the environments in which they prefer to live.

As we have seen, many of the aged still choose to remain in the communities where they have lived most of their lives. Increasing numbers of them are opting to move to more desirable environments. Many move to urban areas, but as compared with their younger migrant counterparts, a larger percentage of them are moving to small communities in areas with mild climates.

That the aged are becoming more free to choose where they will live is encouraging. Some of the choices they make are beset with potential problems, however. Their tendency to move to small communities is one such problem. Many of these communities lack the social and health facilities that will be increasingly necessary as the elderly cohorts grow older. This kind of demographic information is therefore important as nations make policy decisions that affect their aging populations.

REFERENCES

Aiken, Lewis R., *Later Life* (Hillsdale, N.J.: Lawrence Erlbaum Associates, 1989).

Atchley, Robert C. *Social Forces and Aging: An Introduction to Social Gerontology* (Belmont, Calif.: Wadsworth, 1991).

Benet, Sula, "Why They Live to be 100, or Even Older in Abkhasia," in *Aging in America: Readings in Social Gerontology*, eds. Cary S. Kart and Barbara B. Manard (Sherman Oaks, Calif.: Alfred, 1981), pp. 176–88.

Bennett, Neil G., and Lea K. Garson, "Extraordinary Longevity in the Soviet Union: Fact or Artifact?" *The Gerontologist*, 26, no. 4 (August 1986), 358–61.

Bogue, Donald J., and Amy Ong Tsui, "Zero World Population Growth? in *Social Problems: The Contemporary Debates*, eds. John B. Williamson, Linda Evans, and Anne Munley (Boston: Little, Brown, 1981), pp. 392–400.

Bould, Sally, Beverly Sanborn, and Laura Reif, *Eighty-five Plus: The Oldest Old* (Belmont, Calif.: Wadsworth, 1989).

Brown, Arnold S., "The Problem of Housing for the Elderly in Arizona," in *Report of the Arizona 1981 White House Conference on Aging* (Phoenix: Governor's Advisory Council on Aging, 1981), pp. 107–13.

Brown, L. R., P. L. McGrath and B. Stokes, "The Population Problem in 22 Dimensions," *The Futurist*, 5 (October 1976), 238–45.

Bryant , Ellen, and Mohamed El-Attar, "Migration and Redistribution of the Elderly: A Challenge to Community Services," *The Gerontologist*, 24, no. 6 (December 1984), 634–40.

Cowgill, Donald O., *Aging Around the World* (Belmont, Calif.: Wadsworth, 1986).

Davis, Kingsley, "Population Policy: Will Current Programs Succeed?" *Science*, 158 (November 10, 1967), 730–39.

Davis, Kingsley, "Population and Resources: Fact and Interpretation," in *Resources, Environment, and Population: Present Knowledge, Future Options*, eds. Kingsley Davis and Mikhail S. Bernstam (New York: Oxford, 1991), pp. 1–21.

Davis, Kingsley, "The World's Population Crisis," in *Contemporary Social Problems*, eds. Robert K. Merton and Robert Nisbet (New York: Harcourt Brace Jovanovich, 1971), pp. 363–405.

"Demographic Transition and Ageing," in *Population Aging: International Perspectives*, eds. Tarek M. Shuman, E. Percil Stanford, Anita S. Harbert, Marcy G. Schmidt, and Joan L. Roberts (San Diego, Calif.: San Diego State University, 1993).

Donaldson, Peter J., *Nature Against Us* (Chapel Hill, N.C.: The University of North Carolina Press, 1990).

Ehrlich, Paul R., *The Population Bomb* (New York: Ballantine Books, 1968).

Ehrlich, Paul R., and Anne H. Ehrlich, *The Population Explosion* (New York: Simon & Schuster, 1990).

Farley, John E., *American Social Problems: An Institutional Analysis* (Englewood Cliffs, N.J.: Prentice Hall, 1987).

Flynn, Cynthia B., Charles F. Longino, Robert F. Wiseman, and Jeanne C. Biggar, "The Redistribution of America's Older Population: Major National Migration Patterns for Three Census Decades, 1960–1980," *The Gerontologist*, 25, no. 3 (June 1985), 292–96.

Freeman, Joseph T., "The Old, Old, Very Old Charlie Smith," *The Gerontologist*, 22, no. 6 (December 1982), 532–36.

Frey, William H., "Lifecourse Migration and Redistribution of the Elderly Across U.S. Regions and Metropolitan Areas," *Economic Outlook USA*, 2nd qtr. (1986), pp. 10–16.

Fuguitt, Glenn Y., and Calvin L. Beale, "The Changing Concentration of the Older Nonmetropolitan Population, 1960–90," *Journal of Gerontology*, 48, no. 6 (November 1993), S278–88.

Haas, Glenn Y., and William J. Serow, "Amenity Retirement Migration Process: A Model and Preliminary Evidence," *The Gerontologist*, 33, no. 2 (April 1993), 212–20.

Hartjen, Clayton A., *Possible Trouble: An Analysis of Social Problems* (New York: Praeger, 1977).

Haug, Marie R., and Steven J. Folmar, "Longevity, Gender, and Life Quality," *Journal of Health and Social Behavior*, 27, no. 4 (December 1986), 332–45.

Hewitt, John P., *Self and Society: A Symbolic Interactionist Social Psychology* (Boston: Allyn & Bacon, 1991).

Hoover, Sally L., and Jacob S. Siegel, "International Demographic Trends and Perspectives on Aging," *Journal of Cross-Cultural Gerontology*, 1, no. 1 (1986), 5–30.

Ignatius, A.,"Secrets of Bama: In the Corner of China they Live to be 100," *Wall Street Journal* (March 19, 1990), pp. 1,11.

Kart, Cary S., Eileen K. Metress, and Seamus P. Metress, *Human Aging and Chronic Disease* (Boston: Jones and Bartlett, 1992).

Leaf, Alexander ,"Getting Old," *Scientific American*, 229 (September 1973), 45–52.

Lee, Ronald D., "Long-Run Global Forecasting: A Critical Appraisal," in *Resources, Environment, and Population: Present Knowledge, Future Options*, eds. Kingsley Davis and Mikhail S. Bernstam (New York: Oxford University Press, 1991), pp. 44–71.

Livi-Bacci, Massimo, *A Concise History of World Population* (Cambridge, Mass.: Blackwell, 1992).

Longino, Charles F., "Changing Aged Nonmetropolitan Migration Patterns, 1955 to 1960 and 1965 to 1970," *Journal of Gerontology*, 37, no. 2 (March 1982), 228–34.

Longino, Charles F., and Jeanne C. Biggar, "The Impact of Retirement Migration on the South," *The Gerontologist*, 21, no. 3 (June 1981), 283–90.

Longino, Charles F., Robert F. Wiseman, Jeanne C. Biggar, and Cynthia B. Flynn, "Aged Metropolitan-Nonmetropolitan Migration Streams over Three Census Decades," *Journal of Gerontology*, 39, no. 6 (November 1984), 721–29.

Martin, Linda G., "The Aging of Asia," *Journal of Gerontology*, 43, no. 4 (July 1988), S99–113.

Palmore, Erdman B., "Longevity in Abkhazia: A Reevaluation," *The Gerontologist*, 24, no. 1 (February 1984), 95–96.

Peterson, William , *Population* (New York: Macmillan, 1975).

Rives, Norfleet W., and William J. Serow, *Introduction to Applied Demography* (Beverly Hills, Calif.: Sage, 1984).

Ruffie, Jacques, *The Population Alternative* (New York: Random House, 1986).

Schmid, Randolph E., "Census Study Forecasts a Warmer, Older Nation," Associated Press report, *Arizona Daily Sun*, 48, no. 248 (April 21, 1994), pp. 4 and 10.

Schultz, T. Paul, "An Economic Interpretation of the Decline in Fertility in a Rapidly Developing Country: Consequences of Development and Family Planning," in *Population and Economic Change in Developing Countries*, ed. Richard A. Easterlin (Chicago: University of Chicago Press, 1980), pp. 209–88.

Schultz, T. Paul, *Economics of Population* (Reading, Mass.: Addison-Wesley, 1981).

Serow, William J., David F. Sly, and J. Michael Wrigley, *Population Aging in the United States* (New York: Greenwood, 1990).

Teitelbaum, Michael S., and Jay M. Winter, *The Fear of Population Decline* (New York: Academic, 1985).

Treas, Judith, and Barbara Logue, "Economic Development and the Older Population," *Population and Development Review*, 12, no. 4 (December 1986), 645–73.

Weaver, Carolyn L., "Social Security in Aging Societies," *Population and Development Review*, 12, (supplement 1986), pp. 273–95.

Weeks, John R., "The Economic and Social Implications of Population Aging in the Context of Internal and International Migration," in *Population Aging: International Perspectives*, eds. Tarek M. Shuman, E. Percil Stanfod, Anita S. Harbert, Mary G. Schmidt, and Joan L. Roberts (San Diego, Calif.: San Diego State University, 1993), pp.143–62.

Wheeler, R. H., and L. F. Bouvier, *Population: Demography and Policy* (New York: St. Martin's Press, 1981), p. 24.

3

Physical and Psychological Aspects of Aging

INTRODUCTION

The question of why living organisms change with age, eventually lose their capacities to function, and die is not merely an interesting scientific question; rather, it is vital to each of us and to our understanding of the whole meaning of life and death.

Each of us has a very large stake in what happens to us physically and mentally as we grow older. The processes of physical and mental aging, and the results of these processes in terms of the length of our lives, our decreasing abilities to function, and the changes in our appearance are subjects that none of us dares to ignore. It may be difficult for young healthy college students to fully imagine what it is like physically to be a seventy or eighty year old person. Yet, even they have begun to age and can begin to understand the impact of physical aging by asking themselves what they have already had to give up physically. I learned that lesson the hard way when, at age 34, I went on a day of biking with a group of junior high age young people.

Thus, the aging processes have become very important areas of study for gerontologists. They are increasingly significant and challenging areas of study for biological and psychological gerontologists. They are equally significant to those in other areas of gerontology in terms of how they affect the economic, health, and social policies of aging.

The physiology and psychology of aging are of interest to gerontologists in a number of ways. They are important in terms of the knowledge they provide about the age-old question of longevity. Although the question of why we age has not been answered and may never be, biologists and psychologists have provided us with some increasingly informed and promising theories. A great deal is now known about the environmental and dietary factors that make it possible for more people to live and function normally much longer than has generally been true in the past. Studies on these aspects of aging have raised serious questions about physical and mental functioning throughout the life cycle. Physical and mental aging processes also have serious social, psychological, and economical implications, and the study of those aspects of aging are important for that reason as well.

There are many excellent books on the biology and psychology of aging, and it is not our purpose to even attempt to match or duplicate that literature. Instead, the main focuses of this chapter are to (1) analyze the processes of data collection and theory development regarding physical aging and (2) discuss the social and psychological implications of the physical and mental changes that we humans experience as we live our lives.

AGING AND DISEASE

We have become increasingly capable of differentiating between physical and mental changes due to diseases and those due to aging processes themselves. In the past, except for well-known and well-understood acute diseases that young people quite commonly acquired, the distinctions between diseases of the body and mind as compared to the normal physical and mental aging processes were blurred. Some physical and mental problems (particularly chronic problems) were seen as natural consequences of growing old. It was not at all uncommon, in fact, for old age itself to be thought of and treated as a chronic disease and a major cause of death. One of the early theories of biological aging clearly reflected this view. According to this theory, it was assumed that becoming old was simply a matter of "wear and tear." Like a machine, the cells of the human body were thought to be limited to a certain amount of use, and the more active one's life, the faster one's body and mind would wear out and no longer be able to function (Rockstein and Sussman, 1979, pp. 42–43; Wantz and Gay, 1981, p. 43; Sharma, 1988). Sharma criticizes this theory by pointing out that living organisms do not function like machines. Organisms have built-in repair mechanisms that machines do not have.

In more recent years, a much greater distinction between aging and disease processes has been made. Along with that distinction, a very strong belief has developed among biological and medical gerontologists that diseases and other environmental factors—and not aging—cause infirmity and death. Their contention has been that, although the acquisition of chronic diseases and other debilitating factors in the environment may be associated with age (the older one is, the greater the chance of acquiring those diseases and becoming debilitated), age itself does not cause them. As Timiras puts it, "death from 'pure' old age is rare; rather, it may result 'prematurely' from increased pathology superimposed on homeostatic insufficiency" (Timiras, 1988a, pp. 27–42). Chronic diseases can be acquired by people of all ages. Moreover, not all older people acquire these diseases or become debilitated in specific ways.

The distinction between disease and aging has been well articulated by Kohn (Kohn, 1978, p. 10). According to his definitions, the basic difference between disease and aging is that aging involves universal, inevitable, and therefore normal physiological changes, whereas diseases are abnormal in that they do not happen to every member of the species. Troll makes the same distinction in her use of the terms *primary* and *secondary* aging (Troll, 1985, p. 10). She describes primary aging as bodily changes that are "inevitable and universal," and secondary aging as those changes that "are more frequent in the later years of life," but "are not inevitable," such as various kinds of mental and physical illnesses.

Many who have come to make these distinctions will concede that the aging processes themselves do result in diminishing physical, sensory, and cognitive capacities (Troll, 1985, pp. 22–23). However, their contention is that the results of aging happen only gradually and only minimally throughout life and are never the direct causes of physiological malfunction or death. Instead, diseases and environmental factors are the real causes of debilitation and death (Hickey, 1980, p. 3; Marshall, 1973).It is pointed out, for example, that many respiratory problems are the result of pathology rather than of normal aging. Biologists indicate that the respiratory system is the most vulnerable to damage from outside forces, such as air pollution, tobacco smoke, obesity, and respiratory diseases (Dontas, 1984; Rockstein and Sussman, 1979, p. 87). It is difficult to distinguish between the impact of pathological and normal aging factors, but, according to this view of aging, respiratory problems have more to do with the lifestyle one chooses than aging as such.

These kinds of clear distinctions between disease and aging constitute the theoretical perspective of the Duke Longitudinal Studies, as the concepts that were used to guide those studies—"normal aging" and "pathological processes"—illustrate (Busse and Maddox, 1985, pp. 4–8). The expectations of those studies apparently were that the pathological processes would have more to do with functional losses and death than would the normal aging processes.

Torack utilizes this same viewpoint, as it relates to cognitive processes, in his book entitled *Your Brain is Younger Than You Think*. He mentions critically the time when "any serious decline in mental alertness was considered to be a normal consequence of age," in a critical sense. In contrast, he states his belief that "there is no evidence to show that aging per se causes changes in the brain that are responsible for the development of mental illness." In fact, he contends that "the rate of occurrence of mental illness in the elderly should be no greater than that of younger populations" (Torack, 1981, pp. vii–ix).

The distinctions between aging and disease are apparently not as clear-cut as they are sometimes defined (Hickey, 1992). Timiras admits that "it is difficult to isolate the effects of aging alone from those consequent to the disease or to gradual degenerative changes that develop fully with the passage of time." This is particularly difficult to do among the very old (Timiras, 1988a). Stahl and Feller contend that, in reality, even specialists in the biology of aging often cannot "distinguish physical changes attributable to normal aging from those due to detectable disease (Stahl and Feller, 1990, p. 25). Fozard and colleagues make the point that "in the future, studies of aging must better attempt to capture the interplay between disease and aging processes," and that that will take greater commitment to longitudinal studies (Fozard, Metter, and Brant, 1990).

Studies have shown that, beyond the age of 30, the older one is, the less brain mass one tends to have (Rockstein and Sussman, 1979, p. 58). The total difference in brain weight between those who are middle-aged to those who have reached old age is about 7 percent. Elderly persons also tend to have fewer neurons and to have greater amounts of abnormal protein substances within the brain than those who are younger (Santrock, 1985, pp. 121–23). Some researchers conclude from these data that a natural process of brain atrophy occurs with age due to biological deterioration (Takeda and Matsuzawa, 1985). Those who see the environment, rather than aging, as the basic problem point out that almost all of these studies are cross-sectional and that the differences between the age groups are more likely due to the fact that the older people have had, up to now, much less intellectual stimulation and brain usage than those who are younger (Troll, 1985, pp. 47–62).

Spence acknowledges that there are very few longitudinal studies done on the biology of aging, primarily because it is not practical to follow one group of humans throughout their entire life span. It is for that reason that so many of the biological studies are done with other animal species. However, he admits that this is a questionable process. As he puts it, "Data obtained from studies on lower animals may or may not be applicable to humans" (Spence, 1989, pp. 3–4). A good illustration of this kind of questionable application of data from one type of organism to organisms in general is the study of the effects of oxygen supply on the life span of free-living nematodes. Although the authors of this study do not specifically apply their findings to humans, they do so to organisms in general (Honda and others, 1993). Spence does not recognize, though, that most of even the studies done with lower animals are cross-sectional rather than longitudinal. He also ignores another serious methodological problem with the majority of both biological and psychological aging studies. A brief survey of articles in the biology and psychological sections of the *Journal of Gerontology* in issues over a two- or three-year period, reveal that these kinds of research are being done with volunteer rather than with probability samples. Ironically, in the analysis of the data from these studies, significant levels are often quoted and broad generalizations made about what the data means concerning aging in general.

One of the mental capacities that is functionally vital to humans is the ability to remember people, events, and experiences from the past. Without that capacity humans have no means of interpreting or finding meaning in the present. Accounts of our experiences as we observe and interact with our environments are somehow recorded and stored in our brains. Remembering those events requires that those stored records be recalled to consciousness. It has not fully been known whether loss of the ability to remember past events and acquaintances is due to the loss of stored records, the loss of the capacity to recall, or both. A neurosurgeon, Wilder Penfield, shed some light on that question a number of years ago, when he was able to stimulate a patient's memory by means of electronic probes into the brain. The patient suddenly remembered a long-forgotten and uneventful day from her childhood in quite vivid detail ("Exploring the Frontiers of the Mind," 1974). Thus it would seem that most of our past is stored in our brains and remains there throughout our lives, unless we experience some form of neurological damage as a result of trauma or some form of dementia. Our difficulty in remembering the details of the past, then, seems to be related to our inability to recall them (Perlmutter and Hall, 1985, p. 219). Research seems to indicate that, overall, the elderly are less capable than those who are younger of efficiently exercising the recall processes, at least with short-term memory, even when the time and the methods used for recalling is somewhat extended and adjusted from what is normally used in such tests (Craik and Rabinowitz, 1985; Zabrucky, Moore, and Schultz, 1993; Salthouse and Coon, 1993; Fisher and McDowd, 1993).

It needs to be kept in mind, of course, that all of the above-cited studies were based on the cross-sectional research method and a nonprobability sample. Therefore, the findings from none of them can be generalized to the total aging population with any confidence at all. The sampling problem is further compounded by the fact that they are mostly selected from very similar types of people. The younger adults in the studies are typically selected from students, for example. Verhaeghen, Marcoen, and Goossens attempted to overcome this problem somewhat by selecting 122 research projects on loss of memory with aging and using the data from those studies to do secondary analysis (Verhaeghen, Marcoen, and Goossens, 1993). The assumed advantage of that approach was that they would have a much larger number of cases with which to work. This approach in no way overcame the basic nonprobability problem, though, even though their analysis claimed significance levels between variables.

One of the basic problems of cross-sectional research is that it cannot control for the cohort effect that can severely bias the data. This is particularly problematic in aging studies. Cohorts of younger and older individuals have any number of different experiences that have the potential of influencing how they do on laboratory tests. Controlling for such things as level of education does not begin to overcome all of the potentially biasing differences between age groups. The type of educational experiences themselves may well be very different from one age cohort to another, for example. Ryan and See studied and reported on still another problem with this kind of research—that something of a built-in self-fulfilling process is involved. Specifically they have found that elderly people tend to expect that there will be memory loss with age and they tend to apply that perception to themselves as well as to others (Ryan and See, 1993).

Somewhat surprisingly, the elderly tend to have better long-term than short-term memory (Perlmutter and Hall, 1985, pp. 217–19). The reason for this is not clear, but some believe that it is simply because they are more oriented to the past than to either the future or the present. Or, perhaps they most readily recall those events and objects (1) that they share with others in their social environments, (2) that mean the most to them, and (3) that arouse the greatest emotional response (Lindesmith, Strauss, and Denzin, 1977, pp. 201–2; Proust, 1981, pp. 709–10). Once again, environmental circumstances, not aging, are seen as the primary causal factors.

Hickey points out that this is basically an optimistic perspective on aging (Hickey, 1980, p. 2). If disease, and not aging, is seen as causing functional losses and death, then the great advances in medical technology, disease control, and environmental safety over the past 50 years give us plenty of reason to be confident about improving the physical and mental conditions of old age.

This perspective on aging has been labeled "the bioscientific, medical model," (Fries, 1980), presumably because it has been promoted largely by medical science—a branch of science that (1) is oriented to solve medical problems and is unable to accept the notion that aging and death are inevitable and (2) has gone through an era of outstanding advancement. Medical scientists probably want to be able to deny that aging and death are inevitable, and they seem to have plenty of reason to be optimistic. From this perspective, it is believed that the losses of old age not only can be prevented, but they can also even be reversed. Schaie and Willis's experimentation with a program of cognitive training to restore intellectual functioning among elderly persons illustrates this point. Indeed, one of the conclusions they drew from their research was that "cognitive training techniques can reverse reliably documented decline over a 14-year period in a substantial number of older adults" (Schaie and Willis, 1986).

A theoretical expression of this optimistic perspective is the "autoimmune theory" (Walford, 1969; Sharma, 1988; Kart, Metress, and Metress, 1992, pp. 20–21). The contention in this theory is that interaction between the human body and the environment tends to create cellular damage and the failure of the body's immune system. More specifically, the contention is that this results from the production of antibodies that react with normal cells of the body and destroy them (Sharma, 1988). In turn, the failure of the immune system renders us increasingly susceptible to the chronic problems commonly related to old age. Implied in this theory is the assumption that finding ways to protect the body's immune system would help to eliminate the relationship between age and disease. As Sharma says, "the possibility of thyme rehabilitation in old age suggests that lymphoid cells are not inherently defective, but, given the proper stimulus, can return to normal functioning" (Sharma, 1988).

In recent years, the optimistic assumptions about the physical aging process have increasingly been challenged. This challenge is supported by many studies comparing adults at various age levels in virtually every physical and mental function. Data from these studies tend to show a steady and seemingly inevitable loss of the ability to function, both in terms of speed and efficiency. This evidence has led many biologists and psychologists to conclude that, regardless of the presence of diseases, functional losses with age are universal and inevitable among humans as well as all other forms of life. As Fries puts it, "the bioscientific, medical model of disease, our prevalent model, assumes that death is always the result of a disease process; if there were no disease, there would be no death." However, he contends that "this view is hard to defend" (Fries, 1980).

Kohn describes both aging and disease as "progressive processes" that steadily progress toward a final result that is essentially harmful to the person experiencing them (Kohn, 1978, p. 10). Both are harmful in that they result in the loss of functional capacities. In fact, Fries describes chronic diseases as "conditions that originate in early life and develop insidiously" and that are "inescapably linked with eventual mortality" (Fries, 1980). According to this more pessimistic view, aging is ultimately the more devastating of the two processes because aging inevitably results in steadily accelerated losses and death, while diseases are, at least in theory, preventable, treatable, and reversible.

A theory that helps to explain this perspective has been called the "deliberate biological programming theory" (Busse and Blazer, 1980; Zwilling, 1992) or what Rockstein and Sussman termed the "running-out-of-program theory" (Rockstein and Sussman, 1979). It is the contention of this theory that within each normal cell is stored capability to terminate its own life. (Cancer cells are the only ones that are immortal.) It is believed that each human has a genetically programmed life span, and that the closer we come to the end of that life span, the more rapidly we will experience physical losses, purely as a consequence of aging itself (Fries, 1980). While many have contended for some time that diseases were the major causes of death, aging itself is now believed by others to bring inevitable functional losses and eventual death. Zwilling discusses what has been labeled "the error catastrophe theory," which says that functional deterioration of organisms comes from the loss of adequate information to keep somatic cells functioning properly, due to increased mutations and errors within cells. He agrees that this may be happening but argues that it does not adequately explain the aging process. Instead, he believes that "the aging process is determined by a rigid genetic program and not a statistical accumulation of errors" (Zwilling, 1992).

AGING: DECLINE OR DEVELOPMENT?

According to Kohn, aging can be distinguished not only from disease but from development as well. Development is quite the opposite of aging by his definition. Development is the process that brings one to one's highest level of maturity and thus enhances one's functioning capacity. In contrast, aging processes begin at the high point of maturity and cause the functional capacities to continuously diminish (Kohn, 1978, pp. 9–10). Similarly, Rockstein and Sussman divide life into three stages: (1) embryological development, (2) growth and maturation, and (3) senescence. They describe senescence as the stage when "the body's ability to reverse the degenerative changes in structure and function becomes less effective, and ultimately fails" (Rockstein and Sussman, 1979, p. 103). Timiras also divides the stages of the life cycle between the developmental stage, maturity, and aging or senescence. She qualifies how to characterize these stages somewhat by the statement that "it would be unsound, if not physiologically incorrect, to assume that a function is maximally efficient only during adulthood and that differences in the earlier or later years necessarily represent functional immaturity or deterioration, respectively" (Timiras, 1988b). This does not mean that she defines aging differently from the others, however. It is merely her recognition that it begins at different times from person to person, and that those years "are increasingly besieged by pathological events" (Timiras, 1988b). Thus, the ultimate direction of the physical and mental aging processes is toward degeneration and failure. Obviously, this is a negative definition of aging. The most encouraging statement that can be made from this perspective is that the functional losses are gradual for most of the life span and that most people are able to adjust to the changes as they take place unless they are complicated by pathological events.

A number of factors can, and often do, cause degenerative processes to take place rapidly and even quite abruptly. Harmful life habits, accidents, and the acquisition of certain diseases all contribute to degenerative processes. However, it is the view of many biologists today that, regardless of the environmental encounters of the human body, the degenerative aging processes remain inevitable. The available evidence would seem to support the idea that humans do indeed have a finite life span, and that we not only die within a somewhat predictable period of life, but also that our bodies experience several very typical changes as we age.

One typical change that takes place is in the appearance of our bodies. Our skin wrinkles, sags, and develops spots. We tend to become stooped and walk with a shuffling gait. Our hair becomes coarser and loses its color, and our voices change (Rockstein and Sussman, 1979, p. 132; Schulz and Ewen, 1988, pp. 52–58). The evidence indicates that, although these changes are affected by environmental factors (including exposure to the sun and wind, smoking, and diet), internal atrophic processes and cell loss are also involved. Biologists are convinced that these kinds of changes are inevitable, regardless of the use of cosmetics and cosmetic surgery and despite all efforts to avoid environmental exposure. Some living cells and even complex organisms have been found to be immortal (Cunningham and Brookbank, 1988, pp. 34–40; Zwilling, 1992), but humans are not among them.

Another basic characteristic of aging is the declining ability to function physically and mentally and maintain oneself in daily living without assistance. Although the times, rates, and severities of functional decline vary greatly from one individual to another and between different parts of the body, analysts insist that this decline eventually happens to all of us as we grow older and that it happens in all parts of our bodies. The nervous, cardiovascular, respiratory, gastrointestinal, excretory, reproductive, and skeletal systems and the sensory organs all experience functional decline to some degree, and according to some typical pattern, the longer the human organism remains alive (Perlmutter and Hall, 1985, pp. 93–97, 188–89; Rockstein and Sussman, 1979, pp. 65–94; Dontas and others, 1984; Woollacott, 1993; Coggan and others, 1992; Rao and others, 1992). Kohn is adamant that "decline with age in function of the major organ systems responsible for maintaining homeostasis … is unequivocal," and that "every organ system in the body and every physiological process could be discussed in terms of aging" (Kohn, 1978, p. 181).

Some are now challenging the view of aging as the inevitable net loss of function. While no one denies that many physical and mental functions diminish with age, the assumptions that aging results in net functional losses and that aging does not include development or maturing processes are being challenged. Those who challenge these assumptions argue, in fact, that every age represents both functional losses and new functional developments. They would contend that the studies that seem so clearly to support the notion that aging represents net losses have simply ignored those functional capacities that may develop in the later years of life. For example, Kitchener and King found evidence to support their notion that wisdom, in the form of what they defined as reflective judgment, "really does come only with age" ("Can College Teach Thinking," 1987). From this viewpoint, there would be no distinction between development (maturity) and aging.

Ager and others argue for a more positive interpretation of aging in an analysis of what they characterize as "creative aging" (Ager and others, 1983). Their main point is that, contrary to the idea that aging is a process of decline and a deterrent to growth, virtually all aspects of aging are a creative process of continuous adaptation. These analysts might be accused of trying to establish a situation of "mind over matter" as a way of helping elderly individuals to hang onto their capabilities as long as possible before finally having to face the inevitability of decline, or of trying to help individuals adapt to inevitable functional decline and helplessness with as little trauma as possible. Their analysis is much more than wishful thinking, however. They point out that adaptation is an integral part of people's physical and mental constitution. Basic to their argument is what they call the "plasticity" of the central nervous system, which makes it possible for individuals to integrate and adapt to new experiences. They point out that, while the number of neurons in the central nervous system indeed decrease with age, the central nervous system tends to respond to functional demands by sprouting new synaptic endings at given neural junctions. Another adaptive process within the central nervous system is what they term "engram formation," which makes it possible to develop skills through experiential repetition, through a dual process of "divergence" (one neuron influencing multiple other neurons) and "convergence" (each neuron being influenced by multiple other neurons). Kart and colleagues also point out that "the brain has a tremendous amount of reserve tissue" and, therefore, "has a dramatic ability to compensate for neuronal loss." They also report that "some neurons establish new synapses with more distant nerve cells to compensate for the degeneration of adjacent neurons" (Kart, Metress, and Metress , 1992, p. 118). These processes, then, make it possible for one's experiences to compensate for the fact that a slower functional pace accompanies old age.

Physical and mental adaptation is greatly dependent upon the continuous exercising of the physiological and mental functions (Powell, 1974; Kart, Metress, and Metress, 1992, pp. 50–51, 291–93; Cunningham and Brookbank, 1988, pp. 108–11). It is well known that, for people of all ages, physical exercise acts to stimulate metabolic processes that restore and rebuild body tissue. Ager and her colleagues point out that it also brings the neurological processes into play and thus helps individuals to adapt to environmental stresses (Ager and others, 1983, pp. 31–36).

It has been noted that as we age, the speed and accuracy with which we are able to respond to environmental stimuli decreases (Belsky, 1984, p. 85; Evans and others, 1984; Kart, Metress, and Metress, 1992, p. 51). A major factor that is sometimes noted but is seldom stressed in studies of physical and mental aging is that older adults seem to be much more able than younger people to adjust to their physical and mental losses. For example, in studies comparing persons over 60 with younger adults in the length of time to extract information from a display flashed on a screen, it was found that even though the older subjects were slower, they often compensated for their slowness by using cues from their surroundings or by taking advantage of advance information, or both (Perlmutter and Hall, 1985, p. 186). Macht and Buschke found, too, that under given controlled conditions "certain kinds of complex mental processes do not show age-related slowing" (Macht and Buschke, 1984). Apparently then, even in a biological sense, the experience and knowledge that can come only with age are often a distinct advantage.

It is important to note that the functional changes that elderly people tend to experience do not take place at uniform rates and by no means always take place in a steadily declining pattern (Timiras, 1988b, p. 4; Ferrini and Ferrini, 1993, pp. 63–64). Rockstein and Sussman point out that there are two principles to remember about physical aging: (1) In any one organism, all organs do not age at the same rate; and (2) any one organ does not necessarily age at the same rate in different individuals of the same species (Rockstein and Sussman, 1979, p. 10). Furthermore, for many people these declines do not become debilitating until the final months or last few years of their lives (Fries, 1980). Thus, for most people, the degree of decline throughout most of the life span tends to exert a relatively insignificant effect upon their abilities to function—far less significant, at least, than we generally assume. In fact, Chirikos and Nestel found a surprisingly high level of restored functional capability over a five-year period in a longitudinal study (Chirikos and Nestel, 1985).

COMPRESSED AGING

A growing concern in gerontology, and especially among those responsible for setting policy on aging, is how to afford the costs of providing care for the rapidly growing number of aged as the life expectancy continues to increase. This problem is complicated by the fact that the fastest rate of growth is taking place among the very old (those 85 and over). The assumption is that as more and more people live longer and longer, each person will need increasingly intensive care for longer periods of time.

This is an argument that would seem to find support among those who contend that aging itself is a debilitating process which disease control is powerless to stop. According to an analysis by Fries, however, this is an unnecessary worry for the future. He argues instead for what he calls "the compression of morbidity," and "the compression of senescence" (Fries, 1980).

As previously noted, Fries insists that we humans have a somewhat predictable life span, and that "the inevitable result is natural death, even without disease." The "ideal" is for humans to live out their total life span. A statistical analysis (see Figure 3-1) shows that, through the control of disease, progress has already been made toward a "rectangular survival curve," or as Fries explains it, "the elimination of premature death."

It is also Fries' contention, however, that it is basically the acquisition of diseases, rather than aging as such, that creates long-term physical and mental dysfunction during much of the life course. Disease control has the potential of postponing the dysfunctional impact of even chronic (incurable) diseases. Thus, not only is morbidity compressed but so is senescence. Therefore, natural dying and death generally take place in a truncated period of time at the end of the life span. Based on this analysis, Fries foresees a society "in which life is physically, emotionally, and intellectually vigorous until shortly before its close, when, like the marvelous one-hoss shay, everything

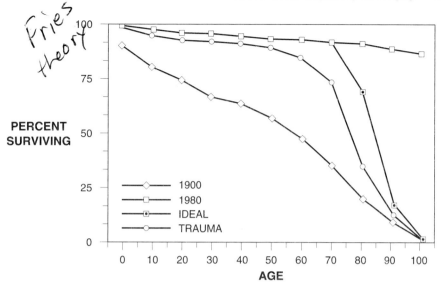

Fries' theory

FIGURE 3-1 The Increasingly Rectangular Survival Curve (SOURCE: J. F. Fries, "Aging, Natural Death, and the Compression of Morbidity," *The New England Journal of Medicine,* 303, no. 3 (July 17, 1980), 130–35, Figure 2.)

comes apart at once and repair is impossible" (Fries, 1980). Furthermore, there is growing evidence that this is beginning to happen ("Shall Age Weary Them?" 1993).

CONCLUSION

Old age in modern society has substantially become a period of life that most people dread. That is due in no small part to how the physical and mental aspects of aging are defined and what the physical aging processes have come to symbolize.

If the assumption is, as much of the research findings would seem to indicate, that growing old inevitably results in the loss of physical and mental capacity to function, then old age is a time of social dependency. One of the most inevitable and most visible age-related physical changes is the change in the skin. Ironically, even though it results in virtually no functional loss, it, more than any other physical change, symbolizes old age as functional loss and almost invariably has negative personal and social consequences. Aside from actual functional losses, the changes in appearance that symbolize old age can serve as the primary source of age-related job discrimination (Brandes, 1986, pp. 112–26).

In addition, actual losses in abilities to function serve as a major source of the loss of social status, even among age peers. According to Rose in his analysis of an emerging subculture of aging, being healthy (functionally active) is one of the most important social values, and the lack of health results in the loss of status within that subculture (Rose, 1965). The psychological results of functional loss, therefore, are apt to be the loss of a sense of self-worth and self-esteem. Kuypers and Bengtson hypothesized, for example, that the elderly become labeled incompetent and eventually internalize that label as a result of the "atrophy of previous skills" and "role loss" (Kuypers and Bengtson, 1973).

A logical extension of the "bioscientific, medical model" of disease and aging, which assumes that disease, rather than aging, causes death, is that every known lifesaving technology ought to be used to keep people alive. This is clearly the prevailing philosophy and policy in modern medicine today. This policy raises practical and ethical questions, however. Is it worth what it costs? Can we continue to afford a practice that serves relatively few people and that increases health care costs? Is it fair that relatively few receive the benefits while many others do not? Does it improve or diminish the quality and dignity of life? Is it even based on realistic assumptions about life and death? Our answer to the latter question is basic to our answers to the others.

The limited life span and compressed morbidity and senescence perspectives on aging have quite different social and psychological implications. Logically, these perspectives raise serious questions about the extent we as a society ought to go in lifesaving techniques. It makes sense to spend a great deal of resources on the prevention and control of diseases in order to keep people as physically and mentally functional as possible throughout the life course. Devices whose only function is to artificially maintain life are logically questionable, however. If we humans have programmed life spans, then we have a right to two basic expectations. First, we have the personal right and the social obligation to remain as physically and socially functional as possible for the duration of that life span. Second, we have the right to die naturally and with dignity. Such a right is increasingly being defined as the right to reject artificial lifesaving technologies and to choose to die in our homes among our loved ones rather than in hospitals. As Fries concludes, "The hospice becomes more attractive than the hospital " (Fries, 1980).

Defining which among all of the available medical technologies are artificial and which are natural is not easy, to be sure. Neither do we know fully which decrements in old age are caused by diseases and which are the results of natural aging processes. We are rapidly moving toward claiming the right to individually define what provides us with or cheats us of our dignity in life and death and to admit that death is as natural as life.

There is much to be learned from a comparison of the theoretical assumptions and practices of modern medicine in the West with those of traditional medicine in the Orient. The basic philosophy on which traditional Chinese medicine is based is in basic agreement with the notion, previously discussed, that humans have set life spans and that this has important implications about the meaning and practices of life.

It is significant that much more emphasis is placed on the prevention of physical problems and less on treatment in the People's Republic of China compared with the United States. For some time the Chinese also deliberately and systematically developed a healthcare system that was much less technologically sophisticated but that was much more readily available to everyone. The results have been that (1) their life expectancy is less than that in the United States, but (2) there are far fewer elderly who are debilitated and dysfunctional. In contrast, Stahl observes that we in the United States are "living longer but are sicker" (Stahl, 1990, p. 15). In China, old age is not perceived as a time of decrements and dependency. The social status of even those in retirement remains in tact and is in some cases enhanced. Death is viewed as a natural process and not something to be feared (Lewis, 1982).

REFERENCES

Ager, Charlene L., Louise W. White, Wanda L. Mayberry, Patricia A. Cristy and Mary E. Conrad, "Creative Aging," in *Annual Editions: Aging*, Fourth Edition, ed. H. Cox (Guilford, Conn.: Dushkin, 1985), pp. 40–44

Belsky, J. K., *The Psychology of Aging: Theory, Research, and Practice* (Monterey, Calif.: Brooks/Cole, 1984).

Brandes, Stanley, *Forty: The Age and the Symbol* (Knoxville: The University of Tennessee Press, 1986), pp. 112–26.

Busse, E. W., and Dan Blazer, "The Theories and Processes of Aging," in *Handbook of Geriatric Psychiatry*, eds. E. W. Busse and Dan Blazer (New York: Van Nostrand Reinhold, 1980), pp. 3–27.

Busse, E. W., and G. L. Maddox, *The Duke Longitudinal Studies of Normal Aging* (New York: Springer, 1985).

"Can College Teach Thinking," *Time*, 129, no. 7 (February 16, 1987), p. 61.

Chirikos, Thomas N., and George Nestel, "Longitudinal Analysis of Functional Disabilities in Older Men," *Journal of Gerontology*, 40, no. 4 (July 1985), 426–33.

Coggan, Andrew R., Robert J. Spina, Douglas S. King, Marc A. Rogers, Marybeth Brown, Patti M. Nemeth, and John O. Holloszy, "Histochemical and Enzymatic Comparisons of the Gasrocynemins Muscle of Young and Elderly Men and Women," *Journal of Gerontology*, 47, no. 3 (May 1992), B71–76.

Craik, Fergus I. M., and Jan C. Rabinowitz, "The Effects of Presentation Rate and Encoding Task on Age-Related Memory Deficits," *Journal of Gerontology*, 40, no. 3 (May 1985), 309–15.

Cunningham, Walter R., and John W. Brookbank, *Gerontology: The Psychology, Biology, and Sociology of Aging* (Philadelphia: Harper & Row, 1988).

Dontas, A. S., D. R. Jacobs, A. Corcondilas, A. Keys, and P. Hannan, "Longitudinal versus Cross-Sectional Vital Capacity Changes and Affecting Factors," *Journal of Gerontology*, 39, no. 4 (July 1984), 430–38.

Evans, Gary W., Penny L. Brennan, Mary Anne Skorpanick, and Donna Held, "Cognitive Mapping and Elderly Adults: Verbal and Location Memory for Urban Landmarks," *Journal of Gerontology*, 39, no. 4 (July 1984), 452–57.

"Exploring the Frontiers of the Mind," *Time*, 103, no. 2 (January 14, 1974), pp. 50–59.

Ferrini, Armeda F., and Rebecca L. Ferrini, *Health in the Later Years* (Madison, Wis.: WCB Brown and Benchmark, 1993).

Fisher, Laurel M., and Joan M. McDowd, "Item and Relational Processing in Young and Older Adults," *Journal of Gerontology*, 48, no. 2 (March 1993), P62–68.

Fozard, James L., E. Jeffrey Metter, and Larry J. Brant, "Next Steps in Describing Aging and Disease in Longitudinal Studies," *Journal of Gerontology*, 45, no. 4 (July 1990), P116–27.

Fries, James F., "Aging, Natural Death, and the Compression of Morbidity," *The New England Journal of Medicine*, 303, no. 3 (July 17, 1980), 130–35.

Hickey, Tom, "The Continuity of Gerontological Themes," *International Journal of Aging and Human Development*, 35, no. 1 (1992), 7–17.

Hickey, Tom, *Health and Aging* (Monterey, Calif: Brooks/Cole, 1980).

Honda, Shuji, Naoaki Ishii, Kenshi Suzuki, and Mitsuyoshi Matsuo, "Oxygen-Dependent Perturbation of Life Span and Aging Rate in the Nematode," *Journal of Gerontology*, 48, no. 2 (March 1993), B57–61.

Kart, Cary S., Eileen K. Metress, and Seamus P. Metress, *Human Aging and Chronic Disease* (Boston: Jones and Bartlett, 1992).

Kohn, Robert R., *Principles of Mammalian Aging* (Englewood Cliffs, N.J.: Prentice Hall, 1978).

Kuypers, Joseph A., and Vern L. Bengtson, "Social Breakdown and Competence: A Model of Normal Aging," *Human Development*, 16 (1973), 181–201.

Lewis, Myrna,"Aging in the People's Republic of China," *International Journal of Aging and Human Development*, 15, no. 2 (1982), 79–105.

Lindesmith, Alfred R., Anselm L. Strauss, and Norman K. Denzin, *Social Psychology* (New York: Holt, Rinehart and Winston, 1977).

Lockshin, Richard A., and Zahra F. Zakeri, "Programmed Cell Death: New Thoughts and Relevance to Aging," *Journal of Gerontology*, 45, no. 5 (September 1990), B135–40.

Macht, Michael L., and Herman Buschke, "Speed of Recall in Aging," *Journal of Gerontology*, 39, no. 4 (July 1984), 439–43.

Marshall, W. A., "The Body," in *The Seven Ages of Man*, eds. Robert R. Sears and Shirley S. Feldman (Los Altos, Calif.: William Kaufmann, 1973).

Perlmutter, Marion, and Elizabeth Hall, *Adult Development and Aging*, (New York: John Wiley, 1985).

Powell, Richard R., "Psychological Effects of Exercise Therapy Upon Institutionalized Geriatric Mental Patients," *Journal of Gerontology*, 29, no. 2 (March 1974), 157–61.

Proust, Marcel, *Remembrance of Things Past*, vol. 3, trans. by C. K. S. Moncrieff, T. Kilmartin, and A. Mayor (New York: Random House, 1981).

Rao, K. Murali Krishna, Mark S. Currie, Jaya Padmanabhan, and Harvey J. Cohen, "Age-Related Alternatives in Actin Cytoskeleton and Receptor Expression in Human Leukocytes," *Journal of Gerontology*, 47, no. 2 (March 1992), B37–44.

Rockstein, M., and Marvin Sussman, *Biology of Aging* (Belmont, Calif.: Wadsworth, 1979).

Rose, Arnold M., "The Subculture of the Aging: A Framework for Research in Social Gerontology," in *Older People and Their Social World*, eds. Arnold M. Rose and Warren A. Peterson (Philadelphia: F. A. Davis, 1965), pp. 3–16.

Ryan, Ellen B., and Sheree K. See, "Age-Based Beliefs About Memory Changes for Self and Others Across Adulthood," *Journal of Gerontology*, 48, no. 4 (July 1993), P199–200.

Salthouse, Timothy A., and Vicky E. Coon, "Influence of Task-Specific Processing Speed and Age Differences in Memory," *Journal of Gerontology*, 48, no. 5 (September 1993), P245–55.

Santrock, John W., *Adult Development and Aging* (Dubuque, Iowa: William C. Brown, 1985).

Schaie, K. Warner ,and Sherry L. Willis, "Can Decline in Adult Intellectual Functioning be Reversed?" *Developmental Psychology*, 22, no. 2 (1986), 223–32.

Schulz, Richard, and Robert B. Ewen, *Adult Development and Aging: Myths and Emerging Realities* (New York: Macmillan, 1988).

"Shall Age Weary Them?" *The Economist*, December 4, 1993, 87–88.

Sharma, Ramesh, "Theories of Aging," in *Physiological Basis of Geriatrics*, ed. Paola S. Timiras (New York: Macmillan, 1988), pp. 43–58.

Spence, Alexander P., *Biology of Human Aging* (Englewood Cliffs, N.J.: Prentice Hall, 1989).

Stahl, Sidney M., and Jacquelyn R. Feller, "Old Equals Sick: An Ontogenetic Fallacy," in *Legacy of Longevity*, ed. S. M. Stahl (Newbury Park, Calif.: Sage, 1990), pp. 21–34.

Stahl, Sidney M., "Introduction: The Legacy of Aging," in *The Legacy of Longevity: Health and Health Care in Later Life*, ed. S. M. Stahl (Newbury Park, Calif:, Sage Publications, 1990), pp. 13–18.

Takeda, Shumpei, and Taiju Matsuzawa, "Age-Related Brain Atrophy, A Study with Computed Tomography," *Journal of Gerontology*, 40, no. 2 (March 1985), 159–63.

Timiras, Paola S., "Aging and Disease," in *Physiological Basis of Geriatrics*, ed. P. S. Timiras (New York: Macmillan, 1988a), pp. 27–42.

Timiras, Paola S., "Introduction: Aging as a Stage in the Life Cycle," in *Physiological Basis of Geriatrics*, ed. P. S. Timiras (New York: Macmillan, 1988b), pp. 1–6.

Torack, Richard M., *Your Brain is Younger Than You Think* (Chicago: Nelson-Hall, 1981).

Troll, Lillian E., *Early and Middle Adulthood*, Monterey, Calif.: Brooks/Cole, 1985).

Verhaeghen, Paul, Alfons Marcoen, and Luc Goossens, "Facts and Fiction about Memory Aging: A Quantitative Integration of Research Findings,"*Journal of Gerontology*, 48, no. 4 (July 1993), P157–71.

Walford, Roy L., *The Immunologic Theory of Aging* (Baltimore: Williams & Wilkins, 1969).

Wantz, Molly S., and John E. Gay, *The Aging Process: A Health Perspective* (Cambridge, Mass: Winthrop, 1981).

Woollacott, Marjorie H., "Age-Related Changes in Posture and Movement," *Journal of Gerontology*, 48, Special Issue (September 1993), 56–60.

Zabrucky, Karen, DeWayne Moore, and Norman R. Schultz, "Young and Old Adults' Ability to Use Different Standards to Evaluate Understanding," *Journal of Gerontology*, 48, no. 5 (September 1993), 238–44.

Zwilling, Robert, "Aging—Still a Mystery," in *Biology of Aging*, ed. Robert Zwilling (New York: Springer-Verlag, 1992), pp. 1–7.

4

A Social Psychology of Aging

INTRODUCTION

We humans are apparently unique among the living organisms of the world in one very important sense: We have an awareness of and curiosity about our environments. We can attempt to understand and assign meaning to the many environmental elements. Even more astounding is the fact that we even learn to become aware of and understand ourselves in the context of our environments. Curiosity is clearly a part of human nature. Human life is full of puzzles that we seem compelled to solve (Lauer and Handel, 1983, p. 4).

Scientific investigation is very much a part of human curiosity and the search for answers about the puzzles of life. Scientists have simply systematized common sense by adding more sophisticated data collection processes and defining concepts more specifically. While other sciences focus on other parts of nature, social sciences ask the puzzling questions and seek explanations about human behavior. Social psychology is one of the branches of social science; as the name implies, it has a focus that draws from two already established social sciences—sociology and psychology.

In order to more fully comprehend what a particular science is all about, we must examine the explanatory factor that is most central to that science. For example, if traditional sociologists were asked what best explains why humans feel and act as they do, they would answer that it is social structure or the social order. It is the social order into which individuals are born and are socialized that influences, and even deterines, individual behavior. Traditional

60

psychologists, on the other hand, contend that the behavior stems from individual personality traits. The difference between these two fields is not so much that they study different phenomena; rather, it is what they see as the most important explanatory factor of human behavior. In that sense there has always been disagreement between the two fields.

Social psychology has emerged because students of both psychology and sociology have recognized the limitations and important emphases of both (Stephan and Stephan, 1990, pp. 15–17). It has become increasingly apparent that individuals influence the social order and that the social order in turn influences individuals. Social psychology is an attempt to find a middle ground and takes both emphases into account. To some extent, though, in attempting to accommodate two somewhat opposing explanatory emphases, it has failed to come up with an explanatory focus of its own (Berkowitz, 1986, p. 13). Nevertheless, social psychology has succeeded in questioning the adequacy of both the psychological and sociological explanations. Specifically, individual personality traits are treated by psychologists as if they were given entities that do not themselves need to be explained. Likewise, sociologists have treated the social order as if it were a given entity that needs no explanation. To fully understand human nature, in fact, both of those phenomena need to be explained, as does any other part of the human environment.

Social psychology with an emphasis on interaction views the human experience as a process of symbolic interaction. According to this theoretical perspective, interaction is the most central explanatory factor. As humans continuously and symbolically interact with one another in all possible situations, both individual identities and social orders are produced. As processes, however, both personalities and social orders are continuously subject to change as the result of further interaction (Hewitt, 1991, pp. 5–8). The interaction perspective offers a dynamic view of all aspects of life, including aging. This is the social psychological perspective that will be utilized in this chapter to analyze the lives of the elderly in various cultural settings. We will examine their sense of self, their relationships, their roles, their attitudes, their feelings about themselves, and how they define the situations in which they find themselves.

CHANGING PERCEPTIONS OF SELF WITH AGE

One of the central social psychological issues related to aging is what characterizes individuals as they age. Social psychologists generally agree that there are individual differences among people in their attitudes, behaviors, and modes of interaction. There are disagreements, however, in conceptualizations of individual differences. Some use *personality* and others use *self* as the concept that best explains individual differences. While the definitions of these two concepts have some aspects in common, there is much variance in their typical treatments. Those who analyze individual differences in terms of personalities tend to categorize them into fairly well-defined and fixed traits that individuals are assumed to possess (Penner, 1986, pp. 99–101). In contrast, those who use the term *self* to account for individual differences tend to define the self as a process and assume that individuals are unique and do not only fit into one category of personal traits or another. This is an important distinction because it helps us to understand what the unit of analysis is in assessing changes in personal characteristics. In analyzing people in terms of the self, the processes through which the self develops constitute the important units of analysis. We must focus on the processes, not on specific characteristics that may be assumed to be related to various ages.

If we assume that the self is a developmental process, then, we need to understand the elements of that process in order to comprehend how the self may change as individuals age. Of first importance is to recognize that the process is a cognitive one. No such phenomenon as the self emerges or becomes a reality without the ability to learn language, to conceptualize and make sense out of the environment, and to interact with others on the basis of how we perceive the world. The use of language is what gives our lives meaning and makes it possible for us to plan and sustain life, and yet it is not a skill with which we are born. It is a skill that we must learn, and we are totally dependent upon others in our social environment to learn it (Hewitt, 1991, pp. 109–16; Lindesmith, Strauss, and Denzin, 1991, pp. 184–85).

It is in an environment of ongoing symbolic interaction that we initially learn the use and the meanings associated with language. We are also largely dependent upon that environment to maintain these cognitive skills throughout our lives. It is in the social realm that the dynamics of life are played out and that our sense of self emerges. Helen Keller's account of her early years illustrates this truth. The symbolic environment in which she lived simply did not reach her because, until she learned a sign language based on touch, she was locked into a world of deafness and blindness in which she simply responded directly to external stimuli just as an animal would (Keller, 1917, pp. 22–24).

Several components of the self emerge from this interactive process. They can be divided into two basic concepts of self: (1) those that provide us with a sense of ourselves as "objects," in relationship to other objects in our midst and give us a sense of our location and (2) those that are evaluative and provide us with a sense of our value or worth (Turner, 1976; Hewitt, 1991, pp. 126–30).

Changes in Self-Awareness with Aging

Probably the most basic self-concept is that of self-awareness. Until we are aware of ourselves as objects or persons separate from but related to others, no other characteristics of the self can develop. Furthermore, to the extent that we lose awareness of ourselves throughout life, we also tend to lose other elements of the self. It has been pointed out, for example, that we often act with very little immediate awareness of what we are doing because many acts become habitual or routine, especially in isolation, where they are never subject to social scrutiny. The result of self-awareness, then, is more accurate self-perceptions (Penner, 1986, pp. 175–76). By implication, the loss of self-awareness will result in less accurate self-perceptions. This is especially applicable to the problem of disengagement among the elderly.

Aside from those among the elderly who suffer dementia-type cognitive losses, loss of self-awareness is actually not as great a problem among this population as many in modern society imagine. The false assumption that aging brings loss of self-awareness was illustrated in a number of television commercials during the 1980s. Particularly offensive were commercials advertising eye clinics in which elderly persons were portrayed as being so unaware of themselves that they became totally dependent upon a son or daughter to explain their problems to them, list their insurance benefits, choose the right clinic, take them to the clinic, and speak for them at the clinic.

As long as 20 years ago this kind of portrayal was described by some as a labeling process, with the effect of creating isolation which, in turn, often does lead to actual loss of awareness, loss of a sense of competence, and even loss of communication skills (Kuypers and Bengtson, 1973). Studies show that this series of events is not typical for most elderly people, however (George, 1980, pp. 41–43).

Loss of awareness among the elderly is often a product of some types of institutionalization, even among those who do not suffer from dementia. For example, Kutner has described the situation of terminally ill patients in hospital wards who had been deliberately isolated from each other and everyone else except hospital attendants. Although none suffered from organic brain damage, typically most had lost confidence, interaction skills, and an awareness of themselves and the world around them. These losses had resulted not from their illnesses, but directly from the isolating practices of the hospitals. Through a specifically designed rehabilitation program, Kutner was able to turn the wards into social groups in which all of the patients actively participated. As a result, their communication skills were effectively restored and they again became keenly aware of and vitally interested in themselves and their environments (Kutner, 1970).

Changes in Self-Perceptions with Aging

Another concept having to do with the self as an object is *self-perception*. Although this concept does not connote a fully developed sense of self, it goes one step beyond a simple awareness of self. With self-perception, individuals are able to take themselves into account much as they do others.

There are two somewhat different ideas of how self-perception contributes to the development of self. Bem has described the process from a purely behavioristic perspective. In essence, he contends that self-perception results from, rather than leads to, behavior (Bem, 1972). According to this theory, humans often act in direct response to external stimuli. They then account for or rationalize their acts by inferring that the actions came from some internal disposition. That inference then becomes part of one's self-perception. This seems to be similar to what Hewitt calls "motive talk"—giving after-the-fact accounts of acts that are questioned (Hewitt, 1991, pp. 183–87)—although it is questionable whether any human behavior ever results from direct responses to external stimuli. Instead, as Hewitt explains it, rationalized, after-the-fact self-perception is more likely to result from situations in which established normative guidelines are absent and actions are based on norms that emerge within the situations themselves (Hewitt, 1991, p. 251). The process is nevertheless a real one, especially for those in the midst of some kind of social adjustment, as many elderly people are in facing such life-changing events as retirement and widowhood. As Cooley explained in presenting his concept, of the "looking glass self," how we experience those kinds of life-changing events depends greatly on how we think others view us (Cooley, pp. 183–85).

The other way of describing self-perception is as the product of actively interacting with oneself. Mead described the self as containing two active elements, the "I" and the "me," which are in constant dialogue with each other. According to Mead, the "me" is that part of the self that represents established values and norms, while the "I" is the impulsive aspect of self and the main source of innovation and creativity (Hewitt, 1991, pp. 85–89). Mead's "I" and "me" should not be confused with Freud's id and superego. The "I" and the "me" are not at war with each other, as Freud depicted the id and superego. Neither is the "I" antisocial as the id was described to be. As Bolton suggests, the "I" is not just a matter of an organism impulsively reacting to stimuli, as a result of some biologically innate drive. Instead it represents an alternative perspective of a situation to that represented by the "me," and may be equally as socially acceptable (Bolton, 1981). The truth is that societies expect individuals to think and even act impulsively as much as they expect them to adhere to established social values. Also, the "me" is not necessarily an internalization of societal norms that have been forced upon the individual, as Freud viewed the superego. Most of all, it is part of the self that may or may not reflect given social values or norms.

In setting forward his ideas of the "I" and the "me," Mead simply wanted to indicate that the processes involved in symbolic interaction themselves work internally, with oneself, as much as they do externally, with others. In that sense the self has all the attributes of a social group. We can talk to ourselves, challenge our own ideas, argue with ourselves, make decisions, and plan our actions. Because we humans have this capability, we are not merely reactive or responsive to our environments, but inevitably and constantly active participants. Even at times when we may outwardly appear to mindlessly respond to environmental stimuli, we are internally actively involved at least to some degree. This is just as true for elderly people as for the young.

It is through the interaction processes, internal as well as external, that we gain a sense of our own identities— what we are like, who we are, where we belong, what we should think, and how we should feel and act. Turner contends that we come to have a "real self"—a core set of feelings, attitudes and values that we are willing to claim as our own—which we cumulatively acquire from all of the interactions in which we have been involved throughout our lives. Having acquired a "real self," we tend to distinguish between those feelings and actions that emanate from us spontaneously but are really foreign to us, and those that come from our real selves. We are ready to claim ownership of the latter but not the former (Turner, 1976).

The real self, according to Turner, tends to be either institutionally or impulsively oriented—to find personal fulfillment either in pursuing the goals of social institutions or in pursuing personal goals. Turner's analysis is limited by a rather narrow definition of institutions, however. The truth is that there are very different types of institutions, and not all of them are committed to established social order. Some, such as the 1960s social revolution (which became quite institutionalized), entrepreneurship, and journalism, exist for the very purpose of challenging the status quo. Others, such as retirement, are structured in a way that, in fact, encourages the pursuit of self-interest. The truth is that all of us are institutionally oriented, and our individual identities are greatly influenced by the particular institutions to which we become attached. Also, when individuals shift their orientations from one type of social institution to another, they can easily become confused about their basic identities.

The quest for "personal identity" is a phenomenon which has emerged only in modern times. Karp and Yoels pointed out in the late 1970s that the search for identity spread rapidly and had by then become something of a social movement (Karp and Yoels, 1979, p. 204). They suggested that this movement had emerged in a time of great geographic and social mobility and of a shift in emphasis in people's social lives from a work ethic to a consumption ethic. Mobility tended to result in a sense of rootlessness, and the consumption ethic pushed people to try to find fulfillment and identity in the consumption of goods and services with built-in obsolescence. The movement was fed by those who promoted and marketed consumption as the answer to the search for identity. These authors contended that this movement especially touched young adults, but today it might well have an even greater impact on the elderly population in the experience of retirement.

Much of the literature on identity crisis is related to aging. Sheehy wrote about identity crises at various points in life that she contended were very predictable (Sheehy 1976, pp. 20–32). Brandes strongly suggests that age 40 is so prominent as a symbol of mid-life crisis that just becoming 40 itself often triggers such a crisis (Brandes, 1986, pp. 3–15). Atchley hypothesizes that identity crises tend to take place in times of such great change that it is difficult to integrate one's experiences into one's sense of self (Atchley, 1987, pp. 100–1). Similarly, George has suggested that in times of social change, adjustment and identity become closely related dynamic processes and not just static states of being (George, 1980, pp. 21–22). It would seem then, that identity would be even more of a problem of older adults than for others. As Atchley puts it, "the longer one has an adult identity, the more times one's theory of self can be tested across various situations" (Atchley, 1987, p. 100).

George points out that our identities are largely related to the statuses, *positions*, we occupy in society and the social roles we perform. Furthermore, the fact of having acquired a sense of identity greatly influences the positions and roles that we continue to select. This selection process in turn serves to solidify our existing identities (George, 1980, p. 18). By the same token, a loss of positions and roles would logically create a loss of identity.

Aging typically brings not only major changes, but also major losses. The combination of both changes and losses would seem to indicate that challenges to identity constitute a particular problem of the aged. This can be illustrated by the experience of becoming widowed, which involves both loss and challenges to one's social identity (Brown, 1974b; Atchley, 1991, p. 228). Most elderly people who are widowed are women and most elderly women today tend to identify themselves in ways intimately connected to marriage and family.

Life-long and Age-Related Self-Identities

What, then, are the facts about identity among the elderly? There are at least two important types of identity issues relating to aging: (1) the extent to which established life-long identities are maintained into old age, and (2) the extent to which individuals take on new age-related identities. With regard to maintaining lifelong identities, many investigators have been convinced that the many changes and related losses experienced in old age would translate into major losses in identity, with consequent negative impacts on self-concept (Rose, 1965a; Kuypers and Bengtson, 1973; Rosow, 1973). However, the available evidence clearly shows that, as a whole, this is not the case (Atchley, 1991, p. 231; George, 1980, p. 21). There is a surprisingly high level of the maintenance of identity among the elderly.

How can identity maintenance in old age be explained? Several factors help to answer that question. One is the emphasis placed on reminiscence among elderly people. Their experiences provide them with much material for self-interaction focused on past accomplishments. Reminiscence is a particular kind of self-interaction that tends to keep elderly people oriented to the past and reinforces their past identities. Lamme and Baars raise the question about reminiscence and why elderly people do so much more of it than younger people (Lamme and Baars, 1993). It is often assumed that they are simply preoccupied with the past because they don't have as much in the present that is worthwhile and have so little future about which to be concerned.

They critique Erickson's notion that reminiscence is an inevitable part of the developmental aging process. According to Erickson, the purpose of reminiscence is for the elderly to work through the issue of "integrity versus despair," the life problem with which elderly people are particularly faced. Lamme and Baars criticize this kind of developmental explanation of reminiscence because it is far too deterministic. They point out that in reality, not all elderly are preoccupied with the past, and there is a lot of differentiation between individuals in how and for what reasons they remember.

They make the case for the idea that remembering the past is "contextual." By and large, it does not take place as an escape from an intolerable present, a hopeless future, and a preoccupation with the past. Instead, it is a part of how individuals interact with their social environments in the present. Specifically, what it does is to make it possible for individuals to reinterpret their history of experiences in order to make sense out of their present situations. Reminiscence is also seen by some as a valuable therapeutic tool to use in helping elderly people overcome depression (Merriam, 1989). This has not been as successful as some thought it would be, mostly because therapists control the subjects on which the reminiscence is focused, rather than the elderly persons themselves, and some subjects tend to prompt unpleasant memories. Burnside contends that reminiscent therapy will work if therapists are careful about the "themes" they choose (Burnside, 1993).

George suggests that another factor related to why elderly people tend to hold onto their lifetime identities may be that the elderly somewhat deliberately select identity-maintaining strategies. Also, identities are inevitably formed and maintained with the encouragement and approval of the significant others in our lives. Aware of the importance of others, many elderly deliberately elect to interact with those who will continue to support them in their established identities (George, 1980, pp. 17–18). Retired teachers may associate with other retired teachers and serve as volunteer tutors enough to maintain their teacher identities, for example.

The contexts in which elderly people adopt new age-related identities, and the extent to which they do so, also deserve to be examined. For example, is it part of being elderly to personally admit the fact of being old and to willingly internalize that identity? Under what circumstances and with what consequences to the sense of self might or might not this happen? A study of this issue was conducted among Yoruba elderly in southwest Nigeria (Togonu-Bickersteth, 1986). A significant positive correlation was found between chronological age and age identification, but there was no relationship between age identification and life satisfaction, as the investigator expected. The Yoruba culture is a rather primitive one in which the older adults never retire and in which roles they perform in old age carry a substantial amount of authority within the family and community. Togonu-Bickersteth speculates that it is likely that the harshness of their lives explains why life satisfaction does not tend to increase with increased old-age identity. In fact, he sees it as at least somewhat surprising that life satisfaction does not decrease with increased-age identity. He concludes that "in Yoruba culture advanced age confers mystical and social privilege" (Togonu-Bickersteth, 1986). Thus, being old is not viewed as socially a negative experience.

Such findings in traditional cultures are probably not surprising, but what about age identification in more modern societies? The People's Republic of China is rapidly becoming an industrially developed country, and some of the Chinese practices related to the aged are similar to those in developed countries. For example, most Chinese citizens retire at even younger ages than in the more industrialized nations. Nevertheless, at least until very recently identification there was certainly not something to be denied or avoided. This was due, in part, to the long tradition of filial piety which has not been totally destroyed during the years of Communist rule. Just as important, though, was the fact that many elderly people in China continued to perform socially significant roles. Although these roles were often quite different from those they had previously performed at work, many of them represented substantial authority (Lewis, 1982).

The situations for elderly Chinese are now dramatically changing, however, primarily due to the economic reforms being instituted in that country. In a recent study of the incidence and consequences of becoming financially dependent on the part of urban, suburban, and rural persons 60 and over in the People's Republic of China, Krause and Liang found that financial dependency is a problem that many Chinese elderly face today. Furthermore, as that happens the emotional support they receive from family members and others tends to decline, and they often experience depressive symptoms as a result (Krause and Liang, 1993). While in China in 1993, I was told that elderly people still tend to perform the same authoritative community roles that they did in the past. Nevertheless, there can be little doubt that economic dependency is severely challenging that authority and subsequently the positive aspects of their old-age identities.

It has long been assumed that there is a strong tendency in the most industrialized countries for the elderly to resist being identified as old as long as possible. In addition, the assumption is that when the aged finally identify themselves as old, they see the identity as a negative one because of the prevailing negative stereotypes about older people (Rosow, 1973, pp. 82–87). Based on his observations of elderly people in Japan in the 1970s, Palmore reported that, despite advanced industrialization in that country, negative stereotypes of the aged did not exist. He concluded that this was because they had effectively adapted their ancient traditions of honoring and respecting their elders to their modern way of life (Palmore, 1975). More recent analyses indicate an increasing breakdown in the application of their traditions and an increase in the amount of negative stereotypes of the aged, however ("The Japanese-Style Welfare System," 1983). Presumably, this trend will also lead to decreased age identification among the aged themselves.

In a recent review of two new books on aging in Japan, Palmore asks the question, "Is aging really better in Japan?" (Palmore, 1993). He concludes that "it depends on your values." He says that "if you value close family ties, abundant employment opportunities, support for families with dependent parents at home, public respect, and relatively high social integration, then your answer will be 'yes.'" However, he also reports that, while public respect for the elderly remains, that fact is balanced by a growing amount of "private negative stereotypes and resentment against the demands and traditional dominance of elders" (Palmore, 1993). It is difficult to determine which of these factors influences old-age identities the most. The fact that many Japanese elderly continue to work would undoubtedly tend to make them maintain their lifelong identities rather than to take on new age-related identities.

Evidence concerning age identity in the United States is mixed. While many elderly Americans view old age more negatively than do the elderly in Oriental societies, Ward found that accepting that identity was related neither to the prevalence of negative stereotypes nor to loss of self-esteem. Instead, age identification was mostly related to actual age-related deprivations (Ward, 1977). In a longitudinal study, Bultena and Powers found substantial denial of age identification among people over 60, but a tendency to accept that kind of identity as those in the sample grew older. There was also a significant tendency for age identification to be seen as positive when respondents assessed their situations as advantageous compared with those of other elderly people with whom they interacted (Bultena and Powers, 1978).

An important factor related to the development and maintenance of one's sense of identity among aging persons is how their bodies continue to function. As Biggs explains, with aging there is "an increasing disjunction between a personal sense of continuity in older age and the discontinuity of the ageing body. The Self grows and develops, whilst the body increasingly lets it down." Also, according to him, another reason that this is important to the sense of self is that, whether negatively or positively, the body serves "as a means of assessing identity" (Biggs, 1993, p. 36).

It has, of course, become commonly known and accepted that all aspects of our bodily functions decline as we age. These kinds of declines, in and of themselves, are generally not drastic enough to seriously debilitate people until very late in life. Nevertheless, they have become a major rationale for eliminating older people from the job market. That is a process that almost inevitably influences elderly persons to reassess their self-image and identity. That kind of reassessment has not proven to be a negative one for most elderly people, however, because retirement from work has become so institutionalized and socially accepted that the changing sense of self that goes with it is seen as problematic to very few people, except those who become disabled. Apparently, the retirement experience itself has come to have its own valued compensations over the years. Therefore, individuals are able to accept themselves as worthwhile human beings in spite of the awareness of their declining physical capabilities. Stevens found, for example, that "feeling useful" was a stronger predictor of life satisfaction among elderly people than having specific productive roles to perform. Instead, feeling useful was related to being respected and continuing to be involved with family, other significant others, and community. Also important was the elderly persons' sense of congruence between what they expected of themselves and what their experiences were (Stevens, 1993).

Aging and Sexuality

One of the bodily functions that seems to be particularly problematic to many elderly persons' sense of self has to do with their sexuality. Research on the subject of sexuality and aging has shown that there are few differences between older and younger people in their desire for, satisfaction in, and enjoyment of sexual activity, but that older people are less sexually capable and have less sexual activity than those who are younger (Schulz and Ewen, 1988, pp. 246–51; Rowland and others, 1993; Ferrini and Ferrini, 1993, pp. 343–48). As Butler and his colleagues explain, "Physiological changes in females (for example, untreated atrophic vaginitis) and prostatic problems in males are some of the possible organic impediments to sexual intercourse." They also indicate that there may be psychological, ethical and fear-related impediments to continued sexual behavior (Butler, Lewis, and Sunderland, 1991, p. 98).

While reviewing the literature on sexuality and aging, one is given the impression that researchers on that topic have a tendency to view the diminished amount of sexual behavior among the aged as abnormal and problematic. They have searched for the possible physical, social, and psychological reasons for that phenomenon, and based on the conclusions they have made about the causes, they have proposed and in some cases implemented various types of interventions (i.e., physical therapy, medical treatments, psychoanalysis, education) to attempt to correct the perceived problem. From a social psychological perspective the assumption is generally made that part of the problem is that society as a whole has imposed the expectation on the elderly that they ought not to be sexually active. However, whenever that point is made, little or no empirical evidence is provided to support it and no explanation is given how elderly people become passive victims of such biases. Mosher did find that religious devoutness was negatively related to the amount of sexual behavior (Mosher, 1994, p. 58), but he made no distinction in his analysis between marital and nonmarital sexual behavior, allowing for the possibility that the lack of sexual behavior may be due to their own moral convictions rather than some societal bias.

Atchley states that many people consider sexual behavior by elderly people as deviant. As evidence of that conclusion he cites the finding in one study that only 5 percent of the public thought that elderly people were "very sexually active." He also reports about individual cases of resistance on the part of administrators of care facilities to allow their institutionalized elderly residents to engage in sexual behavior and to allow their elderly clients to be interviewed about sexuality (Atchley, 1991, p. 320). That is hardly conclusive evidence of a widespread societal bias about sexuality among the aged. Research findings seem to indicate that most elderly are, indeed, not "very sexually active," at least compared to younger people. Besides, even if entire groups of people such as nursing home administrators had such biases, which is doubtful, in fact they represent only one very small segment of society. It may be true that such biases exist but there is little actual empirical evidence to support such an assumption. Yet the idea that the biases do exist continues to be perpetuated in the literature on sexuality and aging. There is just as much evidence that an opposite kind of bias exists among those gerontological investigators who study sexuality and aging. It could well be that their own expectations about correcting such problems serve to create expectations among their elderly respondents about their own sexuality that do not address their own felt needs and that they find increasingly impossible to fulfill, especially when the research continues to compare them to younger people. Libman sums up the inconclusiveness and confusion that exist in the literature about sexuality and aging by stating that, "Sexuality in aging is an area particularly vulnerable to the clash of myth and countermyth" (Libman, 1989).

One of Mosher's respondents made the statement that for the elderly to continue to be sexually active was important because "it keeps us young" (Mosher, 1994, p. 52). That comment in itself ought to give us a clue about how sexuality may be different for older persons than for those who are younger. It is doubtful, for example, that younger persons would ever give "keeping young" as a reason why sex is important to them, but it is undoubtedly a powerful motivating factor among those who are older and feel the need for symbols to show that they are retaining some vestiges of youth as long as possible. It has been discovered, for example, that elderly people tend to consistently hold onto a "youthful bias" when asked how they feel about themselves, how they think they look, what their interests are, and how they act. This kind of biased self-perception does tends to be particularly strong among those whose health is deteriorating. (Staats, Heaphey, Miller, Partlo, Romine, and Stubbs, 1993)

Missing in the literature on sexuality and aging is the possibility that, for one thing, the elderly themselves may be acting on their own strong convictions about when and where sexual behavior is appropriate as much as being influenced by what the rest of society thinks. As Kart and her colleagues put it, "Older people themselves may have many negative attitudes toward sexuality in the aged" (Kart, Metress, and Metress, 1992, p. 263). Another factor that seems to be missing in the literature is the possibility that the sexual needs of elderly people may actually be quite different from those earlier in life.

Part of Mosher's research (discussed earlier) was qualitative, consisting of interviews using open-ended questions to solicit the elderly persons' interpretation of their own sexuality. He found that, in fact, affection in the form of holding hands, kissing, and embracing were much more important to them than it had been earlier in their lives, when their sexuality was more oriented to sexual intercourse. They even included these types of affection as part of their definitions of sexuality. In their interviews, the religiously devout also explained that, even though they believed that sexual intercourse should be confined to marriage, they continued to enjoy having sex with their spouses (Mosher, 1994, p. 51–55). There does seem to be some evidence that the elderly tend to define sexuality and their need for it somewhat differently than younger people do.

From these analyses, it seems apparent that the greatest deterrents to the acquisition of age identity among the elderly are (1) their relative ability to function adequately, compared with others in their own peer group and (2) their relationships with significant others, especially age-related peers. Having meaningful roles to perform and feeling useful in old age, especially as they themselves individually or corporately define those matters, also seem to be important. Generally, the opinions and stereotypes held by the rest of society seem to have very little effect on whether such identities are formed and on whether they are negative or positive.

In the 1960s and 1970s, much emphasis was placed on the negative aspects of old age and its affects on aspects of the self among the aged. It is noteworthy that almost no up-to-date literature exists on the problem of the old-age denial and the unwillingness to be identified as such. Perhaps this is in part because of actual changes in the impact of the negative aspects of aging from then to now. It is also due in part to a fundamental misunderstanding of what is involved in the development of self in old age.

Even in the era of age-related negativism, to which he himself contributed, Arnold Rose hypothesized the development of what he called a "subculture of aging" (Rose, 1965b). As Rose saw it, a central issue in the development of this phenomenon was the increasing interaction of elderly people with one another rather than with those in other age groups. He predicted that, as this happened, regardless of whether it took place as the result of rejection by others or a result of feelings of affinity toward one another, elderly people would begin to establish their own unique set of values and norms. A byproduct of this process would also be an increasing reliance on age-related peer groups for a sense of self-concept and identity. Since the major orientation of this kind of structure is old age, adaptation of age identification would logically be expected on the part of those involved. Perhaps this, more than any other factor, helps to explain why age identification seems to be increasingly prevalent, and why that identification seems to be increasingly positive today.

Self-Worth and Self-Esteem With Aging

Another vital component of the self is the evaluative aspect. This is typically referred to as self-worth or self-esteem and can be defined as the way in which individuals assess their own worth to themselves and to others. The question of whether elderly people maintain a sense of their own personal worth while suffering the many physical, social, and mental losses commonly associated with old age has been a consistent theme of inquiry among gerontologists for many years. In the minds of most social-psychologically oriented gerontologists, it is probably thought of as the most vital factor in the maintenance of a healthy self in old age. It is commonly assessed by the use of a self-esteem scale and is treated as an indicator of life satisfaction and morale. The association between one or more of these measures and every conceivable age-related loss has been studied to determine the impact of the various types of losses on this aspect of the self. The basic assumption behind most of these investigative efforts is that age-related losses lead to negative assessments of personal worth among the aged. Remaining is the question of which of the many losses cause the greatest loss of self-esteem or self-worth.

If this is such a vital issue, then it behooves us to understand it from a theoretical as well as an empirical perspective. Two such perspectives will be examined here. One of the most comprehensive theoretical explanations of the loss of self-worth has been provided by Kuypers and Bengtson (Kuypers and Bengtson 1973). According to this theory, three major losses are typically associated with age: (1) loss of roles, (2) loss of normative guidance, and (3) loss of reference groups. As a result of the loss of productive roles, the elderly become publicly labeled as useless, incompetent, and obsolete. As a result of the loss of normative guidance and reference groups, from which we tend to get clues about actions that are appropriate, elderly individuals become susceptible to and dependent upon public labels. As a result, the aged typically fail to use their functional skills and eventually lose them. The final, defeating result is that the public labels become personally internalized. Elderly persons judge themselves as useless, incompetent, and worthless. These authors expressed their belief that a negative sense of self-worth would predominate among the elderly in the modern world.

As much sense as this may make from the perspective of labeling theory, the prevailing empirical evidence does not tend to support it as the normal pattern among the aged in the United States (George, 1980, p. 43). Self-esteem is consistently found to be high among the aged. In one study, it was found to be almost twice as high among the elderly as among teenagers (Atchley, 1991, pp. 104–5). In fact, evidence indicates that self-esteem tends to increase with age.

One cannot help but wonder about the source of such optimism among the aged. It may be related to their particular perspective on the life course. Based on a recent study on life purposes, it has been suggested, for example, that remembering past accomplishments is an important source of feelings of contentment and a sense of integrity, even among the very old (Recker, Peacock, and Wong, 1987). In addition, evidence does not indicate that there is a major loss of reference groups among the aged, as Kuypers and Bengtson predicted. Peer-group networks are an ever-increasing pattern among the elderly. The formation and maintenance of social networks have been described as "negotiated order" (Fine and Kleinman, 1983). Involvement in such networks is often a result of what the elderly see as needs in new situations. Social networks can easily become the source of new forms of self-esteem and self-worth. In that context, an individual's sense of worth might not be at all apparent to an outsider. For example, this author once observed an elderly lady who came to a senior center daily to do nothing but play Chinese checkers with a few choice friends. She very rarely missed a day. She lived alone and so, on the surface, it appeared that she came purely because she liked the game and to avoid being lonely. Her life seemed to have little or no purpose or worth. However, she related in an interview that, in fact, she was gaining a whole new sense of self-worth by coming to the center each day. She explained that the others with whom she played often told her that they were dependent upon her for their enjoyment of the day's activities. She had come to accept it as her duty to be there every day.

It is clear that self-esteem and a sense of worth among the aged have many possible sources and takes many different forms. Maintaining established or developing new forms of self-worth are dynamic social processes that often cannot be understood without first understanding the social worlds of the elderly themselves.

ROLE TRANSITIONS WITH AGE

Role change is a central issue in the social psychology of aging. As we have seen, roles have a profound effect on an individual's self-concept and sense of worth. They are also vital to the positions of the elderly in society.

In the many analyses of roles among the aged, the concept of loss is an assumption that has consistently been made (Jackson, 1980, pp. 119–25; Kuypers and Bengtson, 1973; Rose, 1965a; Rosow, 1976). The validity of that basic assumption is now being questioned. Perhaps *role transition*, rather than role loss, better represents what people experience as they age. Part of that difference in perspective depends upon how roles are defined.

The definition of roles on which much of the role-loss literature has been based is structural. This is the most prevalent view and one that has been very well articulated in social gerontology by Rosow (Rosow 1976). From this perspective, roles are related to statuses, or the socially defined positions that each person is assigned. Roles are the socially prescribed ways that individuals are expected to act in fulfilling the requirements of their positions. From this perspective, variations in role performances are viewed as deviant.

In analyzing changes in roles through the life course, Rosow explains that role expectations differ from one stage of life to another and that adjustments must be made as we move from one stage to the next. In general, these adjustments are made possible through a well-defined socialization process that rewards individuals for adjusting to the new role expectations of the next stage of life. Leaving the student role behind and becoming a productive worker is rewarded with such things as a paycheck, for example. The one exception to this process is old age. Society provides neither adequate role expectations nor rewards for taking on the old-person status. Old age is the one stage of life for which we are not properly socialized. Consequently, Rosow contends, old age represents a major loss of roles and is seen by the aged themselves as a negative experience that most would prefer to avoid. Not all analysts who have emphasized role loss are structuralists. Yet most have tended to use this kind of description of roles in their analyses.

A very different definition of roles is provided by symbolic interactionists. While they admit that some roles do become fairly well socially established, their contention is that none are ever prescribed fully enough to be considered social structures. Some roles are not defined at all before they are performed. Roles are therefore not social structures that individuals must either conform to or deviate from. Instead, they are negotiated in our interactions with those in our social environments. In order for us to make sense of them, every interaction requires the definition and performance of some kinds of roles. As Turner put it, "The role becomes the point of reference for placing interpretation on specific actions, for anticipating that one line of action will follow another, and for making evaluations of individual actions"

(Turner, 1962). Hewitt explains that humans tend "not merely to accept the guidance of a role but cognitively to structure situations into roles" (Hewitt, 1991, p. 95). We may come to some situations with fairly well-established notions about the roles that we are expected to perform as we engage in interaction. In many other situations, however, the roles have to be negotiated almost entirely from the situations themselves. Regardless of the situations, though, the very processes of interaction include an element of role negotiation. As Colomy and Rhoades explain, "An essential feature of role-taking and role-making processes in the interactionist model is the grouping of behavior into meaningful and intelligible units" (Colomy and Rhoades, 1983). As a professor who has taught a course in sociocultural aging a number of times, for example, I have come to have a good idea of what my role is in teaching that course. From one semester to another, however, the teacher role in that course changes quite drastically, from predominantly lecturing to predominantly discussion, depending upon the number and kinds of comments made by students. According to this perspective, then, the definition and performance of roles are not so much entities that are prescribed in advance but dynamic processes that carry great potential for change even in situations that may seem to be governed by tradition. Viewing the roles of the elderly from this perspective, we cannot assume that the movement out of certain roles will constitute a net loss of roles. Instead, we need to examine more fully their continued interactions to discover what new roles they may be acquiring.

What, then, characterizes the interaction patterns of the aged in the world today? As we will learn in Chapter 7, family relationships continue to be vital to elderly people in all parts of the world. This is particularly true in Oriental countries, but it is also true in the United States and other Western societies. Relationships with spouses are by far the most vital. The evidence is, in fact, that marital satisfaction tends to be at its highest point among couples in retirement (Rollins and Feldman, 1970). As Riley and Riley explain, "In unbroken marriages, the linkages provide the many shared family experiences of aging together from young adulthood to old age. The linkages provide an abiding meeting place for two individuals whose lives are also engrossed in extrafamilial roles—in work, continuing education, or retirement—roles that are also greatly extended by longevity" (Riley and Riley, 1993, p. 186). The elderly also continue to insist on the privilege of having regular contact with their adult children and grandchildren (Brown, 1974a; Shanas and others, 1968, pp. 192–97). This tends to be true even for those who no longer live in close proximity to their children and grandchildren. As a whole, interaction with other extended family members does not seem to be as important. At least part of the reason that family relationships continue is their meaning with regard to role transitions, some of which are viewed positively and some negatively by the aged. In the People's Republic of China, elderly family members who are retired and living with one of their children's families find themselves in partnership with their children in child-rearing roles (Davis-Friedmann, 1983, pp. 47–54). In the West, even though some are unable to do so, elderly parents and their adult children prefer to live in close proximity with one another but not in the same household (Shanas, Townsend, Wedderbaum, Friis, Milho, and Stehouwer, 1968, pp. 192–94). This allows them to interact regularly, to develop new types of nonauthoritative grandparent roles, and, at the same time, to avoid the problem of the role reversal between themselves and their adult children by becoming dependent upon their children in their daily lives. Problems with intergenerational relationships in the family have been noted even in cultural groups in which strong emphasis is placed on the family. This is true in both China (Davis-Friedmann, 1983, pp. 71–84) and Japan (Campbell and Brody, 1985), where a majority of elderly still live with their families in three-generation households. It is also true on the Navajo reservation where intergenerational support is still emphasized (Brown, 1989).

Fear of, and resistance to, becoming dependent is an overriding concern among the elderly, especially in the United States, and it influences both how they interact and with whom (Brown, 1979; Atchley, 1987, pp. 89–91). As a result, a growing tendency among the elderly is to select as friends others who are similar in background and experience. Relationships with people their own age are becoming the most attractive to them (Atchley, 1987, pp. 203–4). These types of relationships are also increasing among those cultural groups in which family intergenerational interdependency is still strongly emphasized, such as in China and among the Navajo elderly.

What, then, are the results of these kinds of relationships with regard to role changes among the aged? For one thing, as discussed earlier, adjustment into retirement (the loss of the work role) has been found to be relatively easy for the vast majority of elderly people. A great deal of evidence on retirement among American workers indicates that their morale and life satisfaction do not decline with retirement, as many have predicted that it would (Brown, 1974b; George and Mattox, 1977). One investigator found that both community involvement and life satisfaction increased following retirement (Bell, 1976). Atchley contends that retirement itself represents a role that includes behavioral expectations (Atchley, 1987, pp. 223–24). Along with societal expectations, the retirement role has also come to encourage peer interaction and activities, such as traveling and recreation. Retirement is becoming a whole new way of life for many elderly people in those communities where retirement has become national policy.

CONCLUSION

We have analyzed the social-psychological conditions of elderly people in the world today. We have examined how their perceptions of themselves and the roles they perform have changed, and we have discussed the interactional situations in which those changes have taken place. It has been noted that in the past, most such analyses have concluded that old age generally means "loss" in the social-psychological sense. However, the available evidence, especially that produced in recent years, shows that what elderly people tend to experience is not so much loss as it is change and transition. The sense of self often changes markedly in old age, but those changes seldom become crisis-oriented even with such experiences as retirement, widowhood, and age-related declines in physical capabilities. Self-perception and self-esteem tend to remain positive and are sometimes even more positive in old age. For increasing numbers of elderly people, the roles of old age are very different than those they had as younger adults. For most of them, retirement does not mean the loss of roles but a transition to new and different roles and relationships, and feeling useful becomes more important to them than performing specific roles.

The elderly are often accused of abnormally living in the past through the process of reminiscence, but in reality that is a process that helps them to deal with their present changing situations. They have a tendency to continue to evaluate themselves from a "youthful bias," and that is often reflected in how they respond to research questions about their physical conditions and activities, particularly related to sexuality. They do, however, tend to define the importance of sexuality from a different set of needs than those who are younger.

The changes and transitions that the aged are experiencing today tend to be mostly positive and are prevalent cross-culturally, and across social classes, despite the vast cultural and class differences. The basically positive nature of social-psychological well-being of elderly people today can be largely attributed to their patterns of interaction. Particularly important is the fact that they increasingly prefer and choose age-peer interaction. Interaction among those in common situations, such as retirement and old age, is a dynamic process that inevitably produces new self-perceptions, new roles, and new relationships that are appropriate and directly applicable to those common situations. To ignore those very dynamic processes in analyzing the social psychology of aging is to misunderstand what becoming old today is really like.

REFERENCES

Atchley, Robert C., *Aging: Continuity and Change* (Belmont, Calif.: Wadsworth, 1987).

Atchley, Robert C., *Social Forces and Aging: An Introduction to Social Gerontology* (Belmont, Calif.: Wadsworth, 1991).

Bell, Bill D., "Role Set Orientations and Life Satisfaction: A New Look at an Old Theory," in *Time, Roles and Self in Old Age*, ed. Jaber F. Gubrium (New York: Human Sciences Press, 1976), pp. 148–64.

Bem, Daryl J., "Self-perception Theory," in *Advances in Experimental Social Psychology*, vol. 6, ed. Leonard Berkowitz (New York: Academic Press, 1972), pp. 2–62.

Berkowitz, Leonard, *A Survey of Social Psychology* (New York: Holt, Rinehart and Winston, 1986).

Biggs, Simon, *Understanding Ageing: Images, Attitudes, and Professional Practice* (Philadelphia: Open University Press, 1993).

Bolton, Charles D., "Some Consequences of the Median Self," *Symbolic Interaction*, 4, no. 2 (Fall 1981), 245–59.

Brandes, Stanley, *Forty: The Age and the Symbol* (Knoxville: The University of Tennessee Press, 1986).

Brown, Arnold S., "A Survey of Elder Abuse of One Native American Tribe," *Journal of Elder Abuse and Neglect*, 1, no. 2 (1989), 17–37.

Brown, Arnold S., "Problems of Dependence and Independence Among the Elderly," unpublished research report presented to the 25th Annual Western Gerontological Society Meeting, San Francisco, Calif., April 1979.

Brown, Arnold S., "Satisfying Relationships for the Elderly and Their Patterns of Disengagement," *The Gerontologist*, 14, no. 3 (June 1974a), 258–62.

Brown, Arnold S., "Socially Disruptive Events and Morale Among the Elderly," unpublished paper presented at the Gerontological Society 27th Annual Meeting, Portland, Oregon, October 1974. Abstract printed in *The Gerontologist*, 14, no. 5, pt. 11 (October 1974b), 72.

Bultena, G. L., and E. A. Powers, "Denial of Aging: Age Identification and Reference Group Orientations," *Journal of Gerontology*, 33, no. 5 (September 1978), 748–54.

Burnside, Irene, "Themes in Reminiscence Groups with Older Women," *International Journal of Aging and Human Development*, 37, no. 3 (1993), 177–89.

Butler, Robert N., Myrna I. Lewis, and Trey Sunderland, *Aging and Mental Health: Positive Psychosocial and Biomedical Approaches* (New York: Macmillan, 1991).

Campbell, Ruth, and Elaine M. Brody, "Women's Changing Roles and Help to the Elderly: Attitudes of Women in the United States and Japan," *The Gerontologist*, 25, no. 6 (December 1985), 584–92.

Colomy, Paul, and Gary Rhoades, "Role Performance and Person Perception: Toward an Interactionist Approach," *Symbolic Interaction*, 6, no. 2 (Fall 1983), 207–27.

Cooley, Charles H., *Human Nature & the Social Order* (New York: Schocken Books, 1964.)

Davis-Friedmann, Deborah, *Long Lives: Chinese Elderly and the Communist Revolution* (Cambridge, Mass.: Harvard University Press, 1983).

Fine, Gary A., and Sherryl Kleinman, "Network and Meaning: An Interactionist Approach to Structure," *Symbolic Interaction*, 6, no. 1 (Spring 1983), 97–110.

Ferrini, Armeda F., and Rebecca L. Ferrini, *Health in the Later Years* (Madison, Wis.: WCB Brown and Benchmark, 1993).

George, Linda K., and George Maddox, "Subjective Adaptation to Loss of the Work Role: A Longitudinal Study," *Journal of Gerontology*, 32, no. 1 (July 1977), 456–62.

George, Linda K., *Role Transitions in Later Life* (Monterey, Calif.: Brooks/Cole, 1980).

Hewitt, John P., *Self and Society: A Symbolic Interactionist Social Psychology* (Boston: Allyn & Bacon, 1991).

Jackson, Jacquelyne J., *Minorities and Aging* (Belmont, Calif.: Wadsworth, 1980).

"The Japanese-Style Welfare System," *Japan Quarterly*, 30 (July-September 1983), 327–30.

Karp, David A., and William C. Yoels, *Symbols, Selves, and Society: Understanding Interaction* (New York: J. B. Lippincott/Harper & Row, 1979).

Kart, Cary S., Eileen K. Metress, and Seamus Metress, *Human Aging and Chronic Disease* (Boston: Jones and Bartlett, 1992).

Keller, Helen, *The Story of My Life* (New York: Doubleday, 1917).

Krause, Neal, and Jersey Liang, "Stress, Social Support, and Psychological Distress Among the Chinese Elderly," *Journal of Gerontology*, 48, no. 6 (November 1993), P282–91.

Kutner, Bernard, "The Hospital Environment," *Social Sciences and Medicine*, 4, sup. 1 (1970), 9–12.

Kuypers, Joseph A., and Vern L. Bengtson, "Social Breakdown and Competence: A Model of Normal Aging," *Human Development*, 16 (1973), 181–201.

Lamme, Simone, and Jan Baars, "Including Social Factors in the Analysis of Reminiscence in Elderly Individuals," *International Journal of Aging and Human Development*, 37, no. 4 (1993), 297–311.

Lauer, Robert H., and Warren H. Handel,*Social Psychology: The Theory and Application of Symbolic Interactionism* (Englewood Cliffs, N.J.: Prentice Hall, 1983).

Lewis, Myrna, "Aging in the People's Republic of China," *International Journal of Aging and Development*, 15, no. 2 (1982), 79–105.

Libman, Eva, "Sociocultural and Cognitive Factors in Aging and Sexual Expression: Conceptual and Research Issues," *Canadian Psychology*, 30, no. 3 (1989), 560–65.

Lindesmith, Alfred R., Anselm L. Strauss, and Norman K. Denzin, *Social Psychology* (Englewood Cliffs, N.J.: Prentice Hall, 1991).

Merriam, Sharan B., "The Structure of Simple Reminiscence," *The Gerontologist*, 29, no. 6 (December 1989) 761–67.

Mosher, Robert F., "The Relationship of Selected Variables to Sexual Knowledge, Attitudes, and Behaviors of the Elderly," unpublished Doctorate of Education Dissertation, Northern Arizona University, 1994.

Palmore, Erdman B., "Is Aging Really Better in Japan?" *The Gerontologist*, 33, no. 5 (October 1993), 697–99.

Palmore, Erdman B., "The Status and Integration of the Aged in Japanese Society," *Journal of Gerontology*, 30, no. 2 (March 1975b), 199–208.

Penner, Louis A., *Social Psychology: Concepts and Applications* (St. Paul, Minn.: West, 1986).

Recker, Gary T., Edward J. Peacock, and Paul T. P. Wong, "Meaning and Purpose in Life and Well-Being: A Life Span Perspective," *Journal of Gerontology*, 42, no. 1 (January 1987), 44–49.

Riley, Matilda W., and John W. Riley, "Connections: Kin and Cohort," in *The Changing Contract Across Generations*, eds. Vern L. Bengston and W. Andrew Achenbaum (New York: Aldine de Gruyter, 1993), pp. 169–89.

Rollins, Boyd C., and H. Feldman, "Marital Satisfaction over the Family Life Cycle," *Journal of Marriage and the Family*, 32, no. 6 (February 1970), 20–28.

Rose, Arnold M., "A Current Theoretical Issue in Social Gerontology," in *Older People and Their Social World*, eds. Arnold M. Rose and Warren A. Peterson (Philadelphia: F. A. Davis, 1965a).

Rose, Arnold M., "The Subculture of Aging: A Framework for Research in Social Gerontology," in *Older People and Their Social World*, ed. Arnold M. Rose and Warren A. Peterson (Philadelphia: F. A. Davis, 1965b), pp. 3–16.

Rosow, Irving, "Status and Role Change Through the Life Course," in *Handbook of Aging and Social Science*, eds. R. H. Binstock and Ethel Shanas (New York: Von Nostrand Reinhold, 1976), p. 462.

Rosow, Irving, "The Social Context of the Aging Self," *The Gerontologist*, 13, no. 1 (Spring 1973), 82–87.

Rowland, David L., Walter J. Greenleaf, Leslie J. Dorfman, and Julian M. Davidson, "Aging, and Sexual Function in Men," *Archives of Sexual Behavior*, 22, no. 6 (1993), 545–57.

Schulz, Richard, and Robert E. Ewen, *Adult Development and Aging: Myths and Emerging Realities* (New York: Macmillan, 1988).

Shanas, Ethel, Peter Townsend, Dorothy Wedderbaum, Henning Friis, Paul Milhoj, and Jan Stehouwer, *Old People in Three Industrial Societies* (New York: Atherton Press, 1968).

Sheehy, Gail, *Passages: Predictable Crises of Adult Life* (New York: Dutton, 1976).

Staats, Sara, Kate Heaphey, Deborah Miller, Christie Partlo, Nanette Romine and Kathy Stubbs, "Subjective Age and Health Perceptions of Older Persons: Maintaining the Youthful Bias in Sickness and in Health," *International Journal of Aging and Human Development*, 37, no. 3 (1993), 191–203.

Stephan, Cookie W., and Walter G. Stephan, *Two Social Psychologies: An Integrative Approach* (Belmont, Calif.: Wadsworth, 1990).

Stevens, Ellen S., "Making Sense of Usefulness: An Avenue Toward Satisfaction in Later Life," *International Journal of Aging and Human Development*, 37, no. 4 (1993), 313–25.

Togonu-Bickersteth, Funmi, "Age Identification Among Yoruba Aged," *Journal of Gerontology*, 41, no. 1 (January 1986), 110–13.

Turner, Ralph H., "The Real Self: From Institution to Impulse," *American Journal of Sociology*, 81, no. 5 (March 1976), 989–1016.

Turner, Ralph H., "Role Taking: Process versus Conformity," in *Human Behavior and Social Processes*, ed. Arnold M. Rose (Boston: Houghton Mifflin Company, 1962), 20–40.

Ward, Russell A., "The Impact of Subjective Age and Stigma on Older Persons," *Journal of Gerontology*, 32, no. 2 (March 1977), 227–32.

5

The Emergence of Social Theories of Old Age

INTRODUCTION

The development and application of social theories of aging by gerontologists in the social sciences have been a very important part of gerontology. These kinds of theorizing activities have helped us to better comprehend the meaning of the many aging-related social problems, as well as the potentially positive aspects of aging. They have also provided many vital insights into how to deal with and even solve many of the problems, both at a societal and a personal level.

Scientific interest in the social aspects of aging is almost exclusively a twentieth-century phenomenon, and much of the early scientific work has lacked a theoretical base. Furthermore, indications are that most of the theoretical work that has been done among social scientists has been initiated in the United States and has only recently begun to be applied cross-culturally. Even the cross-cultural work has been initiated by American scholars. Furthermore, Maddox and Campbell point out that even the social scientific research that has been done and reported internationally has been "national rather than comparative" (Maddox and Campbell, 1985). To understand the important contributions that social theories of aging have made to gerontology, therefore, we must begin first by examining the contexts in which the various social theories have emerged in America, and then examine their cross-cultural adequacy.

Special attention began to be paid to this area of gerontology in the United States during the 1950s. Throughout that decade, U. S. citizens became

increasingly aware and alarmed that the social lives of the aged were changing. It appeared that the elderly were becoming socially isolated and concomi-
tantly seemed to be losing their sense of purpose and self-worth. There seemed
to be no ready or adequate explanations for this, but deep concern for older
people began to pervade society as a whole. There was an underlying suspi-
cion that the rest of society must be at fault, and something of a societal guilt
complex seems to have been partly behind the widespread concern. For example, as a young college student at that time, traveling to and from college, I
often stopped to have a picnic lunch at the park in one of the many small mid-
western towns through which I passed. Typically, I would observe groups of
retired elderly men sitting on the park benches with seemingly nothing to do.
They may have, in fact, been enjoying themselves but in my mind, at the time,
they were to be pitied because of what society was obviously doing to them.

Social gerontology began to develop as a discipline of study during that
era. It became the task of this new discipline to study and provide scientific
explanations for the disturbing phenomena related to aging. As a result of the
work done by social gerontologists from that time until the present, a number
of different and often conflicting theories of aging have been offered as explanations of the social and psychological losses that tended to accompany old
age.

THE GENERATION OF THEORIES IN SOCIAL GERONTOLOGY

The generating of theories of aging since the 1950s has in itself been something of a social process. In a recent article describing the context of the generation of gerontological theory, Hendricks describes it as "part and parcel" of
the particular intellectual milieu in which individual social scientists are
involved. He contends that generating theory, as much as anything, is part of
the process of career building, and that the particular type of theory that an
individual generates depends upon that person's training and the particular
intellectual milieu of which he or she is a part. He provides ample evidence of
the truth of that point (Hendricks, 1992).

More importantly for this analysis, though, is that generating social
gerontological theories is a process that has been very much related to the
changing perceptions of aging and to the social policies related to aging that
have been developed. It has, on the one hand, reflected the changing perceptions and policies of old age and, on the other hand, contributed to those definitions and policies. As the Hendrickses have written about social gerontologists in their earlier textbook, "The crucial dimensions of their conceptual
frameworks are but reflections from the larger social matrix. At the same time,
however, gerontologists strive to reach beyond the world of common sense to
discover consistent patterns of aging in the social world" (Hendricks and
Hendricks, 1979). The theories that have emerged, then, must be analyzed,
not so much as purely scientific work that provides factual explanations, but
more realistically as an integral part of the changing phenomena of aging. In
that sense, then, a comparative look at the major theories of aging and the
social milieu out of which they have risen is an important aspect of the study
of aging in modern society.

It is important here to understand what is meant by theory. The term *theory* is used in two somewhat different ways by social scientists. In one way, it is used synonymously with paradigms. For sociologists, these amount to world views, or more specifically descriptions of what we believe societies are and how they work. Each paradigm or theory emphasizes one aspect of social life which its adherents believe in as the most important factor that needs no explanation but explains the other aspects of social life (i.e., social conflict, social structure, social interaction, social exchange). The particular theory that individuals adopt as their orientation is more a matter of their belief systems or ideologies than the result of scientific evidence. In part, it may be a matter of what they see as the theory that tends to explain the most about social life.

The other meaning of the term theory is that which is made up of sets of specific hypotheses to be tested by scientific research. These theories are used to discover the causes of certain social phenomena, such as the disengagement patterns of elderly people. Not surprisingly, these theories are typically developed from and are based on the paradigms to which the individual investigators are oriented. Structural Functionalists typically use hypotheses that have to do with social structure, for example. Therefore, some of the research of social gerontology has reflected the various sociological paradigms.

Estes and her colleagues argue that social gerontology has been dominated by what they label as the "reigning paradigms" (Estes, Binney, and Culbertson, 1992). They identify these as (1) functionalism and neo-functionalism, which they describe as "rooted in American traditions of individualism, self-reliance, and independence, and posits that cohesion and social harmony are 'natural'"; and (2) biomedicine, which they contend is "based on the notion that there is a biological basis" for understanding what aging is all about. They see these as ideologies that perpetuate the status quo about how aging is defined and the kinds of research that are funded and undertaken. Thus, "gerontological imagination," which they see as vital to the generation of good gerontological theory, has continuously been stymied.

These are important criticisms of gerontology, even though there seem to be some points of confusion and overemphasis in them. To be sure, individualism, self-reliance, and independence are dominant American traditions that have an impact on the elderly. It is difficult to understand how structural functionalism is rooted in those traditions, however. It is also somewhat unfair to assume that all structural functionalists approach that theory as a practicing ideology. Irving Rosow, for example, did not believe that the plight of the elderly, as he depicted it from a structural functionalist perspective, was either right or desirable. Nevertheless, structural functionalism as a paradigm does indeed emphasize social harmony and continues to analyze elements of the social world, such as aging, from that perspective and certainly does have the effect of promoting the status quo.

Even though it is somewhat legitimate to say that structural functionalism has dominated the field of social gerontology, it is not the only sociological theory upon which social gerontological theories have been based. Others have also prominently influenced the development of gerontological theory either by the direct or indirect application of each theory's points of emphasis. These include (1) symbolic interactionist theory, (2) exchange theory, (3) developmental theory, and (4) conflict theory.

Estes and her team of analysts also criticize the field of gerontology for what they call a "crisis mentality" which has prevailed. Dealing with and attempting to correct immediate individual age-related problems with little or no theoretical basis have also served to stymie the generation of general theories of aging, according to them (Estes, Binney, and Culbertson, 1992). Undoubtedly, this is also a legitimate criticism. Nevertheless, the puzzling and pressing problems related to aging, particularly those representing a variety of types of losses, have provided the major impetus for the development of gerontological theories. Therefore, any analysis of the emergence of social theories of aging must take into account both the problems being addressed and the theoretical perspectives of those who have generated the theories.

Hendricks' assessment of the history of the development of social gerontological theory shows how both of those factors are important to consider (Hendricks, 1992). He depicts the process of theory development as a critical dialogue between theorists, moving through the Hegalian dialectical process of thesis, antithesis, and synthesis. In social gerontology, the theoretical *thesis* emerged in the 1960s with an emphasis on the problem of disengagement and activity. He points out that both functionalists and symbolic interactionists provided theoretical analyses of this problem, and that both "looked at the dynamics of adjustment in terms of individual-level attributes." The theoretical *antithesis* took place in social gerontology in the late 1960s and early 1970s, with an emphasis on what was obviously also a growing problem among the aged—the loss of status. Theorists in that stage of theory development turned away from analyses of individual behavior, which were seen as too reductionist, to an almost exclusive emphasis on social structures. Subsequently, the *synthesis* stage of theory development has been emerging since the mid-1970s, with a concern about why people age so differently. According to Hendricks, during this period there has been a growing recognition of the importance of both structure and the individual. As he puts it, "a synthetic view of the situation of the elderly as a composite of his ongoing relationship with society underlies this third generation of theoretical formulations" (Hendricks, 1992).

As this shows, theory development in social gerontology is a matter of dealing with particular emerging issues related to aging as well as the paradigms from which theories come. The following analysis of gerontological theory development will take both of those influences into account. It will also assess the implications of and actual influences that each theory has had on the development of social policies on aging.

THEORIES ON DISENGAGEMENT AND OTHER LOSSES

For over a decade, from the late 1950s and into the 1970s, the social theories of aging concentrated almost exclusively on such social and psychological losses as disengagement, low self-esteem, and decreased life satisfaction.

In the attempts by social gerontologists to find answers to the puzzling questions about these issues, several potentially causal factors became the focus of research. Such obvious contributors to disengagement as physical impairment, mental disorders, and loss of income were repeatedly researched, with the result that it became generally well established that these were indeed major causes. It was soon assumed, however, that the physical, mental and material variables alone could not account for all losses among the aged. Sociocultural and psychological variables such as loss of roles and relations, self-concepts, and personality were, therefore, also investigated. Largely on the basis of these investigations, the major social theories of aging were developed.

When social gerontology began to become an important area of study for social scientists, research was basically descriptive in nature and lacked the discipline of explicit or formalized theory. Most of the social scientists who became interested in aging were involved in providing answers to the practical problems elderly persons faced, often working under the stringent guidelines of a government grant. It soon became clear, however, that the practical answers they provided tended to be based on quite definite theoretical assumptions. One set of these assumptions was later more clearly defined and stated as one of the major social gerontological theories. Since then it has been defended, changed, and even quite severely challenged as other more formalized theories were offered and defended as viable explanations of the social aspects of aging. While the social gerontological theories that have been developed attempted to provide explanations of the losses older people were experiencing, they also sometimes tended to reflect the particular theoretical orientations of those early investigators.

Activity Theory

The early years of the study of aging were somewhat void of formal theory. Investigators were more concerned with solving such problems experienced by elderly people as low levels of happiness, little sense of usefulness, isolation, and inadequate adjustment to life in general (Burgess, 1953–54), than with developing theories of aging. Nevertheless, the work that was done concerning those problems soon became recognized as being consistently based on the underlying assumption that the elderly have the same social and psychological needs to be active as younger adults. This notion was especially emphasized by Burgess, Havighurst, and Tobin at the University of Chicago in the 1950s and was subsequently termed *activity theory* (Havighurst, Neugarten, and Tobin, 1968). According to this theory, remaining active was the key to maintain happy, useful, and successfully adjusting to life in general in old age (Havighurst, Neugarten, and Tobin, 1968).

This was a theory that obviously had very little to do with the theoretical perspectives of the primary investigators. Rather, the major emphasis was a common-sense solution to a major problem. The assumption that elderly people need to remain active was certainly not an original idea with the theorists. It very much fit what most Americans at that time believed and were concerned about in behalf of the elderly people being observed (Matras, 1990, p. 205). It was thus not an empirically established, scientifically tested, or proven theory that had cross-cultural validity. Instead it was a quite popular assumption on which actions in behalf of the aged were being strongly proposed in this country at that time. It did, however, directly influence a major policy effort on behalf of older people at that time. Due to the influence of this theory and in preparation for the 1991 White House Conference on Aging, Arnold Rose at the University of Minnesota was given a research demonstration grant by the federal government to establish senior citizen activity centers in both urban and rural communities throughout the state of Minnesota. The purpose of this program was to study the effects of providing that kind of opportunities to keep the elderly active (Rose, 1963). The results of this and other similar projects in the United States at that time was that establishing activity centers in communities across this country became a major goal of the Older Americans Act in 1965. As characterized by Estes and colleagues, "activity theory lends support to policies that assist in the social integration of the aged" (Estes, Binney, and Culbertson, 1992).

Despite the popular acceptance of this theory and substantial evidence that such social psychological factors as lack of a sense of self-worth were indeed related to low levels of activity (Tobin and Neugarten, 1961), it could not be adequately established that the relationship between those variables was a directly causal one or that the theory was an adequate solution to the problems. Even though there were positive results from the establishment of activity centers for many elderly, the theory turned out to be rather weak as an adequately comprehensive explanation of disengagement and personal loss among the aged. It failed to have the practical results that were anticipated. If the assumption of the theory, that inactivity causes these problems, was sound, then providing opportunities for them to become active in activity centers should have attracted most of the elderly, especially those who had become the most inactive. Yet, not even a majority of the elderly population were reached as participants of activity centers even among the most isolated (Evans and Brown, 1970, pp. 6–8; Moen, 1978). At this point in time we can think of a number of possible reasons that some of the elderly would choose not to participate in activity center programs, but those reasons were not included as activity theory assumptions.

The inadequacy of activity theory was its failure to consider a number of important issues. First, it failed to ask whether or not inactivity among the aged was voluntary on their part or involuntarily thrust upon them. Second, it failed to distinguish among the various types of activities that may have been available to elderly persons and to assess which did and did not provide meaningful roles to perform in later life. Third, it failed to consider the possibility that the activities that middle-aged people value may not be what elderly people value. As Atchley explains, "ample evidence shows that some of the decline in activity levels with age is the result of a desire by older people to have a more relaxed approach to activities" (Atchley, 1991, p. 264). Larson and colleagues found that elderly people with ample opportunities to be as socially active as they wanted to be, in fact, chose and were satisfied to be alone much more of their time each day than younger people. They did not prefer isolation but they enjoyed a surprising amount of solitude (Larson, Zuzanek, and Mannell, 1985). Fourth, it failed to consider what level of activity may be desirable for the aged. Fifth, it failed to analyze the processes of becoming inactive in old age in order to discover the major causal factors of inactivity among the aged.

Disengagement Theory

After a decade in which it had become apparent to most Americans that many of the aged were becoming socially isolated and psychologically troubled, there was an obvious need for some kind of comprehensive explanation to

alleviate some of the national guilt attached to that awareness. Such an explanation was provided by Cumming and Henry in their book entitled, *Growing
Old: The Process of Disengagement*, in which they outlined their *disengagement
theory* (Cumming and Henry, 1961, pp. 210–18). If it had been accepted, it
would have gone a long way toward alleviating the sense of responsibility that
many Americans felt about the plight of older citizens.

Cumming and Henry's book was also a report of an extensive study of
the social lives of the aged conducted in the Kansas City area. Thus, their theory was dignified by the claim of having a solid empirical basis. In analyzing
the validity of the theory, though, it must be realized that it was as much a
product of their structural functionalist frame of reference as it was of the
empirical data they cited as support for the theory. Even though it addressed
the specific age-related problem of disengagement, this was a theory that was
influenced more by the theoretical orientation of the theorists than by the problem that needed to be solved. This was a theory which neatly reflected the
structural functionalist idea that the best way to understand society is to think
of it as a living organism. It is made up of many different working parts that
function harmoniously for the survival and equilibrium of the society as a
whole. There may be situations that seem to be problematic to individuals, but
the ultimate concern is whether that situation is "functional" to society as a
whole. If so, in the final analysis, it also benefits the individuals involved.

Directly challenging the assumptions of activity theory—that elderly
persons have the same need to be active as others—Cumming and Henry contended that social disengagement for the aged is socially and psychologically
functional and a natural part of the processes of aging. As people age, according to their theory, their most basic social psychological needs change from
that of active involvement to that of inactive contemplation about the meaning of life in the face of impending death. This change is mutually advantageous to both society and the aged themselves. For the aged, it means the
opportunity to retreat from the demands of society and quietly contemplate
the meaning of life and death. For the society as a whole, it provides a way to
partially alleviate part of the social psychological trauma of the impairment
and inevitable death of elderly people. By implication, the contention of the
theory is that disengagement is inevitable, typically gradual, and preferred by
and satisfying to the aged. Another implication of this theory was that it
applies universally, and therefore cross-culturally, to all aged persons.

The practical and social policy implications of disengagement theory in
the United States should have been clear. If, as Cumming and Henry proposed, the social and psychological needs of the aged are quite different from
those of the rest of the population, and disengagement is natural and preferred, then feeling guilty about the inactivity of the aged would be useless.
To attempt to keep them active would actually be counterproductive for both
the aged and the society as a whole. The condition of social isolation among
the aged, then, was not something to try to change or about which to despair
but rather was something that ought to be accepted and even encouraged.

Disengagement theory very quickly became well known among gerontologists, but it was accepted and supported by almost none of them. It represented the first comprehensive and definitive social theory of aging, and for
that it was respected. Most social gerontologists simply did not believe it,
however, despite the empirical data the authors provided to support it. In

effect, it became the theoretical orientation for virtually all theorists for many years, primarily because it was the theory to challenge and try to disprove. Many who did the challenging did so with some moral indignation and passion. It was as though we as industrious and socially active Americans could not bring ourselves to believe that social isolation and noninvolvement were right or acceptable for any one, regardless of what evidence there might be to support such an argument. It seemed much better to admit that the condition of old age in the United States was abnormal, to accept the blame, and to do all we could to alleviate the problem. It should have been an explanation that gave societal reassurance about our aged, but it seemed to do precisely the opposite.

The explanation provided by disengagement theory did have verification, as well as nonacceptance problems, however. Cumming and Henry failed to provide adequate evidence that the aged actually prefer to disengage or that they are even satisfied with conditions of disengagement, as the two theorists implied would be true. They also failed to adequately establish that all people do, as they contended, naturally and gradually disengage as they move into old age. Although the statistical analysis of their cross-sectional data made it appear to be a gradual process, subsequent analyses of the actual experiences of the aged have shown that it is socially abrupt and psychologically disturbing process. Furthermore, by no means do all older people disengage (Brown, 1974; Tallman and Kutner 1970). The theory has also been criticized as being simply inadequate as a social theory of aging. As Maddox and Campbell noted, "The theory tended toward biological reductionism and hence dealt inadequately with both the social context of aging and the personal meaning of aging" (Maddox and Campbell, 1985).

Despite the claim that it was universal in scope, disengagement theory has also been criticized because it is culturally bound to the situation of the aged in the United States. In fact, analyses of the theory have been made in at least two other countries, and it was found to be largely invalid in each case because of different cultural characteristics. Simic found, for example, that disengagement simply was not a social pattern among the aged in Yugoslavia. He attributed the difference to the very different socialization patterns in the two countries. According to him, Americans are socialized throughout their lives toward "self-realization, independence, and individualism," all of which are apt to separate the generations and lead to social isolation, especially among elderly people. In contrast, Yugoslavians are socialized toward "kinship corporacy, interdependence, and familial symbiosis and reciprocity," all of which tend to ensure continued intergenerational relationships throughout life (Simic, 1977).

Vatuk studied disengagement in India, where the culture itself tends to emphasize old age as a time of inactivity, or when "one should be able to sit back and let oneself be cared for by others" and when one can disassociate oneself "from direct involvement in the management and direction of household affairs." Presumably disengagement theory ought to apply there if any place. In fact, it was found that elderly people in India typically had personal problems adjusting to the societal expectations of becoming inactive and relinquishing authority, and that their overall levels of social participation did not decline (Vatuk, 1980).

Loss of Major Life Roles Theory

What might be called the *loss of major roles theory* clearly fit the prevailing societal attitude of the early 1960s in the United States much better than did disengagement theory. While the loss of major life roles has never been clearly defined as a theory, it was a major theoretical and socially accepted theme during that time. It emerged in the early 1960s and remained a dominant emphasis for more than a decade.

The loss of major life roles is one of the main explanatory factors developed as a direct challenge to the disengagement theory. It implied that certain social trends and socioeconomic policies of that time were to blame for the existing conditions of the aged. This seemed to be the kind of moral indictment in which the majority of Americans tended to believe and which they were ready to accept. Once again, it is obvious that the issue of the disengagement itself rather than the theoretical orientations of the theorists motivated them to become involved. Symbolic interactionists and structural functionalists alike contributed to the development of the loss of roles theory.

Advocates of this theory challenged the basic assumptions of disengagement theory—that social withdrawal was a natural process of aging and that it was basically satisfying to those who become disengaged. Rather, they claimed, disengagement was a form of behavior imposed upon the aged as a consequence of societal goals in which older citizens were systematically and abruptly denied a part. The result was a severe loss in life satisfaction. Disengagement and the personal losses that tended to be related to it were not primarily a matter of being inactive, as stressed by activity theory. More importantly, the crux of the problem was the loss of those roles in life that provide people with meaning, purpose, and identity.

Specifically, Rose claimed that the policy of compulsory retirement meant that those who retired were suddenly cut off from their major life roles in society—that of employee. By then, compulsory retirement was the policy of virtually all employers in the United States, including the federal government. According to Rose, this was a serious loss, not merely because of the loss of the work role, but also because of its derivative effects on auxiliary roles such as club member and community leader. Typically, personnel for these auxiliary roles were recruited from the ranks of major role participants and almost never from among retirees. The loss of employee roles almost inevitably meant the loss of the auxiliary roles as well. While Rose did not clarify why that kind of role loss should necessarily take place, his research at that time showed that it did take place (Rose, 1965a). At that time Rose was one of the leading symbolic interactionists in the country, and he expressed his desire to apply that theory to the field of gerontology. Yet, it is difficult to distinguish his definition of "roles" from that of Rosow (described below), who was a structural functionalist (Rose, 1965a).

Rosow made a similar point about loss of major life roles a few years later in his book *Socialization to Old Age* (Rosow, 1974, pp. 162–72). Socialization, he said, is the process of society's assigning status (social positions) to its members and outlining the role specifications for those status positions. With the major source of status in our society still being one's occupation and the work that one does, he said, status among the aged is so minor and unimportant that few, if any, roles are specified for them. He contended that they have status of sorts, but that theirs is essentially a roleless status. That was something of the same point Burgess had previously made by referring to old age as a "roleless role" (Burgess, 1960, pp. 352–60). Leisure activities, which had sometimes been mentioned as a possible new source of status for the aged, Rosow claimed, represented not a separate source of status but simply a reward for work. Leisure activities provide prestige only if one's work status is high enough for a person to claim leisure as a part-time reward, according to Rosow. He also made the point that elderly women suffer the loss of roles and fulfilling identity not only when their specific housewife roles decline but even more so as their husbands retire, since their identity is closely related to their husbands' work roles.

Havighurst, Neugarten and Tobin, in arguing against disengagement theory, made the point not only that disengagement is a matter of a lack of role participation among the aged but also that dissatisfaction is a typical correlate of the lack of role activity (Havighurst, Neugarten, and Tobin, 1968). Maddox also found, in studying the relationship between role activity and satisfaction of the elderly, that those who had the least amount of activity were generally the least satisfied with life (Maddox, 1970b).

Lopata made the case that culturally determined loss of major life roles was also applicable to elderly women. She pointed out that at that time most women thought of themselves as housewives. This meant that as their children left home or their husbands retired—typically quite abrupt occurrences in their lives—women's housewife roles suddenly declined in importance and involved them in fewer related community activities. The result of what she called the "life cycle of the social role of the housewife," that typically left women as widows, was that there were no role expectations left for them to perform. They were no longer expected to participate in any of the activities typically related to the housewife role (Lopata, 1966). According to these analysts, then, disengagement and loss of life satisfaction for both men and women resulted from culturally forced loss of those major life roles that tended to provide identity, purpose, and meaning to their lives. Lopata was also a symbolic interactionist whose definition of roles complemented the structural functional definition.

The emphasis on the loss of major life roles as the primary causal factor of disengagement and loss of life satisfaction served to point up the influence that cultural factors seemed to have on these matters. The advocates of this theoretical position convincingly argued that disengagement is much more than a simple lack of activities. They also offered persuasive evidence that quite successfully challenged the notion that disengagement was a natural process preferred by the elderly themselves (Rose, 1965a).

In recent years, Atchley has challenged Rosow's contention that there is nothing to which to socialize the aged, and that the loss of roles results in depression, anxiety, and anomie for the older person. Atchley contends that the role of retired person is not as vague as Rosow claimed. He points out that some retirement roles can be anticipated and prepared for while others are quite successfully negotiated (Atchley, 1991, pp. 119–21).

There is undoubtedly some truth to Atchley's argument that socialization for the aged is not so much toward "packaged" roles as is true for younger people. In part at least, the differences between Rosow's and Atchley's arguments may well be the products of change over time, however. In the early years of mandatory retirement policies in the United States, the loss of major life roles seems to have been very real and quite devastating to many retirees, both personally and socially as well as economically. However, this theory ignored the possibility, as discussed in Chapter 4, that retirement might become institutionalized and that new societal expectations, new roles, and new opportunities for social interaction in old age might develop. Corrective action stemming from the theory itself undoubtedly helped to make disengagement much less culturally forced than it once was and much less of a social problem.

That many elderly people suffered greatly and unfairly from the loss of major life roles became a widely accepted idea during the l960s and 1970s, and there was much concern that something should be done about that problem. Consequently, providing "meaningful roles" for the aged became one of many goal areas that were discussed and for which recommendations for congressional action were made. The result was that the federal government established, and allocated funding for, a number of programs to provide volunteer and paid work opportunities. These included the Retired Senior Volunteer Program (RSVP), Service Corps of Retired Executives (SCORE), Foster Grandparents, the Senior Companion Program, and Title VII of the Older Americans' Act. Volunteerism became an important source of meaningful and fulfilling social roles and personal satisfaction for many retired people. Thus, the loss of major life roles theory tends to be a much weaker theory today than it once was, even in the United States.

The weakness of the loss of major life roles theory is made especially clear when it is applied cross-culturally. Loss of major roles does seem to take place in India. As previously noted, elderly people are expected to eventually relinquish their authoritative work and household roles to those in the next generation. Difficult as it may be for individuals to give up those roles, however, the process apparently does not result in social withdrawal or personal loss (Vatuk, 1980). In the People's Republic of China, there seems to be no pattern of role loss. While retirement at relatively early ages is becoming common, there seems to be no net loss of roles as a result. Instead, socially important and personally meaningful roles are readily available both in the family and the community (Davis-Friedmann, 1983, pp. 80–84). In conversations with officials at the China National Committee on Aging in 1993, I was informed that elderly Chinese still perform authoritative and meaningful roles in their communities in spite of the many social and economic changes currently taking place in that country today. Schweitzer also found that, among two native American tribes in Oklahoma, the roles of elderly tribal members are especially prestigious and powerful. They are culturally functional roles that also keep the elders socially active (Schweitzer, 1983).

The loss of major life roles theory was clearly both time bound and culturally bound. It was at least partially valid during the 1960s in America, but it was less valid as time passed and in other cultures. Nevertheless, the emphasis on this theory did have an effect on how Americans thought of retirement and the conditions of the elderly in general. Aging and retiring became experiences that many Americans came to dread, even though a sizable majority of those who were retired, even in the 1960s, claimed to enjoy retirement and to be highly satisfied with life in old age. This discrepancy in how retired people and others judge old age and retirement still exists today.

Continuity Theory

Some U.S. gerontologists were still unwilling to believe that all of the aged were either willing to disengage or forced to disengage and lose their sense of purpose in life. The evidence indicated that many elderly people did not inevitably disengage as they aged. Many others did so simply as a continuation of "tendencies toward inactivity" that had been established earlier in their lives. Some theorists concluded that neither activity theory, disengagement theory, nor loss of major life roles theory adequately accounted for how people tended to experience old age. Instead, they looked at people's lifetime of experiences and self-perceptions to try to explain the extent to which successful adjustment was part of an individual's old age experience and developed what they called *continuity theory*. Their contention was that the reason that some elderly people disengaged while others did not was that the personalities and lifelong behavioral tendencies of each group influenced them to do one or the other. Some had tendencies to be active, while others had tendencies toward social noninvolvement. Whether people disengaged in old age, then, was due simply to the continuation of these tendencies throughout the life course.

Continuity theory does not seem to be closely related to any of the major theoretical perspectives or put forward by strong proponents of any of those theories. For example, those who have explained the theory come from a variety of theoretical and work backgrounds. It could, in general, be considered a developmental theory but, more than anything, it seems to represent an emergent set of common-sense ideas that have come together over time to counter the commonly held belief that disengagement and poor adjustments to aging were major problems among elderly people and specifically to refute the assumptions of disengagement theory. Atchley has pointed out that "Over the years, various bits and pieces of an alternative perspective called Continuity Theory have appeared" (Atchley, 1989).

When the basic ideas were first introduced as worth considering, it too should have been popular among Americans because it had the potential of alleviating the societal sense of responsibility of causing the commonly perceived problems of isolation and loss of morale among the aged. It basically argued that aging had little or nothing to do with such problems. In the early 1960s Videbeck and Knox were among the first to express concern about continuity. They studied the patterns of social participation of 1,500 adults between the ages of 21 and 69 in the state of Nebraska. Specifically, they examined participation behavior tendencies that were similar on the part of adults of all of the age groups they studied, and which they assumed were "learned" by individuals from their lifetime of experiences. They labeled those tendencies "pre-dispositions" on the part of elderly to participate socially in ways that were consistent with their lifetime patterns. They found that the low levels of social participation on the part of the elderly persons in the sample were primarily true of those with predispositions toward that kind of social behavior, and they concluded that disengagement was totally unrelated to aging as such (Videbeck and Knox, 1965). In 1970, Maddox also reported the importance of considering "the persistence of a lifestyle" when studying the patterns of disengagement (Maddox, 1970a). Neither of these authors used the term *continuity*, nor did they claim that their findings represented a theory of aging, but the assumptions on which they based their conclusions were precisely those that became central to continuity theory. In 1981 Covey tried to explain what continuity theory was about and in doing so explained that lifelong experiences creating "certain predispositions" for social behavior in old age, for example. The extent to which continuity can actually be considered to be a viable theory has been raised. This was addressed in a footnote in Covey's article reportedly about a comment by one of the transcript reviewers (not identified). The reviewer suggested that continuity might better be thought of as an "ideal type" that could be used as a valuable critique of other theories of aging, rather than "a testable theory." Covey and others have made a convincing argument that the kinds of continuity they have outlined indeed do exist. After interviewing many elderly people and letting them "talk about themselves," Kaufman testifies to the fact that "they express a sense of self that is ageless—an identity that maintains continuity despite the physical and social changes that come with old age" (Kaufman, 1993). Nevertheless, there is nothing in the so-called theory that adequately explains their existence. For example, Covey raised the question of what accounts for older persons' success or failure to maintain social roles in old age, and why some do and other do not. His answer was that it basically depends upon how their social environments are structured, that is, the extent to which they are restrictive about social activity and strictly adhere to age-grading practices (Covey, 1981). The problem with that is that, if societal structures determine successful or unsuccessful continuity, then social structure, not continuity itself is the explanatory factor. Atchley (1989) later tried to overcome that problem by defining continuity as having both internal and external components, with the latter having to do with the individual's perceptions of the structure of their social environments, but it still represents an outside influence. Even though he legitimately claims that relatively few elderly have serious problems dealing with the many changes they face, he admits that some do. Continuity is undoubtedly a factor in understanding how most people are able to cope with those changes, and theories of aging ought to take that into account, but it is logically very difficult to understand how continuity explains why some do not cope. Do they have no continuity to draw upon? Gelfand (1994, p. 5) is willing to consider the possibility that continuity is possible among minority people and those of different ethnic backgrounds but believes that some "ethic values may be discontinuous with their past." Atchley admits that there can be "too little continuity," "optimum continuity," and "too much continuity" (Atchley, 1989), but what is not clear is how much is too much or too little and how those variances are accounted for (Fry, 1992).

Fry asks what the implications of continuity theory are for counseling psychologists. Her answer to that question is that coping skills ought to be taught to the elderly (Fry, 1992). In that suggestion, however, she seems to miss the major point of the theory. The overriding assumption of continuity theory is that continuity is not something that can be taught but is acquired in a lifetime of experience. Atchley, for example, makes the point that "Continuity Theory would lead us to expect that neither psychotherapy nor self-help books would sell well among older people and this is indeed the case" (Atchley, 1989). According to him, the reason for that is that part of what psychotherapy is about is trying to change identities that they see as problematic among those being counseled. Some elderly people may indeed need to learn coping skills, but that is not an implication that can be drawn from continuity theory.

An interesting point about continuity theory is that, even though it had little if any influence on either the development of theories on aging or social policies on aging when it was first proposed, it has gained respect in recent years. Atchley, for example, has become a strong advocate and articulator of the theory, having written articles explaining it (1971, 1989) and defended it in his textbook on aging (1991, pp. 103–9, 259–67). It is also now discussed in most other sociology of aging textbooks. Given the number of criticisms of continuity as a viable theory (Fry, 1992, pp. 282–83; Hooyman and Kiyak, 1991, pp. 86–87) and that it does not really apply to the problematic aspects of aging, why has it become a somewhat popular theory? Perhaps the message that most elderly people tend to have enough of their own individual coping mechanisms to adjust to old age is more acceptable today, when those in politics are increasingly calling for cutbacks in programs that serve the elderly.

Socially Disruptive Events Theory

Disengagement is an issue that seems to have declined in importance in recent years. The problem was probably never as widespread as it seemed to be, and programs have been developed and somewhat successfully implemented to alleviate the problem for many elderly people. Nevertheless, disengagement and the loss of self-esteem still prevail on the part of many elderly people. Therefore, the challenge to gerontological theorists is to provide a more generic explanation for this phenomenon than those provided by the previously discussed theories, and one that would have validity over time.

Evidence for such a theory, which most appropriately could be called *socially disruptive events theory,* was produced in research carried out in the late 1960s and early 1970s in two unrelated projects. Research done by Tallman and Kutner showed a clear and strong association between disengagement and what they described as "the stresses of aging" (Tallman and Kutner, 1970). In research carried out by this author a few years later (Brown, 1974), it was discovered that disengagement was related to a number of different events (especially loss of spouse, loss of physical capacity, and retirement) that tended to be severely disruptive of elderly people's lives. It was found that the experience of even one of these events typically resulted in disengagement that was often severe immediately following the event but that eventually tended to be reversed. The accumulation of a number of these events in a short period of time (a pattern more and more prevalent with increasing age), however, almost universally resulted in relatively permanent disengagement and an accompanying loss of morale and sense of self-worth.

The development of this theory obviously emerged out of a concern about disengagement and other problems that were thought to be related to that process, as was true of most of the theories in that time. It also clearly reflected the assumptions of the symbolic interactionist perspective, however, in that the one basic concept of the theory, socially disruptive events, is a product of the interaction processes in which elderly people are involved.

This point becomes clear with an account of how my own research became focused on the issue of the loss of spouse. I had observed a situation, for which there was no easy explanation, of two or three old downtown hotels being filled with individual elderly, most of whom were widowed, living in almost total isolation. They hardly ever even interacted with each other, and that was what I found hardest to understand. In the process of doing open-ended interviews with elderly people of all kinds, I asked one very active widowed lady why she thought that situation existed. She responded with the story of her own experience of dealing with the death of her husband and having to begin living as a widow. She explained that she and her husband had been married for fifty-some years and that almost all of their social lives had become oriented to interacting with other married couples. One illustration she gave of that was being part of a bridge club made up of couples their own age. Talking in the second person, as a way of depersonalizing her story, she said,

> One day you suddenly lose your spouse and go through a time of grief and mourning. But then one day you decide you have to get on with life, so you decide to get back with all of your friends. You go back to bridge club where you have had such close friends, but you feel uncomfortable and a bit out of place. You decide that it's just a matter of getting used to being alone, though, and so you go back again assuming that your friends will help you through that difficult time. But the second time is worse than the first and the third is worse still. You increasingly feel out of place with the very people who have been your best friends. Finally you quit going and find yourself all alone with no one to whom to turn who understands what life as a widow is like, and you become afraid to interact with anyone.

What she was telling me was that the loss of spouse is typically a socially disruptive event that is often extremely difficult from which to recover.

Later while visiting with a middle-aged family friend whose husband had suddenly died, I told her this story and of my conclusions from it about the elderly. When I finished, she looked at me excitedly and said, "For the first time since Lyle died someone understands what I am going through." She had by that time changed her whole social life to the consternation of most of her former friends and had been frustrated by their consternation.

From the perspective of socially disruptive events, disengagement is neither totally voluntary and satisfying, as Cumming and Henry assumed, nor totally forced by social processes as other theories assumed. Rather, it stems from the types of social interaction processes that the aged experience as a result of the disruptive events in their lives. Dissatisfying as it may be, it is part of the social order that is negotiated and accepted in their interactions with others who are associated with those disruptive events (Marshall, 1978–79). Specifically, when one's social life is severely disrupted in a number of different ways in a brief period of time, relationships with others not only change but also tend to become strained and personally disturbing, and social withdrawal becomes the most appropriate response. Once the pattern of disengagement becomes established, it tends to become part of one's social order and becomes increasingly difficult to alter, even though it is not a pre- ferred lifestyle for most people. These are the types of elderly people who are deliberately targeted for recruitment as senior companions in the Senior Com- panion Programs all across the United States. They are extremely hard to find and recruit because they tend to be very isolated. Most of them respond only through some kind of personal contact. Once they are in the program they find, in their words "a new lease on life" (Brown and others, 1991). The Senior Companion Program was formed precisely to reach those kinds of people. Participation in the program changes their whole social lives. Such rehabilita- tion programs as Senior Companion do not fully correct the problem of disen- gagement, however, since elderly people continue to experience socially disruptive events.

The validity of this theory clearly is not confined to the unique cultural experiences of a given time. It provides an explanation of disengagement, when it occurs, that would be valid across time, since it is based on experi- ences especially typical of older persons. As was the case with the others discussed, however, this theory is limited as a comprehensive theory of aging because it, too, focuses on a specific issue and applies to only a small per- centage of older people.

Reconstruction Theory

The rather persuasive belief that the elderly have been unfairly treated in American society and that being old is essentially a negative social experience persisted into and throughout much of the 1970s. Another theory, empha- sizing the impact of labeling processes on old people, was developed in the early part of that decade. It elaborated on the negative aspects of old age even more than did the theories emphasizing socially disruptive events and the loss of major life roles.

Kuypers and Bengtson, the proponents of this theory, which they titled *reconstruction theory*, borrowed Zusman's social breakdown syndrome model of mental illness (Zusman, 1966) to explain the situation of the aged in modern society. The elderly are quite successfully labeled incompetent, they noted, by both societal and self-labeling processes (Kuypers and Bengtson, 1973). They suggested that the primary sources of that very negative label were role loss, lack of reference groups, and ambiguous normative guidance. These experi- ences, which they contended are typical of the elderly, tend to render old peo- ple vulnerable to society's negative labels.

In developing their theory, Kuypers and Bengtson maintained that the labeling processes applied to elderly people in modern society have been quite effective (see Figure 5–1). They concluded that old people (presumably more than others) tend to become dependent upon external, societally established labels for their identity because they lack significant others in their lives with whom to interact. On this basis, old people internalize society's definitions and expectations of them. This, these theorists contend, leads to a "vicious spiral of negativism."

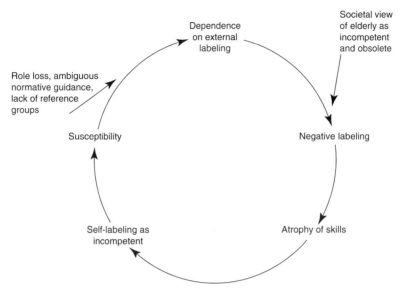

Figure 5–1 System Representation of the Social Breakdown Syndrome as Applied to Old Age, with Negative Inputs from the External Social System (SOURCE: J.A. Kuypers and V. L. Bengston, "Social Breakdown and Competence: A Model of Normal Aging," *Human Development*, 16 (1973), 181–201.)

Kuypers and Bengtson were trying to explain not only disengagement but also the loss of morale and life satisfaction that seemed to be related to social isolation. They elaborated a process that in a sense said what the society already believed: We in the modern society were adding insult to the injury of the experience of being old. We had not only placed the elderly in vulnerable positions, but then we gave them negative labels, which they in their vulnerability tended to internalize as their own perceptions of themselves.

As Kuypers and Bengtson saw it, extensive societal intervention and even quite drastic reconstruction would be necessary to reverse the results of the negative labeling of the aged. Specifically, they called for (1) substantially improving the social services offered to the aged, (2) teaching them how to have better internal control and greater self-confidence, and (3) re-defining the importance of work in society. If labeling, and not sheer survival needs, is the basic problem of the aged, however, one cannot help but wonder how providing further social services would not serve to make them even more, not less, dependent and thus even more vulnerable to the negative labels. Furthermore, the assumption that the aged must be taught by the rest of us to have better internal control and self-confidence would actually seem to be another subtle way of labeling them as incompetent. Ironically, even though these men contended that role loss was part of what makes elderly persons vulnerable to the negative labels, they did not propose the reestablishment of meaningful roles as a way out of the negative dilemma that they described (Kuypers and Bengtson, 1973).

The early 1970s, when reconstruction theory was offered, was probably the culminating time of the negative analysis of old age. At the heart of the 1971 White House Conference on Aging was the desire to do all we could do to overcome the many forms of that negativism. That conference was later described by people preparing for the 1981 White House Conference as covering a "laundry list" of problems associated with being old that needed to be corrected.

Toward the end of the decade of the 1970s, the negative aspects of old age began to be challenged. George's 1980 book, *Role Transition in Later Life*, for example, emphasized the concept of role change rather than role loss. George challenged the negativism of reconstruction theory. She contended that "available evidence suggests that negative self-evaluation in later life is the exception rather than the rule" and that the elderly "meet the demands of personal well-being" and "maintain a positive sense of self" (George, 1980, pp. 41–42). She criticized the social breakdown syndrome (labeling) perspective for not recognizing the importance of what she called "personal resources or coping skills." Crandall also makes the point that individuals can and often do respond differently to the same label (Crandall, 1991, p. 107). As Hewitt explains, "It is important to grasp that individuals do not necessarily or automatically accept the identities that are handed to them." They are often able to reject some unacceptable labels, he says, by "relying on a combination of inner resources, in the form of previously established personal and social identities, and support from others" (Hewitt, 1991, p. 289).

The plight of most of the aged was probably never as negative as Kuypers and Bengtson outlined it. Yet to a very large extent the negative theories were not so much wrong as they were products of the times in which they were conceived. The evidence of later years cited by George does not necessarily disqualify the validity of labeling but only its negative assumptions. The personal resources and coping skills which George discussed but did not even attempt to explain are themselves undoubtedly, at least partially, the products of positive labels that have developed in recent years but that were somewhat missing in the past.

The formation of age-peer groups in recent years is one major source of more positive labels. It is obvious that increasing numbers of exclusively age-related groups and communities are forming and that increasing numbers of the elderly do indeed interact more with each other in those groups than with others. The comparative amount of age-peer interaction itself implies a value preference among those who choose to engage in it and clearly suggests a source of positive labeling and image building. This analysis also suggests the opposite conclusion, that those who choose not to participate in age-related peer interactions are less likely to maintain or reformulate positive self-images.

The labels of "helpless" and "incompetent" are not logically or practically necessary even for the majority of those who are institutionalized. As Kalish has pointed out, becoming dependent in one way does not mean one must become dependent in other ways (Kalish, 1982, pp. 111–12). Most of those in need of long-term physical care are in no way mentally incompetent or incapable of making decisions. Rather, it is the labeling process and policies of long-term care institutions to make decisions for their patients that create conditions of dependency and apparent incompetence among the institutionalized elderly. That long-term care patients can indeed make competent decisions in institutions has been demonstrated by Kutner's environmental therapy program, discussed in Chapter 4, in which chronically ill patients have learned to have some control over their environments (Kutner, 1970).

This analysis of the application of labeling theory to the elderly in the United States today suggests that both negative and positive sources of labeling are present. The negative sources are apparently associated with the ways in which society as a whole tends to respond to the elderly as a group. The positive sources seem to be initiated by the elderly themselves. Ironically, that fact in itself logically refutes the validity of the negative labels that society tends to apply to the elderly. Indeed, aging has been viewed with an increasingly positive emphasis in the United States in recent years. Elderly persons have not only discovered sources of positive labels among themselves, but they, along with a number of gerontologists (Gray Panthers, 1974; Barrow, 1989, pp. 23–40; Comfort, 1976) have also highlighted and challenged what they see as the myths or negative stereotypes of old age.

THEORIES ON THE LOSS OF SOCIAL STATUS

The more that the early gerontologists analyzed the loss of social relationships that elderly people were obviously experiencing in the modern industrialized world, the more they became aware how that drastically contrasted with the past, when older people enjoyed a privileged place in society. Therefore, some of them began to conclude that older people were not merely having fewer social contacts and becoming isolated individually, but as a group they were experiencing a loss of social status. As they began to question why that was happening they developed a number of theories to explain that troublesome phenomenon. Three theories particularly addressed that concern: exchange theory, modernization theory, and age stratification theory.

Exchange Theory of Aging

Exchange theory, one of the major theoretical perspectives of sociology, has been directly applied to gerontology by Dowd (1975; 1980). He presented that theory as an explanation of the loss of status and the experience of being discriminated against among elderly people. In general, exchange theory, as originally outlined by Homans (1961), borrowed from two very unrelated theoretical traditions on the bases of its major premises—behavioristic learning theory and what Hewitt characterizes as "an explicitly economic model of human conduct" (Hewitt, 1991, p. 16). According to this theory, we humans are conditioned or motivated to interact with others on the basis of the rewards for, against what it costs, to do so.

An important component of the theory, especially as it applies to the aged, according to Dowd, is that the rewards received on the part of those involved in exchanges are never equal, due to the amount of power participants bring to the exchange. His basic assumption is that aging means a declining source of power from which to draw. As Dowd puts it, "the aged have very little to exchange which is of instrumental value" (Dowd, 1975), regardless of their physical and mental functional capacities. What matters is how the cohort experiences of the particular elderly generation are defined. For example, typically they end up with deficits in education and with outmoded skills, especially when the exchange takes place between elderly individuals and the society as a whole. In that case, he contends, "the bargaining position of the aged social actor upon retirement quickly deteriorates" (Dowd, 1975). Ferraro believes that this particularly applies to the elderly in ethnic groups. He contends that "their social resources become less valued by younger cohorts both inside and outside the ethnic group" (Ferraro, 1990). In some ways and in some ethnic groups, though, elderly people are seen as having distinct advantages in the exchange process within their ethnic relationships, due to their knowledge of ethnic lore and history, for example (Gelfand, 1994, pp. 3–4).

Dowd readily admits that there is nothing about aging that inherently dictates that old people will necessarily always lack power in their exchange relationships. He indicates that his analysis of exchange theory primarily applies to the situation in the present industrialized world. It may well be different in the future. If that is true, it is not at all clear how exchange theory applies to aging any differently than to those of any other age, and therefore, how it helps to explain aging, beyond what is already covered in modernization theory and age stratification theory (discussed later).

Furthermore, Dowd's assumption that elderly people lack power in their exchanges with society can be challenged on at least two counts. For one thing, they have the power of the vote, which they exercise much more consistently than any other age group. Many of today's politicians have quickly learned how powerful that is when it comes to the rewards they seek in the exchange process, particularly having to do with such matters as health care and social security. For another thing, Markovsky and his colleagues provide evidence that what they label as "weak power" effectively works in exchange situations in favor of those who lack the more formal indicators of power (Markovsky and others, 1993). What they are referring to is any form of exchange that can somehow "'short-circuit' the structural advantages of the strong." An illustration of that kind of power among the elderly, that program planners and service delivery people have been unable to understand, is their simple refusal to participate.

Exchange theory in general, and how it has been applied to aging in particular, has been criticized by others. Hewitt, a symbolic interactionist, acknowledges that it has some things in common with symbolic interaction theory but criticizes it because it has no theory of self. As he explains, "It assumes that something like the self-control of conduct must operate, but it does not give us an explanation of how it is created or how it operates (Hewitt, 1991, p. 18). Atchley suggests that "the exchange process involves elements that are not necessarily either rational or conscious" (Atchley, 1991, p. 293). Hooyman and Kiyak question the application of the theory to aging. They indicate that "more empirical research is essential to attempt to determine the value of exchange theory as an explanation of the aging process" (Hooyman and Kiyak, 1991, p. 97). Furthermore, it is absurd to assume that all interactions between people can be reduced to a simple economic formula.

Modernization Theory of Aging

The early theories of aging emphasized the negative definitions of aging so thoroughly and convincingly that those definitions even became the dominant way of depicting aging in the first efforts to look at aging cross-culturally. Cross-cultural gerontologists focused primarily on the loss of social status among the aged. The assumption was that such a loss was being experienced not only in the United States, but also in Western European countries and indeed in many other places in the world, and always for the same reason. Thus, the idea that old age was a basically negative experience was being defined and treated not just as a culturally bound phenomenon, but as universally applicable.

As the most definitive spokesmen for the loss of status among the elderly on a cross-cultural basis, Cowgill and Holmes developed what they termed the *modernization theory of aging*. They outlined their theory in their book *Aging and Modernization*, published in 1972 (Cowgill and Holmes, 1972). According to this theory, loss of social status was not peculiar to Western societies. Instead, it is a universal experience in all cultures (regardless of economic, religious, political, or social traditions) in which modernization processes are occurring.

These authors based their theory on the findings of their descriptive study of status changes in 15 societies with different levels of modernization. Recognizing their lack of a specific definition of modernization, Cowgill later offered a more definitive restatement and a further defense of the theory (Cowgill, 1981). In making a case for the cross-cultural application of the theory, he selected what he saw as the four "most salient aspects of modernization with reference to aging": (1) the development of health technology, which he claims favors the young by allowing more infants to live into childhood and adult life even though it also results in greater longevity in the long run; (2) economic modernization or development, which he said encourages greater specialization and increasingly complex job skills and leaves the aged not only without work roles but also deprives them of the traditional role of providing vocational guidance to the young (also see Achenbaum, 1983, p. 15); (3) urbanization, which he said tends to separate work from the home and the aged from their younger family members; and (4) formalized education, which he said targets the young and leaves the aged at literacy and educational disadvantages. All of this, wherever it occurs, inevitably leads to an ever-increasing generation gap and a deprived elderly population.

Palmore and Whittington found support for modernization theory in a study carried out in the United States in the early part of the decade of the 1970s (Palmore and Whittington, 1971). They found not only that the aged had lower status than younger adults, but that there had been a significant decline in the status of the aged relative to the rest of the population between 1940 and 1969. The decline of status was worsening, according to the conclusions drawn from these data. These authors believed massive intervention in terms of improved income, work opportunities, and education for the age would be necessary to stop the steady decline of status for the aged in the United States.

Cowgill seemed to be even more pessimistic than Palmore and Whittington. He insisted that the relationship between modernization and declining social status was "not a mere statistical correlation, it is a functional relationship that can be analyzed" (Cowgill, 1974). Loss of status is nothing less than a function of the very structures of modernizing societies, according to this view.

Data gathered from various countries, both modernized and non-modernized, during the 1970s and 1980s seemed to support the theory quite strongly. Some who studied aging in Japan found, for example, that, while tradition called for family and corporate support and respect for the aged, tradition was increasingly being challenged on a practical level (Roth, 1983; Campbell and Brody, 1985).

The modernization theory of aging began to be challenged rather quickly, however. Palmore also studied aging in Japan and concluded that, because of the continued emphasis in that country on the Oriental tradition of honor and respect for the aged, the modernization that had been taking place at a rapid rate since World War II was not causing a decline of status among the Japanese aged (Palmore, 1975). In fact, according to his analysis, even corporations treated workers as family and provided them with lifelong social and economic security. Similarly, in a study of aging in Samoa, Holmes and Rhoads found that respect for the aged among the Samoans had been preserved in the midst of quite rapid and otherwise socially disruptive modernization processes (Holmes and Rhoads, 1983).

The theory has also been criticized because of how the key variables were being defined and how the studies were being conducted. Entire counties were being classified as either modernized, not-modernized, or somewhere in between. Status was typically measured by determining the number of people in those societies who participated in each of the major components of modernization (i.e., occupation held, health benefits received, educational attainment, and being urbanized). If fewer elderly than younger adults, within given modernized countries, were found to have high levels of participation in these objective (nonpersonal) measures of status, the theory was said to be supported. Whole societies were compared to determine whether or not the theory would be supported cross-culturally. Missing from all of this was any consideration of the different levels of modernization within given societies and the more personal aspects of social status such as being respected, which has traditionally also been part of status.

As a way of addressing those concerns, as early as the 1970s, Bengston and his colleagues made a distinction between "modernization," as it had been objectively defined, and "modernity," that emphasized the attitudinal aspects of status (Bengston and others, 1975). To test the importance of this distinction, they conducted a cross-cultural study in which the effects of both could be analyzed, and different levels of modernization could be studied within societies. Six nations were selected, based on their level of per capita industrial output. They included Argentina, Chile, India, Israel, Nigeria, and Bangladesh, and each country was divided among areas that were basically either "rural," "urban nonindustrial," or "urban industrial." In their analysis using the data on modernization, they, indeed, found support for modernization theory. In addition, though, a sample of males between 18 and 32 years of age from each area, who were either farm workers ("cultivators"), urban nonindustrial workers, or urban industrial workers, were interviewed concerning how they perceived the instrumental or educational value of the aged, their attitudes about their own aging, and their acceptance of the norms regarding deference to the aged, to provide a measure of modernity. In that part of the analysis they found that "individual modernizing experiences do not have an important and consistent impact on attitudes toward aging and the aged" (Bengtson and others, 1975). In fact, in four out of the six nations that were studied, rural workers were the least likely of the three types of workers to say they "looked forward to old age."

Also concerned about the subjective aspects of modernization and status among older people, Hong and Keith recently studied what they characterized as "individual modernization," specifically applying these concepts to changes taking place in Korean families (Hong and Keith, 1992). Individual modernization was measured with four attitudinal items on whether (1) children should always obey their parents; (2) women should obey their husbands, (3) women should stay home and not work; and (4) men should not do housework. Status was measured by who makes the final decisions about family finances, grandchildren's education, family events, and other matters related to the home environment.

They studied a sample of partly urban and partly rural elderly men and women in and near Seoul, Korea, all of whom lived in three-generation households, to determine how this particular type of modernization related to elderly persons' status. They found that, in fact, those in rural areas tended to be more modernized than those in urban areas (Hong and Keith, 1992). Apparently, when the subjective component is included as part of the definition of modernization, the elderly are not necessarily disadvantaged. Often, they too become modernized, and if so, they do not tend to lose status.

Another potentially significant and telling criticism of the modernization theory of aging, though, came from a set of data produced in the 1970s that have been treated in a rather low-key manner and with some uncertainty about their meaning. In a study of the loss of status among the aged in a number of societies at various levels of modernization, even while using the traditional objective macrolevel method, Palmore and Manton discovered a tendency for status among the aged to be somewhat regained in the most modernized societies, particularly as status was related to occupation and education (Palmore and Manton, 1974). These data were only a minor part of those produced by the study as a whole, most of which clearly supported the modernization theory of aging. Yet they probably provide as much of a challenge to the theory as anything else. They imply that in the long run, the processes of modernization do not, as proponents of the theory have clearly stated, necessarily lead to ever-declining status for the aged. Instead, the expectation would be that those very processes may well eventually act to restore that status.

Gilleard and Gurkan also found support for modernization theory in a study in Turkey in the 1980s, comparing the status of elderly people in the rural, industrialized, and urban provinces. However, the only measure of education used was whether or not the elderly had completed primary school, and the investigators admitted that, if they had used more sophisticated measures of education and occupational status, the findings would have "appeared to completely refute modernization theory." The reason for that was that most of the highly educated and professionally employed elderly (those with the highest levels of those kinds of status) were found in "the most industrialized and least rural provinces" (Gilleard and Gurkan, 1987).

From a recent study of modernization and status of aged men and women using existing data from 51 nations, Clark reported support for modernization theory, but he used only one measure of modernization (the 1985 per capita gross national product) and one measure of status (occupational). He admitted that education could make a difference in the loss of status of the elderly (Clark, 1992–93).

Modernization theory has also been criticized on other bases as well. For one thing, the assumption that the loss of status on the part of the aged began with modernization that is defined in terms of economic development has been shown by historians to be false (Crandall, 1991, p. 68; Hendricks and Hendricks, 1986, p. 103; Atchley, 1991, p. 49; Hooyman and Kiyak, 1991, p. 68). In addition, some contend that the theory begins with a biased perception about when the conditions for older people were ideal. Passuth and Bengtson state that it has "the world we have lost syndrome" (Passuth and Bengston, 1988), and Ferraro accused the modernization theorists of having "a bias that the world was better in times past and that social and moral entropy is inevitable" (Ferraro, 1990). Crandall also suggests that the theory may suffer from "immaturity." In that regard, he says that even Cowgill himself admitted that a number of factors might, in fact, serve to improve the status of the elderly in the latter states of modernization, such as the softening of the work ethic, increased interdependency and group identity among the elderly themselves, and decreasing amounts of illiteracy among the aged (Crandall, 1991, p. 68).

It would seem, then, that what appeared to be such a strongly predictive theory that would apply across cultures and over time has turned out to also be both time bound, culture bound and somewhat conceptually flawed. It is time bound in that its basic premise is based on how modern societies are structured at present, how they emerged in the West, and how they are being transplanted into other parts of the world. Notions that are particularly apt to change in future modernized societies, and that may serve to date this theory, are that work and occupations are the sole sources of social status, and that formal education will continue to favor young people. Both of these ideas are being substantially challenged in the United States, with an increased importance being placed on volunteer leisure activities, and with the astounding growth in educational programs for senior citizens in recent years. The modernization theory appears to be culturally bound in that its proponents have failed to recognize the power of well-established cultural traditions and to consider the fact that old traditions often take on new forms and are at least somewhat preserved in the midst of change.

Age Stratification Theory

In the early 1970s, Riley led in the development of *age stratification theory* to provide a basis for explaining whatever forms and levels of inequality might exist between the young and old in given societies. Sociologists have usually conceptualized the unequal distribution of social power, prestige, and economic resources in terms of social class distinctions. Riley has contended that age is another important criterion on which inequality is determined. The basic assumption is that societies are inevitably stratified by age as well as by class (Riley, 1971).

The theory did not assume, however, that the conditions of old age are necessarily always the same. They may differ from one society to another. They may also change over time within given societies, as, indeed, they have done and continue to do. According to this theory as it was originally described, the relative inequality of the aged at any given time and in any cultural situation depends upon two types of experiences: (1) their typical life course experiences, due mostly to the physical and mental changes that take place and (2) the historically based experiences they have as part of the age cohort to which they belong. What happens to the members of given age cohorts depends primarily on external events, such as wars, economic changes, and technology that tend to mold their aging experiences, compared to the experiences of the age cohorts that follow them. For example, Riley expressed concern about the effect of "the rapid pace of educational advancement" in this century. She pointed out that "the age pattern of education today is a reversal of that in earlier societies where the old were honored for their great knowledge." While she obviously did not want to be pessimistic about the conditions of today's elderly, she, nevertheless, concluded that, "If one looks ahead from today's knowledge explosion, the information gap between the very young and even the not-so-young is deepening" (Riley, 1971).

Riley has subsequently elaborated on her age stratification theory, in which she identifies three sets of underlying processes: (1) aging and the flow of cohorts; (2) social changes coming from outside the boundaries of the age stratification system; and (3) allocation and socialization that articulate the dual structures of people and roles (Riley, 1985). (See Figure 5-2.) She provides a list of "working principles to help explain what these processes mean and how they work." Seven of the principles refer to age strata: (1) Every society is stratified by age; (2) age strata are produced by both the continuity interplay between social changes and the processes of aging and cohort flow; (3) age strata are interdependent; (4) within each stratum, people tend to share common experiences, perceptions, and interests; (5) integration within age strata can cause conflict with other age strata; (6) individuals within age strata engage in a complex of roles; and (7) individuals in age strata also interact with members of other strata. Four of the principles refer to aging: (1) Aging is a lifelong process; (2) aging is multifaceted, social, and psychological as well as biological; (3) the ways people age are interdependent, influencing and being influenced by each other; and (4) the life-course patterns are influenced by cohort experiences. The last two principles of stratification theory refer to how aging relates to social change: (1) New patterns of aging are both caused by and contribute to social change; and (2) individual aging and social change are

Figure 5–2 Age Stratification System: Conceptual Elements (Source: M. W. Riley, "Age Strata in Social Systems," in *Handbook of Aging and the Social Sciences*, eds. R. H. Binstock and E. Shanas (New York: Van Nostrand Reinhold, 1985), pp. 369–407.)

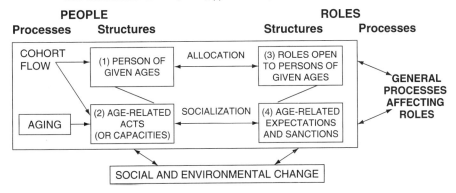

not the same. This set of principles indicates that age stratification theory as it has evolved is a comprehensive theory that seems to take all possible social processes into account in determining the status of particular age cohorts.

As it was originally explained, age stratification theory seemed to allow for changes to occur among age strata that could once again favor the aged. Practically, however, Riley seemed to imply that it is the younger, rather than the older, age cohorts that determine the direction of change (Riley 1971). It also seemed according to the theory, then, that younger cohorts would continue to have the advantage. This conclusion seemed at first to be refuted in Yin and Lai's application of this theory to aging in the People's Republic of China in 1983. They concluded that the existing aged cohort at that time tended to have a power and status advantage over the one that followed. They explained, though, that that advantage was obtained only because of setbacks to the younger cohort due to the cultural revolution, and that future younger cohorts would eventually regain the advantage (Yin and Lai, 1983).

In drawing on later age stratification research findings, Riley has subsequently acknowledged that it is not just theoretically possible for elderly people to gain status, but that actually, even in today's youth-oriented world, "in certain respects, many of those in the older strata are comparatively advantaged." For example, because of a combination of aging and social changes, they have "more leisure time, fewer burdensome responsibilities, and they are more likely than young adults to participate in institutionalized political processes" (Riley, 1985). Still, most of the analysis done from this perspective tends to indicate that age stratification favors younger adults more than the elderly.

An important question to put to stratification theorists, if their theory is to provide an adequate explanation of old age in the future and across cultures, is: What is the nature of the outside factors that tend to determine what the different age strata will be like? From the practical illustrations provided, today's outside influences seem to be parts of what Cowgill conceptualized as "modernization" (Cowgill, 1981). Yin and Lai's analysis indeed reflects an overlapping between the two theories (Yin and Lai, 1983). In a practical sense it is difficult to see how age stratification theory differs much from modernization theory in explaining old age experiences, except that it at least theoretically allows for the restoration of status for elderly people.

Ferraro gives age stratification theory credit for being one of the most comprehensive theories of social aging. He believes it has the potential of integrating the contributions that all of the major sociological theories made to aging, including structural functionalism, symbolic interactionism, and even conflict theory. He also contends that it incorporates both micro- and macro-levels of analysis of social aging (Ferraro, 1990, pp. 122–23).

It is, however, primarily a structural-functionalist–based theory. As such it tends to treat certain societal structures as sociological entities that are taken for granted but not explained. For example, social change is used as an important factor in understanding the conditions in which aging cohorts find themselves. No explanation of where social changes come from is given, however, that would account for why certain kinds of change emerge. Riley does say that aging cohorts are not only influenced by social change but in turn also contribute to it, but does not explain how that takes place (Riley, 1985). The social roles in which individuals perform and how they change with age are important parts of this theory's analysis. They are treated as societally pre-scribed entities into which individuals do or do not fit, though, with no expla-nation of how they come about.

Likewise, the existence of cohorts are described as existing entities, essentially in terms of when groups of people are born and how they are influ-enced by outside forces taking place at that particular time. Cohort analysis is certainly a promising analytical framework (Passuth and Bengtson, 1988), but largely ignored is how individuals are affected differently by the historical events taking place and what accounts for those differences. As Passuth and Bengtson put it, "age stratification's emphasis on differences between cohorts has resulted in a lack of attention to variations within cohorts. The assumption of cohort analysis is that people born in a particular year experience age the same way" (Passuth and Bengtson, 1988). Given the fact that most gerontolo-gists recognize that there is greater diversity among the elderly than that of any other age group, an explanation of that diversity would seem to be impor-tant (Hooyman and Kiyak, 1991, p. 92).

Age stratification is valuable in providing a comprehensive view of aging and in drawing attention to the fact that the situations in which elderly people find themselves do in fact change, in some ways to their benefit and in other ways to their detriment. It also makes it clear that those conditions stem from a variety of sources, social and psychological as well as biological. It is, nevertheless, more of a descriptive than a theoretical system of analysis.

A CONFLICT THEORY PERSPECTIVE

Conflict theory is still another sociological perspective that is represented in the development of gerontological theory. In general, the contention of con-flict theorists is that conflict is so much an integral part of social relationships that it provides the best explanation of what society is and how it operates. Marxism is the classic example of conflict which took the form of economic determinism. The assumption was that conflict over economic development was basic to and determined all other aspects of social life. Marx defined con-flict in terms of a class struggle over economic power which would finally result in a communist state in which there would no longer be social classes.

It needs to be understood, though, that not all conflict theory is Marx-ist. Most of these theories address the issue of unequal power and resource distribution, but few of today's conflict theorists argue for the total destruc-tion of social class. Instead, most believe that the management of conflict and the change that it brings are most basic to societal stability and survival (Brinkerhoff and White, 1985, pp. 17–19).

Political Economic Theory of Aging

This theory attempts to explain the situation in which elderly people find themselves today in terms of the conflict over economic and political power having to do with age-related issues and policies. On the one hand, it analyzes how the policies of providing older retired people with financial resources are actually set to improve the economy and benefit the economically powerful, and, on the other hand, how those policies then become the basis for blaming the relatively powerless elderly for economic crises (Bonanno and Calasanti, 1988). It has also been used to explain how the resources allocated to implement age-related social and health service policies have been used to fund the creation of huge self-serving special interest networks more than to serve the elderly themselves (Estes, 1979; Estes and others, 1984, pp. 23–34). As Passuth and Bengtson put it, "this perspective focuses on the state and its relation to the economy in a capitalist society to explain the plight of the elderly" (Passuth and Bengtson, 1988).

Political economic theorists point out that part of the consequence of this kind of approach is that it tends to create unnecessary dependency among the elderly. According to the Hendrickses, this "stems from interest group politics and deliberate structural arrangements brought about by those who control new components of industrial production" (Hendricks and Hendricks, 1986, p. 110). In part, it also stems from what Wilson characterizes as an "assumptive world" about old age called "the pyramidal model"—that old age is "a time of inevitable and increasing dependence." She points out despite the fact that most of even the oldest of old do not need constant care, the pyramidal model continues to dominate and determine policies on aging (Wilson, 1991).

Political economic analysts report that part of the present debate of those in favor of cutting support programs to the elderly are the claims that the elderly have designed a welfare state to benefit them in old age and that an intergenerational conflict is emerging in which younger adults judge expenditures to the elderly as unfair. In response to that claim, Phillipson offers the following points of rebuttal that apply to both Great Britain and the United States: (1) The British pension legislation and the Social Security Act in the United States were, in fact, passed with "the view that the jobs of older people could be sacrificed to maintain employment for those with families"; and (2) the evidence shows that, in fact, younger adults in both countries continue to support government programs for the elderly. He concludes that this kind of rhetoric does not represent the facts of political economy as it does an ideological bias about "older people in general and retirement in particular" (Phillipson, 1991). In their analysis of the economic situations in Italy and the United States, Bonanno and Calasanti make the further point that social-security–type legislation in both countries created a "deferred wage system" that actually reduced labor expenditures for employers and thus boosted rather than threatened the economies of those countries (Bonanno and Calasanti, 1988).

Passuth and Bengtson identify political economic theory with Marxism and contend that it tends to "overstate the extent to which elderly, as a whole, are impoverished and disenfranchised" (Passuth and Bengtson, 1988). Both of these criticisms reveal a misunderstanding of the major points being made by this theoretical perspective, as demonstrated by what these theorists offer as solutions to the political economic conflicts that they have revealed. For example, Bonanno and Calasanti contend that the solutions to the state's fiscal crisis and problems of the elderly are "through the political process of allocation of power and selection of priorities" (Bonanno and Calasanti, 1988). They in no way call for the establishment of a classless society. Estes and colleagues have not emphasized dependency among the elderly. In fact, quite the contrary, they call for a "gerontological imagination" on the part of gerontologists, that would move us away from the "crisis mentality" into which political economics has tended to lock us (Estes, Binney, and Culbertson, 1992).

This is a theoretical perspective on aging that is badly needed today as a reality test. It also serves as a needed call for basic honesty in the politics and economics of aging. As a social gerontological theory, however, it does not explain all aspects of the aging experience, because politics and economics do not determine everything about aging. For example, it does not explain why there is so much diversity in social participation on the part of those elderly with similar socioeconomic backgrounds and physical and mental capacities. It would seem that some kind of social psychological theory would also be needed for that kind of analysis.

A SYMBOLIC INTERACTIONIST THEORY

Symbolic interaction is another of the major sociological theoretical perspectives. As such, it is based on the assumption that the one most comprehensive explanatory factors about the human experience is that which is universally true of all of us—that we continuously interact with ourselves and others on the basis of concensually validated symbols. It is granted that there is social order to life, but it is more appropriate to think of that order as that which is constantly being negotiated rather than a structure to which we individually must adjust. To be sure, conflict probably permeates and influences most of life's experiences, but it would be difficult to prove that it is universally true; and if there are those exceptions, then conflict itself needs to be explained. Symbolic interactionists contend that both social order (structures) and conflict are the products of interaction.

How then has this theory been applied to aging that helps to account for both the negative and positive aspects of aging—that moves us beyond the prevailing "crisis mentality" about which Estes and her colleagues have expressed concern? As noted before, the emphasis on the labeling theory in Kuypers and Bengtson's reconstructive theory had symbolic interactionism as its basis, but it was used to explain only social losses among the elderly. Many years ago Rose proposed another theory, based on the symbolic interactionist perspective, that was presented as a way of helping us better understand the potential for a more positive view of aging, however (Rose, 1965b).

Subculture of Aging Theory

In the process of bringing elderly people throughout the state of Minnesota together to study senior citizen activity centers experimentally, Rose observed that those people began to interact more with each other than with others in their community (Rose, 1963). On the basis of that observation he predicted that, as the numbers of the elderly continue to grow, increasing numbers of them would come together in groups for two basic reasons: (1) the positive affinity they might feel for each other based on their common interests, and (2) the rejection they experience by younger age groups. Thus, they would inevitably interact more with each other than with others and a subculture of aging would emerge.

He did not predict that all elderly people would become part of such a subculture because of such counterinfluences as continued affiliation with families, continued employment, and the tendency to actively resist being identified as old. Those who would be most apt to become participants in the subculture would be "those in retirement communities, in rural communities from which young people are rapidly emigrating, and in the central parts of big cities" (Rose, 1965b).

According to Rose, the major characteristics of the subculture of aging would be that (1) income would be valued more as an important resource than an object of status; (2) occupational identity would diminish as an important part of status; and (3) physical and mental health would become vital as an object of status. In addition, Rose believed that participants in the subculture of aging would tend to gain a sense of aging group consciousness, join recreational and other expressive associations, and become politically active and a voting block, especially about such vital concerns to them as healthcare.

Some analysts have argued that a subculture of aging has not developed as Rose predicted (Rosow, 1974; Baum and Baum, 1980, p. 82). Longino and his colleagues, for example, contend that groups of elderly people have become retreatist and not politically active (Longino, McClelland, and Peterson, 1980). Nevertheless, it is obvious that increasing numbers of exclusively age-related groups and communities are forming and that increasing numbers of the elderly do indeed interact more with each other in those groups than with others. The comparative amount of age-peer interaction itself implies a value preference among those who choose to engage in it and clearly suggests a source of positive labeling and image building. This analysis also suggests the opposite conclusion: those who choose not to participate in age-related peer interactions are less likely to maintain or reformulate positive self-images.

CONCLUSION

Theories of aging have played an important part in the evolution of the field of social gerontology in the brief history of that area of study. Without them we would be even less sure than we now are of how to interpret the social and psychological meaning of growing old and being old in today's world.

The theories that gerontologists have thus far developed have by no means provided all of the answers to the questions that trouble us and that we would like to have answered about aging. As we have seen, some give different and even conflicting answers to the same questions. Some lack an adequate database to claim much validity and scientific respect, even though most have made substantial practical contributions.

Two basic problems have kept the existing theories of aging from being universally applicable. First, they have largely been time bound and culture bound, finding their validity only in issues related to particular times and places. Second, they have typically addressed specific issues related to aging and being old and have failed to consider the experiences of aging in an inclusive sense. As previously noted, these issues have been largely negative ones. While these problems can never be completely overcome (theorists are as much a part of the times and places in which they live as anyone), what seems to be needed are less time bound and culturally bound theories related to specific issues, and more theories that comprehensively address the experiences of aging and old age.

We have treated the theories from quite a different perspective than they are normally treated. The reason for that was to make the point that the gerontological theories, valuable as they have been and still are, are not so much right or wrong, valid or invalid explanations of the aging experiences; more accurately, they have been products of the particular times in which they emerged. That is, although they may have been valid at one point in time, they tend not to remain valid over time. Instead of merely confining them to history as unimportant relics of particular times, however, we must recognize that many of the theories themselves, because they dealt with the vital issues of their times, have helped to bring about the changes that tended to make them invalid for the future. Loss of major life roles theory, for example, had an unquestionable influence on the U.S. policy of developing volunteer programs for the elderly through which they could begin to find meaningful substitute roles. For that reason alone, these theories have a great deal of practical value to the many people who are training to work as service providers in the field of gerentology today.

While gerontological theory has made an important contribution, it is also important to recognize that there is a dire need for more universal theories of aging that are more comprehensive and valid across cultures and over time. At this point in the evolution of gerontology, that may be too much to expect. The need for such theories is nevertheless a real one, and such theories are worth the search.

REFERENCES

Achenbaum, W. Andrew, *Shades of Gray: Old Age, American Values, and Federal Policies Since 1920* (Boston: Little, Brown, 1983).

Atchley, Robert C., "A Continuity of Normal Aging," *The Gerontologist*, 29, no. 2 (April 1989), 183–90.

Atchley, Robert C., "Retirement and Leisure Participation: Continuity or Crisis?" *The Gerontologist*, 11, no. 1, pt. 1 (Spring 1971), 13–17.

Atchley, Robert C., *Social Forces and Aging: An Introduction to Social Gerontology* (Belmont, Calif.: Wadsworth, 1991).

Barrow, Georgia M., *Aging, The Individual, and Society* (St. Paul, Minn.: West, 1989).

Baum, Martha, and Rainer C. Baum, *Growing Old: A Societal Perspective* (Englewood Cliffs, N.J.: Prentice Hall, Inc., 1980).

Bengtson, Vern L., James J. Dowd, David H. Smith, and Alex Inkeles, "Modernization, Modernity, and Perceptions of Aging: A Cross-Cultural Study," *Journal of Gerontology*, 30, no. 6 (November 1975), 688–95.

Bonanno, Allesandro, and Toni M. Calasanti, "Laissez-Faire Strategies and the Crisis of the Welfare State: A Comparative Analysis of the Status of the Elderly in Italy and the United States," *Sociological Focus*, 21, no. 3 (August 1988), 245–63.

Brinkerhoff, David B., and Lynn K. White, *Sociology* (New York: West, 1985).

Brown, Arnold S., "Satisfying Relationships for the Elderly and their Patterns of Disengagement," *The Gerontologist*, 14, no. 3 (June 1974), 258–62.

Brown, Arnold S., and others, "The Senior Companion Program: An Evaluation," unpublished report of an evaluation of the Northern Arizona Senior Companion Program conducted by Brown and his graduate gerontology class, 1991.

Burgess, Ernest W., *Aging in Western Societies* (Chicago: University of Chicago Press, 1960).

Burgess, Ernest W., "Social Relations, Activities, and Personal Adjustment," *American Journal of Sociology*, 59 (January 1954), 352–60.

Campbell, Ruth, and Elaine M. Brody, "Women's Changing Roles and Help to the Elderly: Attitudes of Women in the United States and Japan," *The Gerontologist*, 25, no. 6 (December 1985), 584–92.

Clark, Roger, "Modernization and Status Change Among Aged Men and Women," *International Journal of Aging and Human Development*, 36, no. 3 (1992–93), 171–86.

Comfort, Alex, "Age Prejudice in America," *Social Policy*, 17 (November-December 1976), 3–8.

Covey, Herbert C., "A Reconceptualization of Continuity Theory: Some Preliminary Thoughts," *The Gerontologist*, 21, no. 6 (December 1981), 628–33.

Cowgill, Donald O., "Aging and Modernization: A Revision of the Theory," in *Aging in America: Readings in Social Gerontology*, eds. Cary S. Kart and Barbara B. Manard (Sherman Oaks, Calif.: Alfred, 1981), pp. 111–32.

Cowgill, Donald O., and Lowell Holmes, *Aging and Modernization* (New York: Appleton-Century-Crofts, 1972).

Crandall, Richard C., *Gerontology: A Behavioral Science Approach* (New York: McGraw-Hill, 1991).

Cumming, Elaine, and William B. Henry, *Growing Old: The Process of Disengagement* (New York: Basic Books, 1961).

Davis-Friedmann, Deborah, *Long Lives: Chinese Elderly and the Communist Revolution* (Cambridge: Harvard University Press, 1983).

Dowd, James J., "Aging as Exchange: A Preface to Theory," *Journal of Gerontology*, 30, no. 5 (September 1975), 584–94.

Dowd, James J., "Exchange Rates and Old People," *Journal of Gerontology*, 35, no. 4 (1980), 596–602.

Estes, Carroll L., *The Aging Enterprise* (San Francisco: Jossey-Bass, 1979).

Estes, Carroll L., Elizabeth A. Binney, and Richard A. Culbertson, "The Gerontological Imagination: Social Influences on the Development of Gerontology, 1945–Present," *International Journal of Aging and Human Development*, 35, no. 1 (1992), 49–65.

Estes, Carroll L., Lenore E. Gerard, Jane S. Zones, and James H. Swan, *Political Economy, Health, and Aging* (Boston: Little, Brown, 1984).

Evans, Idris W., and Arnold S. Brown, *Aging in Montana: A Survey of the Needs and Problems of Older American* (Helena: Montana Commission on Aging, 1970).

Ferraro, Kenneth F., ed., "Sociology of Aging: The Micro-Macro Link," in *Gerontology: Perspectives and Issues*, ed. Kenneth F. Ferraro (New York: Springer, 1990), pp. 110–128.

Fry, P. S., "Major Social Theories of Aging and Their Implicatons for Counseling Concepts and Practices: A Critical Review," *The Counseling Psychologist*, 20 (April 1992), 246–329.

Gelfand, Donald E., *Aging and Ethnicity: Knowledge and Services* (New York: Springer, 1994).

George, Linda K., *Role Transitions in Later Life* (Monterey, Calif.: Brooks/Cole , 1980).

Gilleard, Christopher J., and Ali Arslan Gurkan, "Socioeconomic Development and the Status of Elderly Men in Turkey: A Test of Modernization Theory," *Journal of Gerontology*, 42, no. 4 (July 1987), 353–57.

Gray Panthers Pamphlet (1974); Philadelphia: Gray Panthers, 3700 Chestnut Street, Philadelphia, Penn. 19104.

Havighurst, Robert J., Bernice Neugarten, and Sheldon S. Tobin, "Disengagement and Patterns of Aging," in *Middle Age and Aging*, ed. by Bernice Neugarten (Chicago: University of Chicago Press, 1968), pp. 161–172.

Hendricks, Jon, "Generations and the Generation of Theory in Social Gerontology," *International Journal of Aging and Human Development*, 35, no. 1 (1992), 31–47.

Hendricks, Jon, and C. Davis Hendricks, *Aging in Mass Society: Myths and Realities* (Boston: Little, Brown, 1986).

Hendricks, Jon, and C. Davis Hendricks, "Theories of Social Gerontology," in *Dimensions of Aging*, ed. Jon Hendricks and C. Davis Hendricks, (Cambridge: Winthrop, 1979), pp. 191–208.

Hewitt, John *Self and Society: A Symbolic Interactionist Social Psychology* (Boston: Allyn & Bacon, 1991).

Holmes, Lowell, and Ellen Rhoads, "Aging and Change in Samoa," in *Growing Old in Different Societies*, ed. Jay Sokolovsky (Belmont, Calif.: Wadsworth, 1983), pp. 119–29.

Homans, George F., *Social Behavior: Its Elementary Forms* (New York: Harcourt Brace Jovanovich, 1961).

Hong, Sean-Hee Mo, and Pat M. Keith, "The Status of the Aged in Korea: Are the Modern More Advantaged?" *The Gerontologist*, 32, no. 2 (April 1992), 197–202.

Hooyman, Nancy R., and H. Asuman Kiyak, *Social Gerontology: A Multidisciplinary Perspective* (Boston: Allyn & Bacon, 1991).

Kalish, Richard A., *Late Adulthood: Perspectives on Human Development* (Monterey, Calif.: Brooks/Cole, 1982), pp. 111–12.

Kaufman, Sharon R., "Values as Sources of the Ageless Self," in *Activity and Aging: Staying Involved in Later Life*, ed. J. R. Kelly (Newbury Park, Calif.: Sage, 1993), pp. 19–24.

Kutner, Bernard, "The Hospital Environment," *Social Science and Medicine*, 4, Supplement 1 (1970), 9–11.

Kuypers, Joseph A., and Vern L. Bengtson, "Social Breakdown and Competence: A Model of Normal Aging," *Human Development*, 16 (1973), 181–201.

Larson, Reed, Juri Zuzanek, and Roger Mannell, "Being Alone Versus Being With People: Disengagement in the Daily Living Experience of Older Adults, *Journal of Gerontology*, 40, no. 3 (May 1985), 375–81.

Longino, Charles F., Jr., Kent A. McClelland, and Warren A. Peterson, "The Aged Subculture Hypothesis: Social Integration, Gerontophilia and Self-Conception," *Journal of Gerontology*, 35, no. 5 (September 1980), 758–67.

Lopata, Helena Znaniecki, "The Life Cycle of the Social Role of the Housewife," *Sociology and Social Research*, 51 (October 1966), 5–22.

Maddox, George L., "Persistence of Life Style Among the Elderly," in *Normal Aging* ed. Erdman B. Palmore (Durham, N.C.: Duke University Press, 1970a), pp. 329–31.

Maddox, George L., "Fact and Artifact: Evidence Bearing on Disengagement Theory," in *Normal Aging* ed. Erdman B. Palmore (Durham, N.C.: Duke University Press, 1970b), pp. 324–36.

Maddox, George L., and Richard T. Campbell, "Scope, Concepts, and Methods in the Study of Aging," in *Handbook of Aging and the Social Sciences*, eds. Robert H. Binstock and Ethel Shanas (New York: Van Nostrand Reinhold, 1985), pp. 3–31.

Markovsky, Barry, John Skvoretz, David Willer, Michael J. Lovaglia, and Jeffrey Erger, "The Seeds of Weak Power: An Extension of Network Exchange Theory," *American Sociological Review*, 58, no. 2 (April 1993), 197–209.

Marshall, Victor M., "No Exit: A Symbolic Interactionist Perspective on Aging," *International Journal of Aging and Human Development*, 9 (1978–1979), 345–58.

Matras, Judah, *Dependency, Obligations, and Entitlements: A New Sociology of Aging, the Life Course, and the Elderly* (Englewood Cliffs, N. J.: Prentice Hall, 1990).

Moen, Elizabeth, "The Reluctance of the Elderly to Accept Help," *Social Problems*, 25, no. 3 (February 1978), 293–303.

Palmore, Erdman B., "The Status and Integration of the Aged in Japanese Society," *Journal of Gerontology*, 30, no. 2 (March 1975), 199–208.

Palmore, Erdman B., and Frank Whittington, "Trends in the Relative Status of the Aged," *Social Forces*, 50 (September 1971), 84–91.

Palmore, Erdman B., and Kenneth Manton, "Modernization and Status of the Age: International Correlations," *Journal of Gerontology*, 29, no. 2 (March 1974), 205–10.

Passuth, Patricia M., and Vern L. Bengtson, "Sociological Theories of Aging: Current Perspectives and Future Directions" in *Emergent Theories of Aging*, eds. J. E. Birren and Vern L. Bengtson (New York: Springer, 1988), pp. 333–55.

Phillipson, Chris, "Inter-Generational Relations: Conflict or Consensus in the 21st Century," *Policy and Politics*, 19, no. 1 (1991), 27–36.

Riley, Matilda White, "Age Strata in Social Systems," in *Handbook of Aging and the Social Sciences*, eds. R. H. Binstock and Ethel Shanas (New York: Van Nostrand and Reinhold, 1985), pp. 369–407.

Riley, Matilda White, "Social Gerontology and the Age Stratification of Society," *The Gerontologist*, 11, no. 2 (Summer 1971), 79–87.

Rose, Arnold M., *Aging in Minnesota* (Minneapolis: University of Minnesota Press, 1963).

Rose, Arnold M., "A Current Theoretical Issue in Social Gerontology," in *Older People and Their Social World*, eds. Arnold M. Rose and Warren A. Peterson (Philadelphia: F. A. Davis, 1965a), pp. 359–66.

Rose, Arnold M., "The Subculture of the Aging: A Framework for Research in Social Gerontology," in *Older People and Their Social World*, eds. Arnold M. Rose and Warren A. Peterson (Philadelphia: F. A. Davis, 1965b), pp. 3–16.

Rosow, Irving, *Socialization to Old Age* (Berkeley, Calif.: University of California Press, 1974).

Roth, Judith A., "Timetables and the Lifecourse in Post-Industrial Society," in *Work and Lifecourse in Japan*, ed. David W. Plath (Albany: State University of New York Press, 1983), pp. 248–59.

Schweitzer, Marjorie M., "The Elders: Cultural Dimensions of Aging in Two American Indian Communities," in *Growing Old in Different Societies: Cross-Cultural Perspectives*, ed. Jay Sokolovsky (Belmont, Calif.: Wadsworth, 1983), pp. 168–78.

Simic, Andrei, "Aging in the United States and Yugoslavia: Contrasting Models of Intergenerational Relationships," *Anthropological Quarterly*, 50 (April 1977), 53–63.

Tallman, Margot, and Burnard Kutner, "Disengagement and Morale," *The Gerontologist*, 10 , no. 1 (Spring 1970), 99–108.

Tobin, Sheldon S., and Bernice L. Neugarten, "Life Satisfaction and Social Interaction in the Aging," *Journal of Gerontology*, 16, (October 1961), 344–46.

Vatuk, Sylvia, "Withdrawal and Disengagement as a Cultural Response to Aging in India," in *Aging in Culture and Society*, ed. Christine Fry (New York: J. F. Bergin, 1980), pp. 126–48.

Videbeck, Richard, and Alan B. Knox, "Alternative Participatory Responses to Aging," in *Older People and Their Social World*, eds. Arnold M. Rose and Warren A. Peterson (Philadelphia: F. A. Davis, 1965), pp. 37–48.

Wilson, Gail, "Models of Ageing and Their Relation to Policy Formation and Service Provision," *Policy and Politics*, 19, no. 1 (1991), 37–47.

Yin, Peter, and Kwok Hung Lai, "A Reconceptualization of Age Stratification in China," *Journal of Gerontology*, 38, no. 5 (September 1983), 608–13.

Zusman, Jack, "Some Explanations of the Changing Appearance of Psychotic Patients: Antecedents of the Social Breakdown Syndrome Concept," *The Milbank Memorial Fund Quarterly*, 44, no. 1, pt. 2 (January 1966), 363–88.

6

The Aged In Changing Living Situations

INTRODUCTION

The well-being of the elderly is the paramount concern of gerontologists today. The concern is not only that they should receive the kind of care that allows them to live as long as possible, but also that their lives continue to be meaningful, personally satisfying, and worth living. It is obvious that the situations or conditions of their daily lives are central to their sense of well-being, as college students, whose living situations are often changing, can well understand and appreciate.

As we begin to analyze the living situations of the aged, we are struck with the fact that there is much cross-cultural variation. Even more striking is the realization that living situations of the aged have changed and are apparently still in the process of changing. Their lives as individuals change as they adjust to different stages of the life cycle, and their lifestyles in general have tended to change over time. It is interesting to note further that the two types of changes seem to be interrelated. That is, the fact that living situations change over the life course is itself part of the social changes that are taking place. It is as important for us to understand the characteristics of those changes as it is for us to understand the present living conditions of the aged. Understanding what factors have contributed to the changes and what the processes of change have been give us clues about the adequacy of present conditions.

A deep concern for independence tends to be the most important factor influencing both the changes that have taken place and the present choices that people make about their living situations. This, then, will be the focus of the analysis in this chapter. We will examine the possible sources of the desire for independence, the extent that it prevails cross-culturally, and the potential consequences.

There are essentially five types of living situations that have tended to be prevalent among elderly populations. These situations have tended to reflect certain societal changes, and all forms still exist and seem to be prevalent in given cultures. Furthermore, the rates of change from one to another living situation differ from culture to culture.

EXTENDED FAMILY HOUSEHOLDS

Historically and cross-culturally the most prevalent situation in which elderly people have lived has undoubtedly been in three-generation households. There have been times in the history of almost all economically stable societies when most of the elderly lived with their extended families. Entire extended families have often lived under one roof.

This is the living situation for most of the aged yet today in most Oriental countries (Davis-Friedmann, 1983, pp. 34–46; Palmore and Maeda, 1985, pp. 34–42), in Eastern European countries (Shanas, 1977), to some degree among native American tribes (Brown, 1986), and in many developing countries of the world. This type of living situation is relatively rare, however, in the United States and in Western European countries.

This kind of arrangement tends to prevail in some cultures because of (1) religious/ideological traditions, (2) certain social and economic structures, (3) practical realities, or (4) a combination of these factors. This pattern existed in the past in Western societies when the family was the basic social and economic structure. Those living within a household did not merely share living quarters and family solidarity; they also shared economic goals and responsibilities, and much of the stability of the society depended on how they lived their lives. As discussed more fully in Chapter 7, Zimmerman described this type of family as the "domestic family" (Zimmerman, 1975, pp. 5–12), and elderly people were very much a part of this kind of structure. In fact, they often controlled how the families functioned (Fullerton, 1977, pp. 4–11). For them, social or economical dependence was not an issue they had to face. Instead, they—especially older men—were in control. Age seniority was a fact of life.

The pattern of the elderly living in the same households with the families of their eldest sons has been a strong tradition throughout most of Asia. Studies have also shown that that tradition has largely been maintained in most Oriental cultures up to the present, in spite of some very different political and economic developments that Asian countries have experienced. The kinds of effects these kinds of developments may now finally be having on the traditional living patterns of Oriental elderly is a major gerontological issue in that part of the world today, however.

In a discussion of "Ageing in East and Southwest Asia," Garrett raises the question, "Is family support a viable policy?" (Garrett, 1994). He points out that some countries have made filial care of the elderly a legal obligation, that some countries offer families attractive incentives, and that in all of those countries "the largest proportion of support is provided within household units" (Garrett, 1994). Nevertheless, he recognizes that the increased proportional growth of the aging populations and the increased urbanization of those countries will severely challenge the feasibility of those traditions in the future.

The pattern of Japanese and Chinese elderly living with their adult children has until very recently continued partly because of the strong cultural traditions of filial piety in both of those countries. These traditions have religious as well as cultural connotations and contain twofold expectations with regard to aged family members. First, the aged are respected and venerated. Second, because of that veneration, families (particularly children) are expected to provide whatever care their elderly members need in their old age (Piovesana, 1979, pp. 13–20).

It is noteworthy that even though most Japanese elderly still live with the families of their adult children, there is the beginning of a trend away from that pattern. Also, more and more adult children are expressing feelings of being burdened by having to care for their elderly parents in addition to working and raising their own children. Increasing numbers of elderly are having to and/or are choosing to live separately from their children and grandchildren ("The Japanese-Style Welfare System," 1983).

Analysis of intergenerational households in the People's Republic of China is somewhat complicated by the Communist takeover in that country. Davis-Friedmann has pointed out that after they took over power in 1949, the Chinese Communist Party leaders undermined the patriarchal authority of Chinese elders. Young people were provided jobs by the government and gained economic independence from their families. Marriage laws encouraged young people to ignore the wishes of their families in the choice of mates. Expectations were that the traditions of intergenerational households would be destroyed as a result. Ironically that did not happen, partly because the long tradition of filial piety was culturally too entrenched to be destroyed. More important, as Davis-Friedmann found, "the traditional living arrangements of the elderly are compatible with the Communist revolution" (Davis-Friedmann, 1983, pp. 34–35).

That point needs clarification. Though three-generational households in the early 1980s were similar in composition to what they have always been—elderly parents living with the eldest son and his family—the structure of authority and responsibility was very different. In essence it was a cooperative arrangement between somewhat equal partners. Neither father nor son owned the home and household finances and domestic duties tended to be approximately equally shared. This emphasis was the direct result of, and was compatible with, Communist ideals. In a country in which poverty was widespread, it was also something of an economic necessity. Then too, the fact that there was a serious lack of housing in the People's Republic of China also influenced continuation of the traditional three-generational households in that country. Lack of housing has also been said to be the main reason that the aged in Eastern Europe continue to live in households with their children (Shanas, 1977). Practicality and necessity may be more important than tradition in the continuation of this practice.

Despite all this, however, there are some reasons to believe that the prevalence of the three-generation households may be declining in the People's Republic of China even in the future. For one thing, Davis-Friedmann has reported that there are already cases of elderly parents being rejected as household members by their adult children (Davis-Friedmann, 1983, pp. 43–44). Also, this author was informed by a Chinese official of sentiments among some Chinese elderly in 1984, who were becoming relatively more affluent than most, that they would prefer to live in separate households from their children. It was predicted that these tendencies might well grow if the economic reforms continued and the people as a whole became increasingly affluent. In fact, Yi reported in 1986 that nuclear families versus three-generation families were gaining proportionately in China (Yi, 1986). Indeed, by 1993 it was reported that only 50 percent of the elderly Chinese still live in three-generation households (Hong, 1993).

Knodel, Chayovan, and Saengtienchai argue the conclusion that the elderly in Oriental societies are not declaring independence from their families. They present evidence from the 1990 census in Thailand which shows that there has been no decline at all in the number of elderly people in that country who co-reside with at least one of their adult children. That ancient tradition has been maintained, they point out, despite what they describe as "the rapid and pervasive social and economic development that took place" (Knodel, Chayovan, and Saengtienchai, 1994). Their contention is that these findings are the results of the age-old tradition of intergenerational commitments within families that economic developments cannot change. As they put it, "these findings call into question global assumptions about economic and social change undermining the well-being of the elderly in third world countries." They do not, however, provide any concrete evidence of just how rapid and pervasive the social and economic developments have been in that country. Neither do they analyze such other practical matters as how economic changes may have affected personal and family income or the availability (or lack) of housing. If housing is just not available or if the elderly cannot afford independent housing, they will continue to live in three-generation households as a matter of necessity.

Da Vanzo and Chan studied what kinds of elderly do and do not tend to co-reside with their adult children in Malaysia. This is a country made up of three basic ethic groups (Malays, Chinese, and Indians) with different amounts of emphasis on intergenerational commitments within their families. There were, therefore, some differences in the amount of co-residence found between the aged and their adult children. Much more predictive of the choice to or not to co-reside were such practical matters as the income levels of the elderly persons, housing costs, the health status of the older persons, and whether the elderly people were married or not. Their basic conclusion was that in Asia as well as the West elderly people value privacy and independence (Da Vanzo and Chan, 1994).

The commitments of families to care for their elderly members in Thailand and Malaysia are no doubt still very much intact, as is true in all other parts of the world. However, those commitments are not necessarily related or counter to the growing, and seemingly global, desire of both the aged and their families to live in separate households as that becomes economically possible.

The tendency on the part of Oriental elderly people not to live in extended family situations is even more pronounced among those who migrate to the West. Koh and Bell interviewed a sample of Korean elderly who had migrated to the United States between 1972 and 1982, for example. They found that a large percentage of them had opted not to live with or become overly dependent upon their adult children, even though most of them could not speak English. The investigators concluded that these people, who were still very much steeped in their traditional Oriental culture, had nevertheless, "accepted a pattern of co-existence more characteristic of the United States than of Korea" (Koh and Bell, 1987).

It would seem, then, that there are signs of potential change even in those societies in which the majority of elderly people live with their families. In the industrially developed nations of the West, this pattern has already been abandoned. An important question is why this lifestyle is being rejected. Probably the most prevalent explanation is that it is due to the dynamic influence of modernization processes and economic development. The essence of this argument is that these processes tend to provide younger people with the necessary educational skills to enable them to become economically and socially independent from their families. Thus the aged end up becoming dependent upon their children instead of the other way around, an intolerable situation for both young and old.

This has been a convincing argument in a world currently focused on the importance of modernization. Fischer has provided a quite different and perhaps more profound explanation, however (Fischer, 1978, pp. 72–112). He makes the point that a "revolution in age relations" began in the United States long before the modernization era. The first signs of this revolution began to appear in the United States in about 1750, according to Fischer. Therefore, there must be some other explanation. His contention is that the changes in intergenerational relationships were not the product of economic development at all, but the development of a whole new set of values that severely challenged the existing social and political structure as well as the economic structure. Specifically the radical belief in "equality" and individual "liberty" revolutionized the daily lives of Americans in the mid-nineteenth century. As Fischer explains it, "the growth of those ideas in Anglo-America was caused primarily by the interaction of English Protestant ideas with the American environment" (Fischer, 1978, p. 109). The vast untapped resources in the United States provided practical opportunities for the young to be liberated from the traditional authority of the aged and claim equality with them.

According to Fischer, these values have spread throughout the world and with them the revolution in age relations. It is important to realize that belief in these revolutionary ideas has tended to influence the aged as well as younger people. It is thus very important to the elderly that they remain independent. Consequently, they are probably even more apt than young adults to reject the three-generation household today as a viable living situation.

EXTENDED FAMILY INTERDEPENDENCY

The pattern of multigenerational housing has been overwhelmingly rejected in Western Europe and the United States. It has been rejected by both the aged and their families. Almost the only exceptions to that trend occur when lack of family finances make other options impossible and when the elderly person's need for care becomes critical and families feel obligated to provide it. These exceptions would tend to take place especially on the part of those elderly persons who become widowed. To the extent that it still exists, then, it is practiced, not by preference, but as a result of practical necessity.

The movement away from multigenerational households made the development of other options necessary. The most prevalent option could be characterized as just one step removed. Contrary to the rather common notion that families tend to abandon their elderly members, as a whole, neither younger nor elderly family members have ever declared total independence from each other. They simply prefer not to live together, in order to avoid what could become daily dependence. Consequently, the most prevalent kind of living situation that the aged choose is to live in their own private homes, separate from but near their families. This was the lifestyle pattern found to exist in selected European countries and in the United States by a group of researchers (Shanas, Townsend, Wedderbaum, Friis, Milhoj, and Stenhouer, 1968, pp. 192–97). They characterized this kind of choice as "intimacy at a distance" (Shanas, 1977), indicating that while elderly people and their families wanted to avoid becoming dependent upon one another, they still prized continued and regular intrafamily relationships.

The data show that there was more to the continued family relationship than the need for intimacy, however. Also found were very prevalent mutual helping patterns between the aged and their adult children. They tended to help one another with a number of needs, including finances and domestic tasks (Shanas and others, 1968, pp. 217–25). Therefore, this lifestyle might best be conceptualized as a living situation in which family members are able to avoid total dependency within the family and move instead to family interdependency. Obviously neither the older nor younger adults want to give up the privileges of family membership; they merely want a change in those relationships. In a national survey of the attitudes of both young adults and the aged, Okrahu found more acceptance of the idea of multigenerational residence in 1983 than there had been in 1973 (Okrahu, 1987). The change toward more acceptance of that idea was greater among the younger adults than among the aged, however. These data by no means indicate the beginning of a return to three-generation household living for the aged. Respondents were not asked whether they were willing to live in multigenerational living situations; they were asked only whether they thought it was a good idea. Neither were they asked to distinguish between types of multigenerational residences. Probably the most that can be made of these data is that increasing numbers of people may be willing to consider that kind of living arrangement in a time when adequate care for the elderly is increasingly costly and unavailable, but only if and when necessary. Past evidence has shown that most elderly people still cling to their children and grandchildren more than anyone else for their ultimate care and security (Brown, 1974).

Living in their own private homes is not only by far the lifestyle that most of the aged prefer; it is also probably the one that is also the most feasible for them. In the United States, far more of the aged than any other age group are homeowners (more than 65 percent compared to 40 percent for those under 35). Furthermore, as many as 84 percent of the elderly homeowners actually own their homes outright (Lawton, 1980, p. 54). Most of these homes have been the places of residence of the elderly who own them for many years and are located in communities that they consider their own. This kind of living situation, then, symbolizes their sense of life's accomplishments, a deep sense of security, and a sense of continued independence.

Nevertheless, there are a number of problems associated with this kind of living situation. First, most of the houses that older people own are old; they are often in need of major repairs that are difficult for the aged themselves to make. Second, because their houses were typically purchased at a stage in life when their families were large, they are often too large for elderly couples or single individuals. Belden points out that these kinds of housing problems are particularly true in rural areas. Specifically, it has been found that many more elderly in rural than urban areas live in substandard housing, that there are fewer housing alternatives, and rural housing is worth much less than equivalent urban housing, and the rural elderly are more apt to be poor and unable to improve their housing. This is true even though the rural elderly are more apt to be homeowners (Belden, 1993).

INDEPENDENT LIVING

A sizable minority of the aged in the modern world strongly value their right to remain independent. These are people who not only choose to live in their own private dwellings but also tend to refuse to relate to anyone else upon whom they might become even partly dependent. They typically refuse even the kinds of assistance, from either families or community agencies, that they badly need. In so doing they face the danger of eventually becoming extremely isolated. The older they become, the more likely they are to become widowed and to live alone, and the less able they are to leave their homes to interact with others. At the same time, they will have an increasing need for assistance in daily living. Many who remain in their own homes also live in small communities in which the availability of such help is extremely limited. They must rely on the help of just one or two other people—usually family members—or are forced to enter a long-term care institution. Ironically, the most popular lifestyle choice among the aged often eventually places them in the very kind of dependency that they have tried to avoid by making that choice.

Independent elderly people are found in a variety of living situations. Many live either as couples or alone in their own homes in extreme isolation from both their families and others in their communities. Many live in isolated rural areas, often in primitive living quarters that require heavy labor to maintain. Others live in rental rooms of rundown innercity hotels, and some are among the growing number of homeless living on the streets of our large cities. Ironically, the older these people become, the more adamant they become about refusing help.

This pattern is found even among those whom Frankfather labeled as "confused." In discussing the plight of those who live on city streets, Frankfather said that professionals who deal with them tend to assume that their pitiful situation is due to their having been abandoned by families (Frankfather, 1977, pp. 27–34). In examining their patterns of behavior, we find that their condition is at least partly the product of their continued struggle for independence. In a study of homeless and hotel-dwelling elderly men on the New York City Bowery, for example, Cohen and Sokolovsky found that the one characteristic that distinguished them from other elderly men was their "sociability." They tended to be exceptionally socially isolated and related to others, if at all, "with adherence to a strict norm of reciprocity" (Cohen and Sokolovsky, 1983). The case of Charles E. Perkins in Fairfax, Virginia, illustrates the plight of elderly people's continued struggle for independence. He had been a highly intelligent biochemist, but at 89 he became confused. He challenged the right of law enforcement and welfare personnel to place him in institutional confinement and won. Nevertheless, he finally ended up in a state hospital geriatric ward where he was forced to interact with others who had mental illnesses far more serious than his (Grubisich, 1979).

We in the United States tend to admire the tenaciousness of elderly people who try to maintain their independence. It is generally not a realistic stance on their part, however. They tend to become increasingly isolated and have less capacity to care for themselves as they age. They also tend to neglect their own health and well-being by way of declaring their independence. Thus, the need for care becomes acute earlier than necessary, and they tend to be institutionalized, more prematurely than other elderly people. The lesson these people do not seem to learn is that total independence is impossible, and attempts to live that way are ultimately defeating. Sadly, we as a total society, have not found practical ways of avoiding the negative consequences of emphasizing the extremes of both independence and dependence.

We should not conclude from this, though, that this kind of extreme emphasis on independence typifies all of those elderly who choose to live alone. It does not. Living alone is a living situation that increasing numbers of elderly people are choosing. Arber and Ginn report that "an unprecedented rise in solitary living, and fall in average household size, has occurred in much of Northwest Europe and North America" (Arber and Ginn, 1991, p. 158). According to them, it has increased more in Britain in the past 30 years than in the previous two centuries. In the United States it has increased from 20 percent to 28 percent of the elderly from 1960 to 1980. It is also a trend that is particularly prevalent among those with relatively higher incomes and standards of living and is the most common living arrangement of elderly women (Arber and Ginn, 1991, p. 159). These are not choices that are being made to avoid social relationships or to become socially isolated, however, but rather because of the value being placed on freedom and privacy. Whether or not solo living is satisfying to those who choose it depends most on their health and their financial resources, which make it possible for them to remain socially active (Arber and Ginn, 1991, pp. 170–71).

Gelfand has discovered that living alone is also a pattern among the aged of various ethnic groups in the United States. The evidence in general is that the choice to live alone among nonwhite widows is more determined by the number of children they have and the duration of their widowhood rather than economic factors (Gelfand, 1994, pp. 118–19). Black elderly are the least likely to live alone, and among native Americans those who live off of their reservations are most likely to choose that lifestyle. Some Italian Americans make that choice, but only if they can live in close proximity to family members. Asian-Americans sometimes choose living alone in ethnic communities rather than the traditional pattern of living with their children in order to avoid conflict with their children and to live where they can more readily find friends their own ages and ethnic backgrounds (Gelfand, 1994, p. 119).

With regard to the choice to live alone even among those who are very old, Barer makes the point that men and women age differently (Barer, 1994). She reports that, while the women over 85 in her study tended to be much poorer and were more apt to live alone than the men, they, nevertheless had more contacts with and were more supported by their children. They had also been much less resistant to relocating to retirement housing when that became necessary. Others have similarly analyzed the typical living situations of the oldest old. These analyses are that women over 85 are the most apt of all elderly people to experience poverty, but that living alone is the preferred living arrangement, especially of the unmarried oldest old (Bould, Sanborn, and Reif, 1989, pp. 35–42), and that "most of them care for themselves, see and talk with family and friends, and go about their daily business with relative independence" (Kovar and Stone, 1992).

PEER-GROUP INTERDEPENDENCY

There is no doubt that the family has long been the social group to which elderly people have been oriented and from which they have gained their identities and sense of security. As we have seen, families are still viewed as vital to them. However, the spread of the values of equality and individual liberty and the focus on the importance of independence for the aged have placed important qualifications on their total reliance on family relations. Most elderly would be willing to settle for interdependent relationships with members of their families, but that kind of relationship cannot always be worked out with family members. Interdependency can work only in communities of equals, and relationships between parents and their children do not tend to be equal.

Fischer makes the point that among those who believe in equality and individual liberty, the establishment of communities is possible, but only with those who are "roughly alike" (Fischer, 1978, p. 111). This finding would indicate that, in their common goal of maintaining as much independence as possible for as long as possible, the aged might well increasingly turn to each other. In fact, peer-group participation is increasing among the aged in all parts of the world today. It is also increasing in all other age groups

This pattern of interaction began in the United States in the early part of this century with the development of such groups as the "Townsend movement." Urbanized elderly who shared the common plight of unemployment came together as political advocates to attempt to solve their common economic problems. While this did not represent a holistic, interdependent lifestyle, it served as the beginning of peer-group interdependency.

In the early 1960s, Rose predicted a fully developed "subculture of aging." He believed that as the aged population grew, they would increasingly interact with one another. This interaction pattern would develop partly because of the cohort affinities elderly people would feel for each other and partly because they were being systematically neglected by the rest of society. Out of these peer-group interactions, he said, an age-group consciousness, as well as group values and norms, would take form (Rose, 1965). Others have argued that this would never happen because of the great tendency on the part of those who are aging to resist being identified as old. Resistance to old-age identity does not necessarily preclude a sense of affiliation with one's peer group, however. Even critics of Rose's predictions acknowledge the increased amount of peer-group interactions that are taking place. Communities of the aged in which interdependent relationships exist have materialized out of their interactions.

Peer Group Interaction in Advisory Councils and Advocacy Groups

Elderly peer groups have taken a number of forms in recent years. One form in the United States has been in response to government-sponsored organizations. Local senior citizens' centers have been organized in local communities across the nation through the planning efforts of the federal, state, and local agencies on aging. Elderly people are brought together daily at these centers for a meal, recreation, and informal interaction. Although these centers are professionally administered by local agencies, the government requires that local councils on aging, made up primarily of elderly participants, serve in an advisory capacity to provide input on the centers' operation. These councils often have policy-making power over their local programs.

Similar councils on aging serve as advisory bodies to regional, state, and federal planning agencies. Members on these councils are elected by local bodies, and they often have a great deal of power as direct representatives of the elderly people who have elected them. There are limits to the amount of independence this system allows elderly people to have, however, since it is greatly dependent upon federal funding. Yet it provides abundant opportunities for the elderly to interact with one another and offers potential for them to develop interdependent relationships.

Another form of peer groups among the aged is autonomous advocacy groups, made up of and run by the aged themselves. There are at least three such groups in the United States that are well known and are nationwide: the Gray Panthers, the National Council of Senior Citizens (NCSC), and the American Association of Retired Persons (AARP). All these groups are effective advocates, but of the three, AARP is the best illustration of an interacting, interdependent group. The Gray Panthers and the NCSC have somewhat fixed points of view, are dominated by strong leaders, have members who share the same viewpoints, and promote only limited interactions among elderly people. In contrast, AARP emphasizes local interactive chapters and, in addition to its advocacy work, promotes a variety of activities among its members. This serves as a very practical interdependent peer group for thousands of elderly Americans, and its advocacy work is largely a product of that interdependency. One of the best illustrations of this kind of activity on the part of that organization is their recent involvement in developing the perspective of elderly people on the issue of health care reform. This activity began with a survey of the membership to determine their common perspectives on health care ("Special Report," 1992). Leaders of the organization then formulated a plan that reflected how members had responded. Further comments from members were then once again solicited ("AARP Plan Gets Big Yes Vote," 1992).

There are also local "grass-roots" advocacy groups that serve as interactional interdependent peer groups. In a study of the development of community service programs for the aged, it was discovered that local advocacy groups provided the necessary impetus. In communities in which programs were developed, local elderly people had first informally gathered on the basis of their common interests. They had then become organized in order to act on their common needs, and they advocated for outside assistance in developing programs to meet their needs (Brown, 1985). This is an effective type of interactional, interdependent peer group that has largely escaped our attention until now.

Peer Group Interaction in Age-Concentrated Housing

Probably the most obvious form of interdependent peer group interaction is that found in retirement communities and age-concentrated public housing. It is noteworthy that the demand for both these situations has been increasing among the aged population. There is some disagreement about the extent to which these kinds of living situations contribute to the well-being of those elderly people who are involved. There are many different kinds of age-segregated situations, however, and how participants are affected depends, in part, on which is being considered. In the United States they include a variety of innovative (1) small-scale local housing arrangements, (2) government subsidized housing for low-income elderly, and (3) privately planned retirement communities. It will be helpful to examine each of these approaches in more detail in order to better understand how each contributes to peer-group interdependency.

Malakoff identifies two basic approaches to what she labels as "home sharing" in local communities. One is "match-up home sharing" and the other is "group homes" (Malakoff, 1991, pp. 21–24). She describes the first of these as occurring "when persons with room to spare, share their home with others." Typically, this is a programmed effort on the part of local agencies that match the home providers and the home seekers. The key to the success of this program in promoting peer-group interdependency is how well those involved are matched. As Malakoff explains, "People enter home sharing arrangements with varying goals. Some may be interested in reducing their living expenses; others may be interested in companionship or security. Still others may be interested in exchange of services" (Malakoff, 1991, p. 22). Presumably, compatibility of goals would greatly enhance the interdependency of those involved.

Group homes differ from matchup homes in that they tend to be larger, they are not individually owned, and typically one or more housekeepers are employed. Once again, though, compatibility of goals on the part of participants helps to determine the success of such a program. Malakoff admits that home sharing is not for everyone. It is especially not good for those who value a lot of privacy (Malakoff, 1991, p. 23).

There are two basic types of government subsidized housing for the elderly. One is "planned housing" and the other is "congregate housing." The difference is that planned housing places the emphasis exclusively on housing; congregate housing also provides a variety of services to residents, such as a central kitchen and dining hall and congregate meals (Hooyman and Kiyak, 1991, pp. 350–54). Planned housing projects are typically developed in the form of apartment complexes in which the government subsidizes the rental costs for low-income elderly. Middle- and upper-income elderly are also allowed to rent units in those apartments (with no subsidies) if some units are not rented by low-income people. Thus a variety of elderly people are often involved. In essence, all that this kind of planned housing does to promote peer-group interdependency is to bring them together in one time and place. Whether interdependency emerges depends entirely on the extent that the residents themselves take the initiative to interact with each other. Nevertheless, a study of the residents of one such project revealed that, compared to a control group of nonresidents, they had more improved morale and health, and that they were consistently more active in the community around them, over a nine-year period (Hooyman and Kiyak, 1991, p. 350). A survey of congregate housing residents revealed that one of the benefits they valued the most was access to services that actually permitted them to live more independently than would have been true elsewhere (Hooyman and Kiyak, 1991, p. 354). Apparently peer-group interaction promoted not only interdependency but independence as well.

Peer Group Interaction in Retirement Communities

There are also a great variety of privately planned retirement communities that have emerged in this country in the past 30 or 40 years. They largely fit into three general categories: (1) those that emphasize nature and outdoor recreation; (2) those that emphasize security and social activities; and (3) those that provide a continuum of care. The first of these types of retirement communities are located in environmentally attractive rural areas where the potential for outdoor recreational activities (fishing, boating, etc.) are abundant. These are places that tend to especially attract those in their early retirement years and are relatively affluent. According to Glasgow, these communities have had a major effect on the migration of elderly people to rural areas. She reports that "rural retirement counties are one-fifth of nonmetropolitan counties, but they captured over half of all nonmetropolitan population growth between 1980 and 1986" (Glasgow, 1991). Nevertheless, it is obvious that these communities serve a very limited category of retirees and are able to serve them only for a limited number of years. These communities fail to offer the kinds of services that their residents will eventually need, such as personal and health care.

In spite of the many criticisms that have been leveled against those retirement communities that emphasize security and social activities, such as the Leisure Worlds and the Sun Cities, they continue to attract more and more retirees elsewhere in the world as well as in the United States. According to Gordon, it was estimated as early as 1985 that 1.3 million retired American people over 75 could afford to live in retirement communities, compared to the approximately 200,000 who now live in them. It has also been predicted that there will be a demand for about 812,000 new conventional retirement units by the year 2,000 (Gordon, 1988, pp. 1–2). He offers three basic reasons why these kinds of facilities are attractive to retirees. First, it provides them with specific social and recreational opportunities on which to focus the amount of free time they have in retirement. Second, it gives them a stable living situation with predictable costs for future contingencies that they need as retirees. Third, at least to some degree, it provides them with the potential services they are likely to need as they grow older. Healthcare and long-term care are particular concerns. As Gordon puts it, "Not all seniors need health care or personal care, but all face the growing possibility that an illness or disability will deplete their assets" (Gordon, 1988, p. 12). Increasing numbers of retirement communities are integrating housing with a range of health-related services to help their residents through the transition from independent to dependent status and avoiding the trauma that is so often related to suddenly having to go to a nursing home. In other words, more of them are becoming similar to continuing care retirement communities.

The American Association of Home for the Aging has defined continuing care retirement communities (CCRCs) as organizations that offer "a full range of housing, residential services and health care in order to serve its residents as their needs change over time (Netting and Wilson, 1991). The idea is to promote totally independent living among those who are capable, and at the same time offer every level of services that others need. This is an ever-increasingly attractive option among those who can financially afford it. In 1990 there were 800 such facilities in the United States, serving 230,000 elderly people. By the year 2000 it is projected that there will be as many as 1,500 facilities serving 450,000 (Netting and Wilson, 1991). Problems have been found, however, especially in the attempts being made to accommodate the needs of those at both ends of the continuum. Specifically, providing for the social needs of long-term-care patients is often perceived as undercutting the independence of those who are still capable of that (Netting and Wilson, 1991).

Kinoshita and Kiefer report that similar types of retirement facilities and communities are also rapidly becoming an option to the elderly in Japan (Kinoshita and Kiefer, 1992, pp. 62–79). The 1963 Welfare Act for the Aged made such institutions possible. That act provided the impetus for the development of four different types of facilities: (1) facilities that are similar to American nursing homes; (2) facilities that provide light intermediate care; (3) boarding-house-type facilities that provide residents with daily living services for a small fee; and (4) nonpublic supported residential facilities, for which the residents themselves must pay. According to Kinoshita and Kiefer, the combined total residents in the first three types of facilities grew from 48,186 in 1963 to 238,122 in 1989, and the fourth type of facility "is now a booming industry," despite a media-fed bias against such a movement (Kinoshita and Kiefer, 1992, pp. 74–79).

It would seem, then, that the combination of the various types of retirement communities and facilities are indeed meeting the basic felt needs of the elderly. The question remains, though, about the extent they actually promote peer-group interdependency. Friedan offers a severely negative critique of retirement communities partly in that regard (Friedan, 1993, pp. 59–63 and 381–86). She sees participation in these age-segregated communities as a "denial of age," "passing as young," and the failure to "seek for new functions," all of which deny participants real-life satisfaction and the very kind of intimate and meaningful relationships that they need and want. She also blames promoters of these communities of simply playing on and profiting from "the fear of being old and alone, the specter of age as inevitable deterioration and decline."

There is indeed some truth to her criticisms, if that is all there is to life in retirement communities, and if it is only what promoters advertise them to be. What she overlooks, however, is that day-to-day interactions between residents can produce "zestful improvisation among adventurous aging," who create "new spaces and structures that sustain them" that she so greatly admires, as much in those communities as in any other setting. In response to what they like about the retirement communities in which they live, elderly residents almost inevitably mention the new close friendships they have made (Crandall, 1991, p. 443).

Retirement communities and age-concentrated public housing have been investigated to determine the extent to which they fit Rose's description of the subculture of the aging (Longino, McClelland, and Peterson, 1980; Hinrichsen, 1985). Only limited support for the subculture hypothesis as a whole was found in these studies. Longino and colleagues, for example, found that those who live in retirement communities tend to represent a retreatist lifestyle, rather than the activist lifestyle that Rose had predicted. What is more important to our analysis of peer-group interdependency, however, is the fact that significantly more age-peer social relationships were found among those both in public housing and retirement housing than would have been true in integrated living situations. Obviously, in these situations, elderly people tend to interact more with their peers than with others, and it is in the context of interaction that interdependent relationships become established.

Peer Group Interaction Among Single Room Occupants

Still another illustration of an interactional interdependent peer group is to be found in a very unlikely setting—among single room occupants (SROs) of old inner-city hotels (mostly elderly men). As previously noted, these people tend to be much more isolated than most other elderly people. It has been found, though, that their isolation is by no means complete. They participate in identifiable social networks at least on a limited basis. These networks are typically made up of the occupants themselves in the hotels in which they live. A pattern of interdependency is found between network participants. While this kind of interdependency is limited in scope (the amount of interaction is minimal), it represents virtually the only interaction these people have and the only source of assistance in daily living to which they are willing to turn (Erickson and Eckert, 1977; Cohen and Sokolovsky, 1980; Cohen and Sokolovsky, 1983; Cohen, Teresi, and Holmes, 1985). Peer-group interdependency is clearly a type of interaction to which elderly people from virtually all walks of life are turning.

DEPENDENT LIVING

A fifth type of situation in which elderly people in today's world live is generally conceptualized as dependent living. Two basic questions must be answered in order to analyze this type of living situation. First, how do we define dependency? Second, what particular situations can be treated as dependent?

Investigators of the issue of dependency among the elderly population have tended to apply two basic definitions of dependency. Probably the most prevalent is a functional definition. Various scales based on sets of criteria considered to be normal have been devised that attempt to measure the functioning of individuals in society. Four areas of functioning have been highlighted for analysis: (1) *economic dependency*, which occurs when the older person is no longer a wage earner; (2) *physical dependency*, which occurs as individuals lose the capacity to control their bodily functions and physical environment; (3) *social dependency*, which arises as an elderly person loses meaningful others; and (4) *mental dependency*, which occurs as individuals lose the capacity to make decisions for themselves or solve their own problems (Kalish, 1982, pp. 111–12).

Many of these investigators have focused on just one of these forms of functioning—usually on physical functioning—in order to assess the level and types of care individuals need and the kind of care facilities that may be appropriate for them. These are valuable assessments but they tend to overestimate the extent of dependency. Kalish, for example, makes the very important point that for individuals to be dependent in terms of one type of functioning does not imply that they are also dependent in other ways; yet they are often treated as though that were the case. He suggests that "help with one kind of dependency tends to alleviate problems with other kinds of dependency" (Kalish, 1982, p. 111).

A definition that captures the essence of dependency is that which focuses on the extent that individuals have decision-making control over their own lives and their environments. Obviously, this necessitates that their mental capacities are intact, but an even more important issue is the amount of control over their daily lives that others may impose on them. Since the large majority of the aged do not in fact lose their mental capabilities, it is fair to ask why it is ever necessary to exert total control over them.

An important component of this analysis, then, is to examine the living situations that tend to be categorized as dependent living. Institutional living is the most obvious of these. To a large degree, institutionalization has become the most prominent symbol of the dependent lifestyle for the aged in the Western world. Nursing homes in the United States have come under severe criticism in the media in recent years because of the failure of many of them to provide adequate care. More important to elderly people themselves, though, is that becoming institutionalized represents total and permanent dependency and the loss of control of any part of their lives.

It is assumed that the way nursing homes tend to be managed and the manner in which care is provided serve to foster dependent attitudes and behavior patterns among residents. A number of British nursing homes with different management styles were studied in order to test that assumption. The institutions differed in the amount of freedom of action they allowed their patients to have. It was discovered that the level of dependency was just as great in the institutions allowing some freedom of action as in those with strict controls over patient's activities. The investigator indicated, however, that the differences among institutions' management styles were probably not great enough to make any significant impact on the dependency problem. He concluded that, "some radical departure from current residential practice is required in order to improve the well-being of residents" (Booth, 1986).

Approximately 5 percent of those 65 and over in the United States live in institutions, and assessments indicate that many of them could remain in their own homes if some assistance were available to them. The most prominent sentiment today is that institutionalization ought to be avoided by the aged for as long as possible. However, two very important factors related to dependency tend to be ignored in the prevailing negative attitudes about institutions and positive attitudes about residential living on the part of the aged. On the one hand, as previously noted, remaining in one's own home can create as much dependency as institutional living can. On the other hand, it is clearly possible for forms of interdependency to be created and put into practice even in institutions.

This latter point was illustrated by a program developed and administered by Kutner in the 1960s. This program consisted of helping the terminally ill, institutionalized elderly patients to (1) become sensitized to the institutional environment in which they lived; (2) identify problems related to that kind of environment; and (3) initiate problem-solving processes in cooperation with institutional staff. The patients themselves were often able to help execute the problem-solving plans and even to take charge of the processes involved. They found, in fact, that in some cases they as patients, working together, were able to take care of problems without staff assistance. As a result of this program, life in an institution was literally transformed from one of total dependency, in which some patients had to some degree even lost their interactional skills, to one of vital interdependency with their fellow patients and even the with the institutional staff (Kutner, 1970).

CONCLUSION

Totally dependent living is necessary for only relatively few elderly people. It obviously cannot be avoided on the part of those who suffer from severe dementia. Otherwise, however, dependent living is purely a matter of individual choice, institutional policy, or socially imposed control over the daily lives of elderly people. Furthermore, it is difficult to imagine how unnecessary dependency on the part of elderly people benefits anyone.

Neither is an extreme emphasis on independence a realistic or desirable option. The elderly among us ought to be not only allowed but also encouraged to develop interdependent lifestyles. Given present myths about aging, perhaps the most realistic form of interdependency is with age-related peers. The potential for intergenerational interdependent relationships is just as prevalent and desirable and ought to also be a goal toward which we move.

REFERENCES

"AARP Plan Gets Big Yes Vote," *AARP Bulletin*, 33, no. 10 (November 1992), 1, 14.

Arber, Sara, and Jay Ginn, *Gender and Later Life: A Sociological Analysis of Resources and Constraints* (Newbury Park, Calif.: Sage, 1991).

Barer, Barbara M., "Men and Women Aging Differently," *International Journal of Aging and Human Development*, 38, no. 1 (1994), 29–40.

Belden, Joseph N., "Housing for America's Rural Elderly," in *Aging in Rural America*, ed. C. N. Bull (Newbury Park, Calif.: Sage, 1993), pp. 71–83.

Booth, Tim, "Institutional Regimes and Induced Dependency in Homes for the Aged," *The Gerontologist*, 26, no. 4 (August 1986), 418–23.

Bould, Sally, Beverly Sanborn, and Laura Reif, *Eighty-Five Plus: The Oldest Old* (Belmont, Calif.: Wadsworth, 1989).

Brown, Arnold S., "Grassroots Advocacy for the Elderly in Small Rural Communities," *The Gerontologist*, 25, no. 4 (August 1985), 417–23.

Brown, Arnold S., "Report on Navajo Elder Abuse," unpublished research report submitted to the Navajo Office on Aging, Window Rock, Ariz., Fall 1986.

Brown, Arnold S., "Satisfying Relationships for the Elderly and Their Patterns of Disengagement," *The Gerontologist*, 14, no. 3 (June 1974), 258–62.

Cohen, Carl I., and Jay Sokolovsky, "Social Engagement Versus Isolation: The Case of the Aged in SRO Hotels," *The Gerontologist*, 20, no. 1 (February 1980), 36–44.

Cohen, Carl I., and Jay Sokolovsky, "Toward a Concept of Homelessness Among Aged Men," *Journal of Gerontology*, 38, no. 1 (January 1983), 81–89.

Cohen, Carl I., Jeanne Teresi, and Douglas Holmes, "Social Networks and Adaptation," *The Gerontologist*, 25, no. 3 (June 1985), 297–304.

Crandall, Richard C., *Gerontology: A Behavioral Science Approach* (New York: McGraw-Hill, 1991).

Da Vanzo, Julie, and Angelique Chan, "Living Arrangements of Older Malaysians: Who Resides with Their Adult Children?" *Demography*, 31, no. 1 (February 1994), 95–113.

Davis-Friedmann, Deborah, *Long Lives: Chinese Elderly and the Communist Revolution* (Cambridge, Mass.: Harvard University Press, 1983).

Erickson, Rosemary, and Kevin Eckert, "The Elderly Poor in Downtown San Diego Hotels," *The Gerontologist*, 17, no. 5, pt. 1 (October 1977), 440–46.

Fischer, David Hackett, *Growing Old In America* (New York: Oxford University Press, 1978).

Frankfather, Dwight, *The Aged in the Community: Managing Senility and Deviance* (New York: Praeger, 1977).

Friedan, Betty, *The Fountain of Age* (New York: Simon & Schuster, 1993).

Fullerton, Gail P., *Survival in Marriage: Introduction to Family Interaction, Conflicts, and Alternatives* (Hinsdale, Ill.: Dryden Press, 1977).

Garrett, Mario "Ageing in East and Southeast Asia: Is Family Support a Viable Policy?" *Bold*, 4, no. 3 (May 1994), 13–19.

Gelfand, Donald E., *Aging and Ethnicity: Knowledge and Services* (New York: Springer, 1994).

Glasgow, Nina, "A Place in the Country," *American Demographics*, 13 (March 1991), 24–30.

Gordon, Paul A., *Developing Retirement Facilities* (New York: John Wiley & Sons, 1988).

Grubisich, Thomas, "Aged Wanderer Baffles State," in *Human Services for Older Adults: Concepts and Skills*, eds. Anita S. Harbert and Leon H. Ginsburg (Belmont, Calif.: Wadsworth, 1979), pp. 224–27.

Hinrichsen, Gregory A., "The Impact of Age-Concentrated, Publicly Assisted Housing on Older People's Social and Emotional Well-Being," *Journal of Gerontology*, 40, no. 6 (November 1985), 758–60.

Hong, Guodong, lecture at the American Society on Aging Workshop, Beijing, China, April, 1993.

Hooyman, Nancy R., and H. Asuman Kiyak, *Social Gerontology: A Multidisciplinary Perspective* (Boston: Allyn & Bacon, 1991).

"The Japanese-Style Welfare System," *Japan Quarterly*, 30 (July-September 1983), 327–30.

Kalish, Richard A., *Late Adulthood: Perspectives on Human Development* (Monterey, Calif.: Brooks/Cole, 1982).

Kinoshita, Yasuhito, and Christie W. Kiefer, *Refuge of the Honored* (Berkeley, Calif.: University of California Press, 1992), pp. 62–79.

Knodel, John, Napaporn Chayovan, and Chanpen Saengtienchai, "Are Thais Deserting Their Elderly Parents?" *Bold*, 4, no. 3 (May 1994), 7–12.

Koh, James Y., and William C. Bell, "Korean Elders in the United States: Intergenerational Relations and Living Arrangements," *The Gerontologist*, 27, no. 1 (February 1987), pp. 66–71.

Kovar, Mary G., and Robyn I. Stone, "The Social Environment of the Very Old," in *The Oldest Old* ed. Richard M. Suzman, David P. Willis, and Kenneth G. Manton (New York: Oxford University Press, 1992), pp. 303–20.

Kutner, Bernard, "The Hospital Environment," *Social Sciences and Medicine*, 4 (supplement 1, 1970), 9–12.

Lawton, M. Powell, *Environment and Aging* (Monterey, Calif.: Brooks/Cole, 1980).

Longino, Charles F., Jr., Kent A. McClelland, and Warren A. Peterson, "The Aged Subculture Hypothesis: Social Integration, Gerontophilia and Self-Conception," *Journal of Gerontology*, 35, no. 5 (September 1980), 758–67.

Malakoff, Laura Z., *Housing Options for the Elderly: The Innovative Process in Community Settings* (New York: Garland, 1991).

Netting, F. Ellen, and Cindy C. Wilson, "Accommodation and Relocation Decision Making in Continuing Care Retirement Communities," *Health and Social Work*, 16 (November 1991), 266–73.

Okrahu, Ishmael O., "Age and Attitudes Toward Intergenerational Residence, 1973–1983," *Journal of Gerontology*, 42, no. 3 (May 1987), 280–87.

Palmore, Erdman B., and Daisaku Maeda, *The Honorable Elders Revisited* (Durham, N.C.: Duke University Press, 1985).

Piovesana, Gino K., "The Aged in Chinese and Japanese Cultures," in *Dimensions of Aging: Readings*, eds. Jon Hendricks and C. Davis Hendricks (Cambridge, Mass.: Winthrop, 1979).

Rose, Arnold M., "The Subculture of the Aging: A Framework for Research in Social Gerontology," in *Older People and Their Social World*, eds., Arnold M. Rose and Warren A. Peterson, (Philadelphia: F. A. Davis, 1965), pp. 3–16.

Shanas, Ethel, Peter Townsend, Dorothy Wedderbaum, Henning Friis, Paul Milhoj, and Jan Stenhouwer, *Old People in Three Industrial Societies* (New York: Atherton Press, 1968).

Shanas, Ethel, "Family-Kin Networks and Aging in Cross-Cultural Perspective," in *The Family: Functions, Conflicts, and Symbols*, eds. Peter J. Stein, Judith Richman, and Natalie Hannon (Reading, Mass.: Addison-Wesley, 1977), pp. 300–307.

"Special Report," *AARP Bulletin*, 33, no. 6 (June 1992), 6–10.

Yi, Zeng, "Changes in Family Structure in China: A Simulation Study," *Population and Development Review*, 12, no. 4 (December 1986), 675–703.

Zimmerman, Carle C., *Family and Civilization in the East and the West* (Bombay: Thacker, 1975).

7

The Elderly in the Family

INTRODUCTION

Change has characterized not only the living situations of elderly people, but also the way in which they fit into their families. The family itself has changed in its interactions with other social institutions, particularly the economic and political institutions. The foundations upon which the family rests, its structure and definition, and the kinds of relationships that exist among its members have all undergone basic changes.

There are obviously fundamental cross-cultural differences in the family and how the aged fit into it. How the family has changed within cultures is also different from one culture to another. In the context of change, the family has, at times, appeared to be an extremely fragile institution. Some analysts have even predicted its eventual demise. Surprisingly, though, it has continued to survive as a vital institution in all of its different cultural forms. The elderly member's place in the family in part reflects the changes that have taken place in the family as an institution. What is often overlooked, but is perhaps just as important, is the fact that the elderly have themselves contributed to and influenced the transformation of the family.

In this chapter we will examine how elderly people tend to fit into their families in light of the many changes. Particular attention will be paid to the roles and relationships elderly people tend to have within their families, and to the cross-cultural differences in these relationships.

THE CHANGING FAMILY

Family Changes in Western Cultures

Zimmerman has provided an informative analysis of changes in the family in the Western world over a number of centuries (Zimmerman, 1975, pp. 5–12). According to the analysis, throughout the centuries of ancient and medieval history, the family served both as the seat of political power and as the primary unit of production. These were the times in Western civilization of the "trustee family." Each generation of family members gained identity and social status by serving as trustees of family power and traditions and passing them on to the next generation. An inevitable part of the trustee family, however, was the frequently severe abuse of power.

According to Zimmerman, the trustee family was eventually replaced by the "domestic family." It was characterized as an autonomous, self-contained, economically and socially interdependent unit. While this type of family no longer had political power, societies still depended upon it for the socialization and integration of its citizens. The needs of the family unit were more important than the rights of individuals, but the family was still the source of individuals' identity and social status.

Elderly people tended to have positions of importance in the domestic family. By and large, they owned and controlled the economic (productive) enterprises in which the family was involved. They also served as authoritative heads of households. As long as Western cultures in the modern era remained primarily agrarian, the domestic family remained dominant and the aged continued to be very well integrated into the family system.

As societies became industrialized, the family found itself in competition with two new developments that brought about still another form of family. Corporations began to form and compete with family units as the primary production units upon which the economies of modern societies depended. At the same time, individualism began to take the place of loyalty and commitment to family as the dominant motivating force. As a result, the family lost both its economic function and much of its control over its members and was transformed into what Zimmerman called the "atomistic family." He characterized this type of family as oriented to the needs and aspirations of individuals. The rights of individuals took precedence over the rights of the family as a unit. Families now existed only to serve their individual members.

The nuclear family is the most prominent form of this type of family, and the basis of its strength is the conjugal (marriage) relationship rather than the kinship system. The family exists and serves the needs of its individual members only as long as the conjugal relationship exists. The irony is that the maintenance of the conjugal relationship itself depends upon the extent that it satisfies the needs and the aspirations of the individual marriage partners. These kinds of families do not survive from generation to generation. Instead, the survival of the family as a functional social institution depends upon its being re-created, unit by unit, with each generation. Zimmerman saw this type of family as inevitably self-destructive since self-interest cannot continue over the long haul to create the kind of family solidarity upon which individuals want to depend in order to satisfy their own needs.

   This description of how the family as a social institution has changed is exaggerated, of course. Identity with and commitment to the family by individuals have not disappeared, as Zimmerman's definition of the "atomistic" family would imply. While the extended family has been modified, it has by no means ceased to exist. Nevertheless, there is enough validity to Zimmerman's view of family change to legitimize its use to gain some insights about the place of the elderly in the modern family. As Berger and Berger have aptly described the condition of the modern family, "social changes have had a massive impact on the family, which has shown itself to be a remarkably robust and adaptable institution but which is nevertheless in a state of crisis" (Berger and Berger, 1991). Specifically, Hutter cites "a recurring theme in family sociology—the development of the ideology of family privacy," and that, he says, results in "the separation of the family from the community" and "the lessening of social supports to friends, neighbors, and kin" (Hutter, 1988, p. 433).

   The question for our analysis is how elderly people fit into the atomistic family. Like other individual family members, they would be expected to look to their families for the satisfaction of their felt needs. Logically, however, they could not expect much from their extended families since the nuclear family is the dominant family form. Their greatest source of satisfaction would seem to be the continuance of their own conjugal relationships into old age. The extent this is true today will be examined later.

   A similar description of changing family patterns in the modern era has been offered by Fullerton (Fullerton, 1977, pp. 4–34.) She explains that only 100 years ago, most economic production in the United States was family-dominated. Virtually all families served as economic units, mostly in the form of family farms which they owned and operated. That, probably more than anything else, gave family members common identities, life goals, and a sense of security. Division of labor between men and women and between young and old was pronounced, but everyone in the family had a role to perform and a common stake in the success of the family business. The division of labor was not between production and domestic responsibilities; instead, all the adult roles were blends of both of those types of family responsibilities. Elderly people did not retire from productive roles but simply took on less strenuous work without relinquishing either their share of family responsibilities or their share of the family benefits.

   According to this analysis, changes in family roles and relationships accompanied industrialization. Production moved from the home to the factory, and workers had to leave home and family behind in order to participate in productive work. It was this situation that brought about the division of labor within the family between the provider role for men, the domestic role for women, and virtually no family roles for the aged. In addition, workers now became paid employees, subject to being laid off and retired, especially as they became older. Thus, they were more and more frequently left with neither productive nor domestic family roles.

   It would be a mistake to conclude from this analysis that elderly people were better off in the time the domestic family operated or in the preindustrial era. In fact, those times were harsh, most elderly people worked hard throughout their lives, many were poor, and many workers died young (Fischer, 1978, pp. 59–73) and they were not always secure in their familial support (Hareven, 1992). Neither should we conclude that individuals were passive recipients of the forces of change. Families were made up of individuals, young and old, who were active participants making deliberate choices about such vital matters as working, moving to new communities, getting married, having children, retiring, and living separately from family members. These choices directly affected family roles and relationships and the positions of families in their communities. Together these choices created the changes in families discussed here. Members of today's elderly population were among the active participants. It is not our purpose to pass judgment about whether the changes were good or bad, however. This analysis simply helps us to understand both the processes that have created the changes and the fact that change is a dynamic process in which we ourselves are involved.

Family Changes in Other Cultures

Changes in the family have also taken place and continue to take place in societies with very different cultures from our own. Although the processes of change are based on quite different premises and involve very different players, some are as drastic and far reaching as those in the West. This is true, for example, in both the People's Republic of China and Japan, two Oriental societies which are themselves very diverse from each other.

Families in both the People's Republic of China and Japan have been steeped in the tradition of filial piety for centuries. This tradition specified the positions to be held by elderly people and the ways in which they were to be treated within the family. In addition, it was part of the religious belief system of these societies as well. It was the foundation of their tradition of ancestor worship. According to this tradition, elderly family members held positions of authority, were treated with great respect, and were expected to be taken care of by their families in old age.

Although filial piety was a well-established tradition in the People's Republic of China, it applied almost exclusively to those in the upper class. In a practical sense, poor families had too few resources to make it work (Lewis, 1982). Their whole lives were spent in hard labor in order to survive. The few who lived into old age also had to labor as long as physically possible. The tradition applied primarily to men, even in the upper class. While elderly women were cared for by their families, their authority in the family was mostly over daughters and daughters-in-law. They were subject to and controlled by their husbands, as symbolized by the traditional binding of their feet.

Casual observation of the Chinese family under Communism until very recently seemed to indicate that the filial piety tradition was still intact. Almost all elderly people lived with the families of one of their adult children (usually their eldest sons), and it was stipulated in the national constitution that families were legally responsible to take care of their elderly members. In fact, though, great changes in the family took place during the years of Communist rule in that country, and the elderly member's place in the family became only partly influenced by the tradition of filial piety.

Communism in the People's Republic of China quite effectively challenged the authority of aged males over their family members and the religious beliefs on which that authority rested. As explained in Chapter 6, children were free to marry whomever they chose, and women were liberated from slavery to their husbands. Employment opportunities were also separated from family control (Davis-Friedmann, 1983, p. 34). Although poverty still existed under Communism, the poor received basic benefits from the government or their local work units. Thus, the patterns of family roles and relationships between older and younger family members that developed after 1949 actually changed from the ancient traditions. They conformed more to the ideals of Communism than to the traditions of filial piety.

This point is illustrated by the roles and relationships that were found in the three-generation households not many years ago. The fact that most elderly people lived with their eldest sons and their families was undoubtedly due to the influence of tradition. In direct contrast to tradition, though, is the fact that the authority structure of those households belonged to neither the elderly parents nor their adult children. Instead it was a shared or cooperative authority and an arrangement of mutual benefit to everyone in the household (Butterfield, 1982, p. 219). This practice applied broadly to the entire population. That kind of emphasis represented a substantial change in the place of the aged in the Chinese family.

However, the family situation for the elderly in the People's Republic of China has changed quite drastically in the past decade. The economic reforms that have taken place in that country, and the subsequent financial improvements that so many families have experienced, have dramatically changed how elderly people relate to their families. Improved economics seems to have influenced many elderly people and their children to choose not to live in three-generational families any longer. In a lecture to a group of American gerontologists (of which I was a member) in Beijing in 1993, Hong reported that, in less than a decade, the elderly living in three-generational households had declined from well over 90 percent to one-half. Shi reports from a study of elderly in the rural areas of China that even there only 70 percent of those with three or more children and even fewer (42 percent) of those with less than three children live with children (Shi, 1993). That trend in and of itself severely threatens the amount of family interdependence that is possible. The generations seem to be declaring independence from each other at an alarming rate, at least in their everyday living situations, much the same as they have in most of the Western world. Part of what this means is that the elderly will lose the family role responsibilities, such as child rearing, that they have shared equally with their adult children and that made them a vital part of family life.

A number of people in the People's Republic of China assured me that the Chinese tradition of the importance of elderly people in the family is still intact. The story of a Shanghai family illustrates how continued intergenerational interdependency may still be possible among families that no longer live in three-generational households. In this case, the working parents live near their work in the center of the city, while their son lives with and is cared for by his grandparents during the week. The parents and grandparents also share many of the household costs. Shi also points out that as many as 91 percent of the rural elderly in the sample who live apart from their children still live in the same villages as they do (Shi, 1993). The questions about this are, however, how extensive these arrangements now are, and whether they have become, will ever become, or ever could become well-established patterns. In reality, it seems clear that the rapid trend away from three-generational families is in itself an indication of how quickly family traditions are changing in China, and how those changes will replace interdependency with one-way dependency between the elderly and their adult children. A similar tendency for elderly people to no longer live with an adult child has also been found in Taiwan (Tu, Freedman, and Wolf, 1993).

Changes away from the Oriental tradition of filial piety are also taking place in Japan, but because of very different influences. Japan has undergone the same modernization and economic development that have taken place in the Western world, but even more rapidly and intensely. Those processes have also affected families and the position of the elderly in those families. Changes in the Japanese family are nevertheless different from those that have taken place in the West.

The filial piety tradition in Japan was somewhat different from that in China. While its basic orientation was familial, it also applied to larger communal structures. As Piovesana explains, the family in China was basically a self-contained unit, somewhat independent of larger social structures. Therefore, the tradition of filial piety applied only to family relationships. In Japan, that tradition applied to the larger social structure as well, especially to politics and the military. (Piovesana, 1979). As Japan became industrialized and large corporations developed and grew during the era since World War II, then, it is not surprising that they were organized to include the tradition of filial piety as part of their management-worker relationships. In effect, corporations were conceived of as large families, and workers were treated as family members. As part of this arrangement, corporate heads gave their employees lifetime guarantees of social and economic security. Even though the immediate families are still expected to provide care to their elderly members, they are thus relieved of much of what is expected from the filial piety tradition in Japan. That has affected the kinds of roles and relationships that exist between the generations of the family. According to Palmore, these traditions still apply in a public sense, even though tensions in three-generation households are increasing (Palmore, 1993).

Hashimoto admits that the extended family has gradually decreased in Japan, with as many as a third of the elderly not now living in three-generation households. Nevertheless, he contends that this merely represents "a postponement of coresidence rather than a substantive change in support arrangements for those in advanced age." They expect to move in with adult children "as needed in the future" (Hashimoto, 1993). This does, nevertheless, represent at least somewhat of a change in family traditions.

Meir and Ben-David describe changing family patterns in still another very different cultural situation—that of the Negev Bedouin society, living under Israeli governmental rule since the 1950s (Meir and Ben-David, 1993). As they describe it, during these years society has moved from being purely nomadic through "three quite distinct phases of development." These include (1) seminomadism, or a "shift from pure livestock-based nomadism into a mixed economy of sedentary farming and nomadic pastoralism"; (2) rural sedentarization; and (3) semiurbanization, or living in towns that are larger than villages.

Through those stages the family has changed drastically. As these investigators explain, this was originally a society in which the extended family "behaved as a collective economic unit with a complete collective fund" that supported the elderly, and that fund was controlled by the elderly patriarches in charge of all family matters. In the process of the changes they have experienced, elderly men have lost control over all family economics, and the society itself has lost its ability to economically support its own elderly. Ironically, both older men and women are financially better off today than ever before, because of the availability of government welfare. However, the family structure and traditions have drastically changed and the internal support system that once existed has been progressively severed.

MARITAL ROLES AND RELATIONSHIPS

For the vast majority of elderly people, the marital relationship is the most vital aspect of family life. According to the 1990 census, 77.7 percent of the men and 41.5 percent of the women 65 and over in the United States are married and living with their spouses (Crandall, 1991, p. 49). Most of these couples have lived together for many years, and a major part of their social lives has been oriented to being married regardless of the quality of their marital relationships.

Evidence indicates that how couples divide their family responsibilities and define their respective roles tends to change throughout the course of their marriages. Marriages tend to begin on an egalitarian basis but move toward greater differentiation. This pattern tends to be reversed again in the later years of marriages, mainly as a result of the empty nest and retirement experiences (Troll, 1985, p. 185; Atchley, 1987, p. 185). Marital adjustment and satisfaction through the course of marriage has been an important area of research during the last quarter of the century in the United States. In a cross-sectional comparison of couples at eight different stages of married life, Rollins and Feldman examined a number of facets of marital adjustment (Rollins and Feldman, 1970). Couples in the study were asked to indicate the extent to which they (1) felt their marriages were going well; (2) had negative feelings as a result of interactions with their spouses; (3) enjoyed having positive companionship experiences with their spouse; and (4) felt satisfied with their present marital relationships. The stages of the family life cycle included in the study were (1) beginning families (without children); (2) child-bearing families; (3) families with preschool children; (4) families with school-age children; (5) families with teenagers; (6) families as launching centers; (7) families in the middle years; and (8) aging families.

The findings showed that the older the couples, the more both spouses said their marriages were going well. More aging families felt that way than any of the others. In that sense, elderly men were even more positive about their marriages than their wives. Compared with those at other stages of the family life cycle, elderly couples reported the fewest negative feelings from interactions with their spouses and the greatest levels of marital satisfaction. With regard to marital satisfaction specifically, as many as 82 percent of the elderly wives and 66 percent of the elderly husbands said their marriages were "very satisfying" (see Figure 7-1).

Other studies on marital relationships show similar high levels of marital satisfaction among elderly couples in the United States and elsewhere (Burr, 1970; Stinnet, Collins, and Montgomery, 1970; Stinnet, Carter, and Montgomery, 1972; Atchley and Miller, 1982; Gilford, 1986; Markides and Hoppe, 1985). What this seems to indicate is that the pressures of active parenthood take their toll on marriage. As Collins and Coltrane put it, "the conclusion is hard to escape: children are a strain on a marriage" (Collins and Coltrane, 1991, p. 399). Some have suggested, however, that marital satisfaction among the elderly may simply be because elderly couples represent successful marriages that have survived into old age. The unsuccessful marriages that have ended in earlier divorces are never included. Nevertheless, Gilford found evidence that marital satisfaction among aged couples does not represent just the continuation of previously successful marriages. Instead, there is much potential for marital satisfaction to develop in the context of elderly marriages themselves (Gilford, 1984).

Bengtson and colleagues report that, compared to those who aren't married, married elderly people have "higher levels of morale, life satisfaction, mental and physical health, economic resources, social integration and support, and lower rates of institutionalization" (Bengtson, Rosenthal, and Burton,

Figure 7-1 Percentage of Individuals in Each State of the Family Life Cycle Reporting That Their Present Stage Is "Very Satisfying" (SOURCE: B. C. Rollins and H. Feldman, "Marital Satisfaction over the Family Life Cycle," *Journal of Marriage and the Family,* 32. no. 6 (February 1970), 20–28.)

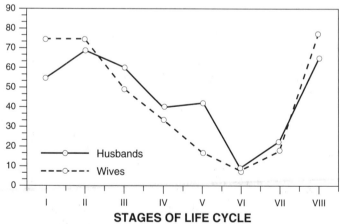

PERCENTAGES

STAGES OF LIFE CYCLE

I = Beginning Families
III = Families with Preschool
    Children
V = Families with Teenagers
VII = Families in the Middle
    Years

II = Child-Bearing Families
IV = Families with School-Age
    Children
VI = Families as Launching
    Centers
VIII = Aging Families

1990). This, they contend, is largely because they are less likely to "engage in high-risk health behavior," and because "spouses provide invaluable care in times of poor health." The elderly report a variety of reasons that the majority of elderly rate their marriages as either "happy" or "very happy," according to these analysts. These reasons include the personal characteristics that they value in their spouse; liking their spouse as a person; having a spouse who is a best friend; agreeing with their spouse on life goals; and maintaining humor in their marital relationships. Bengtson and his colleagues conclude that this list of marital satisfaction items is indicative of the fact that the bases of positive marital relationships change over the life course of the marriage. As they put it, "physical attraction, passion, and self-disclosure are viewed as facilitating the formation of a new relationship, but relations are sustained over the long term by familiarity, loyalty, and a mutual investment in the relationship" (Bengtson, Rosenthal, and Burton, 1990).

In contrast to these positive findings on the marital relationships of elderly couples, Rollins and Feldman found that levels of positive companionship among the elderly were lower than those at any of the other family life-cycle stages. Only 36 percent of the elderly wives and 32 percent of the elderly husbands reported such experiences at least once per day (see Figure 7-2). This raises the question of what the basis of marital satisfaction is for elderly couples. Rollins and Feldman did not address that issue, but subsequent studies have identified four basic reasons that elderly couples give for their positive feelings about their marriages. Ironically, one of the reasons given was com-

Figure 7-2 Percentage of Individuals In Each State of the Family Life Cycle Reporting "Positive Companionship Experiences with Their Spouse At Least "Once a Day." (Source: B. C. Rollins and H. Feldman, "Marital Satisfaction over the Family Life Cycle," *Journal of Marriage and the Family,* 32. no. 6 (February 1970), 20–28.)

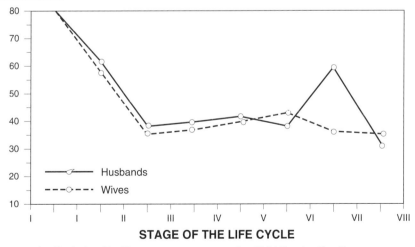

panionship. Stinnet and colleagues found that companionship, seen by both elderly husbands and wives, was the most rewarding aspect of their marriages (Stinnet, Carter, and Montgomery, 1972). This finding would seem to conflict with that of Rollins and Feldman. It may, in fact, simply help to explain the previous finding, however. While Rollins and Feldman focused on the frequency of companionship experiences, the Stinnet data emphasized the quality of marital companionship. Elderly couples may not be as concerned about the number of events that they share as they are about the meanings of what they do together.

Another aspect of marital life that has been identified by elderly couples is that of intimacy (Stinnet, Carter, and Montgomery, 1972; Gilford, 1986; Atchley, 1987, pp, 189–91). Stinnet and his colleagues found that being in love was seen by those in their sample as the most important factor in achieving marital success. Most couples also remain sexually active throughout their lives. In addition, intimacy among elderly couples includes showing mutual affection, respect, and trust (Mosher, 1994, pp. 51–55). They gain much satisfaction from freely and openly sharing feelings, ideas, and opinions. For many older people, especially men, their mates are their only confidants (Lowenthal and Robinson, 1976).

The third reason for marital satisfaction among the aged, very much related to intimacy, is the sense of *belonging* that being married provides. Families, and particularly marriages, apparently become an increasingly important source of identity and of the sense of being important to others as we become older. This would be particularly vital in retirement, with the loss of an active work role.

Still another source of marital satisfaction for elderly couples is interdependency. The sharing of household responsibilities and income is often mentioned as part of their interdependency (Atchley, 1987, pp. 189–91; Gilford, 1986; Kremer, 1985). An even more vital aspect of their interdependence, though, is their reliance on each other for the care they may need in their later years as discussed earlier. Spouses are by far the most preferred caregivers for elderly people (Cantor, 1992), and the knowledge that care by someone as intimate as a spouse is available provides individuals with a great sense of security and satisfaction.

Not all elderly couples are satisfied with their marriages, of course. Factors that tend to be related the most to lack of marital success among the aged are chronic health conditions, lack of mutual interests and values, and lack of companionship (Atchley, 1987, pp. 185–86; Stinnet, Carter, and Montgomery, 1972; Gilford, 1986). It is noteworthy that retirement is hardly ever related to marital problems (Atchley and Miller, 1982).

Cowgill makes the point that very little attention has been paid to marital relationships of elderly people in societies other than Western societies (Cowgill, 1986, pp. 80–81). This does not mean that marriages are unimportant to families in other societies. It does mean, however, that family solidarity in other cultures is not as vitally dependent upon the kinds of relationships married couples have. Likewise, elderly people in non-Western societies tend to be integrated into family life regardless of their marital relationships. Because of these differences, then, attention to the marital adjustment and satisfaction as an important aspect of family life for elderly people is mostly a phenomenon of the Western world.

EXTENDED FAMILY ROLES AND RELATIONS

In the past, the extended family was the most important social context within which the aged were provided with meaningful roles and relationships. During the post-World War II era, students of the family predicted that the extended family would soon cease to exist as a functioning entity in the modern world (Goode, 1963, pp. 179–95). This has not happened. Instead, the extended family itself has substantively changed and remains vital to elderly people. Extended family roles and relationships differ among cultures, but there are similarities as well.

In Western cultures, there has been a move away from the traditional extended family, a kinship system in which there was complete economic interdependence and a daily exchange of goods and services. In its place we have adopted what has become called the "modified extended family." This is a kinship system in which economic resources are controlled by independent nuclear family units, but goods and services are freely and regularly shared and emotional support is provided (Eshleman, 1985, pp. 88–89; Leslie and Korman, 1985, pp. 233–38).

If the modified extended family actually exists in Western societies today, then the aged should have solid family roles and relationships beyond their marriages. During the early post-World War II era in the United States and Europe, it was thought by many that this was not the case and that elderly people were being abandoned by their families. A comprehensive study of the aged in the United States, Great Britain, and Denmark in the mid-1960s, however, clearly showed that almost all elderly people do in fact benefit extensively from a number of different types of relationships within the modified extended family (Shanas, Townsend, Wedderbaum, Friis, Milhoj, and Stehouwer, 1968, pp. 132–57).

Coward and colleagues report that family relations among rural elderly differ from those among urban elderly. In general they have about equal amounts of face-to-face interactions with their adult children, but whether they are "farm" or "nonfarm" rural residents makes a big difference in that regard. Those who are "nonfarm" residents tend to have the least amount of interaction with their children, and the "farm" residents tend to have the most such interaction. However, even that interaction apparently has little or no impact on their personal sense of well-being, such as feeling lonely (Coward, Lee, and Dwyer, 1993).

Because the modified extended family is composed of relatively independent individuals and nuclear family units, it is by nature a voluntary system. Important areas of inquiry, therefore, are (1) what prompts the ongoing relationships between elderly people and their family members; (2) with whom the relationships tend to be; and (3) what the nature of those relationships tend to be.

Family Relational Preferences

One study indicates that many patterns of interaction between the aged and others outside their immediate households are very much related to how satisfied the elderly persons are in relating to those other persons (Brown, 1974). Four types of relationships were compared in this study to determine if and when they tended to disengage from each (see Figure 7-3). These in-

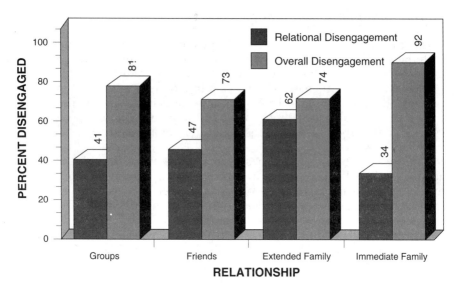

Figure 7-3 Percent of Relational and Overall Disengagement By Type of Relationship (Source: A. S. Brown, "Satisfying Relationships for the Elderly and their Patterns of Disengagement," *The Gerontologist*, 14, no. 3 (June 1974), 258–62.)

cluded (1) group relationships; (2) relationships with friends and neighbors; (3) extended-family relationships (any family members other than descendants of the elderly persons); and (4) immediate family relationships (direct descendants, including sons- and daughters-in-law). It was found that those who expressed some level of dissatisfaction with the first three types of relationships had a distinct tendency to disengage from people in those categories. There were no significant associations between those specific disengagement patterns and overall disengagement, however. As they gave up one kind of relationship, they tended somewhat to develop others to take the place of those that were lost. It is important to note that those in the sample treated extended-family relationships similarly to relationships outside their families. They were given up just as readily when they were no longer personally satisfying.

Relationships with their immediate-family members tended to be different, however. The distinct pattern in that case was that they were much less apt to disengage from their children, sons- and daughters-in-law, or grandchildren, regardless of how satisfying or dissatisfying those relationships might have been. It is interesting, though, that those who expressed less than total satisfaction with immediate-family members tended to demonstrate extensive overall disengagement patterns. It was as though, having withdrawn from most other types of people, they were finally clinging to those relationships that were the most vital to them. Apparently, then, of all extended-family members, descendants are preferred over all others.

Affective, Helping, and Role-Performance Relations

Having children, then, seems to be vital to one's old age experience. Connidis and McMullin point out, however, that studies comparing the well-being of elderly people with and without children show mixed results (Connidis and

McMullin, 1993). They found the advantage or disadvantage of having children tends to depend greatly upon whether or not the elderly parents are emotionally close to their children and whether or not the childlessness of others was a matter of their free choice. There were no significant differences found in their research between these two groups of elderly in terms of their sense of well-being. As they explain this, on the one hand, "the childless by choice develop social support networks which are similar to the networks of close parents in their ability to serve as effective buffers of stress, thereby enhancing well-being." On the other hand, their conclusion is that "children enhance well-being but only if parents view their relationship with them as close" (Connidis and McMullin, 1993). This may be too simple a conclusion because children often provide vital instrumental as well as affective benefits to their elderly parents which contribute to their sense of well-being. Nevertheless, elderly parent-adult children relationships are quite complex. They involve elements of both personal intimacy and role performances on the part of both parties. These relationships are also often beset with problems, even though they have remained persistent over time and across a variety of cultures (Waite and Harrison, 1992). For one thing, as Rossi and Rossi point out, "the parent-child relationship may last 50 or more years and undergo much renegotiation" (Rossi and Rossi, 1990, p. 6).

Relational characteristics between elderly people and their adult children were identified in the cross-cultural study on aging conducted by Shanas and her colleagues in the 1960s (Shanas, Townsend, Wedderbaum, Friis, Milhoj, and Stehouwer, 1968, pp. 195–206). One of those characteristics was that elderly people tended to live in close enough proximity with at least one of their children to have contact with them at least once a week. Data from a study of three other very different countries (Poland, Yugoslavia, and Israel) conducted at about the same time showed similar patterns (Shanas, 1977). A more recent study of weekly contacts between the aged and their adult children in Sweden showed that this interactional pattern still persists today (Sundstrom, 1986). This has been found to be true even for the elderly living in retirement communities (Baker, 1983, pp. 66–67).

Children have clearly been, and continue to be, an important source of intimacy for elderly people even though those in most Western countries prefer to maintain an element of independence from their children. Some types of elderly parent-adult children relations are more important than others. Beckman and Houser studied the other side of this issue—elderly people who have no children with whom to relate. They found that the widowed who were childless had lower feelings of well-being than the widowed with children, particularly if they were in poor health and were socially isolated. This was also more true for Jewish and Catholic widows than Protestants (Beckman and Houser, 1982). It is reported that the mother-daughter relationships tend to be closer and to be characterized by more frequent contact than those of either mothers and sons, fathers and sons, or fathers and daughters (Thurnber, 1982; Troll, 1986).

As noted above, there is much more to elderly-adult children relationships than affection and intimacy, however. Bengtson and colleagues theorized that intergenerational family solidarity or the lack of it was based on three basic elements of compatibility: continuous association or interaction, degree of concensus about values, and affection (Bengtson, Orlander, and Haddad,

1976). In a more recent study of intergenerational solidarity, though, almost no support was found for that theory (Atkinson, Kivett, and Campbell, 1986). Helping behavior, especially by females, rather than either consensus or affection, provided the basis for continued interaction and solidarity. Thus, contacts between elderly people and their adult children involve not only affective relationships but role obligations and responsibilities as well.

Most elderly people and their children readily accept the fact that they have role obligations toward one another and are willing to perform those helping roles. They also understand that the substance of their roles is to provide help when it is needed. Wolfson and colleagues questioned a sample of adult children in Canada about whether they believed that they "should" and "could" provide their elderly parents with needed financial, emotional, and physical support. They found that "all scores were high, with 'should' consistently higher than 'could.'" They concluded that, even though their sense of responsibility was greater than their capacity to carry it out, especially with financial support, nevertheless, "adult children feel a strong obligation to provide care to their elderly parents" (Wolfson and others, 1993).

Johnson and Barer found some variance from this in a comparative study of family support received by inner-city black and white elderly people. They found that neither group received much support from either their spouses or their children (Johnson and Barer, 1990). Part of the reason for this was that they tended to have a number of formal supports such as Medicaid, SSI, formally provided chore workers, transportation, and meals, which their families could not provide. In addition black elderly typically turn to "fictive kinship relationships" (churches, etc.) for the assistance they need (Dilworth-Anderson, 1992; Walls, 1992). As a whole, though, families still provide such care. Also, Troll and Bengtson report that even the old-old tend to make a major contribution to their families as "kin-keepers and enhancers of family solidarity" (Troll and Bengtson, 1992).

Almost never do the parties involved understand the specific duties involved or have a consensus about who is to do what, and when, however. Parent-child relationships may be well understood when children are young, but they become more complicated when both are adults and when parents are in the process of becoming old. Typically, these role obligations must be negotiated in the context of interaction. In all likelihood, role negotiations make up a good part of the interactions between elderly people and their children, and these negotiations are subject to a great deal of misunderstanding and conflict. Interactions are complicated by the fact that what is being negotiated is not just what kinds of help to give to whom at what time, but also who has the power to control the helping processes. Quite often this involves role reversal—a process that neither the elderly parents nor their adult children find desirable.

Evidence of the problematic aspects of elderly parent-adult children relationships was found in a study of the association between intergenerational solidarity and life satisfaction and depression among older Mexican Americans (Markides and Krause, 1985). It was found, contrary to the investigators' expectations, that affection toward them had nothing to do with the extent to which the elderly respondents associated with their children. Association with their children was, in fact, positively associated with depression. At the heart of this relational problem was the extent to which the elderly tended to receive more help from their children than they gave to them.

There are indications that the problematic aspects of elderly parent-adult children relationships may be even more pronounced in Japan than in America. Campbell and Brody studied the attitudes of women in those two countries related to their roles of helping elderly family members. They found that the women of all ages in both countries uniformly agreed that caring for the aged is a family responsibility. However, Japanese women reported fewer positive experiences with older family members than the American women did. In contrast to the American women, they also said that old people in Japan are too powerful (Campbell and Brody, 1985). In reviewing some of the even more recent literature on aging in Japan, Palmore admits that there is a "negative side." Specifically, he recognizes that they can no longer be sure that "their children will take care of them, when and if they become dependent, financially or physically," and that "the public show of respect is apparently balanced by private negative stereotypes and resentment against the demands and traditional dominance of elders" (Palmore, 1993). The lack of positive experiences and the negative attitudes about power in old age among younger Japanese family caregivers results from role negotiations typically taking place in intense household settings.

In the People's Republic of China, the most problematic intergenerational role negotiations have been between mothers-in-law and daughters-in-law, since elderly parents have typically lived with sons rather than daughters. This is still somewhat prevalent but may be less so today than in the past, because fairly well-defined and extensive interdependent helping roles characterize their intergenerational relationships within those situations in which elderly still live in three-generation households. In those cases, it is well understood, for example, that both the men and women will have jobs and that their retired parents will assume the child-rearing responsibilities while the children's parents are at work. Having in-laws to care for their children was generally viewed as a sign of privilege, at least until very recently (Davis-Friedmann, 1983, p. 21) Through these cooperative efforts more income was available to maintain the household, and young and old benefited. Davis-Friedmann reported in the early 1980s that power within Chinese households was determined not by age or tradition, but by who was able to earn the highest income (Davis-Friedmann, 1983, p. 80).

Shi more recently studied the conditions among Chinese elderly in rural areas. It was revealed that as many as 59 percent of the elderly received no income of their own and were, therefore, financially dependent upon their families. In addition, as many as 30 percent of those with three or more adult children and 58 percent of those with fewer than three children no longer lived with any of their children. Most still live in the same villages with their children, however, and there is still a great deal of reciprocal helping behavior but very little with regard to finances. Shi concluded that, as a result of the current one-child-per couple policy, too much strain is beginning to be placed on the increasingly smaller families, and that the tradition of reciprocal elderly-adult child helping processes are eroding in that country (Shi, 1993). A very similar problem exists among the Chinese elderly in Taiwan (Tu, Freedman, and Wolf, 1993).

Much of the literature on relationships between elderly parents and their children treats helping processes as a one-way phenomenon—adult children helping their elderly parents. As the findings from the 1968 cross-cultural study of the aged demonstrated, however, that is only one part of the helping process. Shanas and colleagues found substantial helping behavior in both directions. As Table 7-1 shows, more of the Danish elderly provided help to their children than received help from them, although there were fewer helping relationships in that country than in either the United States or Great Britain. In all three countries there were both types of helping relationships, and in some cases they were reciprocal. Eggebeen reported on a recent national survey of 13,017 respondents to discover the helping patterns of elderly people and their adult children. He found that giving and receiving various types of assistance still go in both directions (Eggebeen, 1992). Among the adult children, 19 percent were "receivers only," 17 percent were advice givers, and only 11 percent were actually "enmeshed in strong exchange networks." Of the elderly included in the survey, 42 percent were advice givers, 29 percent provided childcare, and as many as 33 percent provided financial help to their children, compared to only 3 percent of them receiving financial help from their children. Somewhat surprisingly, only a relatively small percentage of Mexican-American and the African-American children in the sample provided tangible supports to their elderly parents.

Gallagher and Gerstel recently studied the amount and types of helping behavior among a sample of elderly women in the United States. In their study they compared married and widowed women. Their purpose was to test the prevailing stereotypes that elderly people are the ones who receive help from and are dependent upon their families, and that married elderly women provide help to others much more frequently than those who are widowed. They found, in fact, that both groups engage in a surprising amount of helping behavior. It is true that married women spend more time and provide more types of help to those in their kin systems than widows. There are two reasons for this: (1) Widowed women tend to be older and have fewer resources, and (2) they spend more time and provide services to more friends other than kin than married women. The conclusion of these investigators is that "marriage

TABLE 7-1   Proportion of Older Men and Women Giving Help to and Receiving Help From Children

HELPING PATTERNS	DENMARK			BRITAIN		
	MEN	WOMEN	ALL	MEN	WOMEN	ALL
Gave help	24	32	28	40	48	44
Received help	17	21	19	53	63	59

HELPING PATTERNS	UNITED STATES		
	MEN	WOMEN	ALL
Gave help	59	60	60
Received help	61	75	69

SOURCE: Ethel Shanas, Peter Townsend, Dorothy Wedderbaum, Henning Friis, Paul Milhoj, and Jan Stehouwer, *Old People in Three Industrial Societies* (New York: Atherton Press, 1968), pp. 203–6.

privatizes women's help to others" (Gallagher and Gerstel, 1993). Probably it would be more correct to say that widowhood turns the helping process on the part of elderly women away from family to others. In any case, elderly people do in fact engage in the helping process as readily as anyone. While all of this makes elderly people more equal partners in the parent-child relationships than is generally assumed, it undoubtedly serves to complicate the process of role negotiation. The fact that the helping process in most individual situations is one-way, with one or the other party being dependent upon the other, complicates the role negotiation processes even more.

Caregiving as a Family Role Obligation

The caregiver role is an important aspect of the helping process in which many adult children engage in behalf of their aged parents. As Orodenker explains, "commitment to the value of filial responsibility still remains high across all age groups (Orodenker, 1991, p. 4) and this is true in virtually all societies (Winbush, 1992). This is a role that not only must be negotiated but is also problematic in terms of what it requires in performance. It has been discovered that at least 75 percent of the care that elderly long-term-care recipients receive in the United States is being provided by informal caregivers (Cantor, 1983; Goldstein, Regnery, and Wellin, 1981; Branch and Jette, 1983; Orodenker, 1991, p. 4). Most of these are family members, primarily spouses and daughters of the care recipients. The evidence also indicates that the majority of informal caregivers have had no training in, and therefore lack the skills needed for, caregiving (Soldo and Myllyluoma, 1983). While family members generally accept the responsibilities of this role without reservations (Troll, 1986; Campbell and Brody, 1985; Brown, 1989), many become somewhat overwhelmed by what is required in the actual performance of the caregiver role. They often feel frustrated at being unable to do all that needs to be done, heavily burdened by the constancy of the role in competition with other role responsibilities, and guilty about feeling burdened (Orodenker, 1991, p. 9). When these feelings on the part of caregivers are combined with the sense of dependency that elderly parents tend to feel toward their caregiver daughters, caregiving situations can easily threaten parent-child relationships. For one thing, caregivers often develop a heavy sense of burden related to their caregiving responsibilities. Interestingly enough, Thompson and colleagues found that the sense of burden did not relate as much to a lack of support from others in carrying out their caregiver duties as to the need for socializing completely separately from those duties (Thompson, Futterman, Gallagher-Thompson, Rose, and Lovett, 1993).

Affection between parents and children has often been seen as a key to successful caregiving, but Jarrett has suggested that a sense of obligation, somewhat apart from affection, is a more reasonable basis for caregiving (Jarrett, 1985). The role of the caregiver also differs between men and women (Miller and Cafasso, 1992). The relationships between elderly parents and their adult children are obviously vital to elderly people. They are neither consistently negative nor consistently positive but can potentially be both. They involve extremely complex and dynamic processes that can easily result, alternatively, in great personal satisfaction and in frustration.

Part of what complicates the role of the caregiver is having to also hold down a job. This has been analyzed as creating an intensive amount of role conflict for those involved (Cantor, 1992; Leeson and Tufte, 1994). Scharlach found, however, that although some, indeed, felt frustrated in terms of the pressures of time, many experienced a sense of fulfillment and an opportunity to have satisfying relationships with others from their jobs that could never come to them through the caregiver role (Scharlach, 1994).

The Elderly as Grandparents

Elderly persons' positions as grandparents constitute another area of growing interest concerning their place in the family. Limited analysis has been done in this area, with very little cross-cultural comparisons done about it. There are also major disagreements in the literature about the nature of this particular family relationship. Partly at issue are (1) the extent to which grandparents tend to interact with their grandchildren; (2) the importance of being a grandparent; (3) the nature of grandparents' relationships with their grandchildren; and (4) the kinds of role expectations or performances that are connected to being grandparents.

The role of grandparent has changed quite drastically in recent times. As Bengtson and colleagues put it, "grandparenthood is a tenuous role; that is, it has no fixed status from entry to exit" (Bengtson, Rosenthal, and Burton, 1990). Troll points out, the image of grandparents as old people confined to a rocking chair no longer fits reality. Instead, they are active, middle-aged people (Troll, 1985, p. 148). More and more typically, both grandmothers and grandfathers work and many engage in active community roles.

Available statistics show that American grandparents tend to interact with their grandchildren regularly and often, even though very few live in the same households. Troll and co-workers reported in 1979, for example, that nearly half of American grandparents saw at least one of their grandchildren each day and that such interactions were more frequent among blacks than whites (Troll, Miller, and Atchley, 1979, p. 109). Cherlin and Furstenberg also found that grandparents see grandchildren who live near them often even when the grandparents and the children's parents don't get along well (Cherlin and Furstenberg, 1986), although, in part, the grandparent role has to be negotiated with parents as well as the grandchildren (Johnson, 1992). It has been discovered, too, that there tend to be more interactions between grandmothers and granddaughters than between grandfathers and grandsons, perhaps because elderly women have more to share with their granddaughters than elderly men have with their grandsons (Troll, Miller, and Atchley, 1979, pp. 113–14). Interaction with grandchildren tends to be very dependent upon proximity of living, however.

There is some disagreement in the literature about how important relationships with grandchildren are to the aged and how they tend to relate to their grandchildren. The amount of interaction would indicate that they want to have those kinds of interactions, but the question is whether or not or the extent to which they are seen as vital relationships to the elderly. On the one hand, Kornhaber has accused grandparents of living by a norm of noninvolvement and therefore abdicating their responsibility to help their grandchildren in ways that they uniquely could (Kornhaber, 1985). On the other hand, Cherlin and Furstenberg present evidence that, although they tend not to interfere when life for their grandchildren is going well, grandparents have a strong sense of obligation to help in times of crisis. For example, when and if their parents get divorced, many grandparents (men as well as women) take their grandchildren into their homes (Cherlin and Furstenberg, 1986). This is particularly true of many African-American elderly (Burton, 1992). Burton indicates that black grandparents (usually grandmothers) acting as parents "has its reward, but also poses serious challenges"; one of the greatest is the worry about who will raise the grandchildren when they no longer can, due to their own economic and health problems (Burton, 1992; Minkler, 1994). Trout reports that this is also a very prevalent pattern in many Asian and African countries, due, in part to the spread of AIDS in that part of the world (Trout, 1994).

Thomas also presents evidence, in general, that especially the relatively young grandparents readily discipline, care for, help, and offer advice to their grandchildren (Thomas, 1986). There are indications, too, that grandchildren and grandparents deliberately try to influence each other, and both are at least somewhat successful (Wood, 1982). Others characterize the grandparent-grandchildren relationships as "ambiguous" (Wood, 1982), "peripheral" (Troll, Miller, and Atchley, 1979), and "free of normative guidelines" (George, 1980, p. 88; Johnson, 1992). Wood reports that while grandparents may personally enjoy interacting with their grandchildren, few see those relationships as vital. Research findings show that their level of involvement is unrelated to either their life satisfaction or the condition of their mental health (Wood, 1982).

There is much ambiguity in the literature about whether or not grandparenthood today constitutes an identifiable role. Based on their analysis of grandparents helping their grandchildren in times of crisis, Cherlin and Furstenberg conclude that being a grandparent is a deeply meaningful role (Cherlin and Furstenberg, 1986). Neugarten and Weinstein studied grandparents in the early 1960s and reported that they had discovered five basic role models among grandparents: (1) *formal grandparents*, who show interest but whose involvement is limited; (2) *fun-seekers*, who informally share leisure activities; (3) *parent surrogates*, who take on child-rearing responsibilities; (4) *reservoirs* of family wisdom, who serve as authority figures in the family; and (5) *distant figures*, who visit occasionally but are formal and remote (Neugarten and Weinstein, 1964). By and large, however, these categorizations describe the extent and kind of interactional involvement more than they represent defined roles. Parent surrogate could be considered a role, but, according to Neugarten and Weinstein, relatively few American grandparents practice that role, and even fewer prefer it as a grandparenting style.

Many grandparents may interact with their grandchildren in accordance with some selectively defined role, but there is certainly no normatively prescribed roles to which grandparents as a whole are expected to adhere. Many simply prefer to maintain informal and expressive relations with their grandchildren rather than perform some instrumental role. As George concludes, "normative guidelines are so few and so vague that individuals pursue the style of relationship they find the most comfortable (George, 1980, p. 88).

In contrast to grandparenting in the United States, grandparents in the People's Republic of China are oriented almost exclusively to role performance. While much affection may indeed be involved in the grandparent-grandchild relationship, their interactions take place in the context of grandparents' serving as caretakers of their grandchildren, a role they share equally with the children's parents (Davis-Friedmann, 1983, p. 83).

Relations of Elderly Siblings

Another family relationship that has been discussed very little but that is important to many older persons is that of siblings. As people age they have somewhat of a tendency to reestablish relationships even with their siblings with whom they have not been compatible in the past. As Bengtson and his colleagues explain, "sibling relations usually emphasize limited but enduring involvement" (Bengtson, Rosenthal, and Burton, 1990). They don't typically provide each other with any kind of tangible assistance and support, but they become increasingly important as connections to their pasts. Moyer offers five basic bases for the elderly to interact with their siblings: (1) working cooperatively in caring for parents who are still alive, (2) supporting each other, mostly in terms of socializing together, (3) reconciling their past differences, an important issue for some elderly toward the end of their lives, (4) rediscovering each other as travel companions and sources of emotional support, and (5) redefining positions of importance in the family after the death of one or more of other siblings (Moyer, 1992). Indeed, sibling relationships can be a vital part of the sociological aspects of aging.

ELDER ABUSE AS A FAMILY PROBLEM

There is a growing recognition, especially among gerontologists who work with and study the elderly, that elder abuse and neglect represent a major problem in society today (Crystal, 1987; Wilson, 1989; Wolf, 1988; Wolf, 1992). It has been found that it takes place most often, not among strangers on city streets, but in the context of elderly persons' everyday lives, where they live. In recent years it has been discovered that some of the elderly in institutions have been abused (Pillemer and Moore, 1989; Pillemer and Bachman-Prehn, 1991). However, the most alarmingly high rates of elder abuse, especially neglect, take place in the homes of those elderly who still live in their own homes. In both cases the abuse that happens tends to be closely related to the care that is being provided to those elderly people who are the victims (Ross, 1991).

With regard to those elderly who become abused in their own homes, studies based on service provider observations (Phillips, 1983) have focused on what contributes most to the abuse phenomenon. Particular attention has been given to the problems of "informal caregivers" and the vulnerability of the victims (Bookin and Dunkle, 1985; Cantor, 1983; Chance, 1987; Hickey and Douglass, 1981; Kosberg, 1988; Mason and Blankenship, 1987; Pedrick-Cornell and Gelles, 1982; Pillemer and Finkelhor, 1989). According to this perspective, the vast majority of caregivers are spouses or adult female children of those receiving the care, who serve alone as primary caregivers (Baum and Page, 1991), who have not had training in that kind of demanding work, and who typically have been thrust into the caregiver role suddenly (Goldstein, Regnery, and Wellin, 1981; Cantor, 1983; Soldo and Myllyluoma, 1983). Daughters who serve as their elderly parents' primary caregivers often experience severe emotional stress as a result of both role conflict (having to care for their own children, their elderly parents, and having to work at jobs outside the home all at once) (Mui, 1992; Strawbridge and Wallhagen, 1991; Scharlach, Sobel, and Roberts, 1991), and role reversal (Morgan, Schuster, and Butler, 1991; Morycz, 1985). Furthermore, some have defined the informal caregiving role as so demanding and confining, with little if any relief from its demands, that it typically becomes severely burdensome, stressful, and depressing to most of those who perform that role, even when the elderly care recipients require only limited levels of care (George and Gwyther, 1986; McFall and Miller, 1992; Gallagher and others, 1989; Stoller and Pugliesi, 1989). Many have also been observed as feeling isolated and even experiencing a loss of their own individual identities (Zimmer and Mellar, 1982; Zarit, Reever, and Bach-Peterson, 1980). Care-giving has indeed been identified as involving violence and abuse directed toward elderly persons on the part of the caregivers (Pillemer and Suitor, 1992; Brown, 1989). This is often a particular problem when the care recipients have conditions of dementia (Paveza, 1992; Coyne, Reichman, and Berbig, 1993).

Informal caregiving is one of the most serious issues in the field of gerontology today. As we have seen, families are still expected to serve as informal caregivers to provide most of the care that elderly people need throughout the world. The assumption is often made that that kind of in-home care is superior to that provided any other way. What is largely being ignored in both the informal caregiving and elder abuse literature is how those two issues are very much related to each other. In 1985 Bookin and Dunkle reported that there was a great lack of an awareness of the problem of elder abuse and what to do about it even on the part of service providers across the United States (Bookin and Dunkle, 1985), and even more recently a nationwide survey discovered that only three types of service providers were even somewhat helpful in discovering and treating cases of elder abuse and neglect (Blakely and Dolon, 1991). In fact, however, much of informal caregiving within the family situation is an explosive situation that seriously questions the quality of in-home care.

CONCLUSION

It is clear that the family is vital to the aged. The older they become, the more that is true. In a very real sense, elderly people depend upon their families for their social and psychological well-being and survival.

Some of the behavioral tendencies of elderly people would seem to indicate that families are less important to them than was true in the past. Their preferences to live separately from other family members and their increasing tendency to choose age-segregated living situations and daily interactions with nonfamily age peers would seem to be evidence that families are of decreasing importance to the aged.

Evidence indicates, however, that while they increasingly rely on interactions with others for meaning in their daily lives, those relationships tend to be much less vital to the aged than family relationships. We in modern Western societies have modified the extended family, not because it is less important to us but simply to maintain elements of independence between the generations within the family.

In analyzing the place of the aged in the family, it is important to distinguish between family relationships that provide them with needed affection and emotional support and those that represent meaningful roles within the family. In Western societies there tends to be a great deal of confusion about those two aspects of family relationships. Many family interactions between the elderly and other family members include elements of both affection and role performance and negotiation. Probably for that reason, the aged tend to declare a certain amount of independence from those of younger generations.

In contrast, the elderly in Oriental societies tend to emphasize well-defined family roles for their aged. Therefore, they have much less need to live separately from younger generations, although many are clearly moving in that direction in Japan and especially in mainland China. Their attention is centered on the performance of those roles rather than on their needs for emotional support. While emotional support may be as important to their elderly as to ours, they may well think of it as simply a byproduct of their role performance within the family.

We have seen in this chapter that relationships between elderly people and the various family members have different degrees of value for the elderly members. It is clear that marital relations have priority. Most elderly couples have successful marriages which provide them with the kinds of intimacy they want and need and a great deal of social and economic security. Elderly people treat their relationships with their adult children as vital, even though they may be plagued with elements of conflict over the continuing processes of parent-child and authority negotiations. This kind of conflict combined with the extreme stresses of caregiving often even result in various forms of elder abuse. For most elderly people, relationships with siblings and other extended-family members are apparently similar to those with close friends. They are important as long as they are satisfying but are expendable when they are not satisfying. Relationships with siblings apparently take on special meaning among the very old, however.

Relationships with grandchildren in the Western world have much symbolic and affective meaning to the aged. Grandparents in the modern era, though, tend to have very little, if any, authority over the lives of their grandchildren, and relationships do not tend to be as socially or psychologically vital as other family relationships. In Oriental societies, grandchildren are much more a part of the daily lives of elderly people.

REFERENCES

Atchley, Robert C., *Aging: Continuity and Change* (Belmont, Calif.: Wadsworth, 1987).

Atchley, Robert C., and Sheila J. Miller, "Retirement and Couples," *Generations*, 7, no. 2 (Winter 1982), 28–29, 36.

Atkinson, Maxine P., Vira R. Kivett, and Richard T. Campbell, "Intergenerational Solidarity: An Examination of a Theoretical Model," *Journal of Gerontology*, 41, no. 3 (May 1986), 408–16.

Baker, Michael, "The 1982 Sun City Long Term Care Survey: A Statistical Profile of Resident Characteristics, Attitudes and References," unpublished research report at the Arizona Long Term Care Gerontology Center, Tucson, Ariz. 1983.

Baum , Martha, and Mary Page, "Caregiving and Multigenerational Families," *The Gerontologist*, 31, no. 6 (December 1991), 762–69.

Beckman, Linda J., and Betty B. Houser, "The Consequences of Childlessness on the Social-Psychological Well-Being of Older Women," *Journal of Gerontology*, 37, no. 2 (March 1982), 243–50.

Bengtson, Vern L., Carolyn Rosenthal, and Linda Burton, "Families and Aging: Diversity and Heterogeneity," in *Handbook of Aging and the Social Sciences*, eds. R. H. Binstock and L. K. George (San Diego: Academic Press, 1990), pp. 263–87.

Bengtson, Vern L., E. B. Orlander, and A. A. Haddad, "The 'Generation Gap' and Aging Family Members: Toward a Conceptual Model," in *Time, Roles, and the Self in Old Age*, ed. J. F. Gubrium (New York: Human Sciences Press, 1976), p. 257.

Berger, Brigitte, and Peter L. Berger, "The Family and Modern Society," in *The Family Experience: A Reader in Cultural Diversity*, ed. Mark Hutter (New York: Macmillan, 1991), pp. 27–42.

Blakely, B. E., and Ronald Dolon, "The Relative Contributions of Occupation Groups in the Discovery and Treatment of Elder Abuse and Neglect," *Journal of Gerontological Social Work*, 17, nos. 1 and 2, (1991), 183–99.

Bookin, Deborah, and Ruth E. Dunkle, "Elder Abuse: Issues for the Practitioner," *Social Casework*, 66, no. 1 (January 1985), 3–12.

Branch, Laurence G. and Alan M. Jette, "Elders' Use of Informal Long-Term Care Assistance," *The Gerontologist*, 23, no. 1 (February 1983), 51–56.

Brown, Arnold S., "A Survey on Elder Abuse at One Native American Tribe," *Journal of Elder Abuse and Neglect*, 1, no. 2 (1989), 17–38.

Brown, Arnold S., "Satisfying Relationships for the Elderly and Their Patterns of Disengagement," *The Gerontologist*, 14, no. 3 (June 1974), 258–62.

Burr, Wesley R., "Satisfaction with Various Aspects of Marriage Over the Life Cycle: A Random Middle Class Sample," *Journal of Marriage and the Family*, 32, no. 1 (February 1970), 29–37.

Burton, Linda, "Challenges and Rewards: African-American Grandparents as Surrogate Parents," *Generations*, 17, no. 3 (Summer, 1992) 51–54.

Butterfield, F., *China Alive in the Bitter Sea* (New York: Times Books, 1982).

Campbell, Ruth, and Elaine M. Brody, "Women's Changing Roles and Help to the Elderly: Attitudes of Women in the United States and Japan," *The Gerontologist*, 25, no. 6 (December 1985), 584–92.

Cantor, Marjorie H., "Families and Caregiving in an Aging Society," *Generations*, 17, no. 3 (Summer, 1992), 67–70.

Cantor, Marjorie H., "Strain Among Caregivers: A Study of Experience in the United States." *The Gerontologist*, 23, no. 6 (December 1983), 597–604.

Chance, Paul, "Attacking Elderly Abuse," *Psychology Today*, 21, no. 9 (September 1987), 24–25.

Cherlin, Andrew, and Frank F. Furstenberg, "Grandparents and Family Crisis," *Generations*, 10, no. 4 (Summer 1986), 26–28.

Collins, Randall, and Scott Coltrane, *Sociology of Marriage and the Family: Gender, Love, and Property* (Chicago, Nelson-Hall, 1991).

Connidis, Ingrid A., and Julie A. McMullin, "To Have or Have Not: Parent Status and the Subjective Well-being of Older Men and Women," *The Gerontologist*, 33, no. 5 (October 1993), 630–36.

Coyne, Andrew C., William E. Reichman, and Lisa J. Berbi ., "The Relationship Between Dementia and Elder Abuse," *American Journal of Psychiatry*, 150, no. 4 (April 1993), 643–46.

Coward, Raymond T., Gary R. Lee, and Jeffrey W. Dwyer, "The Family Relations of Rural Elders," in *Aging in Rural America*, ed. C. Neil Bull (Newbury Park, Calif.: Sage, 1993), pp. 216–31.

Cowgill, Donald O., *Aging Around the World* (Belmont, Calif.: Wadsworth, 1986).

Crandall, Richard C., *Gerontology: A Behavioral Science Approach* (New York: McGraw-Hill, 1991).

Crystal, Stephen, "Elder Abuse: the Latest 'Crisis,'" *Public Interest*, 88 (Summer 1987), 56–66.

Davis-Friedmann, Deborah, *Long Lives: Chinese Elderly and the Communist Revolution* (Cambridge, Mass.: Harvard University Press, 1983).

Dilworth-Anderson, Peggye, "Extended Kin Networks in Black Families," *Generations*, 17, no. 3 (Summer 1992), 29–32.

Eggebeen, David J., "From Generation unto Generation: Parent-Child Support in Aging American Families," *Generations*, 17, no. 3 (Summer 1992), 45–49.

Eshleman, J. Ross, *The Family: An Introduction* (Boston, Mass.: Allyn & Bacon, 1985).

Fischer, David Hackett, *Growing Old in America* (New York: Oxford University Press, 1978).

Fullerton, Gail P., *Survival in Marriage: Introduction to Family Interaction, Conflicts, and Alternatives* (Hinsdale, Ill.: Dryden Press, 1977).

Gallagher, Dolores, Jonathan Rose, Patricia Rivera, Steven Lovett, and Larry W. Thompson, "Prevalence of Depression in Family Caregivers," *The Gerontologist*, 29, no 4. (August 1989), 449–56.

Gallagher, Sally K., and Naomi Gerstel, "Kinkeeping and Friends Keeping Among Older Women: The Effect of Marriage," *The Gerontologist*, 33, no. 5 (October 1993), 675–81.

George, Linda K., *Role Transitions in Later Life* Monterey, Calif.: Brooks/Cole, 1980).

George, Linda K., and Lori P. Gwyther, "Caregiver Well-Being: A Multidimensional Examination of Family Caregivers of Demented Adults," *The Gerontologist*, 26, no. 3 (June 1986), 253–59.

Gilford, Rosalie, "Contrasts in Marital Satisfaction Through Old Age: An Exchange Theory Analysis," *Journal of Gerontology*, 39, no. 3 (May 1984), 325–33.

Gilford, Rosalie, "Marriage in Later Life," *Generations*, 10, no. 4 (Summer 1986), 16–20.

Goldstein, Vida, Gretchen Regnery and Edward Wellin, "Caretaker Role Fatigue," *Nursing Outlook*, 29, no. 1 (January 1981), pp. 24–30.

Goode, William J., *World Revolution and Family Patterns* (Glencoe, Ill.: Free Press, 1963).

Hareven, Tamara K., "Family and Generational Relations in the Later Years: A Historical Perspective," *Generations*, 17, no. 3 (Summer 1992) 7–12.

Hashimoto, Akiko, "Family Relations in Later Life: A Cross-Cultural Perspective," *Generations*, 17, no. 4 (Winter 1993), 24–26.

Hickey, Tom, and Richard L. Douglass, "Neglect and Abuse of Older Family Members: Professionals' Perspectives and Case Experiences," *The Gerontologist*, 21, no. 2 (April 1981),171–76.

Hutter, Mark, *The Changing Family: Comparative Perspectives* (New York: Macmillan, 1988).

Jarrett, William, "Caregiving Within Kinship Systems: Is Affection Really Necessary?" *The Gerontologist*, 25, no. 1 (February 1985), 5–10.

Johnson, Colleen L., "Divorced and Reconstituted Families: Effects on the Older Generation," *Generations*, 17, no. 3 (Summer 1992), 17–20.

Johnson, Colleen L., and Barbara M. Barer, "Families and Networks Among Older Inner-City Blacks," *The Gerontologist*, 30, no. 6 (December 1990), 726–33.

Kornhaber, A., "Grandparenthood and the 'New Social Contract,'" in *Grandparenthood*, eds. Vern L. Bengtson and J. F. Robertson (New York: Anchor Press/Doubleday, 1985), pp. 97–116.

Kosberg, Jordan I., "Preventing Elder Abuse: Identification of High Risk Factors Prior to Placement Decisions," *The Gerontologist*, 28, no. 1(February 1988), 43–50.

Kremer, Yael, "Parenthood and Marital Roles Performance Among Retired Workers: Comparison between Pre- and Post-retirement Period," *Ageing and Society*, 5, no. 4 (December 1985), 449–60.

Leeson, George, and Eva Tufte, "Concerns for Carers: Family Support in Denmark," *Ageing International*, 21, no. 1 (March 1994), 49–53.

Leslie, Gerald R., and Sheila K. Korman, *The Family in Social Context* (New York: Oxford University Press, 1985).

Lewis, Myrna, "Aging in the People's Republic of China," *International Journal of Aging and Human Development*, 15, no. 2 (1982), 79–105.

Lowenthal, Marjorie F., and Betsy Robinson, "Social Networks and Isolation," in *Handbook on Aging and the Social Sciences*, eds. Robert H. Binstock and Ethel Shanas (New York: Van Nostrand Reinhold, 1976), pp. 432–56.

Markides, Kyriakos S., and Neal Krause, "Intergenerational Solidarity and Psychological Well-Being among Older Mexican Americans: A Three-Generations Study," *Journal of Gerontology*, 40, no. 3 (May 1985), 390–92.

Markides, Kyriakos S., and S. Hoppe, "Marital Satisfaction in Three Generations of Mexican Americans," *Social Science Quarterly*, 66, (March 1985), 147–54.

Mason, Avonne, and Virginia Blankenship, "Power and Affiliation Motivation, Stress, and Abuse in Intimate Relationships," *Journal of Personality and Social Psychology*, 52, no. 1 (January 1987), 203–10.

McFall, Stephanie, and Baila H. Miller, "Caregiver Burden and Nursing Home Admission of Frail Elderly Persons," *Journal of Gerontology*, 47, no. 2 (March 1992), S73–79.

Meir, Avinoam, and Yosef Ben-David, "Welfare Support for Israeli Negev Bedouin Elderly Men: Adaptation during Spatioecological Transformation," *The Gerontologist*, 33, no. 3 (June 1993), 308–14.

Miller, Baila, and Lynda Cafasso, "Gender Differences in Caregiving: Fact or Artifact?" *The Gerontologist*, 32, no. 4 (August 1992), 498–507.

Minkler, Meredith, "Grandparents as Parents: The American Experience," *Ageing International*, 21, no. 1 (March 1994), 24–28.

Morgan, David L., Tonya L. Schuster, and Edgar W. Butler, "Role Reversals in the Exchange of Social Support," *Journal of Gerontology*, 46, no. 5 (September 1991), S278–87.

Morycz, Richard K., "Caregiver Strain and the Desire to Institutionalize Family Members with Alzheimer's Disease," *Research on Aging*, 7, no. 3 (September 1985), 329–61.

Mosher, Robert F., "The Relationship of Selected Variables to Sexual Knowledge, Attitudes, and Behaviors of the Elderly," unpublished Doctorate of Education dissertation, Northern Arizona University, 1994.

Moyer, Martha S., *Generations*, 17, no. 3 (Summer 1992), 55–58.

Mui, Ada C., "Caregiver Strain Among Black and White Daughter Caregivers: A Role Theory Perspective," *The Gerontologist*, 32, no. 2 (April 1992), 203–12.

Neugarten, Bernice L., and Karol K. Weinstein, "The Changing American Grandparent," *Journal of Marriage and the Family*, 26, no. 2 (May 1964), 199–204.

Orodenker, Sylvia Z., *Family Caregiving in a Changing Society: The Effects of Employment on Caregiver Stress* (New York: Garland, 1991).

Palmore, Erdman B., "Is Aging Really Better in Japan?" *The Gerontologist*, 33, no. 5 (October 1993), 697–99.

Paveza, Gregory J., "Severe Family Violence and Alzheimer's Disease: Prevalence and Risk Factors," *The Gerontologist*, 32, no. 4 (August 1992), 493–97.

Pedrick-Cornell, Claire, and Richard J. Gelles, "Elderly Abuse: The Status of Current Knowledge," *Family Relations*, 31, no. 3 (July 1982), 457–65.

Phillips, L. R., "Abuse and Neglect of the Frail Elderly at Home: An Exploration of Theoretical Relationships," *Journal of Advanced Nursing*, 8, no. 4 (July 1983), 379–92.

Pillemer, Karl A., and D. Finkelhor, "Causes of Elder Abuse: Caregiver Stress Versus Problem Relatives, *American Journal of Orthopsychiatry*, 59, no. 1 (January 1989),179–187.

Pillemer, Karl A., and David W. Moore, "Abuse of Patients in Nursing Homes: Findings from a Survey of Staff," *The Gerontologist*, 29, no. 3 (June 1989), 314–20.

Pillemer, Karl A., and J. Jill Suitor, "Violence and Violent Feelings: What Causes them Among Family Caregivers?" *Journal of Gerontology*, 47, no. 4 (July 1992), S165–72.

Pillemer, Karl A., and Ronet Bachman-Prehn, "Helping and Hurting: Predictors of Maltreatment of Patients in Nursing Homes," *Research on Aging*, 13, no. 1(March 1991), 74–95.

Piovesana, Gino K., "The Aged in Chinese and Japanese Cultures," in *Dimensions of Aging: Readings*, eds. Jon Hendricks and C. Davis Hendricks (Cambridge, Mass.: Winthrop, 1979), pp. 13–20.

Rollins, Boyd C., and H. Feldman, "Marital Satisfaction Over the Family Life Cycle," *Journal of Marriage and The Family*, 32, no. 6 (February 1970), 20–28.

Ross, Judith W., "Elder Abuse," *Health and Social Work*, 16, no. 4 (November 1991), 227–29.

Rossi, Alice S., and Peter H. Rossi, *Of Human Bonding: Parent-Child Relations Across the Life Course* (New York: Aldine de Gruyter, 1990).

Scharlach, Andrew E., "Caregiving and Employment: Competing or Complementary Roles?" *The Gerontologist*, 34, no. 3 (June 1994), 378–85.

Scharlach, Andrew E., Eugene L. Sobel, and Robert E. L. Roberts, "Employment and Caregiver Strain: An Integrative Model,"*The Gerontologist*, 31, no. 6 (December 1991), 778–87.

Shanas, Ethel, Peter Townsend, Dorothy Wedderbaum, Henning Friis, Paul Milhoj, and Jan Stehouwer, *Old People in Three Industrial Societies* (New York: Atherton Press, 1968).

Shanas, Ethel, "Family-Kin Networks and Aging in Cross-Cultural Perspective," in *The Family: Functions, Conflicts, and Symbols*, eds. Peter J. Stine, Judith Richman, and Natalie Hannon (Reading, Mass.: Addison-Wesley, 1977), pp. 300–7.

Shi, Leiyu, "Family Financial and Household Support Exchange Between Generations: A Survey of Chinese Rural Elderly," *The Gerontologist*, 33, no. 4 (August 1993), 468–80.

Soldo, Beth J., and Jaana Myllyluoma, "Caregivers Who Live with Dependent Elderly," *The Gerontologist*, 23, no. 6 (December 1983), 605–11.

Stinnet, Nick, Janet Collins, and James E. Montgomery, "Marital Need Satisfaction of Older Husbands and Wives," *Journal of Marriage and the Family*, 32 (August 1970), 428–34.

Stinnet, Nick, Linda M. Carter, and James E. Montgomery, "Older Persons' Perceptions of Their Marriages," *Journal of Marriage and the Family*, 134 (November 1972), 665–70.

Stoller, Eleanor P., and Karen L. Pugliesi, "The Transition to the Caregiving Role: A Panel Study of Helpers of Elderly People," *Research on Aging*, 11, no. 3 (September 1989), 312–30.

Strawbridge, William, and Margaret I. Wallhagen, "Impact of Family Conflict on Adult Child Caregivers," *The Gerontologist*, 31, no. 6 (December 1991), 770–77.

Sundstrom, Gerdt, "Intergenerational Mobility and the Relationship Between Adults and Their Aging Parents in Sweden," *The Gerontologist*, 26, no. 4 (August 1986), 367–71.

Thomas, Jeanne L., "Age and Sex Differences in Perceptions of Grandparenting," *Journal of Gerontology*, vol. 41, no. 3 (May 1986), 417–23.

Thompson, Edward H., Andrew M. Futterman, Delores Gallagher-Thompson, Jonathan M. Rose, and Steven B. Lovett, "Social Support and Caregiving Burden in Family Caregivers of Frail Elders," *Journal of Gerontology*, 48, no. 5 (September 1993), S245–54.

Thurnber, Majda, "Family Patterns Vary Among US Ethnic Groups," *Generations*, 7, no. 2 (Winter 1982), 8–9, 38.

Troll, Lillian E., *Early and Middle Adulthood* (Monterey, Calif.: Brooks/Cole, 1985).

Troll, Lillian E., "Parents and Children," *Generations*, 10 no. 4 (Summer 1986), 23–25.

Troll, Lillian E., and Vern L. Bengtson, "The Oldest-Old in Families: An Intergenerational Perspective," *Generations*, 17, no. 3 (Summer 1992), 39–44.

Troll, Lillian E., Sheila J. Miller, and Robert C. Atchley, *Families in Later Life* (Belmont, Calif.: Wadsworth, 1979).

Trout, Ken, "Grandparents as Parents," *Ageing International*, 21, no. 1 (March 1994), 19–23.

Tu, Edward Jow-Ching, Vicki A. Freedman, and Douglas A. Wolf, "Kinship and Family Support in Taiwan: A Microsimulation Approach" *Research on Aging* 15, no. 4 (December 1993) 465–86.

Waite, Linda J., and Scott C. Harrison, "Keeping in Touch: How Women in Mid-life Allocate Social Contacts among Kith and Kin," *Social Forces*, 70, no. 3 (March 1992), 637–55.

Walls, Carla T., "The Role of the Church and Family Support in the Lives of Older African Americans," *Generations*, 17, no. 3 (Summer 1992), 33–36.

Wilson, Nancy L., "Elder Abuse: Who, What, and How to Help," *The Gerontologist*, 29, no. 5 (October 1989), 711–13.

Winbush, Greta B., "Family Caregiving Programs: A Look at the Premises on Which They are Based," *Generations* 17, no. 3 (Summer 1992), 65–66.

Wolf, Rosalie S., "The Vexing Problem of Elder Abuse [symposium]," *Public Welfare*, 46, no. 2 (Spring 1988), 5–38.

Wolf, Rosalie S., "Making an Issue of Elder Abuse," *The Gerontologist*, 32, no. 3 (June 1992), 427–29.

Wolfson, Christina, Richard Handfield-Jones, Kathleen C. Glass, Jacqueline McClaran, and Edward Keyserlingk, "Adult Children's Perception of Their Responsibility to Provide Care for Dependent Elderly Parents," *The Gerontologist*, 33, no. 3 (June 1993), 315–23.

Wood, Vivian, "Grandparenthood: An Ambiguous Role," *Generations*, 7, no. 2 (Winter 1982), 22–23, 35.

Zarit, Steven H., Karen E. Reever, and Julie Bach-Peterson, "Relatives of Impaired Elderly: Correlates of Feelings of Burden," *The Gerontologist*, 20, no. 6 (December 1980), 649–55.

Zimmer, A. H., and M. J. Mellar, "The Role of the Family in Long Term Home Health Care," paper presented at the 109th Annual Forum of the National Conference on Social Welfare, Boston, Mass., 1982.

Zimmerman, Carle C., *Family and Civilization in the East and the West* (Bombay: Thacker, 1975).

8

Patterns
of Participation
of the Aged
in the Community

INTRODUCTION

Throughout the 1960s and early 1970s in the United States, a movement took place that became labeled "the quest for community." It began among college-aged people but eventually involved people of all ages in some way or another. In essence, it was a response to the growth of large and powerful corporate and governmental structures during the post-World War II period. Big business and big government were perceived as impersonal machines that were taking over the personal lives of individuals. People came to feel as though they were cogs in wheels used to run the machines of business and government; they felt they had no control over their own destinies or even their daily lives (Stein, 1960, pp. 275–303; Sanders, 1975, pp. 3–19).

Prior to that time Mead had used the concept of the *generalized other* to represent the norms and understanding of society as a whole (Mead, 1934, pp. 154–62). His assumption was that all individuals have the ability to understand this kind of societal perspective and take it into account as they decide how to act and interact. As society grew to be increasingly complex and was defined as a *mass society*, however, it became more and more impossible to comprehend. The emphasis thus shifted to the concept of *reference groups* that individuals could define and to which they could actually relate (Hewitt, 1991, pp. 101–102).

The quest for community was manifested in two major emphases. One was the search by individuals to restore personal relationships to their daily experiences. A distinction had been made between primary (personal and intimate) and secondary (impersonal and instrumental) relationships, with an increasing sense that more and more of life was being dominated by secondary relationships. This prompted a deep desire to reemphasize primary groups and reestablish the personal aspects of life.

The second emphasis in the quest-for-community movement was the insistence that individuals and groups of individuals had the right to self-expression and self-determination. There was the overwhelming sense that the power over individuals' daily lives, and even their final destinies, increasingly rested with large, impersonal forces controlled by a few powerful people (Mills, 1956, pp. 1–29).

Even in local communities and bureaucratic structures, power was perceived as being in the hands of small, elite groups who were unaccountable to anybody but themselves (Hunter, 1953, pp. 8–25, 228–61). Much of the revolutionary activity of the 1960s constituted a struggle by individuals and groups for power over their personal lives and their communities as well as over national events. Thus, while it was in part a quest for a sense of community, it was, ironically, also a struggle for individual rights.

As a result of this movement, many types of communal, voluntary, and special-interest groups were formed, some spontaneously and others through a deliberate planning process. Many people, young and old, joined communes and friendship clubs in which they could establish somewhat permanent and intimate ties with others to satisfy their desire for more personal relationships. Others became part of voluntary associations and action groups in an attempt to influence public policy and bring about needed social reform. Grass-roots community action and development projects were organized and implemented across the country. People in small towns and urban neighborhoods met, organized into task forces, and worked together for change (Katz and Bender, 1976).

Another result of this movement was that new meanings were added to the concept of community. A community was not so much a local geographical gathering of individuals and families organized with governmental and institutional entities for their common protection and welfare; more important, it became defined as any group in which individuals felt they belonged and through which their individual rights would be enhanced. We now have the medical, academic, environmental, retirement, and many other communities whose members relate to one another, not so much out of a sense of commitment to their group, but because of a common individual interest that they happen to share. It has been suggested that groups based on self-interest alone last only as long as members continue to have common interests. Kanter observed, for example, that communes quickly cease to exist unless members develop a sense of commitment to the community itself, separate from their own individual goals (Kanter, 1972, pp. 61–74). At best, with the major emphasis being placed on individual rights in the quest for community, we end up with a segmented society made up of many different groups with conflicting values and interests. Age has come to be one of the major factors that has divided us into distinct groups.

Participation in community, then, has largely come to mean the extent to which individuals participate in one or another of the various types of groups.

Particularly important to assess, with regard to the aged, are groups and relationships in which they participate to enhance their personal and social lives, and community action groups and efforts in which they become involved in order to bring about what they see as needed changes.

PERSONAL ENHANCEMENT GROUPS AND RELATIONSHIPS

Relationships with Age-Peer Friends and Neighbors

Having and relating to friends is obviously an extremely important part of the social lives of elderly people. To be sure, as was noted in Chapter 7, relationships with family members are generally viewed by the elderly as more permanent and ultimately more reliable in times of crisis and for need fulfillment than are friendships. Friends are important to them, however, in helping them find meaning in their daily lives. In this respect, as was also noted in Chapter 7, elderly people tend to very much prefer having friends among their age peers. Friendships among their cohorts with whom they share common values, interests, and experiences would understandably provide them with the greatest satisfaction in their search for life enhancement (Jerrome, 1992, p. 72).

Jerrome discusses the particular meaning that friendships among their peers have for the elderly in Great Britain. She points out that those kinds of friendships are primarily expressive and intimate rather than an emphasis on some kind of instrumental relationship. They are vital to older people because that particular kind of intimacy acts as a buffer against the age-related losses that they have in common, and because the very existence of friends is in itself a "measure of social success" and a sign to them of "continuing vitality and social involvement." They can also serve as substitutes for the instrumental roles they have had to give up in retirement and important sources in the construction of the new social realities that are needed in old age (Jerrome, 1992, pp. 72–74).

The distinction between friends and neighbors is an important one. The elderly do not, of course, consider all of their neighbors as friends, nor do neighbors as a whole relate to elderly people indiscriminately. Cantor has optimistically suggested that friends and neighbors can be counted upon to offer needed support to elderly people when family members are not available (Cantor, 1979). O'Bryant found, however, that neighbors do not necessarily tend to provide support to those with the least family support. She compared the amount of support offered by neighbors to three types of widowed elderly people: (1) those with children living in their communities, (2) those with children but none in their communities, and (3) those with no children. Ironically, of the three types of widows, neighbors tended to give the least assistance to those with no children (O'Bryant, 1985). In all probability, neighbors are more inclined to respond more to the elderly people who are socially active than to respond according to their level of needs, and, as O'Bryant suggests, having had children may have helped them to be more socially active in their neighborhoods. As important as some neighbors are to some elderly in particular situations, they cannot always be depended upon to offer assistance, even when it is badly needed. Nevertheless, friends are generally chosen by the aged from among their neighbors. Lawton points out that proximity is one of the most important determinants of the establishment of active friendships among the aged (Lawton, 1980, p. 40).

Friendships among old people tend to form into friendship networks made up largely of age peers. Substantial research has been done on the importance of social networks to aging. This research tends to focus on two basic questions: (1) Do they tend to provide needed support to those involved? and (2) Do they contribute to the overall sense of well-being of those involved?

It has been discovered that social networks in at least some situations do, in fact, provide support to old people with special needs. A group of investigators studied elderly residents in a number of single-room occupancy hotels in Manhattan to determine the extent to which social networks existed there, and, if they did, whether or not members of those networks tended to help one another when needs arose (Cohen, Teresi, and Holmes, 1985). They found that even in an environment in which social interaction tends to be limited, social networks not only exist, but they also help individuals in two important ways. To some degree they contribute directly to meeting needs, and they help individuals cope with their problems. An earlier, similar study, however, showed that network interventions into people's problems are not always effective (Cohen and Adler, 1984). Many individuals had needs that were too immediate and they were too distrustful of others to rely on network responses. Many also cared more about their privacy than about being helped by friends in the network.

The amount of support that individuals receive from social networks in these types of settings also depends greatly on the attitudes the network members have about helping their friends. In a study of relationships among older residents in retirement housing, Goodman identified three types of helping neighbors: (1) high helpers (willing to help anyone without regard to reciprocation); (2) mutual helpers (willing to help based on reciprocal exchange); and (3) neighborhood isolates (the disengaged who did not participate in the helping processes) (Goodman, 1984).

Ironically, as was found to be true in traditional neighborhoods, those with the most need for assistance seem to be the most ignored by the social networks in public housing for the aged. Paris found that those who were the most isolated in planned housing projects tended to be those who were the most chronically ill. Whatever support network they had was composed of people from outside the projects (Stephens and Bernstein, 1984). Sheehan also found that the frail elderly living in public housing did not tend to be supported by the existing informal network of residents. Her data indicated that the attitudes and behaviors of both the frail and the healthy residents tended to keep them from interacting with each other. The frail elderly often deny that they have needs and distance themselves socially from in-housing neighbors as a mechanism for maintaining that denial. Healthy residents tend to ignore their frail neighbors out of the fear that interactions with them will sap too much of their energy. Thus they tend to confine their interactions to those who can reciprocate (Sheehan, 1986). As noted in Chapter 6, this same pattern has been found among residents of continuing care retirement communities in recent years (Netting and Wilson, 1991).

Ward reports that there is very little evidence to show that social networks contribute to the general well-being of those in old age (Ward, 1985).

Rook reports that, in fact, interactions with friends often have more negative results than positive. Some interactions are downright unpleasant and even cause stress. In a study of elderly widows, she found that friends and relatives had made life more difficult for over two-thirds of the respondents (Rook, 1984).

Ward makes the point, though, that social support of the aged is not static but dynamic, and in order to understand the importance of support networks, we need to examine those dynamic processes and not just note whether or not they exist (Ward, 1985). For example, widowhood is often very socially disruptive and few peers who have not experienced it are able to comprehend or relate to the problems involved (Brown, 1974b).

There is no doubt that individual friendships and those found within social networks among the aged are valuable sources both of practical assistance and a sense of well-being for many of those who participate. Not all age-peer relationships are positive or beneficial, however. Old people are probably more diverse than any other age group. They differ in terms of their past experiences as well as their present living conditions. Those differences as well as others influence the extent to which peer group interactions are or are not rewarding. An especially important factor that seems to influence whether or not elderly people will have positive interaction with one another is the extent to which those interactions are potentially reciprocal and thus preserve the common desire for elements of independence in their lives.

Age-Specific Voluntary Community Group Participation

Participation in voluntary community groups is another important source through which elderly people look for meaningful and satisfying personal relationships. It is true, as reported in Chapter 7, that older people have a tendency to become dissatisfied with groups in general and disengage from those types of social relationships (Brown, 1974a). There is, however, a growing tendency for them to join and actively participate in various types of age-specific groups in which they can interact with others on the basis of shared values and interdependent relationships.

In the study of group participation of elderly people in Great Britain cited above, Jerrome observed a tendency on the part of elderly members of heterogeneous groups to mix very little, take a peripheral place, and form into subgroups based on age. Participation in age-peer groups is characterized as an intensity of interaction (Jerrome, 1992, pp. 35–37). These kinds of groups tend to be more expressive than instrumental, especially those involving elderly women. Most participants gave as their primary reason for participating in peer groups that they needed the social contacts that the group provided. As Jerrome concluded, "membership is indeed a strategy for dealing with loneliness and the lack of activity." The groups she observed typically engaged in rituals that were expressions of allegiance to the group and provided participants with a sense of belonging and personal security. There was also a great deal of overlapping of membership among a number of similar groups within communities and this tended to provide individuals with even larger peer support networks (Jerrome, 1992, pp. 38–51).

A 1969 survey of the aged in the state of Montana identified a number of types of community organizations in which elderly people were members

(Evans and Brown, 1970, pp. 3–10). These organizations included lodges, church-related groups, and professional groups in which they shared membership with adults of all ages. With the exception of churches, participation in these organizations decreased with age. The other major type of organization that was identified in the survey was specifically for senior citizens. Some of these were small clubs that met weekly. More importantly, there were also a total of 14 senior citizens' centers in the state at that time with a total membership of 6,750. With the exception of religious groups, rates of attendance in the age-specific groups were generally higher than in the integrated groups.

It has consistently been found that, as a whole, the aged in the United States participate more in religious groups and activities than in any other type of group activity in the general community (Koenig, George, and Siegler, 1988; Hooyman and Kiyak, 1991, p. 412). Evidence shows, however, that church attendance itself has not consistently been associated with life satisfaction or personal adjustment (Van Haitsma, 1986). This does not mean, of course, that religious involvement is not important to those who participate. The fact is, as discussed in Chapter 15, religious groups are quite different from other groups to which elderly people tend to belong. Church membership is often made up of very diverse types of people with many different views. The purpose of participation in religious activities is not merely to have compatible and satisfying interactions, but to worship, learn spiritual truth, and share in the mission of the group. Controversy, and even conflict, are not at all uncommon in church meetings, and conflict can be expected to be negatively related to such things as morale and life satisfaction. Probably the most comforting aspect of religious participation is how it relates to what individuals believe. As Young and Dowling have explained, "religious involvement (whether private or formal) is noteworthy in that it reveals a direct connection between beliefs (attitudes) and behavior" (Young and Dowling, 1987). Indeed, Haitsma found that intrinsic religious orientation among the elderly was related to their level of life satisfaction (Van Haitsma, 1986).

Jerrome observed religious age-peer participation as well as others in Great Britain (Jerrome, 1992, pp. 54–68). Based on the patterns of participation in these groups, she concluded that they were different from other groups, in that they "cannot be isolated from the religious and specifically Christian context in which they operate." She labeled these groups as "fellowship" rather than "friendship" groups because the content of the meetings were largely devotional and oriented to particular religious themes. Particularly meaningful to the elderly group members were discussions about how the declining aspects of aging ought to be understood in the context of such religious concepts as regeneration and life-giving and life-preserving forces. Emphasis was also placed on the value of conciliation with and commitment to group members and the church to which they belong. As Jerrome explains, this kind of group participation is "the antithesis of self-interest" (Jerrome, 1992, p. 67).

Participation in Senior Citizen's Centers

There has been a growing demand for senior citizens' centers in the United States since their inception in the early 1960s. Krout reports that by the late 1970s there were about 5,000 centers nationwide, by 1985 the number had grown to about 10,000 (Krout, 1986), and by 1989 to perhaps as many as 12,000, serving between 5 and 8 million participants (Krout, Cutler, and Coward, 1990).

Nevertheless, it has been found that even senior citizens' centers with elaborate activity programs and meals program attract only a minority of the elderly in their communities. For example, it was found that in 1975, only 18 percent of elderly Americans participated in seniors' centers (Krout, 1986), and even fewer (15 percent) in recent years (Krout, Cutler, and Coward, 1990).

Why there is such a low percentage of the elderly in the United States who take advantage of the many senior center facilities available to them has been a continuing issue among gerontologists in this country. It may be partly due to the fact that such centers are not accessible to those with serious health problems as some have suggested (Krout, Cutler, and Coward, 1990). It is doubtful that making them accessible to that part of the elderly population, however, would raise the percentage of participation much if at all.

Krout provides an optimistic perspective of senior centers in rural areas, that they should attract many of the elderly. He reports that centers in rural communities not only provide a "wide range of health, social, recreational, and educational services," but they also "serve as resources for the entire community," and provide opportunities for elderly people "to contribute their knowledge and leadership skills" (Krout, 1994). However, while senior center participation is relatively high in non-farm rural communities, it is lower than anywhere else in farm communities. In addition to the promising factors related to centers in rural areas, Krout reports that the users of those centers tend to be confined primarily to females, those who live alone, and those who are older and poorer. He also points out that, relative to urban centers, the rural centers have lower budgets, less staff, fewer services, smaller facilities, and fewer increases in programs in recent years (Krout, 1994).

When considering senior centers as a whole, it has furthermore been noted that they progressively got "older" during the 1980s as their regular participants "aged in place," and those who were younger became less inclined to attend (Krout, Cutler, and Coward, 1990). A recent national survey of participants in senior centers in general reveals that those who used the centers over a year's time tended to be (1) older, although not the oldest old; (2) those with low income, but not the lowest; (3) those with high levels of social interaction; (4) those with good health, but not the best; (5) those with education, but not with the highest levels; and (6) women (Krout, Cutler, and Coward, 1990). This represents a relatively narrow set of elderly people, and an explanation is needed as to why attendance tends to be confined to them.

There has been a growing concern for a number of years among professional planners, that senior centers ought to be more responsive to the needs of frail elderly and those with special unmet needs (Guttman and Miller, 1972; Krout, Cutler, and Coward, 1990). As a way of addressing that issue the 1973 and 1978 revisions of the Older Americans Act stipulated that, where feasible, senior centers should become designated as "multipurpose centers" and as "focal points" in their communities with attempts to provide services to all elderly with special needs.

McClain and colleagues report on a special effort to transform senior centers in four rural communities in Nebraska into effective focal points on behalf of all of the elderly in those communities (McClain and others, 1993). The approach was to first form a "Statewide Resource Council" to plan the project, then to form a "Community Resource Council" to make the people in the targeted community aware of the importance of community focal points, and then to hire "Community Focal Point Developers" in each of the four communities to "market the focal point concept to Senior Center Boards of Directors" and implement the project. The conclusion by the authors who reported on this project was that, "There are strong indications that the organization activities at both state and community levels have generated a permanent commitment to senior center focal point development in rural areas of the State of Nebraska" (McClain and others, 1993). It is noteworthy, though, that how this effort may have negatively or positively affected the rates of participation on the part of the elderly people themselves in those communities was not even mentioned by the authors.

Krout contends that the data on who tends to participate in senior center programs do not support the argument that centers should be especially responsive to the needs of the frail elderly for three practical reasons: (1) Centers are not staffed to serve their needs; (2) they lack the necessary facilities; and (3) they are typically not adequately located. Furthermore, he and his colleagues make the point that "the development, growth, and survival of senior centers in America has been due in no small part to the fact that centers are not seen as serving the poor, the very sick, and minorities in some communities" (Krout, Cutler, and Coward, 1990).

What has often been overlooked in these noble efforts is the fact that the elder population is a diverse group in many more ways than just age, and that those who differ typically choose not to interact with each other on a daily basis. Their reluctance to participate is understandable when we also realize that individuals are recruited on the basis of how the program is supposed to benefit them, and that becomes their main motivation to participate. Thus, individuals with such differences as socioeconomic, racial, and ethnic backgrounds, and especially with different health conditions, often do not feel personally rewarded by interacting with one another. It has been found in the past that individual centers tend to attract mostly one type of elderly people or another. Some have tended to serve one type and others served other types of senior citizens, but few, if any, were able to serve more than one or two types of populations. Even in homogeneous communities, differences among individuals keep some elderly persons from participating in center activities. Participants were compared to nonparticipants in a study in a Burbank, California, center in the early 1970s, for example. They differed in three respects: (1) level of activity, (2) mental condition, and (3) physical condition (Hanssen and others, 1978).

While professional planners see senior citizens' centers as multipurpose agencies providing a variety of services to all elderly people with unmet needs, by and large, the senior citizens themselves see the centers as opportunities to interact and share experiences with those they consider to be their peers. This distinction is evident in a study of five senior citizens' centers in Crawford County, Arkansas, a predominantly rural, low-income county. To the obvious disappointment of the service provider-oriented investigators, those with the greatest need were not primarily the ones who participated in the centers' programs. Instead, participants tended to be those who were relatively healthy and already active (Schneider, Chapman, and Voth, 1985).

Participation in Retirement Homes and Communities

The choices that elderly make to live in retirement homes and communities and age-segregated housing also reflect their desire to establish a sense of community with their peers. There are, of course, a number of practical reasons that such choices are made, such as economics and safety, but the desire to live in an environment in which elderly individuals can regularly interact with their peers seems clearly to be part of those choices. For example, as noted in Chapter 6, senior citizens' housing projects have been constructed with government subsidies for the primary purpose of providing affordable housing for the elderly poor, yet Varady found that the most economically needy are not the ones who tend to apply or even express interest in such housing. It is noteworthy that black elderly, who tend to be disproportionately represented among the poor, did not tend to be interested because they tend to be more integrated into their extended families than others. The Varady study does not deal with specific motivations for applying for public housing, but the primary motivation clearly was not economic need (Varady, 1984).

Another possible alternative motivation is the desire on the part of the elderly to live close to and interact with peers. Further evidence of the importance of peer relationships to the aged is provided in a study by Longino, McClelland, and Peterson of why retirement-community residents prefer age-based interaction and housing (Longino, McClelland, and Peterson, 1980). They found what they labeled a "retreatist" style of life among the residents. One of the major aspects of that style, as they expressed it was "the warm companionship of those like themselves" that they enjoyed in retirement communities.

Cross-Cultural Differences In Peer Group Participation

It is important to note that little or no cross-cultural literature is available about such variables as individual life satisfaction and its relationship to friendships or group involvement. That may simply be an oversight by investigators. More likely, though, it means that those types of data are unimportant to the aged in many other parts of the world. People of most other non-Western countries do not seem to be engaged in the search for personal identity and a sense of community that we in the West seem to be. In other cultures, being part of a community may be taken for granted, and personal identity is seen as a natural consequence of community integration. Jerrome makes the point, about many non-Western societies, that relationships are formal, structured, and do not involve freedom of choice about relational preferences and satisfactions (Jerrome, 1992, p. 73).

In Communist China, for example, communities, not individuals, are emphasized as the more important part of society. People were for some time identified with and treated as members of communes or organized work units (Lewis, 1982). Regardless of how individuals felt about this, it nevertheless provided them with a sense of where they belonged and who they were. They were also dependent upon their communities for their daily welfare. In that kind of social context, the pursuit of individual identities and interests is simply not culturally appropriate. Even now, after all communes and government-mandated work units have been dissolved, those in the urban areas still live in highly organized neighborhoods, to which they are identified. With the economic and social changes taking place in that country, however, this may well change in the relatively near future.

In a different way, the Japanese elderly are also, to a great extent, oriented to culturally defined groups rather than to individual concerns. While this is beginning to change somewhat there as well, they still tend to be integrated into their extended families and many still have lifetime identities with the companies for which they work ("The Japanese-Style Welfare System," 1983; Palmore, 1993). A good part of their social contacts are presumably oriented to those groups. Again, membership in these groups has, at least until recently, provided individuals with welfare, identity, and a sense of belonging.

Data on the relationship between interpersonal involvement and personal feelings of life satisfaction among the elderly are also largely missing from some culturally unique minority groups in the United States. The Navajo Indian tribe is an example. Many senior citizens' centers have now been developed across the reservations, and the Navajo elderly readily participate. For most of them, however, involvement is not motivated by a desire to interact with their age peers as a way of improving their own sense of well-being apart from their families. At least for the most traditional Navajo elders, families have always been the source of personal identity and social well-being. The centers simply provide them with needed services and a supplementary source of social contact. The maintenance of these cultural traditions by Navajo elderly was discovered in a resent study of elder abuse on the reservation (Brown, 1989).

COMMUNITY ACTION GROUPS AND EFFORTS

An increasing amount of the involvement of elderly people in community groups today is motivated not only by the need for meaningful interaction, but also by what is perceived as the need for action. According to some analysts, on the one hand older people have been ineffective and reluctant political activists (Binstock, 1972; Hudson and Strate, 1985). Matras, on the other hand, contends that older people in the United States have "engendered one of the largest and strongest political constituencies and coalitions ever in American politics" (Matras, 1990, p. 226). It is probably true that many of them would not choose to be involved in politics as such, but increasing numbers of them are realizing that some of their needs could be met by community-based programs. They are often willing to join groups that work to initiate those programs and to bring about change. This kind of community involvement has largely been ignored in the gerontological literature and unrecognized in modern societies that tend to view the aged as dependent.

The processes by which elderly people become involved in community action were discovered in a study in northern Arizona of how programs for the aged in small communities are developed (Brown, 1985). It was found that these programs became a reality mostly by the actions, not of professional planners, as might be expected, but of groups of the elderly people themselves, almost none of whom would have identified themselves as political activists. Several stages were found to characterize the way in which these groups became involved in this particular form of community action. The first stage in the process was just *getting together*. It turned out that this was a very dynamic event. In the small towns under study, elderly folks had known one another before, but coming together as cohorts of elderly people, prompted a keen awareness of their common interests as older persons. The importance of getting together became particularly apparent when about 20 elderly people were brought together in one small northern Arizona community. They had obviously known each other for many years but had never met as a group of elderly people until that day. They were meeting at the request of state and county officials as part of a statewide effort to prepare for the 1981 White House Conference on Aging. I attended as an observer to study the results of a first-time meeting of elderly people. The topic addressed at the meeting was how to define the special needs of the elderly in that community, a topic which that group had never before even considered. In fact, as individuals, they had previously resisted any suggestions that they had special needs as older persons. From the introductory remarks by those in charge of the meeting, those present learned that other small communities in the state already enjoyed programs that served older people in those communities. That prompted the quick question from one of the elderly gentlemen present, of why no such programs existed in that community. The answer was that no one from there had ever requested any, and that individuals from there had said that none was needed. The elderly gentleman's immediate response was, "Then, I guess we had better get organized." It is noteworthy that those present began the process of becoming organized before that meeting ended. It was apparent that that would not have happened unless and until those elderly people had met together for whatever reason.

The second stage was that of *getting organized*. Without that formalization step, such groups either eventually disbanded or remained casual friendship groups. In becoming organized, the groups chose leaders and began to think in terms of what the group should be doing and what activities they could plan. Long-range goal setting and planning were not involved, however. At this stage, groups simply planned those activities in which they as group members were interested and that they could achieve with their own resources. They were generally not yet ready to engage in community action projects.

The third stage can be characterized as *identifying needs*. Typically, this was not a process in which the group members deliberately engaged. Instead, as they interacted with one another and tried to recruit other elderly people into their groups, unmet needs among the aged in their communities became apparent. With the recognition of needs, the desire typically grew within the groups to do something about them. It was at this point that the groups began to become oriented to community action.

The final stage in this process was *seeking outside help*. Groups soon understood that developing programs to meet the needs of a whole segment of the communities' populations required resources beyond what those in the groups could provide. The search for help typically took them to town and county governments and eventually to the Area Agency on Aging.

Another form of community involvement typical of many aged in the United States today follows almost naturally from involvement in the local grass-roots groups described above. As local service programs are developed from Area Agency on Aging funds, and as staff are hired to administer the programs, advisory councils on aging are required to advise the administrative staff. Members of the local groups of aged are usually asked to serve in that capacity. Although their role is advisory, members of these councils are sometimes able to exert a great deal of influence over the policies and operations of such programs. Some individuals have been thrust into new careers in their retirement years by serving on regional, state, and even national councils on aging.

It is important to realize that, contrary to the rather common myth that the aged are relatively uninvolved in their communities, involvement among the aged is actually quite substantial. More of their participation than we might suppose also involves action to bring about change. Much of their community participation, however, as we have seen, is oriented to their own concerns. In that sense, though, they are not different from the rest of the population in the growing trend toward power by special interest groups.

Community involvement by the aged in the People's Republic of China, by comparison, is very different from that in the United States. It is true that in large urban neighborhoods, increasingly elderly can be observed getting together at neighborhood centers for recreational activities similar to those at seniors' centers in the United States, as I did in 1984 and again in 1993. This does not represent a predominant type of community participation for elderly Chinese, however. Rather, their community participation generally involves performing important community leadership roles. Some of these roles, in fact, provided them with a great deal of influence and even power within their communities, especially in the 1970s and early 1980s (Treas, 1979). According to Lewis, more elderly women than men served as community leaders (Lewis, 1982). Lewis identified a number of roles that retired people tended to perform, including dispute settlement, work consultant, neighborhood cleanup, child care, neighborhood study groups, health and welfare service provision, community watching, and mentoring. These were roles that they were uniquely qualified to perform for two basic reasons: (1) Because they were retired, they were more consistently available within the neighborhoods; and (2) they often had years of work experience to qualify them for particular assignments. Neighborhoods in Chinese cities were organized into a system of committees that managed the neighborhood residents and offered various types of services to neighborhood residents. To a large extent, retired people made up those committees.

According to Yin and Lai, the role of mentor was a particularly vital one in the early 1980s. They point out that children and adolescents were denied formal educational opportunities during the Cultural Revolution and thus moved into young adulthood with educational deficits. Elderly people were relatively well educated, especially in Communistic doctrines and the history of the revolution (Yin and Lai, 1983). Thus they could uniquely serve as effective mentors. This role may well have been the most socially vital of them all at that time. Obviously, the participation of elderly Chinese in those roles involved them directly in the mainstream of the society. That kind of involvement was probably the major source of the maintenance of their social status. As Yin and Lai predicted, however, that role has undoubtedly already diminished as a vital part of the educational system.

With regard to the neighborhood leader roles, elderly people still serve in that capacity. However, the amount of authority those roles provide them has already begun to diminish and will probably continue to do so. This is due primarily to the changes that are taking place related to the economic reforms. In the past, under Communist rule, all aspects of the social lives of the Chinese people were organized and meticulously controlled by an elaborate system of work units (communes, etc.) The organized neighborhoods in the cities were part of that social system, and they controlled where people worked, where they lived, how they related to each other, and the welfare they received. During the latter part of the 1980s, however, all government mandated work units were disbanded as part of economic reform in that country.

In a 1993 interview in Shanghai, a government worker who lived in an inner-city neighborhood provided information about how neighborhood committees function today. He explained that neighborhoods are still organized as they were before, and that retired elderly still serve on the neighborhood committees. He also explained, however, that the economic reforms have seriously undermined the effectiveness and authority of those roles. The essence of the problem is that workers are now encouraged to seek employment wherever they can find it. Consequently, they are free to travel widely and move to the places where they find employment. Even though they are still required to be registered as residents of the neighborhoods where they live, they often do so only if and when they need the welfare benefits available to those who are registered. As a result of these new kinds of freedoms, it is increasingly difficult for neighborhood workers to locate the residents in their neighborhoods and to administer neighborhood policies with any kind of authority.

THE AGED AS STUDENTS

Active academic involvement is a rapidly growing type of community participation on the part of older people today. This is a phenomenon found not only in the United States but elsewhere in the world as well. The different emphases in this kind of activity in the two particular countries, the United States and the People's Republic of China, further illustrate their different lifetyles.

Many services that are available to the elderly population have been initiated by others. In contrast, educational opportunities for the aged have in this country gradually developed as a result of the demands made by elderly people who are relatively well educated and who value further educational experiences to improve themselves and to interct with their academic peers. Those who lack formal education rarely participate.

Two different approaches of providing education for elderly students have emerged in the United States. Some elderly students prefer to enroll as regular students at colleges and universities. They share classes with students of all ages. An important part of their learning process, according to them, is the intergenerational interaction in which they become involved. The second approach to education for the aged in the United States is best illustrated by the Elderhostel Program. Elderhostel was organized as a nationwide program that offered classes exclusively for older students on many college and university campuses across the country, and it now has expanded to other countries as well. This program offers at least two attractive opportunities: (1) the chance to learn and (2) the chance to interact with other elderly people on an academic level.

In the People's Republic of China, Shandung Province founded "The Old People's University of Shandung Province" in 1983 at the Red Cross University in Jinan. The emphasis in this program, in contrast to education for the aged in the United States, is on completing an established curriculum. The basic intent is not so much to enable individual students to pursue their own academic interests, but to better prepare the aged to live in the retirement years in ways to benefit society as a whole ("A Brief Introduction...," 1984). These kinds of educational programs are now available to the Chinese elderly in many of the major cities in the People's Republic of China. The subject of the aged as students is discussed further in Chapter 12.

THE AGED AS VICTIMS

As we look at elderly persons' patterns of participation in their communities we need to understand that in some ways that puts them at-risk. An increasing amount of gerontological literature describes how they are being victimized and abused. As we have seen in Chapter 7, most elder abuse takes place in the homes and is family related. Far too much also takes place in community settings, however.

There is some confusion from reports on the extent that elderly Americans are actually the victims of crime today. Statistics show, in fact, that in general elderly people are much less likely to be victimized in this way than younger adults. As Fattah and Sacco report, "aging brings with it a significant and dramatic decline in the risk of criminal victimization." They also report on data from a Canadian survey which showed that the elderly were victims of personal crimes such as assault, sexual assault, personal theft and robbery at one-sixth the rate of adults as a whole (Fattah and Sacco, 1989, pp. 169–70). These kinds of statistics do not, however, tell the whole story of the seriousness of elderly victimization.

The elderly, in fact, tend to be the primary targets of some crimes. In particular, they are susceptible to crimes that are motivated by economic gain such as fraud and con games (Fattah and Sacco, 1989, p. 169; Rykert, 1994). When and where the crimes are committed and by whom are also important considerations. Specifically, they tend to happen during the day, at times when they are alone, in public buildings or near the victims' own homes, and by strangers (Fattah and Sacco, 1989, pp. 172–74). According to Rykert, "elderly individuals are twice as likely as younger individuals to be victimized at or near their homes" (Rykert, 1994).

The fact that the elderly are often victimized at or near their homes by strangers makes them feel particularly vulnerable and contributes to what Rykert characterizes as the "fear continuum." This is perhaps the most serious aspect of victimization because as Rykert indicates, it "often reduces the quality of life more than the actual threat of crime" (Rykert, 1994). The fear continuum includes various levels of fear, ranging from "apathy" to "tormented and terrorist fear." The last two levels can even be dangerous in that they can sometimes produce unwarranted violence on the part of the elderly victims. At the least they almost certainly lead to severe loss of freedom and quality of life. This kind of fear is especially experienced by elderly persons when they are victimized at or near their homes.

A particular form of victimization among somewhat confused elderly is financial exploitation by those who have been appointed by the courts as their "guardians" and/or "powers of attorney." The basic problem with that is that neither the legal system nor the courts provide potential victims with protection (Mathis, 1994).

Victimization of the elderly has been seen by law enforcement officials as serious enough to focus specific attention on the problem. They have deliberately engaged in a series of organizational efforts at both national and local levels. For one thing, a number of city police departments across the country have added "law enforcement gerontologists" to their staffs (Rykert, 1994). These are specialists who usually receive the training that is necessary for the kind of work they do from the National Crime Prevention Institute and/or from the crime prevention training program provided by the American Association of Retired Persons. Much of their work is focused on crime prevention. Their typical approach is to (1) build rapport with the older citizens in their communities; (2) work cooperatively with the organizations and agencies that are primarily concerned about aging issues to pinpoint specific crime-related problems; and (3) enlist elderly people themselves in crime prevention projects.

A program called "Triad" was formed at the national level in 1987 at a meeting of representatives of the International Association of Chiefs of Police (IACP), the National Sheriff's Association (NSA), and the American Association of Retired Persons (AARP). These three national groups have worked together to provide program guidelines, a training program, and other resources needed to establish Triad programs in local communities.

The primary focus of this program, as Cantrell explains, is on "crime prevention and victim assistance for seniors and seniors' need for security and reassurance" (Cantrell, 1994). The impetus for beginning a Triad program locally comes when police departments, sheriff's departments, and senior citizen groups cooperatively become concerned about victimization among the elderly in their communities. Again an important part of this program is the involvement of elderly volunteers. Cantrell contends that this kind of program is "most successful when seniors volunteer their time and expertise to help" (Cantrell, 1994). Senior volunteers are recruited to do such things as lead neighborhood watch groups, conduct home security surveys, make presentations to senior organizations about the program, and provide information and support to crime victims.

INTERGENERATIONAL RELATIONSHIPS IN THE COMMUNITY

As noted in Chapter 1, much has been made of what has been seen by some as an impending intergenerational crisis in this country. Rosenbaum and Button found evidence of substantial negative attitudes toward elderly people in

Florida, at the community level, especially in those counties with the larger proportion of older residents (Rosenbaum and Button, 1993). It is noteworthy, though, that these attitudes did not come from actual interactional episodes between younger and older people. Instead, investigators explain that the criticism of the aging among the younger respondents "was generalized and diffuse, unanchored to specific community acts or events" (Rosenbaum and Button, 1993).

Out of concern about and attempts to combat the growing trend toward these kinds of negative intergenerational attitudes, a movement is developing to promote various types of positive intergenerational relationship (Newman, 1989). At the heart of this movement is the organization of programs that bring the elderly and young people together in ongoing mutually beneficial interactions.

Advocates of these programs genuinely believe that they benefit the individual elderly and young participants in very substantial ways. They provide the participants with badly needed services that are often not available by any other means, a unique type of companionship, and a new sense of meaning to their lives (Moody and Disch, 1989; Kingson, 1989). According to Nee, such programs can also capture the "deep desire for community" that is true of most people and is difficult to find in today's world (Nee, 1989). Beyond the benefits to those involved, Moody and Disch also contend that these kinds of programs "have public importance." Depending on the specific institutional focus, they can help to build support for public education, or help overcome racial and ethnic conflict, for example (Moody and Disch, 1989).

Newman provides us with a history of the development of intergenerational programs in the United States, where apparently most of them exist (Newman, 1989). According to her, the movement began in 1963, when the Office of Economic Opportunity (OEO) started the Foster Grandparents Program as a Community Action Project. It soon became one of the permanent volunteer service programs under ACTION, an agency of the federal government. In this program, low-income elderly are recruited to work with children with special problems and needs. A number of federal and state level programs are listed that promote many different kinds of non-family intergenerational relationships. Some emphasize young people helping elderly persons, but most provide the elderly with opportunities to work with and help children and youth. The National Student Volunteer Program (now the Student Community Service Program) is a program in which college students provide weekly services to the elderly in the communities where they are in school. It was begun in 1969 and at one time students at 50 different universities participated. An example of programs in which elderly people work with children and youth is the Generations Together Program that was inaugurated at the University of Pittsburgh in 1978. Especially featured in this program are mentorship projects in which retired professional people are recruited as academic mentors to children and youth in the Pittsburgh public schools and to college students at the University of Pittsburgh.

Tout reports that efforts have been made to develop intergenerational programs in developing countries in various parts of the world, especially in those countries in which families are breaking up and the elderly are being rejected (Tout, 1989). Typically, these are countries that are experiencing budgetary cutbacks and funding for the intergenerational programs has had to come from a variety of volunteer sources, such as the Help Age organization. That organization, for example, has organized "Adopt-a-Grandparent" projects in India, Sri Lanka, Kenya, and Columbia. In those programs, school children visit their adopted grandparents on a regular basis. One activity that many of the children engage in is to read to their elderly partners because many of the elderly participants are illiterate. It has been noted that this activity has had the effect of motivating some of the elderly to "acquire the rudiments of literacy," something adult professionals have not been successful in doing. Reciprocally, the elderly in these projects have shared "rich stories of cultural traditions, memories, songs, dances, games," which had never been recorded in written form (Tout, 1989).

CONCLUSION

Participation in community activities on the part of the aged is substantial in both the United States and the People's Republic of China. The patterns of participation are quite different between the two countries, however.

The search for community and personal satisfaction has provided the basic orientation of those in the United States. Their basic motivation for community involvement has been to gain a sense of self-fulfillment. The important focuses of community involvement have been on pursuing friend-ships among like-minded age peers, joining groups that provide personal relationships and meaningful recreational opportunities, and moving to re-tirement homes where they can live near age peers. Many elderly Americans have also participated in community action efforts that focus on meeting the needs of their own population. Elderly Americans are rapidly becoming inter-ested in education and intergenerational relationships, with an emphasis, again, on individual self-interest. It is obvious in all of this that elderly Amer-icans fit very nicely into the overall American culture, which places great value on the pursuit of self-interest. Community involvement does, however, often place them at risk of being victimized in a variety of ways, a problem that is increasingly being addressed by those in law enforcement.

In contrast, the community involvement among the Chinese elderly and those of other cultures is clearly focused on maintaining their integration into the community. Community participation, in fact, still provides them with opportunities to exert influence and power over others in the changing world around them. Opportunities to interact exclusively with peers may represent enjoyable experiences but are by no means central to their community activi-ties. The emphasis of their educational program also reflects the importance of community integration rather than the pursuit of personal interests. This, too, is consistent with the culture of which they are a part.

REFERENCES

Binstock,Robert H., "Interest-Group Liberalism and the Politics of Aging," *The Gerontologist*, 12, no. 3, part 1 (Autumn 1972), 265–80.

"A Brief Introduction of the Red Cross Old People's University of Shandung Province," unpub-lished paper presented at meeting of an American Gerontology team, sponsored by People to People International, at Jinan Red Cross University, June 9, 1984.

Brown, Arnold S., "Grassroots Advocacy for the Elderly in Small Rural Communities," *The Gerontologist*, 25, no. 4 (August 1985), 417–23.

Brown, Arnold S., "A Survey on Elder Abuse at One Native American Tribe," *Journal of Elder Abuse and Neglect*, 1, no. 2 (1989), 17–37.

Brown, Arnold S., "Satisfying Relationships for the Elderly and Their Patterns of Disengagement," *The Gerontologist*, 14, no. 3 (June 1974a), 258–62.

Brown, Arnold S., "Socially Disruptive Events and Morale Among the Elderly," unpublished paper presented at the Gerontological Society 27th Annual Meeting in Portland, Oregon, October, 1974. Abstract printed in *The Gerontologist*, 14, no. 5, pt. II (October 1974b), 72.

Cantor, Marjorie, "Neighbors and Friends: An Overlooked Resource in the Informal Support System," *Research on Aging*, 1, no.4 (December 1979), 434–63.

Cantrell, Betsy, "Triad: Reducing Criminal Victimization of the Elderly," *FBI Law Enforcement Bulletin*, 62, no. 2 (February 1994), 19–23.

Cohen, Carl I., and Arlene Adler, "Network Interventions: Do They Work?" *The Gerontologist*, 24, no. 1 (February 1984), 16–22.

Cohen, Carl I., Jeanne Teresi, and Douglas Holmes, "Social Networks and Adaptation," *The Gerontologist*, 25, no. 3 (June 1985), 297–304.

Evans, Idris W., and Arnold S. Brown, *Aging in Montana: A Survey of the Needs and Problems of Older Americans* (Helena: Montana Commission on Aging, 1970).

Fattah, Ezzat A., and Vincent F. Sacco, *Crime and Victimization of the Elderly* (New York: Springer-Verlag, 1989).

Goodman, Catherine Chase, "Natural Helping Among Older Adults," *The Gerontologist*, 24, no. 2 (April 1984), 138–43.

Guttman, David, and Phyllis R. Miller, "Perspectives on the Provision of Social Services in Senior Citizen Centers," *The Gerontologist*, 12, no. 4 (Winter 1972), 403–6.

Hanssen, Anne M., Nicholas J. Meima, Linda M. Buckspan, Barbara E. Henderson, Thea L. Helbig, and Steven H. Zarit, "Correlates of Senior Center Participation," *The Gerontologist*, 18, no. 2 (April 1978), 193–99.

Hewitt, John P., *Self and Society: A Symbolic Interactionist Social Psychology* (Boston: Allyn & Bacon, 1991).

Hooyman, Nancy R., and H. Asuman Kiyak, *Social Gerontology: A Multidisciplinary Perspective* (Boston: Allyn & Bacon, 1991).

Hudson, Robert B., and John Strate, "Aging and Political Systems," in *Handbook of Aging and the Social Sciences*, eds. R. Binstock and E. Shanas (New York: Van Nostrand, 1985), pp. 554–85.

Hunter, Floyd, *Community Power Structure* (Chapel Hill, N.C.: University of North Carolina Press, 1953).

"The Japanese-Style Welfare System," *Japan Quarterly*, 30 (July-September 1983), 327–30.

Jerrome, Dorothy, *Good Company: An Anthropological Study of Old People in Groups* (Edinburgh: Edinburgh University Press, 1992).

Kanter, Rosabeth Moss, *Commitment and Community* (Cambridge, Mass.: Harvard University Press, 1972).

Katz, Alfred H., and Eugene I. Bender, "Self-Help as a Social Movement," in *The Strength in Us: Self-Help Groups in the Modern World*, eds. A. H. Katz and E. I. Bender (New York: New Viewpoints, 1976), pp. 24–33.

Kingson, Eric, "The Social Policy Implications of Intergenerational Exchange" in *Intergenerational Programs: Imperatives, Strategies, Impacts, Trends*, eds. Sally Newman and Steven W. Brummel (New York: Haworth Press, 1989), pp. 101–10.

Koenig, Harold G., Linda George, and Irene C. Siegler, "The Use of Religion and Other Emotion-Regulating Coping Strategies Among Older Adults," *The Gerontologist*, 28, no. 3 (June 1988), 303–10.

Krout, John A., "Senior Center Linkages in the Community," *The Gerontologist*, 26, no. 5 (October 1986), 510–15.

Krout, John A., "Senior Centers in Rural Communities," in *Providing Community-Based Services to the Rural Elderly*, ed. J. A. Krout (Thousand Oaks, Calif.: Sage, 1994), pp. 90–110.

Krout, John A., Stephen J. Cutler, and Raymond T. Coward, "Correlates of Senior Center Participation: A National Survey," *The Gerontologist*, 30, no. 1 (February 1990), 72–79.

Lawton, M. Powell, *Environment and Aging* (Monterey, Calif.: Brooks/Cole, 1980).

Lewis, Myrna, "Aging in the People's Republic of China," *International Journal of Aging and Human Development*, 15, no. 2 (1982), 79–105.

Longino, Charles F., Jr., Kent A. McClelland, and Warren A. Peterson, "The Aged Subculture Hypothesis: Social Interaction, Gerontophilia and Self-Conception," *Journal of Gerontology*, 35, no. 5 (September 1980), 758–67.

Mathis, E. McRae, "Policing the Guardians: Combating Guardianship and Power of Attorney Fraud," *FBI Law Enforcement Bulletin*, 62, no. 2 (February 1994), 1–4.

Matras, Judah, *Dependency, Obligations, and Entitlements: A New Sociology of Aging, the Life Course, and the Elderly* (Englewood Cliffs, N.J.: Prentice Hall, 1990).

McClain, John W., J. Michael Leibowitz, Stephen B. Plumer, and Karin S. Lunt, "The Senior Center as a Community Focal Point: A Strategy for Rural Community Development," in *Aging in Rural America*, ed. C. Neil Bull (Newbury Park, Calif.: Sage, 1993), pp. 59–70.

Mead, George H., *Mind, Self, and Society* (Chicago: University of Chicago Press, 1934).

Mills, Wright, *The Power Elite* (New York: Oxford University Press, 1956).

Moody, Harry R., and Robert Disch, "Intergenerational Programming in Public Policy," in *Intergenerational Programs: Imperatives, Strategies, Impacts, Trends*, eds. Sally Newman and Steven W. Brummel (New York: Haworth Press, 1989), pp. 101–10.

Nee, David, "The Intergenerational Movement: A Social Imperative," in *Intergenerational Programs: Imperatives, Strategies, Impacts, Trends*, eds. Sally Newman and Steven W. Brummel (New York: Haworth Press, 1989), pp. 79–90.

Netting, E. Ellen, and Cindy C. Wilson, "Accommodation and Relocation Decision Making in Continuing Care Retirement Communities," *Health and Social Work*, 16 (November 1991), 266–93.

Newman, Sally, "A History of Intergenerational Programs," in *Intergenerational Programs: Imperatives, Strategies, Impacts, Trends*, eds. Sally Newman and Steven W. Brummel (New York: Haworth Press, 1989), pp. 1–16.

O'Bryant, Shirley L., "Neighbors' Support of Older Widows Who Live Alone in Their Own Homes," *The Gerontologist*, 2, no. 3 (June 1985), 305–10.

Palmore, Erdman B., "Is Aging Really Better in Japan?" *The Gerontologist*, 33, no. 5 (October 1993), 697–99.

Rook, Karen, "The Negative Side of Social Interaction: Impact on Psychological Well-Being," *Journal of Personality and Social Psychology*, 46, no. 5 (May 1984), 1097–1108.

Rosenbaum, Walter A., and James W. Button, "The Unquiet Future of Intergenerational Politics," *The Gerontologist*, 33, no. 4 (August 1993), 481–90.

Rykert, Wilbur L., "Law Enforcement Gerontology," *FBI Law Enforcement Bulletin*, 62, no. 2 (February 1994), 5–9.

Sanders, Irwin T., *The Community* (New York: Ronald Press, 1975).

Schneider, Mary Jo, Diana D. Chapman, and Donald E. Voth, "Senior Center Participation: A Two-Stage Approach to Impact Evaluation," *The Gerontologist*, 25, no. 2 (April 1985), 194–200.

Sheehan, Nancy W., "Informal Support Among the Elderly in Public Senior Housing," *The Gerontologist*, 26, no. 2 (April 1986), 171–75.

Stein, Maurice R., *The Eclipse of Community* (New York: Harper & Row, 1960).

Stephens, Mary Ann Parris, and Murray D. Bernstein, "Social Support and Well-Being Among Residents of Planned Housing," *The Gerontologist*, 24, no. 2 (April 1984), 144–48.

Tout, Ken, "Intergenerational Exchanges in Developing Countries" in *Intergenerational Programs: Imperatives, Strategies, Impacts, Trends*, eds. Sally Newman and Steven W. Brummel (New York: Haworth Press, 1989), pp. 67–77.

Treas, Judith, "Socialist Organization and Economic Development in China: Latent Consequences for the Aged," *The Gerontologist*, 19, no. 1 (February 1979), 34–43.

Van Haitsma, Kim, "Intrinsic Religious Orientation: Implications in the Study of Religiosity and Personal Adjustment in the Aged," *The Journal of Social Psychology*, 126, no. 5 (October 1986), 685–87.

Varady, David P., "Determinants of Interest in Senior Citizen Housing Among the Community Resident Elderly," *The Gerontologist*, 24, no. 4 (August 1984), 392–95.

Ward, Russell A., "Informal Networks and Well-Being in Later Life: A Research Agenda," *The Gerontologist*, 25, no. 1 (February 1985), 55–61.

Yin, Peter, and Kwok Hung Lai, "A Reconceptualization of Age Stratification in China," *Journal of Gerontology*, 38, no. 5 (September 1983), 608–13.

Young, Gay, and Winifred Dowling, "Dimensions and Religiosity in Old Age: Accounting for Variations in Types of Participation," *Journal of Gerontology*, 42, no. 4 (July 1987), 376–80.

9

Politics and the Emergence of Policies on Aging

INTRODUCTION

Throughout the twentieth century, old age has become an issue in which the politics of many nations of the world have increasingly become involved in the establishment of age-related policies. The politics of aging has involved a variety of social and political motivations, interactions, and actions in defining why such policies were needed, in the first place, and what kinds of policies were called for, in the second place. Whether or not those involved in the political arena seriously considered and subsequently took action to set policies in behalf of the elderly depended upon three basic processes. These include (1) defining old age as a "public issue" (Mills, 1959, pp. 1–18) or as a social problem; (2) the emergence of effective advocacy mechanisms related to aging; and (3) consideration of other, closely related political agendas.

In this chapter we will examine these processes as they apply especially to the United States, but also how they apply to the other very different cultures as well. We will also discuss the key pieces of legislation that have been passed that represent the established age-related policies. These will include Social Security, Medicare, and the Older Americans Act. The challenges to us as students of gerontology are to carefully examine the facts about the policies that have been set, separate those facts from the many myths about those policies, and then determine how fair and appropriate they are today.

DEFINING OLD AGE AS A SOCIAL PROBLEM

Growing old has never been without its problems in any society throughout history, but even the age-related debilitating experiences were seen as problems only to the elderly individuals who experienced them, and not to the elderly population as a whole. Defining old age as problematic began in the latter part of the nineteenth century in Europe and the United States (Fischer, 1978, pp. 158–61; Conner, 1992, p. 45). With the many social changes accompanying the industrialization process throughout the Western world in particular, however, problems of growing old have increasingly taken on social and economic as well as physiological and psychological dimensions, and the problems usually associated with aging have tended to increase. Thus, growing old itself, especially since the 1930s, has become defined as a social problem that requires the collective social actions of whole nations (Johnson and Williamson, 1980; Conner, 1992, pp. 38–50). Harris also makes the further point that "the major social institutions have not kept pace with the rapid increase in the number of older people nor made the necessary adaptations to their needs" (Harris, 1990, p. 332).

Societal Values as a Source of Defining Old Age as a Social Problem

Defining old age as a social problem has in part sprung from a set of values that has dominated the attitudes, aspirations, and behaviors of Western cultures for many years. Sociologists generally agree that one of the most dominant values in modern industrialized societies is the work ethic (Kando, 1975, pp. 8–15; Brinkerhoff and White, 1985, p. 399), or the "protestant ethic" as Weber called it because it had a strong religious as well as social connection (Weber, 1958, pp. 53–54; Macionis, 1993, p. 471). Arber and Ginn explain that "the classical sociological theories shared a conception of modern industrial societies as 'work societies,'" and they contend that, as a result, sociology has neglected later life ever since (Arber and Ginn, 1991, pp. 22–26). When discussing aging in Japan, Kinoshita and Kiefer make a similar point. They contend that "neither Japan nor the United States has a viable philosophy on which to base social policies for the aged." What they mean specifically is that "the rationalism that was the propelling philosophy of industrialization in Japan as well as America appears, with all its benefits, to be dysfunctional when it comes to coping with the mass of dependent elderly." It is a philosophy that judges individuals on the basis of their productive capabilities (Kinoshita and Kiefer, 1992, pp. 5–6). Although the validity of the work ethic may be effectively challenged in the future, as some have suggested (Ward, 1984, pp. 364–65), it, more than any other, has until now been the value that has defined the status and worth of individuals in modern societies, and if individuals, for whatever reason, fail to perform some productive role, they have lacked status and have tended to be labeled and treated as socially unworthy (Harris, 1990, pp. 264–65).

A second prominent value in Western cultures emphasizes that those relatively well off ought to act benevolently and do what they can to help the

poor who are unable to provide for their own needs. This has been emphasized as a religious duty that has influenced national policies toward the poor
and has resulted in elaborate welfare institutions designed to help those
people who are unable to survive independently.

The consequences of societal responses to this combination of values
have been that nonachievers not only lack status and social worth but are also
seen as dependent burdens to the societies in which they live. How these two
values sometimes influence the interactions between people, and lead to the
perpetuation of the idea that elderly people are dependent, is illustrated by
Betty Friedan's account of her involvement in a seminar on "Health, Productivity, and Aging." Attendants included a variety of young professional people.
She reports that "despite the announced focus of the seminar, there was a stub-
born resistance to the very notion of 'productive aging.' Day after day, when
the participants broke into discussion groups after each lecture, they only
wanted to talk about Alzheimer's, senility, and nursing homes. They vehemently objected to discussing age in terms of any kind of 'productivity.'" Her
response, as an older person interested in the possibility and importance of
elderly persons being productive, was "Deliver me" (Friedan, 1993, pp. 25–26).
The situation for nonachievers is also complicated by their tendency to internalize the labels of being dependent and unworthy and to continue to act
accordingly. Perceived dependency and lack of self-worth tend to perpetuate
themselves (Kuypers and Bengtson, 1973; Estes, 1979, p. 13).

In the Western world, the elderly, more than any other identifiable group,
tend to be labeled as dependent and as nonachievers (Ward, 1984, pp. 364–65;
Sarason, 1977, p. 264). While it is expected that younger nonachievers will be
trained to take on productive roles some time in the future, the aged are viewed
as permanent nonachievers and social dependents (Sarason, 1977, pp. 264–65).

Indications are that elderly people today are beginning to question the
application of these traditional social values to their situations (Ward, 1984,
pp. 365–66). Neither do they tend to internalize the labels of being dependent
or unworthy to any significant extent (George, 1980, p. 43). Nevertheless, the
dominant social values of achievement and independence still constitute one
of the strong orientations of most elderly today (Kaufman, 1993) and have
historically provided the framework for defining old age as a social problem
in Western societies. Hooyman and Kiyak also make the point that the prevailing social values, especially of policy makers, often determine who among
the elderly receive the services that are available and how those services are
delivered (Hooyman and Kiyak, 1991, p. 501).

A comparison of Western and Oriental cultures with regard to the influence of values on treatment of the aged reveals both similarities and differences. The People's Republic of China, for example, is not only an Oriental
society but also has very different ideological and political bases. Nevertheless, a set of values similar to that in the West seems to be at work there, but
with somewhat different results.

The importance of work was a major tenet of the Chinese communist
revolution under the leadership of Mao Tse Tung. It was seen not merely as
the means of producing needed goods and services and of stimulating the
economy; labor was also central to the Communist ideologies of preventing
alienation between humans and of building human character. During Mao

Tse Tung's reign, all physically able citizens were not only expected but were required to work (Lewis, 1982). Ironically, however, retirement for able-bodied elderly people began in the People's Republic of China as early as the 1950s and has now become a widespread policy throughout the country, with no apparent loss of status (Lewis, 1982; "Growing Old in China," 1981).

The idea that those without adequate resources to care for their own needs ought to be cared for has also been an important value in Communist China. The guiding philosophy was that everyone should be "eating from the same big pot" and was until recently quite broadly practiced throughout that country since 1949 (Tian, 1986). Welfare, in fact, was available not only to people in emergency situations but to all citizens throughout their lives (Mok, 1983). Most of the care for elderly people who need it is provided by their families, according to both cultural tradition and as a requirement of the national constitution (Mok, 1983). Under the Chinese socialist system, then, welfare has been viewed not as an act of benevolence to the poor on the part of those who are not poor, but as a right for everyone. Thus, it obviously did not carry the stigma of unworthiness for recipients that it tends to in Western capitalist societies. Partly for that reason, Chinese elderly have tended to retain social status, even though they generally did not participate in economically productive work. With the new economic reforms now being established in the People's Republic of China, however, something of a shift in values is taking place. According to Vice-Premier Jiyun Tian, the reforms call for less emphasis on the equalitarian idea of "eating from the same big pot" and increased emphasis on the more competitive idea of "to each according to his work" (Tian, 1986). This inevitably raises the question of whether the relatively high status that elderly people now enjoy will be maintained under Chinese socialism. *not communism?*

Indications are that both the work ethic and the benevolency norm are also applicable to the aged in Japan, another, but very different, Oriental society. Even though it does not have the religious base that it once had in the West, the work ethic seems to be as strongly imbedded in Japan today as in any other modernized, industrialized nation, if not more so (Casassus, 1986). By the early 1970s Japanese workers were being described as "workaholics" (Roscoe, 1985). Yet many employers in Japan expect people to retire at relatively early ages (Casassus, 1986; Maeda, 1980).

Providing care for those who need it, particularly for the elderly, is also very much a part of the tradition of Japanese culture, and that tradition has apparently been maintained in the modernized Japan. Although government welfare provisions for the elderly are not yet as well developed in that country as they are in most of the Western industrialized nations, the tradition of filial piety, of families being responsible for the care of their elderly members, has at least until very recently been shared by some employers. Japanese workers, therefore, are said not only to have their specific welfare needs taken care of, but have lifelong security as part of their work commitments. The claim has been that this system of care for the aged reflects a commitment to the elderly people that is unique in modernized societies.

Such a claim has been seriously questioned, however. For example, Maeda has pointed out that retirement pensions tend to be so low that a majority of retirees must try to find other jobs, most of which offer lower pay and lower social status than those from which they retired (Maeda, 1980). It has also been noted that the adult children of the aged increasingly view their sense of duty to their elderly parents as a burden that they are less and less willing to bear. Kinoshita and Kiefer conclude that "Japan has adopted many core values of American culture" (Kinoshita and Kiefer, 1992, p. 7).

Provision of Services as a Source of Defining Old Age as a Social Problem

The public provision of services is another factor in defining old age as a social problem. In virtually all societies, caring for the aged has traditionally been a private matter, with families shouldering most of the responsibility. Increasingly, however, in economically developing as well as developed nations, the aged as a group are being highlighted as having financial, physical, and social needs great enough to require a public response. This has led many national governments to adopt policies of service provision specifically targeted for elderly. It is especially in this sense that old age is being treated as a social problem. It is important to note, however, that the public provision of services is not just a sign that old age is being viewed as a social problem; it also contributes to such a perception, as the following analysis will show.

The passage of the Social Security Act in 1935 in the United States clearly contributed to the view of old age as a social problem. In the early years of this century, there was a growing recognition that poverty was a serious problem among the elderly, and eventually the Social Security Act of 1935 was passed in response to that recognition. While it did little to solve the economic problems of the elderly in that day, the passage of Social Security legislation did significantly contribute to the process of defining old age as a social problem. First, it began the process of official societal acceptance of the responsibility for the care of the elderly. Second, it made retirement conceptually synonymous with old age (Rose, 1965). Third, it provided a working social definition of who in society would be identified and treated as old. The aged became an identifiable and socially visible group that included all of those who were over age 65 and retired. As a group, they were beginning to be seen as having special needs.

The phenomenon of public provision of services for the aged has become a pattern in many other nations throughout the world, largely for the same reasons and with very similar results. As noted above, public provision of services in the People's Republic of China has not been confined to the elderly but universally applied, and that would seem to prevent the elderly from being stigmatized. Yet, increasingly and in a number of ways, the aged are being singled out for special attention. The aged population is growing rapidly ("Forecasting on the Aging Population," 1986; Shujun, 1984; Harper, 1992), and more government-supported homes for the especially needy aged were being built with public support in both rural and urban areas across the country (Renzhi, 1984). These changes have led to a growing understanding of the problems related to old age in that country (Caiwei, 1993).

In recent years the Japanese have also become painfully aware that they have the fastest growing aged population in the world and that this is already beginning to undermine their reliance on their nonpublic welfare system. Furthermore, it is projected that the problems of that system will rapidly worsen in the future. Public services have already begun to be provided, especially in the form of free health services for those 65 or over and increases in pension benefits provided by the National Pension Plan (Maeda, 1980; "The Japanese-Style Welfare System," 1983; Shiro, 1983). Ironically, the more their traditional system fails and the more they move to publicly supported services, the less the elderly are favored in the work place and the more old age is being defined as a social problem.

Retirement Policies as a Source of Defining Old Age as a Social Problem

Post-World War II retirement was a contributing factor helping to define old age as a social problem. During World War II, in which all of the world's major countries were involved, it is safe to assume that none of the nations of the world considered old age a social problem. All able-bodied workers, including the elderly, were needed and used in their country's war efforts. For the relatively short period of the war, therefore, viewing old age as a social problem was deferred. In the post-World War II era, however, being old once again became a social problem, and with much more intensity than ever before.

In the United States, almost universal mandatory retirement by employers took place across this country within less than a decade after the war. Following the war, the job market was flooded by young men returning to civilian life from the armed forces, and fewer jobs were available for a dramatically increased work force. It became necessary to eliminate people from the work force if the United States was not to be faced again with the disastrously high unemployment rates of the Great Depression. Mandatory retirement policies provided the simplest way of easing the keen competition for jobs. With almost no voices of opposition, mandatory retirement policies spread among employers, including the federal government. By 1960, nearly 70 percent of U.S. citizens over 65 were retired (Atchley, 1976, p. 17).

Primarily as a direct result of these policies, the aged increasingly became perceived as financially dependent, as having lost their major life roles, and as socially disengaging or withdrawing at alarming rates (Rose, 1965). In the eyes of much of the American public, these became problems that the vast majority of the elderly shared and problems over which they had no control. The aged seemed incapable of charting the course of their own destiny. They were seemingly unable to cope with the rapid social and economic changes that were eliminating them from productive participation in society's mainstream.

In neither the People's Republic of China nor Japan were the patterns of retirement as rapidly established as in the United States. Only in the last 15 to 20 years has retirement become widespread throughout China, and even then the Chinese tended to take a more positive view of those who were retired because many of them performed social roles and made financial contributions that were vital to their families and communities (Davis-Friedmann, 1983). It is also apparent that the Chinese population is still young enough and the size of the younger work force is still large enough to easily support the retired population ("Forecasting on the Aging Population," 1986). Nevertheless, it has been projected that families will soon begin to feel the burden of caring for their elderly members and that the nation as a whole will begin to be burdened with the economic support of its aged, as a result of the strictly imposed population-control policy in that country. It is likely that retirement policies in China will contribute to the notion of old age as a social problem in that country also in the near future (Renzhi, 1984). The Japanese are having to face the fact that they are rapidly becoming an old population (Kinoshita and Kiefer, 1992, p. 5; Komine, 1990), and as a result, old age is indeed becoming a social problem.

Changing Family Relationships as a Source of Defining Old Age as a Social Problem

Another factor contributing to the definition of old age as a social problem is the changing patterns of family roles and relationships. An overwhelming majority of elderly parents in the Western world live separately from their adult children and their grandchildren and avoid interfering in the family lives of their adult children (Shanas, 1967; Troll, Miller, and Atchley, 1979, pp. 84–92). As a result, the elderly are left with diminished family roles (Eshleman, 1985, pp. 537–38). While the roles of parent and grandparent are important roles to many of the elderly (Brown, 1974), those roles lack substance or authority beyond informal friendships and occasional helping relationships with adult children and grandchildren (George, 1980, pp. 84–88; Troll, Miller, and Atchley, 1979, pp. 110–19). Of particular importance are the facts that the housewife role tends to diminish and even disappear for elderly women (Lopata, 1966), that the head-of-the-household status for elderly men tends to diminish (Hutter, 1988, pp. 432–32), and that the tendency for older persons to live alone in increased isolation has become a distinct pattern (Hochschild, 1977). These patterns have contributed greatly to the definition of old age as a time of special need and thus a problem that the total society should address.

As discussed in Chapter 7, family roles and relationships of the aged in Oriental societies are also changing. The warning is already being issued that, with most couples being allowed to have only one child, the burden of caring for the aged will soon be too much for young families to bear in mainland China (Shujun, 1984; Renzhi, 1984). Similar patterns are also developing in both Japan (Shiro, 1983) and Taiwan (Tu, Freedman, and Wolf, 1993). Thus, changing family roles will undoubtedly contribute to the designation of old age as a social problem in all those countries, as has been the case in the United States and elsewhere.

Life Expectancy and Health as Sources of Defining Old Age as a Social Problem

Increasing life expectancy and changing health problems are also factors in defining old age as a social problem. Technological advances in disease control and health maintenance in this century have substantially raised the life expectancy of people in many countries around the world. Consequently, the number of people reaching old age has dramatically increased. In addition, recently declining fertility rates have drastically increased the proportion of the total population who are elderly.

The fact that increased numbers of people are living into old age indicates that they have survived the many acute health problems that once took the lives of many at relatively younger ages. As a result, increased numbers of elderly people are suffering from chronic diseases (Hickey, 1980, pp. 2–3; Wantz and Gay, 1981, p. 81; Matras, 1990, pp. 279–81). Particularly in the United States, this has served to refocus much of the health care for the elderly from rehabilitative to long-term care. Although the percentage of elderly people with severe chronic health problems is relatively small, it is large enough to make them quite visible. Those suffering from chronic health problems are particularly visible because many are institutionalized in nursing homes, where the media have portrayed them as pathetically helpless. Thus the general image of the elderly as physically dependent has resulted (Hickey, 1980, pp. 92–95).

The image of the aged as sick and physically helpless is not yet nearly as prominent in the People's Republic of China. This is primarily due to two factors: (1) the emphasis in the Chinese healthcare system is more on preventive measures and less on the extensive rehabilitative and lifesaving methods that characterize Western medicine; and (2) much of the care of elderly Chinese who are impaired is provided in their homes by family members and neighborhood health care paraprofessionals ("barefoot doctors"). Consequently, although Chinese people tend not to live as long as Americans, they tend to remain relatively healthy and physically functional. Thus, they often avoid developing crippling chronic problems in their later years, and they almost never end up in institutions for the severely physically impaired.

Different types of institutions are available for the aged in Japan, depending upon the levels of care they need (Palmore, 1975b; Kinoshita and Kiefer, 1992, pp. 64–69). Because of the prevailing tendency for the aged to live with their adult children, however, only a total of 1.7 percent of them are institutionalized (Kinoshita and Kiefer, 1992, p. 67). Thus, although the Japanese population is aging rapidly, a trend which may soon result in institutionalization of many more elderly people, the public image of the aged in general still seems to be that they are integrated into family life rather than that they are physically impaired and helpless (Palmore, 1975a).

DEVELOPMENT OF THE NEED FOR ADVOCACY FOR THE AGED

With the definition of old age as a time of life characterized by unique needs has come the recognition that advocating is also necessary. In the United States, in fact, advocacy has become so vital to the elderly that it became defined as one of their basic needs (*Guide to AoA Programs*, 1980; Fritz, 1979). Before we analyze how advocacy is so vital to the elderly, though, we need to understand what is meant by advocacy and how it works in behalf of sets of people like the elderly.

Definitions of advocacy that have been given include the "marshalling of resources for the benefit of a clientele constituency" (Fritz, 1979); activities "designed to enable special-interest groups to acquire and use power effectively to produce desired changes in society" (Berger, 1976); and "efforts to represent the interests of specific populations, to reallocate resources in their

favor, or to provide services for them" (Lauffer, 1978, p. 289). These definitions of advocacy raise a number of key questions that are important in
analyzing advocating activities in behalf of the elderly. It is important to ask
of advocates: By what authority? with what accountability? by whom? for
whom? by what means? toward what ends? and with what results?

Lauffer has recognized potential problems concerning the answers to
some of these questions. He has drawn a distinction between legal and social
advocacy (Lauffer, 1978, p. 289). He pointed out that the authority of *legal* advocacy is prescribed by law and is an integral part of the legal system, and
that, by legal definition, accountability is directed to those individuals or
groups that constitute the clientele. It is primarily *social* advocacy, however,
that relates to the sociology of aging, and this is not nearly as clearly defined
in terms of either authority or accountability. The authority of social advocacy
may come from such a variety of sources as legislative mandate (as in the case
of the Older Americans Act), the specified purposes and goals of local organizations or agencies, and the will of groups of aged themselves. Furthermore,
social advocacy invariably takes place in the political arena and is very much
oriented to what is politically acceptable and feasible. Because of that, ironically, social advocacy is often oriented as much to the politics of social control
and the ideological and survival concerns of organizations, agencies and programs as to the interests and needs of the client populations.

If the questions of authority and accountability cannot be clearly
answered or taken at face value when dealing with social advocacy, neither
can the questions of who is doing the advocating, by what means, for whom,
and to what ends. The latter questions logically follow from those of authority
and accountability and require careful analysis.

It may be asked why advocacy for the elderly is necessary in today's
societies. There are two other basic factors that help explain why advocacy for
elderly persons seems to be necessary today: (1) the growing tendency in
many countries to define old people as a group with special unmet needs
(Berger, 1976); and (2) the extremely complex ways that we attempt to meet
those needs.

In the United States, defining the elderly population as a group with
special unmet needs began with the emergence of industrialized job-related
poverty, especially among elderly workers, in the early part of the twentieth
century. Pay was insufficient to allow industrial workers to save for old age,
and elderly workers were more vulnerable to losing their jobs. This led to a
widespread advocacy movement for the establishment of pension plans to
provide for their economic needs (Fischer, 1978, p. 157–82).

The definition of the aged as people with special unmet needs grew in
more recent years to include a whole array of need areas. Besides the recognition that economic poverty was still very prevalent, the delegates to the 1961
and 1971 White House Conferences on aging in their roles as advocates, identified the following need areas: physical and mental health, housing and environment, nutrition, education, employment, retirement roles and activities,
transportation, and spiritual well-being (Lowy, 1980, pp. 31–32). Virtually all
aspects of the lives of the aged were seen as being inadequately addressed by
local community institutions. Conference delegates, contending that meeting
these needs was the responsibility of the nation as a whole, called for a

"national policy on aging" (Lowy, 1980, p. 31; "U.S. Subcommittee on Aging," 1973, p. 153).

With the passage of the Social Security Act in 1935, the Older Americans Act in 1965, and the numerous revisions of these pieces of legislation, provision for the many perceived unmet needs of the elderly increasingly became the responsibility of the federal government. However, it is one thing to establish policy and say that the federal government is responsible, and quite another for the federal government to carry out those responsibilities effectively. Two basic practical problems have progressively hampered the efforts of the federal government to fulfill its defined responsibility to elderly people: (1) mustering and coordinating the necessary resources to do the job, and (2) locating and reaching all of the eligible elderly constituents. It has been impossible to fulfill either of those goals given the limited amount of money allocated to support programs for elderly people and the kind of benefit-delivery systems that have been created (Schulz, 1980).

In fact, the government did not guarantee that all elderly people would receive the benefits that were available to them. Instead, an "eligibility-claims benefit-provision system" was created. That required those who wanted to receive any of the available services to prove eligibility, claim the right to participate, and plan the necessary service programs. In fact very few elderly people have had the skills or even the will to perform those kinds of tasks (Lowy, 1980, p. 193; Moen, 1978). Advocacy for the aged has become necessary (1) to influence social policy; (2) to acquire, coordinate, and consolidate the necessary resources; and (3) to implement existing program benefits on as equitable a basis as possible.

Advocacy has also become important for the elderly in a culturally different group within the United States where, although the circumstances are different, the end results have tended to be similar. Navajo elderly are the recipients of many of the same programs that apply to the rest of the American aged. Government aging services were historically of little concern to them because few elders reached an age at which support services were needed. Life expectancy has now greatly increased, however, and a great many more Navajo people are experiencing many of the same aging problems as others (Brown and Timmreck, 1984). As their numbers have increased and the traditional family support systems have diminished, professional and formalized provider systems began to be developed in response to these defined needs. Needless to say, they, even more so than their Anglo counterparts, were ill-equipped to cope with or use those formal systems. Thus, the need for advocates in behalf of the Navajo has been even more acute than for other elderly Americans.

Advocacy as Influencing Social Policy and Public Opinion

Advocating for the purpose of influencing public opinion and social policy in behalf of elderly people has involved very different processes from one culture to another. As would be expected, the results are also different but in some ways all are at least somewhat similar. By comparing United States advocacy efforts with those in the People's Republic of China, we will gain a sense of some of those cross-cultural differences and similarities.

In the United States, this kind of advocacy is clearly a twentieth-century phenomenon. As was noted earlier, trying to influence public opinion and policy in behalf of the aged began in the 1920s as groups of elderly people in urban areas became organized to make the public aware that increasing numbers of them were unemployed and living in poverty with little or no chance of improving their economic conditions. Most political analysts agree, however, that this effort had very little influence on public policies related to the elderly. They claimed to have had a direct influence on the passage of the Social Security Act in 1935 (Lowy, 1980, p. 191), but other more important issues had much more to do with making that a reality (Fischer, 1978, p. 183).

A much more effective policy-related advocacy began to emerge shortly after World War II, especially with the development of the tradition of holding White House conferences on aging every 10 years. This tradition grew out of the National Conference on Aging in August of 1950, held to (1) help professional workers who served elderly patients; and (2) to promote the Truman administration's hope of establishing a national health plan (Pratt, 1978). It is significant that none of the delegates were elderly.

Delegates to the 1961 and 1971 White House Conferences on Aging were selected on the basis of state representation and representation of a number of newly formed age-related special-interest organizations. The organizations that were represented included such groups as the National Council of Senior Citizens (NCSC), the American Association of Retired Persons (AARP), the National Association of Retired Teachers (NART), the National Council on Aging, and the Senate Subcommittee on Aging. Only a few such groups had been formed by 1961, and their influence was limited. They had become more influential by 1971, but it is noteworthy that, with the exception of AARP and NART, none of the groups was exclusively made up of elderly people and some had no elderly members at all. No care was taken at either the 1961 or 1971 conferences to assure that any elderly people would be present (Pratt, 1978).

Delegates at both the 1961 and the 1971 White House Conferences claimed to speak for the aged. They outlined what they saw as unmet needs among the aged and recommended that a national policy on aging be established, focused particularly on providing special health care, nutrition, and social- and support-service programs. Clearly, a pattern of relying on special-interest groups to advocate for social policy on aging had been established. This pattern continued and even expanded throughout the 1960s and 1970s as more and more age-related special-interest groups came into existence. These organizations were formed for the sole purpose of advocating for policy from the perspective of quite specific special interests (Estes, 1979, pp. 73–74).

It is important to understand the policy-related problems of that advocacy approach. One clear problem is the vested interests those groups have in their own continued existence. Consequently, Estes has contended, "the needs of the aged are replaced by the needs of the agencies formed to serve the aged, and this transposition turns the solution into the problem" (Estes, 1979, p. 74). Another, perhaps more serious consequence of the special-interest group advocacy approach is its almost exclusive emphasis on the definition of the aged as people with unmet needs. Virtually all of the age-related legislation that has been passed (Social Security, the Older Americans Act, and the

Medicare revision of the Social Security Act), and the agencies and programs that have resulted from those congressional acts are products of advocacy that may not represent, as Estes puts it, "the interests of the aged, as perceived by the aged themselves" (Estes, 1979, p. 74). There have been both positive and negative consequences of this. On the positive side, many practical benefits have been provided to the aged that are vital to many of them. The negative consequences have been that the needs-oriented advocacy has led to needs-oriented policy and practice, by and large ignoring the valuable contributions that older people make to the society. The needs of the aged (not the importance of their social contributions) are, ironically, the major emphases in the implementation even of such volunteer programs as the Retired Senior Volunteer Program (RSVP) and Service Corps of Retired Executives (SCORE).

The effective involvement of the elderly themselves in policy-related advocacy has, in fact, dramatically increased in recent years. This has taken place at both state and federal levels. An event that took place in the state of Arizona some years ago serves to illustrate this phenomenon at the state level. It was the advocating activities that led to the passage of the Arizona Older Americans Act in 1980. It is very significant that it was almost exclusively involving retired people, advocating in their own behalf. The movement began when a retired member of a regional council on aging from a small rural community initiated a petition calling for funding from the state government for aging programs. A statewide planning and advocacy group was eventually formed under the auspices of the Governor's Advisory Council on Aging, a well-organized advocacy group made up primarily of retired people. The group wrote the law and lobbied for its passage in the state legislature. The law passed relatively easily even though no such law had ever before even been considered in Arizona.

Advocacy activities by elderly persons have also increased dramatically at the national level. This is probably best illustrated by what took place at the 1981 White House Conference on Aging. For the first time in the history of White House Conferences on Aging, regulations stipulated that a majority of delegates would be chosen from the elderly. Then, at the conference itself, the claim of the age-related special interest groups that they spoke for elderly people was effectively challenged by those representing the Reagan administration at the conference. The elderly delegates themselves stood squarely behind such elderly spokesmen as Representative Claude Pepper (not even an official delegate) and Charles Schottland (retired delegate from Arizona), who fought for issues that were universally vital to elderly people, especially the continuation of Social Security benefits and adequate health care. It has clearly been the overwhelmingly strong voice of the elderly people themselves, and not the voices of others who claim to speak for them, that has thus far made it politically unfeasible for anyone in the political arena to drastically change or cut Social Security benefits, even in times when the national economy is in crisis and most social programs are being cut. In addition to the elderly themselves are middle-class adult children who, as Atchley puts it, "recognize that they could not meet the income security and health care needs of older family members without help from social insurance" (Atchley, 1991, pp. 354–55).

A look at advocating in behalf of the special needs of elderly persons in the People's Republic of China reveals a quite different set of circumstances.

Singling out the aged as a group having special needs began at a grass-roots level having to do primarily with the issues of work, retirement, and providing care to the aged. A large labor surplus has existed in China for many years, and retirement for the aged has emerged as a need. According to "Mr. Wang," an official of the Chinese Association of Science and Technology (Brown, 1984), soon after the Cultural Revolution, elderly workers and their families began to make requests to the production units to which they belonged that the elderly members be allowed to retire. Agreements were often made between family members and production unit officials that the younger workers in the families would do the work, and that the elderly persons would retire and continue to receive a percentage of their salaries. In a situation of surplus labor and large families, this plan placed little or no burden on family members. In fact, as noted in Chapter 7, having elderly retired grandparents available to help with child care and home maintenance was distinctly beneficial to families. In addition the retired elderly were also able to help their families take advantage of the small-scale free-enterprise opportunities allowed under the new economic reforms under way in that country at that time. Elderly people and their families, in effect, initiated a retirement system that became general policy first within production units and eventually across much of the nation. To a large extent, then, the Chinese aged themselves have in the past had a major voice in defining their own needs, have acted as their own advocates, and have been able to influence policy in their own favor. It remains to be seen how long the authority of the aged will last in the current period of economic reform and modernization, however. The present extent and pace of economic reform toward privatization, the intense demand for the elderly to retire at relatively young ages, and increased dependency upon their families (in place of the family interdependency of the past), together will inevitably diminish their political power in the future.

Advocacy to Acquire, Coordinate, and Consolidate Resources

The acquisition of resources to meet the needs of the elderly has been a particular problem in the United States. In passing the Older Americans Act in 1965, Congress made the federal government responsible for the overall welfare of the aged in the United States (Gelfand, 1993, p. 263–64). To fulfill that responsibility two things were necessary: (1) the planning and implementation of programs, and (2) the acquisition of the resources necessary to implement such programs. The dilemma has been that the first requirement is dependent upon the second, and the federal government has always been unwilling or unable to allocate enough funds to provide adequate resources for the programs promised in the Older Americans Act (Atchley, 1985, p. 330).

In order to solve the dilemma of accepting the responsibility but not providing the necessary resources, Congress created an agency, the Administration on Aging (AoA), with the dual mandate: (1) to plan and implement needs-providing programs, and (2) to advocate for resources (Fritz, 1979). One of the functions assigned to the Administration on Aging was to "stimulate more effective use of existing resources and available services for the aged and aging" (Binstock, 1971).

One implication of this responsibility was that the AoA would have the authority to review all programs related to the aged being planned by other federal agencies and to coordinate interagency implementation efforts, and to coordinate efforts with nongovernment age-related groups (Fritz, 1979). In addition, the 1973 Older Americans Act revisions called for the establishment of substate Area Agencies on Aging (AAAs) and part of their function was to advocate for the acquisition of local resources.

Some analysts contend, though, that those advocacy efforts that have been made by AoA and the aging network to acquire and coordinate resources have been spasmodic, unsystematic, and relatively ineffective. Fritz cites several reasons for this. For one thing, AoA is located at too low a level of the federal bureaucratic structure to have the authority to function as an interagency coordinating organization. In addition, the advocacy role was too poorly defined. Whether and how to act as advocates largely depended upon the interests and whims of the individuals working in AoA at any given time (Fritz, 1979). Furthermore, advocating work has had to compete with program planning activities within the network, and it has consistently been given second priority. It may also be that planning and advocacy are perceived as somewhat incompatible roles for an agency to perform. From the perspective of agencies it would be somewhat risky to support truly independent groups of senior citizens engaged in resource acquisition advocacy (Cohn, 1976). It is too likely that the advocacy would be directed back to the agencies providing the support rather than elsewhere. Consequently, advocacy to acquire needed resources, no matter to whom the job has fallen, has been only minimally successful.

Advocacy to Implement Program Benefits Equitably

One of the basic concerns in the provision of services for the welfare of the elderly is that services be provided on an equitable basis to those who need and want them. There have been problems with this kind of advocacy for the aged in very different cultural settings.

In the United States, the systems of service provision by the AoA and the whole aging network have themselves created inequities. Great numbers of eligible and particularly needy individuals have not been served, because the needed services were not available. Whole neighborhoods, communities, and geographical areas have been denied service programs that were readily available in other similar areas, because of the ways service programs have been planned and implemented.

For individuals to receive any of the available services under the Older Americans Act, local agencies must be organized and must follow a very complex and technical planning process (according to elaborate federal guidelines) to create the necessary service programs. Without the existence of these organizations and their successful planning efforts in local communities, no services are available even to individual elderly people who may need them. Even within neighborhoods and communities where service programs have been organized and supported by Older Americans Act funds, there is by no means equal access to services.

This problem was recognized in the 1973 revision of the Older Americans Act. That revision mandated that all states be divided into planning districts and that an area agency on aging be formed in each planning district, and area agency on aging (AAA) staff members were expected to advocate for the potential elderly recipients throughout their respective areas. The Older Americans Act revision also mandated the creation of a system of advisory councils in each area, made up of a majority of elderly members. These included project councils, county councils, and regional councils. Theoretically, these councils gave elderly people the opportunity to advocate in their own behalf for equal access to services as well as for needed resources (Cohn, 1976). It is important, though, to ask about the extent to which this system has actually given the aged a voice, and about whether it has made service provision more equitable.

In a study of advocacy for the aged in the rural area of Northern Arizona as mentioned in Chapter 8, it was discovered that there were definite limits on any attempts to provide services equitably in rural communities (Brown, 1985). Members of county councils either did not understand their equitable-oriented advocacy role or were frustrated with trying to make it functional. Those who understood it and took it seriously reported two problems connected with that kind of advocacy work. First, travel funds needed to reach unreached communities were not available. Second, the few attempts that were made either by council members or AAA staff to reach communities without programs were often met with indifference and even opposition on the part of leaders in those communities.

The Northern Arizona advocacy study revealed that program development and the provision of services in given communities came as a result of a localized, grass-roots advocacy process. Local leaders recognized the needs of the aged in their communities and persistently helped the aged themselves to organize in order to meet those needs. From the perspective of the AAA and the larger aging network, then, the development of new programs is not the result of mandated advocacy on their part. Rather it is their response to the grass-roots advocacy emanating from local neighborhoods and communities. Kaiser and Camp report that there is also "evidence of the increased recognition that older Americans are a crucial cog in rural economic development efforts." They found this to be true in two specific economic development projects; one in the Dominican Republic and the other in the state of Kansas (Kaiser and Camp, 1993). In any case, the official system of advocacy has not functioned as it was expected to function to make services equitably accessible to the needy aged. Thus, advocacy to provide equitable access to services has by no means yet been accomplished.

Similar grass-roots advocacy processes to provide elderly persons with needed services seem to have also been operating in the two other cultural situations that we have been examining in this chapter. Advocacy for the aged among the Navajos began in the early 1970s when a small group of elderly people organized themselves into the Navajo Council on Aging and began investigating sources to fund and develop programs to serve the Navajo elderly population. At first the Navajo Council on Aging was an autonomous group with no attachment to any official tribal organization. Acting largely on their own, the council members acquired funding to develop and staff a number of service programs for the aged in selected chapters (regions into which the Navajo reservation is divided) of the reservation. The need for coordination of existing programs and for systematic planning for more programs soon became apparent, however, and an Office of Aging Services was established and located in the Division of Health Improvement Services of the Navajo Tribal Government. Tribal government eventually took over the official responsibility for aging services among the Navajos and the Council on Aging became merely an advisory group.

For a time, the Office of Aging staff and the Council on Aging worked closely together to advocate for program expansion and the acquisition of new programs that would be culturally compatible. Within less than a decade two nursing homes were built and became operational on the reservation, nutrition sites were opened in 36 of the 60 chapters across the reservation, meals on wheels programs were functioning in a number of places, two experimental group homes were opened to provide temporary respite care for elders with special health care needs in the chapters where they were located, and a home health care program was planned in one selected area of the reservation. A system of support from a combination of four federal agencies (AoA, the Bureau of Indian Affairs, Indian Health Service, and ACTION), and the Navajo Tribal Council, was established.

Despite this initial success, however, there are clear limitations to the advocacy processes for Navajo aged, similar to those for other aged Americans. Although the initial advocacy efforts were made by the elderly themselves, that aspect of their work has subsequently diminished as their role became advisory. The responsibility to advocate for all Navajo elderly has largely become the responsibility of the Office of Aging staff, but they now have many existing programs to maintain in a time when support for social services is declining. Thus, many Navajo elderly still have no access to services that they badly need because no services exist in many of the chapters (Brown and Timmreck, 1984).

As explained above, advocacy in behalf of elderly people in China began with the elderly people themselves, their families, and production unit officials at the grass-roots level and spread to have an influence on national policy. However, these advocacy efforts have not been successful in providing equal access to the benefits that are available to many of the aged in that country. According to the present Chinese constitution, care of all elderly people is not only promised but guaranteed. Still, no national commitment of resources has yet been made to support that guarantee, except to those who have worked directly for the government. Instead, the national government now expects that families of the aged will provide the resources for their care (Caiwei, 1993). Until recently, the poorer production units, especially in rural areas, often simply did not have the resources to provide the kinds of social and health services available to those in more wealthy production units. The privatization of production in recent years raises further questions about how services will be provided.

The Chinese national government has a relatively generous retirement policy for government workers and is now planning for a nationwide social security program (Hong, 1993). Nevertheless, it has not yet become a mandated policy of the national government and was never established at all in some financially poor production units in rural areas. A structure of gerontology committees has been formed throughout the country at national, provincial, and city levels to advocate and plan for needed services for the aged. Yet not only are services still not offered equitably to all aged, but no plans have yet been proposed as a means of doing so.

THE FORMATION OF AGE-RELATED POLICIES

Partly as a consequence of defining old age as a social problem and a time of dependency and the advocacy efforts discussed above, political actions in behalf of the elderly have taken place and policies have been set. Part of what prompted those actions were other political agendas that existed at the time. In the United States there have been three basic pieces of legislation, the combination of which constitutes American social policy on aging. These include Social Security, Medicare, and the Older Americans Act. We will discuss how each of these came about and how they have changed as a result of further advocacy efforts and the changing times.

Attempts to provide financial support for the elderly poor in the United States began with the development of pension plans by a few states as the result of pressure from a number of grass-roots organizations. By 1933, most states had enacted at least modest pension plans despite the opposition of conservative politicians and judges (Fischer, 1978, p. 174). With the advent of the Great Depression in the 1930s, however, state pensions did almost nothing to stop the spread of poverty among the aged. Finally, in 1935, Congress passed the Social Security Act, part of which was the establishment of a social insurance program that became the backbone of financial support for older people in this country.

Part of the motivation for passing Social Security, to be sure, was to alleviate at least some of the economic woes of poverty-stricken, unemployed older workers. Politicians in the era of President Roosevelt's New Deal could no longer be insensitive to that kind of problem. Advocates from the Townsend Movement no doubt did have some influence on this action. As Conner concludes, "it sent the clear message to politicians that the day of publicly financed pensions for older Americans had come" (Conner, 1992, p. 64). An even more pressing problem in the depths of the Great Depression, though, was the fact that nearly one-fourth of the entire American work force was unemployed, and the economic structure of the nation was threatened with collapse. Young adults by the hundreds of thousands needed work to provide food and shelter for their families. Social Security would eliminate many of the older people from the unemployment lists as cheaply as possible. To be sure, the initial benefits were by no means sufficient to lift any older persons out of poverty, but it at least gave them a small monthly income and took them out of competition for the few jobs that were available. As Schulz explains, "Old age pensions were provided to help the elderly financially but also to encourage them to leave or remain out of the work force" (Schulz, 1988, p. 122). This was initially, and has remained, a basic reason for the establishment and maintenance of the Social Security. Thus, advocacy by and in behalf of older people had only a small part, if any, in its passage.

In recent years a new struggle of advocacy has emerged between two opposing groups. On the one hand are those who contend that the elderly are once again needed in the work force, due to drops in the birth rate, and that we can, therefore, no longer afford to support them in retirement (Sheppard and Rix, 1977, pp. 1–35). This kind of argument was the driving force behind the 1983 amendments to the Social Security Act. One of the important changes that was made at that time was that beginning with those retiring after the year 2003 individuals will not be eligible for full retirements before the age of 67 (Schulz, 1988, pp. 151–52).

On the other hand are those who see no such crisis and are claiming their right to retire and receive benefits from the social security fund into which they have paid throughout their lives. It is true, of course, that the number of workers paying into the fund relative to those receiving benefits from it are decreasing at the same time that those retiring and receiving benefits are growing. Ironically, however, the social security retirement benefit fund continues to have an increasing surplus from which the government borrows to pay its bills. Furthermore, employers continue to offer special incentives to their employees to retire early, because it is economically sound to do so. Apparently, the job market continues to be more competitive than some would believe.

As noted earlier, the situation with regard to retired people in the People's Republic of China has changed dramatically as a result of economic reforms. Consequently, the pressures to establish a national system of support for those retiring is being felt. In response to that, Hong reports that the State Planning Committee, an agency of the national government, is now developing a nationwide, comprehensive social security system to provide all retired workers with needed income (Hong, 1993). As it is now being planned, funds to finance the program will be provided by individual worker contributions (beginning with a 3 percent tax on wages), contributions from business enterprises (private and state-run), and state subsidies. It is explained that, not only will this program provide the elderly with needed support, but it will also serve "to change people's concepts of preferring male children for their support in old age and to promote the implementation of family planning policies" (Hong, 1993).

Another increasingly vital concern about which older people have advocated is health care. This has been a major concern of employers and workers for some time as well. As the United States became industrialized and urbanized, employers became increasingly dependent upon a healthy work force in order to compete in the marketplace. They therefore began to work to mold the health care system to meet their needs (Estes and others, 1984, pp. 17–18). Maintaining people's physical and mental functional capabilities has thus become one of the main goals of the modern health care system, with little or no attention being paid to the health needs as individual consumers might define them.

In that regard, more than a decade ago, Inglehart accused business and government of beginning "to look at medical care as more nearly an economic product than a social good" (Inglehart, 1982). Carlson has also contended that the decisions about health care allocations were being made "far more for political, social, and economic reasons than therapeutic ones" (Carlson, 1983).

The present existing health care system is the result of negotiations that have been carried out in the political arena since World War II. Those negotiations were rife with conflict between those representing the medical community and those advocating for a publicly supported national health care system. Due to the lobbying efforts of those in the medical professions, especially members of the American Medical Association, the goal of labor and others to form a publicly supported and administered national health care system was never realized. Instead, private health insurance companies were created to provide financial services to unions and businesses for compulsory health care coverage for their workers. Services were provided by established health care systems. Thus, a health-related business enterprise was created that provided substantial support to modern medicine and the professional people in it.

While the primary focus of the health care system that emerged in the United States following World War II was on those in the work force, two overlapping segments of the American population, both of which were growing in numbers and political importance, were left out. The poor and the aged had little or no promise of adequate health care coverage. In the War on Poverty era of the 1950s and 1960s, though, a great deal of sentiment existed to provide needed services to both of those populations. Politicians favoring a national health care system pushed for special health care legislation for the poor and the aged as a first step toward national health care for everyone. Consequently the 1965 revisions of Social Security included Medicaid for the poor and Medicare for the aged. Both programs are designed to pay for the health care services according to funding criteria set by the government. The actual provision of services is left to health professionals, who get reimbursed by annual government allocations made for those programs.

Medicare is a national health insurance program for Americans 65 years of age and older. The bias toward workers in building a system of health care, discussed earlier, is also demonstrated in this law. Eligibility to receive benefits is limited to participants in the Social Security retirement program. Others who are 65 and over must pay monthly premiums in order to participate. It was not designed as a welfare program but as an "earned right" for years of productive work (Estes and others, 1984, p. 50). As such, it also serves as an added incentive for individuals to retire and leave the work force.

The Medicare program, discussed more fully in Chapter 12, is divided into two parts, one compulsory and the other voluntary. Part A, the compulsory component, is the hospital insurance program, the benefits of which are paid for out of a Social Security Administration fund created for that purpose out of worker payroll taxes. The amount of hospital costs that are covered under Part A, however, are limited by a designated "deductible," which participants, themselves, must pay for each incident of hospital care before they are allowed to receive Medicare coverage.

Part B is a supplementary medical insurance program to cover 80 percent of physicians' fees and certain other, designated, out-of-hospital medical costs. This part of the Medicare program is also subject to an annual "deductible," which participants themselves must pay. This part of the program is voluntary and is financed by monthly premiums that participants must pay.

Medicaid provides funds to states to help them cover the health care costs of their poor, many of whom are typically also elderly. Individual states have the option to participate in the program or not. If they choose to participate, they must provide a certain percentage of the program costs with state funds, based on their per capita income levels. Within federal guidelines, states may set eligibility standards and determine how the money will be spent. It is up to participant states to administer this program within their borders. Needless to say, coverage under Medicaid varies greatly from state to state. Generally, though, it is the major source of public funding for long-term care in this country (Gelfand, 1993, p. 61). Some support is given to provide in-home medical care, but much more goes for institutional, nursing home care. Thus, to a large extent, Medicaid has helped to build the nursing home industry as a sizable business enterprise in the United States.

The third major piece of legislation passed in the United States in behalf of elderly persons was the Older Americans Act, originally passed in 1965. This was enacted in an almost direct response to the recommendations made by the delegates at the first White House Conference on Aging, held in Washington, D. C. in 1961 (Gelfand, 1993, p. 11). As was pointed out before, those recommendations came from others than the elderly and emphasized the notion that being old constitutes a stated dependency. That same kind of emphasis is made in the statement of purpose of the Older American Act that reads, "AN ACT TO provide assistance in the development of new or improved programs to help older persons" (Gelfand, 1993, p. 263).

With the Older Americans Act and its 11 subsequent revisions, the last of which was made by Congress in 1992, the Administration on Aging and a vast network of state, area, and local agencies were formed. These agencies were then charged with planning and implementing an array of service programs for the elderly in local communities. Provisions were made to establish senior centers; nutrition programs (including both congregate meals and "meals on wheels" delivered to those confined in their homes); support services in the form of such needs as transportation, housing assistance, residential repairs, an ombudsman program for those living in institutions, legal services and counseling, personal counseling, translation services, and outreach programs. In addition, funding for training, research, and discretionary projects, and employment for low-income elderly was provided through this act.

Eligibility for elderly persons to participate in all of these programs except the one to provide employment was based solely on age. The assumption has been that these programs represented the needs of all elderly regardless of their socioeconomic situations. As noted above, not only the provision of the services themselves, but how they have been delivered as well, have served to perpetuate the idea that elderly people are basically dependent, despite how vital the services have been to many of the elderly.

CONCLUSION

As this chapter has indicated, policies on aging that have been generated across cultures have depended upon two basic processes: (1) defining old age as a social problem, and (2) the development of advocacy in behalf of older people. On a practical level, we have discovered a mixed bag of social problem definitions, political motivations, advocating approaches, and policy results.

With regard to defining old age as a social problem, the set of factors that, together, have created that kind of definition have also created the public image in America that the elderly are dependent, helpless, and even incompetent (Kuypers and Bengtson, 1973). They had been retired partly because they were characterized as less competent than younger workers. They were eliminated from productive roles in society and visibly left with few, if any, socially useful roles to perform. Many were seen as being forced into financial dependency upon those still working, and the elderly as a group were seen as economic burdens to the rest of the population. More and more of them have been found to be physically dependent, in need of long-term care, and confined to institutions, where their visibility has created the image of helplessness. Their increasing numbers made them even more visible in their dependent situations, and they became defined as people whose special needs were extensive enough to demand the attention of the entire society.

Public concern for the elderly in this country grew rapidly throughout the 1950s and defining their specific needs and providing services to meet those needs became political issues. As early as 1950 the Truman Administration organized and held a National Conference on Aging and just a decade later, a full-fledged White House Conference on Aging was held to discuss the special needs of the aged and to recommend congressional action in their behalf. As a result of this kind of political activity in behalf of the elderly in the United States, the Older Americans Act was passed in 1965. One provision of the Older Americans Act was the establishment of a federal bureaucracy, the Administration on Aging with a vast planning and service-delivery network. It was the responsibility of this "aging network" to plan and implement social-service programs for all of the elderly in every local community across the country.

One of the network's primary goals has been to help solve the problem of dependency among the aged, but analysts today claim that it has instead served to perpetuate dependency and contribute to the definition of old age as a social problem (Estes, 1979, pp. 2–3; Estes and others, 1984, pp. 71–72). For one thing, the planning perspective of those in the network has largely been that old people are dependent and relatively helpless (Hudson, 1981). From this perspective, it was appropriate for the planners and providers in the network to assume paternalistic or maternalistic attitudes and approaches to their work. Without a doubt, this approach has served to perpetuate the image of the elderly as dependent. Another part of the problem is what Estes describes as a tendency for agencies to serve as agents of social control. Although their work is defined in terms of "helping," they also exert power over the lives of those being served (Estes, 1979, p. 25). The aging network itself has, thus, contributed to the continued definition of being old as a social problem.

Those serving the elderly populations in the People's Republic of China and Japan have apparently not been organized as elaborately or with the same attitudes as the U.S. "aging network." It is also true that the view of old age as a time of dependency and helplessness, and thus as a social problem, is not nearly as well developed in either of those countries as it is in the United States. This is true for at least two basic reasons. First, both of these Oriental societies still place great emphasis upon their traditions of filial piety and, to a large extent, rely upon families to care for the aged who need special care. Second, more of the aged in China and Japan either remain in the work force or fill societally vital roles in retirement than is true in this country. Nevertheless, there are clear indications that the social-problem perception of old age is also developing in both of these Oriental countries. In both countries far more emphasis is placed on economic development than on concern for the elderly. In both countries the elderly population is growing rapidly and the sense of burden of their care is being felt and expressed. As these trends continue, the view of the aged as dependent is bound to increase.

It is apparent from this analysis that the social problem of old age as it has been defined has not been solved. Although the attempted solutions may have improved the quality of life for many elderly people, they have also served to perpetuate the public perception that to be old in modern society is to be dependent, helpless, and in need of special services. Ironically, even though, as discussed in Chapter 1, the opposite kind of image, of the elderly as a privileged class of people, is now emerging, the dependency image still dominates the professional world of gerontology and still largely controls policies on aging.

With the emergence of the definition of aged persons as "dependent" has come the growing assumption that they need someone to advocate for them. This assumption has been prevalent in countries with very different cultural backgrounds and political structures. Informal grass-roots systems of advocacy involving elderly people themselves, as well as formal systems involving government and agency personnel, have been at work in behalf of the elderly. In the United States, professional workers and groups have assumed the advocate role in behalf of the aged. However, they have historically been relatively ineffective in actually representing the needs of all of the elderly or in meeting the needs as defined by the aged themselves. For example, age-related special-interest groups have claimed to advocate for the aged in terms of influencing policy, but they have often advocated as much for their own vested interests as for the actual needs of the aged as they themselves might define them. That kind of advocating has, in fact, tended to perpetuate the view of the aged as dependent and helpless.

The legislatively mandated system of advocacy in which federal, state, and area agencies and their advisory councils have been expected to acquire and coordinate needed resources and equitably provide services to the aged has by no means functioned as expected. While the aging network has planned and delivered many vital services to elderly people, it has done little to muster additional resources beyond those provided by the Older Americans Act itself. Neither has it delivered services on any kind of equitable basis.

In fairness to those in the aging network, it is probably unreasonable to expect them to fulfill such a role. Their advocacy roles have not been well defined. They have not been given an adequate power base within bureaucratic structures to be able to function as advocates. In addition, it seems clear that the planning and service-provision roles are somewhat incompatible with the advocacy role. Effective advocates must be independent of the service-providing agencies and have the potential of reaching all communities and all eligible elderly people.

Logically, it would seem that the aged themselves ought to act as their own advocates. They have not had great success at this in the past, however, at least in the United States. Many of them have not understood how to advocate, nor have they even had the desire to be involved in advocacy activities. Furthermore, with the great economic and social divergence among their population, they have lacked group consensus about their needs. Given their social positions of economic dependency, they have also lacked the political power to advocate effectively for themselves.

Recent indications are, however, that many of them are becoming their own most effective advocates, at least in the United States. They are beginning to recognize that there are issues that touch them all. With the formation of large independent groups made up almost exclusively of elderly members, they are finding that they now have great political power, and they are beginning to advocate quite successfully in their own behalf.

As the aged take over their own advocacy, a substantial shift will undoubtedly take place in how their needs are defined and what concerns will emerge as policy issues. Much less emphasis will be placed on dependency-building, stereotyping, needs-providing issues. Much more emphasis will be placed on their capabilities and potential contributions to society, and on the provision of opportunities to perform meaningfully productive roles, both in and outside of retirement. This is an emphasis that has been made by such groups as the Gray Panthers for some time (Long, 1981). An example of this kind of shift in priorities is Moody's discussion of the "policy significance of productive aging." He anticipates that the need to be productive on the part of increasing numbers of elderly people will require policy decisions in the future. According to him, the kinds of issues that policies may be asked to address include age discrimination, empowerment and training, creation of special productive programs and opportunities, and the provision of benefit incentives to encourage participation among the elderly (Moody, 1993).

Increasing demands are also being made for the rights of the aged themselves to plan and control their own life activities and destinies, in terms of such matters as financial stability, social activities, health care, and retirement. In addition, the elderly are increasingly recognizing the importance of advocating to combat the stigmas and myths of aging. Self-advocacy on the part of the elderly themselves will almost certainly result in a dramatic change in our social policies on aging, in the rest of the society's view of them, and the roles and relationships they enjoy.

In the People's Republic of China, as compared with the United States, elderly people have enjoyed relatively greater social and political power in the past and were thus considerably more successfully involved in defining their own needs and in influencing age-related policies. Navajo elderly have also been successfully involved in advocating for themselves, at least initially and in terms of acquiring services that were previously nonexistent. Neither the Chinese nor Navajo self-advocacy efforts have as yet succeeded in creating equitable systems of service provision, however. In fact, effective advocacy in both of those societies has diminished recently.

As a whole, much has been accomplished due to the advocating efforts on behalf of elderly people in the world today. Much remains to be accomplished, however.

REFERENCES

Arber, Sara, and Jay Ginn, *Gender and Later Life: A Sociological Analysis of Resources and Constraints* (Newbury Park, Calif.: Sage, 1991).

Atchley, Robert C., *Social Forces and Aging: An Introduction to Social Gerontology* (Belmont, Calif.: Wadsworth, 1985).

Atchley, Robert C., *Social Forces and Aging: An Introduction to Social Gerontology* (Belmont: Calif.: Wadsworth, 1991).

Atchley, Robert C., *The Sociology of Retirement* (New York: Wiley, 1976).

Berger, M., "An Orienting Perspective on Advocacy," in *Advocacy and Age*, ed. Paul A. Kerschner (Los Angeles: University of Southern California Press, 1976), pp. 2–13.

Binstock, Robert, *Planning Background Issues: White House Conference on Aging Report* (Washington, D.C.: U.S. Government Printing Office, 1971).

Brinkerhoff, David B., and Lynn K. White, *Sociology* (St. Paul: West, 1985).

Brown, Arnold S., "Grassroots Advocacy for the Elderly In Small Rural Communities," *The Gerontologist*, 25, no. 4 (August 1985), 417–23.

Brown, Arnold S., "Satisfying Relationships for the Elderly and Their Patterns of Disengagement," *The Gerontologist*, 14, no. 3 (June 1974), 258–62.

Brown, Arnold S., "Social Policy of Aging in Mainland China," unpublished report of an informal study of the social policy on aging in China done while in China, summer 1984.

Brown, Arnold S., and Thomas Timmreck, "Summary Report of a Survey on the Navajo Nation Long Term Care and Aging Policy," unpublished paper submitted to the Arizona Long-Term Care Gerontology Center, the University of Ariz., Tucson, Ariz., 1984.

Caiwei, Xiao, China National Committee on Aging, Beijing, China, correspondence with Arnold S. Brown, December 19, 1993.

Carlson, Rich, "Health Promotion and Disease Prevention," *Generations*, 7, no. 3 (Spring 1983), 10–12, 72.

Casassus, Barbara, "The Fight to Weave Silver Threads into a Golden Age, *Far Eastern Economic Review*, 130 (December 19, 1986), 74–75.

Cohn, J., "Advocacy and Planning: Its Strength, Potential and Future," in *Advocacy and Age*, ed. Paul A. Kerschner (Los Angeles: University of Southern California Press, 1976), pp. 74–76.

Conner, Karen A., *Aging America: Issues Facing an Aging Society* (Englewood Cliffs, N.J.: Prentice Hall, 1992).

Davis-Friedmann, Deborah, *Long Lives: Chinese Elderly and the Communist Revolution* (Cambridge, Mass.: Harvard University Press, 1983).

Eshleman, J. Ross, *The Family: An Introduction* (Boston: Allyn & Bacon, 1985).

Estes, Carroll L., *The Aging Enterprise* (San Francisco: Jossey-Bass, 1979).

Estes, Carroll L., Lenore E. Gerard, Jane S. Zones, and James H. Swan, *Political Economy, Health, and Aging* (Boston: Little, Brown, 1984).

Fischer, David Hackett, *Growing Old in America* (New York: Oxford University Press, 1978).

"Forecasting on the Aging Population," *Beijing Review*, 27 (March 10, 1986), 25–34.

Friedan, Betty, *The Fountain of Age* (New York: Simon & Schuster, 1993).

Fritz, Dan, "The Administration on Aging as an Advocate: Progress, Problems and Perspectives," *The Gerontologist*, 19, no. 2 (April 1979), 141–50.

Gelfand, Donald E., *The Aging Network: Programs and Services* (New York: Springer, 1993).

George, Linda K., *Role Transitions in Later Life* (Monterey, Calif.: Brooks/Cole, 1980).

"Growing Old in China," *Beijing Review*, 43 (October 26, 1981), pp. 22–28.

Guide to AoA Programs, Publication No. (OHDS) 80–20176 (U. S. Department of Health and Human Services, 1980), pp. 3–5.

Harper, Sara, "Caring for China's Ageing Population: The Residential Option—A Case Study of Shanghai," *Ageing and Society*, 12 (1992), 157–84.

Harris, Diane K., *Sociology of Aging* (New York: Harper & Row, 1990).

Hickey, Tom, *Health and Aging* (Monterey, Calif.: Brooks/Cole, 1980).

Hochschild, Arlie, "Communal Living in Old Age," in *The Family: Functions, Conflicts, and Symbols*, eds. Peter J. Stein, Judith Richman, and Natalie Hannon (Menlo Park, Calif.: Addison-Wesley, 1977), pp. 404–9.

Hong, Guodong, "Support for the Elderly in China—Gradual Improvements in Social Security," in *Population Aging: International Perspectives*, eds. Tarek M. Shuman, E. Percil Stanford, Anita S. Harbert, Mary G. Schmidt, and Joan L. Roberts, (San Diego, Calif.: San Diego State University, 1993), pp. 433–40.

Hooyman, Nancy R., and H. Asuman Kiyak, *Social Gerontology: A Multidisciplinary Perspective* (Boston: Allyn & Bacon, 1991).

Hudson, Robert B., "The 'Graying' of the Federal Budget and Its Consequences for Old-Age Policy," in *The Aging in Politics: Process and Policy*, ed. Robert B. Hudson (Springfield, Ill.: Charles C. Thomas, 1981), pp. 261–81.

Hutter, Mark, *The Changing Family: Changing Perspectives* (New York: Macmillan, 1988).

Inglehart, J. K., "Health Care and American Business," *The New England Journal of Medicine*, 306, no. 2 (January 1982), 120–24.

"The Japanese-Style Welfare System," *Japan Quarterly*, 30 (July-September, 1983), 327–30.

Johnson, Elizabeth S., and John B. Williamson, *Growing Old: The Social Problems of Aging* (New York: Holt, Rinehart and Winston, 1980).

Kaiser, Marvin A., and Henry J. Camp, "Beneficiaries and Contributors to Rural Community and Economic Development," in *Aging in Rural America*, ed. C. Neil Bull (Newbury Park, Calif.: Sage, 1993), pp. 45–58.

Kando, Thomas M., *Leisure and Popular Culture in Transition* (Saint Louis, Mo.: C. V. Mosby, 1975).

Kaufman, Sharon R., "Values as Sources of the Ageless Self," in *Activity and Aging: Staying Involved in Later Life*, ed. John R. Kelley (Newbury Park, Calif.: Sage, 1993), pp. 17–24.

Kinoshita, Yasuhito, and Christie W. Kiefer, *Refuge of the Honored: Social Organization in a Japanese Retirement Community* (Berkeley, Calif.: University of California Press, 1992).

Komine, Takao, "The Aging of the Labor Force in Japan," in *The Promise of Productive Aging: From Biology to Social Policy*, eds. Robert N. Butler, Mia R. Oberlink, and Mal Schechter (New York: Springer, 1990), pp. 116–17.

Kuypers, Joseph A., and Vern L. Bengtson, "Social Breakdown and Competence: A Model of Normal Aging," *Human Development*, 16 (1973), 181–201.

Lauffer, Armand, *Social Planning at the Community Level*, (Englewood Cliffs N.J.: Prentice Hall, 1978).

Lewis, Myrna, "Aging in the People's Republic of China," *International Journal of Aging and Human Development*, 15, no. 1 (1982), 79–105.

Long, Christina, "Gray Panthers: Some Grassroots Projects," *Generations*, 6, no. 2 (Winter 1981), 28–29.

Lopata, Helena Z., "The Life Cycle of the Social Role of the Housewife," *Sociology and Social Research*, 51 (1966), 5–22.

Lowy, Louis, *Social Policies and Programs on Aging* (Lexington, Mass.: Lexington, 1980).

Macionis, John J., *Sociology* (Englewood Cliffs, N.J.: Prentice Hall, 1993).

Maeda, Daisaku, "Japan," in *International Handbook on Aging: Contemporary Developments and Research*, ed. Erdman B. Palmore (Westport, Conn.: Greenwood Press, 1980), pp. 253–70.

Matras, Judah, *Dependency, Obligations, and Entitlements: A New Sociology of Aging, the Life Course, and the Elderly* (Englewood Cliffs, NJ: Prentice Hall, 1990).

Mills, C. Wright, *The Sociological Imagination* (New York: Oxford University Press, 1959).

Moen, Elizabeth, "The Reluctance of the Elderly to Accept Help," *Social Problems*, 25, no. 3 (February 1978), 293–303.

Mok, Bong-ho, "In the Service of Socialism: Social Welfare in China," *Social Work*, 28, no. 4 (July-August, 1983) 269–72.

Moody, Harry R., "Age, Productivity, and Transcendence," in *Achieving a Productive Aging Society*, eds. Scott A. Bass, Francis G. Caro, and Yung-Ping Chen (Westport, Conn.: Auburn House, 1993), pp. 27–40.

Palmore, Erdman B., "Is Aging Really Better in Japan?" *The Gerontologist*, 33, no 5 (October 1993), 697–99.

Palmore, Erdman B., "The Status and Integration of the Aged in Japanese Society," *Journal of Gerontology*, 30, no. 2 (March 1975a), 199–208.

Palmore, Erdman B., "What Can the USA Learn from Japan about Aging?" *The Gerontologist*, 15, no. 1 (1975b), 64–67.

Pratt, J. J., "Symbolic Politics and the White House Conference on Aging," *Society*, (July/August 1978), pp. 67–72.

Renzhi, Du, "Old People in China: Hopes and Problems," *Beijing Review*, 27 (April 16, 1984), 31–34.

Roscoe, Bruce, "The Search for an Antidote to Workaholism," *Far Eastern Economic Review*, 130 (December 19, 1985), 76–78.

Rose, Arnold M., "A Current Theoretical Issue in Social Gerontology," in *Older People in Their Social World*, eds. Arnold M. Rose and Warren A. Peterson (Philadelphia: F. A. Davis, 1965), pp. 359–66.

Sarason, Seymour B., *Work, Aging, and Social Change* (New York: Free Press, 1977).

Schulz, James H., *The Economics of Aging* (Dover, Mass.: Auburn House, 1988).

Schulz, James H., "The Future of Social Security and Private Pensions or Does Social Security Have a Future?" *Generations*, 4, no. 1 (May 1980), 21–23.

Shanas, Ethel, "Family Help Patterns and Social Class in Three Countries," *Journal of Marriage and the Family*, 29 (May 1967), 257–66.

Sheppard, Harold L., and Sara E. Rix, *The Graying of Working America: The Coming Crisis in Retirement-Age Policy* (New York: The Free Press, 1977).

Shiro, Hashimoto, "Population Trends in Japan," *Japan Quarterly*, 30 (April-May, 1983), 194–200.

Shujun, Zhou, "Prospects for China's Population in 2000," *Beijing Review*, 27 (April 2, 1984), 20–23.

Tian, Jiyun, "Will Reform Lead to Capitalism?" *Beijing Review*, 29 (February 3, 1986), 15–17.

Troll, Lillian E., Sheila J. Miller, and Robert C. Atchley, *Families in Later Life* (Belmont, Calif.: Wadsworth, 1979).

Tu, Edward Jow-Ching, Vicki A. Freedman, and Douglas A. Wolf, "Kinship and Family Support in Taiwan: A Multisimulation Approach," *Research on Aging*, 15, no. 4 (December 1993), 465–86.

U.S. Subcommittee on Aging of the Committee on Labor and Public Welfare and the Special Committee on Aging United States Senate, *Post-White House Conference on Aging Report*, 1973 (Washington, D.C.: U.S. Government Printing Office, 1973).

Wantz, Molly S., and John E. Gay, *The Aging Process: A Health Perspective* (Cambridge: Winthrop, 1981).

Ward, Russell A., *The Aging Experience: An Introduction to Social Gerontology* (New York: Harper & Row, 1984).

Weber, Max, *The Protestant Ethic and the Spirit of Capitalism*, trans. Talcott Parsons (New York: Scribner's, 1958).

10

The Extent of Economic Dependency Among the Aged

INTRODUCTION

It is generally assumed in the modern world today that elderly people are economically dependent and represent an unfair burden on younger workers. Those over 65 and under 16 years old are compared with those 16 through 65 by economists and demographers to analyze what they term the *dependency ratio* of a given population, for example. The idea behind this concept is that children, youth, and old people are being totally supported by young and middle-aged adults, and that this is placing an increasing and unfair burden on the rest of the population (Sheppard and Rix, 1977, pp. 13–35).

The challenges to all of us, young and old, are to determine the validity of this concept and to judge the extent to which that sense of burden is fair in light of the facts. To analyze the extent of economic dependency among the aged, then, we need first of all to understand what is meant by economics, how the economic system is assumed to work, and how the notion of old age dependency emerged. We will also see how the notion of economic dependency of the aged is being avoided in other nations.

ECONOMICS AND THE ECONOMIC SYSTEMS

We have a tendency today to think of money whenever economics is discussed. Money does not define economics, however. In essence, economics has to do with the production, distribution, and consumption of goods and services needed by given societies. Money is involved merely as the basic tool to enhance those processes in today's complex societies.

Historically, human labor has been needed to produce and distribute necessary goods and services. In fact, in the hunting and fishing as well as in the agricultural societies, in which the level of technology has been limited or non-existent, all of the available human labor has been needed for these purposes. The very survival of many such societies is constantly threatened if enough human labor is not available. Therefore, in these kinds of societies, those unable to do the work required in the productive or distributive processes become dependent upon those who can and do perform those kinds of tasks.

The burden of the dependency of those unable to perform physical labor, especially the aged, has been found to be too great for some hunting and fishing societies living in particularly harsh environments. Sharp reports, for example, that old age in the Chipewyan tribe in the subarctic area of northern Canada is despised and feared. If the aged are no longer able to hunt, they are left out of social life, feel useless and powerless, and are sometimes even abandoned. Subsistence for the Chipewyan is so precious that the tribe simply cannot support those aged who become economically dependent (Sharp, 1981).

Sheehan compared the place of the aged in three types of "traditional" societies located in various parts of the world: (1) those that were geographically unstable (seminomadic); (2) tribes that lived in relatively permanent villages; and (3) those living in peasant communities and engaged in agriculture. His data showed that the status of the aged in the geographically unstable societies largely depended on each individual's ability to continue to contribute to the group's survival. Among the relatively stable tribes, older people typically had positions of importance, but priority was still given to younger members of the tribes. Among the agricultural peasant groups, older people were held in high esteem (Sheehan, 1976).

In agricultural societies, production has developed beyond the level of simple subsistence, and the accumulation of family assets becomes possible. A division of labor is typically worked out, with management positions becoming important. Land ownership also develops, with owners holding positions of control over others. Far from being treated as dependent, the aged in these types of societies tend to continue to participate in the productive processes throughout their lives, with increasingly important and powerful positions. They often own the land and manage production while younger family members provide the hard labor. As Williamson and his colleagues explain, "The institution of property rights gave the elderly considerable control over those who were younger; particularly their children" (Williamson, Evans, and Powell, 1982, p. 5). Fischer has reported that land ownership contributed greatly to the veneration and economic power of the aged in the United States from colonial days at least through the eighteenth century (Fischer, 1978, pp. 51–58). Actually, remnants of economic power among the aged in rural parts of the United States have survived to the present day.

Production and distribution of goods and services in hunting and fishing as well as in agricultural societies are controlled and carried out by family or kinship units. In these kinds of situations, the economic security of older people depends primarily on whether or not the accumulation of resources is possible. As we have seen, that is clearly most possible in those societies in which agriculture has been developed. Even then, however, old age itself does not guarantee economic security. That comes only to those who are able to acquire and control resources within their families and communities. It is just that economic power among older people is most possible in agricultural settings.

The economic status of the aged is strengthened not merely because they are able to control economic resources, but also because they tend to continue participating in production. While the work they do tends to be less physically demanding as they age, they nevertheless continue to contribute vital efforts to production. Thus, the work ethic is upheld as much by elderly family members as others, and human labor continues to be emphasized as the most important determinant of economic status.

Much has been made of the loss of productive roles experienced by the aged in industrialized societies. It is assumed that economic status declines and economic dependency sets in as a result of their retirement from those active roles. It is assumed that, because they are retired, the aged make no contributions to the productive processes of society and that their dependency is the burden of those who remain in the work force. This kind of analysis is based on the notion that human labor is still the primary factor that makes production possible. To assess the validity of this notion, we need to examine the economic system prevalent in the industrialized world.

Two factors about modern economics are important in analyzing the economic status of the aged today. One is the importance of technology in the actual productive processes, and the other is the importance of capital in the capitalist system that dominates production today.

It is obvious that the functions of modern economic systems are extremely complex. In agrarian societies, both production and distribution are relatively simple processes. In some cases distribution is nonexistent; families tend to be economically autonomous, producing what they themselves consume. In contrast, distribution is as vital as production in industrialized societies, and both of these processes are extremely complex. It is not at all uncommon, for example, for many goods and services to be shipped thousands of miles from where they are produced to potential consumer markets through a complex system of wholesale and retail companies. Adding to the complexity of this kind of system is also the fact that both production and distribution depend upon increasingly sophisticated technology.

There are two important things to consider with regard to the development of the technology involved in modern economics. First, it is eliminating much of the need for human labor in the production and distribution of goods and services. Machines are now available not only for those tasks that once required manual labor but for mental tasks as well. Second, technology requires money. Relying on labor-saving technology is generally more profitable for businesses than relying on human labor. Machines are faster and more efficient. Nevertheless, acquiring the needed machinery typically requires initial capital. The need for capital, then, is a vital part of the modern economic system.

The use of technology and the need for capital in modern economic systems are both important to understand if we are to get a true picture of the extent to which the aged are economically dependent in the industrial world today. The specific issues are (1) the extent to which their elimination from the work force actually creates an economic burden of dependency for those in the work force, on the one hand, and may enhance the economic situation for those in the work place, on the other hand, and (2) the extent to which and the ways in which the aged may actually contribute positively to today's economic conditions. These are issues that are largely ignored in today's gerontological literature.

DEVELOPMENT OF FINANCIAL SUPPORT FOR THE AGED IN THE UNITED STATES

As the United States moved into the twentieth century, the last areas of the great western frontier were being settled. For over 200 years, the frontier movement had been a major source of economic development. As land for new frontiers diminished, though, economic expansion moved in a very different direction. The nation rapidly became industrialized. With an abundance of natural resources and the growing technology to transform those resources into usable products, factories were built and an ever-expanding array of goods were produced. Jobs in the city factories were readily available to individuals who chose to leave the drudgery of farm work. Jobs in industry became an increasingly attractive alternative to that of eking out livings on small acreages of farmland, especially to young adults. Pay tended to be better, the working hours were fewer, the chances for advancement were greater, and the living conditions in the cities were far less primitive and harsh (Achenbaum, 1983, pp. 9–10).

Ironically, although industrialization greatly benefited the rest of the American population economically, it had a negative effect on many elderly people. They no longer owned or controlled their work situations. Instead, their economic conditions depended entirely upon them being employed by others (usually large corporations). Whether or not they were employed as they aged was controlled by employers whose primary concern was to produce as many goods as possible in order to make as much profit as possible. Employers tended to assume that older workers were not as efficient or productive as younger workers (Olson, 1982, pp. 33–34). Thus, increasing numbers of elderly people became unemployed, especially during the 1920s. At the very time when much of the rest of the society enjoyed relative economic prosperity, increasing numbers of old people were experiencing poverty. The older they were, the poorer they tended to be (Achenbaum, 1979, pp. 21–37). Fischer reports that 23 percent of elderly Americans were economically dependent in 1910; by 1922, that figure had risen to 33 percent, and it was as high as 40 percent by 1930 (Fischer, 1978, p. 174).

Attempts to provide financial support for the elderly poor in the United States began with the development of pension plans by a few states, as the result of pressure from a number of grass-roots organizations. By 1933, most states had enacted at least modest pension plans despite the opposition of conservative politicians and judges (Fischer, 1978, pp. 175–76). With the advent of the Great Depression in the 1930s, however, state pensions did almost nothing to stop the spread of poverty among the aged. As Steuerle and Bakija explain, these pension plans "were not very safe or reliable." They could not be transferred from one job to another, most of them were not sufficiently funded, and many went bankrupt, leaving "many employees with no pensions and no recourse" (Steuerle and Bakija, 1994, p. 27). That fact plus the many bank failures convinced the people that "the private market was failing to accommodate the needs not only of the poor but also of the middle class" (Steuerle and Bakija, 1994, p. 27). The American public was finally convinced that it was up to the federal government to correct the existing economic situation. Finally, in 1935, Congress passed the Social Security Act, part of which was the establishment of a social insurance program that became the backbone of financial support for older people in this country. Ever since then, Social Security has been the major source of retirement income even though the number and size of pensions have grown and become more stable and other sources of income have also develped. Figure 10–1 shows how the percentages of elderly relying on the various sources of income changed from 1962 to 1990.

FIGURE 10-1   Percent of Aged Receiving Income from Various Sources, 1962 and 1990. (Source: "Income of the Aged Population," in *Fast Facts & Figures* (Washington, D.C.: Social Security Administration, Office of Research & Statistics, 1993, U.S. Government Document # HE 3.94: 993), pp. 4–8.)

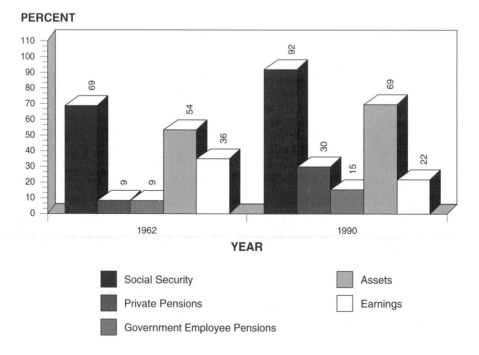

RETIREMENT BENEFITS THROUGH SOCIAL SECURITY

According to Steuerle and Bakija, the Social Security Program in the United States was developed by utilizing a set of principles from the prevailing theory of public finance as guidelines, for the primary purpose of helping the elderly poor (Steuerle and Bakija, 1994, pp. 12–25). Following is a list of those principles and how they were applied to the Social Security Act.

The Economic Principles on which Social Security was Based

The first principle was "Progressivity" or "Vertical Equity." Myers refers to this as "social adequacy" (Myers, 1993, p. 10). The goal of this principle was to reduce economic inequality in society, by addressing the special needs of those experiencing inequality (in this case, the elderly). This called for some form and level of income redistribution which was part of what Social Security attempted to do, at least to some small but significant extent.

The second economic principle that was considered was "Individual Equity." This principle holds that the taxes that individuals pay to the government in support of the program should be somehow directly related to the benefits that they receive from the program. From an economic point of view, then, it ought not to just simply be a welfare program. Instead, for it to work, benefits needed to be available to all who participated. It is this principle that is being emphasized when Social Security is called "social insurance." Now, basically, this principle conflicts with the first one. As Steuerle and Bakija point out, a strict application of it "precludes any redistribution by government to reduce inequality or ameliorate need" (Steuerle and Bakija, 1994, p. 18). The Social Security law was developed, however, as a compromise between the two principles by confining it to employees, requiring all employees to contribute a certain percentage of their wages to the program, making them eligible for financial benefits upon retirement, and establishing a fixed minimum benefit level to address the needs of the poorest workers. Myers believes that social adequacy (vertical equity) is the one most emphasized (Myers, 1993, pp. 10–11), but that would be hard to substantiate.

The third principle taken into account in developing Social Security was "Horizontal Equity." The idea here is that participants in the program whose circumstances are equal should be treated equally. Employees born the same year and earning equal amounts of wages, for example, should be taxed equally and receive the same amount of benefits if they retire at the same ages, for example. This principle is what makes the Social Security system as fair as it is possible to make it and one to which the program has quite consistently adhered.

The fourth and last principle on which Social Security was built was "Economic Efficiency." This principle stipulates that, "an economy ought to operate so that individuals can achieve the maximum well-being with their limited resources" (Steuerle and Bakija, 1994, p. 13). That, of course is how the free market is supposed to operate, but when it does not, as was certainly true during the Great Depression, then governmental intervention is appropriate to make the economy more efficient again. This means, though, that an intervention focused on one particular problem area, in this case the poverty among the elderly, must be limited so as not to ignore other societal needs.

This kind of theoretical analysis of the United States Social Security program is valuable in understanding how the program was developed. It may also be helpful in making needed changes in the program in the future, as Steuerle and Bakija suggest. We need to recognize, though, that it is basically a theoretical analysis and is limited in the practical world of working conditions and politics. Specifically, it ignores much of the political motivation behind the passage of the Social Security Act of 1935.

The Practical Principles on which Social Security was Based

It is also important to examine more thoroughly the political motivation of the passage of this piece of legislation and the practical principles on which it was structured, in order to understand its effect on the economic status of elderly people today. As discussed in Chapter 9, the unemployment rate in the middle of the Great Depression of the 1930s required that as many people as possible needed to be eliminated from the work force as cheaply as possible. Social Security was one of many pieces of legislation that would do that and help overcome the economic crisis that was crippling society. It was deliberately designed, as Schulz has said, "to encourage older people to leave and remain out of the work force" (Schulz, 1988, p. 122). Steuerle and Bakija argue that unavailability of jobs is not a legitimate reason for the establishment and continuation of Social Security (Steuerle and Bakija, 1994, pp. 30–31). Theoretically, that may be a reasonable argument, but one has to wonder how the millions of unemployed people in the depression and young people today would view the problem of competition for jobs. Except for the time of World War II, job competition has been an increasing fact of life for workers in the industrialized world.

That keeping older people out of the work force was initially, and has remained, a basic reason for the establishment and maintenance of Social Security becomes apparent when we examine the very practical principles on which the program was built. Those principles also show us the place that elderly people have in financing the program.

The old-age pension part of the Social Security program has consistently operated on six basic principles, as outlined by Schulz (Schulz, 1988, pp. 125–26). First, participation in the program is *compulsory*. With only a few exceptions, such as those who were self-employed, all American workers were required to contribute to the Social Security fund out of their monthly pay checks. By paying into the fund, they were then eligible to receive retirement benefits from it when they retired. This principle does not mean that retirement itself was compulsory. The Social Security program has never made retirement mandatory for anyone, even though one of the purposes of the law was clearly to encourage retirement from the work force.

The second principle of operation of Social Security is that it is an *earnings-related system*. This program has been referred to by many people as a type of welfare for the aged. This principle clearly shows that assumption to be false. No one receives retirement benefits from the program except those who have first paid into it and their dependents, and each person contributes an amount based on earned wages. Subsequently, the amount received in benefits upon retirement is based on salary earned while working.

The third principle states that Social Security is simply *a floor of protection*. The intention is not to cover all of the financial needs of retired individuals. Workers were expected to prepare financially for their retirement years beyond the benefits they would be eligible to receive from Social Security. Given the level of poverty among the elderly and even younger workers in 1935, this was certainly an unrealistic expectation. Nevertheless, it was all that could be hoped for at the time from a political perspective. As Fischer has observed, "the astonishing fact about Social Security was not that it was passed in so conservative a form, but rather that it was passed at all in so conservative a nation" (Fischer, 1978, p. 184).

The fourth operational principle of Social Security is that the funds for the program are to come from *contributions* made by the workers themselves and their employers ("Social Security Programs in the United States," 1991). Again, this was not meant to be a welfare program, but a social insurance program. Eligibility based on need has never been the major part of Social Security. Instead, all participants have earned the right to receive benefits because of having contributed as workers. This does not mean that the contributions that individuals make to the Social Security retirement trust fund in the form of taxes are reserved exclusively for their individual retirement benefits. Instead, the program is partially, and sometimes fully, financed on a pay-as-you-go basis. This basically means that current employees are taxed at a high enough level to fund the benefits of present retirees (Steuerle and Bakija, 1994, p. 18). The amount of Social Security taxes workers must pay per year is figured on the basis of a certain percentage of their wages up to a given maximum level and the retirement benefits participants ultimately receive in retirement are based on those same wages, plus the number of years having worked. Any amount of income made by individuals above the maximum is considered neither in Social Security taxes having to be paid nor the amount of retirement benefits subsequently received. Benefits are also adjusted annually to compensate for increases in the cost-of-living experienced the previous year. Cost-of-living increases for 1992 were 3.0 percent and for 1993 it was 2.6 percent ("Social Security in Review," 1993).

Relative to the rest of the population, both the percentage of Social Security taxation and the maximum amount of income subject to that taxation have dramatically increased over the years that the program has been in operation because Social Security is basically a pay-as-you-go system and because of the fact that the aged population has been rapidly growing . It is also true that increasing numbers of benefit recipients eventually receive more in payments from the retirement trust fund than they have contributed to it in taxes. As Quinn explains, "cohorts who have retired thus far have received benefits well in excess of what their and their employers' contributions would have yielded" (Quinn, 1993). The maximum amounts of income on which social security taxes are paid in given years have been compared to the average annual wages among workers in those same years. As Figure 10–2 shows, the maximum earnings on which taxes are figured have consistently been higher than the average wages for that year. It is noteworthy, though, that the difference between those figures has progressively increased over the years. Obviously, as the taxes from ordinary laborers were not sufficient to keep the trust funds solvent, it has become necessary to tax more and more of the wages

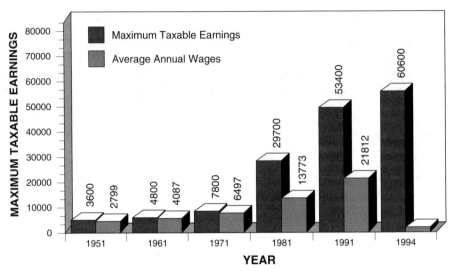

FIGURE 10-2   Maximum Taxable Earnings for Social Security Purposes and Average Annual Wages By Year (Source: Adapted from Table 2.A8, *Social Security Bulletin*, 56, no. 4 (Winter 1993), 89.

of higher income workers. Ironically, of course, that has the effect of also increasing the amount of benefits they have a right to receive in retirement. That constitutes an added demand on what many analysts see as an already inadequately financed trust fund ("Actuarial Status...," 1994; Eastaugh, 1994, pp. 204–5).

The program's fifth principle is what has been called *social adequacy.* Lower-income workers are to be somewhat favored. Therefore, a minimum income benefit has been set, which all eligible participants are guaranteed regardless of the level of income they have had as employees. According to Myers, this kind of benefit can only be provided in such a compulsory and large program such as Social Security (Myers, 1993).

The last of the practical principles on which Social Security is based was that a *retirement test* is required before individuals can receive the income benefits for which they are eligible. It is clear from this that one of the major purposes of this program has consistently been to remove the aged from, and keep them out of, the work force. The retirement test has been somewhat liberalized since the 1930s. As of 1991, those under 65 who are already on Social Security may earn only $7,080, above which one for each two dollars earned from employment is subtracted from their monthly checks. Those 65–69 are docked one for each three dollars earned in employment over $9,720. Those 70 or older may now earn as much in wages as they can without being penalized ("Social Security Programs...," 1991). Nevertheless, the retirement test as it has been defined has always been strictly followed. It is important to note that there are no restrictions on the amount of income individuals are allowed to earn in retirement as long as that income is not earned from employment. They may, for example, earn substantial income through investments, as those with money typically do. This very pointedly illustrates the fact that the modern economic system needs capital more than it needs workers in order to function.

Middle-Class Workers as the Primary Target of Social Security

The Old Age Insurance pension part of the Social Security began and has continued to be a program that targets ordinary middle-class workers, not the rich. They pay a higher percentage of their income in social security taxes and the benefits they receive represent a higher percentage of their retirement income. To assure that that would be true, the social security law has continuously capped the dollar amount of people's annual income on which both social security taxes and retirement benefits would be based. That cap has increased over the years, from $3,000 in 1936 to $60,600 in 1994. The point is that any income individual workers earn above those amounts is not subject to social security taxation and is not considered in determining his or her retirement benefits. At present, for example, those earning $60,600 pay the same amount of social security taxes per year as those with incomes of any amount over that. Also, when they retire, they will receive the same amount of income benefits from Social Security. This program was clearly not created to make people rich in retirement, nor does it. Rather, it was to provide ordinary workers with enough retirement income to encourage them to retire from an extremely competitive work force.

The Solvency of the Social Security Program

Many people have contended since the 1970s that the Old Age Insurance and Disabled Insurance (OAIDI) Social Security trust funds are in financial trouble in the years ahead. Consequently, in 1985 Congress made a number of amendments to the Social Security Act, that greatly improved the financial situation for a number of years. Changes that were made included (1) postponing the dates when already-approved employee tax rate increases would go into effect; (2) increasing the self-employment tax rates; (3) taxing up to half of the Social Security benefit income of upper-income beneficiaries, with the resulting revenues being appropriated to the OAIDI Trust Funds; (4) expanding the coverage of the Social Security program to include federal civilian employees hired after 1983, and all non-profit organization employees; and (5) gradually increasing the age of eligibility for full benefits as follows: (a) from 65 to 66 for those 62 in 2000–2005, and (b) from 66 to 67 for those 62 in 2017–2022 ("Actuarial Status," 1994).

As a consequence of those changes a surplus immediately began to accrue in the OAI Trust Fund. These funds are, as stipulated in the law, invested in interest-bearing government securities. This practice has been a bone of contention for many people. It has led some to erroneously conclude that in fact there is actually no surplus at all but is being used up to pay for other government programs. In fact, a surplus does exist in much the same way that I have a balance in my bank savings account, which the bank is obviously investing elsewhere. Trust fund surplus investments receive annual interest payments, in the same way that bank accounts do. It is said that all of that is only "on paper" (Eastaugh, 1994, p. 204), but to some extent so are bank accounts and private investments of all kinds. Others object to the Trust

Fund's being invested in the government for two basic political reasons. First, investments elsewhere would earn more interest. Second, it makes it appear as though the federal debt is less severe than it actually is. This is mostly what prompted Senator Moynihan, a few years ago, to propose that Social Security employee taxes be lowered and the system be moved back more to a pay-as-you-go program again. These are arguments that have merit and, if they ever have enough political support behind them, changes in the law will undoubtedly be made. In the meantime, the surplus funds will continue to be invested in government securities and will continue to earn interest, as has always been the case.

In spite of the present balance in the Social Security Trust Funds, however, it is becoming clear that, unless and until further changes are made fairly soon, the program will again be in financial trouble. According to a 1993 Social Security Board of Trustees report to Congress, the various trust funds will be depleted and begin showing deficits as follows:

- Old-Age and Survivors Insurance (OASDI)—To be depleted in 2036
- Disability Insurance (DI)—To be depleted in 1995
- Hospital Insurance (HI) (Medicare Part A)—To be depleted in 2001

In order to correct this set of problems, in 1994 the Trustees proposed to Congress both short- and long-term solutions. First, they propose that a larger portion of the combined OASDI funds be allocated to the DI part of the program, with a somewhat smaller portion going to the Old Age and Survivors (OAS) part than is now the case. If this proposal is approved both of those funds would be solvent until 2029. Second, the Trustees are urging Congress to again address how the long-range deficit problems in all of the funds can be solved ("Actuarial Status...," 1994).

The Old Age Assistance Aspect of Social Security

In addition to the Old Age Insurance (OAI) pension program, the Social Security Act of 1935 also established Old Age Assistance (OAA), a welfare program for the elderly poor. Under OAA, states received federal grants to provide income assistance to their elderly poor. Within broad federal guidelines, states were allowed to set their own standards for eligibility and amount of assistance. Consequently, there was a great lack of uniformity from state to state as to whom received the benefits and how adequate they were ("Supplemental Security Income," 1991). Thus, in the 1974 Social Security Act revisions, the OAA program was changed to the Supplemental Security Income program (SSI). Under this new program, eligibility criteria were set and a nationwide formula for benefits was standardized. Administration of the program was assigned to the Social Security Administration. In essence SSI established a minimal guaranteed income of a specified amount for all elderly Americans. If they have no other source of income, that total specified amount is provided from SSI funds. If individuals receive small amounts of income from other sources, then SSI will make up the balance to bring their total incomes up to the specified amount. That amount does not lift recipients out of poverty, however. The maximum any individual could receive per month from SSI in 1994 was set at a mere $446 (an increase of $12 from 1993), and $669 for couples (an increase of $17 from 1993) ("Social Security in Review," 1993). That amount is severely cut for those living in someone else's household, (payments are cut by a third), and those in Medicaid-approved institutions, who receive a maximum of $30 per month. Assets worth a maximum of $2,000 for individuals and $3,000 for couples are not counted in determining whether individuals are eligible for payments. The kinds of assets that are allowed are houses in which the elderly recipients live, automobiles they use for necessities, and a certain amount of personal goods ("Supplemental Security Income," 1991).

Many people confuse the SSI and OAI programs. They are, however, very different. SSI is a welfare program funded out of the general federal budget (not from any of the Social Security trust funds). In contrast, OAI is a social insurance program, the benefits of which are reserved for those who have participated by contributing to the fund as discussed above. About the only similarities between the two programs are that (1) they both target elderly people, and (2) both are administered by the Social Security Administration.

RETIREMENT BENEFITS THROUGH PENSION PROGRAMS

An increasing amount of financial support for the older population today is coming from private pension programs. Pension programs are provided by private employers, government agencies, labor unions, and professional groups as part of the benefit packages for their worker constituents. Employers have been willing to develop pension programs and even make contributions to pension funds in behalf of their employees for a variety of reasons. According to a number of analysts, pension programs are not only beneficial to workers as an important source of income security when they retire. Just as importantly, employers have long recognized that such programs were useful to them as a mechanism of social control over their workers. In explaining how pensions for railroad workers in both the United States and Great Britain began as long ago as the late 1880s, Schulz and Myles list several reasons that the companies were willing to provide those plans. In addition to the altruistic motivations that sometimes existed they list five ways that pensions were useful to employers. They were functional in: (1) promoting the retention of workers they wanted to keep (especially white-collar professionals); (2) promoting greater efficiency in the productive process; (3) helping them to adjust the company's work force to shifting demands; (4) facilitating and even compelling the retirement of workers they considered no longer capable as workers; and later (5) helping them be able to contain labor unrest and union power (Schulz and Myles, 1990). Mitchell and Rappaport contend that pension programs today also, in some cases, serve to encourage workers "to more closely align their work efforts with company objectives" (Mitchell and Rappaport, 1993). Bodie and Papke summarize these points in stating that employers "use pension plans as a device to attract, retain, and motivate employees, and eventually to encourage them to retire" (Bodie and Papke, 1992). Partly for these reasons, some predict that pensions will continue to be a major institution throughout the industrialized world in the future, in spite of the many criticisms of the systems (Schulz and Myles, 1990).

For a number of years there were serious problems with many private pension programs in the United States. The practice of employers providing pension plans to their employees began in the United States in the latter part of the nineteenth century first among railroad companies. In Great Britain the first pensions were also among railroad workers as well as government civil service employees. Increasing numbers of large companies followed suit with plans of their own into the 1920s. In most of the countries where pension plans have been formed, government workers have been the first ones to be targeted (Schulz and Myles, 1990). However, all of these efforts combined did not begin to overcome the problems related to the economic security of workers. They covered only a small percentage of the labor force (Dailey and Turner, 1992). Furthermore, some of those that were developed were too small and too poorly managed to guarantee their continued existence. There were no eligibility standards or controls. Consequently, many workers who had paid into pension funds for years found upon retirement that either no funds were available for their pensions or that they were not eligible to receive them (Olson, 1982, p. 5). Then, as Schulz and Myles explain, "the Great Depression put most plans under great financial strain; many did not survive" (Schulz and Myles, 1990).

This set of circumstances finally led to the conclusion by many that what was needed was to "nationalize" pension programs. The first movement in that direction was the passage of the Railroad Retirement Act in 1935. Then, to set standards on all private pension programs, the United States Congress passed the Employment Retirement Income Security Act (ERISA) in 1974. Among other provisions, this legislation (1) outlined vesting programs (specifications of when participants have been in the plan long enough to receive full benefits) to be followed by all pension plans; (2) required that certain funding standards be set to guard against the fund's unnecessarily going bankrupt; (3) required annual reporting to participants; and (4) established the Guaranty Benefit Corporation with a government-controlled fund to guarantee benefits if given pension funds went bankrupt (Olson, 1982, p. 5). This has not only made it possible for employees to plan for their retirements with much greater confidence, but it has also increased the amount of money accumulated in pension funds across the country. The amount of money in pension funds has increased enormously in the past two or three decades. For example, between 1960 and 1980, the amount accrued in retirement funds grew from $73 billion, representing 4 percent of outstanding stock in the United States, to $653 billion, representing between 20 and 25 percent of total stocks of companies listed on the New York and American exchanges (Olson, 1982, p. 100). Bodie and Papke also reported in 1992 that "pension funds now own a substantial portion of the stock in U. S. corporations," so much so that "their voting power can profoundly affect corporate policy" (Bodie and Papke, 1992).

The number of workers covered by private pension plans has also dramatically increased during the past 20 years. It has been reported, for example, that as early as 1979, 40 percent of the women and 55 percent of the men working in the private sector in the United States were covered by private pension plans (Olson, 1982, p. 81). In numbers of workers the report is that "pension plan participants covered under one or more private-sector plans grew from 30.7 million workers in 1975 to 40.5 million in 1985" (Andrews and Hurd, 1992).

Nevertheless, despite this amount of growth, less than 50 percent of all workers in the United States, and fewer yet in other industrialized countries, are covered by private pensions (Dailey and Turner, 1992). Also, as Andrews and Hurd report, "pension plan participation has just kept pace with the growth in the labor force," and pension participant rates among employers in the United States have actually "declined precipitously in recent years"—from 87 percent in 1979 to 76 percent in 1986 (Andrews and Hurd, 1992).

The extent to which pension program participation is found on the part of workers, however, depends in part on the kind of program that is in effect. There are basically two very different types of plans. One type has been labeled the *defined benefit* plan and the other the *defined contribution* plan. Table 10–1 provides a brief description of the differences between these types of pension programs.

Defined benefit plans have in the past been the more common of the two. In this type of plan, participants in a particular work situation (i.e., all state employees) make regular contributions to a common fund. None of those funds accrue to individual participants. Instead, retirement benefits are determined on the basis of an established formula which considers such things as salary and the length of time the individual has worked for the particular employer in the situation. The program and the fund are owned and man-aged by representatives of the organization sponsoring the program. Problems have often developed in this kind of retirement plan when they are either underfunded or develop surpluses. If underfunded they may fail, and if there are surpluses, sponsors may use some of the surplus funds for other purposes unrelated to retirement. When government agencies are the sponsors, these purposes are often the promotion of particularly political agendas. According to Mitchell and Rappaport, the problems related to these kinds of programs were particularly addressed in the Tax Reform Act of 1986. Consequences of the regulations legislated in that act were that "pension benefits rose for lower-paid, and/or were reduced for higher-paid employees," and

TABLE 10–1   Major Differences between Defined Benefit and Defined Contribution Pension Plans

PLAN FEATURE	DEFINED BENEFIT	DEFINED CONTRIBUTION
Benefit accrual pattern	Higher in later years	Higher in earlier years
Cashouts for early leavers	Not usually	Lump sum
Retirement benefit payments	Annuity until death	Lump sum or annuity
Early retirement subsidy possible	Yes	Not usually
Postretirement benefit increases	Often	Not usually
Investment risk	Borne by employer	Borne by employee
Benefits fully guaranteed	No	Yes
PBGC benefit guaranteed	Yes	No
Employee makes asset allocation decision	No	Often

SOURCE: O. S. Mitchell and A. M. Rappaport, "Innovations and Trends in Pension Plan Coverage, Type, and Design," in *Future of Pensions in the United States*, ed. Ray Schmitt (Philadelphia: University of Pennsylvania Press, 1993), pp. 53–91, adapted from Table 4.

"employers' abilities to reward higher-paid employees with tax-qualified benefits" were limited (Mitchell and Rappaport, 1993). One major problem still remains with these kinds of programs, however—they are not portable. As a result many workers who change jobs lose many, if not all, of the benefits they have accrued (Andrews and Hurd, 1992).

In defined contribution plans, typically, a percentage of employees' regular pay checks is placed in pension funds that are reserved for them. Records are kept of the amounts individuals or their employers, or both, have paid into the fund. The accumulated funds plus the interest they earn throughout individuals' working years become available to them as retirement income. Participants have a lot of control over not only when and how to receive those funds in payments, but increasingly how the funds are invested (Rowland, 1994).

At retirement, individuals typically have three types of options for receiving the money they have accrued. First, most programs give individuals the option of taking their pension funds out in one lump sum. Almost no one chooses this option for the simple reason that the tax rate on that much money makes it prohibitive. A second option is to divide the available money over a fixed number of years and take it out in monthly payments. This type of option involves the risk that a person may live beyond the fixed number of years, during which no pension income will be available to them. A third option for individual retirees is to settle for somewhat lower monthly incomes, but with the promise that they will continue to receive monthly checks for the rest of their lives. This option represents almost no risk to the fund itself since monthly payments are usually set on the basis of only the interest being earned on those funds. The total amount of individually accrued funds remains available to the sponsoring organization of the program for investment (insurance companies, banks, employer organizations, unions, professional groups, and so on).

These kinds of programs are now becoming more and more popular and available to workers compared to defined benefit programs. Andrews and Hurd report, for example, that "the number or participants in defined contribution plans increased from 3.9 million in 1975 to 11.6 million in 1985," while those having coverage from a defined benefit plan fell from 87 percent in 1975 to 71 percent in 1985" (Andrews and Hurd, 1992). The problem is, though, that too much of the risk may be placed on individual participants who have inadequate knowledge, experience, or available help to make the strategic decisions they must make. As Rowland has dramatically put the problem, "the rules for withdrawing money from retirement accounts are so obscure that few banks, brokers, or even employers understand them. The penalty for making mistakes is high" (Rowland, 1994).

CHANGING ECONOMIC CONDITIONS OF THE ELDERLY IN AMERICA

It is obvious that, despite a number of improvements in providing financial support for older people in the United States in recent years, the adequacy of that support remains in question. On the one hand, a number of cross-sectional studies have reported that the financial condition of the elderly population in general has improved in recent years. Harris studied the income statistics of elderly people between 1945 and 1980 and concluded that there were no declines throughout that period. In fact, he reported improvements of incomes of the aged relative to others, especially between 1967 and 1977. He attributes these statistics to improvements in Social Security and pension fund benefits (Harris, 1986). Similarly, Moon looked at changes in income levels of the aged compared to others in the United States between 1980 and 1984. She found that the elderly suffered far less of a decrease in income benefits than other groups. She also assumed that this was due to improvements in Social Security (Moon, 1986). In 1992, Andrews and Hurd also reported that, as a whole, "elderly are found to be as well off as the nonelderly."

On the other hand, studies of the economic conditions of specific groups of older people and longitudinal studies of the economics of old age reveal a much less optimistic picture. The rates of poverty among minority elderly people are much higher than those of the white majority. In 1977, for example, only 11.9 percent of elderly whites were poverty stricken compared to 21.9 percent of Hispanics and 36.3 percent of blacks (Jackson, 1980, p. 144).

Poverty has also been found to be much more prevalent among elderly women, especially widows, than among men (Andrews and Hurd, 1992). Warlick has provided evidence for her statement that poverty in old age "has become and will continue to be largely a woman's problem." She found that the basic reason for the relative deprivation of elderly women in this country is that when they become widowed, the retirement systems, upon which they must rely for income, fail to provide the support necessary. As she points out, "Social Security benefits are reduced" and "private pensions may cease altogether" (Warlick, 1985). Another study of changes in the incomes of older women from 1960 to 1980 found that, in absolute terms, older women tended to have higher incomes in 1980 than in 1960. More important, though, the drop in incomes that the elderly women tended to experience in 1980 as they moved into old age was much greater than they had been in 1960. In terms of the living standards represented by their incomes, elderly women today are not really any better off than they were in 1960 (Uhlenberg and Salmon, 1986). Schulz and Myles make the point that, "pensions have been slow to adjust to the new realities of female family roles and labor force participation." Specifically, survivor protection has been uneven, and vesting regulations have ignored women's work schedules (Schulz and Myles, 1990). Another reason that women are financially worse off than men is that they often have family caregiver responsibilities, both with children and with aging parents, that interfere with their schedules as workers (O'Grady-LeShane, 1993). In addition, it has long been recognized that widowhood is closely associated with poverty among elderly people.

It has generally been assumed that women are financially hurt but that men are not. One study has shown that this assumption tends to be misleading, however. Zick and Smith conducted a longitudinal study of financial changes that a group of nonpoor elderly couples experienced over a 12-year period. They found that those in the sample who tended to suffer severe economic losses were those who became widowed. Nearly half of those who experienced the loss of a spouse during the 12-year period spent at least one year out of the first five years of widowhood in poverty. Surprisingly, widowers and widows suffered similar financial losses. Neither group recovered those losses quickly (Zick and Smith, 1986). The study provides no evidence of why the widowed experience such financial losses. One possible explanation that tends to be ignored in the literature on widows is the cost of caregiving that often precedes the loss of one's spouse, in terms of such things as medical treatment and loss of jobs. Regardless of the costs of widowhood, though, financial losses are apparently as much related to the processes of becoming widowed as they are to the differential treatment between males and females. Gonyea analyzed the usefulness of the "feminization of poverty" concept as related to aging, and she concluded that that concept was limited in part because of its "exclusion of poverty" among some men (Gonyea, 1994).

Furthermore, it has been discovered that poverty is still much more related to old age in general than much of the cross-sectional data on poverty rates would indicate. Evidence of this was provided by a longitudinal study of the changing income patterns of a nationwide sample of over 4,000 elderly heads of households. Respondents were interviewed every two years over a 10-year period between 1968 and 1978. It was found, once again, that women tended to be plunged into poverty with the loss of their husbands. As many as 80 percent of them also eventually escaped from poverty during the 10 years, however. It was discovered, too, that poverty was by no means confined to widowhood. Couples often experienced it just before one of them became widowed. In addition, even among the continuously married couples, as many as 20.9 percent of them experienced at least one time of poverty during the 10-year study period. The overall conclusions from the study were that (1) there is considerable movement in and out of poverty among the elderly, including both couples and those who are widowed; and (2) while most people do eventually escape from poverty, that escape tends to be temporary (Holden, Burkhauser, and Meyers, 1986).

Obviously, the risks of poverty among the aged in the United States are much greater than annual poverty-rate statistics would lead us to believe. In addition, Uehara and colleagues have found that, even though the actual cash benefits of elderly welfare recipients were not cut as much as were benefits for others on welfare in the 1980s, they have endured even more cutbacks in terms of other benefits, such as food stamps and health care (Uehara, Geron, and Beeman, 1986).

CHANGING RELATIONSHIPS BETWEEN THE ECONOMY AND THE ELDERLY

The question still remains of whether allowing elderly to retire from the work force, and providing them with billions of dollars of pension money on which to live, is good or bad economic policy. Can we continue to afford it, or is it just too much of a burden on those still working? Does it serve to stimulate or depress the economy? As stated above, the answers to those kinds of questions depend upon the extent to which the modern economic system needs human labor to function and on how pension funds relate to the economy.

With regard to the need for human labor, it is noteworthy that while some analysts contend that elderly people are badly needed in the work force due to the declining younger population, most employers continue to encourage their older workers to retire as early as possible. It may be that some employers are motivated out of personal bias or self-interest as Johnson, Conrad, and Thomson (1989) have suggested, but the practice is too widespread for that to be an adequate overall explanation. In essence, it is good economics to do so in part because the salaries of those replacement workers are lower than those retiring, and also because the retirement funds which support their retirees are unrelated to their operational budgets. The practice of retiring elderly workers is not even an option, of course, unless either their positions are no longer needed or younger replacements are readily available. The fact that both of these cases readily exist today is evident from the widespread personnel cutbacks going on among large employers today for their companies to become economically sound. Clearly, the elderly are not needed in the highly technical modern work force of today and it would economically be a mistake to insist that they stay in it. Atchley makes an important point when he says that, "without retirement, the unemployment rate would be much higher than it is today" (Atchley, 1991, p. 344).

But what about all of the money it takes to finance their retirement years? It is assumed by some that that is a burden which stymies the financial development of younger workers. For example, Johnson, Conrad, and Thomson refer to providing retirement income to the elderly, in whatever form, as a "welfare" system, and they state that it is "inevitable that the interaction of current demographic trends and current welfare policies will impose a large, growing, and possibly unsustainable fiscal burden on the productive populations in developed nations" (Johnson, Conrad, and Thomson, 1989). In fact, though, even if we were to accept the notion that the retired population constitutes a financial burden to the younger employed population, indications are that it is not a growing problem at all. As Schulz and Myles report, "Total age-dependency ratios—the ratio of all people (at any age) not working to the working population—have not risen in the 1980s," and, in fact, they are "declining in industrial countries and will generally continue to do so until early in the next century" (Schulz and Myles, 1990).

In recent years, much has been made of the idea that the baby boom generation has been particularly financially disadvantaged as a result of the burden of the elderly population. To discover whether or not that is a valid assessment of the situation, Easterlin, Macunovich, and Crimmins did a comparison of the general economic status of the baby boom generation and that of elderly people. Part of what they studied was the extent to which individuals of each group responded to adverse conditions with what they called "life cycle decisions"—that is, whether and when to get married, have children, and temporarily live in less desirable but cheaper situations. They found that, in fact, "the baby boomers have been able to maintain their relative economic status because of life cycle decisions." Furthermore, they found evidence that the baby boomer generation will, in fact, be better off in retirement than any previous generation, because "each younger generation—including the baby boomers—starts out better off than its predecessor, and that advantage is maintained throughout the life cycle" (Easterlin, Macunovich, and Crimmins, 1993).

Part of what determines whether or not elderly on retirement pensions represent a financial burden on others is how pension funds relate to the economy. As noted above they are not funds that come out of employers' operating budgets. Instead they are investments that workers make, and their employers make in their behalf, as part of their total benefit packages. In addition, as cumulative funds they represent sources of capital that are vital to companies competing in a growing economy. Instead of being a burden on the economy, then, they are a vital part of it. Furthermore, by-and-large those funds are not depleted by the monthly payments that are made from them to the retired recipients. As Olson has stated, "rather than assuring adequate retirement income and economic security for the vast majority of older people, a major goal of private, state, and local trusts is capital formation" (Olson, 1982, p. 100). Clearly the capital that pension funds represent is much more important economically than the participation of elderly persons in a highly competitive labor force.

ECONOMICS OF AGING IN OTHER CULTURES

That old people are dependent is by no means a universally shared phenomenon. Neither is the discrepancy between the financial situations of elderly men and women universal. With regard to sexual equality of financial resources of the aged, a comparative study of 10 different nations between 1960 and 1980 was conducted. It was found that the financial situation of both men and women improved over the 20-year period. In 5 of those countries (Australia, West Germany, the Netherlands, New Zealand, and the United Kingdom), there was absolute financial parity between men and women; but in the other 5 (Finland, France, Switzerland, Sweden, and the United States) men improved much more than women (Tracy and Ward, 1986). Parity is generally achieved by establishing pension benefits on the basis of either flat rates for retirees or those that reflect a share of material economic growth. The countries that favor men tend to base pensions, at least in part, on the work histories of retirees. These systems have generally provided increased benefits for both men and women but have benefited men much more than women because of disparities in employee salaries. These disparities were not reflective of either the adequacy of old people's incomes or the extent they were financially independent, however.

In 1976, Pendrell noted that early retirement was becoming a pattern not only in the United States but throughout the world. This, she contended, means mounting social costs that are alarming economists and government workers of the nations of the world (Pendrell, 1976). This type of analysis reflects the rather common notion, which has prevailed in the United States for some time, that equates the provision of pensions for the aged with inadequate labor, depression of economies and economic dependency of older people. Many gerontologists have also made this assumption. Pendrell quoted Cottrell as saying, for example, that "business is simply not going to take adequate care of most of the aging," when reflecting on these concerns. Likewise, more recently, Johnson, Conrad and Thomson express their strong belief that providing pensions and other services to the older population will increasingly "impose a large, growing, and possibly unsustainable fiscal burden on the productive populations in developed nations" (Johnson, Conrad, and Thomson, 1989). They recognize that most employers today, in fact, support, and if possible, practice early retirement policies, but they dismiss this phenomenon as pure self-interest or selfishness on the part of both those who offer it and the elderly who accept it. Their moral judgment of this practice is that "a higher level of labour force participation among older people, which would be in the interest of all western societies now facing the problem of aging, seems not to be in the interest of any of the parties involved in the decision—a clear case perhaps of the public good and individual self-interest in conflict" (Johnson, Conrad, and Thomson, 1989).

In discussing the issue of the impact of pensions on labor force participation, Schulz and Myles admit that, indeed, "public and private pensions are a major factor associated with the dramatic decline in labor force participation rates in various industrialized countries" (Schulz and Myles, 1990). They do not conclude, however, that this fact translates into a depressed economy. Whether or not the elderly are needed in the labor-force for the sake of the economy is not the issue. Instead, according to them, the issue for the future is whether working-age populations "will accept this change (of the existing demographic age mix) and its consequences." They believe the answer will be "yes," because many observers see no alternative (Schulz and Myles, 1990). An issue that even they do not address, though, is the question of to what extent it is fair to label elderly people who are no longer employed and are receiving pension benefits as dependent.

The Economics of Aging in Japan

Undoubtedly, the dependency perspective is largely determined by the cultural contexts in which the provision of financial support for the aged takes place. It also depends upon the extent to which the provision of financial old-age benefits are personalized or collectivized. The elderly in Japan represent an informative study in this respect. On the one hand, as explained in Chapter 9, the claim has been made that employers provide their workers with lifetime economic security. If that were true, workers would tend to stay with their employers throughout their careers and would enjoy economic security in old age. Indeed, Palmore and Maeda report that the average family income for households headed by persons 65 and over in 1955 amounted to 90 percent of the average of all Japanese households in 1982. They also report that more elderly people in Japan than in any other industrial nation claim to have adequate incomes (Palmore and Maeda, 1985, pp. 71–76). On the other hand, Levine reports findings to show that lifetime relationships with employers are actually not typical of Japanese workers. They seem to have little or no reluctance to change jobs in order to pursue new career opportunities. Lifetime relationships may once have been a cultural ideal, but they are no longer widely practiced (Levine, 1983). Furthermore, the relative financial well-being of elderly people's households in Japan is undoubtedly due to the fact that many of the elderly remain employed. In 1981, over half of those 65 to 69 years old, and almost 40 percent of those 70 to 74 were still in the work force. As many as

18 percent of even those 80 and over were still working (Palmore and Maeda, 1985, p. 50). For those who live on pensions, the wage-replacement value of those pensions averaged only 41 percent, about the same for retirees in the United States and less than for those in West Germany (Palmore and Maeda, 1985, p. 78). Palmore and Maeda also report that a shift has been occurring among the Japanese elderly away from the idea that economic security is a family responsibility and toward a dependency on social security, pensions, and savings (Palmore and Maeda, 1985, pp. 74–75). Concepts of economic dependency among the aged, similar to those in the United States, seem to be developing in Japan.

The Economics of Aging in the People's Republic of China

An analysis of the economic situation of the aged in the People's Republic of China provides important insights as well. A combination of the influences of Oriental traditions and socialism served to create a rather unique economic situation for the older population at least until very recently. As Treas has pointed out, there were forces in that country since the communist takeover in 1949 that increased the power and prestige of younger people. Laws were passed and official practices established to eliminate the filial piety traditions and to undermine the economic authority of the elderly within families. The whole Cultural Revolution, much of which was aimed at the final elimination of traditional authority, was carried out by youth (Treas, 1979). Nevertheless, elderly people in China under strict communist domination tended to retire at ages 55 or 60 with pensions that equaled from 70 to 90 percent of their employment wages. Furthermore, their retirement benefits were viewed neither as burdens on the younger employed population nor as symbols of dependency.

There were three basic reasons that the Chinese elderly were not viewed as economically dependent, as those in industrialized nations tend to be. First, they typically contributed financially to their families on an approximately equal basis with their adult children. Their retirement income, from which they contributed to household maintenance, was often equal to the salaries of their adult children with whom they lived. In most households in which the elderly lived, four salaries were contributed to the costs of those households. Younger couples who lived with elderly parents therefore tended to be financially better off than those who did not (Treas, 1979).

The second reason that the aged in the People's Republic of China were not generally viewed as dependent was related to the way retirement benefits were then financed. They were not provided out of funds that came from taxes on individual workers' incomes, as was the case in many capitalist countries. Neither did they come from the national government. Instead, they were paid out of profits made by the collective production units to which workers belonged. Therefore younger workers perceived no sense of burden, since their work-related incomes were not directly involved and many of them directly benefited from their parents' retirement pensions (Brown, 1984).

The third reason that the elderly in the People's Republic of China were until recently not considered to be economically dependent is related to how the economic reforms began to be instituted in that country a few years ago. Families in urban areas were allowed to develop small businesses, and those in rural areas were permitted to farm plots of land for their own profit even while they still lived in collectives. These businesses and farms tended to be cooperative intergenerational family ventures. Retired members of the families often did much of the work of the family businesses while younger adults were at their jobs.

Although the elderly people in the People's Republic of China tended to retire from paid jobs at relatively young ages and received relatively generous financial benefits, they were not generally viewed as dependent. They made direct and obvious economic contributions to their families and, in turn, to their communities. In addition, they were eliminated from an increasingly competitive labor force.

As discussed in Chapter 7, though, drastic economic and social changes have taken place in the People's Republic of China that are severely challenging both the status and the economic situation of the elderly. With the dissolution of all communes and similar organized work units and the shift to a private enterprise economic system, only the elderly who work for the government are guaranteed pensions when they retire. At this time, those who have no pensions to rely upon are expected to turn to their families for financial support. It is unclear how many are presently found in that kind of situation, but as economic reforms move forward, their numbers will almost certainly increase. In anticipation of that future problem, as pointed out in Chapter 9, the government has formed a national planning committee to develop a comprehensive social security that will be financed by taxing workers' wages, similar to the United States system (Hong, 1993). When implemented elderly Chinese will again have some level of financial security, but they will almost certainly become vulnerable to the burden-of-dependency label being applied to the aged throughout the world.

The Economics of Aging among Native Americans

The financial situation of still another very unique cultural group provides further insights about the relative dependence of elderly people. Native Americans in the United States are often lumped together as one of many minority groups, but each of the native American tribes also has a unique culture. An analysis of the elderly in the largest of these tribal groups, the Navajos, in terms of both their minority status and their cultural traditions, provides us with some valuable information.

Culturally, the kinship system has been the center of their social and economic lives. Family and clan relationships were built around the sharing of all of the available resources and around mutual obligations to care for one another. These traditions of sharing and family interdependence are still very prevalent today, particularly among the older members of the tribe. The Navajos also have some of the same minority-group characteristics as other minorities. The younger generation has increasingly become dependent upon jobs for financial support, and relatively few jobs are available to them on the reservation. Consequently, the unemployment and poverty rates among them are extremely high. Many younger adults have little or no sources of income.

As a twist of fate, many elderly Navajos are eligible to receive minimum amounts of income in the form of either Social Security or SSI benefits.

Those small amounts of monthly income give them something important to share with their needy family members. As Foner explains, "In poor communities where cash is hard to come by, old-age pensioners provide a steady source of income for their households, sometimes becoming the mainstay of their domestic economy" (Foner, 1984, p. 218).

There is a tendency on the part of some service workers to define this as exploitation on the part of the family members involved. In a 1986 survey of Navajo elder abuse, however, every one of the elderly persons, who admitted that some of their money had gone to family members, said that they had voluntarily shared what they had. They insisted that that was what they wanted to and should do. The family members who received the help often provided the elderly persons with needed care. The survey showed, in fact, that, by and large, Navajo families respond in whatever ways they can when their elderly members need care (Brown, 1989).

Even though the majority of Navajo elderly fall below the poverty line, they are not as yet viewed as economically dependent by either their families or the tribe. Instead, they are seen as financially independent and even as making important financial contributions to their families. The relationships are generally characterized as mutual dependency or interdependency. If and when economic development is enhanced on the reservation, they will also become vulnerable to the "dependent" label, however.

CONCLUSION

Four basic issues have been dealt with in this chapter: (1) the financial well-being of elderly people; (2) the sources of their financial support; (3) the public view of their economical dependence or independence; and (4) their financial contribution to the economies of the nations in which they live. There are major cross-cultural differences regarding each of these concerns.

Ironically, the financial situation of the elderly, relative to others in their societies, until recently has been better in the poorer of the cultural groups we have examined. It is also in those cultural groups that elderly people were recognized as making important economic contributions and were not defined as economically dependent and burdensome. As economic developments have begun to take over in those societies, however, the financial situations of the elderly are beginning to be threatened there as well.

In the highly industrialized and economically affluent societies, the tendency is to fund old age support from taxes on individual salaries and to politicize the processes of providing pensions. One of the consequences of this tendency has been to define the older population as a burden and to provide inadequate support. Part of that definitional process has been the tendency among some analysts to characterize social security and pension benefits as income redistribution. While that may be somewhat of a consequence of those kinds of programs, that was clearly not the intent of their development. Instead, the intent was related to problems that were only secondarily related to income redistribution. There were basically two reasons for the development of those programs: (1) to encourage older people to leave the increasingly competitive work force and make room for younger workers, and (2) to provide older people with a convenient method of saving for their retirement years. Obviously, those purposes are as valid today as they have ever been.

There are, of course, some in retirement who are financially better off than their younger counterparts, partly because of the retirement programs in which they participate. That is clearly not the case for by any means all, or even a majority, of the elderly, though. As we have seen, elderly minorities and women are especially apt to experience poverty, the older they become.

This is not to say that we in the modern world of today do not have income distribution problems on the part of increasing numbers of younger children and adults. It may also be legitimate to make the case that elderly people who are relatively wealthy should somehow contribute their fair share of what it will take to redistribute income in favor of those younger families with special income needs. What is a falacious assumption, though, is the idea that they ought to do so because the lack of financial resources among younger people has been caused by them.

The problem is that much of the rationale for defining the elderly as economically burdensome is based on false assumptions. Sheppard and Rix, for example, made the case in the 1970s that as the American population grows older, it will be increasingly impossible for the nation to support older people in retirement (Sheppard and Rix, 1977, pp. 13–35). Despite these kinds of arguments that have multiplied ever since, there is still a distinct tendency for employers in this country to encourage early retirement because they see it as economically beneficial. The policy also continues to be favored by younger workers seeking jobs and fighting for promotions. In fact, even as the older population continues to grow, the competition for jobs also seems to be increasing.

Three important factors are ignored in the argument that old people are an economically dependent and burdensome part of the population. First, with an increasingly technologically based system of production, less, not more, human labor is needed. Elderly people are simply not needed in the work force. In fact, their continued participation in it tends to stifle the economic advancement of younger adults. Second, modern production companies need available capital far more than they need labor. As we have seen, the aged are making a major contribution to this aspect of the overall economy in the form of pension funds. This in itself ought to be enough for the rest of society to recognize that most older people are not economically dependent and burdensome. Third, the highly productive units of modern societies badly need markets. Consumer markets probably constitute a greater source of stimulation to the economy than anything else. Obviously, consumerism is an important part of retirement today. Leisure among the retired populations of the world has created large and vital consumer markets.

REFERENCES

Achenbaum, W. Andrew, *Shades of Gray: Old Age, American Values, and Federal Policies Since 1920* (Boston: Little, Brown, 1983).

Achenbaum, W. Andrew, "The Obsolescence of Old Age," in *Dimensions of Aging: Readings*, eds. Jon Hendricks and C. Davis Hendricks (Cambridge, Mass.: Winthrop, 1979), pp. 21–37.

"Actuarial Status of the Social Security and Medicare Programs," *Social Security Bulletin*, 57, no. 1 (Spring 1994), 53–59.

Andrews, Emily S., and Michael D. Hurd, "Employee Benefits and Retirement Income Adequacy: Data, Research, and Policy Issues," in *Pensions and the Economy: Sources, Uses, and Limitations of Data*, eds. Zvi Bodie and Alicia H. Munnell (Philadelphia: University of Pennsylvania Press, 1992), pp. 1–30.

Atchley, Robert C., *Social Forces and Aging: An Introduction to Social Geronotlogy* (Belmont, Calif.: Wadsworth, 1991).

Bodie, Zvi, and Leslie E. Papke, "Pension Fund Finance," in *Pensions and the Economy: Sources, Uses, and Limitations of Data*, eds. Zvi Bodie and Alicia H. Munnell (Philadelphia: University of Pennsylvania Press, 1992), pp. 149–72.

Brown, Arnold S., "A Survey on Elder Abuse at One Native American Tribe," *Journal of Elder Abuse and Neglect*, 1, no. 2 (1989), 17–37.

Brown, Arnold S., "Social Policy of Aging in Mainland China," unpublished report of an informal study of the social policy on aging in China done while in China, summer 1984.

Dailey, Lorna M., and John A. Turner, "The Use of International Private Pension Statistics for Policy Analysis," in *Pensions and the Economy: Sources, Uses, and Limitations of Data*, eds. Zvi Bodie and Alicia H. Munnell (Philadelphia: University of Pennsylvania Press, 1992), pp. 205–20.

Eastaugh, Steven R., *Facing Tough Choices* (Westport, Conn.: Praeger, 1994).

Easterlin, Richard A., Diane J. Macunovich, and Eileen M. Crimmins, "Economic Status of the Young and Old in the Working-Age Population, 1964 and 1987," in *The Changing Contract Across Generations*, eds. V. L. Bengston and W. A. Achenbaum (New York: Aldine De Gruyter, 1993), pp. 67–85.

Fischer, David Hackett, *Growing Old in America* (New York: Oxford University Press, 1978).

Foner, Nancy, *Ages in Conflict* (New York: Columbia University Press, 1984).

Gonyea, Judith G., "The Paradox of the Advantaged Elderly and the Feminization of Poverty," *Social Work*, 39, no. 1 (January 1994), 35–44.

Harris, Richard, "Recent Trends in the Relative Economic Status of Older Adults," *Journal of Gerontology*, 41, no. 3 (May 1986), 401–7.

Holden, Karen C., Richard V. Burkhauser, and Daniel A. Meyers, "Income Transitions at Older Stages of Life: The Dynamics of Poverty," *The Gerontologist*, 26, no. 3 (June 1986), 292–97.

Hong, Guodong, "Support for the Elderly in China—Gradual Improvements in Social Security," in *Population Aging: International Perspectives*, eds. Tarek M. Shuman and others (San Diego: San Diego State University, 1993), pp. 433–40.

Jackson, Jacquelyne J., *Minorities and Aging* (Belmont, Calif.: Wadsworth, 1980).

Johnson, Paul, Christoph Conrad, and David Thomson, "Introduction" in *Workers Versus Pensions: Intergenerational Justice in an Aging World*, eds. Paul Johnson, Christoph Conrad, and David Thomson (New York: Manchester University Press, 1989), pp. 1–16.

Levine, Solomon B., "Careers and Mobility in Japan's Labor Market," in *Work and Lifecourse in Japan*, ed. David W. Plath (Albany: State University of New York, 1983), pp. 18–33.

Mitchell, Olivia S., and Anne M. Rappaport, "Innovations and Trends in Pension Plan Coverage, Type and Design," in *The Future of Pensions in the United States*, ed. Ray Schmitt (Philadelphia: Pension Research Council, Wharton School of the University of Pennsylvania, 1993), pp. 53-101.

Moon, Marilyn, "Impact of the Reagan Years on the Distribution of Income of the Elderly," *The Gerontologist*, 26, no. 1 (February 1986), 32–37.

Myers, Robert J., *Social Security* (Philadelphia: University of Pennsylvania Press, 1993).

O'Grady-LeShane, Regina, "Changes in the Lives of Women and Their Families: Have Old Age Pensions Kept Pace?' *Generations*, 17, no. 4 (Winter 1993), 27–33.

Olson, Laura K., *The Political Economy of Aging: The State, Private Power, and Social Welfare* (New York: Columbia University Press, 1982).

Palmore, Erdman B., and Daisaku Maeda, *The Honorable Elders Revisited* (Durham, N.C.: Duke University Press, 1985).

Pendrell, Nan, "Old Age Around the World," *Social Policy*, 7, no. 3 (November/December 1976), 107–10.

Quinn, Joseph E., "Is Early Retirement an Economic Threat?" *Generations*, 17, no. 4 (Winter 1993), 10–14.

Rowland, Mary, "Pension-Payout Headaches," *Modern Maturity*, 37, no. 4 (July-August 1994), pp. 51–53, 77–78.

Schulz, James H., *The Economics of Aging* (Dover, Mass.: Auburn House, 1988).

Schulz, James H., and John Myles, "Old Age Pensions: A Comparative Perspective," in *Handbook of Aging and the Social Sciences*, eds. R. H. Binstock and L. K. George (San Diego: Academic Press, 1990), pp. 398–414.

Sharp, Henry S., "Old Age Among the Chipewyan," in *Other Ways of Growing Old: Anthropological Perspectives*, eds. P. T. Amoss and S. Harrell (Stanford, Calif.: Stanford University Press, 1981), pp. 99–109.

Sheehan, Tom "Senior Esteem as a Factor of Socioeconomic Complexity," *The Gerontologist*, 16, no. 5 (October 1976), 433–40.

Sheppard, Harold L., and Sara E. Rix, *The Graying of Working America: The Coming Crisis in Retirement-Age Policy* (New York: Free Press, 1977).

"Social Security in Review," *Social Security Bulletin*, 56, no. 4 (Winter 1993), 85–88.

"Social Security Programs in the United States," *Social Security Bulletin*, 54, no. 9 (September 1991), 2–19.

Steuerle, C. Eugene, and Jon M. Bakija, *Social Security for the 21st Century: Right and Wrong Approaches to Reform* (Washington, D. C.: Urban Institute Press, 1994).

"Supplemental Security Income," *Social Security Bulletin*, 54, no. 9 (September 1991), 64–67.

Tracy, Martin B., and Roxanne L. Ward, "Trends in Old-Age Pensions for Women: Benefit Levels in Ten Nations, 1960–1980," *The Gerontologist*, 26, no. 3 (June 1986), 286–91.

Treas, Judith, "Socialist Organization and Economic Development in China: Latent Consequences for the Aged," *The Gerontologist*, 19, no. 1 (February 1979), 34–43.

Uehara, Edwina S., Scott Geron, and Sandra K. Beeman, "The Elderly Poor in the Reagan Era," *The Gerontologist*, 26, no. 1 (February 1986), 48–55.

Uhlenberg, Peter, and Anne P. Salmon, "Change in Relative Income of Older Women, 1960–1980," *The Gerontologist*, 26, no. 2 (April 1986), 164–70.

Warlick, Jennifer L., "Why is Poverty After 65 a Woman's Problem?" *Journal of Gerontology*, 40, no. 6 (November 1985), 751–57.

Williamson, John B., Linda Evans, and Lawrence A. Powell, *The Politics of Aging: Power and Policy* (Springfield, Ill.: Charles C. Thomas, 1982).

Zick, Cathleen D., and Ken R. Smith, "Immediate and Delayed Effects of Widowhood on Poverty: Patterns from the 1970's," *Gerontologist*, 26, no. 6 (December 1986), 669–75.

11

Retirement as a Social Institution and a Process

INTRODUCTION

Retirement is rapidly becoming an institutionalized part of the modern world. More and more people in many societies are moving into retirement, and it is increasingly accepted as an inevitable part of the cycle of life. Fur-thermore, in contrast to common misconceptions, a fairly large majority of people today actually look forward to it and enjoy it. Then, too, it serves a fairly well-defined societal need in those societies in which it is practiced.

Retirement is a concept that requires definition. There is a great deal of confusion in the gerontological literature about how to define it, depending upon the perspective from which it is discussed. Part of the definitional confusion has to do with the relationship of retirement to three other concepts: (1) work, (2) leisure, and (3) volunteerism. Retirement must be defined and discussed in terms of not only *from what,* but also *to what* people retire.

Part of the definitional problem is also how those concepts tend to relate to one another in the context of old age experiences. A historical analysis of each of these concepts and their relationship to one another will help us to understand more about the meaning of retirement to the elderly. Just as importantly, it may provide us with some insights about potential future meanings of retirement, and therefore what meaning it already has for those of younger ages. On a personal level, it will be well for readers to ask themselves how they anticipate their own retirement, as they read this chapter.

CHANGING CONCEPTS OF WORK AFFECTING THE AGED

Work and how it has affected people's lives, especially during the twentieth century, are central to the meaning of retirement. Work has always been, and still is, a vital part of the daily lives of people of all cultures. Yet what is considered as work and how individuals experience the world of work have changed quite drastically.

Work is often equated with activity—keeping busy physically or mentally. That kind of definition does not capture the essence of what work is all about, however. Work has economic, social, psychological, and even religious significance.

First and foremost, work has been an economic necessity throughout history. Primitive and modern societies alike have depended upon the physical and mental efforts of their members to produce the goods and services for their survival. Work, then, is not merely human activity, but activity that has productive purpose and is conducted with an economic obligation.

Marx contended that economics was the basis of all human life, and that workers were the most vital part of economics. As Campbell explains Marx's social theory, "Marx is a materialist, not because he values material goods above all else,... but because he held that the laws of tendencies which describe, explain and, to an extent, predict how societies work, are laws of economics" (Campbell, 1981, p. 118). He referred to economics as the ship of life and all other aspects of life as merely the superstructure, built on top of and totally dependent upon the economic structures. In the final analysis, it is economics that determines human values, beliefs, and norms, and human labor was central to economics (Campbell, 1981, p. 119).

As important as economics may be to our lives, however, it is by no means the only reason that work has been important to the human experience. Weber challenged Marx's ideas. His contention was that religious beliefs, more than its economic significance, gave meaning to work, at least in that particular time and place. According to Weber the theological perspective of Protestant Christianity had come to determine the European attitudes about work. For most Europeans, especially those who were Protestants, work amounted to nothing less than a calling by God (Weber, 1958, pp. 47–78). In that context, more than anything, work was the symbol of their commitment to God and of their faithfulness to that calling. Their success in their work provided a sign that God had indeed called them and was blessing them. That they also produced necessary goods and services for secular societies in which they lived was of only secondary importance to them. From the perspective of what Weber termed "the Protestant ethic," as well as from an economic perspective, it was important that everyone worked. Pursuit of their Christian calling was as vital to the Protestant Christians' sense of religious well-being and relationships with God as worship or any other part of their religious lives.

Much of this particular religious connotation of work has been lost today. Nevertheless, its influence is still felt. The work ethic is still very much intact. In effect it says that work, for its own sake, is important, regardless of its social or economic utility. A general norm seems to exist that, regardless of the kind of work people do, it is important that they work. As Morse and

Weiss discovered in a 1950s study on the function and meaning of work, "for many individuals, commitment to working is much deeper than commitment to their particular jobs" (Morse and Weiss, 1955).

The Marxist idea of work was not religious, but it was certainly ideological. It was an integral part not just of economics in general, but a particular economic philosophy. The idea was that everyone should work not merely to produce needed goods and services but because the division between workers and capitalists was wrong. That kind of division caused alienation within individuals and within society as a whole and created inevitable and serious social conflict. The economic structure in the People's Republic of China under Mao Tse Tung illustrates this philosophy. Everyone belonged to work units and everyone who was able worked, regardless of whether that much labor was really needed. Technology that would have advanced productivity and stimulated economic growth was never allowed to develop under Mao because it was important that everyone would work.

Very closely associated with the religious and ideological orientation of work is the social psychological significance of work. Due to its religious importance in some societies and because of its economic importance in all societies, work is generally an important part of most societal value systems. From the societal perspective, work is part of the behavior expected of all able-bodied individuals. Some form of sanctions tend to be applied to those who fail to comply with that expectation, and rewards are given to those who comply. The division of labor is one of the most important parts of social structure.

From the perspective of individuals, work is a major source of social status, power, and prestige as well as a means of making a living in order to provide for self and family. It typically becomes not merely a social obligation to individuals but a major life orientation—a career. It provides individuals with a sense of belonging, a personal identity, and a sense of purpose. Working is often thought of as a right that individuals do not want to lose. For some the loss of the right to work represents the loss of self.

Retirement, then, would seem to be a major adjustment problem for people in most societies. Gratton and Rotondo indicate that this was not the case in the United States at the end of the nineteenth and the beginning of the twentieth centuries because it was a gradual process and because families took care of what financing was necessary (Gratton and Rotondo, 1992). Recently, though, studies show that adjustment to retirement may be a problem. A study in Great Britain in 1977 of the attitudes of men and women, aged 50–72, revealed that as many as 65 percent of them were either unhappy or ambivalent about the prospect of retiring (Parker, 1982, p. 67). In the People's Republic of China today, in an era of economic reform, women are expected to retire five years earlier than men. This is a country in which work outside the home was not even available to women before 1949. Yet many Chinese women today are protesting the expectation that they retire any earlier than men. Sixty-two percent of the women questioned about this in a survey said they wanted to postpone their retirements ("Should Women Retire Earlier Than Men?" 1986).

Even in the United States where retirement has become quite widely accepted, one study shows that as many as 23 percent of men 65 to 69 and

18 percent of those 70 to 74 choose to remain in the labor force, at least on a part-time basis (Hayward and Liu, 1992). Some undoubtedly do so primarily out of the need for further income, but certainly some are motivated by a continued belief in the work ethic. Even among fairly well-adjusted retirees, Ekerdt has observed that the work ethic directly influences their behavior patterns. While their lives may no longer be directly controlled by the work ethic, they tend to act on the basis of something very much akin to it—namely "the busy ethic" (Ekerdt, 1986). This behavioral approach to retirement has a number of purposes, according to Ekerdt. First, it makes retirement more closely fit mainstream social values. Second, it symbolically defends against the appearance of aging. Third, it tends to legitimize some leisure activities in retirement.

There can be little doubt that work has been a vital part of the human experience, both from an individual and societal perspective. It has always been so for men, and it has become increasingly so for women. This raises an important question about the acceptance of retirement: How is it possible to reconcile work and retirement, either conceptually or experientially? Part of the answer to that dilemma has to do with the changing nature of work.

Two historical technological developments related to economics have brought about drastic changes in how humans perform their work and what work means to them. Agricultural technology made it possible to produce more goods and services with less work than was possible in hunting and gathering societies. Families were able to settle into stabilized communities. A division of labor became possible, and specialties in work began to develop.

Societies were now lifted a step above simple survival. Few able-bodied persons were exempted from the need to work. Yet certain types of work required little physical strength and some luxuries became possible. It was also possible to incorporate limited amounts of pleasurable activities, unrelated to work, into the lifestyles of families and communities. Leisure as a reward for work was possible and became part of the orientation of life.

Agricultural technology by no means diminished the importance of work for individuals or societies. In fact, it made it possible for elderly people to continue to work and enjoy long careers even after hard physical labor was no longer possible. It also introduced leisure as an integral part of life albeit on a very limited basis. As Miller has explained, "The preindustrial culture based on an agricultural economy and rural in character ... did not separate work and leisure, nor did the demands of labor segment the life of the person into a world of work and another of the family" (Miller, 1965). Gratton and Rotondo point out also that, in the early 1900s, with the support of families, the elderly were often able to reduce their work efforts without fully retiring (Gratton and Rotondo, 1992).

Industrial technology is the second development that has tended to change the nature and meaning of work. With industrialization both the place of work and the types of work have changed. The place of work moved away from the home setting to the office, the factory, and the marketplace. The type of work changed progressively from hard, unskilled labor toward that demanding the technical skills needed to run the increasingly sophisticated industrial machinery. The division of labor was increased dramatically, with specialization being more strictly defined in narrower and narrower terms.

Training and education became increasingly necessary to perform the specialized labor, and further technology soon made existing specialties obsolete.

Where, when, and how individuals worked was controlled, not by the workers themselves, but by bosses and corporate managers. As early as the 1950s, Bendix characterized industrial work as a situation in which "American employers came to make their own absolute authority within the plant so central a tenet that the compliance of the workers became ideologically a far more important value than his independence and initiative" (Bendix, 1956, p. 274). Thus workers could no longer plan and implement productive processes from beginning to end. Instead, they tended to be confined to just one aspect of those processes, and work became extremely routinized. Brinkerhoff and White have made the point that this is true not only of blue-collar and white-collar workers, but of professionals, who are typically thought of as having a high degree of autonomy as well. As they put it, increasingly, people in the professions work for others within organizational structures that constrain many of the most characteristic aspects of professionalism" (Brinkerhoff and White, 1985, p. 396).

Kando has described the way in which industrialization changed the nature of work as follows:

> Scientific technology led to the Industrial Revolution. During the successive stages of a revolution that has yet to be concluded, handcraft was first superseded by mechanical production of commodities; subsequently machines were built that built other machines; finally machines were built to regulate themselves. As mechanization, automation, and finally cybernation succeeded each other, man's role could be expected to be reduced, or elevated, to that of decision maker rather than operator. (Kando, 1975, p. 4)

Work in industrial settings has become extremely monotonous and competitive, even in the service industries. Labor unions have been formed to make jobs more secure and improve working conditions, but they have done nothing to alleviate the problems of either the monotony of work or the competition for jobs. Both of these problems at least potentially undermine the meaning and importance of work to individuals. Competition inevitably informs workers that their skills are no longer necessary in the production of goods and services. The meaning of work to them, then, is confined to one or more of the following: (1) the intrinsic value of the particular job to the individual; (2) its value as a means of providing for self and family; or (3) its value as a means of keeping active. If there is no intrinsic value to the work one does, and there are other, more challenging ways of providing for self and family and keeping busy, we in the modern world would presumably be inclined to opt for the alternatives. Given the competition in training for and acquiring jobs, it is little wonder that retirement has become attractive to elderly people in today's industrial and postindustrial world, since older adults seldom have the advantage in training and job competition. Hayward and Liu found, for example, that while some men stay at work after they are eligible to retire, many others retire before they become eligible for social security benefits (Hayward and Liu, 1992).

THE EMERGENCE OF RETIREMENT POLICIES AND SYSTEMS

What is retirement and what does it mean to elderly people who retire? First, the emergence of and the institutionalization of retirement in the world today is very much related to the changing nature of work. Specifically, retirement policies have been developed by employers as the most feasible means of solving today's labor-related problems. More than anything else, therefore, retirement means the separation of individuals and groups from the labor force. That was the basis on which the initial retirement policies were set, and it remains the rationale for their continuation today. To be sure, retirement holds other, more subjective, meanings for those who anticipate and experience it, but those meanings are generally by-products of its relationship to the labor force. According to that kind of definition, those who are still part of the official labor force are not retired, while those outside that group can rightfully be considered retired. It is from that perspective that we will begin our analysis of the emergence of retirement. From there we will look at what else it has become.

Retirement is often treated from what Graebner terms "the mythology of individual responsibility." It is as though the aged initiated it and continue to support it for the benefits it offers them. He points out that its real beginnings and its actual economic functions have largely been ignored. The result has been "a form of blaming the victim" (Graebner, 1980, pp. 234–36). This approach is well illustrated by the emphasis in recent literature on the concept of the dependency ratio and the great economic burden that it is said to represent as discussed in Chapter 10. Over the last two decades or so there have been those who have argued about the burden of the dependency of older people in the United States and elsewhere in the world (Sheppard and Rix, 1977, pp. 135–55; Rix and Fisher, 1982, pp. 18–28; Johnson, Conrad, and Thomson, 1989). Ironically, the basis for these analyses is not actual finances but the demographics of aging—the ratio of those over 65 to those 16 to 64—and the fallacious assumption that that defines economic dependency.

In fact, retirement policies were developed precisely for the benefit of economics and were initiated by those in charge of the corporate structures. As Graebner explains, "The history of retirement reflects the changing methodologies of American capitalism in the nineteenth and twentieth centuries" (Graebner, 1980, p. 13). Before corporations controlled the productive process and the labor on which they depended, retirement was not a well-developed concept. There was an informal expectation that older workers would voluntarily retire, or at least take on less demanding types of jobs, when they could no longer perform the work that was required. No mandatory retirement policies existed, however.

By 1885, corporations had largely become the basic economic units, and retirement policies began to emerge, with the agreement of leaders in both business and labor. According to Graebner, this was very much related to the problems of an increasing labor surplus and the assumption that young people were more efficient workers. As he puts it, "For business, retirement meant reduced unemployment, lower rates of turnover, a younger, more efficient, and more conservative work force; for labor, it was in part a way of transferring work from one generation to another in industries with a surplus of workers" (Graebner, 1980, p. 13). Similarly, in studying retirement in Great Britain,

Parker concluded that it is "not something that has been fashioned by human aspirations. It is closely associated with the growth of bureaucracy, government organizations, and large companies which have their own reasons for 'retiring' older employees" (Parker, 1982, p. 19).

An important component of the rationale for retiring older workers has been the assumption that they are less efficient in their work than younger workers. Yet in periods when labor for industry was in short supply, the push for retirement policies was eased and older workers were, in fact, encouraged to remain at work. During World War II, for example, elderly workers staffed defense factories and the production of military supplies flourished. After the war, when there was once again an abundance of workers, strict mandatory policies were put in place and older workers were once again labeled as less efficient. Graebner contends that retirement policies and age discrimination emerged at the same time, not by coincidence, but because retirement was the easiest means available to deal with the problem of surplus labor. It was both impersonal and gave the appearance of being egalitarian (Graebner, 1980, p. 53).

Early in the process of setting retirement policies, pensions were developed to legitimize them. Weak and inadequate as many of them were, they provided incentives for individual workers to retire, and they promised retirees financial support. Some were private pensions provided by employers, and others were public, provided by government entities. The types of financial supports (private pensions, public pensions, publicly provided old-age assistance) have been related to society's defining the aged as economically dependent. As in the United States, government support for the aged in Great Britain has come from both contributory pension programs and noncontributory old-age assistance. Even though both government support and private pensions were provided as an incentive to retire, government support, especially in the form of old-age assistance, as Parker puts it, "brought an abrupt transition from independence to dependence" on the part of those in retirement (Parker, 1982, p. 17).

A slightly different pattern has taken place among elderly workers in modern, industrialized Japan. The larger firms in particular have promised their workers pensions to support them throughout their lives and have tended to set mandatory retirement policies at relatively young ages, typically 60 years of age for men and 55 for women. According to Maeda, as pointed out in Chapter 9, the problem is that the pensions are hardly ever enough for retirees to live on, and pensioners are therefore forced to find other, lower paying jobs (Maeda, 1980). Then, to make the matter worse, more recently Komine has reported that in Japan, "those laid off from long-term jobs will have trouble finding new jobs, for firms prefer to employ and offer on-the-job training for younger workers" (Komine, 1990). It is ironic also that, as Cowgill has observed, people in developing nations are asked to retire at even earlier ages than in the developed nations (Cowgill, 1986, p. 125).

It would seem, from this historic analysis of retirement, that elderly workers are being victimized and that they might therefore be expected to resist retirement policies. Evidence that this may be true comes from the struggle to pass antimandatory retirement legislation in the United States in the 1970s. The fact that legislation was passed in 1978 to severely restrict mandatory retirement policies before the age of 70 would seem to indicate something of a victory for resistance to retirement. Graebner provides quite a different interpretation of what was behind that legislation, however. He makes the point that it was passed "only when influential elements within American capitalism had concluded that retirement as then constituted was unduly costly as well as inefficient in allocating labor" (Graebner, 1980, p. 270). It might be more correct to assume that such legislation became possible when government officials began to see the elderly as dependent and too costly to support. Furthermore, there are indications that very few elderly people actively supported the bill. Most supported it in principle, but left it to key political figures like Claude Pepper to fight for it.

Ironically, indications are that older workers, instead of opposing the retirement systems that seem to have been imposed on them, have largely accepted them. They have generally welcomed the pension plans and supported the reality of retirement (Graebner, 1980, p. 267). Maeda reports that the same is true in Japan (Maeda, 1980). The question of why this is true leads us to an examination of the subjective meaning of retirement.

SUBJECTIVE MEANING AND ATTITUDES ABOUT RETIREMENT

What then has the institution of retirement come to mean to elderly people themselves? Why have they retired? What have their attitudes been as they have faced retirement and after they have become retired?

Why Elderly People Retire

Most elderly, in fact, choose to retire (Palmore and others, 1985, p. 36). An important question, though, is, why? Some benevolent reasons are often overlooked. In the early days, when retirement was just beginning to be considered, no substantial financial support systems had been established and poverty was typical among retirees. Yet even then, many elderly people were willing to sacrifice their own jobs in favor of younger workers (Graebner, 1980, p. 266). Through the Townsend movement during the 1920s, for example, their struggle was not to restore lost job opportunities, but to gain financial support in retirement.

Motivation on the part of older workers to retire can be analyzed from two perspectives: (1) objective factors that correlate with their retirement patterns, and (2) the reasons they themselves give for retiring. We will look at data from both of these perspectives.

Palmore and a group of associates reviewed and compared a number of longitudinal studies on retirement that had been conducted in the 1960s and 1970s. Their analyses provide us with many insights about both the causes and consequences of retirement. The group found five major factors that had been emphasized as potential predictors of retirement: (1) demographic characteristics, such as age, marital status, and number of dependents; (2) socioeconomic status; (3) health; (4) job characteristics; and (5) attitudes toward work and retirement.

Data from these studies indicated that of those five variables, by far the strongest predictors of retirement were socioeconomic status and job characteristics. Contrary to findings from some cross-sectional studies, though, health and attitudinal variables were relatively unimportant as predictors of retirement at age 65. Instead, poor health was found to be a major reason for early retirement (Palmore and others, 1985, pp. 23–36). Those with poor health not only tended to retire early, but they also tended to have poorer attitudes about retirement. Thus, poor health is not a result of retirement, as it is often assumed (Ekerdt, 1987). Instead, when retirees have poor health, it has typically been a precondition of, and even a reason for, their retirement. The negative attitudes about retirement associated with early retirement also tend to be more a result of the poor health than of retirement itself. It has often been supposed that having to retire is causally linked to acquiring health problems and even dying. As Robinson and her colleagues point out, these suppositions are based on clinical impressions without solid evidence of real causal relationships, but they have nevertheless had an influence on some key aging issues (Robinson, Coberly, and Paul, 1985). Longitudinal studies, such as those reviewed by Palmore and co-workers, are therefore important in that they clearly show that the causal linkage tends to be in the opposite direction. Keith also discovered, in a longitudinal study on retirement among unmarried elderly people, that poor health was especially hard on those who had never been married. Because they tended to lack adequate family support groups, health problems threatened their ability to maintain a semblance of independence (Keith, 1985).

As noted, socioeconomic status and job characteristics turned out to be the strongest predictors of retirement in the longitudinal studies. Specifically, those with greater socioeconomic resources in their work situations generally tended to be more reluctant to retire. This very much depended upon the kinds of jobs they held, however. Not surprisingly, individuals tended to retire more regularly if retirement was mandatory or if they were covered with pensions than if those conditions did not exist. Kilty and Behling found, also, that characteristics of the jobs themselves were important predictors of retirement. They studied retirement patterns among four types of professional workers: (1) attorneys, (2) social workers, (3) high school teachers, and (4) college professors (Kilty and Behling, 1985). Although all of these people had professional careers, their retirement patterns tended to be quite different. Lawyers tended to be the least positive about the prospects of retirement and the most apt to want to postpone it. Most high school teachers said they would be ready to retire at relatively young ages. Social workers and college professors tended to be more reluctant than high school teachers to retire early. These differences were largely related to a form of alienation from work. Although none of these workers were dissatisfied with their careers, those who had put in many years in the same job routines tended to become disenchanted with their work. High school teachers were much more apt to have accumulated many years of work at earlier ages than the other professionals.

It is true, of course, as noted above, that not all workers retire as soon as it is possible for them to do so. Depending on the type of work they have done, some workers have a tendency to keep working longer before retiring and to even reenter the work force after they have retired. Hayward and Grady collected longitudinal data on the histories of labor force behavior, patterns of retirement, becoming disabled, and eventual mortality, from 2,816 men, from 1966 to 1983. They found that these patterns differed greatly from one type of worker to another. Among other things, they discovered that of all types of workers, self-employed and farm laborers worked the longest before retiring, had the shortest time in retirement, were the most apt to reenter the labor force after initially retiring, and were most apt to become disabled early in life (Hayward and Grady, 1990). As they explain these differences, it does not mean that these workers have any more desire to keep working than other workers. The situation is rather that they simply do not have as much access to pension income and other support services in retirement as both blue-collar and white-collar workers who receive these benefits as a part of their employment benefit packages. Nevertheless, it is true, as they put it, that "retirement is not a one-time event in many people's lives" (Hayward and Grady, 1990).

Arber and Ginn also make the case that retirement for women is quite different from that of men (Arber and Ginn, 1991, pp. 61–65). They identify two modern-day views of what retirement is all about today. One has been expressed by those they label as "conflictual ageists" who argue that the generous retirement pension benefits allow elderly workers to escape a highly competitive labor force into a comfortable life in retirement, at the expense of younger workers. The other view is based on what they call "structural dependency theory." The argument here is that retirement serves to force elderly people into dependency and eventual poverty. According to these analysts neither of these views take into account what retirement means to women. For one thing, the conflictual ageist "rosy view" of how comfortable retirement is "is hard to reconcile with the poverty in which many elderly people, especially women, live." Specifically, because women's work histories tend to be spasmodic, they have a harder time achieving occupational goals and typically suffer greater loss of income in retirement. Also they are expected to retire at about the same time as their husbands, and typically do so even though many receive either very low paying private pensions or none at all (Hayward and Liu, 1992). Furthermore, they are more apt then men to experience both retirement and widowhood in a short period of time, and that often means postponing retirement for two or more years, and not planning to retire at all, for some (Morgan, 1992). Thus, they are usually more frustrated with having to retire than men. For another thing, having to face financial dependency in retirement is nothing new to them. For most of them, that began earlier in life when they got married.

An important difference between women and men on what retirement means to them is in terms of how it relates to family responsibilities. Hatch and Thompson examined the relationships between those two variables (Hatch and Thompson, 1992). They found that neither race nor level of income were predictors of retirement among women. Factors that were somewhat related to retirement included (1) receiving income from pensions and Social Security, (2) having to put less time into work force experience, (3) reporting poor health, and (4) just becoming older. The greatest predictor of retirement among women, however, was having an ill or disabled household member who required assistance. Having children and/or parents living with them did not tend to prompt retirement. What did was one or more of them needing special care.

These kinds of complications often interfere with plans that elderly couples might have to coordinate the times when they retire. To analyze the effect when dual-working couples retire in relationship to each other, O'Rand, Henretta, and Krecker examined what they called couples' "pathways to retirement" (O'Rand, Henretta, and Krecker, 1992). They found their respondents in one of four different situations, relative to retirement: (1) those in which husband and wives had retired jointly, (2) those in which the husbands had retired but the wives were still working, (3) those in which the wives had retired but the husbands were still working, and (4) those in which both were continuing to work. The tendency was for those in the three latter situations to be economically and socially disadvantaged, making it necessary for one or both to remain in the work force. They were often plagued with having to live on relatively low wage and pension support, and sometimes having someone in the household for whom to provide care. The authors characterized those who had been able to retire jointly as having "an economically and maritally advantaged state, because, as they put it, they had obviously made "early and sustained investment ... to work and family" (O'Rand, Henretta, and Krecker, 1992). This, of course, does not mean that not retiring together, as such, is detrimental to a good adjustment to retirement. Rather, it means that joint retirement is symbolic of lifetime investments in work and family that typically lead to good retirements.

Obviously decisions about whether to retire and when to retire are much more dynamic processes than much of the scientific literature would indicate. Important interactional negotiating patterns are involved, as are the influences of such variables as types of jobs. Data from the longitudinal Normative Aging Study begun in 1963 in Boston show, for example, that the ages at which men preferred to retire and the ages they planned to retire differed (Ekerdt, Bosse, and Mogey, 1980). Five age-level worker cohorts said they would prefer to retire at earlier ages than they actually planned to retire. Furthermore, the older the cohorts, the higher they set both their preferred and planned retirement ages and the closer together those two ages became.

Further analysis of the data from the Normative Aging Study revealed that part of the dynamic involved in retirement decisions was what was labeled "preretirement involvement behavior." It was discovered that the closer men came to the time when retirement tended to be expected of particular worker cohorts, the more frequently they talked to wives, relatives, friends, and co-workers about retirement, and the more they read about it (Evans, Ekerdt, and Bosse, 1985). Robbins, Lee, and Wan also discovered that the two most basic factors related to adjustment in retirement, for those who had retired early were (1) goal continuity, and (2) social support. Surprisingly, neither health status nor social class (socioeconomic status or SES) were found to relate to adjustment at significant levels (Robbins, Lee, and Wan, 1994). Presumably, involvement with significant others tends to have a great influence on how people view retirement. These kinds of interactional patterns seem to have become fairly well established for those facing retirement and constitute what has come to be thought of as "anticipatory retirement."

In that regard Bernheim found that, in general, workers do, indeed, "think seriously about future events," such as retirement, and that they are "reasonably competent at making relatively accurate forecasts" (Bernheim, 1989). Gender, education, and wealth were particularly related to how accurate people are in their expectations about retirement. Men, those with the most education, and those with the most wealth tend to be the most accurate, according to that investigator. Perhaps those factors have more to do with individuals' abilities to manipulate desired circumstances than they do simply with expectations, however. One noteworthy finding discovered by Bernheim, is that workers, in situations in which retirement was mandatory at specific ages, were particularly prone to retire earlier than was required.

Anticipation of Retirement

Vinick and Ekerdt recently studied how well couples facing retirement anticipated what retirement would be like. The specific focus of their study was how the elderly respondents expected various activities in their lives to change with retirement (Vinick and Ekerdt, 1992). The activities included in the investigation were (1) husbands' and wives' household tasks, (2) social and couple-oriented leisure activities, and (3) husbands' and wives' personal pursuits. To discover the accuracy of the expectations of those facing retirement, their answers were compared to how those activities had actually changed for a group of couples who had already retired (see Table 11–1).

With regard to household tasks, both husbands and wives quite accurately expected that the level of women's involvement in that kind of activity would change very little. Interestingly, though, retired couples actually reported more increase in husband involvement in household tasks than either not-yet-retired husbands or wives (especially the wives) said they expected. In terms of social and couple-related leisure activities, the investigators reported that two patterns emerged. First, husband and wife answers were almost identical within each group of respondents. Second, though, couples not yet retired anticipated increases in these kinds of activities to a far greater extent than the retired couples reported as actually taking place. The area in which expectations quite accurately match outcomes had to do with wives' personal pursuits. A majority of all respondents said that that would essentially remain the same. However, the not-yet-retired husband much too optimistically anticipated an increase in terms of their own personal pursuits. A conclusion of the investigators from these data was that "the higher number of respondents who predict expansion of couple-only leisure activities (as well as joint social activities) implies a strong normative component underlying the expectation of increased companionship in retirement." They do admit, though, that the lack of accuracy in that regard and also, with regard to husbands' anticipated personal pursuits, may be the source of serious adjustment problems.

A word of caution concerning this particular study must be made, as the researchers themselves provide. It was a cross-sectional study. Therefore, the possibility of bias due to cohort effect could not be controlled. Part of the difference in the answers given by the two groups could well be due to how those groups differed from each other in ways besides being and not being retired. Nevertheless, it undoubtedly provides at least some valid insights into problems related to anticipatory retirement.

TABLE 11–1   Change in Activities Anticipated by Percent of Working Couples and Reported by Percent of Retired Couples

	ANTICIPATED CHANGE (N=125)		REPORTED CHANGE (N=92)	
	(A)	(B)	(C)	(D)
Activity	HUSBAND	WIFE	HUSBAND	WIFE
Husband's Household Tasks				
Less	1	2	6	6
Same	44	59	31	35
More	55	39	63	59
Wife's Household Tasks				
Less	21	18	27	36
Same	66	71	64	56
More	13	11	9	8
Joint Social Activities				
Less	4	2	9	14
Same	42	46	65	65
More	54	52	26	21
Couple-Only Activities				
Less	1	1	3	5
Same	18	19	45	48
More	81	80	52	47
Husband's Personal Pursuits				
Less	10	9	18	10
Same	38	50	48	46
More	52	41	34	44
Wife's Personal Pursuits				
Less	15	30	26	40
Same	65	55	61	51
More	20	15	13	9

SOURCE: Barbara H. Vinick and David J. Ekerdt, "Couples View Retirement Activities: Expectations Versus Experience," in *Families and Retirement*, eds. Maximiliane Szinovacz, David J. Ekerdt, and Barbara H. Vinick (Newbury Park, Calif.: Sage, 1992), Table 8.1, p. 138.

Part of the decision-making process related to retirement, in addition to when to retire and activities in which to engage, is where to live. It has been pointed out that that kind of decision is especially related to the family life of retirees. At the heart of that kind of decision is whether or not to move or age in place. In that regard Cuba studied a group of retirees who decided to migrate to two communities at Cape Cod, Massachusetts. The primary purpose of the study was to determine: (1) "to what extent family issues influence retirement migration," and (2) "to what extent retirement migration affects family life" (Cuba, 1992). In general, he found that most respondents had moved from communities that were relatively near, and that they had chosen to move where they did in order to be able to stay in touch with their families and lifelong friends. Families had obviously influenced their migration decisions. That would, of course, not apply to all retirement migrants (i.e., those deciding to migrate to Florida or Arizona). He also found an important way in which the migrant's decision to migrate affected family life.

Even though an important reason for the choice they made was to hold onto family relations, it did, nevertheless preclude ever relying on family members for the care they might eventually need. Most respondents indicated that their decision to move where they did was permanent, and they were not near enough to their families to expect any kind of care from them.

How Retirement Turns Out for Retirees

How retirement tends to turn out is another important aspect of the processes involved in retirement. What happens to them in terms of personal economics might seem to be a key to other considerations. In that regard, it has long been recognized that, on the average, the incomes of people who retire are drastically cut. Conclusions drawn from cross-sectional studies on retirement income have been that people's incomes are cut in half, on the average, when people retire. Those kinds of data are misleading, however, because the incomes of given cohorts of retirees are compared to other cohorts rather than to their own preretirement incomes. Longitudinal studies, which compare individuals' own incomes before and after retirement, reveal that the actual average loss of income due to retirement amounts to only about one-fourth (Palmore and others, 1985, p. 47). In the People's Republic of China today, retirement benefits range from 60 to 90 percent of preretirement wages ("Growing Old in China," 1981).

Questions about the adequacy of retirement income remain, however. The cross-sectional studies show that the retirement income improves for each succeeding generation of retirees. Thus, the older people become, the less income they will have, relative to others who retire later. Retirees' financial status relates to more than just what they made before they retired, of course. It was found in one study, for example, that, because of such income support mechanisms as Social Security, SSI, and food stamps, the incomes of the elderly poor tended to improve, while the incomes of those who had enjoyed middle-level and relatively high salaries tended to decline. The relatively wealthy were able to maintain quite comfortable and satisfying lives, while the financially marginal, whose incomes had been insufficient to allow them to save for their retirements, were hurt the most. They had the benefits of neither life savings nor of government subsidies. The conclusion from these findings was that retirement has an income-leveling effect (Fillenbaum, George, and Palmore, 1985).

The income levels among those in retirement are, nevertheless, very much related to both gender and marital status. In a longitudinal study of elderly people over a 10-year period, for example, Hurd and Wise found that, of the poor elderly, 80 percent were widows or other single individuals, and that as many as 30 percent of widows and other singles, compared to only about 8 percent of those still married, were poor (Hurd and Wise, 1989). It is also noteworthy that the poverty of many of those widows was related to the poor health and death of their husbands. More than three-fourths of them had not been poor prior to their husbands' deaths. Poverty for some also followed a period of poor health on the part of their husbands before they died. The combination of poor health and the death of their husbands left many of them without such things as private pension income, life insurance or savings income, and housing wealth that helped to keep others out of poverty. Some were also left with expenses related to their husbands' illnesses and death.

The social and psychological adjustments that people make in their retirement years have been a major area of concern of gerontologists. Much of the attention paid to this concern has focused on satisfaction among the elderly with life in general and with various aspects of being retired. In this regard, Davies likens the experiences of retirees to those of younger people who are being relegated to positions of permanent unemployment due to technological developments. He depicts the experiences of both the unemployed and retirees as characterized by alienation, lack of direction, economic dependence on the general public, and aimless expenditure of time (Davies, 1985). His contention is that, in order for these people to positively adjust to their nonproductive situations, society would have to redefine the importance of the work ethic.

There are indications that the experiences of semipermanent unemployment are, indeed, socially and psychologically devastating. In a study of unemployed professional men, Powell and Driscoll found that long periods of unemployment caused respondents to become cynical, to lose confidence in their professional competence, and to develop feelings of malaise (Powell and Driscoll, 1979). There is little evidence that these experiences are typical of those in retirement, however.

Adjustment to retirement has not been nearly as negative as it was thought to be even in the early days of mandatory retirement in the United States (in the 1950s and 1960s). It is true that high percentages of retirees expressed negative feelings about retirement in a 1960s international survey. Retired men in the United States, Great Britain, and Denmark were asked, among other questions, what they liked about retirement. Sizable percentages, especially in Denmark answered "nothing." It was also found, however, that many of them, particularly in Denmark, also answered "nothing" to the question of what they missed about their work. Furthermore, many of the negative feelings about retirement were expressed by those with relatively poor health (Shanas and others, 1968, pp. 330–40). Few negative attitudes about retirement have been found in subsequent surveys (Atchley, 1991, pp. 201–2). As Cowgill suggested, retirement has been the most difficult for the first cohorts of retirees (Cowgill, 1986, p. 129).

Indications of the high level of adjustment to retirement were found in the National Longitudinal Surveys in the United States. The 1976 part of that survey, based on a sample of both black and white males, revealed high levels of satisfaction with a number of aspects of aging (Parnes and Nestel, 1981). As many as 89 percent of the whites and 84 percent of the blacks expressed some level of happiness with retirement in general. Nearly half of the blacks (47 percent) and slightly more than half of the whites (51 percent) said they were "very happy." Health was found to be the least satisfying of any of the factors under study, which included housing, area of residence, standard of living, and leisure activities. It is especially noteworthy that a slightly higher percentage of the healthy retirees than those in the sample who had not yet retired reported being very happy with life in general.

To be sure, some experiences that elderly people have tend to be related to low levels of life satisfaction or morale. It was noted many years ago, for example, that disengagement was associated with lack of life satisfaction (Havighurst, Neugarten, and Tobin, 1968). It was generally assumed, therefore, that disengagement was a cause of low morale (Maddox, 1970). A later study compared disengagement related to widowhood and disengagement related to retirement. It was discovered that while disengagement related to widowhood was associated with substantial loss of morale, that related to retirement was almost totally unrelated to morale (Brown, 1974). It was concluded from this study that elderly people experience loss of morale when events in their lives are socially disruptive. While little can be done to prepare for becoming widowed, retirement can now be anticipated, planned, and experienced with relative ease.

One's social contacts and interactions especially with families, appear to be key factors in determining successful adjustment in retirement. Sagy and Antonovsky found this to be true among a sample of Israeli retirees from very different circumstances (i.e., some from Kibbutz and some not) (Sagy and Antonovsky, 1994). Much has been made of the impact of retirees' attitudes about work and retirement on whether or not they make satisfactory adjustments. Foner and Schwab have suggested that thinking about when to retire and having positive preretirement attitudes may influence adjustment to retirement even more than actual planning for it (Foner and Schwab, 1981). The question that arises, though, is what the sources of the preretirement attitudes are. Sheley found that attitudes about work and retirement among those living in retirement communities tended to be especially conducive to positive adjustments in retirement. This was true because the retirement community dwellers lived in an atmosphere in which emphasis on work is largely missing and a sense of belonging exists for those who are retired (Sheley, 1974).

Adjustment to retirement is not automatic, nor is it instantaneous. Retirement represents change, regardless of whether major losses are involved, and regardless of whether those changes may be welcome. Ekerdt and his colleagues investigated differences in overall life satisfaction among men who had been retired for various lengths of time. Those retired for less than 6 months were compared to those retired 7 to 12, 13 to 18, 19 to 24, 25 to 30, and 31 to 36 months. It was found that life satisfaction tended to be high for those retired 6 months or less but diminished for subsequent cohorts. The lowest measure of life satisfaction was found among those retired between 13 and 18 months, but it tended to increase among those retired longer than 18 months. The investigators concluded that adjustment to retirement typically involves a letdown period but tends, overall, to be a positive life experience (Ekerdt, Bosse, and Lewkoff, 1985).

A vital part of adjusting to retirement is how retirees relate to their families. Not only are families important in anticipating retirement, but also in how it turns out. As discussed in Chapter 7, marital relationships are particularly important. In the past, some analysts have conjectured that the adjustments to retirement are so drastic that the marriages of those involved would surely suffer as a result of retiring. Studies throughout the last quarter century of the marital satisfaction of elderly couples, compared to those of younger ages have, however, consistently reported the opposite results. It is true that the validity of these studies has been somewhat questioned because almost all of them were cross-sectional rather than longitudinal—the marital satisfaction of different age groups were compared instead of determining how the marital satisfaction of a single group changed over time. Therefore, we cannot be sure that how the elderly feel about their marriages at one point in time will be how those who are younger feel when they are elderly.

Atchley has recently reported the results of a longitudinal study on the effects of marital satisfaction in retirement, beginning with a sample of those who were 50 years old and older in 1975. The data from this study reveal a somewhat different pattern between husbands' and wives' expressions of marital satisfaction (Atchley, 1992). For men, the only significant predictor of being extremely satisfied with their marriages was age, or the length of time they had been married. For women, surprisingly, the only significant predictor of their being extremely satisfied with their marriages was the experience of a nonserious "recent disability," on the part of the husband or wife. Atchley's explanation of that indicates how marital satisfaction is indeed especially related to retirement. As he puts it, "caregiving gave the caregiver a sense of satisfaction and purpose, and care receiving gave the recipient a sense of security and being cared for" (Atchley, 1992).

SOCIAL ROLES IN RETIREMENT

Social status in modern societies is described by sociologists as *achieved* rather than *ascribed*. That is, we gain our sense of identity not by virtue of the family or clan into which we are born, but by the positions we come to hold and the roles we play due to our own efforts. Therefore, an analysis of roles in retirement is important to our understanding of retirement.

In 1960, Burgess described retirement as a "roleless role" (Burgess, 1960, p. 352–60), because it appeared in those days that, while elderly people were being forced to retire, they were given no meaningful roles to perform. This was a reasonable perception to have of retired people at that time. The aged could be observed daily gathered in city parks, hotel lobbies, local barber shops, and the like, with nothing apparent to do that would be meaningful to them.

Rosow provided a comprehensive explanation for this phenomenon. He contended that the problem was that modern society was failing to provide the aged with adequate socialization into retirement and old age (Rosow, 1974, pp. 162–72). He explained that socialization for those at younger ages typically involves assigning social positions (mostly in the form of well-defined occupations), prescribing the roles related to those positions, and providing rewards for performing the roles. In contrast, while elderly people are assigned the position of retired persons, no roles are specified for them, nor are they rewarded for becoming retired. Instead, they experience a major loss of status. Disengagement would thus be a typical response on the part of older persons. This is obviously a basically negative perspective of retirement roles. It depicts socialization as a process that is controlled and implemented by society. Thus, as Davies implied, any improvement of the lives of people in retirement would depend upon a major shift in the societal value of work (Davies, 1985).

While this perspective provides us with a good introduction to the concept of retirement roles, it has severe limitations. From the perspective of retired people themselves, for example, retirement is generally not perceived as a negative experience, as we have already noted. In addition, this perspective overlooks the fact that roles are generally acquired and assumed not so much from set prescriptions imposed by society, but from a negotiating process, through the individuals' interactions with the social entities of which they are part (Lindesmith, Strauss, and Denzin, 1991, pp. 230–31).

Even from the perspective of societal expectations of retirement, it is not fair to assume that retirees are expected to disengage and do nothing. Instead, it was precisely that apparent tendency among those in retirement that became disturbing to the American public in the 1960s. It is probably more accurate to say that the society provides those in retirement with freedom from the social obligations of previous roles. In the context of that freedom, the societal expectation is that they will negotiate their own roles. In that sense, disengagement may be tolerated but is certainly not encouraged.

This does not mean that each individual retiree necessarily defines a unique role or that there are no roles common to retired persons in general. It is the nature of the role-negotiating process that common role patterns will emerge. We can rightfully expect that retirement roles are indeed being negotiated, that they will be substantially different from preretirement roles, and that they will generally be adopted by many of those in the retired population. Part of this discussion is the extent and ways that the elderly are willing to and do, in fact, engage in productive activities. Danigelis and McIntosh compared the amount of productive work that was done by a sample of elderly (60+) white men, black men, white women, and black women. They asked how many hours per week each respondent did of (1) paid work, (2) unpaid work at home, and (3) unpaid work outside the home (Danigelis and McIntosh, 1993). They hypothesized that those with the greatest amount of resources (i.e., income, physical abilities, education, being married and having others in the household as support, etc.) would be found to spend the most hours in productive activities. However, what they found was that, while white men clearly had more resources than the others, black people were nearly as productive as whites and that women were significantly more productive overall than men, especially as related to unpaid work both in the home and outside the home (See Figure 11–1). Dorfman has reported that, while some studies find that husbands in retirement are doing more household tasks that have traditionally been defined as women's work, the husbands still tend to define it as "helping the wives" (Dorfman, 1992). Keith, Wacker, and Schafer also report that, while retired men in their study were more active in "feminine household tasks" than employed men, this "did not foster perceptions of greater equity" between husband and wives (Keith, Wacker, and Schafer, 1992). Danigelis and McIntosh concluded, somewhat to their surprise, that resources were not "universal, positive contributors to productive activity." The one resource variable that turned out to be the most predictive of all kinds of productive work among all respondents was their physical ability (Danigelis and McIntosh, 1993).

What, then, characterizes the emerging retirement roles? There is much disagreement in the gerontological literature about this. The main issue of disagreement is whether leisure constitutes a viable role for the elderly and whether, in fact, they are even willing to adopt it.

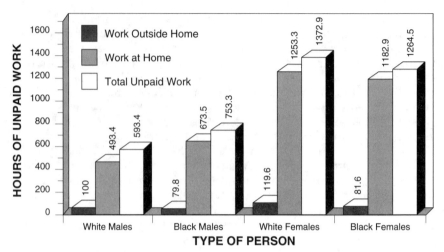

FIGURE 11-1   Average Yearly Hours of Unpaid Work by Type of Elderly Person (Source: Nicholas L. Danigelis and Barbara R. McIntosh, "Resources and the Productive Activity of Elders: Race and Gender as Contexts," *Journal of Gerontology*, 48, no. 4 (July 1993), S192–203, adapted from Table 2.)

Gerontologists in recent years have discussed the viability of leisure as a role for the aged. The problem in those discussions, however, has been the definition of leisure. Leisure has been viewed simply as the negative side, or absence, of work. Much emphasis, for example, has been placed on "free-time" (Cox, 1988, p. 187), and on what people with time on their hands do with that time. Rosow defined leisure negatively, as a reward for work, and he therefore contended that it could never be a viable role for retired people (Rosow, 1968).

In some societies in the past, leisure was given a positive definition. The classical Greek definition of leisure, for example, was that it consisted of the cultivation of self. It was viewed as a viable role of the privileged class, and it called for such pursuits as meditation and the development of true spiritual freedom (Kando, 1975, pp. 19–24). Freedom is a central part of most definitions of leisure. It is noteworthy that probably the one aspect that retirees most often say they enjoy about retirement is the freedom that it offers them. By this they do not mean simply "free time," but freedom from the obligations of the work from which they have retired, which many refer to as "the rat race," and the freedom to pursue their own individual interests and preferred associations (Brown, 1972, pp. 91–94).

In analyses of leisure among retired persons, the focus is often on the kinds of activities in which they engage. In that sense, it has been noted that retirees often simply engage in activities similar to those they engaged in in their work, and that is seen as evidence of their continuing orientation to the work ethic (Parker, 1982, pp. 138–45). What is missing in this analysis is that even though the activities may be similar, when they are done as leisure they are done from the perspective of freedom from the social obligation of work and the pursuit of their own individual interests.

This perspective on retirement is increasingly found among retirees today. There is also evidence that it is not confined to those in higher socioeconomic classes. In one study it was found, to the surprise of the investigators, that both retired professionals and individuals who had worked as day laborers saw retirement as a positive experience because of the freedom it offered them, provided there were opportunities for them to pursue their individual interests (Evans and Brown, 1970, pp. 27–28).

Three specific types of roles are rapidly emerging among retired people today that fit under the umbrella of leisure: (1) volunteer (Pepper, 1981), (2) student, and (3) pursuer of arts and crafts. Among these three types of roles there is great potential for the aged to make creative contributions to the cultures of which they are a part.

Elderly volunteers are quickly becoming seen by governments as valuable community resources, and increasing resources are being offered toward their support and recognition. Some of these roles represent social needs that the elderly are better able to fulfill than other people. Two examples, one from the People's Republic of China and the other from the United States, will illustrate how vital these kinds of roles are to communities as well as to the elderly participants.

In the People's Republic of China, women, particularly those in urban areas normally retire at age 55. At that time, as mentioned earlier, many of them volunteer to work in various types of community services (Lewis, 1982). They somewhat uniquely have the time and skills to perform these types of roles. Many of these women become members of neighborhood committees that serve as both welfare and social-control agents. These roles are vital to the community and are meaningful to those who fill them (Treas, 1979). While the amount of authority of these positions has somewhat diminished due to recent economic and social changes in that country, those kinds of community roles still exist for elderly people.

One of many similar volunteer roles that have been developed exclusively for the aged in the United States is that of "senior companion." It functions under a program sponsored by the federal government. Senior companions are recruited from among able-bodied, low-income elderly, most of whom have become relatively isolated. They serve as companions to other frail elderly people to help them with activities of daily living. Those who serve the homebound make particularly important contributions. The record of their work reveals that lives have literally been saved and many elderly have been kept from being prematurely institutionalized. Senior companions almost universally testify that their senior companion roles have provided them with new leases on life (Brown, 1991).

Still another of what might be categorized as a volunteer role for elderly persons comes from a very traditional culture. As a participant observer, anthropologist Schweitzer analyzed what old age was like among the Oto-Missouri and Ioway Indian tribes in Oklahoma (Schweitzer, 1983). She found, in contrast to the prevailing negative definitions of aging in the dominant American culture, that the prevailing definition of old age in these tribes continued to be positive. What provided that basically positive definition was the "functional" roles that those tribes reserved for their elderly members. Based on their knowledge of "tribal ways and traditions," elders of the tribes served as "ritual specialists" and "religious specialists" in tribal ceremonies, and as teachers of tribal traditions. These are not required roles for all who are old, but they represent positions of honor, prestige and power in these tribes.

Volunteerism indeed provides new and vital roles for the elderly in today's world. Many of these roles resemble work roles in that they contribute to societal productivity. Yet because they are voluntary, they also represent the freedom that characterizes leisure roles. Their value to those who perform them is primarily for self-improvement and secondarily that of productivity.

Volunteerism is apparently not a role that is universally enjoyed by retired people in all cultures. Cowgill reports, for example, that volunteers are neither respected nor treated with dignity or appreciation in Sweden. Although some who are retired do volunteer work, they typically complain that they are given tasks that are menial, inconsequential, and boring (Cowgill, 1986, p. 131).

The second rapidly emerging role among elderly people today is that of learner. This kind of role is so new that it is only now beginning to be discussed in the gerontological literature. Interest in education among the aged population was, from all appearances, almost nonexistent any place in the world in the early 1970s. As late as 1978, in an article "An Overview of Gerontological Education," Peterson ignored this aspect of age-related education in favor of education for professionals serving elderly people (Peterson, 1978). Since then, the demand for educational opportunities among older adults has mushroomed in a number of different cultural settings. According to Hately, there are basically three types of educational programs for the elderly. The first and most prominent is "reaching out," with the focus on learning about other cultures, places, and things. The second is "reaching in," emphasizing an understanding of self. The third type of program is called "reaching up," which is centered on religious and spiritual concerns (Hately, 1987–88).

The forms that this phenomenon has taken illustrate why it is fair to identify it as an important leisure role for older adults. With few exceptions, older adults are clamoring for educational opportunities, not for the purpose of meeting the requirements for a degree or learning a marketable skill, but merely to learn and share the learning process with other students. The only instrumental goal they may have is to learn to cope economically, politically, socially, psychologically, and spiritually as older adults.

In the United States, the primary structure of older-adult education is epitomized by the Elderhostel program (discussed in Chapter 8). Administered by a nationwide private organization, week-long educational programs exclusively for elderly people are offered at many colleges and universities across this country and in other parts of the world as well. Classes included in each program are selected purely on the basis of student interest, with no attempt to develop any kind of comprehensive curriculum. Participants in each week's program are treated as cohort groups. As a rule, all participants attend all of the courses being offered each day. Courses are not offered for credit since the students enroll simply to learn and to share what they learn with their fellow students. The program has become quite popular and is well attended.

As also explained in Chapter 8, in the People's Republic of China a program called "the Old People's University" was begun in 1983 at the Red Cross University in Jinan, sponsored jointly by that university and Shandung Province. It is administered by a president, 7 full-time staff members, and 8 part-time vice presidents. During the first year of operation, there were 48 part-time volunteer teachers in the program. Some 37 of the teachers were professors at the university, and the others were recruited from the community.

The guiding principle of the program is that of "taking good care of the old people to improve their health and to prolong their lives and providing a chance for them to study to increase their knowledge to enable them to continue to serve for the society" ("A Brief Introduction...," 1984). To accomplish these goals, a full two-year curriculum has been developed. The curriculum includes courses on health care and physical exercises; courses in such academic areas as history, geography, philosophy, and literature; and creative-expression courses such as calligraphy, painting, photography, gardening and music. Although courses are not for credit in the usual sense, elderly students who complete the two-year program receive a certificate of recognition from the university. During the first year of operation (1983 to 1984) a total of 980 students were enrolled. The majority of them were between 60 and 69 years old; the oldest was 86. Those from other parts of the People's Republic of China lived at the university along with other regular students.

Another illustration of educational programs for older people is found in Kyoto, Japan (Thornton, 1987–88). It was begun in 1969 for those 60 years old and older, under the sponsorship of the Hyogo prefectural government. There are three major program areas, each with an elaborate and well-established curriculum. Included are (1) The Senior Citizens College, a four-year course of study with emphases on learning about aging and other interests, making new friends, and reaching out to the community; (2) The Leadership Training Program, a two-year curriculum preparing leaders "to help organize and direct community club activities for elderly people throughout the prefecture;" and (3)The Senior Citizen University of the Air, a one-year correspondence course of study, in which some of the courses from the other programs are taught in weekly radio broadcasts to students who are unable to leave their homes.

The third type of leisure role that has emerged among the elderly today is that of pursuers of arts and crafts. Those involved in this type of role range from those who take courses on various kinds of crafts at senior citizens' centers and do crafts as hobbies, to those who are or become accomplished artists. There are those among the accomplished artists who did not discover their artistic abilities until after they retired and began to pursue art as an area of personal interest (Kastenbaum, 1991). As previously noted, art classes are part of the curriculum at the Old People's University in Jinan, China. This author had the privilege of observing displays of sculpture that some of these elderly students had done at the Red Cross University in Jinan in 1984.

Admittedly, by no means have all elderly people taken on leisure roles. There are those who do indeed experience a net loss of roles as they age, and who disengage from active social participation. This is particularly true of those with the least amount of formal education and who have particularly low incomes. Nevertheless, it is significant that the number of elderly people who are opting for one or more of the leisure roles is rapidly growing. Increasing numbers are becoming active volunteers. This type of role is increasingly involving many poor and uneducated elderly people, especially through federally mandated programs.

It is important to understand that these roles are largely leisure roles, in the classical sense, in that they are freely chosen by individuals for the primary goal of self-improvement. Precisely because they are leisure roles, they carry great potential for creativity and innovation. In addition, individuals who are involved make many vital contributions to their communities that all too often go unrecognized or unappreciated.

CONCLUSION

Retirement is becoming an increasingly well-established social institution and social process. It exists with basic systems of support in the developed nations of the world. It is also quickly becoming an established part of society in most of the developing nations. Only in those areas where the environments tend to be harsh and economic conditions are still undeveloped is it mostly nonexistent.

The institution of retirement has become possible in today's world largely because of the changing nature and the meaning of work. Throughout much of history, work, in the form of productive human labor, was economically necessary, and had religious and ideological meaning. It was also a primary source of individual identity and self-worth. With the great advancements in technological development in the modern era, however, machines have rendered much of human labor not only unnecessary but obsolete. Much of the work that is still needed has become routine, tedious, and even boring. To be sure, much of work remains important for its intrinsic value and especially as a means of making a living. It has, however, largely lost its religious and ideological meaning, and most jobs have become extremely competitive. Only the highly trained and skilled are able to compete.

In the modern technological world, retirement began, not so much as a system of support benefits for a needy or indulgent older population, as we might be led to believe, but as an economic necessity. It has been imposed on the aged population by the executives of corporations and employment organizations as the easiest way of dealing with the problem of surplus labor.

The argument that older workers are less efficient and competent than younger workers has never been substantiated. Nevertheless, it has been used as a rationale to legitimize mandatory retirement policies. In cases when surplus labor is not an issue and older workers are employed, for example, no such complaints are made.

Ironically, retirement has also largely become not only accepted but welcomed by the world's older populations. It is true that many of those among the early cohorts of people upon whom mandatory retirement policies were imposed had serious adjustment problems. It is also true that a minority of people with poor health, financial difficulties, and strong orientations to the work ethic still have adjustment problems. Most who are retired today, though, express much satisfaction about both retirement and life in general.

Part of the subjective meaning of retirement has to do with the growing role opportunities available to retirees. Contrary to the many arguments against leisure as being meaningful to retired people, the classic definition of leisure is precisely the orientation that most elderly people adopt in accepting retirement roles. They are free from productive obligations, and they take on roles primarily for their own self-improvement. Analyzing leisure simply in terms of specific activities misses that important point. Activities are leisure activities, not by virtue of the types of activities they are, but by virtue of how they are approached.

Leisure for those in retirement is becoming a way of life for both rich and poor. Volunteer programs of various kinds today have made this possible. Such programs as the Senior Companion Program in the United States, which is specifically designed for the elderly poor, illustrates that point. Creative activities in the forms of education and artistic work are also increasing among those in retirement. These roles are not only meaningful to those who adopt them, but they are also beginning to provide the aged with new and important identities.

In conclusion, retirement is not only a firmly established social institution, but it may well be one of the most valuable social inventions of the modern era. Admittedly, associated problems such as poor health, poverty, and adjustment difficulties remain. Still, a leisure class that is free from productive obligations and is oriented to self-improvement can prove to be socially valuable. As the ancient Greek philosophers, who were part of a privileged leisure class, demonstrated, these kinds of leisure activities have great potential to add significantly to the world's body of knowledge and to contribute to artistic beauty. While this kind of potential is now only beginning, these kinds of accomplishments will almost certainly multiply as the educational level of the retired population increases.

REFERENCES

Arber, Sara, and Jay Ginn, *Gender and Later Life: A Sociological Analysis of Resources and Constraints* (Newbury Park, Calif.: Sage, 1991).

Atchley, Robert C., "Retirement and Marital Satisfaction, in *Families and Retirement*, eds. Maximiliane Szinovacz, David J. Ekerdt, and Barbara H. Vinick (Newbury Park, Calif.: Sage, 1992), pp. 145–58.

Atchley, Robert C., *Social Forces and Aging: An Introduction to Social Gerontology* (Belmont, Calif.: Wadsworth, 1991).

Bendix, Reinhard, *Work and Authority in Industry: Ideologies of Management in the Course of Industrialization* (Berkeley, Calif.: University of California Press, 1956).

Bernheim, B. Douglas, "The Timing of Retirement: A Comparison of Expectations and Realizations" in *The Economics of Aging*, ed. David A. Wise (Chicago: University of Chicago Press, 1989), pp. 335–55.

"A Brief Introduction of the Red Cross Old People's University of Shandung Province," unpublished paper presented at a meeting of an American gerontology team, sponsored by People to People, International, at Jinan Red Cross University, June 9, 1984.

Brinkerhoff, David B., and Lynn K. White, *Sociology* (Los Angeles: West, 1985).

Brown, Arnold S., *Northern Arizona Senior Companion Program Evaluation Report*, submitted to ACTION agency in 1991.

Brown, Arnold S., "Socially Disruptive Events and Morale Among the Elderly," unpublished paper presented at the Gerontological Society 27th Annual Meeting in Portland, Oregon, October, 1974. Abstract printed in *The Gerontologist*, 14, no. 5, pt. 2 (October 1974), p. 72.

Brown, Arnold S., "The Elderly Widowed and Their Patterns of Social Participation and Disengagement," unpublished doctoral thesis, University of Montana, 1972.

Burgess, Ernest W., *Aging in Western Societies* (Chicago: University of Chicago Press, 1960).

Campbell, Tom, *Seven Theories of Human Society* (New York: Oxford Press, 1981).

Cowgill, Donald O., *Aging Around the World* (Belmont Calif.: Wadsworth, 1986).

Cox, Harold, *Later Life: The Realities of Aging* (Englewood Cliffs, N.J.: Prentice Hall, 1988).

Cuba, Lee, "Family and Retirement in the Context of Elderly Migration," in *Families and Retirement*, eds. Maximiliane Szinovacz, David J. Ekerdt, and Barbara H. Vinick (Newbury Park, Calif.: Sage, 1992), pp. 205–21.

Danigelis, Nicholas L., and Barbara R. McIntosh, "Resources and the Productive Activity of Elderly: Race and Gender as Contexts," *Journal of Gerontology*, 48, no. 4 (July 1993), S192–203.

Davies, Christopher S., "The Throwaway Culture: Job Detachment and Rejection," *The Gerontologist*, 25, no. 3 (June 1985), 228–31.

Dorfman, Lorraine T., "Couples in Retirement: Division of Household Work," in *Families and Retirement*, eds. Maximiliane Szinovacz, David J. Ekerdt, and Barbara H. Vinick (Newbury Park, Calif.: Sage, 1992), pp. 159–73.

Ekerdt, David J., "The Busy Ethic: Moral Continuity Between Work and Retirement," *The Gerontologist*, 26, no. 3 (June 1986), 239–44.

Ekerdt, David J., "Why the Notion Persists that Retirement Harms Health," *The Gerontologist*, 27, no. 4 (August 1987), 454–57.

Ekerdt, David J., Raymond Bosse, and Sue Lewkoff, "An Empirical Test for Phases of Retirement: Findings from the Normative Aging Study," *Journal of Gerontology*, 40, no. 1 (January 1985), 95–101.

Ekerdt, David J., Raymond Bosse, and John M. Mogey, "Concurrent Change and Planned and Preferred Age for Retirement," *Journal of Gerontology*, 35, no. 2 (March 1980), 232–40.

Evans, Idris W., and Arnold S. Brown, *Aging in Montana: A Survey of the Needs and Problems of Older Americans* (Helena, Mont.: Montana Commission on Aging, 1970).

Evans, Linda, David J. Ekerdt, and Raymond Bosse, "Proximity to Retirement and Anticipatory Involvement: Findings from the Normative Aging Study," *Journal of Gerontology*, 40, no. 3 (May 1985), 368–74.

Fillenbaum, Gerda G., Linda George, and Erdman B. Palmore, "Determinants and Consequences of Retirement Among Men of Different Races and Economic Levels," *Journal of Gerontology*, 40, no. 1 (January 1985), 85–94.

Foner, Anne, and Karen Schwab, *Aging and Retirement* (Monterey, Calif.: Brooks/Cole, 1981).

Graebner, William, *A History of Retirement: The Meaning of An American Institution, 1885–1978* (New Haven, Conn.: Yale University Press, 1980).

Gratton, Brian, and Frances M. Rotondo, "The Family Fund: Strategies for Security in Old Age in the Industrial Era," in *Families and Retirement*, eds. Maximiliane Szinovacz, David J. Ekerdt, and Barbara H. Vinick (Newbury Park, Calif.: Sage, 1992), pp. 51–63.

"Growing Old in China," *Beijing Review*, 43 (October 26, 1981), 22–28.

Hatch, Laurie Russell, and Aaron Thompson, "Family Responsibilities and Women's Retirement," in *Families and Retirement*, eds. Maximiliane Szinovacz, David J. Ekerdt, and Barbara H. Vinick (Newbury Park, Calif.: Sage, 1992), pp. 99–113.

Hately, B. J., "Reaching In, Reaching Up," *Generations*, 12, no. 2 (Winter 1987–88), 42–45.

Havighurst, Robert J., Bernice Neugarten, and Sheldon S. Tobin, "Disengagement and Patterns of Aging," in *Middle Age and Aging*, ed. Bernice Neugarten (Chicago: University of Chicago Press, 1968), pp. 162–72.

Hayward, Mark D., and William R. Grady, "Work and Retirement Among a Cohort of Older Men in the United States," *Demography*, 27, no. 3 (August 1990), 337–56.

Hayward, Mark D., and Mei-Chun Liu, "Men and Women in Their Retirement Years," in *Families and Retirement*, eds. Maximiliane Szinovacz, David J. Ekerdt, and Barbara H. Vinick (Newbury Park, Calif.: Sage, 1992), pp. 23–50.

Hurd, Michael D., and David A. Wise, "The Wealth and Poverty of Widows: Assets Before and After the Husband's Death," in *The Economics of Aging*, ed. David A. Wise (Chicago: University of Chicago Press, 1989), pp. 177–99.

Johnson, Paul, Christoph Conrad, and David Thomson, "Introduction," in *Workers Versus Pensions: International Justice in an Aging World*, eds. Paul Johnson, Christoph Conrad, and David Thomson,(New York: Manchester University Press, 1989), pp. 1–16.

Kando, Thomas M., *Leisure and Popular Culture in Transition* (Saint Louis: C. V. Mosby, 1975).

Kastenbaum, Robert, "The Creative Impulse: Why it Won't Just Quit," *Generations*, 15, no. 2 (Spring 1991), 7–12.

Keith, Pat M., "Work, Retirement, and Well-Being Among Unmarried Men and Women," *The Gerontologist*, 25, no. 4 (August 1985), 410–16.

Keith, Pat M., Robbyn R. Wacker, and Robert B. Schafer, "Equity in Older Families," in *Families and Retirement*, eds. Maximiliane Szinovacz, David J. Ekerdt, and Barbara H. Vinick (Newbury Park, Calif.: Sage, 1992) pp. 189–201.

Kilty, Keith M., and John H. Behling, "Predicting the Retirement Intentions and Attitudes of Professional Workers," *Journal of Gerontology*, 40, no. 2 (March 1985), 219–27.

Komine, Takao, "The Aging of the Labor Force in Japan," in *The Promise of Productive Aging: From Biology to Social Policy*, eds. Robert N. Butler, Mia R. Oberlink, and Mal Schechter (New York: Spring, 1990), pp. 116–17.

Lewis, Myrna, "Aging in the People's Republic of China," *International Journal of Aging and Development*, 15, no. 2 (1982), 79–105.

Lindesmith, Alfred R., Anselm L. Strauss, and Norman K. Denzin, *Social Psychology* (Englewood Cliffs, N.J.: Prentice Hall, 1991).

Maddox, George L., "Fact and Artifact: Evidence Bearing on Disengagement Theory," in *Normal Aging*, ed. Erdman Palmore (Durham, N.C.: Duke University Press, 1970), pp. 324–26.

Maeda, Daisaku, "Japan," in *International Handbook on Aging: Contemporary Developments and Research*, ed. Erdman B. Palmore (Westport, Conn.: Greenwood Press, 1980), pp. 253–70.

Miller, Stephen J., "The Social Dilemma of the Aging Leisure Participant" in *Older People and Their Social World*, eds. Arnold M. Rose and Warren A. Peterson (Philadelphia: F. A. Davis, 1965), pp. 77–92.

Morgan, Leslie, "Marital Status and Retirement Plans," in *Families and Retirement*, eds. Maximiliane Szinovacz, David J. Ekerdt, and Barbara H. Vinick (Newbury Park, Calif.: Sage, 1992), pp. 114–26.

Morse, Nancy C., and Robert S. Weiss, "The Function and Meaning of Work and the Job," *American Sociological Review*, 20, no. 2 (1955), 191–98.

O'Rand, Angela M., John C. Henretta, and Margaret L. Krecker, "Family Pathways to Retirement," in *Families and Retirement*, eds. Maximiliane Szinovacz, David J. Ekerdt, and Barbara H. Vinick (Newbury Park, Calif.: Sage, 1992), pp. 81–98.

Palmore, Erdman B., Bruce M. Burchett, Gerda G. Fillenbaum, Linda K. George, and Laurence M. Wallman, *Retirement: Causes and Consequences* (New York: Springer, 1985).

Parker, Stanley, *Work and Retirement* (London: George Allen and Unwin, 1982).

Parnes, Herbert S., and Gilbert Nestel, "The Retirement Experience" in *Work and Retirement: A Longitudinal Study of Men*, ed. Herbert S. Parnes (Cambridge, Mass.: MIT Press, 1981), pp. 155–97.

Pepper, Claude, "Senior Volunteerism: Alive and Well in the 80's," *Generations*, 5, no. 4 (Summer 1981), 6–7.

Peterson, David A., "An Overview of Gerontology Education," in *Gerontology in Higher Education: Perspectives and Issues*, eds. Mildred Seltzer, Harvey Sterns, and Tom Hickey (Belmont, Calif.: Wadsworth, 1978), pp. 14–26.

Powell, Douglas H., and Paul F. Driscoll, "Middle-class Professionals Face Unemployment," in *Socialization and the Life Cycle*, ed. Peter I. Rose (New York: St. Martin's Press, 1979), pp. 309–19.

Rix, Sara E., and Paul Fisher, *Retirement-Age Policy: An International Perspective* (New York: Pergamon Press, 1982).

Robbins, Steven B., Richard M. Lee, and Thomas T. H. Wan, "Goal Continuity as a Mediator of Early Retirement Adjustment: Testing a Multidimensional Model," *Journal of Counseling Psychology*, 41, no. 1 (January 1994), 18–26.

Robinson, Pauline K., Sally Coberly, and Carolyn E. Paul, "Work and Retirement," in *Handbook of Aging and the Social Sciences*, eds. Robert H. Binstock and Ethel Shanas (New York: Van Nostrand Reinhold, 1985), pp. 503–27.

Rosow, Irving, "Retirement, Leisure and Social Status," in *Duke University Council on Aging and Human Development*, (Durham, N.C.: Duke University Press, 1968), pp. 249–57.

Rosow, Irving, *Socialization to Old Age* (Berkeley, Calif.: University of California Press, 1974).

Sagy, Shifra, and Aaron Antonovsky, "The Reality Worlds of Retirees: An Israeli Case-Control Study," *Journal of Psychology*, 128, no. 1 (January 1994), 111–28.

Schweitzer, Marjorie M., "The Elders: Cultural Dimensions of Aging in Two American Indian Communities," in *Growing Old in Different Societies: Cross-Cultural Perspectives*, ed. Jay Sokolovsky (Belmont, Calif.: Wadsworth, 1983), pp. 168–78.

Shanas, Ethel, Peter Townsend, Dorothy Wedderbaum, Henning Friis, Paul Milhoj, and Jan Stehouwer, *Old People in Three Industrial Societies* (New York: Atherton Press, 1968).

Sheley, Joseph F., "Mutuality and Retirement Community Success: An Interactionist Perspective in Gerontological Literature," *International Journal on Aging and Human Development*, 5, no. 1 (1974), 71–77.

Sheppard, Harold L., and Sara E. Rix, *The Graying of Working America: The Coming Crisis in Retirement-Age Policy* (New York: Free Press, 1977).

"Should Women Retire Earlier Than Men?" *Beijing Review*, 29, no. 17 (April 28, 1986), 9–10.

Thornton, James E., "Third-Age Colleges in Japan and Canada," *Generations*, 12, no. 2 (Winter 1987–88), 52–54.

Treas, Judith, "Social Organization and Economic Development in China: Latent Consequences for the Aged," *The Gerontologist*, 19, no. 1 (February 1979), 34–43.

Vinick, Barbara H., and David J. Ekerdt, "Couples View Retirement Activities: Expectations Versus Experience," in *Families and Retirement*, eds. Maximiliane Szinovacz, David J. Ekerdt, and Barbara H. Vinick (Newbury Park, Calif.: Sage, 1992), pp. 129–44.

Weber, Max, *The Protestant Ethic and the Spirit of Capitalism*, (New York: Charles Scribner's Sons, 1958).

Health and Health Care
for the Aged

INTRODUCTION

In the mid-1960s, Rose predicted that good physical and mental health was becoming a major component of the value system of the rapidly growing elderly population. Everyone wants to be healthy, but for elderly people, health is also an important symbol of social status. It is more important, in fact, than such traditional social status symbols as income and occupation. This would be true, according to Rose, especially among those elderly people who become part of the "subculture of the aging" that he said was developing (Rose, 1965).

Indeed, the maintenance and restoration of health have become two of the highest priority concerns of the elderly people today. They are two of a very few subjects about which virtually all of the aged tend to agree. Rich and poor alike see health care as a common need. Consequently, health care for the retired population has become one of the major expenditures of individual elderly people and the governments of the industrialized world.

Given the vital nature of this topic to the aged, it is important to explore the answers to a number of questions. First, what, precisely, do we mean by health and how has it become so vital to the aged? How is it related to aging, to illness or disease, and to everyday living? What are the basic types of health problems with which the aged must deal? What are the processes in which they must become involved in the pursuit of their own health status?

hat kinds of governmental health care policies have been developed to support them in their health needs? How do these elderly compare cross-culturally with regard to health care? What are the typically positive and negative consequences to the lives of elderly persons in their pursuit of good health? We will deal with these kinds of issues in this chapter.

CHANGES IN THE HEALTH PROBLEMS OF THE AGED

In the past, before science had been extensively applied to the problems of health, the health problems of elderly people were not very different from those of any other age group. In those times, few people lived into their sixties. Many died in early childhood. Most others died either in adolescence or as relatively young adults of accidents, communicable diseases, or any number of other acute ailments. Individuals were susceptible to any of these kinds of often fatal problems throughout their lives. Many at every age level suffered from them. Those who lived longer than others did so primarily because they had been fortunate enough to have escaped health-related problems or were strong enough to overcome them without much, if any, professional help.

Infectious diseases posed the most serious threat to health. Epidemics of such diseases as cholera, yellow fever, and smallpox took many lives in countries that were becoming industrialized and urbanized as late as the latter part of the nineteenth century (Carlson, 1983).

In the past, health status was typically thought of quite differently than it is today. Science had not yet been applied to areas of health in providing practical remedies for illness. As Carlson points out, "Medical practice was largely an art" (Carlson, 1983). Thus, many perceived health and the problems of health from a religious perspective. It was a matter of individuals' relationships with God and God's benevolence toward them. For many others, good health was simply a matter of good luck, and most families used home remedies to treat illness. Carlson also points out that homeopathic medicine was practiced in the past. That is, health problems were treated by attempting to stimulate the body's capacity to recover (Carlson, 1983). As we shall see later, that is the basic difference between Oriental and Western approaches to medicine.

Those few who lived to be very old were indeed plagued with different mental and physical problems from those of the rest of the population. Those problems were not even viewed as health problems that called for any kinds of remedies, however. Instead, they were thought to be simply the natural consequences of old age.

Dramatic changes have come about during the twentieth century, first in the Western industrialized world and now in many other parts of the world as well, in people's orientation to health and the conditions of their health. These changes have had a major impact on the lives of elderly people. It was essentially the application of modern science to solve the problems related to health that brought about the changes. Modern science transferred the focus of health maintenance from a religious or fateful orientation to an almost total emphasis on the disease concept. In attempting to define health, for example, someone at the World Health Organization proposed that it is "a State of complete physical, mental, and social well-being and not merely the absence of disease or infirmity" (Liang and Whitelaw, 1990). Likewise, DuBois has said that it is unrealistic to think of health as the absence of disease. A healthy society, he believes, in one that "successfully adapts to diseases" (DuBois, 1965, pp. 344–51). This concept has been so all-encompassing that it has also been widely applied to such areas as mental disorders, drug abuse, criminal behavior, and the debilitating problems of old age (Mechanic, 1978, pp. 99–105; Stahl and Feller, 1990).

At the heart of the meaning of the concept of disease is causation. Diseases are not seen as matters of religion or fate. Neither do they need to be fatal when acquired. Instead they have causes that, if and when discovered, can be eliminated through specified treatments. Thus, the diseases themselves can be cured and their debilitating effects corrected through technology. Scientific advancements have been made, then, in three basic areas: (1) the study and discovery of the causes of diseases, (2) the creation of treatment and disease control methods, and (3) the development of corrective and lifesaving technologies.

Particular attention was paid, in the latter part of the nineteenth and the early part of the twentieth centuries, to the causes of contagious diseases that had taken the lives of people of all ages. The discovery of bacteria as the cause of these diseases and the reason for their contagiousness was a particularly important scientific breakthrough. Knowledge of the causes of diseases led to (1) the establishment of public health programs that effectively controlled the contagion processes, (2) the development of immunization procedures that virtually eliminated a number of diseases, and (3) the discovery of treatments that helped to cure many diseases. In addition, a great deal of progress was made in developing many forms of technology that would correct the debilitating effects of many accidents and diseases and replace the functions of a number of the vital organs of the body.

The scientific use of the concept of disease has thus had dramatic results in the maintenance of physical health and the preservation of life. Consequently, that concept has been widely applied to other human conditions and problems. Of particular importance to our analysis of the health of the elderly are mental disorders and long-term physical problems typically found among the aged. These problems become defined as diseases rather than as the inevitable products of aging itself. Even though the causes of most of these ailments have not yet been established, and thus no cures have been developed, it has become something of a matter of scientific faith that the causes and cures will eventually come.

As a result of this kind of scientific perspective, a distinction has been made between two very different types of diseases: acute and chronic. This distinction has very important practical implications for health and health care among the aged. *Acute* diseases have been defined as "physical conditions with a specific onset and limited duration," and *chronic* diseases as "conditions that persist over time" (Hickey, 1980, p. 175). Another distinction between them today is that acute illnesses tend to be curable while chronic problems tend to be incurable. In the past, however, the acute more than the chronic diseases were the ones that were fatal. The speed with which they develop and their durations are the most important distinctions between them. Chronic problems are long term and often even permanent conditions with which the elderly especially must live (Eustis, Greenburg, and Patten, 1984, p. 7).

The important consequences of the scientific successes in the field of health care are that increasing numbers of people have survived the danger of infant mortality, avoided fatal involvement with infectious diseases, avoided or survived other acute illnesses, and lived safely into old age. The longer they live, however, the more apt they are to acquire chronic problems that require some level and form of long-term care. In old age, the incidence of acute problems usually diminishes and the probability of acquiring chronic problems grows. Thus, in contrast to the past, the health problems of the aged today tend to be quite different from those of the rest of the population. That is a fact that the present health care system has so far tended to ignore, as we will discuss later.

ALZHEIMER'S AND OTHER DEMENTIA DISEASES AS A SPECIAL HEALTH PROBLEM OF THE AGED

Alzheimer's disease, along with other similar forms of dementia, is probably the most serious health problem faced by older people today. It is undoubtedly the one most dreaded and frightening disease that it is possible for older people to acquire. It also presents a seemingly impossible and burdensome challenge for both professional and informal caregivers to meet. Furthermore, it represents one of the major national health care expenditure burdens that exists, not only now but also increasingly so in the future.

There are no specific statistics on the total number of people who suffer from Alzheimer's disease. Informed estimates have been made, however, and they indicate that there are presently as many as anywhere between 2.5 to 4 million in the United States. It is also estimated that, if present trends continue, by 2025 or 2030, when baby boomers have joined the over-65 population, their numbers will swell to at least 7 million and perhaps as many as 9 million. Statistic estimates also show that the older people become the greater the chances are that they will acquire Alzheimer's disease or some other form of dementia (Brownlee, 1992; Butler, Lewis, and Sunderland, 1991, p. 154; Weiss and Lonnquist, 1994, pp. 77–78). Evans and his colleagues report, for example, that only about 3.9 percent of those between 65 and 74 have Alzheimer's while as many as 16.4 percent of those 75 to 85 have it, and probably as many as 47.55 percent of those 85 and over are afflicted with it. As a whole, 11.3 percent of those 65 or older are estimated to have it (Evans and others, 1990). They also projected increases in the number of Alzheimer's disease victims into the future, using census data. Table 12-1 and Figure 12-1 show the increase in numbers by age group over 65 from 1980 to 2050 that can be expected to acquire Alzheimer's. It is noteworthy that the numbers in the 65 to 74 age group are expected to increase very little over the 60-year period, while the number of those 75 to 84 will almost double, and those 85 and over will increase by nearly 700 percent. There are two basic reasons for these projected differences. First, although aging does not cause dementia, as we have seen, the longer one lives the more apt he or she will experience it. Second, the 85 and over age group is growing and will continue to grow faster

TABLE 12-1   **Estimated Number (in millions) of Persons in the U.S. with Alzheimer's Disease, 1980 through 2050, by Age Group**

YEAR	65–74	75–84	85+	TOTAL AGED 65 AND OVER
1980	0.61	1.25	1.02	2.88
1990	0.59	1.57	1.59	3.75
2000	0.54	1.65	2.32	4.51
2010	0.54	1.61	2.98	5.12
2020	0.73	1.68	3.22	5.62
2030	0.86	2.40	3.73	6.99
2040	0.74	2.84	5.49	9.07
2050	0.74	2.46	7.06	10.20

Source: Denis A. Evans and others, "Estimated Prevalence of Alzheimer's Disease in the United States," *The Milbank Quarterly*, 68, no. 2 (1990), pp. 267–89, adapted from Table 1.

than any other age group. We do need to remember, of course, that these figures only represent rough estimates of the numbers of both present and future cases of dementia. Also, as we pointed out earlier, the future estimates are expected to be somewhat close to reality, only if present trends continue; that is if medical science fails to accomplish a breakthrough in discovering causes of and effective treatments for the number of dementia diseases that exist. Nevertheless, Alzheimer's disease is a serious problem that deserves all of the attention we as a society can give it.

FIGURE 12-1   Projected Number of Persons 65 and Older with Probable Alzheimer's Disease in the U.S. from 1980 through 2050 by Age (Source: Denis A. Evans and others, "Estimated Prevalence of Alzheimer's Disease in the United States," *The Milbank Quarterly*, 68, no. 2 (1990), pp. 267–89, Figure 2.)

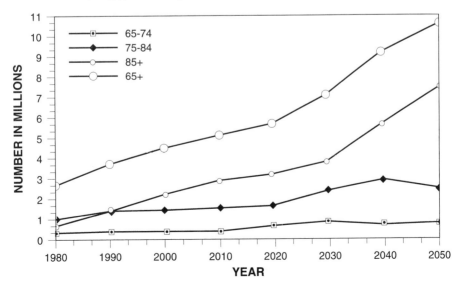

The seriousness of this disease is illustrated by the progressively worsening symptoms of the disease as well as by its prevalence among the elderly population. The most commonly known symptom of any is the loss of memory. This typically happens gradually and for a time does not appear to be abnormal. After all, everyone is forgetful at times, especially as they become older. However, for Alzheimer's victims, the loss of memory progressively and irreversibly gets worse, because of damage to that part of the brain that controls the cognitive process by which we as humans think, talk, and communicate with each other (Kart, Metress, and Metress, 1992). Other related symptoms that often eventually develop include impaired cognition, disorientation about times, place, and identities, decline in task performance, decrease in verbal abilities, blunting of emotional feelings, depression, and even at times unpredictable and violent behavior (Hamdy, 1994). What Helmchen and Linden found out about the relationship between dementia, depression, and aging is noteworthy. Dementia and depression were differentially related to aging. While dementia closely correlated with age, depression did not. Depression was found as prominent among young as older adults. Part of that was due, however, to the effect of dementia itself. It was discovered that dementia actually tended to "suppress the expression of depressive symptoms" (Helmchen and Linden, 1993). Obviously, Alzheimer's and other forms of dementia are so destructive that they eventually blot all forms of consciousness, including both positive and negative. In the final stages of the disease, for those who live long enough, individuals lose their ability to control any of their bodily functions (Weiss and Lonnquist, 1994, pp. 155–59). As Brownlee so aptly puts it, "harmless forgetfulness gives way to a cruel and capricious insanity" (Brownlee, 1992).

When close family members observe their elderly members going through these kinds of tortuous experiences and at times becoming people with an entirely different personality, they often experience their own psychological trauma. This is particularly true of those who also take on the increasingly difficult responsibilities of being the caregivers of their elderly family members. Without a doubt, caring for Alzheimer's disease victims is the most difficult caregiving responsibilities anyone could experience. What makes it even more difficult than it might otherwise be is that within families the re-sponsibility is typically left to one person, usually a woman who becomes socially isolated (Caserta, Lund, Wright, and Redburn, 1987). Therefore, it should not be surprising that many of these caregivers have been found to also suffer depression, poor health, and low life satisfaction (Weiss and Lonnquist, 1994, pp. 78–79). Wright compared elderly couples in which both spouses were healthy with those in which one spouse had Alzheimer's disease. As a whole the data showed that among the well couples "spouses increasingly value each other as unique persons." In contrast, the marital relationships of the couples with one having Alzheimer's was described as "a committed-dependent relationship that spans outcomes of adaptation and control, as well as distortion and disorder" (Wright, 1993, pp. 111–12). Kiecolt-Glaser and Glaser studied the impact that caregiving has on the health of family members who provide care to Alzheimer's patients, and concluded that, "in spousal caregivers, who are old, chronic stress could have long-term, potentially irreversible consequences" (Kiecolt-Glaser and Glaser, 1994). These kinds of problems related to caring for Alzheimer's patients at home have led to the development of a nationwide organization called the Alzheimer's Disease and Related Disorders Association (ADRDA). Increasing numbers of communities now have local chapters that form self-help groups made up of caregivers of Alzheimer's patients that meet regularly (typically weekly) for sharing of experiences and mutual support. Many chapters also make respite services available to their local caregivers (Hooyman and Kiyak, 1991, p. 272). The kinds of services this organization provides are vital to many caregivers across the country (Caserta, Lund, Wright, and Redburn, 1987).

Increasingly, the populations of nursing homes are becoming elderly people with one or another form of dementia. One study, for example, of a number of nursing homes found that almost 70 percent of the residents were demented. This led one practitioner to comment that, "these are mental institutions, except we call them nursing homes" (Brownlee, 1992). The irony of that is that few nursing homes have psychiatrists or psychiatric nurses on staff or even provide training on problems of dementia for the staff they have. What they, therefore, fail to realize is that "some of the most bizarre of unmanageable behavior exhibited by people with Alzheimer's can be diverted with surprisingly simple technique," as Brownlee was informed. In some cases, all that it takes is making the effort to keep patients busy with simple and easy to perform activities (Brownlee, 1992). Indeed, even though neither causes nor cures of serious forms of dementia have yet been discovered, the study of those diseases has led to some effective ways of working with their victims. Objectively diagnosing individuals as having Alzheimer's disease often leads to the assumption that "nothing can be done" and that, therefore, all that can be done with them is to simply control their behavior and take care of their physical needs. Cotrell and Lein contend that out of all the concern shown for the caregivers, very little attention has been paid to "enhancing the quality of life for the dementia victims" (Cotrell and Lein, 1993). As Dawson, Wells, and Kline report, though, studies have revealed some important facts. For one thing, many individuals with dementia symptoms have been found to have what has been identified as "excess disability"—individuals exhibiting greater disabilities than their actual capabilities would call for, simply because they are never expected to act on their own. These can be corrected with the right kinds of interventions. That group of investigators have also learned that the type of environment in which elderly people live greatly influences how adequately Alzheimer's patients are able to function. The more complex the environment the less able they are to function (Dawson, Wells, and Kline, 1993, pp. 4–11). Controlling the environment so that it matches the individual patient's mental capabilities, then, is one of the keys to enhancing his/her ability to remain functionally active (Butler, Lewis, and Sunderland, 1991, p. 154).

Dawson and her colleagues have developed an impressive program which they have entitled "Enablement," for use by nursing home patients. The purpose of this program, as they explain it, is to make a shift away from "the traditional preoccupation with the disease" and to "foster meaningful life experiences for individuals despite the presence of cognitive impairments" (Dawson, Wells, and Kline, 1993, pp. 2–3). The program begins with a thorough assessment of participants' "self-care," "social," "interactional," and "interpretative" abilities. That is followed by the attempt to create an environment that is complex enough to challenge the client but simple enough to allow them to function according to their level of capability. Then, staff follow an "ability-enhancing" process as they work and interact with their elderly patients. What they are attempting to do is "to promote the continued use of retained abilities" (Dawson, Wells, and Kline, 1993, p. 6). In this program seemingly lost capabilities are sometimes found to be restored to individual participants. Even though they are aware that some of the mental losses they are experiencing are irreversible, being helped in this way to remain at least somewhat active is encouraging to them. This is particularly true if what they do benefits others. One lady, for example, could still read, even though she had almost no comprehension of what she read. Despite that handicap, she gained encouragement by just being able to read to a blind man.

There are no known causes of Alzheimer's disease, but there is a variety of theories. They range from the idea that it results from an excess amount of aluminum concentrated in the brain, to its being genetically inherited, to its being a slow form of virus. Some theorists even believe that it is the consequence of "accelerated aging" (Butler, Lewis, and Sunderland, 1991, pp. 163–65; Kart, Metress, and Metress, 1992, p. 121). If this were true, then, everyone would eventually have the disease if they lived long enough. This idea tends to be rejected by most investigators, however, because some of those who live the longest have never experienced any such damage to their brains and have not lost their memories. Furthermore, the results of tests on such things as memory loss among those with Alzheimer's differ greatly from other elderly people. As Sloan explains it, "memory loss in patients with Alzheimer's disease is multifactorial, and changing performance in memory patterns over time indicates that multiple independent systems are deteriorating" (Sloan, 1994).

Obviously this is a devastating disease, negatively affecting an ever-increasing number of elderly, their families, and whole societies. There are those who contend, however, that it is not gaining the attention of research funding agencies because of the competition it faces with other serious diseases concentrated among younger people. As Brownlee points out, "the total annual federal budget for Alzheimer's research is $230 million, a fraction of the $1.7 billion for AIDS" (Brownlee, 1992).

MENTAL DISORDERS AMONG THE AGED

The likelihood and frequency of mental disorders among elderly people is an increasingly important health concern among gerontologists. It is commonly acknowledged that, in general, there are fewer cases of mental illness in the older population than among younger adults (Wykle and Musil, 1993; Koenig, George, and Schneider, 1994; Butler, Lewis, and Sunderland, 1991, p. 116). It is also true, however, that many of those in nursing homes are especially afflicted with at least one type of mental disorder (Wykle and Musil, 1993), and that some of them have more than one such problem (Tariot, Podgorski, Blazina, and Leibovici, 1993). Also, while there are fewer incidences of such mental problems as depression, anxiety, schizophrenia, phobias, or substance abuse (Ferrini and Ferrini, 1993, p. 241; Wykle and Musil, 1993), they experience severe cognitive impairment much more frequently than younger adults (Wykle and Musil, 1993; Ferrini and Ferrini, 1993, p. 241). Part of the problem regarding mental disorders among older people is that they are much less likely to seek and receive professional help to deal with their problems. Wykle and Musil report, for example, that while estimates indicate that at least 7.8 percent of them need professional help, only 2.5 percent ever get it (Wykle and Musil, 1993). Some (2.4 percent) turn to their physicians, but that still leaves many without the help they need. Similarly, Butler and his colleagues report that from 15 to 25 percent suffer from symptoms of mental illness to some degree, but only 4 percent of patients who receive treatments are elderly (Butler, Lewis, and Sunderland, 1991, p. 116).

Older people today, just as those who are younger, suffer from a variety of mental disorders, but the three problems that plague them the most are cognitive impairments (discussed earlier), depression, and substance abuse (particularly in the form of alcoholism). The extent that older people suffer from such chronic mental disorders as schizophrenia, for example, is very minimal—only about one percent of those over 65—and many of them acquired those problems earlier in life and have never been cured (Ferrini and Ferrini, 1993, p. 246). Depression, on the other hand, is considered to be a functional problem and has been found to exist among elderly people, not so much as a disease with organic origins, but primarily as a consequence of the many losses they experience as they age and the stress those losses create for them (Butler, Lewis, and Sunderland, 1991, p. 89; Ferrini and Ferrini, 1993, p. 237; Gurian and Goisman, 1993; Kahana, Stange, and Kahana, 1993).

The types of losses that seem to be the most stressful to elderly persons and are the most apt to make them depressed include declining finances, death of loved ones (especially one's spouse), declining physical and mental capabilities, the acquisition of chronic diseases, and the decreasing ability to live and act independently (Ellison, 1994; George, 1993; Evans, Buckwalter, and Fulmer, 1993). Among the "very old," Roberts, Dunkle and Haug found that the two most frequent and troubling life events were the illness and subsequent death of the significant others in their lives and the recent physical changes they had experienced (Roberts, Dunkle, and Haug, 1994). Matt and Dean found, in fact, that the loss of friends and stress have a vicious-cycle relationship among the very old. As they put it, "the old-old are particularly vulnerable to psychological distress when losing friend support, and are vulnerable to losing friend support when experiencing psychological distress" (Matt and Dean, 1993).

The loss of friends and loved ones, then, is not merely one of the many losses that older persons typically face. Even more importantly, it is somewhat of a key to how they respond to the other relatively permanent losses they are forced to endure, such as physical impairments (Hughs, DeMallie, and Blazer, 1993). This is a particular problem on the part of those who sustain multiple losses over a short time period (Ferrini and Ferrini, 1993, p. 241), and among those in nursing homes (Ferrini and Ferrini, 1993, p. 241). The basic problems with the nursing home environment, in this regard, are that "the nursing home often seeks 'medical solutions' to 'socialpsychological problems,'" and that "the staff in nursing homes are often inadequately prepared to respond to residents' mental health needs" (Evans, Buckwalter, and Fulmer, 1993). The lack of social support is apparently what seems to make elderly men more vulnerable to psychological distress than elderly women (Matt and Dean, 1993).

Drug abuse in general and alcoholism in particular are increasingly also seen as serious mental disorders among older people. Ferrini and Ferrini, as well as Dunlop, report that the major substance abuse problem for the elderly is a combination of the overuse of prescription drugs, such as tranquilizers, and alcohol (Ferrini and Ferrini, 1993, p. 248; Dunlop, 1992). That is true, not only because both types of those drug-related behaviors are in fact abuses and can lead to addiction problems. In addition, when both types of drugs are concurrently and excessively used by elderly individuals, serious physical and psychological complications almost invariably develop. As Lamy explains, it is possible that any or a number of the following problems could result: loss of a sense of reality; loss of correct self-judgment; a psychiatric syndrome, including fear and depression; deficiencies in attention, memory, or other cognitive functions; and finally conflict in family relations. His very apt conclusion is that, "alcohol misuse and abuse present a clear danger to older people, particularly those with multiple diseases, whether prescription or non-prescription and medications" (Lamy, 1988).

Alcohol abuse and alcoholism specifically, is defined by some as deviant behavior. When that is the case, special attention is paid to elderly alcoholic men on skid row. Atchley reports that these kinds of people are largely ignored and left alone by authorities, as long as they do not bother the public on the streets (Atchley, 1991, pp. 319–20). That perspective on the problem means that how alcohol use among the aged may be somehow related to mental problems is totally ignored. Since they cause few social disturbances, they tend to be "out of sight and out of mind." Thus, their real problems are never addressed. Mostly, the literature on alcohol abuse among the aged, though, defines it as a major health problem, and particularly as a mental health problem. Drinking, particularly alcoholism, has been found to be less frequent among the elderly than younger people (Ferrini and Ferrini, 1993, pp. 248–49; Alexander and Duff, 1988). Speculations are that there is less alcohol abuse with age for two basic reasons: (1) Many of the heavy drinkers of the present cohorts of elderly people have already died or are presently institutionalized, and (2) some elderly may choose to drink less to avoid health problems that could result from it (Ferrini and Ferrini, 1993, p. 249). Another obvious reason is that an increasing percentage of each cohort of elderly people are women, the older they become. By far fewer women than men drink and become alcoholic (Ferrini and Ferrini, 1993, pp. 248–49; Butler, Lewis, and Sunderland, 1991, p. 209; Alexander and Duff, 1988).

There has been a great deal of dialogue about the possible causes of alcoholism. Butler and his colleagues categorize the theories between those that contend genetics is the determining factor and those that place the emphasis on learned behavior, particularly as individuals try to adapt to such problems as psychological stress (Butler, Lewis, and Sunderland, 1991, p. 210). The latter type of theory would seem to best explain alcoholism among the aged. It has been found, for example, that a substantial number of elderly who engage in alcohol abuse fit into the "late-life onset" category. That is, they began heavy drinking as older adults, largely in reaction to such experiences as the loss of spouse, retirement, moving, loss of income, impaired health, pain, loneliness, boredom, and/or depression (Schonfeld and Dupree, 1992; Butler, Lewis, and Sunderland, 1991, p. 211). Schonfeld and Dupree compared the drinking patterns of the "late-life onset" drinkers with those who fit into the "early onset" group (those who had begun heavy drinking earlier in life) and found them to be quite similar. Both groups tended to drink alone at home, in response to such negative emotional states as sadness, loneliness, boredom, and depression. Most were widowed or divorced, and had minimal social support networks with which to relate (Schonfeld and Dupree, 1992). It would seem, then, that heavy drinking and alcoholism among the aged tend to be mostly related to the many physical and mental health problems they tend to face.

Alexander and Duff, however, found a very different pattern of drinking among those living in retirement communities. They interviewed a random sample of 260 residents in three relatively large retirement communities with regard to their drinking patterns. In contrast to what other studies have shown, they found that those who were the most isolated were the least likely to drink heavily. The more active respondents were, the more likely they were to be heavy drinkers and to have increased the amount of drinking they were doing since moving to that community. There were people who did solitary drinking, but they were among those who also drank socially. These analysts concluded that drinking in those kinds of communities is not done out of the problems residents face without social support networks. Instead, it seems to be something that is promoted as part of the leisure subculture. This is alarming, given the serious consequences to their health that are apparently being ignored (Alexander and Duff, 1988).

How to treat alcohol abuse among the elderly is an important gerontological issue today. The Ferrinis report that older alcoholics are more likely to successfully complete treatments than younger people, when/if they enter programs (Ferrini and Ferrini, 1993, p. 250). Part of the problem, though, is that symptoms are often difficult to identify as necessarily related to alcohol abuse. As they explain, "alcoholism has more subtle manifestations in elders than in younger groups" (Ferrini and Ferrini, 1993, p. 249). Many of the physical signs, such as depression and dementia-like reactions can easily be attributed to other things. Dunlop has reported on a treatment program for elderly alcoholics at a hospital in Portland, Oregon. It has a very comprehensive schedule of events beginning with an ambitious effort at outreach and assessment, and including educational and group counseling components. It concludes with outpatient group counseling on a weekly basis for an extended period of time. Still another part of the program is the expectation that participants will attend Alcoholics Anonymous (AA) sessions at least once per week for the duration of their involvement in the program. The success of this program is not at all clear. The only evaluative report made consisted of positive comments made by a few of the participants (Dunlop, 1992). What success it has could be due to participants' involvement in AA. Butler and his colleagues state that, overall, AA "has an impressive record of achieving sobriety," with 63,000 active groups around the world, and as many as two million current members (Butler, Lewis, and Sunderland, 1991, p. 212).

The problem of mental disorders in its numerous forms among the elderly is at present serious enough, but it is projected to reach crisis proportions in the future. As Koenig and his colleagues point out, by the year 2020 the "baby boom" generation will become 65 and take their place in the older population. That will mean that the size of that part of the population will increase dramatically. In addition, and even more importantly, the rate of mental disorders among them will almost certainly also increase since, as Table 12–2 indicates, they already have a much higher incidence of those kinds of psychological problems (Koenig, George, and Schneider, 1994). What will also feed the seriousness of this crisis are the reimbursement cutback trends in Medicare and private health insurance programs. For example, Medicare will now approve only $68 per 50 minute therapy session with psychologists and psychiatrists, for which they would typically receive at least $110 from private patients (Koenig, George, and Schneider, 1994). These authors speculate about possible solutions to this impending crisis, and conclude that prevention programs would perhaps be the best approach. Specifically, they point to an already existing and growing church-sponsored interdenominational program, entitled "Shepherd Centers." These centers are organized and administered by the elderly themselves and emphasize education, self-help support groups, and recreation (Koenig, George, and Schneider, 1994).

DEVELOPMENT OF HEALTH CARE SYSTEMS

Few would argue with the observation that an elaborate and effective health care system has been put in place in this country. It is also true that important components of that system have been targeted toward the aged. The health of millions of people has been preserved even into old age, and many lives have been saved as a direct result of the application of our system of health care. Some would argue that it is a system that is second to none in the world in terms of the benefits it offers, especially to the older population.

Despite its many, and often spectacular, accomplishments, however, some analysts are challenging such an optimistic assessment of the U.S. health care system today. Critics contend that it has serious limitations in terms of the care it provides those of all ages and older people in particular.

In order to gain a true picture of our health care system, we must analyze it from at least three perspectives: (1) the economic perspective, (2) the political perspective, and (3) the medical perspective. As we will see, it has been

TABLE 12-2   **Rates of Major Psychiatric Disorders among Community-Dwelling Adults (1980–81)**

	AGE			
PSYCHIATRIC DISORDER	18–24 %	25–44 %	45–64 %	65+ %
Alcohol abuse/dependence	4.1	3.6	2.1	0.9
Drug abuse/dependence	3.5	1.5	0.1	0.0
Major depression	2.2	3.0	2.0	0.7
Dysthymia	2.2	4.0	3.8	1.8
Anxiety disorders	7.7	8.3	6.6	5.5

SOURCE: Harold G. Koenig, Linda K. George, and Robert Schneider, "Mental Health Care for Older Adults in the Year 2020: A Dangerous and Avoided Topic," *The Gerontologist*, 34, no. 5 (October 1994), 674–79, Table 1.

developed not merely to provide consumers with the best medical care available, but also to comply with political and economic demands.

It is somewhat ironic and puzzling that health care in the United States has always been offered from an economic as well as from a medical basis. While other service-providing institutions, such as education, law enforcement, and welfare, have operated on the basis of public support, health care has largely functioned on the basis of private enterprise. Individual practitioners and organizations in the system (physicians, hospitals, and so on) have generally been motivated by profit.

In the era of our history when the United States was essentially an agrarian society, the health care system was rather simple. Families served as the basic economic production unit and maintaining health was largely a family concern. Ailments were treated with home remedies, and families were responsible for the care of their older members. To the extent that they were available, physician and hospital services were utilized in cases of emergency situations on a fee-for-services basis.

As the United States became industrialized and urbanized, health maintenance was not only an individual and family concern. Employers also became increasingly dependent upon a healthy work force in order to compete in the marketplace. They therefore began to work to mold the health care system to meet their needs. According to Estes and her colleagues, those in the private sector have even influenced the way in which health is defined today. They point out that although it would be in an individual's best interest to define health in terms of their ability to control their own destiny, those concerned about economics have influenced it to be defined in functional terms, or in terms of individuals' capacities to produce (Estes and others, 1984, pp. 17–18). Maintaining people's physical and mental functional capabilities has thus become one of the main goals of the modern health care system, with little or no attention being paid to the health needs as individual consumers might define them.

The health care system that has emerged as a result of the political influences of the medical profession and industry has been labeled a "medical industrial complex" (Relman, 1987). Two major emphases have characterized this system. First, care is provided in the context of what has been called the "medical-engineering model of health and illness," or the medical model. This model focuses almost exclusively on the biological causes of diseases and functional disability. Ignored is the relationship between the social, environmental, and intellectual aspects of life (Estes and others, 1984, p. 18; Kart, Metress, and Metress, 1992, pp. 302–5).

The second characteristic of the modern health care system is the economic commercialization of health care. A number of analysts contend that health care has moved from the simple fee-for-services system of the past to a system that is controlled primarily by business and government policies for the purpose of making money. Iglehart accuses business and government of beginning "to look at medical care as more nearly an economic product than a social good" (Iglehart, 1982). Carlson points out that allocations for purposes of health care are almost exclusively allocated for "a medical care system focused on the agents of disease." He believes that the decisions for these kinds of allocations are made "far more for political, social, and economic reasons than therapeutic ones" (Carlson, 1983).

The presently existing health care system is the result of negotiations that have been carried out in the political arena since World War II. Those negotiations were rife with conflict between those representing the medical community and those advocating for a publicly supported national health care system. President Truman and his administration fought especially hard for the passage of national health care in the 1940s. One of his biographers, Monte Poen, has reported that Truman's motivation was as much personal as it was political. As a young man he was at times unable to get adequate health care and could not go to West Point because of health reasons. He believed strongly in preventive health care, and referred to medical people and Republicans who opposed a national health program as uncaring "high hats" (Poen, 1982). The fear on the part of many was that a national, publicly supported and administered health care program, as most European countries had adopted, would have taken the control of health care away from those in the medical profession. The legislation that resulted not only allowed those in the medical profession to continue to define and control health care, but also helped it to become a lucrative business enterprise. The emergent system clearly serves both the medical and business interests in a collaborative way.

As explained above, the basic orientation of the medical model of health has been on the control and cure of disease. Of central importance to that orientation are hospitals, where the latest medical technology is available and health care professionals are able to control the treatment process. This concept of health care was greatly affirmed and supported by the federal government with the passage of the Hill-Burton Hospital Survey and Construction Act of 1946. Substantial subsidies were provided to the private sector for the construction of hospitals and nursing homes across the country (Eustis, Greenburg, and Patten, 1984, pp. 17–18). The act also provided the major impetus for the establishment of health care as a private business enterprise (Estes and others, 1984, pp. 18, 60.) The medical model has also been boosted by the biomedical research financed through federal grants from the National Institutes of Health; such research has concentrated almost exclusively on what makes people sick rather than why they may remain healthy (Carlson, 1983).

Due to the effective lobbying efforts of those in the medical professions, especially members of the American Medical Association, the goal of labor and others to form a publicly supported and administered national health care system was never realized. Instead, private health insurance companies were created to provide financial services to unions and businesses for compulsory health care coverage for their workers. Services were provided by established health care systems. Thus, still another health-related business enterprise was created that provided substantial support to modern medicine and the professional people in it.

As the above discussion indicates, the primary focus of the health care system that emerged in the United States following World War II was on those in the work force. It was in the best interest of both business and labor that industrial workers remain as physically and mentally functional as possible. Two overlapping segments of the American population, both of which were growing in numbers and political importance, were left out, however. The poor and the aged had little or no promise of adequate health care coverage. In the War on Poverty era of the 1950s and 1960s, though, a great deal of sentiment existed to provide needed services to both of those populations. Politicians favoring a national health care system pushed for special health care legislation for the poor and the aged as a first step toward national health care for everyone. Consequently the 1965 revisions of Social Security included Medicaid for the poor and Medicare for the aged.

Both of these pieces of legislation were vehemently opposed by those in the medical profession. Ironically, however, they, more than any other health-related entities, have helped to create a health care system that serves the interests of both business and professional medicine. Both programs are designed to pay for the health care services according to funding criteria set by the government. Once again, the actual provision of services is left to health professionals, who get reimbursed by annual allocations made for the programs.

Medicare is a national health insurance program for Americans 65 years of age and older. The bias toward workers in building a system of health care, discussed earlier, is also demonstrated in this law. Eligibility to receive benefits is limited to participants in the Social Security retirement program. Others who are 65 and over must pay monthly premiums in order to participate. It was not designed as a welfare program but as an "earned right" for years of productive work (Estes and others, 1984, p. 50). As such, it also serves as an added incentive for individuals to retire and leave the work force, at least when they reach the age of 65.

The Medicare program is divided into two parts, one compulsory and the other voluntary. Part A, the compulsory component, is the hospital insurance program, the benefits of which are paid for out of a Social Security Administration fund created for that purpose out of worker payroll taxes. The amount of hospital costs that are covered under Part A, however, are limited by a designated "deductible," which participants, themselves, must pay for each incident of hospital care before they are allowed to receive Medicare coverage.

Part B is a supplementary medical insurance program to cover 80 percent of physicians' fees and certain other, designated, out-of-hospital medical costs. This part of the Medicare program is also subject to an annual "deductible," which participants themselves must pay. This part of the program is voluntary and is financed by monthly premiums that participants must pay.

Medicaid provides funds to states to help them cover the health care costs of their poor, many of whom are also elderly. Individual states have the option to participate in the program or not. If they choose to participate, they must provide a certain percentage of the program costs with state funds, based on their per capita income levels. Within federal guidelines, states may set eligibility standards and determine how the money will be spent. For example, they may decide to include or exclude coverage of the medical expenses of the "medically needy" elderly—those whose incomes do not qualify them for other welfare benefits (110 percent of poverty as of 1991 and 120 percent of poverty beginning in 1995). They are, however, required to use their Medicaid funds to pay for all Medicare premiums, copayments, and deductibles for Medicare beneficiaries in their state who are below the poverty line. It is up to participant states to administer this program within their borders with consideration given to those kinds of freedoms and restrictions. Needless to say, coverage under Medicaid varies greatly from state to state. Generally, though, it is the major source of public funding for long-term care in this country (Gelfand, 1993, pp. 59-62) Some support is given to provide in-home medical care, but much more goes for institutional, nursing home care. Gelfand reports that in 1989 as much as 69 percent of Medicaid expenditures for the elderly went to nursing homes (Gelfand, 1993, p. 61). Thus, to a large extent, Medicaid has helped to build the nursing home industry as a sizable business enterprise in the United States.

PRESENT CONDITIONS OF HEALTH AND HEALTH CARE FOR THE AGED

The life expectancy of elderly Americans has increased dramatically in this century and continues to increase. That means that the very old constitute an ever-increasing percentage of the population. It might be expected, therefore, that an increasing percentage of the elderly would be functionally disabled and institutionalized. Instead, the percentage of them who are institutionalized has remained about the same for many years, which means that the health status of elderly Americans has improved, largely as a result of the many forms of medical achievements made in recent years.

Nevertheless, there are serious problems related to the present health care system in this country in terms of the adequacy with which it serves the health needs of the aged. Part of the problem is related to the medical model on which the existing system is based. As previously explained, the medical model basically defines health problems in terms of diseases which require advanced professional knowledge to understand. A further assumption of this model is that the best treatments and corrective measures are those that are technologically developed external to the body. From this perspective, then, the diagnostic and treatment processes for health care must be controlled and administered by medical specialists. Furthermore, for those processes to be effective, they must be carried out in the most technologically advanced settings—namely physicians' offices and hospitals.

As valid as many of the basic assumptions of this model may be, Carlson criticizes it for essentially ignoring other health-related factors. For example, there are aspects of modern life that are unrelated to disease, but that directly effect health. Stresses that are not yet understood or even identified, certain lifestyles and environmental conditions, and the loss of social support groups may all directly affect health. Yet they receive little or no attention in either medical research or practice (Carlson, 1983). Kart and his colleagues make the point that medical professionals also tend to concentrate on just one condition or dysfunction, while elderly clients almost always have multiple conditions that contribute to the health problems they are experiencing. In addition these authors challenge the claim of objectivity that health care professionals tend to make in making diagnoses and prescribing treatments to older patients. Instead, they conclude that "there is considerable evidence that such objectivity is a questionable assumption underlying the medical model" (Kart, Metress, and Metress, 1992, p. 302).

Health Care as Creating Dependency

Equally as severe a criticism that can be leveled against the medical model is that it tends to create and foster dependency among the client populations. To be sure, this is not serious when acute problems, typical of younger people, are being diagnosed and treated. In that case the dependency period is short and it tends to be reassuring to clients that competent professionals are diagnosing and treating the problem. For those with chronic problems for which there are few, if any, promises of cure, however, dependencies tend to become long term and even permanent and often lead to a sense of hopelessness for elderly clients.

It might seem that the great advancements in spectacular, lifesaving technology would represent renewed hope. In fact, that kind of technology often has precisely the opposite effect. For many, technology represents the ultimate form of dependency and indignity. Increasing numbers, in fact, are willing to die rather than experience the kinds of indignities that often result from lifesaving technologies.

Medical sociologists have analyzed some of the negative effects of the sense of dependency that elderly people with chronic problems tend to experience. These analysts have long recognized a quite well-established behavior pattern related to acute illness, which they have identified as the "sick role" (Mechanic, 1978, pp. 84–89; Cokerham, 1986, pp. 127–48; Kart, Metress, and Metress, 1992, pp. 61–62). This is a socially sanctioned set of behaviors typical of those who recognize some kind of physical or mental problem. As originally conceptualized, the sick role included a set of four social norms: (1) sick persons are exempt from their "normal" roles while they are sick, relative to the seriousness and length of the illness; (2) they are not responsible for their sick conditions and need help to get well; (3) they will do all they can to get well as soon as possible; and (4) they will seek help from and cooperate with medical professionals (Weiss and Lonnquist, 1994, p. 134). In part, this was seen as a form of social control to keep the members of a society as functional and productive as possible, with physicians serving as the basic agents of control by controlling and administering the diagnostic and treatment processes related to health care (Cokerham, 1986, pp. 130–36). Assuming the sick role helps to alleviate the psychological stress that is often related to illness, though it also constitutes something of a coping response to illness for many people (Mechanic, 1978, pp. 84–89).

However, Cokerham indicates that the sick role concept has been criticized for a number of reasons. Two of those reasons particularly relate to older people. First, it has been pointed out that while it fits acute types of illnesses, it does not fit chronic illnesses. Second, the fact is that by no means all individuals who are thought to be ill are either willing to admit to being ill or to cooperate with their physicians (Cokerham, 1986, pp. 137–40; Weiss and Lonnquist, 1994, p. 135). The point is that, for elderly people with chronic illnesses, taking on the sick role is entirely different than doing so for younger people with acute illnesses. As Hickey puts it, for the elderly, the sick role typically becomes transformed into an "at-risk role" (Hickey, 1980, pp. 93–96). The sick role is socially acceptable in the case of acute health problems because these kinds of problems are temporary. The sick-role behavior pattern has become quite clearly institutionalized, with well-established resolutions to the problems. In contrast, chronic problems are long term, behaviors connected to them have not been institutionalized, and there are no resolutions. The basic problem here is, as explained by Kart and his colleagues, that "despite its advances, modern medicine is still incapable of effectively treating most chronic diseases of the type commonly experienced by older adults" (Kart, Metress, and Metress, 1992, p. 62). To take on the sick role on a permanent basis in response to chronic problems is not socially acceptable. Chronic patients tend to receive inconsistent social support from both their families and health practitioners (Hickey, 1980, p. 95). Elderly people with serious chronic problems are therefore said to be socially at risk.

In a study of patients with chronic multiple sclerosis, for example, Stewart and Sullivan discovered a number of negative results stemming from being caught in a relatively permanent sick-role performance. They found (1) a tendency to avoid medical treatments even for other acute ailments, (2) a great deal of conflict between patients and medical professionals, (3) a tendency for patients to reject physicians' diagnoses, and (4) a great deal of emotional stress on the part of patients, which often led to a variety of psychosomatic symptoms (Stewart and Sullivan, 1987). Therefore, instead of being expected to eagerly seek medical help, they could well be expected to avoid seeking help.

Health Care as Failing to Provide Long-Term Care

In addition to the problem of dependency-building, the program designed exclusively for the aged largely fails to cover their most salient health care needs. The Medicare legislation was passed by Congress as a health insurance program specifically to cover the costs of elderly persons' medical needs, over the vehement objections of those in the medical professions. It is, therefore, ironic that, while the professional and economic interests of the medical community were carefully safeguarded, the worst health care problems of older people were not even addressed in the program's structure. Medical professionals were allowed to maintain control over the diagnostic and treatment processes, while the long-term care needs were systematically ignored.

Specifically, while Medicare takes care of acute ailments quite adequately, it barely begins to cover chronic problems. This is clearly illustrated by Part A of the Medicare provisions ("The Medicare 1994 Handbook," 1994, p. 39). Medical coverage for each ailment requiring hospitalization decreases the longer the problem lasts. For the first 60 days of hospitalization, Medicare covers all hospital costs, less the amount of the deductible ($696 in 1994). Then, on the 61st day of hospitalization, elderly patients must begin to pay as much as $174 per day; and on the 91st day, twice that much ($348 per day). If their hospitalization lasts beyond 150 days, they are forced to bear the total cost of their care for the duration of their hospitalization. Most elderly long-term patients are transferred from hospitals to skilled nursing homes as soon as possible if they need institutional care beyond 60 days. The problem with this, though, is that Medicare will support their stay in nursing homes for even fewer days than in hospitals. They are supported fully for only the first 20 days in skilled nursing facilities. For 80 days after that, they are individually charged as much as $87 per day, and they must cover the total costs of their care beyond 100 days.

Medicare will now fully support, on an indefinite basis, whatever medical services are needed among homebound elderly long-term patients. It will not cover any of the support services these people typically need in order for them to live at home, however. The program simply is not designed to meet the long-term care needs of the many elderly who suffer from chronic diseases. A bill to provide for the long-term care needs of the aged was voted down by Congress in June 1988.

Health Care as Profit Oriented

Another part of the problem related to the health care system on which elderly Americans must depend is an economic one. As we have seen, the system has been developed to foster profit-making businesses that are expected to provide the needed health benefits. As Estes and colleagues put it, "The goals of the health service industry are not only to improve the health status of the population and to protect a plurality of vested interests, but also, and more importantly, to strengthen and preserve the private sector in different ways" (Estes and others, 1984, pp. 61–62).

From a business perspective, those services that require the most advanced scientific technology and professional knowledge legitimize the highest charges and are, therefore, the most profitable. Therefore, if we insist that our health care system operate from a private-sector, business-oriented model, we have to expect that it will follow those health care procedures that will be the most profitable. It should not be surprising when businesses indeed act like businesses. Medical research and practice have focused on increasingly sophisticated, technological, lifesaving techniques, not merely to advance medicine and save lives, but to make more money. A point in all of this that many in the medical profession choose to ignore is that the medical services that cost the most serve only an extremely small minority, and the extent to which the quality of even their lives is improved is seriously being questioned today.

The result of this approach to health care has been an enormous escalation of the costs of health care in recent years. Costs have increased at such an accelerated rate that many in government have become alarmed that Medicare and Medicaid will be unable to bear the costs of supporting the elderly to the extent that they have in the past. Cost-cutting measures are being sought for both programs today.

One way of cutting costs in recent years is to turn to home health, on the assumption that it will be cheaper to provide services to people in their own homes than in expensive institutions. The accuracy of this assumption has not yet been established, but it is noteworthy that, for home health to gain Medicare approval, it must be delivered by a professional "participating home health agency" ("The Medicare 1994 Handbook," 1994, p. 18). Increasing numbers of such agencies are also profit-making businesses.

Another clear trend in the Medicare program is to shift more and more of the costs to individual clients who are eligible for coverage under that program. One method that has been used has been to raise the deductible amount under Part A, which represents the amount elderly patients must pay out of their own pockets, each time they are hospitalized. As Figure 12–2 shows, that amount has increased by 209 percent since 1965, and as much as 206 percent during the nine-year period between 1979 and 1988.

Still another cost-cutting measure has been the development, under Medicare, of *diagnostic-related groups* (DRGs). Under this policy, hospitals are reimbursed for services by Medicare, not on the basis of "reasonable costs" (as

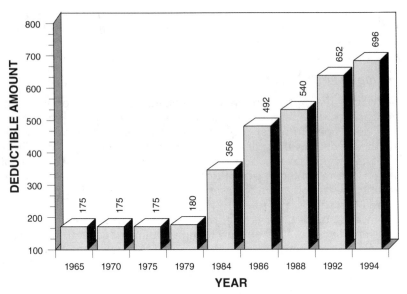

FIGURE 12-2 Increase in Medicare, Part A, Deductible, 1965–1994 (Source: Compiled from publications from Health Care Financing Administration, U.S. Department of Health and Human Services.)

they were before), but on the basis of flat fees established by the government for each type of service. In cases in which allowable fees do not cover the actual costs, hospitals have been expected to absorb the difference. Critics of this approach contend that the policy has simply invited hospitals to discharge patients prematurely and endanger their lives (Dolenc and Dougherty, 1985).

The cost of all forms of health care is becoming prohibitively high for increasing numbers of elderly Americans, particularly for those with debilitating chronic conditions. Coverage of institutionalized care on an extended long-term basis is available only under Medicaid to those living in poverty. Consequently, many aged who require full-time skilled care quickly use up what financial resources they have and are forced into poverty in order to get the care they need. This situation compounds their condition of dependency. Sometimes almost overnight they move from a situation of relatively secure independence into a permanent condition of both financial and physical dependency. Supplemental, private, long-term care insurance policies are available to guard against this type of eventuality, but most of them have a number of exclusions and many elderly simply cannot afford the high monthly premiums (Weiner, Ehrenworth, and Spence, 1987). One study indicates, for example, that only about 50 percent of those 65 and over can afford to insure their health with private programs. Many of them can only do it if they spend their assets (Cohen, 1987).

The health care system that has unfolded in the United States during the post-World War II years has served both the medical community and the business world well. Many profitable private-sector businesses have been created and sustained from the expenditure of public funds. Likewise, the program has continued to allow medical professionals to control both the definition and practice of health care. This point is illustrated by the "peer review organizations" under Medicare. Each state has one of them. They decide whether a given individually requested care "is reasonable, necessary, and provided in the most appropriate setting" and also whether it "meets the standards of quality generally accepted by the medical profession." These organizations are made up entirely of "practicing doctors and other health care professionals" ("The Medicare 1994 Handbook," 1994, p. 3). The existing system has also supplied physicians, hospitals, and nursing homes with an ever-increasing and virtually certain client constituency. At the same time, however, the existing system has failed to serve the elderly population either adequately or appropriately. It has failed to address the most prevalent health problems of older people and has tended to place them into situations of permanent dependency.

Health Care Reform Attempt

The Clinton Administration came into office in 1993 promising to reform the health care system in the United States. Their basic goals in this effort were to (1) provide universal health care coverage, so that all American citizens would have access to the health care they needed, and (2) cut the ever-increasing costs of health care. In November they presented the Health Security Act to Congress as the "Clinton Plan" of how these goals could best be accomplished. Subsequently, as the congressional debate on health care reform proceeded, a number of other plans were submitted, most of which were alternatives to, changes, and/or compromises of the "Clinton Plan." It was that plan, however, that prompted the increasingly heated debate that took place not only in Congress but in the media and especially on the part of such special interest groups as the private health care insurance industry and the American Association of Retired People. President Clinton's hope was to have a comprehensive health care plan with universal coverage enacted sometime in 1994. Obviously, that was not accomplished, and, given the extremely contentious political situation that followed, there was and remains very little possibility that any kind of comprehensive and cost containment reform would be enacted any time soon. However, understanding some of the basic features of the Clinton proposal provides some important insights about the present state of health care in this country and especially how it applies to aging today.

In essence, the Clinton Administration proposed a dual rather than a single health care support system—one to serve the elderly and the other to serve the rest on the population. Under that plan all elderly people would be covered by keeping Medicare pretty much intact as it is (Health Security Act, 1993, p. 14), adding insurance coverage for prescription drugs (Health Security Act, 1993, pp. 334–80). Medicaid, which now provides the elderly poor with long-term care provisions would have been canceled (Health Security Act, 1993, pp. 786–88), and long-term care coverage for all elderly would have been limited to that which now exists in the Medicare program (Gerety, 1994). Health care for everyone else would be provided by forming alliances to which all individuals (with a few exceptions) would belong based largely on where they lived and/or where they worked (Health Security Act, 1993, pp. 115–221). For example, those employed by a number of small businesses along with the unemployed in a given area would form an alliance. Representatives of each alliance would collectively negotiate with private health insurance companies for the best coverage they could get at the cheapest cost possible, much as many large employers and labor unions already do on behalf of their employees and members. The idea behind this approach was "managed competition," which would cut the costs of health care by forcing health insurance companies to compete with each other for contracts with large alliances. All employers would have been required to pay the health insurance premiums for all of their employees (called the "employer mandate"), and the government would have subsidized those who were unemployed (Health Security Act, 1993, pp. 298–314).

Even though the elderly generally supported the efforts of the Clinton Administration to reform health care in the United States, gerontologists have been critical of the Health Security Act approach in terms of specific ways that elderly people would probably be effected. For one thing, as Gerety has stated, "No provisions are made in the Clinton plan or any other plan under serious consideration in Congress to include institutional long-term care as an integral part of a new health care system" (Gerety, 1994). In addition, Moon discusses what she sees as "perceived inequities" (Moon, 1994). Specifically, she cites a weakness of Medicare having to do with its cost sharing structure. As she explains it, Medicare "beneficiaries now pay a hospital deductible of $696 for each 'spell of illness' and a $100 deductible for physician and ambulatory services. This compared to a $200 deductible for all services under the Clinton proposal" for others. Thus, individuals turning 65 and retiring, many with a loss of income, would be faced with a substantial increase in what they themselves would have to pay for health care, in terms of deductibles alone (Moon, 1994). This is just one illustration of how most of the reform plans proposed to partly pay for their plans by "savings" in the Medicare program.

HEALTH AND HEALTH CARE IN OTHER CULTURES

Cultures differ greatly in their definitions of health and illness, the health status of their aged, and the types of health care systems they have. With more and more cross-cultural interactions regarding matters of health and health care, however, cross-cultural accommodations are beginning to be made.

How health is defined is basic to other differences that exist between cultures. In that respect, societies might be divided between those that emphasize "traditional" and those that emphasize "modern" definitions of health. A number of societies are influenced by a combination of both definitions. As discussed above, the modern medical model most basically defines both physical and mental health from the perspective of diseases. While other environmental factors, such as accidents and stress, can impede one's physical and mental conditions, the most essential definition of health is the absence, or at least the effective treatment, of disease. As we have seen, this model has largely determined how individuals' health conditions are assessed and how they will be treated in the United States. The influence of this perspective is spreading into other parts of the world as well.

Nevertheless, traditional definitions still exist and are even dominant in some societies. Indications are that there may also be a resurgence of this type of definition throughout the world. While traditional definitions differ somewhat from culture to culture, they all tend to define health from what has come to be called a *holistic* approach (Sobel, 1979, pp. 15–19). Health is seen as much more than the process of the body's being invaded by harmful and destructive matter from the outside. Instead, it is a matter of how the total body functions in a state of equilibrium and harmoniously relates to its environment. One's state of health, therefore, cannot be determined merely by diagnosing the presence or absence of specified diseases, but more adequately by assessing all of the elements of life (social, psychological, economic, political, spiritual, as well as biological and mental).

This essentially captures the meaning of health for the people of two separate and quite different cultures that we will examine here: the Navajos and the Chinese. To the Navajo people, health has a distinct spiritual or religious connotation. Their traditional religious belief is that they as humans have emerged out of the earth and that their health is dependent upon living close to and in constant harmony with the earth. Being ill means being out of harmony with nature as a whole. Treatment is therefore placed in the hands of medicine men, who are also religious practitioners. Their job is to restore individuals to a proper state of harmony with the natural environment through ceremonies that symbolize that process. As Sandner discovered, those who are believers are often, indeed, cured of their ailments (Sandner, 1979), although there is little empirical evidence to indicate the extent that process is effective or which kinds of illnesses it best serves. Limited as this may seem to us as an effective healing process, it nevertheless focuses our attention on at least two important elements of life obviously important to health and well-being: the spiritual component of life and our relationship to the rest of nature. Traditional medicine is especially important to elderly Navajos who are still oriented to the traditional culture.

Modern medicine is also very prevalent in the Navajo nation, provided by the Indian Health Service, an agency of the U.S. federal government. Therefore, in essence, they have two quite separate health care systems. Many elderly Navajos use both systems, and yet there are only minimal attempts to establish working relationships between the two systems, and little has been done to discover a way in which they may be compatible or complimentary. Many still go to medicine men, not only because they believe in them but also because they are much more immediately accessible. This would particularly be true of the elderly who live in isolated areas. In contrast to the rest of the Americans, Navajos living on the reservation (as well as all native American tribes in the United States) enjoy health care that is provided through a publicly supported system. Health care provided by the Indian Health Service without charge to individuals is part of the agreements made with Indian tribes in treaties made between them and the U.S. government.

Provision of health services needed by elderly Navajos is basically ignored by Indian Health Services, however. That agency does not provide for long-term care, for example. In an attempt to provide for that special need among their elderly people, therefore, the tribal government has opted for a system of care similar to that in the rest of the country. In part, they have contracted with private nursing homes off the reservation to provide the skilled care needed by some of their aged. They have also contracted with a private company to build and operate three nursing homes on the reservation. This kind of program is even more devastating to the Navajo aged than it is to white Americans. It creates the same type of dependency in their daily lives. In addition, it is much more culturally incompatible to them than for other Americans. It removes them from their extended families, upon whom they have traditionally depended for their security. It also separates them from the land that is culturally vital to their sense of well-being.

Two special programs have recently been developed under tribal sponsorship to provide alternatives to institutionalization for those with long-term care needs. One is a home health program and the other is a group home health program in which those in temporary need of continuous care may live for a limited time. Neither of these programs has been developed across the reservation, however. Many Navajo elderly long-term care patients still become institutionalized either on or off the reservation. (This discussion of the Navajo health care systems is based on observation by the author during over 10 years of involvement with the Navajo Office on Aging at Window Rock, Arizona.)

In no other place in the world today is traditional medicine more alive than in the People's Republic of China. It is not based on superstition or ancient religious beliefs, as is often supposed, but on a well-developed theory of natural phenomena. Health is defined in terms of how the human body is structured and is affected by the forces of the natural environment, including the whole cosmos (Porkert, 1979).

The theory on which traditional Chinese medicine is based says that all natural phenomena are composed of and function in terms of opposite forces: *yin*, which is basically a positive force, and *yang*, which is basically a negative force. All of nature is made up of and subject to these forces. According to this theory, the human body is divided into identifiable functions and has an elaborate system of conduits, along which energy moves throughout the body, with sensitivity points along those conduits.

Humans can be negatively as well as positively affected by the natural forces around or within them. The most appropriate treatments for mental or physical problems, therefore, are those that come from nature itself and that focus on the sensitivity points of the body. Medicines used consist of carefully selected herbs. Two treatments widely used in Chinese traditional medicine are massage and acupuncture. Many in Western medicine have very little respect for Chinese medicine because they contend it has no established scientific basis. Porkert disagrees, noting that, "the traditional medical practices of Chinese medicine continue to stand up remarkably well in the diagnosis and treatment of certain types of disease" (Porkert, 1979). In fact, he suggests that it may offer better rational diagnoses and therapies than Western medicine for some functional diseases for which the record of effective treatment in the West is poor. It is noteworthy that the Chinese elderly prefer the treatments of traditional medicine for chronic ailments.

Western medicine has also made its way to the People's Republic of China and is now practiced widely there. The two types of approaches to medicine, according to Porkert, are potentially not only compatible but complimentary (Porkert, 1979). Western medicine tends to be more effective with acute diseases, for example. Yet, the practitioners of the two approaches have little recognition or respect for each other. In some places in China they are not even practiced in the same hospitals. Also, the diagnoses of some problems that have been identified in one are changed to fit the cultural definitions of the other, and the practices originated in one are given different rationales before they are used in the other. On the one hand, for example, Kleinman found that the emotional problem called neurasthenia has been found to be very prevalent in China today but has been diagnosed as a physical disease there (Kleinman, 1986). On the other hand, Wolfe reports that before medical doctors would approve the practice of acupuncture in the United States, they had to find some logical scientific explanation for it, even though it has clearly been an effective treatment in China for centuries (Wolfe, 1987). There is one exception to the lack of coordination between the two models. Acupuncture is now used by many surgeons in China to provide anesthesia.

Until very recently, the health care system in the People's Republic of China differed from the system in the United States in three basic ways: (1) the manner in which it is financially supported, (2) the kinds of care that were administered, and (3) how and to whom it was delivered. Improving and maintaining the health of all Chinese citizens, regardless of age, was a very high priority of the Communist government (Lewis, 1982). Health care became established under a system of public support soon after the People's Republic of China was founded in 1949. A few years later it was stipulated as a right for elderly people in the "five guarantees" promised to them in the national constitution ("Growing Old in China," 1981).

This does not mean that a national health care system was established and funded by the national government. Neither did it mean that all citizens enjoyed equal coverage. The national government provided health care to those who fought in the revolution and those who worked for the government. Otherwise, the government mandated that local work units build and support their own systems of health care as long as those units existed. The level of health care provided by each brigade or commune depended upon their financial capability.

Nevertheless, in the past some level of health care has been available to all Chinese. Much of the care provided in rural areas was administered by "barefoot doctors," who were somewhat equivalent to paramedics in the United States. Their training was minimal and mostly concentrated on traditional medicine. They also relied to some extent on the knowledge they gained from their experiences caring for their local clients. They were, in fact, often trusted more than better-trained medical people because they had a keener understanding of the local people and the environments in which they live (Li lecture, 1986). Even though health care was not equally available to all Chinese on a daily basis, it was available for those with critical ailments. As Lewis pointed out when universal health care still existed in that country, "If the ailment is complicated, confusing, or requires more sophisticated treatment, the person is sent on to the next level of care" (Lewis, 1982).

The health care facilities and services themselves have changed very little in the People's Republic of China. Traditional and modern medicine are both still widely practiced and municipal as well as state owned and operated hospitals are readily available, at least in the urban centers. What has changed, as a result of the economic reforms in that country, is how health care for the elderly, as well as others, is financed. They no longer have universally guaranteed health coverage. The government still provides health care for its present and past (retired) employees, but other workers have coverage only if their employers choose to provide it. No program yet exists that requires them to do so. Health care for the unemployed and non-government retired elderly must rely, either on their own resources or the help of their families. Families are still held legally accountable to provide the care their elderly members need. That, however, creates two very serious potential problems. First, their families may not have sufficient resources either. Second, it typically results in a one-way dependency relationship between younger family members and their elderly parents, a situation that very seldom existed in China before now (Caiwei, 1993). In the rural areas, reliance on barefoot doctors is undoubtedly as prevalent, if not more so, than it was in the past.

Geriatrics has not yet been developed as a medical specialty among medical professionals in the People's Republic of China to any degree. Part of the reason for that is that health practitioners have paid much more attention to preventing the onslaught of debilitating ailments than to developing and using lifesaving technology. (Lewis, 1982). Major efforts have been made to overcome the problems of hunger and malnutrition with a great deal of success. Beyond that, regular exercising among the aged is encouraged and has become a part of the way of life of a large percentage of them. It has been estimated by the secretary general of the Chinese National Gerontology Committee, Yu Guanghan, that at least 40 percent of the nation's aged participate daily in organized exercise programs (Guanghan lecture, 1984). The parks in all of the Chinese cities are packed with elderly people doing their exercises every morning. Also, as was noted above, the treatments of Chinese traditional medicine tend to be relatively effective in treating the chronic problems of the aged.

What are the consequences of these quite different emphases on health care in the People's Republic of China compared to the United States? On the one hand, not as many Chinese people live to advanced ages as in the Western industrialized nations. As noted in Chapter 2, the life expectancy in China is somewhat lower than in the United States. On the other hand, as a whole, Chinese elderly people who are fortunate enough to have great longevity appear to be healthier than their counterparts in this country. For example, as Lewis has pointed out, there are few long-term care institutions such as our nursing homes (Lewis, 1982), and it is rare to find any public place in China where the aged are permanently bedridden. There are frail and chronically ill elderly in China, but they tend to remain in their homes and to be cared for by their families until they die. That increasingly places a heavy burden on families, yet it is precisely the kind of situation for which more and more American elderly are advocating.

TRENDS IN HEALTH CARE FOR THE AGED

It is not the purpose here to attempt to predict what health care of the aged will be like in the future, either in terms of specifics or even in terms of general directions. Even if human behavior itself were subject to that kind of prediction, the personal, professional, and political issues involved in health care for the aged are far too complex to warrant such an attempt. Instead, we will simply explore the beginnings of a number of trends that could well influence the future of this vital gerontological issue.

The rising cost of health care in the United States has prompted a number of potentially innovative approaches to improving and maintaining the health of elderly people. For one thing, some attempts are being made at prevention. Some senior citizens' centers and individual volunteers, for example, sponsor exercising programs and conduct health fairs and other types of programs to assess the health status of elderly people and provide opportunities for them to have assessments of various aspects of their health. Valuable as these efforts are, however, they are not mandated by any authoritative agencies and they do not, as yet, seem to represent a major growing trend.

Nutrition programs, on the other hand, are widespread, and have become a central and permanent part of Older American Act programs across the country. These programs typically provide hot, nutritiously approved meals to millions of elderly Americans, including the homebound, on a daily basis. The importance of this emphasis to the maintenance of health, if not the prevention of illness, is recognized by virtually everyone concerned about aging. The social relationships resulting from the meals programs are another valuable benefit that undoubtedly also contributes to the health of the elderly participants.

An emphasis on home health care has been growing in recent years in response to public criticisms of the costs and quality of care in many nursing homes. The basic assumption has been that home health care costs less than institutional care and that the quality of care is as good if not better than that provided in institutions. As previously noted, Medicare now provides for home health coverage, but only for those services that are delivered by health professionals from Medicare-certified home health agencies. These services, of course, represent only a small percentage of those provided in institutions. If the costs of such services as meals, housekeeping, and assistance with personal care were added to the more specifically defined health services, home health care might well be as costly as institutional care. All of these kinds of services are often necessary on a daily basis to enable elderly long-term care patients to remain at home, but housekeeping and personal care assistance are rarely, if ever, provided by home health agencies. In some communities, publicly supported social-service agencies provide some homemaker services to elderly clients, but the amount they are able to provide is limited and often does not meet the need.

The great bulk of care received by elderly people is, in fact, provided by informal caregivers. It has been found that over 80 percent of all care for the aged comes from the elderly persons' own natural support systems (family members, neighbors, and friends) (Cantor, 1983). Most of this kind of care comes from female family members, typically the wives and daughters of those receiving the care. Not surprisingly, the pattern of families caring for their elderly members has been found to be prevalent in such diverse cultural groups as the Navajo tribe in North America (Brown, 1986) and the Japanese. It may be surprising to learn, however, that the commitment to caregiving on the part of American women is as great as among Japanese women (Campbell and Brody, 1985). When it is called for, working daughters provide care to their elderly parents as readily as nonworkers (Brody and Schoonover, 1986).

A great deal of concern has been expressed about "cost containment" of medical expenditures for the aged in the United States in recent years. It has become a political issue among gerontology planners, policy makers, and the aged themselves. There have been two basic responses to the cost containment issue. One has been for the government to set specific amounts that they will reimburse elderly people for each medical service under Medicare and Medicaid. The hope is that hospitals and physicians will charge patients only the amount of the reimbursement figure, but they are not obligated to do so. Insurance companies have begun to follow a similar cost containment policy. If the fees being charged are more than the insurance coverage allows, the elderly patients are obligated to pay the balance. As noted above, some hospitals have been accused of discharging elderly patients prematurely as a way of complying with this policy and ensuring that they still make a profit. Cost containment was a major objective of the Clinton health care reform proposal.

Another response to the cost containment issue has been the formation of health maintenance organizations (HMOs). Those participating in an HMO pay a set annual fee to, and sign a contract with, the organization, which guarantees that all of their health needs for the year will be taken care of by the HMO medical staff. The claim made by HMO staff is that that kind of system cuts costs while making it possible for participants to practice preventive medicine. The rationale is that under this system, physicians have no incentive to perform unneeded medical procedures since they would have to pay for such procedures. Furthermore, checkups are encouraged since they often help to prevent the need for more expensive remediation.

The major problem associated with HMOs, however, is that there is no guarantee that patients who require health care will receive prompt or adequate attention. The legitimacy of that concern was demonstrated in a study in the early 1980s, comparing Medicare-eligible cancer patients who enrolled in HMOs with those who were treated under the fee-for-services system. The data revealed that there was a significantly longer period of time between being diagnosed as having cancer and the beginning of treatment for HMO patients than those not participating in HMOs (Greenwald, 1986). Among a significant number of physicians the profit-making incentive would seem to take some precedence over that of providing care even among patients with the most vital need to be treated. HMOs may indeed cut costs but whether they ensure quality care is in question.

Cost containment efforts will undoubtedly continue, but those efforts are also likely to be scrutinized in terms of the adequacy of the care they provide. It ought to be clear that, as long as a medical industrial complex is allowed to control whatever health care programs we create for the elderly population, cost containment and quality of care will be in continuous tension. With profit as a major reason for providing services, we cannot expect to be able to cut costs without also sacrificing services.

Another trend today is a set of challenges to the prevalence of the medical model of health. Central to that challenge today is the idea that emphasis ought to be placed on holistic medicine. The notion behind this concept is that poor health cannot be explained by a narrow focus on the biological disease processes and specific physiological functions. To get at the problems involved, close attention must be paid to all aspects of people's lives and the environments in which they live. Treatments that are prescribed must also take all aspects of life into account and must consider the relationship between human life and the environment, as much of the cross-cultural data indicate. A change in lifestyle or attitude may be as crucial, or more so, to improved health as taking medicine. As Teegarden, a physician, explains, "Rather than focusing only on the malfunctioning body part, it also explores the broader dimensions of the patient's life—physical, nutritional, environmental, emotional, spiritual, and life-style" (Teegarden, 1985). Teegarden contends that medical practitioners and the public as a whole are moving toward this kind of perspective of health and health care. Indeed, something of a movement is under way to promote the holistic approach to medicine. Heading that movement is the organization called the American Holistic Medical Association.

This movement is not only based on the belief that the holistic model results in better health than the medical model; it also represents a challenge to what is seen as too great a reliance on the medical model. Its proponents basically reject "lifesaving technology" in favor of "health-preserving technology" for elderly patients, for example. On the one hand, the net effect of lifesaving technology has often been to sustain people's lives "in a miserable, unhealthy state." On the other hand, life-preserving technology promises longevity on the basis of "prolonged and productive involvement in family and community affairs ... , and an enduring sense of meaning and purpose of life itself" (Bliss, 1985).

The holistic approach does not deny the validity of the specific practices of the medical approach. Rather, the challenge is to the attitude that the biochemical approach either has all of the answers to existing health problems or that no answers are available. That medical practitioners ought to control all diagnostic and treatment processes is also being challenged. From the holistic perspective other practitioners (such as social workers, religious counselors, nutritionists, and educators) and especially patients themselves and their families have the right to control much of the treatment processes for the restoration and maintenance of health. One does not need an appointment with or a prescription from a physician, for example, to engage in such vital "medicine" as regular physical activity and learn that it improves circulation, helps get rid of toxic substances, and burns off excess body fat (Bliss, 1985).

The basic concepts and tools are readily available to apply the holistic-medicinal model to aging in a very realistic and practical way. Three such concepts, representing steps that can be taken, are particularly important in this effort. The first step in applying holistic medicine to the aged is health assessment. From the holistic perspective, this involves much more than determining which particular ailments the patient may or may not have. Instead, as in the case of the "Older-American Resources Survey" (OARS), developed at Duke University in the early 1970s, their social, mental, economic, and environmental situations, as well as their physical conditions are assessed. In addition, an account is taken of the resources that are already available to them (Hickey, 1980, pp. 73–75).

The second step in applying holistic medicine to the aged is the development of a case management program. This means (1) determining individuals' needs in order to restore and maintain their lives at maximum functional levels, (2) identifying the resources already available to them, and others that are needed, and (3) assigning responsibility to appropriate people in applying resources to the needs. Central to case management is that the elderly persons are the most important players in defining their own needs and taking on as much of the responsibility to help themselves as possible.

The third step in applying the holistic approach to the health of the aged is to base caregiving on the principle of reciprocity or interdependency. The assumption here is that most elderly people with health care needs also possess talents that can potentially be used to benefit others who are younger (for example, retired teachers can serve as tutors to younger students, even from a sick bed). To match young and old in reciprocating helping relationships helps to keep elderly patients in a useful, productive mode that is an important component of a healthy life.

CONCLUSION

As we have seen, the health care system in the United States has been built on the assumption of the medical model, that health basically has to do with the control of the disease processes. It has also been oriented to and controlled by profit-making enterprises. However, holistic medicine is a concept in which increasing numbers of people believe. It represents a growing movement. To some extent it has been and continues to be applied to the health care of the elderly population. Ironically, though, it has not tended to influence the policies that are being set regarding health care for the aged. Medicare and Medicaid legislation, in all of their revisions since 1965, have continued to favor practices prescribed and controlled by those still very much oriented to the medical model.

For an answer to the question of why the medical model continues to dominate policy decisions about health care for the aged, we must turn to the economics and politics involved. Making policy decisions is not so much based on ethical considerations as it is determined by a political process that is very much influenced by the vested interests of those with economic and political power. The truth of the matter is that it is in the best economic interest of both medical professionals and those in the business end of health care for the aged for the medical model to remain dominant. This so-called medical industrial complex constitutes an effective lobby in favor of their own interests.

Innovative ideas and demonstrations about how holistic medicine would improve the health care system indeed provide definitive and rational bases for change. Cross-cultural data also strengthen that rationale. Vital as the new ideas may be for the future well-being of elderly people, however, they will only be translated into actual policy through the political processes. That will necessitate the formation of coalitions of those willing and able to advocate for the kinds of change needed. At present there are few indications that such a coalition is forming. It remains to be seen whether the pressures of such issues as health care costs and dependency among the aged will prompt the necessary political activity to bring the needed changes.

REFERENCES

Alexander, Francesca, and Robert W. Duff, "Drinking in Retirement Communities," *Generations*, 12, no. 4 (Summer 1988), 58–62.

Atchley, Robert C., *Social Forces and Aging: An Introduction to Social Gerontology* (Belmont, Calif.: Wadsworth, 1991).

Bliss, Shepherd, "Enhancing and Prolonging Life," in *The New Holistic Health Handbook: Living Well in a New Age*, eds. Shepherd Bliss, Edward Bauman, Lorin Piper, Armand I. Brint, and Pamela A. Wright (Lexington, Mass.: Stephen Greene Press, 1985), pp. 285–87.

Brody, Elaine M., and Claire B. Schoonover, "Patterns of Parent Care When Adult Daughters Work and When They Do Not," *The Gerontologist*, 26, no. 4 (August 1986), 372–81.

Brown, Arnold S., "Report on Navajo Elderly Abuse," unpublished research report submitted to the Navajo Office on Aging, Window Rock, Ariz., Fall 1986, pp. 14–15, 18.

Brownlee, Shannon, "Alzheimer's: Is There Hope?" in *Annual Editions: Aging*, ed. Harold Cox (Guilford, Conn.: Duskin, 1992), pp. 115–20.

Butler, Robert N., Myrna Lewis, and Trey Sunderland, *Aging and Mental Health: Positive Psychological and Biomedical Approaches* (New York: Macmillan, 1991).

Caiwei, Xiao, China National Committee on Aging, Beijing, China, correspondence with Arnold Brown, December 19, 1993.

Campbell, Ruth, and Elaine M. Brody, "Women's Changing Roles and Help to the Elderly: Attitudes of Women in the United States and Japan," *The Gerontologist*, 25, no. 6 (December 1985), 584–92.

Cantor, Marjorie H., "Strain Among Caregivers: A Study of Experience in the United States," *The Gerontologist*, 23, no. 6 (December 1983), 597–604.

Carlson, Rick, "Health Promotion and Disease Prevention," *Generations*, 7, no. 3 (Spring 1983), 10–12, 72.

Caserta, Michael S., Dale A. Lund, Scott D. Wright, and David E. Redburn, "Caregivers to Dementia Patients: The Utilization of Community Services," *The Gerontologist*, 27, no. 2 (April 1987), 209–14.

Cohen, Marc A., "The Financial Capacity of the Elderly to Insure for Long–Term Care," *The Gerontologist*, 27, no. 4 (August 1987), 494–502.

Cokerham, William C., *Medical Sociology* (Englewood Cliffs, N.J.: Prentice Hall, 1986).

Cotrell, Victoria and Laura Lein, "Awareness and Denial in the Alzheimer's Disease Victim" *Journal of Gerontological Social Work*, 19, no. 3/4 (1993), 115–79.

Dawson, Pam, Donna L. Wells, and Karen Kline, *Enhancing the Abilities of Persons with Alzheimer's and Related Dementias* (New York: Springer, 1993).

Dolenc, Danielle A., and Charles J. Dougherty, "DRGs: the Counterrevolution in Financing Health Care," *Hastings Center Report*, 15, no. 3 (June, 1985), 19–29.

DuBois, Rene, *Man Adapting* (New Haven, Conn.: Yale University Press, 1965).

Dunlop, Jean, "Peer Groups Support Seniors' Fighting Alcohol and Drugs," in *Annual Editions: Aging*, ed. Harold Cox (Guilford, Conn.: Duskin, 1992), pp. 112–14.

Ellison, Christopher G., "Religion, the Life Stress Paradigm, and the Study of Depression," in *Religion in Aging and Health*, ed. Jeffrey S. Levin (Thousand Oaks, Calif.: Sage, 1994), pp. 78–121.

Estes, Carroll, Lenore E. Gerard, Jane S. Zones, and James H. Swans, *Political Economy, Health, and Aging* (Boston: Little, Brown, 1984).

Eustis, Nancy, Jay Greenburg, and Sharon Patten, *Long–Term Care for Older Persons: A Policy Perspective* (Monterey, Calif.: Brooks/Cole, 1984).

Evans, Denis A., and others, "Estimated Prevalence of Alzheimer's Disease in the United States," *The Milbank Quarterly*, 68, no. 2 (1990), 267–89.

Evans, Lois, Kathleen Buckwalter, and Terry Fulmer, "The Mosaic of Needs for Elderly With Mental Concerns," *The Gerontologist*, 33, no. 2 (April 1993), 280–81.

Ferrini, Armeda F., and Rebecca L. Ferrini, *Health in Later Years* (Madison, Wis.: WCB Brown and Benchmark, 1993).

Gelfand, Donald E., *The Aging Network: Programs and Services* (New York: Springer, 1993).

George, Linda, "Depressive Disorders and Symptoms in Later Life," *Generations*, 17, no. 1 (Winter/Spring 1993), 35–38.

Gerety, Meghan B., "Health Care Reform from the View of a Geriatrician," *The Gerontologist*, 34, no. 5 (October 1994), 590–97.

Greenwald, Howard P., "Cost Containment and Initiation of Care for Cancer in a Medicare–Eligible Population," *Public Administration Review*, 46 (November/December 1986), 651–56.

"Growing Old in China," *Beijing Review*, 43 (October 26, 1981), 22–28.

Guanghan, Yu, lecture given in Beijing, June 14, 1984.

Gurian, Bennett, and Robert Goisman, "Anxiety Disorders in the Elderly," *Generations*, 17, no. 1 (Winter/Spring 1993), 39–42.

Hamdy, Ronald C., "Clinical Presentation," in *Alzheimer's Disease: A Handbook for Caregivers*, eds. Ronald C. Hamdy and others (Chicago: Mosby, 1994), pp. 102–16.

Health Security Act (Washington, D.C.: U.S. Congress Printing Office, 1993).

Helmchen, Hanfried, and Michael Linden, "The Differentiation Between Depression and Dementia in the Very Old," *Ageing and Society*, 13 (1993), 589–617.

Hickey, Tom, *Health and Aging* (Monterey, Calif.: Brooks/Cole, 1980).

Hooyman, Nancy R., and H. Asuman Kiyak, *Social Gerontology: A Multidisciplinary Perspective* (Boston: Allyn & Bacon, 1991).

Hughs, Dana C., Diane DeMallie, and Dan G. Blazer, "Does Age Make a Difference in the Effects of Physical Health and Social Support on the Outcome of a Major Depressive Episode?" *American Journal of Psychiatry*, 150, no. 5 (May 1993), 728–33.

Iglehart, J. K., "Health Care and American Business," *The New England Journal of Medicine*, 306, no. 2 (January 1982), 120–24.

Kahana, Eva, Kurt Stange, and Boaz Kahana, "Stress and Aging: The Journey from What, to How, to Why," *The Gerontologist*, 33, no. 3 (June 1993), 423–35.

Kart, Cary S., Eileen K. Metress, and Seamus P. Metress, *Human Aging and Chronic Disease* (Boston: Jones and Bartlett, 1992).

Kiecolt-Glaser, Janice K., and Ronald Glaser, "Caregivers, Mental Health, and Immune Function," in *Stress Effects on Family Caregivers of Alzheimer's Patients*, eds. Enid Light, George Niederehe, and Barry D. Lebowitz (New York: Springer, 1994), pp. 64–75.

Kleinman, Arthur, "Social Origins or Distress and Disease: Depression, Neurasthenia, and Pain in Modern China," *Current Anthropology*, 27, no. 5 (December 1986), 499–509.

Koenig, Harold G., Linda George, and Robert Schneider, "Mental Health Care for Older Adults in the Year 2020: A Dangerous and Avoided Topic," *The Gerontologist*, 34, no. 5 (October 1994), 674–79.

Lamy, Peter P., "Actions of Alcohol and Drugs in Older People," *Generations*, 12, no. 4 (Summer 1988), 9–13.

Lewis, Myrna, "Aging in the People's Republic of China," *International Journal of Aging and Human Development*, 15, no. 2 (1982), 79–105.

Li, Jing-Fang, lecture given at Northern Arizona University during summer 1986.

Liang, Jersey, and Nancy A. Whitelaw, "Assessing the Physical and Mental Health of the Elderly," in *The Legacy of Longevity*, ed. Sidney M. Stahl (Newbury, Calif.: Sage, 1990), pp. 35–54.

Matt, Georg E., and Alfred Dean, "Social Support from Friends and Psychological Distress Among Elderly Persons: Moderator Effects of Age," *Journal of Health and Social Behavior*, 34 (September 1993), 187–200.

Mechanic, David, *Medical Sociology* (New York: Free Press, 1978).

"The Medicare 1994 Handbook," U.S. Department of Health and Human Services, Health Care Financing Administration, (Washington, D.C.: Publication No. HCFA 10050, 1994).

Moon, Marilyn, "Lessons from Medicare," *The Gerontologist*, 34, no. 5 (October 1994), 606-

Poen, Monte M., "The Truman Legacy: Retreat to Medicare," in *Health Insurance: The Continuing Debate*, ed. Ronald L. Numbers (Westport, Conn.: Greenwood Press, 1982), pp. 97–113.

Porkert, Manfred, "Chinese Medicine: A Traditional Healing Science," in *Ways of Health: Holistic Approaches to Ancient and Contemporary Medicine*, ed. David S. Sobel (New York: Harcourt Brace Jovanovich, 1979), pp. 147–72.

Relman, Arnold S., "The New Medical–Industrial Complex," in *Dominant Issues in Medical Sociology*, ed. Howard D. Schwartz (New York: Random House, 1987), pp. 597–608.

Roberts, Beverly L., Ruth Dunkle, and Marie Haug, "Physical, Psychological and Social Resources as Moderators of the Relationship of Stress to Mental Health of the Very Old," *Journal of Gerontology*, 49, no. 1 (January 1994), S35–43.

Rose, Arnold M., "Subculture of the Aging: A Framework for Research in Social Gerontology," in *Older People and Their Social World*, eds. Arnold M. Rose and Warren A. Peterson (Philadelphia: F. A. Davis, 1965), pp. 3–16.

Sandner, Donald F., "Navajo Indian Medicine and Medicine Men," in *Ways of Health: Holistic Approaches to Ancient and Contemporary Medicine*, ed. David S. Sobel (New York: Harcourt Brace Jovanovich, 1979), pp. 117–46.

Schonfeld, Lawrence, and Larry W. Dupree, "Older Problem Drinkers —Long–Term and Late–Life Onset Abusers: What Triggers Their Drinking?" in *Annual Editions: Aging*, ed. Harold Cox (Guilford, Conn.: Duskin, 1992), pp. 108–11.

Sloan, Patrick, "Neuropsychological Assessment of Dementia," in *Alzheimer's Disease: A Handbook for Caregivers*, eds. Ronald C. Hamdy, James M. Turnbull, Linda D. Norman, and Mary M. Lancaster, (Chicago: Mosby, 1994), pp. 44–64.

Sobel, David S., *Ways of Health: Holistic Approaches to Ancient and Contemporary Medicine* (New York: Harcourt Brace Jovanovich, 1979).

Stahl, Sidney M., and Jacquelyn R. Feller, "Old Equals Sick: An Ontogenetic Fallacy," in *The Legacy of Longevity*, ed. Sidney M. Stahl (Newbury Park, Calif.: Sage, 1990), pp. 21–34.

Stewart, David C., and Thomas J. Sullivan, "Illness Behavior and the Sick Role in Chronic Disease: The Case of Multiple Sclerosis," in *Dominant Issues in Medical Sociology*, ed. Howard D. Schwartz (New York: Random House, 1987), pp. 40–51.

Tariot, Pierre N., Carol Ann Podgorski, Linda Blazina, and Adrian Leibovici, "Mental Disorders in the Nursing Home: Another Perspective," *American Journal of Psychiatry*, 150, no. 7 (July 1993), 1063–69.

Teegarden, David, "Holistic Health and Medicine in the 1980's," in *The New Holistic Health Handbook: Living Well in a New Age*, eds. Shepherd Bliss and others, (Lexington, Mass.: Stephen Greene Press, 1985), pp. 14–19.

Weiner, Joshua M., Deborah A. Ehrenworth, and Denise A. Spence, "Private Long-Term Care Insurance: Cost, Coverage, and Restrictions," *The Gerontologist*, 27, no. 4 (August 1987), 487–93.

Weiss, Gregory L., and Lynn E. Lonnquist, *The Sociology of Health, Healing, and Illness* (Englewood Cliffs, N.J.: Prentice Hall, 1994).

Wolfe, Paul R., "The Maintenance of Professional Authority: Acupuncture and the American Physician," in *Dominant Issues in Medical Sociology*, ed. Howard D. Schwartz (New York: Random House, 1987), pp. 580–94.

Wright, Lore K., *Alzheimer's Disease and Marriage* (Newbury Park, Calif.: Sage, 1993).

Wykle, May L., and Carol M. Musil, "Mental Health of Older Persons: Social and Cultural Factors," *Generations*, 17, no. 1 (Winter/Spring 1993), 7–12.

The Development and Provision of Long-Term Care for the Aged

INTRODUCTION

Long-term care is increasingly becoming one of the most important and vital issues in the field of gerontology today, even though, in effect, it has not existed as a meaningful concept to elderly people for more than 50 years. It was clearly not an issue that was considered to be important when Medicare was passed in 1965, for example. Why, then, has it now come to demand so much of our attention in recent years?

For the most part, long-term care has emerged as a vital concern because of the dramatic increases in life expectancy and the very different health problems related to that phenomenon. Life expectancy has risen to a large extent because most people are now able to survive the acute ailments that once took the lives of many individuals at relatively young ages. As pointed out in Chapter 12, however, the longer they live, the more apt they are to acquire chronic conditions that are mostly incurable and permanently disabling. Furthermore, becoming old typically often results in the acquisition of multiple chronic conditions. Many older people, therefore, do not just have to be cared for only temporarily but require it on a long-term and usually permanent basis.

Long-term care has become an issue today also because of the politics and rapidly accelerating costs of health care provision in the United States. Specifically, in this regard have been the almost exclusive reliance on the institutionalization of chronic patients (the most expensive form of long-term care), the lack of support for long-term care in general, and the increased awareness of long-term care due to government actions.

There are a number of different approaches to long-term care that have been developed and that are being used, ranging from the very informal to the professional and institutionalized. First, and by far the most frequent type of care is that which is provided by informal caregivers in the homes where the elderly care recipients live. This is the type of care being provided for over 80 percent of the elderly receiving some level of care, not only in the United States but also in such other countries as Australia and Canada (Van Nostrand, Clark, and Romoren, 1993). A second form of care that is becoming more and more prevalent is that which is delivered by professionally trained providers (nurses, social workers, etc.) to the elderly in their own homes. These providers do not, however, tend to provide such needed support services as housekeeping, which are done either by informal caregivers or not at all. A third level of care, the least utilized in this country, is that provided in supportive houses. These are houses in which a number of elderly live together, and in which support service staff are present at all times. A fourth type of care is provided in institutions in which only a minimal amount or no skilled nursing care is provided. The fifth level of care is provided in skilled nursing care institutions. This form of care is utilized by less than 5 percent of the elderly in nearly all modern nations of the world.

There are a number of deeply felt and interrelated concerns about long-term care that keep attention focused on that subject. These include (1) the projected increases in demand on families and institutional systems for such care in the future that appear to be impossible to meet with the numbers of those above age 85 growing faster than those in any other age category; (2) the necessity to somehow contain the costs especially of this kind of care; (3) the fear among the elderly of losing what support they now have for this type of care; (4) the quality of the care that is provided to them; and (5) elderly persons' dread of becoming totally dependent.

THE INCREASING NEED FOR LONG-TERM CARE FOR THE ELDERLY

There is a growing sense of alarm about what seems to be an ever-increasing need and demand for long-term care especially on the part of analysts who specialize on that aspect of gerontology. It is obvious that not only does the present level of need present the nations of the world with an overwhelming challenge, but also that the need for long-term care in the very near future will multiply. The questions being raised have to do with the welfare of elderly people and possibly overtaxing societal resources.

Statistical projections of the uses of long-term care resources provide us with a graphic picture of how dramatically this age-related phenomenon is growing. Atchley reports, for example, that in 1980 approximately 440,000 85 and older elderly people were relying on some level and type of long-term care. Given that year's rate of utilizaton, he then reports that by the year 2000 at least 1 million in that age bracket will be the recipients of long-term care, by 2020 the number will be 1.5 million, and by 2050 that number could double to as many as 3 million (Atchley, 1991, pp. 385–86). What complicates the matter even more is the realization that, as Atchley also points out, at age 85 and over the "care needs increase dramatically and are not as likely to be amenable to in-home services" (Atchley, 1991, p. 386).

According to other analysts, these figures are much too conservative. Clair, in fact, reports the projection that by the year 2000 as many as 2.3 million elderly people 65 and over will be living in institutions alone, to say nothing of those receiving long-term care in other settings (Clair, 1990). At least half of that 2.3 million will be 85 years old and older, since 45 percent of all those 65 and over needing some level of personal assistance are 85 and over (see Figure 13–1).

Another indication that the 1980 utilization figures may be much too conservative as a base of projection about long-term care needs in the future is the fact that projections of the future growth of the elderly population as a whole have consistently been underestimated. For example, Manton reports that in December 1972, the over-65 population was projected to be 24.1 million in 1980, but the actual 1980 population figures showed a total of 25.7 million over 65. This was an error of 6.6 percent or of 1.6 million people in just eight years. Since everyone over 65 in 1980 was obviously already alive in 1972, how could that much of a miscalculation have been made? As Manton explains, "this discrepancy was due to the inability to anticipate the decrease of mortality rates" (Manton, 1982). Simply put, many more elderly people than expected remained alive. Census data show that these kinds of underestimations have been made ever since the 1950s. What is probably the surprising part of the decreases of the mortality rate in this country is that they are more than twice as high among those over 85 than among those younger (Manton, 1982; Manton, Corder, and Stallard, 1993). Even though the death rate among those over 85 obviously remains much higher than among those who are younger, the percent of decrease in that rate each year is greater.

FIGURE 13-1 The Need for Personal Assistance Increases with Age (Source: Armeda F. Ferrini and Rebecca L. Ferrini, *Health in the Later Years* (Madison, Wis.: Brown and Benchmark, 1993), Table 13.1, p. 404.)

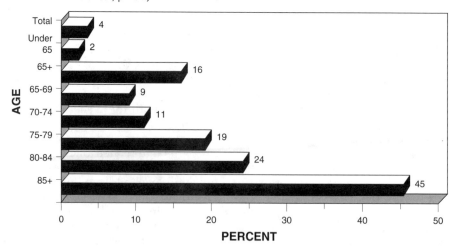

The question this leaves is, how do all of these facts relate to the need for long-term care? One might conclude that mortality among the oldest old is declining because in general health is improving, and that that should result in fewer demands on the long-term care system.

As discussed in Chapter 3, Fries has, in fact, theorized that the need for long-term care will eventually decline. His "compressed morbidity" theory of aging is based on the idea that humans have a biologically determined life span and that death at the end of the life span is a relatively short-term not a long-term process. It is dying as a consequence of chronic diseases that requires long-term care. Therefore, as these kinds of diseases are eliminated long-term care will become less of a problem to the elderly and less of a drain on the resources of society (Fries, 1980; Fries, 1989).

However, others argue that life expectancy is not continuing to increase and morbidity is not declining because of compressed morbidity. Instead, those population changes are taking place precisely because of the availability of long-term care and advancements in medical technology. Chronic degenerative diseases are not being either prevented or even retarded. The only thing that is happening, according to this argument, is simply postponing the fatal consequences of those diseases, or "prolonging their average duration" (Gruenberg, 1977). Therefore, the longer people live, the more dependent they become on long-term care, and the older the population becomes the greater will be the demand for increasingly technical types of long-term care.

Still others contend that the progress that has been made in declining mortality has come more from improved lifestyles, hygiene, nutrition and the efforts of public health than from medical technology or disease control. However, the need for long-term care continues to grow because of the growing danger of such modern-day factors as environmental deterioration and occupational stress (Manton, 1982).

Finally, both Manton and Clair believe that viewing the human organism from the perspective of single factors such as biological makeup, diseases, or environment fails to reveal the dynamic aspect of human life. As Clair sees it, even though all of the components of physical life undergo functional decline with age, "no one system is often sufficiently compromised to result in death in the absence of disease." Instead he submits that "a morbidity process generates death via an interactive process." Specifically, he contends that "one specific disease may give rise to several particular impairments and social functional disability." As a result of this kind of interaction process, he pessimistically predicts that among elderly people, "for each active functional year gained an expected 3.5 compromised years can be added to the life span. In other words, "an increase in life expectancy does not necessarily mean greater health" (Clair, 1990). Consequently, from this perspective, the future growth in long-term care will be dramatic.

Manton's perspective is not a pessimistic one, but he too predicts a dramatic expansion of long-term care in the future. He also believes that all aspects of human life are dynamically involved in what happens to the body as we age. He presents four basic principles that explain that dynamic process: (1) The human organism is a complex multicomponent system, with each component having its own aging rate; (2) the failures of components can be identified with major chronic degenerative diseases (separating chronic diseases from mortality as Fries partly does is a mistake); (3) the tendency for individual components to fail with age is only partly dependent upon the tendency for other components to fail (but they are at least partly related, as Clair contends); and (4) analyses of mortality must take both individual behavior and environmental risks into account. Manton conceptualizes the interaction of the components of the human organism as a process of "dynamic equilibrium," which helps to explain both the incidence and duration of chronic diseases, and how those diseases relate to mortality reductions among the elderly. As he puts it, "dynamic equilibrium" suggests that "if incidence is unchanged, then mortality reductions leading to life-expectancy increases can only occur by increasing the duration of the disease and, consequently, its prevalence" (Manton, 1982).

A number of implications related to long-term care stem from this way of viewing human aging. First, the need for long-term health care will increase rather than diminish in the future. Manton warns that "health care costs will be incurred in reducing the severity of the chronic disease, or slowing its rate of progression, in order to reduce mortality risks" (Manton, 1982). Second, the encouraging part is that increased amounts of long-term care do not just prolong the miseries of elderly people suffering from chronic diseases, as Clair seems to suggest. They do, in fact, result in declining mortality rates, greater life expectancy, and improvements in the functional capabilities of people at older and older ages. The point is that lower rates of disability and mortality at given ages directly depend upon "how the natural history of disease is altered," through prevention and improved treatment (Manton, Corder, and Stallard, 1993). The third implication that is drawn from this analysis, again, provides us with a reason to be optimistic about the future. The clear implication is that, along with increased life expectancy, as a result of continued long-term health care, "productive life span will also increase and potentially lead to greater economic productivity" (Manton, 1982). From the societal perspective, and perhaps also from the perspective of most elderly persons themselves, that is the ultimate payoff that makes the increasing amount of long-term care worth what we invest in it.

In his 1989 restatement of his idea that morbidity is becoming more compressed, Fries presents an even more optimistic perspective of the future than that presented by Manton. He would certainly agree that the potential for more and longer productivity is great. He also presents evidence from experimental studies on preventive measures related to specific chronic diseases showing that while appropriate preventive efforts had little or no effect on mortality rates, they were directly related to improvements in morbidity. Those who practiced prevention were ill significantly less time but did not tend to live any longer than those who did not. In addition, he presented evidence to show that individuals at all ages who die from the same chronic diseases have about an equal length of time in morbidity. Morbidity seems to be more prolonged among the elderly only because more of them are apt to have chronic diseases. According to Fries, the key to better health and productivity among the elderly is not costly technological disease control efforts and prolonged long-term care, but the establishment of effective preventive procedures. As he puts it, "if we continue to emphasize high technology and replacement of worn-out body parts, costs will increase. There is a potential option for a healthier and perhaps a less-expensive future, but our response to the choice is not yet recorded" (Fries, 1989).

THE INSTITUTIONALIZATION OF LONG-TERM CARE

Most of the policy and expenditure on long-term care in the United States have been focused on the institutionalization of those elderly in need of such care. This has been true even though only a small minority of the elderly live in institutions at any given time, and despite the fact that providing that kind of care has been extremely expensive and continues to become even more so. The major form of long-term care institution is the nursing home, although other types are now being developed. The emphasis on nursing homes has been so prevalent that *long-term care* and *nursing home* have become synonymous in the minds of many Americans (Manson, 1989a).

Institutionalization of elderly people is by no means a new phenomenon in America. It began as long ago as colonial times with the establishment of almshouses and public poor houses, in which all kinds of poor were placed as wards of the government. According to Gelfand, these kinds of facilities became increasingly popular, and they served to severely isolate the aged and the infirm from the rest of society. This kind of institutionalization of elderly poor continued through most of the nineteenth century (Gelfand, 1993, pp. 222–23).

The practice of isolating elderly people in institutions changed in the 1930s with the passage of the Social Security Act. The philosophy behind that legislation was to provide individual elderly persons with a floor of financial support to make it possible for them to remain in the community with their families (Gelfand, 1993, p. 223). The Social Security Act of 1935 also established grants-in-aid to states so that they could provide financial assistance to helpless elderly for whom they were responsible (Stahlman, 1992). What happened to many of these people, especially those with no families to support them, was that they became housed in boarding homes. Eventually these homes began to add registered nurses to their staffs in response to the growing need for that kind of care. That was the beginning of the "nursing home" movement (Gelfand, 1993, p. 223). All of this has prompted Stahlman to conclude that the Social Security Act of 1935 "signaled the end of the poor farms and almshouses," and, even though that was not the intent of that act, it nevertheless, was "instrumental in the creation and development of the modern day nursing home" (Stahlman, 1992). The spread of the nursing home movement was further helped by the federal government in the 1940s and 1950s. Particularly important, as discussed in Chapter 12, were the provisions made available through the Hill-Burton Act of 1946. This act authorized loans and grants to be made to states to construct and equip over 6,000 health care facilities across the country, including many nursing homes and other long-term care institutions (Gelfand, 1993, p. 224; Stahlman, 1992).

Undoubtedly the greatest impact that the federal government had on the institutionalization of long-term care was the passage of Medicare and Medicaid in the 1960s. According to Gelfand, these two programs "opened new and major funding sources for the long-term care institutions" (Gelfand, 1993, p. 224). Because the purpose of these programs was to provide health care coverage to the elderly and the poor, the services that were included were defined in medical terms. Consequently, long-term care became defined almost exclusively as a medical problem (Estes, Swan, and Associates, 1993, p. 3), and hospitals and similar institutions became favored as the preferred settings at which services were to be provided. Nursing homes were, thus, treated not as residential facilities for impaired elderly, but as quasi-hospitals. Medicare has had only a limited impact on the institutionalization of long-term care, since, as discussed in Chapter 12, it was designed primarily to take care of the acute, not the chronic, health problems of elderly people. Only a limited coverage has ever been provided for institutionalized long-term care elderly through Medicare (Estes, Swan and Associates, 1993, p. 3; Wright, 1993, pp. 108–9; Ferrini and Ferrini, 1993, p. 405). Medicaid, on the other hand, was created to cover an unlimited amount of long-term care in institutions for the elderly recipients, but only if they were poor (Wright, 1993, p. 109). As Ferrini and Ferrini report, "Medicaid is the principal public mechanism for funding nursing home care" (Ferrini and Ferrini, 1993, p. 405). Evidence of that is the fact that a total of 52.1 percent of Medicaid expenditures in 1988 went for nursing home care (Stahlman, 1992), and, as indicated in Figure 13–2, in 1989 Medicaid covered 42 percent of the $45 million spent on nursing homes (Butler, Lewis, and Sunderland, 1991, p. 370).

It is important to recognize that long-term care institutions in the United States have undergone substantial changes over the past 50 or 60 years, due in large part to changing characteristics of the elderly population and the ever-changing, reactive age-related policies of the federal government. For

FIGURE 13-2　Percent of Nursing Home Costs by Source in 1989 (Source: Robert N. Butler, Myrna Lewis, and Trey Sunderland, *Aging and Mental Health: Positive Psychosocial and Biomedical Approaches* (New York: Macmillan, 1991), p. 370.)

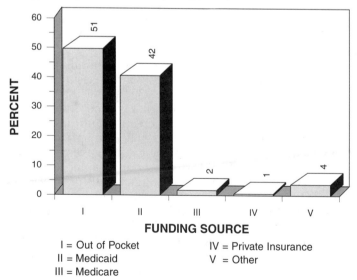

one thing the characteristics of the client population of long-term care institutions (particularly those in nursing homes) have become quite different from the way they were in the past. These changes partly reflect the fact, as discussed earlier, that the fastest growing segment of the population is among those 85 years old and older, and that the ratio of men to women is smaller in that age bracket than any other. The changes are also, in part, a reflection of the fact that nursing homes have become basically identified as medical facilities, as was also discussed earlier.

Typically, the current long-term residents of nursing homes have been identified as being mostly poor, generally female, mostly white, mostly single with little or no family support, generally very old, mostly having one or more crippling disabilities, and many suffering from behavioral and/or mental disabilities such as Alzheimer's disease (Stahlman, 1992). In the past many other somewhat functional and younger elderly people also lived in nursing homes simply because there were few other options besides becoming burdens to their families. If or when these types of people are admitted to nursing homes or hospitals, their length of stay has decreased dramatically, due in large part to cost containment measures that serve to seriously limit treatments, that are needed (Stahlman, 1992). Lin and Manton, for example, report that 40 percent of the admissions to nursing homes as early as from 1982 and 1984 were for only short stays (Lin and Manton, 1989). According to Close and others, these measures have also meant a dramatic increase of what they call "workload intensive clients," or those needing the greatest amount of constant care (Close, Estes, Linkins, and Binney, 1994). Consequently, the Ferrinis point out that nursing homes in the United States have a bad reputation and have come to be seen as "a last resort—a place to die," and that having to go to one "is usually accompanied by trauma for both the elderly and family" (Ferrini and Ferrini, 1993, p. 417). According to Gelfand, nursing home care largely ignores the social and psychological needs of residents and gives priority to medical care. As he explains the situation, "long-term care residences are increasingly being used for care of very old patients" and are "closer to being *chronic disease hospitals* for physically and mentally impaired elderly than care centers and homes for ambulatory aged who are not self-sufficient" (italics added) (Gelfand, 1993, p. 225). Evidence of this trend is the percentage of the elderly who are found to be institutionalized above ages 65, 75, and 85 (see Table 13–1). In spite of these changed client characteristics, the

TABLE 13–1 Percentage of Elderly Over Ages 65, 75, and 85 In Institutions

AGE	PERCENT
Over 65	5%
Over 75	10%
Over 85	22%

SOURCE: Robert N. Butler, Myrna Lewis, and Trey Sunderland, *Aging and Mental Health: Positive Psychosocial and Biomedical Approaches* (New York: Macmillan, 1991), p. 359.

nursing homes have increased by leaps and bounds, both in terms of their numbers and the size of their clientele. Gelfand, for example, reports that the number of long-term care institutions grew from approximately 1,200 in 1939 to as many as 25,646 in 1986 and that the client population of those institutions grew from about 25,000 to 1,700,000 during that time (Gelfand, 1993, pp. 223–24). Then, Ferrini and Ferrini report that the nursing home population is projected to grow to as many as 3 million by the year 2025 (Ferrini and Ferrini, 1993, p. 416).

Another way that long-term care institutions have changed is that they have become increasingly business oriented. The Reagan administration deliberately introduced competition into the nursing home industry, presumably as a cost containment measure. According to Estes and others, however, costs continued to escalate and "health care was redefined as an economic rather than a social good" (Estes, Swan, and Associates, 1993, p. 6). The problem was that the Medicaid and Medicare guaranteed payment reimbursement procedures made the nursing home industry into a "no-lose proposition," so much so that even physicians, despite obvious conflicts of interest, have invested in and become owners of their own nursing homes (Butler, Lewis, and Sunderland, 1991, p. 371). Even the introduction of recent cost containment regulations have done more to either deny patients needed services or shift the costs to them than to make private nursing homes less profitable (Estes, Swan, and Associates, 1993, pp. 6–12). The number of profit-making nursing homes has tripled in the last 30 years (Ferrini and Ferrini, 1993, p. 416), as an estimated 75 to 80 percent of all nursing homes in the United States are now for-profit organizations (Abel, 1991, p. 15; Close, Estes, Linkins, and Binney, 1994; Gelfand, 1993, p. 231) and they have forced many non-profit institutions to, as Estes and others have put it, "embrace expansionary growth and engage in for-profit ventures to remain solvent in the new competitive health care marketplace" (Estes, Swan, and Associates, 1993, p. 11).

Several special problems have been identified with relying on long-term care being provided in institutions. One particular area of concern relates to the decision to become a resident of such an institution. There are at least two factors related to that, which are problematic: (1) the "risk" involved, and (2) the move, once the decision has been made. Thinking of having to move to a nursing home is commonly thought of as a "risk" (Conner, 1992, pp. 150–52), but what precisely is the risk? Much has been made in the gerontology literature of the lack of quality care and the amount of neglect in many institutions, and that is undoubtedly part of the risk involved. More than anything else, though, the elderly themselves dread life in institutions because they see that as the ultimate and final loss of their independence. As Hickey put it, "refusal to acquiesce to institutional long-term care may reflect a fear of yielding to others all residual control over one's life" (Hickey, 1980). Then too, actually making such a move is often in itself a source of serious trauma (Eustis, Greenberg, and Patten, 1984, p. 78). It has been found to be related to serious illness and even death of some older persons (Butler, Lewis, and Sunderland, 1991, pp. 364–65). Having some control over the decision certainly helps some in this regard, however.

Assuring quality care in nursing homes has become a major concern with regard to the institutionalization of long-term care. To a large extent that concern has to do with the adequacy of the staff of the institutions. There are requirements that nursing homes have nursing staff on duty at all times, and that physicians must be available for regular visits with the residents of their homes who need physician care (Ferrini and Ferrini, 1993, pp. 419–20). However, quality of care depends mostly upon who provides the care that resdents need on a continuing hour-by-hour and day-by-day basis. In that respect, Gelfand reports that between 80 and 90 percent of all of the care provided in nursing homes is provided by aides and orderlies (Gelfand, 1993, p. 233). As a whole these are workers who (1) are uneducated; (2) have little or no training for that kind of work; (3) work at extremely low wages (at or about minimum wage); (4) are often only part-time workers; (5) have few if any benefits; (6) have an unbelievably heavy work load; and (7) have virtually no career advancement opportunities. It should not come as a surprise, then, that there is a high degree of "burnout" (Turnbull, 1994) and a personnel turnover rate of about 75 percent each year (Gelfand, 1993, p. 233) among these kinds of workers, or that the quality of care in nursing homes is often seriously compromised. A Nursing Home Quality Care Amendment to the Omnibus Budget Reconciliation Act was passed by the United States Congress in 1987 that put some tough operational standards in place for nursing homes and established some basic resident rights (Somers and Spears, 1992, pp. 55–56). How to implement those standards at the practical level remains to be resolved, however.

LONG-TERM CARE AT HOME

It is ironic that long-term care has become almost exclusively identified with such institutions as nursing homes and that by far the most long-term care money has been spent in this country for institutionalized care (Gelfand, 1993, p. 195). In fact, though, the great bulk of the long-term care delivered to elderly people has been and still is administered to them in their own homes. Therefore, any discussion of long-term care for the elderly must recognize that it also includes care in the home and community (Butler, Lewis, and Sunderland, 1991, p. 313).

There is, however, a growing recognition that long-term care does, in fact, take place in the homes of the elderly and that it is a potentially important care providing resource. This is particularly true on the part of policy makers concerned about the soaring costs of health care (McAuley, Travis, and Safewright, 1990; Estes, Swan, and Associates, 1993, p. 156; Applebaum and Flint, 1993). The basic assumptions that are made by those who tend to promote home care are that it is a cheaper form of long-term care, and that it is a better quality care than that provided in nursing homes. Kropf, for example, when discussing home care of frail elderly women concludes that, "even if nursing home placement would be a less-costly alternative, the quality of her life would not be proportionate to the financial saving" (Kropf, 1992). Inasmuch as most of the care that the elderly receive at home is provided by untrained, heavily burdened, and sometimes even abusive caregivers, that would seem to be a conclusion that is difficult to support across the board. There are no guarantees about quality of care in either setting, and not everyone agrees that home care is any less expensive than institutional care. Butler, Lewis, and Sunderland, in fact, make the case that all things considered it is even more expensive. As they put it, "home-and-community-based care, together with the services that support them, actually raise overall health-care service costs" (Butler, Lewis, and Sunderland, 1991, p. 322).

Nevertheless, it is true that home care, especially by family members, is much preferred over professional and institutional care, by the elderly themselves (Kropf, 1992, p. 178). In spite of the potential problems connected with it, there are apparently some good reasons for this preference. For example, Tennstedt, Kinlay, and Kasten studied the extent that elderly people's needs for assistance in their activities of daily living (ADLs) changed over a four-year period. They wanted to find out if (1) the needs that were being met at the beginning were still being adequately met at the end; (2) unmet needs they had had at the beginning were finally being met at the end; (3) all of their needs continued to be met throughout the four-year period; and (4) there were unmet needs at the end that were not there at the beginning. The overall results are shown in Figure 13–3. One important finding from this was that those who were the most likely to have developed new unmet needs during the four years were those with caregivers other than family members and those whose primary source of care had changed from the informal caregiver system to the formal system (Tennstedt, McKinlay, and Kasten, 1994).

Professionally Provided Community-Based Care

Both in-home and other forms of community-based care constitute a growing part of long-term care in the United States. Butler, Lewis, and Sunderland explain something of what that means economically when they report that, "home care is a growing consumer market that is creating many new jobs and a whole new service industry" (Butler, Lewis, and Sunderland, 1991, p. 319). This kind of growth has also effected government expenditures. For example, according to Estes, Swan, and Associates, "During the 1980s, home health care constituted the fastest growing component of Medicare spending" (Estes, Swan, and Associates, 1993, p. 3).

This part of long-term care has not only grown in terms of expenditures and numbers of older people served, however. In addition, the array of types

FIGURE 13-3   Changes in Unmet Need over Four Years for Community Residing Frail Elders (n=235) (Source: Sharon Tennstedt, John McKinlay, and Linda Kasten, "Unmet Need Among Disabled Elders: A Problem in Access to Community Long Term Care?" *Social Science and Medicine*, 38, no. 7 (April 1994), Figure 1, p. 920.)

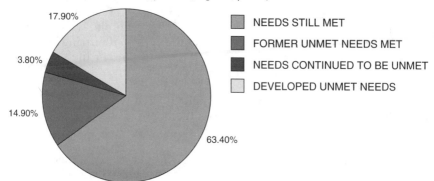

of services now being provided in the community is impressive. Attempts have been made in some communities to provide a community-based continuum of care through a variety of programs, some with and some without sources of funding. Rabins offers a useful categorization of community-based services to provide an understanding of what the continuum of care means on a practical level (Rabins, 1994). Some services fit into what he identifies as "primary interventions," which are basically ways to help prevent the development of potentially functional disabilities. Probably the best illustration of this kind of service is the nutrition program for elderly Americans in most communities across the country, in the form of both daily congregate meals and meals-on-wheels programs of the homebound elderly. These are funded through Title III of the Older Americans Act and are available to everyone 60 years old and older. The congregate meals serve a dual purpose. As Kropf explains, they "address both the nutritional and social aspects of eating" (Kropf, 1992, p. 186).

The second type of community-based services identified by Rabins is what he called "secondary interventions." In this category are programs provided to those who are experiencing the early stages of some kind of disability. According to Rabins, the largest number of services found in the community fall into this category (Rabins, 1994), and are offered in the attempt to keep the elderly recipients as independently functional as long as possible, and to diminish their "risk" of becoming institutionalized. Included here are such programs as homemakers, home health aides, adult day-care centers, and hospice care (Ferrini and Ferrini, 1993, pp. 407–10), the costs of which may now (since 1982) be covered under Medicare, if recipients meet the rather strict eligibility criteria (Butler, Lewis, and Sunderland, 1991, p. 345). Specially designed housing for the aged is also provided in some communities, which offer enough types of care to allow them to remain in their homes longer than they would be able to otherwise. These include congregate housing, boarding houses, and continuum of care retirement homes, which provide various levels of care according to resident needs (Butler, Lewis, and Sunderland, 1991, pp. 345–46).

"Tertiary interventions," according to Rabins, constitute the third kind of caregiver services. They are applied "after morbidity occurs," as Rabins puts it. They emphasize what needs to be done to minimize the effects of whatever ailments individual elderly may have (Rabins, 1994). The idea that in-home health care could compete with skilled-care nursing homes to adequately care for the needs of those with serious, disabling illnesses, and do so less expensively, has led to more and more funding for home health care through Medicare. This provision clearly defines the problems to be covered as medical problems and stipulates that medical practitioners will be in charge, however. The four criteria on which eligibility for reimbursement are based make that clear. The criteria are that (1) "the care needed includes intermittent skilled nursing care; (2) the person is confined to his or her home; (3) a doctor determines that home health care is needed and sets up a home health plan; and (4) the home health agency providing services is participating in Medicare" (Butler, Lewis, and Sunderland, 1991, p. 325). Tertiary interventions, then, typically provide for the involvement of medical personnel in the community, including regular visits to the homes of patients in need of their services. These sometimes include physicals, nurses, dentists, physical therapists, speech therapists, and even occupational therapists (Ferrini and Ferrini, 1993, pp. 407–08).

Much progress seems to have been made in the development and implementation of community-based long-term care along a broad continuum of needs, in recent years, at least from a professional perspective. Of course, few areas enjoy the entire array of community-based services that are possible. The ideal would be for given individual communities to provide services at each level of the continuum of care. Some programs have been identified as models toward that end. One of them is the "Nursing Home Without Walls Program" (NHWW, also known as the Lombardi Program) established in the state of New York in 1977. Following is a comprehensive description of this program:

> A viable alternative to institutional care, both providing and coordinating the delivery of nursing-home level services to the chronically ill and disabled so they may be cared for at home. A comprehensive range of health, social, and environmental services is tailored to patients' individual needs and managed on a 24-hour, 7-day-a-week basis. Care is provided by approved hospitals, residential health care facilities, and certified home health agencies and is available to any patient determined medically eligible for placement in a skilled or intermediate care nursing facility and who can be appropriately maintained at home. NHWW has allowed families to remain together and has provided care in a more personalized and compassionate manner. Many patients already hospitalized have been able to return home; at-risk community residents have avoided further deterioration; some patients have been rehabilitated. At the same time that it helps meet the increasing need for long-term care, NHWW helps contain the high costs to public and private payers. Patient care costs are approximately half of what institutional facilities charge for comparable care. Lombardi services cannot cost over 75 percent (or in some cases 100 percent) of the average cost of care in a residential health care facility. (Butler, Lewis, and Sunderland, 1991, pp. 352–53).

The question is often raised, however, how well the elderly in rural areas are being served in terms of the need for a continuum of care. Salmon, Nelson, and Rous recently investigated that issue in a number of rural counties in North Carolina. They discovered that overall, rural counties fare as well as, and in some ways better than, the urban areas of the state. Specifically, rural counties had received greater per capita funding from state and federal funds (with the exception of Medicare) for in-home services, but less so for adult day care. Also, about equal numbers of institutional beds per 1,000 people over 65 years old were available to rural and urban elderly. They did find, though, that the most isolated rural counties were more deprived than either the other rural counties or the urban counties (Salmon, Nelson, and Rous, 1993). Kenney used Medicare records to compare the use of home health services among rural and urban elderly on a national basis. Based on these data she also presents an encouraging perspective on health care among the rural elderly. She reports that the gap between urban and rural use rates narrowed considerably from 1983 to 1987. In fact, she found that "home health use rates grew more from 1983 to 1987 in the thinly populated, outlying rural areas than in the urbanized rural areas" (Kenney, 1993).

Provision of Care by Informal Caregivers

Despite all of this attention to the professionalization of community-based long-term care, it is a fact of life that the great bulk of care at all levels of need is still being provided at home by informal caregivers, most of whom are family members (Ferrini and Ferrini, 1993, pp. 406 and 412; Kropf, 1992) (see Figure 13–4). Furthermore, the costs of that part of long-term care have not even begun to be calculated. Most of the informal caregivers are also women, with daughters of the elder recipients of the care carrying most of burden of that type of care (Estes, Swan, and Associates, 1993, p. 157). Abel reports, for example, that "women represent 72 percent of all caregivers and 72 percent of the children providing care" (Abel, 1991, p. 4).

Given the fact that the quality of in-home care, most of which is provided by women who are members of the family of the elderly persons being cared for, cannot be guaranteed, as discussed above, the wonder is why there is still so much of it. There are three basic answers to that question. For one thing, Estes, Swan, and Associates contend that it is in part being forced on families by a health care policy that dismisses elderly clients from the expensive institutions of care "sicker and quicker" than they ought to be. Specifically, the "prospective payment system" (PPS) Medicare policy "sets hospital payment amounts in advance for particular conditions or diagnosis-related groups (DRGs) and pays the hospital a fixed cost before the care is given and regardless of actual cost" (Estes, Swan, and Associates, 1993, p. 160). Thus, for financial reasons, as discussed in Chapter 12, hospitals are inclined to dismiss clients before they have fully recovered, and if they or their families cannot afford professional community-based health care that may be available, they have no choice but to rely on the informal care from their families or others from their support networks. Estes and her colleagues characterize this system as creating a "no-care zone," and a reliance on "unpaid labor" (Estes, Swan, and Associates, 1993, pp. 160–61). As evidence that the system does indeed function in that way, these analysts report that "the result in the first year of the PPS alone was an annual transfer of 21 million days of care previ-

FIGURE 13-4 Percent of Caregivers by Types (Source: Robert N. Butler, Myrna Lewis, and Trey Sunderland, *Aging and Mental Health: Positive Psychosocial and Biomedical Approaches* (New York: Macmillan, 1991), p. 321.)

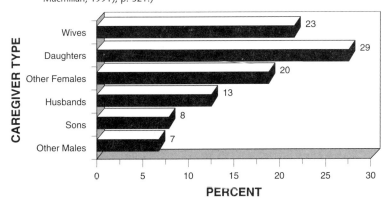

ously rendered in the hospital and financed by the government to the home and community" (Estes, Swan, and Associates, 1993, p. 160).

While it is not really accurate to claim that the present health system has created the informal caregiving phenomenon, it is certainly fair to assume that recent policies were adopted to fully take advantage of, and even exploit it. Nevertheless, there are also motivational and preferential explanations of informal care, on the part of both elderly recipients and those who are willing to become caregivers. Clearly, the vast majority of elderly people want to remain in their homes regardless of the condition in which they find themselves. Kropf insightfully explains, "An important part of psychological adjustment to receiving services is the value that older people attach to their home environment. Most older people desire to remain in their own homes and communities—places which have real and symbolic value" (Kropf, 1992, p. 177). In addition, elderly people not only prefer to be cared for by their own descendents, but they also feel that they have the right to rely on family members in times of need.

What, then, motivates family members, especially adult children to become the providers of care to their elderly family members? Some analysts have made the assumption that a major part of the motivation of adult children is to reciprocate for all that their elderly parents have done for them (McAuley, Travis, and Safewright, 1990), and this has been used as a legitimate reason for society to expect adult children to become the caregivers of their elderly parents (Estes, Swan, and Associates, 1993, p. 157). In in-depth interviews with a number of daughters who were serving as primary caregivers, however, Abel reports that most of them "did not perceive themselves as giving payment for services rendered. They were rendering care "in spite of rather than because of their treatment as children" (Abel, 1991, p. 91). Their basic motivation was an overwhelming sense of responsibility for their parents' lives. As Abel explains it, "once women had begun to make decisions on their parents' behalf, they felt accountable not just for the consequences of their decisions but for virtually every aspect of their parents' lives" (Abel, 1991, p. 74). Part of caregivers' motivation is undoubtedly often also to save money and to keep their elderly members from having to go to nursing homes (Ferrini and Ferrini, 1993, p. 412).

In spite of the nobility of caregivers' motivations, though, that role in the family is beset with numerous unresolvable problems. Abel noted that the women she interviewed faced a deep-felt dilemma related to their great sense of accountability. They also often felt powerless to do what needed to be done for them to protect their parents and preserve their dignity (Abel, 1991, p. 76). They typically experience role strain and outright conflict, with regard to the demands from having to fulfill such incompatible roles as employee, parent, as well as caregiver to an elderly parent, all at the same time (McAuley, Travis, and Safewright, 1990). Also, caregivers often experience stress from what are often responsibilities as caregivers that are beyond their skill levels and time limits. In addition, caregiving, especially by women, often results in quite severe financial losses, both in terms of income and benefits such as health insurance. What tends to add insult to injury about such hardships, according to Estes and her colleagues, is that "the magnitude of the sacrifices entailed by women's caregiving is unrecognized because family labor tends to be viewed as free labor" (Estes, Swan, and Associates, 1993, p. 158). Similarly, Applebaum and Flint make the point that rationalizing caregiving as self-sacrifice and personal dedication is simply incompatible with the business world which has become the primary orientation of health care today. He contends that authorities "continue to confuse the objective of good care with profitability" (Applebaum and Flint, 1993), and that confusion takes it toll on caregivers with the sacrifices they are expected to make. Also, the burdens of caregiving often extend to changes in overall family relationships (Mellins and others, 1993). Furthermore, Lund makes the point that caregiving by adult children sometimes negatively affects their "lifelong developmental process." For example, data from a 3-year longitudinal study done at the University of Utah Gerontology Center show that women between 30 and 40 years old who become caregivers of their parents are often forced to give up their jobs and find it difficult to resume their careers later (Lund, 1993).

Other family members besides children of the elderly who need care serve as caregivers, of course. Spouses are, in fact, preferred by most elderly as the person they would choose to take care of them when they need it (Abel, 1991, p. 4), but some have questioned the ability of spouses to adequately fulfill the role of caregiver since many of them are also afflicted with one or more chronic conditions. Wright recently studied the effectiveness of 30 spouses who had taken on the role of caregiver for their husbands or wives who had been diagnosed as having Alzheimer's disease, over a two-year period. The specific goal of the study was to discover the amount of positive interactions there were between the spouses and how that related to whether the spouse with Alzheimer's either (1) remained at home for the two-year period; (2) had gone into a nursing home during that time; or (3) had died. It was found that continued interaction between the spouses, continued commitment to the marital relationship, and the continued good health of the caregiver spouse were positively associated with the afflicted spouse remaining at home. Nursing home placement was related to caregivers' level of education, low level of marital happiness, and low level of commitment to the future of the marital relationship. Fewer positive interactions, lack of commitment to the marital relationship, and poorer health on the part of the caregiver spouses were associated with the death of the Alzheimer's victims during the two years. Wright's basic conclusion was that "that data seem to suggest that something other than Alzheimer's pathology is occurring, that afflicted persons are 'giving up' or something is 'shutting down'" (Wright, 1993). The most vital aspect of the spouse's caregiver role may well be continued positive interaction rather than instrumental roles.

Connidis studied still another close relative, siblings, to discover the extent that they serve as caregivers. Of the total sample of 678 elderly people needing assistance, who were interviewed, slightly less than a quarter had ever been cared for by a sibling. They were more apt to have had sibling caregivers if their sibling was a sister and not married. Also, having only one sibling meant that they were more likely to have requested them to help and received it when they needed it (Connidis, 1994). Clearly, elderly people in need of care do not assume that family members other than their spouses or children are morally obligated to provide that kind of care. In all likelihood helping patterns between siblings would usually be based on some type of reciprocal understandings.

Considering the many problems related to informal caregiving, due in part to the time-consuming, demanding, and intense characteristics of that kind of work, programs to provide respite care have been increasingly developed. The assumption behind these programs is that, if caregivers are allowed to be relieved of their caregiver duties with the assurance that those who depend upon them are not being neglected, the sense of burden the caregivers feel will be lifted. Indeed, in a survey of 244 information and referral agencies throughout the state of Michigan concerning services which were the most available and needed for dementia patients and their families, it was discovered that "respite and adult care were least available and most needed" (Shope, Holmes, Sharpe, Goodman, Izenson, Gilman, and Foster, 1993). Lawton and others have evaluated respite care programs, especially designed to provide respite for caregivers of Alzheimer's disease patients, to learn the extent that kind of benefit is realized. In this case the respite was provided by professional workers at day-care centers, and an evaluation was conducted over a 12-month period to determine the program's effectiveness. It was found that while the caregivers' social lives were somewhat improved, and that there were some favorable outcomes for the impaired persons (Lawton and others, 1989), there was relatively little if any evidence that caregiver's basic mental health improved (Lawton, 1994). As disappointing as that finding may be, it is probably not too surprising, considering the comprehensive sense of responsibility and powerlessness that family caregivers tend to feel, as discussed above. There simply is no time-off for that kind of burden. Nevertheless, when it is possible to effectively provide it, respite is extremely valuable to caregivers. Lund, Hill, Caserta, and Wright have recently developed and experimentally tested a unique form of respite, which they call "video respite." Video messages from the caregivers of Alzheimer's disease patients are taped and then played for the Alzheimer's patients to watch, sometimes on a daily basis. As many as nearly 67% of the caregivers involved in the experimental study said that, aside from the value it was to elderly persons being cared for, it provided them (the caregivers) valuable respite time (Lund, Hill, Caserta, and Wright, 1995).

With all of the emphasis placed on the dependency of elderly people who have become functionally disabled in one way or another and to some degree or another, we seem to have lost sight of a very important factor—that most if not all of those people still practice a great deal of "self-care." According to Kart and Engler, "self-health care" is the most predominant form of primary health care. Although very little is made of it, it is an important way for them to hang onto some control of their own lives (Kart and Engler, 1994). In a recent study of this phenomenon among a nationwide sample of people 55 years and older, it was discovered that as many as 86.3 percent of them had had at least one illness in a six-month period for which they had done their own diagnosis and prescribed their own treatment without consulting a physician. Also, it was found that those who were the oldest and were females in the sample tended to practice self-health care the most and were the most satisfied with the results (Kart and Engler, 1994).

A form of self-care has been formalized and taught to elderly people with chronic ailments by the MidPeninsula Health Service organization in the San Francisco Bay area. The goal of this program, which was titled "self-management," is to help the participants become active partners with the professional health care providers, and make it possible for the elderly to improve their own health status with less utilization of the formal health care system. The classes do not try so much to educate the participants about the diseases themselves, but to teach them about such things as problem solving, utilization of what resources are readily available to them in their daily lives, behavioral techniques to compensate for their physical limitation, and efficacy enhancing strategies. Lorig reports on the results of this kind of class specifically designed for those elderly with arthritis. One important result was that those participants who had received the efficacy enhancement training, compared to those who had not, began to feel that they had control over the symptoms of their disease and consequently actually experienced less pain, were less disabled, and were less depressed (see Figure 13–5). In addition, their general health status was enhanced (Lorig, 1993).

There are obviously both positive and negative aspects of both the formal and informal community-based caregiving systems. In order to maximize the best and minimize the worst of both systems, perhaps more interfacing ought to be done between them, as suggested by Kropf (1992, p. 183). This is being done at least somewhat successfully on a small scale. For example, Anne McKinley has been using a community development process in some of the small rural communities in Yavapai County, Arizona, to provide training for informal caregivers and tie the formal and informal care-providing systems together in a cooperative, mutually support the effort (Brown, 1985). Community-based care effectiveness will be greatly improved if/when those kinds of efforts are multiplied across the country.

LONG-TERM CARE IN OTHER CULTURES

The policies and practices of long-term care are changing in many parts of the world today. This is happening in Communist and former Communist countries, and in a number of democratic nations as well. An analysis of what has

FIGURE 13-5 Arthritis Self-Management Course Percentage Improvement over 4 Months with and without Enhancement of Efficacy Training (Source: Kate Lorig, "Self-Management of Chronic Illness: A Model for the Future," *Generations*, 17, no. 3 (Fall 1993), 11–14.)

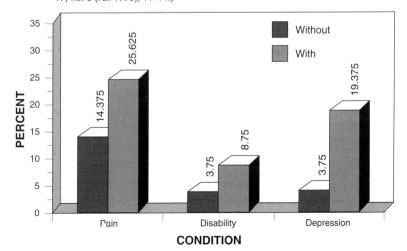

happened or is happening in the People's Republic of China, Russia, Northern Europe, and Northern Africa will provide us with a picture of the kinds of changes that are taking place.

In 1984 a team of gerontologists, of which I was a member, visited an institute for the elderly who had no families with whom they could live, in an organized worker residential neighborhood of Shanghai, China. The staff of that institute included nurses who provided 24-hour a day medical services when and if they were needed by any of the residents. Many of the organized city neighborhoods and communes in the urban areas had developed these kinds of institutes. They are still in operation and, though they are not skilled nursing homes, they are the nearest thing to nursing homes that exist in China. Nevertheless, at the Shanghai Institute that we visited, only one person was bedridden. She was the only person in any situation that we visited who was that disabled. That is not to assume that few elderly Chinese are disabled, of course. What it does mean is that long-term care is a family responsibility and that those in need of continuous care are found at home. That is so much a part of the tradition of Chinese culture that it is doubtful that long-term care is even a meaningful concept to them.

As a member of another group of American gerontologists in 1993, I learned that the institutes that were developed to care for the elderly without families now must be self-supporting and are open to any elderly persons. Some elderly with families may choose to live there if they or their families will cover the costs of their residency and care. At a time when collective organizations (communes, etc.) no longer exist and the state no longer has a policy of universal health care coverage, care of the elderly disabled falls even more heavily on families. Informal caregivers are increasingly carrying the burden of long-term care in that country as much as in America.

The long-term care situation in the former Soviet Union is even more problematic than in the People's Republic of China. On a tour of that country in 1991, with still another group, to study health care, I was privileged to spend a number of hours in the home of a family of medical doctors in the city of Novosibirsk in Siberia. The mother, her two daughters, and both of the daughters' husbands were all doctors, employed at one or the other of the hospitals in that city. One of the daughters served as a home health professional in a community-based outreach program of one of the hospitals to their elderly homebound patients. She explained that there was a limit to how adequately she could meet their needs because of the great lack of the right kinds of health-related supplies. Particularly lacking were drugs. Even at that time when the country was still under Communist rule, the whole health care system was in a state of crisis. Since the collapse of Communism and the breakup of the Soviet Union, it is not clear what has happened to such community-based programs as that doctor was administering. If they still exist, in all likelihood the clients or their families are required to pay for the services, which very few of them would be able to afford. Again, as elsewhere, responsibilities for long-term care in that country, where family solidarity has not been a strong cultural tradition for some time, tend to fall back onto the family.

The countries in Northern Europe, where relatively elaborate public supported and professionally run systems of care have been in effect for many years, are in the process of changing the way they do community-based long-term care (Evers and Leichsenring, 1994). Virtually all of them have either already adopted or are seriously considering the adoption of some form and level of "care allowance" or "attendance allowance" programs, in which informal caregivers (family members or others) are either directly or indirectly paid to take on the caregiver role in behalf of frail and disabled elderly people in the place of professional care providers. In the case of "attendance allowances," those needing the care are given the allowance and, therefore, have control over whom to hire. The United Kingdom and Ireland have both developed nationwide allowance programs, while most of the Scandinavian countries are experimenting with various forms of such programs.

According to Evers and Leichsenring, there are three ideological arguments that are driving the debate over this kind of change in policy. First, there are conservatives who insist that caregiving is already the responsibility of family members, especially women, and public payments should be reserved for only residual situations. Second, social democrats also tend to be against allowances because they believe that professional service providers are needed in order to both reduce the burdens of informal caregivers and to assure that the elderly are adequately cared for. Third, there are the growing demands made by such organizations as the Independent Living Movement in Sweden, that are fighting for the right of all elderly to remain independent and have control over their own lives, regardless of their physical conditions. In addition, practical considerations are pushing the European nations toward the adoption of allowances: (1) They are reaching the limits of being able to "substitute professional services for family care;" (2) the general shift toward home care has revealed the importance of informal caregiving; (3) the existence of a growing and vital debate on the role of the family; and (4) the women's movement's insistence that household and family responsibilities be given greater value (Evers and Leichsenring, 1994). Leeson and Tufte also point out the need for greater coordination of formal and informal resources in order to assure that informal caregivers and volunteers are not exploited (Leeson and Tufte, 1994).

Institutional care is still the dominant form of long-term care internationally as well as nationally. Van Nostrand, Clark, and Romoren have reported on a comparative study of the prevalency of nursing homes in five countries: (1) Australia, (2) Canada, (3) the Netherlands, (4) Norway, and (5) the United States. As shown in Figure 13–6, all five countries rely heavily on institutions to take care of the long-term care needs of their elderly people, with the United States having the highest percent living in nursing homes and the Netherlands and Norway having substantially lower percentages than the other three (Van Nostrand, Clark, and Romoren, 1993). This is reflective of the emphasis on home care in Europe discussed above. In the Netherlands, it was found that 15 percent of the elderly were disabled and lived at home and were given the care they needed from the formal care system. The same was true of as many as 20 percent of the elderly in Norway. Major differences between the United States and Norwegian nursing homes are that, while 75 percent of those in the United States are for-profit and relatively large institutions, 85 percent of those in Norway are nonprofit and relatively small.

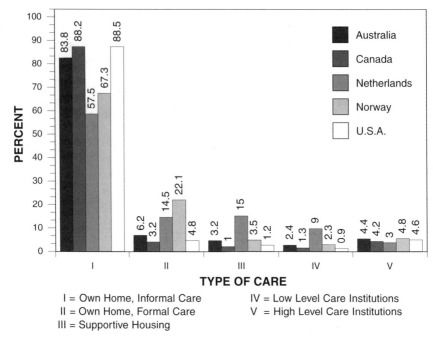

FIGURE 13-6   Comparison of Percent of Elder (65+) by Long-Term Care Setting in Five Countries (Source: Joan F. Van Nostrand, Robert F. Clark, and Tor Inge Romoren, "Nursing Home Care in Five Nations," *Ageing International*, 20, no. 2 (June 1993), Table 1.)

Cattell has analyzed the situation of the elderly in the "sub-Saharan" nations of Africa, with particular attention paid to their long-term care needs (Cattell, 1993). The nations that are included in this analysis are Botswana, Ghana, Nigeria, Kenya, South Africa, and Zimbabwe. This is an area of the continent that has experienced a great deal of political unrest and has undergone cultural changes as a result of Western influence for some period of time. Also, poverty is widespread throughout that region.

Traditionally, older people were highly respected because the older they became the more they were identified with ancestors. However, in some cases this had a negative effect. Becoming very old was sometimes a sign that it was time to join the ancestors. Thus, Cattell explains that "there is little philosophical or religious support for clinging to the last vestiges of life" (Cattell, 1993). Changes that have particularly affected elderly persons in need of long-term care, according to Cattell, have been the response of the population "to wage employment and labor migration, the growth of cities and national politics, and the spread of Christianity, literacy and medicine." A major effect of these influences has been to take away much of the decision-making power of older people and make them basically dependent upon others.

The conditions of the elderly in the region tend to add to their dependent situations, especially their dependency on their families. Very few receive pensions, have health insurance, or even have access to health care. Most live with their children and grandchildren or other kin in multigenerational households. This kind of situation is complicated, however, by the fact that families have increasingly become spread out geographically in their search for jobs. Thus, fewer family members are available as caregivers to those who need it. A few community-based programs and very small institutions (but no nursing homes) have been developed to serve those with long-term care needs, but they are few in number, and serve only a very small fraction of the needy elderly. By and large, the long-term care of this older population is almost exclusively dependent upon families. Cattell indicates that research confirms over and over that, despite all of the problems involved, "families (particularly, but not only, spouses, sons, daughters-in-law, and daughters) are providing support and care to aging relatives" (Cattell, 1993). This situation is an almost totally parallel situation to that which has been found to exist on the native American reservations in the United States. The similarities include the traditional respect for the elderly, the widespread poverty among the populations as a whole, the changing political and economic situations, the lack of accessibility to medical resources, and the dependency and reliance upon families for the care needed on the part of the elderly (Manson, 1989b; Brown, 1989).

CONCLUSION

It is clear that long-term care policies and practices are changing not only in the United States, but also in many other places in the world. There are differences between cultures, to be sure, but what is the most amazing are the similarities. The similarities are particularly surprising, considering how different the cultural traditions are and where nations stand with regard to economic development and modernization. Where nations differ the most does not seem to be as much a reflection of cultural traditions or the goals nations want to accomplish in providing long-term care for their older citizens, but how far they have progressed. Institutionalized care is, by and large, accepted as a necessary part of long-term care, even though neither among policy-makers, the elderly themselves, nor their families like it, at least in terms of how institutions (particularly nursing homes) now function. They tend to create unacceptable and seemingly unnecessary amounts of dependency, and, therefore, avoiding institutionalization has in effect become a dominant and widespread gerontological norm. It is ironic then, that the great bulk of long-term expenditures, at least in the nations with long-term care budgets, is spent on institutional care, and nursing homes have become part of big business.

Community-based care is also increasingly becoming accepted as an important part of long-term care. It is viewed as either a means of helping older people to avoid institutionalization as long as possible, or as a total alternative to institutionalization. The cost involved is one of and perhaps the major motivation behind the push to develop community-based programs. The assumption is that community-based long-term care is cheaper. However, it is not at all clear that community programs elaborate enough to serve as an alternative to nursing homes are much if any less costly. Nevertheless, they do tend to be much more acceptable to the elderly recipients and so they continue to be defended on that basis by some. Thus, a great deal of home health care has also become big business and administered by professional staffs. Ironically, the formal system of community-based long-term care has a distinct tendency to also create dependency among those elderly who participate. The elderly recipients have little if any say in the what, when, or how about the services they receive. Nevertheless, these kinds of programs are found to some extent in virtually all parts of the world, even in such undeveloped areas as sub-Saharan Africa.

Probably the one most common form of long-term care throughout the world is the reliance on informal caregivers, particularly on the part of the families of those needing the care. This is by far the most prevalent form of long-term care in all societies. As we have seen, in the richest nations, in which formal long-term care systems flourish, informal caregiving is increasingly being relied upon. In fact, for example, this is happening in the People's Republic of China precisely as, and to some degree because, their economy improves. As we have seen, the informal caregiver system has its own set of problems that potentially affect the quality of the care being provided and the well-being of the caregivers themselves. This is so much so that some see the increased emphasis of that form of long-term care as an exploitation of families.

Perhaps the most promising aspects of long-term care today are those programs that attempt to improve the effectiveness of the existing caregiving systems. Included in this category are such programs as respite, day care, and community organizations that build cooperative linkages between agencies as well as between formal and informal caregivers.

REFERENCES

Abel, Emily K., *Who Cares for the Elderly?: Public Policy and the Experiences of Adult Daughters* (Philadelphia: Temple University Press, 1991).

Applebaum, Robert, and William Flint, "Stuck in Adolescence: Will Home-Care Ever Come of Age?" *The Gerontologist*, 33, no. 2 (April 1993), 278–80.

Atchley, Robert C., *Social Forces and Aging* (Belmont, Calif.: Wadsworth, 1991).

Brown, Arnold S., "Increasing the Effectiveness of the Informal Support System in Rural Areas," ERIC Document Reproduction Service, No. ED 261 279, 1985.

Brown, Arnold S., "A Survey of Elder Abuse at One Native American Tribe," *Journal of Elder Abuse and Neglect*, 1, no. 2 (1989), 17–37.

Butler, Robert N., Myrna Lewis, and Trey Sunderland, *Aging and Mental Health: Positive Psychosocial and Biomedical Approaches* (New York: Macmillan, 1991).

Cattell, Maria G., "Caring for the Elderly in Sub-Saharan Africa," *Ageing International*, 20, no. 2 (June 1993), 13–19.

Clair, Jeffrey M., "Old Age Health Problems and Long-term Care Policy Issues," in *The Legacy of Longevity: Health and Health Care in Later Life*, ed. Sidney M. Stahl (Newbury Park, Calif.: Sage, 1990), pp. 93–114.

Close, Liz, Carroll L. Estes, Karen W. Linkins, and Elizabeth A. Binney, "A Political Economy Perspective on Frontline Workers in Long-Term Care," *Generations*, 18, no. 3 (Fall 1994), 23–37.

Conner, Karen A., *Aging America: Issues Facing an Aging Society* (Englewood Cliffs, N.J.: Prentice Hall, 1992).

Connidis, Ingrid Arnet, "Sibling Support in Older Age," *Journal of Gerontology*, 49, no. 6 (November 1994), S309–17.

Estes, Carroll L., James H. Swan, and Associates, *The Long-Term Care Crisis: Elderly Trapped in the No-Care Zone* (Newbury Park, Calif.: Sage, 1993).

Eustis, Nancy, Jay Greenberg and Sharon Patten, *Long-Term Care for Older Persons: A Policy Perspective* (Monterey, Calif.: Brooks/Cole, 1984).

Evers, Adalbert, and Kai Leichsenring, "Paying for Informal Care: An Issue of Growing Importance," *Ageing International*, 21, no. 1 (March 1994), 29–40.

Ferrini, Armeda F., and Rebecca L. Ferrini, *Health in the Later Years*, (Madison, Wis.: WCB Brown and Benchmark, 1993).

Fries, James F., "Aging, Natural Death, and the Compression of Morbidity," *The New England Journal of Medicine*, 303, no. 3 (July 17, 1980), 130–35.

Fries, James F., "The Compression of Morbidity: Near or Far?" *Milbank Quarterly*, 67 (1989), 208–232.

Gelfand, Donald E., *The Aging Network: Programs and Services* (New York: Springer, 1993).

Gruenberg, Ernest M., "The Failures of Success," *Milbank Memorial Fund Quarterly*, 55 (1977), 3–24.

Hickey, Tom, *Health and Aging* (Monterey, Calif.: Books/Cole, 1980).

Kart, Cary S., and Carol A. Engler, "Predisposition to Self-Health Care: Who Does What for Themselves and Why? *Journal of Gerontology*, 49, no. 6 (November 1994), S301–308.

Kenney, Genevieve M., "Rural and Urban Differentials in Medicare Home Health Use," *Health Care Financing Review*, 14, no. 4 (Summer 1993), 39–57.

Kropf, Nancy P., "Home Health and Community Services," in *Gerontological Social Work*, eds. Robert L. Schneider and Nancy P. Kropf (Chicago: Nelson-Hall, 1992), pp. 173–201.

Lawton, M. Powell, "Broad-Spectrum Service Program Effect on Caregivers," in *Stress Effects on Family Caregivers of Alzheimer's Patients*, eds. Enid Light, George Niederche, and Barry D. Lebowitz (New York: Springer, 1994), pp. 138–55.

Lawton, M. Powell, Elaine M. Brody, and Avalie R. Saperstein, "A Controlled Study of Respite Service for Caregivers of Alzheimer's Patients," *The Gerontologist*, 29, no. 1 (February 1989), 8–16.

Leeson, George, and Eva Tufte, "Concerns for Carers: Family Support in Denmark," *Ageing International*, 21, no. 1 (March 1994), 49–53.

Lin, Korbin, and Kenneth G. Manton, "The Effects of Nursing Home Use on Medicaid Eligibility," *The Gerontologist*, 22, no. 1 (February 1989), 59–66.

Lorig, Kate, "Self-Management of Chronic Illness: A Model for the Future," *Generations*, 17, no. 3 (Fall 1993), 11–14.

Lund, Dale A., "Caregiving," in *Encyclopedia of Adult Development*, ed. Robert Kastenbaum (Phoenix, AZ: Oryx Press, 1993), pp. 57–63.

Lund, Dale A., Robert D. Hill, Michael S. Caserta, and Scott D. Wright, "Video Respite[TM]: An Innovative Resource for Family and Professional Caregivers and Persons with Dementia," an unpublished paper being reviewed for possible publication (1995).

Manson, Spero M., "Provider Assumptions About Long-Term Care in American Indian Communities," *The Gerontologist*, 9, no. 3 (June 1989a), 355–58.

Manson, Spero M., "Long-Term Care in American Indian Communities: Issues for Planning and Research," *The Gerontologist*, 29, no. 1 (February 1989b), 38–49.

Manton, Kenneth G., "Changing Concepts of Morbidity and Mortality in the Elderly Population," *Milbank Memorial Quarterly*, 60, no. 2 (1982), 183–244.

Manton, Kenneth G., Larry S. Corder, and Eric Stallard, "Estimates of Change in Chronic Disability and Institutional Incidence and Prevalence Rates in the U. S. Elderly Population from the 1982, 1984, and 1989 National Long-Term Care Survey," *Journal of Gerontology*, 48, no. 4 (July 1993), S153–66.

McAuley, William J., Shirley S. Travis and Maria Safewright, "The Relationship Between Formal and Informal Health Care Services for the Elderly," in *Legacy of Longevity: Health and Health Care in Later Life*, ed. Sidney M. Stahl (Newbury Park, Calif.: Sage, 1990), pp. 201–16.

Mellins, Claude A., Mindy J. Blum, Sandra L. Boyd-Davis, and Margaret Gatz, "Family Network Perspectives on Caregiving," *Generations*, 17, no. 1 (Winter/Spring, 1993), 21–24.

Rabins, Peter V., "Clinical Interventions with Alzheimer's Caregivers: A Conceptual Approach," in *Stress Effects on Family Caregivers*, ed. Enid Light (New York: Springer, 1994), pp. 133–37.

Salmon, Mary Anne P., Gary M. Nelson, and Sarah G. Rous, "The Continuum of Care Revisited: A Rural Perspective," *The Gerontologist*, 33, no. 5 (October 1993), 658–66.

Shope, Jean T., Sara B. Holmes, Patricia A. Sharpe, Cheryl Goodman, Sanford Izenson, Sid Gilman, and Norman L. Foster, "Services for Persons with Dementia and Their Families: A Survey of Information and Referral Agencies in Michigan," *The Gerontologist*, 33, no. 4 (August 1993), S29–33.

Somers, Anne R., and Nancy L. Spears, *The Continuing Care Retirement Community: A Significant Option for Long-Term Care in the United States* (New York: Springer, 1992).

Stahlman, Stephen D., "Nursing Homes," in *Gerontological Social Work: Knowledge, Service Settings, and Special Populations*, eds. Robert L. Schneider and Nancy P. Kropf (Chicago: Nelson-Hall, 1992), pp. 237–73.

Tennstedt, Sharon, John McKinlay and Linda Kasten, "Unmet Need Among Disabled Elders: A Problem in Access to Community Long Term Care? *Social Science and Medicine*, 38, no. 7 (April 1994), 915–24.

Turnbull, James M., *Alzheimer's Disease: A Handbook for Caregivers* (St. Louis: Mosby-Year, 1994).

Van Nostrand, Joan F., Robert F. Clark, and Tor Inge Romoren, "Nursing Home Care in Five Nations," *Aging International*, 20, no. 2 (June 1993), 1–5.

Wright, Lore K., *Alzheimer's Disease and Marriage* (Newbury Park, Calif.: Sage, 1993).

14

Social-Service Provision in the Aging Network

INTRODUCTION

A major concern about elderly people in America in recent years has been the quality of their social lives. Regardless of what social status they may have enjoyed earlier in their lives, they tend to lose that status as they grow older and experience a great deal of ambivalence in their lives in terms of how they fit into society. As noted in earlier chapters, on the one hand they are increasingly hearing the message that they represent an unfair burden to the younger population. On the other hand, they are treated as though they are socially, as well as physically and economically, helpless and dependent. Their very competence in relating especially to their families and professional people is increasingly under question. It seems to many that, left to their own devices, they typically become socially isolated and even lose their social skills.

The prevailing assumption is that social intervention, as well as other kinds of interventions, is necessary. Consequently, we Americans have made it a policy to develop social-service programs for our aged, have made them available to those who fit that category, and have even encouraged them to participate at the same time that they are told how much of an undue burden they are. It is significant that the social relationships that are emphasized in these efforts are within age-peer groups, while, as a whole, little is done to maintain or reestablish intergenerational relations.

In analyzing this aspect of the lives of the aged today, it is important to note that the view of them as socially dependent and burdensome represents a drastic change in perspective from that of the past. Clearly, there was a time in American history when older citizens were seen as more socially capable and respectable than any others in society. Far from being socially dependent, they were looked to as social leaders. To better understand how that has changed, younger readers might ask themselves when, if ever, they have thought of older persons as social leaders, or if they have ever turned to an elderly person for counsel.

In light of the great changes in society's view of elderly people, then, two basic questions have become crucial to our understanding of their social standing today and in the future. First, what are the essential factors that have brought about such a switch in views about social standing of the elderly? Second, what are the consequences to the elderly of the provision of social services, on the one hand, and being treated as unnecessary burdens, on the other hand?

PROCESSES IN DEFINING THE AGED AS SOCIALLY DEPENDENT

For over 100 years of American history, older people, as a whole, held especially honorable social status in the communities in which they lived. This can best be illustrated by the situation among the Puritans in Massachusetts Colony. Drawing upon the Puritans' literary writings and historical records, Fischer has reported that except for the poor, the ungodly, and widowed women, elderly people were not only highly respected and honored, but also treated with much veneration (Fischer, 1978, pp. 30-40). The environment in which they lived was relatively harsh, and very few lived to be old. Therefore, those who were able to live into old age were respected partly just for having survived. The longer they lived, the more they were respected.

More importantly, though, their respected and venerated positions in society were based on their Puritanical religious beliefs and orientation. Old age was an important sign to them that God had elected and blessed them to be among his chosen followers. From that religious perspective, then, elders also held special positions of power. The young readily rallied behind and obeyed the leadership of elderly "gray champions" in family matters, community affairs, religious practices, and even into battles when necessary. The positions of power of the elderly patriarchs were also secured by the fact that they owned the land and controlled the economic processes.

There were problems and limitations to the social situations of elderly Puritans, however. For one, they, like everyone else, were very much subject to religious authority. Male heads of the households, no matter what their ages, were strictly held accountable to the church for how they ran their households and how their family members behaved. They lived in what has been called "closed communities and open families." Religious leaders in the strictly controlled communities had the right to enter the homes at any time to discipline family members, especially the heads of the households. Also, any family members had the right, and even the duty, to report any failures of the male heads to comply with the rules of the church (Martinson, 1970, pp. 17–22).

Another problem with the social status of elderly Puritans is that they tended to experience what Fischer described as "psychic infirmity" (Fischer,

1978, pp. 72–73). While they tended to be respected, venerated, and obeyed, elders among the colonial Puritans were kept at an emotional distance from those under their control. They were treated as strangers even among their closest relatives, and they enjoyed little or no social support for their authoritative actions. Younger people often resented their authority, and many elders were plagued with continual anxiety. Thus, there were strains in the system of social standing that elderly people in the colonial era enjoyed. Eventually, social change effectively challenged that system.

There have been different analyses of how age relations were challenged in the United States. Fischer contends that it has not been, as some have said, a modern phenomenon at all. Instead, he presents evidence that it began in revolutionary times with a radical redefinition of ideas. The concepts of both equality and liberty were defined as individual rights (Fischer, 1978, pp. 108–12). At least in principle, young adults no longer needed to feel compelled to follow the dictates of their elders.

These were not really new concepts that suddenly emerged in the United States in the mid-eighteenth century. European philosophers, particularly Immanuel Kant, were arguing that individuals were capable of controlling their own destinies through the use of reason (Jones, 1952, pp. 808–10). Also, as Fischer acknowledges, these ideas were an inherent part of Protestant Christianity which began in Europe and spread to the American colonies. Long before the days of the American Revolution, Roger Williams and others were expelled from Massachusetts Bay Colony for claiming the right of individual freedom. As early as 1636, Williams founded the colony of Rhode Island with a charter establishing individual freedoms (Latourette, 1953, p. 953).

To a large degree, however, opportunities for the practical application of equality and liberty were rare in the colonial era. There were too many life-threatening dangers among white people in the New World for them to challenge the collective and hierarchical authority of the colonies. The Revolutionary War era was important because opportunities to expand beyond the colonies were becoming increasingly available, making it possible to challenge the colonial hierarchies. As Fischer analyzes the situation, "Once those great principles were set loose in the world, they developed an irresistible power" (Fischer, 1978, p. 110). The result of this emphasis on equality and individual liberty was a revolution of age relationships. According to Fischer's analysis, the years that followed saw the establishment, not only a cult of youth, but a defiance of the authority of elders. Old age was increasingly viewed with disdain and disrespect. By the early part of the twentieth century, American literature portrayed the aged as pathetic, empty, and absurd (Fischer, 1978, pp. 113–56).

Achenbaum analyzes the loss of social status and respect among elderly people in the United States in terms of forces that have brought on "the obsolescence of old age." According to Achenbaum, these forces have been at work since the Civil War. They include (1) the theoretical and practical developments in medical science, (2) the increased social reliance on "experts" who base their expertise on the accumulation of knowledge rather than on experience, and (3) the increased reliance on what was believed to be the efficiency of youth compared to that of older people (Achenbaum, 1979). Debilitating diseases and the deteriorating results of physiological and mental aging challenged not only the physical capabilities of old people but also the idea that they were in any way intellectually superior to younger people. Instead of being viewed as wise, they were increasingly seen as "old fogies" who were set in their ways and unable to learn new things and keep up with the growing body of knowledge. In that context, a lifetime of experience was seen as irrelevant compared to the knowledge that younger experts were able to gain through the educational and training processes.

Cowgill has argued that the processes involved in the modernization of societies have brought about the loss of status among elderly people. As explained in Chapter 5, he cites four key variables to explain this phenomenon (Cowgill, 1981). First, he points out that the development of health technology is an important component of modernization that has had a detrimental effect on the social standing of older people. Health technology has made it possible for most people to live longer than they did in the past. Old age is therefore no longer rare and deserving of great respect by the young. Instead, it has become a symbol of dependency. The second part of modernization that Cowgill says hurts old people's social standing is economic technology. With progressively newer productive technologies, work skills quickly become obsolete, leaving older workers at a continuous disadvantage. Retirement policies have by and large accentuated the loss of status among elderly workers. Urbanization is the *third* aspect of modernization that contributes to social losses among the aged, according to Cowgill. This, more than anything else, breaks up the extended-family system as a unit of intergenerational interdependency. While family relationships continue, independence of the generations is fostered, again leaving the aged at a social disadvantage. The *fourth* process related to modernization from which Cowgill claims old persons experience loss of status is education. Each generation of people must learn more skills and accumulate more knowledge than the previous generation. As Achenbaum also pointed out, this renders the skills of each cohort of elderly people obsolete and even challenges the notion that wisdom rests with the lifelong experiences of the aged. In general, as each of these factors illustrates, modernization is characterized by social change and Cowgill explains that "rapid social change tends to undermine the authority and status of the elderly generation" (Cowgill, 1986, p. 198).

The notion that the past was ideal for older people has been challenged in recent years, however. Analyses have shown that not all societies have honored their elders and that not all old people in any society at any one time have been respected (Williamson, Evans, and Powell, 1982, pp. 51–71). There are elements of truth to that idea, but few would deny that, in general, the aged have experienced a loss of social status and that the emphasis on the burden of their social dependency has increased. The foregoing analyses provide at least part of the explanation for that phenomenon. It is clear from these analyses that the loss of status among old people is not merely an accident of recent history. Instead, it is the product of a long history of changing values and social relationships.

By the mid-1960s in the United States, the wisdom of the aged had effectively been challenged and their authority in society been denied; moreover, they began to be seen as socially incompetent. Observations of the older population seemed to indicate that they were increasingly isolated, suffered from low self-esteem, and were often afraid and unable to interact meaningfully with others. They were looked on as somewhat pathetic, as having lost their social skills, and in need of professional help to have their social lives stabilized and reestablished (Kuypers and Bengtson, 1973).

DEVELOPMENT OF SERVICE-PROVIDING NETWORKS

Concern for elderly Americans intensified throughout the 1950s. Their numbers were increasing dramatically and more and more of them were poor and in need of long-term health care. Furthermore, they generally appeared to be becoming progressively inactive and they seemed to be losing their sense of purpose in life. Old age quickly became an issue with which the federal government felt compelled to deal. A National Conference on Aging was held in 1950, an interdepartmental Committee on Aging and Geriatrics was soon formed, and the first official White House Conference was planned for 1961 (Rich and Baum, 1984, pp. 25–26).

As explained in Chapter 9, the inactivity of the aged became a particular area about which it was assumed some kind of intervention was needed. It seemed that the federal government ought to be able to somehow help to restore elderly people to social activity.

Consequently, in partial preparation for the 1961 White House Conference on Aging, the federal government funded a research demonstration project in Minnesota to organize and evaluate the effectiveness of senior citizens' activity centers. Under the leadership of Arnold Rose, sociologist at the University of Minnesota, centers were developed in five counties throughout the state. Elderly people were located, invited to participate, and the effect on their social lives were studied. It was found that while by no means all elderly people responded, center programs positively impacted the social lives of those who did (Nash and Bloedow, 1963).

Their social lives were given new meaning in the context of peer-group relationships and activities. Rose saw this as a dynamic process from which a subculture of aging (explained in Chapter 5) would eventually materialize (Rose, 1965). This prediction has received little support among gerontologists, however. It rests on a view of the aged as possessing the kinds of interactional and social skills and initiatives that few people believed they had.

Restoring the social lives of the aged and keeping them active through programs of intervention was a major goal in the United States during the 1960s. Senior citizens' centers were developed in local communities across the country. They served to draw elderly residents together in social activities and to deliver a variety of services that elderly people were assumed to need.

The Older Americans Act was passed in 1965 in response to the recommendations made by the delegates of the 1961 White House Conference on Aging. This piece of legislation committed the United States government, in cooperation with the states, to make it possible for older people "to secure equal opportunity to the full and free enjoyment" of income, health, housing, meaningful activities, social assistance, and a variety of community services (Gelfand, 1993, p. 263).

Title II of the Older American Act called for the creation of the Administration on Aging (AoA), a new federal agency responsible for programs on aging mandated by Congress. In provisions of the original and subsequent revisions of the Older Americans Act, many federal, state, regional, and local community agencies were tied together with the AoA into an interdependent working relationship. These agencies were expected to be run by trained planning personnel and were responsible to one another in a hierarchical order, from the top, down (Canter and Little, 1985).

The AoA was responsible for (1) developing program guidelines for each of the services outlined in the Older Americans Act and making them available to state agencies; (2) setting funding allocations for the states based on old-age population figures and their written plans (annual, three-year, five-year, and so on); and (3) monitoring state agencies' allocation expenditures and accomplishments. State agencies, in turn, were responsible for (1) developing written plans outlining what programs would be implemented, where they would be implemented, and what would be spent on each program; (2) setting funding allocations for each area agency (AAA) within their states, based on written plans submitted by the AAAs; (3) monitoring how AAAs spent their allocations and what was accomplished in their respective regions; and (4) submitting regular reports of accomplishments to the AoA. AAAs were, likewise, responsible for (1) developing written plans for their regions; (2) setting funding allocations to local community agencies based on program proposals submitted by the local agencies; (3) monitoring how local agencies spend their funds and meet their program goals; and (4) submitting regular reports of accomplishments. Finally, local community agencies are responsible for (1) submitting proposals requesting needed funds and outlining how services to the aged will be administered; (2) implementing and administering services to the aged in their communities; and (3) submitting regular reports of accomplishments to the AAAs.

The kinds of service programs typically provided for elderly people by local agencies with Older Americans Act support include activity centers, nutritional meals (congregate and meals-on-wheels), transportation, homemaker services, telephone reassurance, information and referral, legal services, and outreach. Probably the two most vital parts of this set of services are the centers and the meals programs.

As noted in Chapter 8, there is a growing concern about the fact that those who participate in senior citizen center programs tend to increasingly be older and poorer women (Krout, Cutter, and Coward, 1990; Miner, Logan, and Spitze, 1993; Krout, 1994). Speculations as to why that is true include the ideas that: (1) present participants are those who started coming a number of years ago and have simply "aged in place" (Krout, Cutter, and Coward, 1990); (2) center programs are poorly organized in terms of clearly defined procedures and outcomes (McClain, Leibowitz, Plumer, and Lunt, 1993); (3) directors have simply failed to continuously recruit the younger members of the elderly population (Miner, Logan, and Spitze, 1993); and (4) many centers are not available and accessible to many who would otherwise participate (Logan and Spitze, 1994). There is little if any empirical evidence to show that these factors explain the present aging of participants problem at senior centers, however. For example, Logan and Spitze report findings that accessibility, in fact, does not tend to be part of the problem. Their research showed that, as they put it, "where the problem is one of an older person's getting to a service site, people are reasonably able to solve this problem on an individual basis" (Logan and Spitze, 1994). More to the point seems to be how the elderly people tend to characterize senior centers and what motivates them to participate or not.

Senior centers began as places to provide opportunities for elderly people to become and remain socially active. However, planners soon began to view them from a different perspective. They saw them as ideal places at which and from which many social services could be delivered. The focus was thus changed from what Taietz called the original "voluntary association model," with the major emphasis on social activities, to the "social agency model," with the major emphasis on outreach and provision of services to the frail elderly with a variety of needs, as well as others (Taietz, 1976; Krout, Cutler, and Coward, 1990). The social agency model has been mandated in Older Americans Act revisions and government policies. In the 1973 amendments to the act, centers began to be referred to as "multipurpose senior centers," and in 1976, Older Americans Act funds began to be made available for the construction of those kinds of centers (Lowy, 1980, pp. 163–64). As a consequence of this emphasis, those who now attend most frequently tend to be the elderly who need the services provided (Miner, Logan, and Spitze, 1993). Evidently, the younger elderly prefer centers that would emphasize the importance of contacts with their age peers (Logan and Spitze, 1994).

Among other things, seniors' centers have become nutrition sites where congregate meals are provided for senior citizens. Meals programs are the focus of a large percentage of Older Americans Act expenditure. They are seen as vital not only as a way to maintain the health of elderly people, but also as a form of social intervention in their lives as well. It has been pointed out that meals have important cultural as well as nutritional significance. As Kart explains, "Food is important in the expression of group identity or solidarity" (Kart, 1985, p. 222). For most people, therefore, meals are social events that take place either with families or other culturally meaningful groups. However, many elderly people live alone and lack a social incentive to plan and prepare good meals. Wantz and Gay made the point that "some older people feel so rejected and lonely that they lose the incentive to eat alone" (Wantz and Gay, 1981, p. 287). There are also practical reasons, such as lack of income and transportation, that many elderly people do not provide themselves with adequately nutritious meals. Therefore, congregate meals and meals-on-wheels programs for older people have become a vital part of the package of social services provided through the Older Americans Act. Meals are prepared according to strict nutritional guidelines, and transportation is provided to bring elderly people to the nutrition sites to participate in the congregate meals and to deliver the meals to the homebound.

INFLUENCES OF THE AGING NETWORK ON THE AGED

The services provided with Older American Act funds and the planning efforts of the aging network have indeed helped to meet some well-established needs of many older Americans. Many elderly people have come to rely on those services on a regular basis. For a good many of them, daily participation, especially in seniors' center activities and the meals programs, has become an enjoyable way of life upon which they depend. Lowy describes these centers as follows:

> The philosophy of the senior center is based on the premises that aging is a normal developmental process; that human beings need peers with whom they can interact and who are available as a source of encouragement and support; and that adults have the right to have a voice in determining matters in which they have a vital interest. (Lowy, 1980, p. 164)

However, important as they may seem to be and as institutionalized as they are today, by no means would all senior citizens agree with Lowy's optimistic assessment about the quality of services provided at seniors' centers. Evidence of that is the fact, as discussed before, that a substantial percentage of older people in virtually every community in the United States choose not to participate in any of the programs offered at seniors' centers. Attention has been given to the problem of the underutilization of services by eligible elderly people. Holmes and his colleagues noted that this problem was reported especially among minority elderly. They conducted a survey of community-based programs serving minorities to determine the extent to which they were participating. They discovered that utilization of services was somewhat greater in those programs in which outreach efforts were carried out. Most important, though, was the extent to which there were minority members on the program staffs. The questions of whether or not potential elderly participants might define the services as necessary or appropriate and whether they were being delivered in acceptable ways were neither raised nor included as part of the survey. The primary conclusion of the project was that minority staff ought to be recruited (Holmes, Holmes, Steinbach, Hausner, and Rocheleau, 1979).

Underutilization of transportation services was also discovered in a special research-demonstration project in the early 1970s. The most troublesome factor was that those who obviously needed the services the most—people isolated in their homes—were mostly the ones who failed to use the services. This was true even though part of the transportation system was specifically designed to target that group of elderly (Brown, 1972).

It has been discovered that, while there are elderly people from all ethnic, racial and social class groups who take advantage of senior citizens' center programs, few, if any, specific centers serve elderly people with different backgrounds. Fewer still serve the frail or confused elderly (Frankfather, 1977, pp. 36–39).

It is noteworthy that there seem to be two basic assumptions in the lack-of-utilization literature that do not seem to even be questioned. First, it is assumed that the social services will better meet the needs of the elderly recipients if they are planned and administered by professionals. Contrary to what Lowy reports about center programs allowing seniors a voice in matters that are vital to them, in reality, they generally neither control nor participate in the planning of the programs designed for them. Instead, program guidelines come from the government and are locally administered by professionals. It is true that some elderly people serve on advisory councils and in that role may exert a small amount of influence, but only within the limits set by professionally developed guidelines and agency policies. In her critique of the professional approach to assessing elderly client needs, for example, Hill points out that from the perspective of professionals, the only ways in which client behavior can be regarded is in terms of either "utilization" or "compliance" (Hill, 1993).

The second basically unchallenged assumption that seems to be made in the lack-of-utilization literature is that failure to take advantage of the services is somehow unreasonable and even irrational. At best, the basis of non-compliance responses of the aged is assumed to be misunderstandings or unfounded fears about the real value of the programs.

The typical response of program planners and administrators is to improve their outreach efforts, add more services, or improve the service-delivery system. They attempt to make their programs even more professionally administered. According to Hill, "promoters of aging services again assert that what is needed is fine-tuning of the system and improvement in the ability to demonstrate its effectiveness" (Hill, 1993). In a study comparing seniors' centers in rural and urban areas, for example, Krout found that centers in rural areas offered fewer services because the sizes of their budgets and staffs were inadequate (Krout, 1987). Taietz and Milton had found these kinds of rural-urban discrepancies and recommended that rural centers needed more staff, help from outside consultants, and seminars on grantsmanship (Taietz and Milton, 1979). In another study, Krout also discovered that even centers with large budgets were experiencing barriers to the goals of serving as a community "focal point" in behalf of the aged. Their efforts to develop linkages with other community agencies and to thereby serve more elderly people were also meeting with resistance. He concludes that ways need to be found to overcome the problem of linkages in order to make it possible for centers to more adequately serve as community focal points (Krout, 1986). Schneider investigated what kept elderly people from participating in nutrition programs in Virginia, where an intensive outreach project had been carried out. He found that there was a combination of personal (attitudinal), environmental (racial differences), and programmatic barriers involved. His basic recommendation was that outreach workers needed to be better organized and informed about the community and the program (Schneider, 1979).

In response to the problem of utilization in rural areas of Nebraska, as discussed in Chapter 8, McClain and colleagues reported on a statewide reorganizational effort on the professionally oriented service-delivery system to the elderly (McClain, Leibowitz, Plumer, and Lunt, 1993). The Pennsylvania Office on Aging also responded to the problem that they identified as a "fragmentation of services" with a statewide organizational effort in the late 1970s. Their approach was focused on what they called "service management." Trained service managers were added to all of their AAA staffs throughout the state, professional consultants were made available, and all staff were trained in the service-management procedures. Each AAA could choose between two possible service-management models, depending on how they wanted to process their clients (Ishizaki, Gottesman, and MacBride, 1979). Gottesman and his fellow planners concluded that such a system is obviously "of real help" to clients since "it takes a professional with several years of experience to know when and how to access services" (Gottesman, Ishizaki, and MacBride, 1979).

It is obvious from this analysis that the aging network operates almost exclusively from a professional orientation. Indeed, that is the orientation that was recommended by the 1971 White House Conference on Aging delegates. Even though they recommended "involvement of older people and independent agencies and organizations in the making of policies and in all aspects of planning," the more basic part of the recommendation was that "primary responsibility for planning and coordination of health, welfare, and other services for the older population should be placed in a public service agency with divisions at the federal, state, and local level with strong administrative authority and funding controls and the capability of functioning across departmental lines" ("1971 White House Conference on Aging").

To be sure, the professional approach to service delivery has accomplished much in identifying some types of needs and efficiently providing vital services to the elderly. Two things tend to be overlooked with this approach, however. First is the extent that the scientific, professionally oriented approach to the assessment of needs actually reflects the needs of elderly people as they themselves define them. Hill characterizes this way of defining needs as a "rational, technoscientific stance toward the definition of need," and suggests that "there is a lot of 'lost' information" in the process (Hill, 1993). The second factor that is largely overlooked with this approach, though, is the effect that professionalism itself can have on the social and psychological lives of the elderly recipients. Specifically, attention needs to be paid to the ways in which it tends to create a sense of helplessness, powerlessness, and dependency. As Hill also explains, behind the professional needs assessment approach is the basic assumption that a "continuum of care" is being dealt with, and underlying that is the assumption of "the relative dependency of the older individual" (Hill, 1993). From that perspective, it ought to be obvious that decisions not to accept available services by elderly persons who are constantly sensitive to the risk of losing their independence are entirely rational and deserve to be respected.

The professional approach to the planning and delivery of social services to elderly persons tends to be a dependency-creating process. That in itself raises serious questions about the validity of the ways in which professional service providers tend to not only define but also attempt to meet the social needs of older people. It is commonly recognized that elderly people are overwhelmingly concerned about maintaining as much of their independence as possible. An increasingly prevalent way of trying to satisfy that concern today on the part of the aging network's professionally oriented personnel is to enable elderly people to remain in their own homes, a situation that has become labeled, and presumed to epitomize, "independent living." This is made possible by professionally planned and delivered in-home services. Elderly individuals are thus enabled to remain at home by accepting given packages of services that are not at all unlike those they might receive in institutions (meals planned by someone else and delivered at specified times, housekeeping and friendly visitor services scheduled at the initiative and convenience of the service providers, and so on). While this approach may well be an acceptable and even necessary alternative to institutionalization, it is difficult to understand the logic of the claim that it always represents independent living. It simply does not inevitably meet the desire to remain independent. In fact, the more isolated these older people become in their homes, the more dependent they become on those from whom the services come.

CROSS-CULTURAL COMPARISONS IN SERVICE PROVISION

A search of the cross-cultural literature on the provision of social services to older people reveals some patterns that are quite similar to those in the United States. This is especially true of the industrially developed nations of Europe and North America.

In the survey on aging of three industrial societies, (Denmark, Great Britain, and the United States), carried out in the 1960s by an international team of investigators, it was discovered that social-service programs for older people had already been developed in all three countries. It is important to note that they were reported as welfare programs, included in the existing general welfare systems. Undoubtedly, that represents the prevailing view of elderly people in those countries (Shanas, Townsend, Wedderbaum, Friis, Milhoj, and Stehouwer, 1968, pp. 102–31). The welfare perception of social services still prevailed in European countries in the 1980s (Cantor and Little, 1985).

As reported in the 1960s international study, even though a majority of the social services were provided by the family members of the elderly, they were supplemented by community agencies. No matter who provided them, though, survey respondents reported a reluctance to accept assistance with personal matters even when they needed that kind of help. Many said they would rather go without. The investigators interpreted that kind of response as an "obstinate" attempt to "preserve their independence" (Shanas, Townsend, Wedderbaum, Friis, Miljoh, and Stehouwer, 1968, p. 115). While older people would perhaps prefer that such services come from family members than outsiders, they are apparently seen as a threat to independence regardless of the source.

In more recent years the provision of services has become increasingly professionalized in other modern Western societies besides the United States. In fact, in the middle of the 1980s, Kane and Kane believed that we Americans could well learn from the professionally run system of care provided to elderly Canadians. They reported that in three Canadian provinces (Ontario, Manitoba, and British Columbia), social workers and nurses, functioning as case managers, controlled social and other services to the aged (Kane and Kane, 1985, pp. 263–64). The services provided were free to the elderly participants. Because of this, some worried that too great a demand would be made on the social service system. It was reported, though, that this did not happen, because case managers basically controlled which services were used and when they were used (Kane and Kane, 1985, p. 263). Kane and Kane presented this system of care as one that the United States might well adopt because it demonstrated that the kinds of services needed by elderly people can be provided when and where they are needed at affordable prices to the general society and certainly to the elderly people themselves. From the perspective of concern about accelerating costs and growing need for various levels of care on the part of the elderly, this is certainly a compelling argument. Case management is rapidly becoming seen as an efficient and effective professional system in the welfare service-delivery system. Nevertheless, it is a professionally controlled and administered system. As a system, it assumes that the elderly recipients, or "clients," are not capable of defining their own needs. Such a system fails to consider one of the most important social psychological needs of older people: the maintenance of their sense of independence. It is, instead, a dependency-creating system.

In a number of other cultures, until recently there was much less emphasis on the provision of social services as such for older people, and less loss of social status and independence with age. Three aspects of older people's lives seemed to directly contribute to those differences. One important factor was the intimate involvement of older people in the three-generation households with their adult children. In that case, their social lives were basically oriented to their families, and their social needs were provided for by family members.

As we have already noted, a large majority of elderly Japanese have traditionally lived with their children, and their social status seemed to be higher than it is for those in the industrialized nations of the West. The three-generation household was not only a tradition in Japan, but it also became a part of government policy ("The Japanese-Style Welfare System," 1983). Over a decade ago Maeda reports that the government had offered a number of incentives to families to encourage three-generational households: (1) tax deductions, and even exemptions, (2) loans for house remodeling, (3) provision of special equipment, (4) provision for short-term stays in nursing homes for emergencies, (5) day care programs for the impaired elderly, (6) community home-help assistance, and (7) visiting nurses (Maeda, 1983).

Despite these efforts, the trend in Japan is, nevertheless, for fewer and fewer older people to live with their children. According to Maeda, between 1970 and 1980, the portion of the older population living with their children dropped from 76.9 percent to 68.7 percent, while those living with only their spouses rose from 12.1 percent to 18.9 percent, and those living alone increased from 5.5 percent to 8.2 percent. During that same decade, the number of beds for elderly in institutions more than doubled (Maeda, 1983). An even more recent statistic on elderly in three-generation households is that the proportion of Japanese elderly aged 65 and over living with their children fell from 87 percent to 50 percent between 1960 and 1990 (Ogawa and Retherford, 1993). It is also true that, while respect for and authority of the elderly may still be an observed cultural tradition in Japan, the attitudes of many younger people seem to represent a challenge to that tradition. As early as 1985, Campbell and Brody found, for example, that women—who were basically responsible for the care of elderly family members—tended to feel that old people were too powerful and did not gain in wisdom with age (Campbell and Brody, 1985).

More recently Ogawa and Retherford theorized that in modernized societies in which normal filial obligations have been formalized in religious doctrine or civil law, such as Japan, adjustments of those norms to the demands of modernization will not be gradual but will happen in spurts. In research to test that theory, they collected longitudinal data from a national sample of elderly married women who were under 50 years of age in 1963, when the study began. One of the questions they were asked was how they felt about children being expected to care for their elderly parents. They were asked if they thought this was a "good custom," just a "natural duty," merely "unavoidable," or "not a good custom" at all. Their findings showed that "norms of filial care for elderly parents were fairly constant from 1963 until 1986, when a major weakening of norms began" (Ogawa and Retherford, 1993). As Figure 14–1 indicates, there was a gradual shift from the percentage of those seeing that obligation as a "good custom" to those viewing it as just a "natural duty" and merely as "unavoidable." Then, as Figure 14–2 shows, after 1986 there was a sudden shift from the percentage of those who saw it as a "natural duty" to those seeing it as either "unavoidable" or just plain "not a good custom" at all. That very abrupt shift was apparently sparked by the government establishing public support for the elderly and then announcing cut-backs. According to the investigators, it also represents a relatively sudden change away from the traditional norm of filial responsibility to a modern view of family relationships. As these kinds of trends continue, it is reasonable to expect that elderly Japanese people will increasingly find themselves in dependency modes similar to those in modern Western nations.

The situation for the aged in Hong Kong is similar to that in Japan. Historically they have lived in the homes of their children, and this pattern was made government policy in 1965. There seemed to be no need for special social-service programs for the older population (Chow, 1983). As their numbers grew and households were increasingly confined to nuclear units, however, government policies on aging changed. Many "care in the community" service programs have been developed and made available to older residents, including community nursing, home help, day care, laundry and canteen

FIGURE 14-1 Distribution of Responses About Caring for Elderly Parents as a Good Custom and a Natural Duty (Percentage) (Source: Noahiro Ogawa and Robert D. Retherford, "Care of the Elderly in Japan: Changing Norms and Expectations," *Journal of Marriage and the Family*, 55 (August 1993), 585–97, Table 1.)

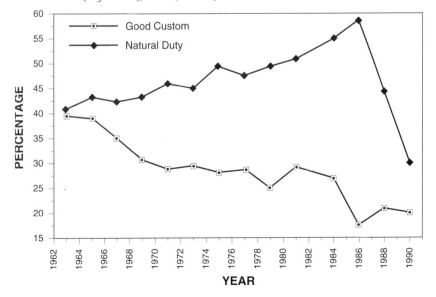

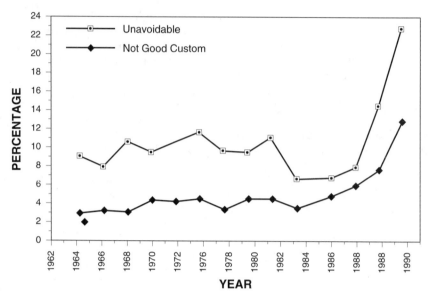

FIGURE 14-2   Distribution of Responses About Caring for Elderly Parents as Unavoidable or Not a Good Custom (Percentage) (Source: Noahiro Ogawa and Robert D. Retherford, "Care of the Elderly in Japan: Changing Norms and Expectations," *Journal of Marriage and the Family*, 55 (August 1993), 585–97, Table 1.)

services, social and recreational activities at centers for the aged, and sheltered employment. Those over the age of 70 are now also eligible for a monthly income allowance (Chow, 1983).

Clearly, the pattern of decreasing emphasis on families to provide for the social needs of the elderly and increasing reliance on publicly supported social-service programs also prevails in Hong Kong. The perception of the elderly as dependent will undoubtedly be a product of that trend. The growing perception of dependency does not merely stem from public supported services, however. The situations of older people in Japan and Hong Kong indicate, in fact, that it probably begins with the younger family members, who increasingly tend to view their older members as burdens, particularly in societies in which individual achievement is stressed. For that reason, it must be realized that intimate, daily involvement of older persons with their families does not necessarily help to maintain their social status or keep them from becoming treated as dependent. It may, in fact, contribute to the perception that they are dependent.

Another aspect of elderly people's lives that tends to create a more positive perception of their social worth has to do with the systems of care under which they live. The American system of welfare has always placed, and continues to place, the emphasis on those with special needs. This sets welfare recipients apart from others and stigmatizes them as less competent and less worthy. In contrast, other nations have adopted welfare systems that are accepted as part of the everyday lives of all citizens. The philosophy behind this kind of system of care is that, like education, welfare serves basic, universal human needs. No one can do without it and no one independently has the resources that are necessary to meet those needs. In those countries that have developed systems of care based on this philosophy, the typical approach is to provide publicly supported, comprehensive, cradle-to-grave welfare programs at no charge or at minimal charge to recipients.

Many nations have established these kinds of health care systems, and virtually all socialist and communist countries have provided all forms of social services on this basis. The advantage to elderly people of this kind of system of care has been that it did not set them apart from the rest of the population as people with needs with which they were incapable of dealing. Being a recipient of welfare has had no stigma attached to it. In fact, it has been pointed out that in the People's Republic of China in the past, welfare to families and individuals of all ages was so much a part of their daily lives that elderly people were not only the recipients of it but also often dispensed it to families in their neighborhoods (Mok, 1983). As it has already been pointed out, however, the provision of services to the Chinese elderly quite drastically changed during the 1980s as a result of the economic reforms that have taken place in that country. The government no longer requires or provides the elderly with retirement income, health care coverage, or any other welfare services. If employers fail to provide such services, families are expected to do so. Krause and Liang report that consequently many elderly now have to rely on their families for financial assistance. In a survey of 2,774 older adults in Wuhan City, China, they examined the relationship between receiving financial support and being emotionally supported by families and other significant others. They found that not only did emotional support diminish but also that negative interaction increased between the elderly and those from whom they received financial support. By way of explanation, Krause and Liang suggest that "financial strain may disrupt social network ties because it is a source of stigma, embarrassment, and unwanted dependence on others" (Krause and Liang, 1993).

The third aspect of elderly people's lives that helps to maintain their social competency is the extent to which they are involved in interdependent and reciprocating relationships with others in their social settings. In the United States, elderly retired people offer their services in millions of hours of volunteer work. Yet the public perception of being old as a state of dependency and social incompetence continues partly because the elderly are seldom involved in direct reciprocal relationships. In contrast, the aged in a number of other societies do have those kinds of relationships in their daily lives, particularly with their families.

Kerns did an in-depth study of the Black Carib elderly in Belize, along the Caribbean coast of Central America (Kerns, 1980). She found an inconsistency between the attitudes of the people about old age and how they actually related to old people. On the one hand, they almost universally expressed negative attitudes about old age. On the other hand, most of them felt affection and a deep sense of obligation toward their elderly parents. As Kerns put it, "Filial responsibility to parents is a cultural ideal espoused by all" (Kerns, 1980). The key to this sense of responsibility, though, is not so much that cultural tradition demands it. Instead, it is based on mutual helping relationships between parents, especially mothers, and their children that are developed over their years of living together. Widowed mothers, who typically have no source of economic security of their own, generously offer their help-ing services to their children as a base from which they can expect reciprocal help from their adult children when they need it. Thus, the elderly Black Carib are not treated as socially incompetent or dependent but as interdependent partners.

Much is made of the idea that the ancient tradition of filial piety is still being practiced in the People's Republic of China, and that older people are therefore respected and maintain high social status. This no doubt helps in part to explain the amount of social respect they still enjoy. Perhaps more impor-tant, though, is the fact that until recently they generally had all three of the previously mentioned living situations that enhanced their social competence. Along with the loss of those situations by many in the last few years will un-doubtedly be the loss of a sense of competency as well.

As we learned in Chapter 11, in the past when elderly Chinese retired, they typically received relatively high pensions. In addition, they continued to receive free medical and welfare services along with the rest of the popula-tion. They were thus no more economically dependent upon their children than their children were upon them. As we have also noted, almost all of them lived in three-generation households with the family of one of their chil-dren. There they had roles that were vital to the welfare of the family. Besides child-care and housekeeping activities that they performed while their sons and daughters-in-law were at work, they also contributed on about an equal basis to family expenditures. Even though there were families in which there may have been serious intergenerational problems on a personal level, (such as between mothers-in-law and daughters-in-law), the relationships were characteristically interdependent and reciprocal.

This does not mean that life among Chinese elderly was ideal. Many of them lived in poor financial and environmental conditions. However, they did not tend to be singled out and treated as though they were socially incom-petent and dependent. As the study by Krause and Liang show, however, those kinds of relationships no longer exist for many Chinese elderly.

POTENTIAL FUTURE TRENDS IN SOCIAL-SERVICE PROVISION

What, then, is the future of the provision of social services for the aged? It cannot be denied that many of them do have special social needs, or that the programs of intervention that have been devised in recent years have helped to revitalize the social lives of many. This point can be illustrated by citing the example of a program in which this author was involved in the early 1970s in Butte, Montana.

Elderly participants could request a special bus, with stewards on board, to pick them up at their homes, deliver them to their destination, and return them home later. The purpose was to offer transportation to individuals who otherwise lacked it at a cost they could afford. In analyzing the utilization data from this project, it was learned that for many, the rides themselves became meaningful social events that they would not otherwise have had (Brown, 1972). Almost certainly, the lives of most of those individuals once again became socially isolated when that part of the program was not refund-ed and had to be discontinued.

Perhaps, then, elderly people in the United States who have social needs that they cannot satisfy on their own are simply doomed to live out their lives in an essentially dependent mode. As Green puts it, "receipt of care—especially pure, unsolicited, unilateral care—confers dependency on the recipient" (Green, 1993, p. 76). Perhaps, as some trends already indicate, elderly people in other nations will be forced into that same dependency as their numbers grow and their social needs multiply. If that is indeed the inevitable future condition of older persons, then their lives will not only be affected negatively, but the burden of their care can do nothing but increase. The truth is that the more our service-providing systems promote dependency among the aged, the more dependent the aged become. This is true because, if and when we humans lose our decision-making and planning skills, we cease to use them. Those kinds of skills keep life at any age vital and prevent us from becoming burdens to society. They make it possible for us to continue to make valuable social contributions.

A cross-cultural analysis reveals that older people in many societies continue to be intimately involved with and are respected by their families. This seems to keep them from becoming dependent upon societal benevolence for their social needs. Family involvement is still a prevalent tendency even among some American ethnic groups. Johnson found this to be true, for example, in the immigrant environment of Italian Americans in Syracuse, New York (Johnson, 1983). Elderly Italian Americans are still respected and allowed to enjoy control over younger family members, even over those who have become educated, successful professional workers. This is accomplished by a strict, family-oriented socialization that begins early in their lives, and by constant reminders by the family elders of younger members' family obligations.

This kind of family involvement on the part of elderly members has long been rejected by most elderly and younger family members alike in the United States, however. Decisions not to live with and not to interfere in the family affairs of their adult children constitute compliance with what has become a well-established social norm among elderly Americans. It is doubtful that traditionally oriented ethnic groups, such as Italian Americans, will be able to ignore that norm for very many more generations. Furthermore, family involvement alone by no means assures elderly people that they will not be placed into situations of premature dependency. Indeed, the evidence seems to indicate that in most cases, family members are the first ones to express the idea that elderly people represent burdens of care rather than social assets to their families. This type of attitude seems to emerge in particular societies as the numbers of older people increase, even when it represents a serious break with centuries-old traditions, as is beginning to happen, especially in Japan, for example. To be sure, families still offer elderly people a vital sense of security that is not available to them elsewhere (Bosse, Aldwin, Levenson, Spiro, and Mroczek, 1993). Families also often push older members into states of social dependency, however.

It has been proposed that chronological age should no longer be used as the criterion by which individuals become eligible to participate in publicly supported social-service programs. According to this argument, actual, documented needs would be a better way of determining the populations to whom to target such programs (Neugarten, 1982). The logic of this position is two-fold: (1) Making services available to all older people is too expensive, and (2) by doing so, we tend to reinforce the negative perceptions of old age. As Neugarten notes, that process may end up "stigmatizing rather than liberating older people from the negative effects of the label, 'old'" (Neugarten, 1982).

Compelling as this argument may seem, there are good reasons that it is neither conceptually nor practically feasible. Conceptually, as the primary advocate for using need instead of age as the criteria, Neugarten fails to recognize how relative "needs" are to existing situations and our definitions of those situations. As Lindesmith, Strauss, and Denzin point out, needs basically "arise in interpersonal interaction" (Lindesmith, Strauss, and Denzin, 1991, p. 200). Neugarten implies, but fails to adequately establish, that there are no needs that are unique enough to old people to warrant special attention in behalf of that population. Cook raises the issue of "specialness" in determining need among the aged with regard to victimization. She correctly reports that they are no more victimized than those of any age in terms of physical or financial losses, but that their level of fear about being victims of crime is indeed special for the aged (Cook, 1982). Such experiences as retiring and becoming retired are unique enough to old age to be considered as special, and both are associated with serious social adjustment problems. Practically, these are real situations that elderly people face today, and they represent some level of social need for many. The question is not whether elderly people do or do not have social needs (they do), but how those needs are treated.

Providing for the social needs of the elderly without also making them dependent may be close to impossible, given the present set of social and political circumstances. From a societal perspective, for example, there may be an important rationale for making elderly people dependent and treating them as dependent. From that perspective, formalized and professionalized provision of services for the aged becomes not so much a way of meeting their individual social needs as a form of social control. As Williams and his colleagues explain it, the public provision of services to elderly Americans has made it possible for them to remain somewhat independent of their adult children, but it did not make them less dependent. What has taken place is "an increase in dependence on and control by the state and its representatives in various government bureaucracies" (Williamson, Evans, and Powell, 1982, p. 215). Similarly, Arber and Ginn observe that, "in recent years, state provision of resources have been pitted against provision by individuals, their family or community in both Britain and the US," and that all of these forms of services create dependency (Arber and Ginn, 1991, p. 71). They do so because they tend to eliminate the element of choice in elderly persons lives, which is what Rubinstein, Kilbride, and Nagy have identified as the essence of independence (Rubinstein, Kilbride, and Nagy, 1992, p. 3). As the number of elderly retired people grows, they inevitably represent threats to many components of the existing societal power structures. Providing strictly controlled services to at least those who are the most apt to agitate for change make them dependent on those providing the services. Creating that kind of dependency is an extremely effective way of exerting social control over a population. Dependent people seldom become change agents.

This is not to say that our systems of services were created as a conspiracy to control elderly troublemakers. Neither do professionals perform their duties with that as their basic motivation. Nevertheless, the systems of care are indeed organized to operate that way. Service providers believe that they must control the service-delivery processes for the sake of efficiency. If advisory boards are added to give elderly recipients a voice in how the programs will function, they become one more element of the process to manipulate and control. To be sure, our service-provision systems work efficiently and deliver important services to our elderly citizens. We need to understand, though, that they do not deal with one of the most basic social concerns of today's older population: the fear of becoming dependent.

The existing system of social-service provision is well institutionalized and thus could not easily be changed. An even more basic issue, however, is whether it is even possible to provide such services without making the elderly participants basically dependent. Providing services to individuals is a form of intervention into their lives, and the very notion that any form of intervention is necessary implies that, at least in that sense, they are dependent. The fact is, people of all ages are subject to some forms of intervention and dependency. It happens to all of us as a normal part of life, as college students of all ages well know. The issue with elderly people, then, is not whether they experience a certain amount of dependency or not. Rather, it is whether dependency permeates so much of their lives that they become labeled "dependent," and begin to see themselves as, and act as if they are, socially incompetent. Intervention, as such, does not bring this about, but some kinds and amounts can and do. As Rubinstein, Kilbride, and Nagy explain, all of the possible choices we humans can make for ourselves can not be completely taken from us. However, "when big decisions have already been made in life or are limited or become few," all that are left are small decisions, which "increase in importance" (Rubinstein, Kilbride, and Nagy, 1992, p. 8).

Clearly, if social services are to be offered to the elderly today in ways that enhance rather than diminish their social competency, then new approaches are necessary. At least two promising approaches are already available and deserve consideration. One promising approach is what has been referred to as the self-help movement. Essentially, this means creating situations in which elderly people themselves are given the major responsibility of planning and even conducting the social services they need. One such approach, called a "network model," was put into operation in a residential area of San Francisco where over 20 percent of the residents were elderly people (Ruffini and Todd, 1979). Of central importance to the success of the program, called the Senior Block Information Service (SBIS), is a newsletter that provides a vital link to the social network for virtually all elderly people in the neighborhood. The newsletter provides information about available services and people in the network. Elderly volunteers are recruited from the neighborhood, and they provide much of the leadership in planning monthly meetings and special events. In reporting on this unique program, Ruffini and Todd conclude that, "the network model, as represented by SBIS, works for a range of people … Furthermore, it provides a latent structure that may be activated when necessary to mobilize large numbers in a crisis" (Ruffini and Todd, 1979).

Another promising approach for the enhancement of elderly peoples' social competency is to place special emphasis on intergenerational relationships that are reciprocal and interdependent. This is probably the most important lesson we can learn from the cross-cultural literature on the social standing of elderly people. In those societies in which the elderly are viewed as socially competent, they have family or community roles, or both, to fill in addition to being the recipients of needed services. To some extent reciprocal roles continue to tie together the older and younger generations in the People's Republic of China, for example, in interdependent relations and mutual respect. Johnson reports that interdependent relations were also part of the basis for continued intergenerational respect among Italian Americans (Johnson, 1983). While most reciprocal relationships reported in the literature have taken place in the family setting, this approach could just as well be applied in the context of publicly supported social-service programs. This has already been suggested as a valuable additional emphasis in the aging programs in Hong Kong (Chow, 1983).

CONCLUSION

In our critique of the aging network in planning and providing services to the aged in the United States, we find reasons to be both optimistic and pessimistic about the condition of the aged in the future. The network has been criticized by some for inconsistency and inefficiency. Given the complexity of its structure, the enormity of its tasks, and the diversity of its clientele, its record on those counts is a relatively good one. Both the structure and the operational approaches of the network have become institutionally entrenched as part of the American service-provision system. Changes may be needed in social-service delivery methods, but they will not be made merely because new approaches may be more meritorious than existing ones.

Whether approaches such as those we have discussed here are considered for adoption will depend upon active advocacy on the part of those who are concerned about the social well-being of elderly people. It has been pointed out that older people have very little power or influence over policy issues related to them. Indeed, the dependency-creating forces that exist today may continue to effectively deny them the power needed to make the changes that they see as important. There are some indications, however, that they may now be beginning to take the necessary initiative to advocate effectively in their own behalf. If so, that in itself will help to demonstrate their social competencies to the rest of society.

REFERENCES

Achenbaum, W. Andrew, "The Obsolescence of Old Age," in *Dimensions of Aging: Readings*, eds. Jon Hendricks and C. Davis Hendricks (Cambridge, Mass.: Winthrop, 1979), pp. 21–38.

Arber, Sara, and Jay Ginn, *Gender and Later Life* (Newbury Park, Calif.: Sage, 1991).

Bosse, Raymond, Carolyn M. Aldwin, Michael R. Levenson, Avron Spiro III, and Daniel K. Mroczek, "Change in Social Support after Retirement: Longitudinal Findings from the Normative Aging Study," *Journal of Gerontology*, 48, no. 4 (July 1993), P210–17.

Brown, Arnold S., "Final Report: The Problems of Mobilizing the Elderly with a Special Transportation Project," unpublished report of demonstration-research grant #93-P-75063/8-02 to Title IV Research and Development Grants Program, Administration on Aging, Social and Rehabilitative Service, Department of Health, Education, and Welfare, Washington, D.C. 20201, October, 1972.

Campbell, Ruth, and Elaine M. Brody, "Women's Changing Roles and Help to the Elderly: Attitudes of Women in the United States and Japan," *The Gerontologist*, 25, no. 6 (December 1985), 584–92.

Canter, Marjorie, and Virginia Little, "Aging and Social Care," in *Handbook on Aging and the Social Sciences*, eds. Robert H. Binstock and Ethel Shanas (New York: Van Nostrand Reinhold, 1985), p. 768.

Chow, Nelson Wing-sun, "The Chinese Family and Support of the Elderly in Hong Kong," *The Gerontologist*, 23, no. 6 (December 1983), 584–88.

Cook, Fay Lomax, "Age as an Eligibility Criterion," in *Age or Need? Public Policies for Older People*, ed. Bernice L. Neugarten (Beverly Hills, Calif.: Sage, 1982), pp. 171–203.

Cowgill, Donald O., "Aging and Modernization: A Revision of the Theory," in *Aging in America: Readings in Social Gerontology*, eds. Cary S. Kart and Barbara B. Manard (Sherman Oaks, Calif.: Alfred, 1981), pp. 111–32.

Cowgill, Donald O., *Aging Around the World* (Belmont, Calif.: Wadsworth, 1986).

Fischer, David Hackett, *Growing Old in America* (New York: Oxford University Press, 1978).

Frankfather, Dwight, *The Aged in the Community* (New York: Praeger, 1977).

Gelfand, Donald E., *The Aging Network: Programs and Services* (New York: Springer, 1993).

Gottesman, Leonard E., Barbara Ishizaki, and Stacey M. MacBride, "Service Management—Plan and Concept in Pennsylvania, *The Gerontologist*, 19, no. 4 (August 1979), 379–85.

Green, Bryan S., *Gerontology and the Construction of Old Age* (New York: Aldine De Gruyter, 1993).

Hill, Ann, "Defining Needs, Defining Systems: A Critical Analysis," *The Gerontologist*, 33, no. 4 (August 1993), 453–60.

Holmes, Douglas, Monica Holmes, Leonard Steinbach, Tony Hausner, and Bruce Rocheleau, "The Use of Community-Based Services in Long-Term Care of Older Minority Persons," *The Gerontologist*, 19, no. 4 (August 1979), 389–97.

Ishizaki, Barbara, Leonard E. Gottesman, and Stacey M. MacBride, "Determinants of Model Choice for Service Management Systems," *The Gerontologist*, 19, no. 4 (August 1979), 385–88.

"The Japanese-Style Welfare System," *Japan Quarterly*, 30 (July–September 1983), 328–30.

Johnson, Colleen Leahy, "Interdependence and Aging in Italian Families," in *Growing Old in Different Societies: Cross-Cultural Perspectives*, ed. Jay Sokolovsky (Belmont, Calif.: Wadsworth, 1983), pp. 92–101.

Jones, W. T., *A History of Western Philosophy* (New York: Harcourt, Brace, 1952).

Kane, Robert, and Rosalie Kane, *A Will and a Way* (New York: Columbia University Press, 1985).

Kart, Cary S., *The Realities of Aging: An Introduction to Gerontology* (Boston: Allyn & Bacon, 1985).

Kerns, Virginia, "Aging and Mutual Support Relations Among the Black Carib," in *Aging in Culture and Society*, ed. Christine L. Fry (New York: J. F. Bergin, 1980), pp. 112–25.

Krause, Neal and Jersey Liang, "Stress, Social Support, and Psychological Distress Among Chinese Elderly," *Journal of Gerontology*, 48, no. 6 (November 1993), P282–91.

Krout, John A., "Rural-Urban Differences in Senior Center Activities and Services," *The Gerontologist*, 27, no. 1 (February 1987), 92–97.

Krout, John A., "Senior Center Linkages in the Community," *The Gerontologist*, 26, no. 5 (October 1986), 510–15.

Krout, John A., "Senior Centers in Rural Communities," in *Providing Community-Based Services to the Rural Elderly*, ed. John A. Krout (Thousand Oaks, Calif.: Sage, 1994), pp. 90–110.

Krout, John A., Stephen J. Cutler, and Raymond T. Coward, "Correlates of Senior Center Participation: A National Survey," *The Gerontologist*, 30, no. 1 (February 1990), 72–79.

Kuypers, Joseph A., and Vern L. Bengtson, "Social Breakdown and Competence: A Model of Normal Aging," *Human Development*, 16 (1973), 181–201.

Latourette, Kenneth S., *A History of Christianity* (New York: Harper and Brothers, 1953).

Lindesmith, Alfred R., Anselm L. Strauss, and Norman K. Denzin, *Social Psychology* (Englewood Cliffs, N.J.: Prentice Hall, 1991).

Logan, John R., and Glenna Spitze, "Informal Support and the Use of Formal Services," *Journal of Gerontology*, 49, no. 1 (January 1994), S25–34.

Lowy, Louis, *Social Policies and Programs on Aging* (Lexington, Mass.: Lexington Books, 1980).

Maeda, Daisaku, "Family Care in Japan," *The Gerontologist*, 23, no. 6 (December 1983), 579–83.

Martinson, Floyd M., *Family in Society* (New York: Dodd, Mead, 1970).

McClain, John W., J. Michael Leibowitz, Stephen B. Plumer, and Karin S. Lunt, "The Senior Center as a Community Focal Point: A Strategy for Rural Community Development," in *Aging in Rural America*, ed. C. Neil Bull (Newbury Park, Calif.: Sage, 1993), pp. 59–70.

Miner, Sonia, John R. Logan, and Glenna Spitze, "Predicting the Frequency of Senior Center Attendance," *The Gerontologist*, 33, no. 5 (October 1993), 650–57.

Mok, Bong-ho, "In the Service of Socialism: Social Welfare in China," *Social Work*, 28, no. 4 (July-August 1983), 269–72.

Nash, Bernard E., and Gerald Bloedow, "The Five-County Demonstration Project," in *Aging in Minnesota*, ed. Arnold M. Rose (Minneapolis: University of Minnesota Press, 1963), pp. 21–33.

Neugarten, Bernice L., "Policy for the 1980s: Age or Need Entitlement?" in *Age or Need? Public Policies for Older People*, ed. Bernice L. Neugarten (Beverly Hills, Calif.: Sage, 1982), pp. 19–32.

"1971 White House Conference on Aging," an unpublished report to the delegates from the Conference Sections and Special Concerns Sessions, p. 50.

Ogawa, Naohiro, and Robert D. Retherford, "Care of the Elderly in Japan: Changing Norms and Expectations," *Journal of Marriage and the Family*, 55 (August 1993), 585–97.

Rich, Bennett M., and Martha Baum, *The Aging: A Guide to Public Policy* (Pittsburgh: University of Pittsburgh Press, 1984).

Rose, Arnold M., "The Subculture of the Aging: A Framework for Research in Social Gerontology," in *Older People and Their Social World*, eds. Arnold M. Rose and Warren A. Peterson (Philadelphia: F. A. Davis, 1965), pp. 3–16.

Rubinstein, Robert L., Janet C. Kilbride, and Sharon Kagy, *Endless Living Alone: Frailty and the Perception of Choice* (New York: Aldine De Gruyter, 1992).

Ruffini, Julio L., and Harry F. Todd, "A Network Model for Leadership Development Among the Elderly," *The Gerontologist*, 19, no. 2 (April 1979), 158–62.

Schneider, Robert L., "Barriers to Effective Outreach in the Title VII Nutrition Programs, *The Gerontologist*, 19, no. 2 (April 1979), 163–68.

Shanas, Ethel, Peter Townsend, Dorothy Wedderbaum, Henning Friis, Paul Milhoj, and Jan Stehouwer, *Old People in Three Industrial Societies*, (New York: Atherton Press, 1968).

Taietz, Philip, "Two Conceptual Models of the Senior Center," *Journal of Gerontology*, 31, no. 2 (March 1976), 219–22.

Taietz, Philip, and Sande Milton, "Rural-Urban Differences in the Structure of Services for the Elderly in Upstate New York Counties," *Journal of Gerontology*, 3, no. 3 (May 1979), 429–37.

Wantz, Molly S., and John E. Gay, *The Aging Process: A Health Perspective* (Cambridge, Mass.: Winthrop, 1981).

Williamson, John B., Linda Evans, and Lawrence A. Powell, *The Politics of Aging: Power and Policy* (Springfield, Ill.: Charles C. Thomas, 1982).

15

Religion as a Vital Aspect of Aging

INTRODUCTION

Religion is a very prevalent and vital part of the lives of a large portion of today's elderly population. Because of this, it would be impossible to get a comprehensive view of the social lives of elderly people today without carefully examining this aspect of their lives in terms of what it means to them and how their religious orientations relate to the other elements of their lives. Another important part of this analysis is to discover how religions tend to define the aging processes compared to the views of science and the modern secular world.

Evidence of the extent of the religious influence in the lives of elderly people is plentiful. A 1987 Gallup Poll report, as well as other more recent data, for example, shows that attendance at religious services on a weekly basis increased steadily with age ("Church Attendance," 1987; Achenbaum, 1985; Glass, 1990). As Figure 15–1 indicates, nearly half (49 percent) of those 65 years old and older, compared to only 45 percent of those between 50 and 64, 39 percent of those 30 to 49, and 33 percent of those 18 to 29, reported that they attended religious services at least once each week. This is an especially important finding when it is recognized that many of the very old are no longer physically capable of attending public gatherings.

In addition, the Gallup Poll compared the elderly with the other age groups in terms of a subjective assessment of religion. They were asked how "important" religion was to them in their daily lives. What was found was

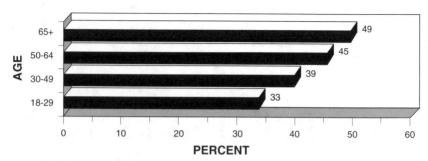

FIGURE 15–1   Percent Attending Religious Services Weekly by Age (Source: "Church Attendance," *Gallup Report, 259* (April 1987), 38–39.)

that as many as 67 percent of the elderly, compared to only 44 percent of those between 18 and 29, answered that it was "very important" ("Importance of Religion," 1987). A similar but more specific measure of subjective religion was included in a 1982 national survey of elderly people. Subjects were asked how much God influenced their lives, as well as how important an influence their religious faith was in their lives. The results were that as many as 75 percent said that God was "very influential" in their lives, and 80 percent said that their religious faith was the "most important" influence in their lives (Hooyman and Kiyak, 1991, p. 412).

Some analysts have speculated that the differences between age groups may simply be the result of the differences between age cohorts rather than the effect of aging. The present cohort of elderly people may have always been religiously oriented, whereas those who are now younger may not now be and will never be as religious. In other words, it may simply be a specific example of the continuation of a particular social pattern throughout life, as continuity theory explains many of the social patterns of the elderly. To some degree that may well be true as at least one longitudinal study indicates (Hooyman and Kiyak, 1991, p. 412). Another possible explanation of these generational differences, based on activity theory, is that the higher levels of religious participation among the elderly is because it is a readily available way of keeping socially active.

There are indications, though, that aging itself may also have some association with religious experiences. For one thing, the 1991 records of weekly attendance at religious services show increases on the part of those 18 to 29 (from 33% to 36%) and those 30 to 49 (from 39% to 41%), but stayed the same (47%) for those 50 and older ("Church Attendance," 1987; "The Faithful Return to Church," 1991). For another thing, in a discussion of how religion affects elderly people who are disabled, Koenig reports the finding, from a sample of 850 elderly hospitalized men, that a third of them said they had had a "life-changing religious experience at some time in their lives" and that "more than 40 percent reported that this event occurred after they had reached the age of 50" (Koenig, 1994). Based on these kinds of realities among elderly Americans, J. Conrad Glass at North Carolina State University recently raised what would seem to be a valid question. "Given these facts, it seems strange that so often books that are purported to address various factors related to older adults overlook the area of religion and aging" (Glass, 1990).

RELIGIOUS AND SCIENTIFIC DEFINITIONS
OF AGING COMPARED

As was discussed earlier, in the past, in Western as well as Oriental societies, being old meant not only being respected and honored, but also having authority and even being venerated. For over 100 years of American history, especially during the colonial era, older people tended to hold especially privileged social status in the communities in which they lived. Among the Puritans in Massachusetts Colony, for example, as described in Chapter 14, the elders held special positions of power and the elderly were so elevated in status that many experienced "psychic infirmity" (emotional distance from those under their control) (Fischer, 1978, pp. 72–73). This was carried even a step further in China and Japan when the aged became part of the social and religious traditions of filial piety and ancestor worship (Piovesana, 1979, pp. 13–20).

Two historic movements in the Western world have been identified as doing the most to change these views of aging to very opposite views. First, as also discussed in Chapter 14, was the revolutionary development in the right of individual "liberty" and "equality," in the late 1700s. This, according to Fischer, was "caused by the interaction of English Protestant ideas with the American environment" and created a "revolution in age relations" (Fischer, 1978, p. 109). It is ironic that these ideas, which seem to have emerged from a religious emphasis, provided the challenge to the wisdom, functional value, and authority that elderly people had enjoyed in the very religious bodies from which the revolutionary ideas came. Indeed, Haber challenges the idea that even the great sense of religious calling among the elderly devout Puritans in the Colonial era had much to do with their power and prestige. Instead, she contends that basically they had power and were considered wise only if they were land owners and exerted control over their families. She explains that, even though it rarely happened, the transfer of land resulted in the established hierarchy being reversed. As she put it, "the aged, rather than being respected without question," then "assumed the subservient role in the relationship" (Haber, 1985, pp. 8–21). It is noteworthy, also, that apparently no such revolutionary movement took place in Japan or China, at least until Communism took over in China only in relatively recent years. But even Communism has not basically changed the idea that the elderly are wise, even though there was an attempt to do so by passing some new laws to counter the power of older people.

The second movement that has helped to redefine the meaning of old age has been "modernization." As explained in Chapter 5, Cowgill has argued that the processes involved in the modernization of societies have brought about the loss of status among elderly people, wherever in the world it has taken place. Particularly important in this regard are the processes of technological development, economic development, urbanization, and modern education, all of which isolate the elderly and leave them at social and intellectual disadvantages.

In general, modernization is characterized by social change and Cowgill contends that "rapid social change tends to undermine the authority and status of the elderly generation" (Cowgill, 1986, p. 198). In spite of the cultural differences between Western and Oriental societies, there are signs of the beginnings of the loss of social status among the elderly in Japan, as that country has become modernized (Roth, 1983; Palmore and Maeda, 1985, pp. 74–75), and even in China, as that country has begun the processes of modernization (Hong, 1993).

The emphasis on aging as decline and loss, which seems to be supported by the current scientific data on all aspects of aging, stands as an effective challenge to the possibility that there may be developmental aspects to aging among humans and that the elderly may be uniquely equipped to perform certain socially vital roles. This current view of aging as decline implies a cyclical concept of the way that we humans experience time. We are born, go through a developmental and maturing time, and then decline and die. This is in stark contrast to the Biblical linear concept of time in which we humans are seen as continuing to move toward an ultimate, eternal destiny. According to this view there is never a time of life that we humans are not moving toward that eternal destiny. All of this earthly life involves active participation that moves us toward whatever eternal destiny is in store for us. In old age, just as at any age, we may move toward either an evil or a holy destiny, but we never just naturally decline, become irrelevant, and fade away. Some Christian theologians, for example, have characterized old age as a time of spiritual growth rather than nothing but decline. As Lyon has put it, "while the body suffers deterioration with aging, the spirit or soul may yet grow in old age" (Lyon, 1985, pp. 42–43). The question this raises about the elderly, especially about those whose destiny is holy, is, what is the nature of their active participation?

Just what is the relationship between religion and aging? For one thing, it has been found that the older people become, the more apt they are to believe in God, to believe in immortality, and as indicated above, to feel that being religious is important to them. Up to age 80, after which age they are less able to do so, as we also discovered earlier, the older people become the more apt they are to regularly attend religious services. In addition, the life satisfaction among those who are religiously active tends to be higher than among those who are not (Cox and Hammonds, 1988; Guy, 1982; Ellison, Gay, and Glass, 1989).

It is a fair question to ask why there tends to be a positive correlation between religious involvement and life satisfaction. Markides, and Cox and Hammonds conclude that it is because church becomes a focal point of social integration activity for these elderly, providing them with a sense of community and well-being (Cox and Hammonds, 1988; Markides, 1983). One has to wonder about that kind of purely sociological conclusion, however. A great deal of evidence exists that modern churches have done very little to include elderly people into their ongoing activities (Achenbaum, 1985).

Why life satisfaction tends to be related positively to participation in religious life undoubtedly has more to do with what they believe religiously and how strongly they believe it (i.e., that God forgives, protects, and provides for them regardless of existing social conditions) than the sociological circumstances related to church life. It has been found, for example, that intrinsic religious orientation among the elderly is especially related to their level of satisfaction in life (O'Connor and Vallerand, 1990). Rosik also compared intrinsically and extrinsically religious widowed elderly with regard to the levels of grief and depression they were experiencing. All of the

respondents were attending support groups at the time they were interviewed. Extrinsic religiosity was defined as endorsing religion to find social
and emotional support rather than adhering to a specific set of beliefs. He
found that those more extrinsically religious showed more signs of grief and
depression than the intrinsically religious group (Rosik, 1989). Bearon and
Koenig also found that prayer in the lives of religious elderly people tended
to be related to their state of health. They believed that prayer was a vital
source of help, as well as their physicians, in matters of health (Bearon and
Koenig, 1990). Kinoshita and Kiefer told about a close-knit group of elderly
Japanese Christians in a retirement home in Japan that met weekly for worship, prayer, and study. They observed that, "the mere fact of Christian belief
seems to create strong interpersonal bonds" among them (Kinoshita and
Kiefer, 1992, p. 164). Krause and Van Tran studied the relationship between
both organizational religious involvement (church attendance) and nonorganizational religious involvement (prayer and religious feelings) as each was
related to stress among black elderly. They found that not only did those with
the most religious involvement have less stress but also that self-esteem was
greatly enhanced regardless of whether or not they were experiencing stress
in their lives (Krause and Van Tran, 1989). Levin reports that religious involvement and subjective religious attitudes or beliefs also consistently promote better health among elderly people (Levin, 1994). In addition, Pressman
and his colleagues found that greater religiosity was associated with lower
levels of depression among a sample of hospitalized elderly women being
treated for broken hips (Pressman, Lyons, Larson, and Strain, 1990). Muldoon
and King have also proposed that just being spiritual, by which they mean
approaching life holistically, promotes greater well-being among the chronically ill. They do not, however, provide tangible evidence of that assumption
(Muldoon and King, 1991). Spirituality is a term that is used in the context of
religion, but it tends to be so broadly defined that it is difficult to know just
what it is, whether or not it is related to religion, and certainly how it may
affect the lives of frail elderly people.

The question of what specifically there is about religion that tends to
produce the positive results among elderly people has been studied. The
answers that have been provided deal with some substantive elements that a
number of religions have in common and which are emphasized in the activities in which they engaged. One of those emphases is that of hope. In that
regard, Koenig explains that in the Judeo-Christian religions, the ritualisti-
cally supported promise that God not only loves us as individuals but makes
it possible for us and expects us to reach out to others in love, is an enormously powerful source of hope and consequently of self-esteem, especially
to disabled elders. As he puts it, "Out of a love relationship with God, then,
the elderly may begin to feel that he or she is worthwhile and is an important
and vital part of this world" (Koenig, 1994). Other ways to think of this point
are (1) that "God has put the *awareness* of eternity into our mind" (Hulme,
1986, p. 84), and (2) that "it is because God redeems our lives from final mean-
inglessness that the blessing of age carries the force that it does" (Lyon, 1985,
pp. 116–17).

Another substantive component of many religions that has been highlighted as being especially meaningful to elderly persons is the promise of

forgiveness. Kaplan makes the point that forgiveness is "deeply woven into the Judeo-Christian traditions, indeed much of religion," and that "religious rituals normally include the rituals of forgiveness as healing" (Kaplan, 1992). He and his colleagues recognize that religion can, and often does, have negative as well as positive effects on people and the world. It has at times produced resentments and violent forms of revenge, but those have been forms of religion of which forgiveness had no part in their traditions and rituals. In contrast, when forgiveness is a central component of religion, it liberated individuals from resentment and vengeance—sentiments that are easy to develop through the aging processes (Kaplan, Monroe-Blum, and Blazer, 1994). As Achenbaum put it, "a religious commitment entails and facilitates a continuous assessment of one's life in a way that does not impel doubt and criticism, for a living faith simultaneously requires one to review past mistakes and wrongdoing and to look forward." To be sure, this is not a very happy process, but the point is that, "religion has provided, and continues to offer, vital directions and support for an older person putting life into perspective" (Achenbaum, 1985).

With a growing number of studies on the relationship between religious involvement and such outcomes as health and life satisfaction, a concern has developed to develop a more comprehensive measure of religiosity. Particularly important has been the inclusion of subjective aspects of religion as well as such purely behavioral measures as frequency of attendance at services (Ainlay and Smith, 1984; Krause, 1993; Thomas and Eisenhandler, 1994). Consequently, recent studies have used measures of religiosity that include (1) organizational religiosity (i.e., attendance and other forms of active involvement), (2) nonorganizational religiosity (i.e., tithing, praying, and reading scripture), and (3) subjective religiosity (i.e., how strongly religious respondents feel they are).

In addition to these more traditional expressions of and experiences with religion, Levin also studied what he called "mystical experiences" (Levin, 1993). These included (1) being in a new place with the sense of having been there before, (2) being in touch with someone far away, (3) having a vision of an event far away as it takes place, (4) being in touch with someone who has died, and (5) having an out-of-body experience. Specifically, he wanted to find out how these kinds of experiences related to the traditional forms of religious experiences on the part of those in four different age groups: 18–30; 31–40; 41–50; and over 60.

He found that, in general, the over 60 group reported having significantly fewer such experiences than any of the other groups (see Figure 15-2). It is probably not too surprising that the two types of mystical experiences the elderly respondents reported having had as frequently as the others were being in touch with someone who had died and out-of-body experiences. It was also found that having mystical experiences was positively related only to the nonorganizational and/or subjective aspects of religiosity among all of the age groups. Overall, participation in organized religious activities was negatively correlated with having mystical experiences. Individualized religiosity was all that was related to having mystical experiences. It may well be that it is the isolated and frail elderly, with strong general feelings of being religious, who are most apt to have a sense that they are corresponding with deceased

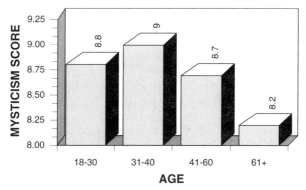

FIGURE 15-2   Age Differences in Mystical Experience by Mean Score (Source: Jeffrey S. Levin, "Age Differences in Mystical Experiences," *The Gerontologist*, 33, no. 4 (August 1993) 507–13, from Table 2.)

loved ones and having out-of-body experiences. Undoubtedly, those still an active part of organized religion, which is ritually focused on the substantive aspects of religion, would tend not to have those kinds of experiences. As Levin explains, he suspects it may be that "regular participation in public worship discourages paranormal involvements" (Levin, 1993). What is not known about mystical experiences is the extent that they may or may not benefit individual elderly persons' self-esteem and health, as does traditional religious participation.

REVISITING THE CONCEPT OF WISDOM AS RELATED TO AGING

Of particular importance to a discussion of religion and aging is the relationship between old age and wisdom and how the elderly may perform valuable roles in the context of religion. Few today would doubt that there is a slowing down of the physical and mental capacities with age, even though Wintraub and Shneidman have recently discovered that some "gifted" men in their seventies and eighties scored as high or higher on mental capacity (memory, attention, visual perception, calculation, and reasoning) as younger men, and that they increased their vocabularies in their seventies. This finding was obviously only true of the most gifted ("Some Get Sharper with Old Age," 1991). The question is, however, whether or not the usual slowing down processes necessarily eliminate the possibility that a certain type of wisdom may come with aging. This is a question that is very seldom even raised, in the current gerontological literature (Schulz and Ewen, 1988, p. 163; Moberg, 1971, pp. 223–33). When the question is raised it is typically dealt with as a relic of the past. When asked, many people say that they believe the elderly possess wisdom, but few treat them as though they are wise (Richman, 1977; Taranto, 1989).

The concept of wisdom, itself, as it is dealt with today by philosophers and psychologists, suffers from a lack of how to define it. As Taranto puts it, "wisdom as a concept appears about as ethereal as rarified air and … it is a notion that is obviously difficult to grasp let alone hold onto" (Taranto, 1989).

It is described by some as creativity (Hooyman and Kiyak, 1991, pp. 219–20), by others as the accumulation and application of knowledge (Clayton, 1982), and by still others as "the highest level of cognitive development" (Moody, 1983). It is defined by Luce, one of the organizers of SAGE, as "an awareness of the larger whole" and as "the melting of boundaries and concepts" (Luce, 1981, p. 41) and by Salk as "the art of the disciplined use of imagination, exercised at the right time and in the right measure" (Salk, 1973, p. 72). The philosopher, Jonathan Jacobs, describes wisdom as "practical," by which he means the ability to discern what is objectively moral in human nature, in contrast to the rather common idea in the secular world that morality is relative (Jacobs, 1989). Kitchner and King have conceptualized wisdom as "reflective judgment" and have devised tests to measure it. They have found that this kind of wisdom is indeed developmental and "comes only with age." Their research samples included only subjects to age 55, however. There is no indication that their theory would cover anyone beyond that age ("Can Colleges Teach Thinking?" 1987).

The Ericksons identify their last life cycle stage as wisdom. Working through the struggle between integrity and despair, and ending up with integrity involves the kind of wisdom that is unique to older persons. As Joan Erickson explains, "Old age is a time for remembering and weaving together many disparate elements, and for integrating these incongruities into a comprehensive whole." She also contends that, ironically, wisdom, rather than resulting in persons who know it all, inevitably leads the older person to a point of "genuine humble curiosity" (Erickson, 1988, pp. 103–4).

The questions that remain are how the different religions define wisdom and whether the study of the religious perspective of aging may reveal a type of wisdom that comes uniquely with aging and that the scientific perspective of aging has simply missed. Sontag contends that there is a universality about the way that the religions and philosophies of the world define the ethically ideal man. In essence he believes that, with the exception of the evolutionary philosophy of Marxism, the one most important universal aspect is "the stress on the mean between extremes." His claim is that "East and West agree on the desirability of moderation" (Sontag, 1990). Specifically he believes that the moral order, by which he means the social structure, is fixed and the human ethic is following it, not overturning it by revolution. Highest in that moral order are "those born wise." He admits that Christian ethics does have a revolutionary element to it, but that only applies to the end of time. Clearly he fails to fully understand how the message of both Judaism and Christianity are expected to apply to and transform human life in the here and now. Consequently, in contrast to Sontag's analysis, how wisdom is defined is very different from one religion to another.

In her article on "Shamanism and Aging," Halifax described the role of the wise shaman as "the channel for the knowledge of the Ancients, the means for the wisdom of the Elders and Elements to be transmitted to the community" (Halifax, 1981, pp. 49–60). This defines the wisdom of the elderly in terms of the roles they play in the transmission of culture from one generation to the next. This is a typical definition of wisdom among native American elderly (Schweitzer, 1983) as well as how Confucius described it with his emphasis on the importance of maintaining family harmony in Oriental cultures (Chai and Chai, 1965, pp. 1–18; Novak, 1994, pp. 119–20). As Hall and Ames point out, though, Confucius saw the sage as operating in a much more dynamic way than merely performing a prescribed cultural role (Hall and Ames, 1987, pp. 268–300). Instead, he was a "master of communication," one who learned the art of communicating, an artistic and creative process (Novak, 1994, pp. 131–33). He first had to learn how to listen and become "attuned" to the world around him, and from that sense of attunement he communicated through both language and music to create and recreate harmony. His use of language is not a matter of understanding the meaning of abstract concepts, as would be true in Western cultures, but of using names that appropriately describe the elements of nature. Good communication depends upon what Confucius called "the ordering of names." This, he said, was absolutely vital to harmonious life, because without it there would be no harmony.

It is important to understand that transcendence is not a part of Confucianism, and that, therefore, wisdom was not a matter of understanding anything like a transcendent god. Rather, the future of human existence was a matter of creating and maintaining harmony in life. It is also explained that it was not until he was 60 years old that he had really learned to listen and become attuned. This kind of definition of wisdom was very much supported in Oriental societies because of the importance placed on families as the most vital social entity, and because of the religious concept of ancestor worship (Kinoshita and Kiefer, 1992, p. 51). A similar social and religious system can be found among many African tribes, as is still true in Zaire (Mpolo, 1984). Confucianism and its emphasis on the wisdom of those who are old is being challenged by some today at least in modern Japan, but even there, as well as in Korea, overall those traditions are still quite strong (Loughman, 1991; Sung, 1990).

In contrast to defining wisdom in terms of roles that elderly play in transmitting culture or in creating and maintaining harmony in life, Judaism and Christianity define it quite differently. These are religions that emphasize the vital importance of a transcendent God who dominates all of human life. Novak characterizes Judaism, for example, as "the evolution of a people in the grip of two toweringly great ideas. The first is the idea of God—imageless, primordially creative, and utterly transcendent—who, nevertheless, cares for the creation. The second is the idea of human dignity: men and women become fully human only by responding to the moral intuitions divinely etched in their hearts" (Novak, 1994, p. 176). Here, then, wisdom is seen first and foremost as residing in God, who actively reveals himself to his people and who gives wisdom as a special gift to certain individuals among his followers (Hamilton, 1990).

Gladson and Lucas report that for some time Biblical theology largely ignored the concept of wisdom because it was seen to have no revelatory or redemptive emphases. Recent research has challenged that assumption, however. Theologians have recently begun to recognize that the Biblical approach to wisdom, especially as depicted in late Old Testament times, became decisive in the formation of both rabbinical Judaism and Christian theology. According to these authors the fundamental premises underlying this type of wisdom were that (1) the world operates according to an order established by the Creator; (2) this order appears implicit in the way both positive and negative deeds (i.e., "compassion toward the poor finds favor") come back to the doer; (3) the fear of the Lord leads to life; and (4) ultimate human plans must be bent to divine order (Gladson and Lucas, 1989). Concerning the importance of wisdom in the Judeo-Christian tradition, Blech also makes the point that the command to respect wisdom itself is found in Leviticus 19:32 (Blech, 1981).

So what place do the elderly have in all of this? Isenberg has studied the place of older people throughout the long history of Judaism and has found both positive and negative "strands" (Isenberg, 1992). On the one hand, some of the ancient Old Testament literature depicts being old as "the ripening of what had been seeded," "a time for sharing the wisdom of experience," and "a reward for keeping the covenant requirements." On the other hand, other parts of that literature emphasize old age as "dissipated power," the "loss of autonomy, respect, and self-worth," and even as "punishment for not living in accord with God's will." Moses illustrates these kinds of contrasts concerning the place of the elderly in Judaism. He was blessed in old age as a great leader of his people, but was also finally punished and not allowed to enter the Promised Land. The point here is that age itself is not an adequate measure of wisdom. Rather, "true wisdom is rooted in the fear of God" (Isenberg, 1992). According to Novak, what happened to Moses was not so much punishment for unfaithfulness as it was to emphasize the point that God himself was the true source of wisdom. The fact that Moses is said to have died "away from his people, in an unknown grave," guarded against "the temptation to deify him" on the part of the Israelites (Novak, 1994, p. 191).

Minois offers a similar viewpoint of the Biblical view of wisdom and the elderly, but with additional insights (Minois, 1989, pp. 25–42). He points out that during the nomadic period of the Israelites, the older men were seen as wise and the natural leaders of the people. Especially in the period of the Judges, they formed into councils of wise men to whom the leaders were accountable. After the monarchical state was formed, however, even though councils of elders remained, their influence declined. Their wisdom and counsel were increasingly challenged in favor of that of younger men. It was recognized that not all older people were necessarily wise and members of the councils of elders were selected more because they were individually seen as wise rather than because they were old. Apparently this trend continued in the period of the early Christian church. The church inherited the institutions of councils of elders, but even less attention was given here to the age of their members than was true among those in the Jewish synagogues. Christian elders were those in the community who were judged as "renowned in wisdom," regardless of how old they were (Minois, 1989, pp. 34–35). Nevertheless, there are a number of references in the New Testament calling for elderly to be respected, and obeyed, especially in reference to parents (Knapp, 1981).

Obviously, not all religions agree about what constitutes wisdom nor who has it. It depends greatly upon what their messages are to the world and who can best communicate that message. The message of many religions is that we human beings must live out our lives in harmony with nature and the social institutions of which we are a part. In those cases, it takes wisdom to know how that can be done, and elderly people are generally most apt to have that kind of wisdom, with their years of cultural experiences. The message of Judaism and Christianity has been one of hope for a better life than this world offers, made possible by a compassionate and merciful God. The kind of wisdom needed for that kind of religious emphasis can come only from God himself and given to whomever he chooses.

Nevertheless, a study of the history of both Judaism and Christianity reveals that elderly people have traditionally been considered to be wise more often than those who are younger. To be sure one is not wise simply because he or she is old, but the experiences that come with aging have undoubtedly been assumed to make those with the gift of wisdom even wiser.

Achenbaum and Orwoll studied the Book of Job for insights into how wisdom and age are related from a Biblical perspective. They apply Job's story to a "psycho-gerontological" theoretical model of wisdom that was recently developed. According to this model, which they contend is thoroughly supported by Job's experiences, the essential features of wisdom are "intense introspection, a willingness to penetrate and deflate conventional ideas with searching questions, and an ability to change one's views on the basis of interactions with others" (Achenbaum and Orwoll, 1991). Therefore, according to this view, growing wiser takes time, and wisdom is much more apt to be found among the old than the young. Specifically, their claim is that the process of becoming wise takes place at three levels of experience: intrapersonal, interpersonal, and transpersonal, and "is manifested in feelings, thoughts, and actions." Unless changes occur at all of these levels and in all of these ways, a person is not truly wise (see Figure 15–3). As these authors analyze what happened to Job, in his long and painful dialogue with God, he was eventually forced to face up to his own intrapersonal imperfections. As a consequence of that and of the misery he was experiencing he came to identify or empathize interpersonally with the downtrodden, and have a sense of humility over what his experiences meant at a more universal level.

Through his experiences of losing everything and struggling with God, Job eventually accepted the fact that what he knew and could do on his own was severely limited relative to the power of God. Specifically related to his own deep concern, he finally accepted the reality that the problem of evil was beyond human solution. As Achenbaum and Orwoll conclude, "fathoming the limits of cognition is the beginning of wisdom." Eventually, Job gained "integrity" and "maturity" in the kinds of compassionate interactions he came to

FIGURE 15-3   A Synthetic Model of Wisdom (Source: W. Andrew Achenbaum and Lucinda Orwoll, "Becoming Wise: A Psycho-gerontological Interpretation of the Book of Job," *International Journal of Aging and Human Development*, 32, no. 1 (1991), pp. 21–39, Figure 1.)

	INTRAPERSONAL	**INTERPERSONAL**	**TRANSPERSONAL**
AFFECT	Self-Development	Empathy	Self-Transcendence
COGNITION	Self-Knowledge	Understanding	Recognition of Limits of Knowledge and Understanding
CONATION	Integrity	Maturity in Relationships	Philosophical/Spiritual Commitments

have with others, as well as a new spiritual commitment, and his life was redeemed from the state of misery he had experienced. What is noteworthy about his redemption, though, is that it was not due merely to his repentance but came after he had also interceded before God in behalf of his "friends," who had previously severely judged him. As Achenbaum and Orwoll summarize what the Book of Job teaches us about wisdom, "Growing wise requires knowledge and reflection, but not these alone: one matures in wisdom through a concatenation of self expression and compassionate deeds, as well as conversations and interactions with others" (Achenbaum and Orwoll, 1991).

With regard to this kind of a description of wisdom, I am reminded of the story one of my fellow students in graduate school told about her father that illustrates the process of gaining wisdom in the secular world. She explained that, as a highly successful and high-level executive at the Lockheed airplane plant in Seattle, his attitude about people on welfare and the whole idea of welfare was one of condemnation. Then one day the company lost a contract with the federal government, he lost his job, and was unable to find employment elsewhere. Out of that humiliating experience, he not only had to eventually apply for welfare himself for a time, but he also became an enthusiastic advocate of the poor and of the provision of welfare in their behalf. His daughter expressed a great deal of admiration for what she saw as a wise and compassionate person.

Lampe makes a similar point about the Apostle Paul in his words about what wisdom is really all about in his first letter to the Corinthian Church. Paul's experiences in life somewhat paralleled those of Job. He was a fully educated, dedicated, and highly respected Jewish theologian. As such, he had dedicated his life to stamping out Christianity, what he saw as a heretical and dangerous movement. The movement had been established in Damascus as well as Jerusalem and he set out for Damascus to put a stop to it. On the road he had some kind of traumatic experience in which he went temporarily blind. After a time of struggling with this humiliating experience which made him a helpless individual, he defined the incident as being confronted by Christ, face to face. Finally, he ended up, not only as a defender of the very people he had previously persecuted, but also as a dedicated missionary of Christianity to the Gentiles, among the Greeks.

Among the many Greek cities in which he later established churches, one of them was Corinth. As the membership of that church grew, it became a greatly diverse group. There were those with both Gentile and Jewish backgrounds as well as rich and poor. There were also those who claimed to be followers of different famous Christian leaders such as Paul, Apollos, and Cephas, and quarrels developed over which group was right, and represented true wisdom. Finally Paul wrote to challenge all of them about their conventional ideas about wisdom. He accused both Jews and Greeks of distorting the truth about God in their demands toward each other for "signs" on the part of the Jews and for "wisdom" on the part of the Greeks. Interpreting Paul's words to all of them, Lampe concludes that, "The Jewish demand for signs and the Greek demand for wisdom evidently have in common that they call for proof supporting divine truth. With that, Jews and Greeks, 'set themselves up as an authority that can pass judgment upon God ... They expect

God to submit himself to their criteria'" (Lampe, 1990). In his letter to the Corinthians, Paul tried to make it clear that even he claimed no such wisdom as they were claiming. Instead, he had gone to them in the first place "in weakness, fear, and much trembling." As Lampe puts it, "when the cross is proclaimed and through this act a community is founded, human wisdom and strength do not contribute anything to it" (Lampe, 1990). It is the humble wisdom born out of the honest and active struggle for the meaning of life and death that really counts.

Post has also criticized how Christianity offers meaning to life in old age. He argues against what he calls "the contemporary myth of eternal bodily life and of youthful old age" which, he submits, "are tragic and finally painful for the very persons they are intended to inspire." In contrast, he says that "the Christian will find meaning by transcending his or her despair through faith in the continuing reality of a merciful and just God, through hope in everlasting life, through acts of authentic other-regarding love, and through a continued interior search for the peaceful presence of God" (Post, 1992). True as this discussion of Christianity is, nevertheless, he makes this final phase of the Christian pilgrimage appear to be an extremely lonely one, almost as though disengagement is called for in order that the individual older person can come to grips with the meaning of life and death, as depicted in disengagement theory. Missing is what the elderly uniquely have to contribute to the family of believers, such as the wisdom gained through a lifetime of faith, as suggested by Achenbaum.

PRESENT-DAY MINISTRIES FOR THE AGED

It was noted above that far too little is being done by today's religious organizations to include older people in their ongoing activities. Only recently have seminaries begun to include gerontology as part of their training of pastors (Lewis, 1991; Moberg, 1980; Payne, 1989; Powers, 1988), and only recently have churches begun to pay any special attention to their older members. This has come in part because such organizations as the Interfaith Coalition on Aging and the American Association of Retired Persons have exerted a major effort to encourage seminaries and churches to develop programs for the elderly in recent years (Powers, 1988). The major rationale given for this has been because of the growing numbers of elderly and the great need they have for special services (Hendrickson, 1986; Oliver, 1987; Tobin, 1986, pp. 27–37; Worthington, 1989). The provision of services, then, has been the major focus of how churches have responded to their older members, even though some religious leaders have resisted even this approach, giving as their rationale that their organizations exist to serve the spiritual needs of all ages of people equally. In that regard, Glass makes the point that professional religious leaders have basically relied on findings from behavioral science to identify what services elderly people need (Glass, 1990). Thus, much of what has been done for them in churches tends to simply reflect the scientific perspective that older people are essentially dependent.

Not much information about the extent that individual churches and synagogues across the United States provide services is available. However, it is well known that some local groups have developed fairly elaborate programs of service to their older people. In addition, a number of nationally organized religious groups have focused special attention on the needs of senior adults, as illustrated by the "Aging Today and Tomorrow" program of the American Baptist Churches of the USA (Cruz-Griffith, 1991). The types of services provided by local religious groups have been divided between "primary" and "secondary" (Tobin, 1986, p. 29). The primary activities are those that focus on communicating the belief systems of the particular religion involved, through such functions as worship and scriptural study groups, sometimes specifically targeting the elderly. As noted earlier, these kinds of services tend to be especially meaningful to the elderly. With regard to worship, Holmes makes the point that it "requires the accumulation of memories" and that "the richer the evocation of the past reaching back to childhood, the greater is its ability to open to us the possibilities of life now and in the future." Accordingly, he makes a distinction between "poor liturgy," which he labels as nothing but "sentiment" to make people feel good at the moment, and "good liturgy" that presents important symbols from the past and applies them to the present and the future (Holmes, 1981). According to Clements, this kind of emphasis on memories or "reminiscence" has the important psychological as well as religious effect of "dissonance reduction" and "life review" (Clements, 1979, p. 501). Glass believes that the study or educational religious activity focused on aging is particularly vital, and contends that "education about aging is for every age group." In addition, "education for the aging" helps them to look ahead to the challenges they may encounter and at the same time "enables them to express their potential more fully" (Glass, 1990).

The secondary activities in behalf of the elderly by religious organizations involve providing for their specific social and psychological needs. In some cases the participation of the religious organization is simply to provide the space for another community social service agency to operate such programs as a day-care or a senior citizen center for the older people from the whole community (Glass, 1990). In other cases the religious body administers the services themself, providing such services as visitation to the home-bound and hospitalized elderly, telephone reassurance to elderly who need it, meals, and housekeeping to the homebound, advocacy, and referral (Tobin, 1986, pp. 30–31; Glass, 1990). Some churches or synagogues are motivated to provide these kinds of services to fill in gaps of needed services not being provided by other community social service agencies. Others provide them basically for their own older members and in ways that fit their own belief systems. In still other situations several religious groups in the community work cooperatively in an interfaith effort to provide services to the whole older population of the community (Tobin, 1986, pp. 27–37). An example of the interfaith approach to service provision is the development and implementation of the "Shepherds Center" in Kansas City. According to Koenig, this is a program that is supported by 25 local churches and synagogues as well as local businesses, foundations, and individuals. It serves several thousand elderly people and is administered primarily by a staff of several hundred volunteers who are elderly themselves. The services provided focus mostly on the "mental, emotional, and spiritual dimensions" of the elderly persons' lives as well as health maintenance and preventive care (Koenig, 1986). This program has now spread to many other communities in the United States.

ROLES IN RELIGIOUS LIFE FOR THE AGED

In spite of all the positive aspects of religious participation and of being the recipients of valuable services provided by religious institutions, there are barriers to participation on the part of elderly people. Glass, for example, identifies such practical physical barriers as poor health and the lack of such things as transportation, hand rails, ramps, and elevators. Perhaps even more important, though, are such relational and attitudinal barriers as no longer being "asked to serve on committees," experiencing "the congregation's negative attitude toward older people," and not being "looked to for wisdom, knowledge, and leadership." Glass gives an insightful observation about the relationship of elderly persons and religious organization. He suggests that, "even with best intentions, we may do an injustice, and perhaps serious damage, to older people in the church if we only think about ministry to them and for them. We may be contributing to the future isolation, dependence, and devaluing with such a philosophy" (Glass, 1990). Furthermore, Jones accuses the religious community of "squandering the contribution which makes the aged unique and inexpendable" (Jones, 1987). Much of the religion and aging literature reflects that sentiment by suggesting the kinds of meaningful roles older people are especially qualified to fill.

Most of the roles being suggested in the literature on aging and religion, by the scholars of that area of concern, basically come from studies of religious traditions. Special attention, for example, has been paid to how the elderly fit in religiously throughout the long history of Judaism and Christianity, that is, Old Testament times, the Early Christian church era, Reformation times, and colonial times in America. The primary focus of this analysis is how the religiously oriented wisdom that has been attributed to older people in the past can be applied to religious bodies in modern times.

Practically speaking, suggesting roles for anyone to play in any group or organization such as churches or synagogues does not in itself make a reality. As Wimberley points out, "role-identity" is a necessary part of role-fulfillment, and that comes about, in large part, from the "expectations for appropriate behavior, which are generally shared by the individual who occupies the corresponding position and by those with whom the individual interacts in that position" (Wimberley, 1989). An illustration of this point is the case of a 90-year-old lady who had suffered from cancer for years. She often informed people (young and old) in her congregation who had special unfulfilled needs, that she prayed for them every day. Eventually, others in the church began to refer to her as "a prayer warrior" and to provide her with special prayer requests. That became a vital role that she was seen as uniquely qualified to fulfill. It wasn't that others could not and did not also offer prayers for people in the congregation, but that her prayers were seen as particularly vital because of her age, her loving spirit, and her great faith in the face of her own difficulties and suffering. Sadly, that lady's case is rather rare in religious life in the modern era. As noted before, it is commonly recognized that older members are expected to make very few substantive contributions to church life today (Achenbaum, 1985). That is, of course, not to say that older members are never called on to hold leadership positions in churches or synagogues. They are, but there are few if any expectations that older people may have something special to offer. An important part of the case that is being made by religiously oriented gerontologists to change that, then, is to educate both lay and professional religious leaders about what older congregational members may uniquely have to offer (Lyon, 1985, p. 33; Glass, 1990).

It is recognized by all who are making the case for religious roles among the aging that aging in and of itself does not make people qualified leaders. By no means are all elderly people wise. What it is that qualifies them as wise and able to contribute their wisdom to religious communities, therefore, is of first importance in identifying the roles they can be expected to play. In that regard, a crucial qualifying element is what in the older persons' individual lives has contributed to and strengthened their religious convictions. In particular, this has to do with how they integrated all of the many experiences of their lives (good and bad, successes and failures, painful and painless) into their religious faith.

Applying this specifically to Christians, Lyons highlights the importance of prayer, introspection, and meditation which are characterized first of all by "reminiscence" (Lyon, 1985, pp. 48–53). Reminiscing among the aging is sometimes seen as either an unhealthy way of living in the past, when life was easier and more pleasant, or as an important therapeutic process which keeps them from dwelling on their present problems. For religious purposes, though, Lyons describes it as "not simply a 'pleasant work' ... "but more importantly "to determine as best they can 'how things stand between God' and themselves" (Lyon, 1985, pp. 48–50). Other essential parts of that process, according to Lyon, are (1) the recognition of human weakness, (2) repentance, and (3) the necessity of depending on and relating to a caring and forgiving God (Lyon, 1985, pp. 48–50). Wisdom and the religious roles of the elderly that emerge from that wisdom, then, are not based on great amounts of knowledge about human existence but on the humble faith by which they have learned to live. Continuing to become educated about one's religious traditions and issues, as a lifetime, never-ending process, is also seen as leading to similar results (LaPorte, 1981), but also, in a broader sense to help the elderly critically think through the "historic claims" of the religious traditions on their constituents, in terms of how they may currently apply (Lyon, 1985, p. 53).

Reed provides a somewhat similar analysis of wisdom from a less religious perspective. She discusses what she calls "self-transcendence." As she describes it, this consists of "the expansion of one's conceptual boundaries" through three types of behavioral patterns: (1) inward introspection, by which the individual contemplates how to integrate the physical and other changes they are experiencing as older people into their overall sense of self; (2) temporal activities, by which they consider how to integrate perceptions of their past and future in order to enhance the present; and (3) outward activities in which they become concerned about and become actively involved with helping others. She studied the effect of these processes on elderly subjects between the ages of 80 and 97 and found substantial improvements in their mental health. Particularly important in that regard was "body-transference." As she concluded, they "displayed active integration and flexibility in attitudes toward their health problems" (Reed, 1991).

On the basis of the wisdom gained through lifetimes of religious experiences, as outlined above, and the traditional role expectations from the past, several roles for elderly people are suggested for consideration on the part of religious groups in this modern day and age. For one thing, they should be uniquely qualified to act as the "bearers of the living tradition" of the religious body of which they are part. According to Knierim, that is a role that was assigned to the elderly in Biblical times (Knierim, 1981), and it is certainly just as valid today as it ever was. In that same vein Clements calls on the elderly church members to diligently help their churches to "take the past seriously" and "value the process of building memories of value in its people" (Clements, 1981).

Throughout much of the history of Judaism and Christianity, elders have been responsible to instruct the younger members of those religious communities. As Knierim says, in discussing the place of the elderly throughout Old Testament times, "Old people specifically represented the linkage ... the generations" (Knierim, 1981). It is hard to imagine elderly people in today's churches and synagogues being expected or even allowed to have the primary responsibility of providing religious instruction of young people. Neither the younger nor the older people would agree to that. Establishing certain kinds of helping relationships between them, however, has been proposed and would be feasible. LaPorte reports, for example, that the elderly in the Early Church often served as "wise counselors of the young" (LaPorte, 1981), and that is true to some degree in some churches still today. This is the same kind of relationship that is programmed in a growing number of intergenerational programs across the United States with a great deal of success. Simmons discusses the motive for young and old participating in "intergenerational support systems" within religious congregations in ethical terms—it would be wrong not to do so (Simmons, 1991). In addition, though, analyses of communitywide intergenerational programs show that they are seen by both young and old participants as mutually rewarding experiences (Newman, 1989).

One further religious role that has been proposed in which the elderly ought to be expected to participate is to help their religious institutions understand where they stand on ethical issues being faced in the larger community. These would include such matters as the "right to die" movement; "the continuing responsibilities for elderly citizens" (Clements, 1981); and the involvement of the religious community in civil affairs (Achenbaum, 1985).

It is obvious, from this analysis of the potential and suggested religious roles for today's elderly people, that many of them have a great deal to uniquely contribute. It is not being proposed that they should necessarily compete with younger people for positions that the younger people are perfectly qualified to fill. Rather, what is being called for is the recognition that there are some vital functions of religious life for which older people with lifelong spiritual experiences are particularly qualified.

CONCLUSION

Obviously, religion is an important part of a sizable majority of elderly people's lives today. Studies also show that those who participate regularly in religious activities out of strong religious convictions greatly benefit in both physical and mental well-being. What that means, then, is that in order to discover why religion has those kinds of positive results among the elderly we need to do more than pay attention to their participation patterns, as has been true of many investigators in the past. The substance of the belief systems, and how older people tend to respond to them, are equally if not more important to understand. Examining how modern science and religion tended to define aging and characterize old age differently is also helpful in this sense. For that kind of information, the writings of both theologians and social scientists have been utilized in this chapter.

As we have seen, scientifically oriented gerontologists have largely defined aging as physical and mental decline and loss, with little or no allowance for any kind of development or growth. While many admit that modern health technology has done much to prolong and slow down the declining processes, few believe that further growth is possible in old age. Consequently, old age has largely been characterized as a time of increasing dependency. It is almost exclusively on the basis of this characterization that services targeting the elderly have been developed and delivered. This, at least in part, has had the effect of serving as a self-fulfilling prophecy.

In contrast, as we have seen, religious scholars (i.e., theologians) have tended to define aging as a maturing, growing process throughout the human life span, one that at least has the potential of making older persons particularly wise. This is true of such very diverse religions as Confucianism, found in the Orient, and Judaism and Christianity in the West, even though these two religious traditions differ greatly in terms of what they mean by wisdom. On the one hand, wisdom as Confucius defined it is a matter of learning through a lifetime of experience all there is to know about life in the universe that maintains environmental and family harmony, and understanding how we humans are and ought to be part of the environment in which we exist, and remain part of in death. On the other hand, Judaistic and Christian scholars have informed us that wisdom for followers of those religions comes from a history of relating to and becoming dependent upon the one transcendent Father God in whom they believe as the one who both created the universe and continues to love and care for that creation. Particularly important in the development of wisdom on the part of individual believers are experiences of diversity and suffering, out of which faith in God has been tested and strengthened. For many elderly people today these experiences include the many physical, psychological, and social struggles they have in aging itself.

Parker discusses a process that she labels as "The Great Escape" that has nothing to do with religion, but involves some of the same experiences by which older religious people are said to gain wisdom. As she describes "The Great Escape," it involves what she sees as "the major themes of life" among the elderly: "the importance of life review, intergenerational conflict and resolution, loss of control and renewed control of one's destiny, and acceptance of our own mortality" (Parker, 1991). What this process especially does for the elderly persons who go through it is to prepare them for a peaceful death, according to Parker. What she does not address, though, is how frequently elderly people actually experience it and how they find the moral strength and motivation to endure it. For religious people that comes from the substance of their faith, and one of the results is that they become particularly qualified for such roles as special counselors and mentors to the young.

Today's church and synagogue leaders have been criticized for failing to recognize the qualifications many elderly people in their congregations have for those kinds of special roles, and how important those roles are to older and younger people alike. The tendency is for many religious leaders to see elderly people in their congregations as dependent (Achenbaum, 1985). The potential exists, however, and there does seem to be a growing recognition of the importance of mutual helping intergenerational relationships both within religious organizations and also in the larger communities.

REFERENCES

Achenbaum, W. Andrew, "Religion in the Lives of the Elderly: Contemporary and Historical Perspectives," in *Values, Ethics and Aging*, ed. Gari Lesnoff-Caravaglia (New York: Human Sciences Press, 1985), pp. 99–115.

Achenbaum, W. Andrew, and Lucinda Orwoll, "Becoming Wise: A Psycho-gerontological Interpretation of the Book of Job," *International Journal of Aging and Human Development*, 32, no. 1 (1991), 21–39.

Ainlay, Stephen C., and D. Randall Smith, "Aging and Religious Participation," *Journal of Gerontology*, 30, no. 3 (May 1984), 357–63.

Bearon, Lucille B., and Harold G. Koenig, "Religious Cognitions and Use of Prayer in Health and Illness," *The Gerontologist*, 30 (April 1990), 249–53.

Blech, Benjamin, "Judaism and Gerontology," in *Aging and the Human Spirit: A Reader in Religion and Gerontology*, eds. Carol LeFevre and Perry LeFevre (Chicago: Exploration, 1981).

"Can Colleges Teach Thinking?" *Time*, 129, no. 7 (February 16, 1987), 61.

Chai, Ch'u, and Winberg Chai, *The Humanist Way in Ancient China: Essential Works of Confucianism* (New York: Bantam, 1965).

"Church Attendance," *Gallup Report*, 259 (April 1987), 38–39.

Clayton, Vivian, "Wisdom and Intelligence: The Nature and Function of Knowledge in Later Years," *International Journal of Aging and Human Development*, 15, no. 4 (1982), 315–20.

Clements, William M., *Care and Counseling of the Aging* (Philadelphia: Fortress, 1979).

Clements, William M., "Introduction: The New Context for Ministry With the Aging," in *Ministry With the Aging*, ed. William M. Clements (New York: Harper & Row, 1981), pp. 1–20.

Cowgill, Donald O., "Aging and Modernization: A Revision of the Theory," in *Aging in America: Readings in Social Gerontology*, eds. Cary S. Kart and Barbara B. Manard (Sherman Oaks, Calif.: Alfred, 1981).

Cowgill, Donald O., *Aging Around the World* (Belmont, Calif.: Wadsworth, 1986).

Cox, Harold, and André Hammonds, "Religiosity, Aging, and Life Satisfaction," *Journal of Religion and Aging*, 5, no. 1/2 (1988), 1–22.

Cruz-Griffith, Martha, "Growing Old Gracefully," *The American Baptist*, 189, no. 7 (September 1991), 15–18.

Ellison, Christopher G., David A. Gay, and Thomas A. Glass, "Does Religious Commitment Contribute to Individual Life Satisfaction?" *Social Forces*, 68, no. 1 (September 1989), 100–123.

Erickson, Joan M., *Wisdom and the Senses: The Way of Creativity* (New York: Norton, 1988).

"The Faithful Return to Church at Easter," *The Gallup Poll Monthly*, 306 (March 1991), 57–58.

Fischer, David Hackett, *Growing Old in America* (New York: Oxford University Press, 1978).

Fischer, Kathleen, *Winter Grace: Spirituality for the Later Years* (New York: Paulist Press, 1985).

Gladson, Jerry, and Ron Lucas, "Hebrew Wisdom and Psychotheological Dialogue," *Zygon*, 24, no. 3 (September 1989), 357–76.

Glass, J. Conrad, "Religion and Aging and the Role of Education," in *Introduction to Educational Gerontology*, eds. Ronald H. Sherron and D. Barry Lumsden (New York: Hemisphere, 1990), pp. 109–34.

Guy, Rebecca Faith, "Religion, Physical Disability, and Life Satisfaction in Older Age Cohorts," *International Journal of Aging and Human Development*, 15, no. 3 (1982), 225–32.

Haber, Carole, "Aging in Colonial America," in *Beyond Sixty-Five: The Dilemma of Old Age in America's Past* (New York: Cambridge University Press, 1985).

Hall, David L., and Roger T. Ames, *Thinking Through Confucius* (New York: State University of New York Press, 1987).

Halifax, Joan, "Shamanism and Aging: The Elders and the Elements," in *Wisdom and Age*, ed. John-Raphael Staude (Berkeley, Calif.: Wright Institute, 1981).

Hamilton, Gary G., "Patriarchy, Patrimonialism, and Filial Piety: A Comparison of China and Western Europe," *British Journal of Sociology*, 41, no. 1 (March 1990), 77–104.

Hendrickson, Michael C., *The Role of the Church in Aging for Policy and Action* (New York: Haworth, 1986).

Holmes, Urban T., "Worship and Aging: Memory and Repentance," in *Ministry With the Aging*, ed. William M. Clements (New York: Harper & Row, 1981), pp. 91–106.

Hong, Guodong, "Support for the Elderly in China—Gradual Improvements in Social Security," in *Population Aging: International Perspectives*, eds. Tarek M. Shuman, E. Percil Stanford, Anita S. Harbert, Mary G. Schmidt, and Joan L. Roberts, (San Diego: San Diego State University, 1993), pp. 433–40.

Hooyman, Nancy R., and H. Asuman Kiyak, *Social Gerontology: A Multidisciplinary Perspective* (Boston: Allyn & Bacon, 1991).

Hulme, William Edward, *Vintage Years: Growing Older with Meaning and Hope* (Philadelphia: Westminster, 1986).

"Importance of Religion," *Gallup Report*, 259 (April 1987), 13–15.

Isenberg, Sheldon, "Aging Judaism: 'Crowning of Glory' and 'Days of Sorrow,'" in *Handbook of the Humanities and Aging*, eds. Thomas R. Cole, David Van Tassel, and Robert Kastenbaum (New York: Springer, 1992), pp. 147–74.

Jacobs, Jonathan, "Practical Wisdom, Objectivity and Relativism," *American Philosophical Quarterly*, 26, no. 3 (July 1989), 199–209.

Jones, W. Paul, "Theology and Aging in the 21st Century," *Journal of Religion and Aging*, 3, no. 1/2 (Fall/Winter 1987), 17–32.

Kaplan, Berton H., "Social Health and the Forgiving Heart: The Type B Story," *Journal of Behavioral Medicine*, 15, no. 1 (1992), 3–14.

Kaplan, Berton H., Heather Munroe-Blum, and Dan G. Blazer, "Religion, Health, and Forgiveness," in *Religion in Aging and Health: Theoretical Foundations and Methodological Frontiers*, ed. Jeffrey S. Levin (Thousand Oaks, Calif.: Sage, 1994), pp. 52–77.

Kinoshita, Yasuhito, and Christie W. Kiefer, *Refuge of the Honored: Social Organization in a Japanese Retirement Community* (Berkeley, Calif.: University of California Press, 1992).

Knapp, Kenneth R., "Respect for Age in Christianity: The Base of Our Concern in Scripture and Tradition," in *Aging and the Human Spirit: A Reader in Religion and Gerontology*, eds. Carol LeFevre and Perry LeFevre (Chicago: Exploration, 1981), pp. 420–44.

Knierim, Rolf P., "Age and Aging in the Old Testament," in *Ministry With the Aging*, ed. William M. Clements (New York: Harper & Row, 1981), pp. 21–36.

Koenig, Harold G., "Religion and Hope for the Disabled Elderly," in *Religion in Aging and Health: Theoretical Foundations and Methodological Frontiers*, ed. Jeffrey S. Levin (Thousand Oaks, Calif.: Sage, 1994), pp. 18–51.

Koenig, Harold G., "Shepherd Centers: Helping Elderly Help Themselves," *Journal of the American Geriatrics Society*, 34 (1986), 73–74.

Krause, Neal, "Measuring Religiosity in Later Life," *Research on Aging*, 15, no. 2 (June 1993), 170–97.

Krause, Neal, and Thanh Van Tran, "Stress and Religious Involvement Among Older Blacks," *Journal of Gerontology*, 44, no. 1 (January 1989), S4–13.

Lampe, Peter, "Theological Wisdom and the 'Word About the Cross': The Rhetorical Scheme in I Corinthians 1-4," *Interpretation*, 44, no. 2 (April 1990), 117–31.

LaPorte, Jean B., "The Elderly in the Life and Thought of the Early Church," in *Ministry With the Aging*, ed. William M. Clements (New York: Harper & Row, 1981), pp. 37–55.

Levin, Jeffrey S., "Age Differences in Mystical Experiences," *The Gerontologist*, 33, no. 4 (August 1993), 507–13.

Levin, Jeffrey S., "Investigating the Epidemiologic Effects of Religious Experience: Findings, Explanations, and Barriers," in *Religion in Aging and Health: Theoretical Foundations and Methodological Frontiers*, ed. Jeffrey S. Levin (Thousand Oaks, Calif.: Sage, 1994).

Lewis, Albert M., "The Middle Aging in America: Spiritual and Educational Dilemmas for Clergy Education," *Journal of Religious Gerontology*, 7, no. 4 (1991), 47–53.

Loughman, Celeste, "The Twilight Years: A Japanese View of Aging, Time, and Identity," *World Literature Today*, 65 (Winter 1991), 49–53.

Luce, Gay Gaer, "SAGE and Wisdom," in *Wisdom and Age*, ed. John-Raphael Staude (Berkeley, Calif.: Wright Institute, 1981), p. 41.

✝ Lyon, K. Brynolf, *Toward a Practical Theology of Aging* (Philadelphia: Fortress, 1985).

Markides, Kyriakos S., "Aging, Reliogisty, and Adjustment: A Longitudinal Analysis," *Journal of Gerontology*, 38, no. 5 (September 1983), 621–25.

Minois, George, *History of Old Age: From Antiquity to the Renaissance*, trans. Sarah Hanbury Tension (Oxford, U.K.: Polity, 1989).

Moberg, David O., "Aging and Theological Education," *Theological Education*, 16, no. 3 (Special Issue, Winter 1980), 283–93.

Moberg, David O., *Spiritual Well-Being—Background and Issues for 1971*, White House Conference on Aging, 1971.

Moody, Harry R., "Wisdom in Old Age: The Highest Level of Cognitive Development," paper presented at the 36th Annual Meeting of the Gerontological Society of America, November 1983. Abstract in *The Gerontologist*, 23 (Special Issue, October 1983), 263.

Mpolo, Masamba ma, *Older Persons and Their Families in a Changing Village Society: A Perspective from Zaire* (Washington, D.C.: International Federation on Aging and the World Council of Churches Office of Family Education, 1984).

Muldoon, Maureen H., and J. Norman King, "A Spirituality for the Long Haul: Response to Chronic Illness," *Journal of Religion and Health*, 30, no. 2 (Summer 1991), 99–108.

Newman, Sally, "A History of Intergenerational Programs," in *Intergenerational Programs: Imperatives, Strategies, Impacts, Trends*, ed. Sally Newman (Binghamton, N.Y.: Haworth Press, 1989), pp. 1–16.

Novak, Philip, *The World's Wisdom* (New York: HarperCollins, 1994).

O'Connor, Brian P., and Robert J. Vallerand, "Religious Motivation in the Elderly: A French-Canadian Replication and an Extension," *Journal of Social Psychology*, 130, no. 1 (February 1990), 53–9.

Oliver, David B., *New Directions in Religion and Aging* (New York: Haworth, 1987).

Palmore, Erdman B., and Daisaku Maeda, *The Honorable Elders Revised* (Durham, N.C.: Duke University Press, 1985).

Parker, Marcie, "The Great Escape: The Meaning of the Great Escape Theme in the Humanities and Gerontology," *Educational Gerontology*, 17, no. 1 (January-February 1991), 55–61.

Payne, Barbara, "Introduction and Suggestions for Use," *Journal of Religion and Aging*, 6, no. 1/2 (1989), pp. 3–13.

Piovesana, Gino K., "The Aged in Chinese and Japanese Cultures," in *Dimensions in Aging: Readings*, eds. Jon Hendricks and C. Davis Hendricks (Cambridge, Mass.: Winthrop, 1979), pp. 13–20.

Post, Stephen G., "Aging and Meaning: The Christian Tradition," in *Handbook of the Humanities and Aging*, eds. Thomas R. Cole, David Van Tassel, and Robert Kastenbaum (New York: Springer, 1992), pp. 127–46.

Powers, Edward A., "Pastoral Care," in *The Aging Society: A Challenge to Theological Education*, ed. Edward A. Powers (Washington, D.C.: Interreligious Liason Office, American Association of Retired Persons, 1988).

Pressman, Peter, John S. Lyons, David B. Larson, and James J. Strain, "Religious Belief, Depressions, and Ambulation Status in Elderly Women with Broken Hips," *American Journal of Psychiatry*, 147, no. 6 (June 1990), 758–60.

Reed, Pamela G., "Self-Transcendence and Mental Health in Oldest-Old Adults, *Nursing Research*, 40, no. 1 (January/February 1991), 5–11.

Richman, Joseph, "The Foolishness and Wisdom and Age: Attitudes Toward the Elderly as Reflected in Jokes," *The Gerontologist*, 17, no. 3 (June 1977), 210–19.

Rosik, Christopher H., "The Impact of Religious Orientation in Conjugal Bereavement Among Older Adults," *International Journal of Aging and Human Development*, 28, no. 4 (1989), 251–60.

Roth, Judith A., "Timetables and the Lifecourse in Post-Industrial Society," in *Work and Lifecourse in Japan*, ed. David Plath (Albany: State University of New York Press, 1983), pp. 248–59.

Salk, Jonas E., *The Survival of the Wisest* (New York: Harper & Row, 1973).

Schulz, Richard, and Robert B. Ewen, *Adult Development and Aging: Myths and Emerging Realities* (New York: Macmillan, 1988).

Schweitzer, Marjorie, "The Elders: Cultural Dimensions of Aging in Two American Indian Communities," in *Growing Old in Different Societies: Cross-Cultural Perspectives*, ed. Jay Sokolovsky (Belmont, Calif.: Wadsworth, 1983), pp. 168–78.

Simmons, Henry C., "Ethical Perspective on Church and Synagogue as Intergenerational Support System," *Journal of Religious Gerontology*, 7, no. 4 (1991), 17–28.

"Some Get Sharper with Old Age," *Arizona Daily Sun* (February 16, 1991), p. 3.

Sontag, Frederick, "The Analects of Confucius: The Universal Man," *The Journal of Chinese of Philosophy*, 17, no. 4 (1990), 427–38.

Sung, Kyu-taik, "A New Look at Filial Piety: Ideals and Practices of Family-Centered Care in Korea," *The Gerontologist*, 30, no. 5 (October 1990), 610–17.

Taranto, Maria A., "Facets of Wisdom: A Theoretical Synthesis," *International Journal of Aging and Human Development*, 29, no. 1 (1989), 1–21.

Thomas, L. Eugene, and Susan A. Eisenhandler, "Introduction: A Human Science Perspective on Aging and the Religious Dimension," in *Aging and the Religious Dimension*, eds. L. Eugene Thomas and Susan A. Eisenhandler (Westport, Conn.: Auburn House, 1994), pp. xvii–xxi.

Tobin, Sheldon S., *Enabling the Elderly* (Albany: New York State University Press, 1986).

Wimberley, Dale W., "Religion and Role-Identity: A Structural Symbolic Interactionist Conceptualization of Religiosity," *The Sociological Quarterly*, 30, no. 1 (Spring 1989), 125–42.

Worthington, Everett L., "Religious Faith Across the Life Span: Implications for Counseling and Research," *Counseling Psychologist*, 17 (October 1989), 555–612.

16

Dying and Death
as Experiences
of the Aged

INTRODUCTION

As a child growing up on a farm in northern Montana, this author lived in the midst of death on an almost daily basis. Watching wild animals of many types die was a common experience. Many pets died of accidents or problems of aging. Watching, and even participating in, the killing and butchering of domestic animals were also part of the rural life of those days. Neither did human death escape my farm-boy experiences. A 26 year old neighbor boy who lived only half a mile away suddenly got bronchial pneumonia one cold winter day and died before his parents could get him to the hospital 40 miles away. Only a year later, I was suddenly afflicted with the same disease and rode the 40 miles in an unheated automobile afraid that I would not make it in time either. Death was no stranger in that neighborhood. It was something that happened to young and old alike. It took place where people lived, in their homes or places of work, more than anywhere else. Those who died were buried ceremoniously with the participation of the whole neighborhood, and survivors went on with their lives.

How different are the experiences of death and dying today? By and large, death now occurs among those who are old, and it is typically preceded by a somewhat extended period of dying. Furthermore, few people nowadays die either at home or where they work. Death has thus become an important subject in which gerontologists have become keenly interested. We want to explore how the experiences with death have changed and how those changes have affected older people and their relationships.

DEATH AS A COMMON EXPERIENCE OF THE PAST

Many of today's students of death and dying point to the past as the time when death was not avoided but dealt with realistically, meaningfully, and effectively. When the United States was basically an agrarian nation and technological development was limited, it was indeed difficult for most people to avoid direct experiences with death. The loss of family members, close friends, and neighbors of all ages was also almost inescapable. Furthermore, people in the past typically died in their homes or work places, in the midst of family and friends who knew them intimately. Thus, survivors were often present as their loved ones died.

One distinct advantage that people in rural communities of the past had when someone close to them died was that they were almost always surrounded by the support of others. Families tended to be large, neighbors were often close friends, and communities were made up of people in daily contact with each other. Experience with death was rarely a lonely event. Even neighbors who were not close would pay their respects and express concern. Survivors were comforted, helped to make some common-sense meaning of death, and encouraged to move on with their lives.

Funerals tended to be highly meaningful events in rural America. They were events at which the total attention of communities was focused on the needs of survivors. They were also times when the lives of those who had died, even those not well liked, were ceremoniously honored and even celebrated. Their lives were put into the best possible perspective, providing assurances that they had not lived in vain but had made contributions to their families and communities.

To be sure, experiences with death in those kinds of settings in the past were real and vital. We must be careful, however, not to depict that as the ideal with regard to matters of death and dying. It was far from it. The frequency of experiences with death in our past history by no means made them easy. The loss of close relatives and friends in death was traumatic and highly dreaded. Grief was shared, but it was nevertheless harsh and often viewed as unfair. The trauma of so much unpredicted death was neither easy nor understood, and was devastating to whole communities (Baum and Baum, 1980, p. 195). Baum and Baum suggest that, contrary to what is assumed in today's literature on death and dying, avoidance of the problems of death was probably more prevalent in the past than it is today. Elaborate funerals were perhaps more a way of avoiding death than actually coming to grips with it (Baum and Baum, 1980, p. 195). Moving through the rituals undoubtedly helped people to put the "why" questions aside unanswered and allowed them to get on with the problems of making a living and surviving.

People did not pursue the meaning of death or of the dying process. Dying as an elongated process was something few experienced. The few who did had little understanding of the agony involved and found little or no community support or empathy. People in the past faced death because they had very little choice, and dealt with it in practical ways that somewhat helped to alleviate the personal agony and the societal hardship. However, we would be mistaken if we supposed that they were any more emotionally or philosophically comfortable with death than we in modern societies are.

DYING AS AN OLD-AGE EXPERIENCE

A number of basic changes in our perception and experience of death have taken place in recent years. These changes, to a large extent, are directly related to the advancements that have been made in medical technology, particularly in the area of disease control. As a result of these advancements, the major causes of death have changed quite drastically.

In the not-too-distant past, the leading causes of death in the United States were acute, infectious diseases such as diphtheria, typhoid fever, and smallpox. Other acute problems, such as pneumonia and tuberculosis, also were common causes of death. Only a relatively few people survived all of the possible acute causes of death. As a result of the advances made in disease control technology and policies during this century, (including immunization, vaccination, drugs, infection control, and so on), not only do few if any people die from these diseases (see Table 16-1), but also fewer and fewer are even afflicted with them. Few acute diseases take people's lives in modern societies.

Thus, while the death rate was once high among infants and spread across the age spectrum, death is now largely reserved for those who are old. Also, since there are fewer deaths at younger ages, more and more people live into old age and there are increasing numbers of deaths among the older population (Backer, Hannon, and Russell, 1994, p. 5).

Our experiences with death changed not only in terms of who dies but also in terms of how they tend to die. The major causes of death have largely shifted from acute to chronic health problems. Gee refers to this shift as the "epidemiological transition" and explains that, "when death rates are high and life expectancy low, the major takers-of-life are infectious diseases, which tend to select young victims. As death rates decline and life expectancy increases, the degenerative diseases of old age predominate" (Gee, 1987). That transition is shown in Table 16-1. Wolinsky and his cohorts recently did a study of what particular factors in elderly people's lives put them at risk of being placed in nursing homes and of death. They discovered that the two most prevalent risk factors of both being institutionalized and of dying relatively young were more bodily functional limitations and having a history of such diseases as rheumatic heart disease or cancer. They concluded that

TABLE 16-1   Three Leading Causes of Death and Percentage of Deaths by Each, 1900 and 1980

1900		*1980*	
CAUSE	PERCENT	CAUSE	PERCENT
Pneumonia, influenza, bronchitis	14.4	Heart disease	38.2
Tuberculosis	11.3	Cancer	20.9
Diarrhea and enteritis	8.1	Strokes	8.6

SOURCE: E. M. Gee, "Living Longer, Dying Differently," *Generations*, 11, no. 3 (Spring 1987), 5.

"there can be little doubt that deteriorating health status is an important index of the risks for nursing home placement and death" (Wolinsky and others, 1993). Chronic problems are generally those that require long-term care and elongate the dying process. Thus, the "dying trajectory" has become an important part of the whole death syndrome (Glaser and Strauss, 1968, pp. 5–6). For many elderly people today, the suffering of dying is much worse than death itself.

Other factors, other than diseases, have also been identified as related to death in recent studies. Sugisawa, Liang, and Liu, for example, studied the relationship between the social lives of Japanese elderly and their patterns of mortality. They examined three different measures of social behavior including "social contact" (interactions with family and friends), "social participation" (attendance at organized gatherings), and "marital status" (whether or not they were currently married). In addition they included a measure of self-rated health status as a control factor. Surprisingly, they found, on the one hand, that neither marital status nor social contacts were directly or even indirectly related to if/when they died. On the other hand, social participation was found to have a strong impact on mortality. As the investigators explain, it had "indirect effects on the mortality of Japanese elders through its linkages with functional status and self-rated health" (Sugisawa, Liang, and Liu, 1994). Attendance at group meetings undoubtedly tends to be what is sacrificed as individuals develop declines in functional capacity. However, on the positive side, not only do Japanese elderly rarely discontinue interactions with family members and friends, regardless of health status, but, according to these analysts, there is a dynamic effect from the other forms of social relations. As they put it, "more social support leads to improved self-rated health, which in turn reduces the chance of dying" (Sugisawa, Liang, and Liu, 1994).

The discovery of another factor related to mortality that is difficult, if not impossible to explain, comes from a recent longitudinal study of the income levels of retired Canadian men. Data for this study came from the Canadian Pension Plan records of the 545,769 males who turned 65 years old in 1979, when the nine-year study began. The developmental history of these men's incomes and the death rates among them were examined. It was found that slightly over 10 percent of the group had died by 1988 when the study was completed. Also, a direct linear association was found between increases in incomes and mortality—the greater the increase and the amount of income the less apt the subjects were to have died. Each extra dollar earnings added to what the investigators called a "protective effect" (Wolfson and others, 1993).

These data did not provide a specific answer to the question of why income tends to be related to mortality, but the authors suggest a couple of possibilities. Differences in access to health care would be a clear possibility, except for the fact that everyone in Canada has a universal health care system, providing equal access. Another possibility is that poor health early in life may be the cause of both loss of income and death at a relatively early age. Wolfson and his fellow analysts explain, however, that the association between income and death changed very little even when health status was controlled for (Wolfson and others, 1993). This study leaves us with some unanswered questions, but it does raise the clear probability that other factors besides health status contribute to death among the older population.

One result of the growing recognition that death has become mostly a phenomenon of old age may be that it has also become socially more acceptable. Gadow describes three quite common ways of defining death among the aged: (1) as inevitable, (2) as natural, and (3) as peaceful. She suggests that it is, in fact, no more inevitable, natural, or peaceful in old age than at any age (Gadow, 1987). There is some evidence that would seem to support the notion that death tends to be more socially acceptable among the aged than it is among young people. Mumma and Benoliel, for example, compared the life saving efforts that were made in behalf of various types of dying patients. Among other findings, they noted that the older the patients were, the less the lifesaving efforts that were exerted in their behalf (Mumma and Benoliel, 1984–85).

We need to be aware, though, that the so-called social acceptability of death is related to other factors as well as to age. Mumma and Benoliel found, for example, that the extent to which lifesaving treatments were provided was also related to how long the patients had been in the hospital and to the cause of dying. If they had had a relatively long stay in the hospital, and if they were afflicted with cancer, fewer efforts were made to save their lives (Mumma and Benoliel, 1984–85). It should not be too surprising that we are more willing today to accept the inevitability of death among those with chronic problems from which cures are relatively rare than among those with acute and correctable problems. Indeed, a movement for the right to reject many lifesaving practices and to die without having to endure the trauma of long dying trajectories is gaining widespread support today. Since death from chronic problems is more prevalent among the aged than others, it quite understandably does become more acceptable among them than among others. That does not mean, of course, that any form of death among the elderly is acceptable, at least on the part of the aged themselves. That form of ageism undoubtedly exists to some degree in modern society, however.

OLDER PEOPLE AND DEATH BY SUICIDE

Death by suicide is an especially salient issue related to death among the older population. A much greater percentage of elderly people commit suicide than of any other age group (Valente, 1993–94; Carney, Burke, and Fowler, 1994; Brant and Osgood, 1990). As Valente explains, "They die by suicide at a rate of 22 per 100,000 compared with 13 per 100,000 for the general population" (Valente, 1993–94). Another way of describing the difference is that, "persons aged 65 and older, who comprise nearly 13 percent of the US population commit 17 to 25 percent of annual reported suicides" (Brant and Osgood, 1990).

One of the most perplexing factors related to suicide among elderly people is the typical inability of family members and professional people to anticipate or predict that/when an elderly person is contemplating suicide. In contrast to younger people, who usually display some kind of cries for help, the elderly, as Rosowsky puts it, "seldom gesture and more often 'just do it'" (Rosowsky, 1993). This has led some to typify elderly suicide as "rational suicide." According to this idea, when the elderly commit suicide they tend to do so on the basis of a clear cognitive process, rather than being driven to it out of their own intense emotional state. Furthermore, the option of suicide is chosen on the basis of the set of circumstances that characterizes their lives at the time, rather than a history of some kind of mental disorder, such as depression.

Valente discusses the concept of rational suicide as though it is a process that is being promoted by proponents who see suicide as an acceptable option to people in certain circumstances. In opposition to that, she complains that such proponents fail to consider "the impact of suicide on family or loved ones" (Valente, 1993–94). There are, of course, those who promote suicide as an acceptable option, but "rational suicide" as an operating procedure is in itself not a promotional program. It does, however, imply that much more attention needs to be paid to how elderly people tend to define the set of circumstances in which they often find themselves, and less attention to simply devising controls over their self-destructive behavior and diagnosing them as fitting into some kind of mental disorder. Shneidman, of the UCLA Neuropsychiatric Institute, makes the point, for example, that, "the problem of suicide should be addressed directly, phenomenologically, without the intervention of the often obfuscating variable of psychiatric disorder." Specifically, he suggests that "physicians and other health professionals need the courage and wisdom to work on a person's suffering at the phenomenological level and to explore such questions as 'How do you hurt?' and 'How may I help you?'" (Shneidman, 1992).

What then are the particularly peculiar circumstances of elderly people who tend to decide to take their own lives? In an attempt to answer that kind of question, a comparison was made of what characterized those in three age levels who had committed suicide in San Diego over one full year. Compared were those 16 to 30, 31 to 59, and 60 and over. From interviews with family members and others, it was found that, relative to the others, those 60 and over tended to (1) live alone and be socially isolated; (2) have attempted suicide before less often; (3) be less apt to have drug problems; (4) have experienced interpersonal losses; and (5) have serious health problems. Somewhat surprisingly, financial problems were less of a problem for them than of those in either of the younger groups (Carney, Burke, and Fowler, 1994). In a discussion of suicides among nursing home residents, Rosowsky identified the following characteristics which she labeled as "red flags": (1) the recent death of someone close; (2) being diagnosed as having a major illness; (3) having to move some place where they do not want to go; (4) frequently moving to new situations; (5) experiencing the loss of independence and sense of purpose; and (6) feeling hopeless and powerless. To illustrate the combination of all of these characteristics, she gave a case history of a 76-year-old man who very calmly took his own life the day after being admitted to a nursing home and being placed in a room with another man in advanced stages of dementia (Rosowsky, 1993). Brant and Osgood offer a similar list of characteristics related to suicides in long-term care institutions, but with one important addition: namely, being abandoned and/or rejected by their families (Brant and Osgood, 1990). Zweig and Hinrichsen likewise emphasize how much interpersonal factors tend to be related to attempted suicides. In their investigations, they also found that "attempters" of suicide tend to "occupy a higher average social class position" than non-attemptees living in similar circumstances (Zweig and Hinrichsen, 1993).

Evidence is overwhelmingly found that the above set of circumstances are related to the incidences of suicide among the aged. That should not be surprising to anyone. In most cases of elderly suicides, though, it would be a mistake to assume that depression is the major cause of suicide. Much more to the point are how older people tend to define their dire circumstances relative to whether or not life is still worth living. How to help them change the circumstances in which they live and make their lives worthwhile once again would seem to be a more appropriate deterrent to elderly suicide than simply controlling their suicidal behavior.

PROFESSIONALIZING AND INSTITUTIONALIZING DEATH AND DYING

Death has increasingly become both professionalized and institutionalized. That is, how we die has largely come to be controlled by medical professionals, and death now takes place most often in medical institutions, mostly hospitals and nursing homes (Marshall and Levy, 1990). The history of these trends is important.

These changes have taken place as a result of the development of modern medicine in the Western world. The emergence of the hospital as the place where modern medicine is administered and ailments are cured has been part of the change that has taken place. There was a time when people's homes were considered the best environment for recuperation. Centuries ago in Europe, hospitals began as lodging houses for travelers, and they were sponsored by religious organizations. They gradually turned into refuges for the poor and homeless, many of whom were physically ill, and health care began to be provided (Backer, Hannon, and Russell, 1994, pp. 86–88). They also became opportune centers for medical research, and the poor and homeless readily available experimental subjects. Thus, hospitals eventually became the primary locations of the latest medical technology, and subsequently replaced people's own homes as the preferable places for rich as well as poor sick patients to receive the best medical care.

In the United States, the importance of hospitals in offering professional health care was greatly enhanced by the passage of the Hill-Burton Act in 1946. As explained before, it was under the provisions of this legislation that federal money was provided to build hospitals and to equip them with the best medical technology available. That legislation, and the Medicare and Medicaid laws, helped to make hospitals and nursing homes the acceptable places for elderly people with long-term chronic problems to turn for the care they needed (Rabin and Stockton, 1987, pp. 113–16).

Medical institutions have not only become the places where health care is expected to be administered, but the provision of health care has also become more and more professionally oriented. Those in the practice of medicine became increasingly successful at curing illnesses and saving lives. Their expertise became unquestionably established. They, and they alone, diagnosed medical problems, operated the medical technology, and administered the appropriate treatments. Being cared for in the concerned and loving environment of their own homes became less and less important to the welfare of those who were ill. Access to the latest medical technology and professional treatments was what was vital.

Despite their increased success at curing the diseases and saving the lives of younger people, though, the lingering deaths of older people suffering from chronic diseases became a serious and troublesome dilemma for the practitioners of modern medicine. From their perspective, the inevitability of those kinds of deaths increasingly represented a failure of medical science, on which their expertise was based.

It has seemed logical that, because death tends to result from health problems, medical personnel would be the best qualified to deal with dying patients. It is true that their diagnostic expertise is important in determining whether or not patients' conditions are terminal. Ironically, however, evidence indicates that they are no more qualified than many other types of people to provide appropriate care for the terminally ill. They are no better prepared than anyone else to deal with their own emotions concerning death. Indeed, the very goals of their professional work and the training they receive may make them even less qualified than other people to provide appropriate care for those who are dying (Backer, Hannon, and Russell, 1994, pp. 49–75).

There are at least three types of evidence that tend to challenge the professionalization and institutionalization of death and dying: (1) the appropriateness of the institutional environments, (2) attitudes of doctors and nurses about death, and (3) the kinds of relationships doctors and nurses tend to have with dying patients.

For some time now, the idea of hospitals as appropriate environments for dying patients has been challenged. Part of the reason for this is that the overriding purpose of hospitals is to cure ailments as quickly and efficiently as possible, and they are highly organized toward fulfilling that purpose (Backer, Hannon, and Russell, 1994, pp. 86–87). Mauksch has made the point that dying patients in that kind of setting tend to threaten the hospital and its personnel, and that the "routine orders, the predictable activities, when applied to the dying patient, cease to be meaningful, cease to be effective, and above all, cease to be satisfying either to the people doing them or to the patients who receive them" (Mauksch, 1975). Ironically, even though nursing homes are rapidly becoming the most typical place for dying people to spend their time before their deaths, they are essentially organized and operated from a hospital model.

There is evidence that the functional aspects of hospitals do, in fact, influence the attitudes of hospital workers about dying patients. Thompson studied nurses' attitudes about working with dying patients, for example. He found that whether their attitudes tended to be negative or positive depended more upon the unit of the hospital in which they worked (palliative, surgical, or pediatric) than on the amount of experience they had had with dying people (Thompson, 1985–86). As might be expected, those assigned to the palliative unit, which provided hospice services, expressed the most positive attitudes. As Thompson explains, "Each unit approaches its work with the dying with its own philosophy or 'sentiment order,' where the emotional climate in a unit encourages a particular affective reaction to death" (Thompson, 1985–86).

The attitudes of medical practitioners about death is partly personal as well as structural. The advisability of relying upon doctors and nurses as the primary caregivers for the elderly and others who are dying has been challenged on the basis of the practitioners' own personal anxiety or fear of death. Studies have shown, in fact, that fear of death tends to be greater among physicians than among lay people and that many avoid thinking about or dealing with it in their own personal lives (Backer, Hannon, and Russell, 1994, pp. 68–69).

The basic assumption is that, if medical practitioners have not come to grips with their own personal feelings and attitudes about death, then they will be inclined to avoid dealing with dying patients except as medical technicians. Glaser and Strauss observed that many physicians did, in fact, visit their dying patients only intermittently and briefly. They also reported that many nurses refused to talk to their patients about death because that meant to them that their patients had given up on life (Glaser and Strauss, 1965, p. 45).

It may be, however, that those kinds of avoidance behaviors have more to do with the given circumstances concerning dying patients than with the fear of death physicians and nurses may feel. The avoidance behaviors reported by Glaser and Strauss, for example, were observed in the context of whether or not patients were aware of their terminal condition. Avoidance in these kinds of circumstances may have more to do with ambivalence about whether, when, and by whom patients ought to be told they are dying than to physicians' and nurses' own fears of death.

Regarding that issue, physicians in general have tended to change their opinions since the 1950s. The majority in the 1950s would not tell their patients that they were dying, but by the mid-1960s, about half were disclosing terminal diagnoses to patients (Baum and Baum, 1980, p. 190). In a survey of family physicians and medical students, Eggerman and Dustin discovered that a large majority of both groups believed that dying patients ought to be told and that physicians were the ones that should inform patients. Nevertheless, both physicians and students were found to have substantial levels of death anxiety (Eggerman and Dustin, 1985–86).

Indeed, death anxiety and fear on the part of caregivers may not be a predictor of avoidance behavior at all. Thompson found, in fact, that nurses with the most experience with dying patients and the greatest willingness to work with them had the highest levels of death anxiety (Thompson, 1985–86). Momeyer contends that, contrary to the common notion that fear of death is abnormal, it is in fact a universal human experience. He also proposes that being anxious about one's own death can make a caregiver even more sensitive to dying patients' fears (Momeyer, 1985–86).

From the viewpoint of philosophical theory, Momeyer's point makes good sense. Practically, though, it probably does not follow that the higher the level of fear and anxiety about death, the more understanding the practitioner will be of dying patients. Whether fear of death is normal or not, excessive amounts of it are functionally debilitating. It may be true, of course, that physicians and nurses are no more adversely affected by fear of death than other groups.

The issue about medical professionals is not so much whether their personal attitudes about death and dying are better or worse than anyone else's. The question is whether they are the best qualified to structure and control the situations in which elderly people will live through the dying trajectory. Given their goals as professionals and their lack of training in both gerontology and thanatology, it seems doubtful that they are. It was the judgment of one trained thanatologist that most of the physicians who treated his father during his dying experience "failed miserably." His father, he said, had come to see them as "simply uninterested in him as a dying, aged person" (Leviton, 1986–87).

RELATIONSHIPS OF PUBLIC WITH DEATH AND DYING

How do most people in modern society relate to death and dying? What are their experiences with the processes of dying and with death itself? What are their attitudes and feelings about dying and death? These are questions to which a great deal of the thanatological literature is oriented.

Some authors have made the judgment that the United States is by and large a death-denying society (Becker, 1973). Indications of this attitude include such tendencies as (1) speaking of the dead as "departed" or "deceased" rather than "dead," (2) letting people die in hospitals rather than at home with their families, (3) turning the management of dying and death over to professionals in preference to family involvement, and (4) having morticians use cosmetics to make corpses appear as life-like as possible. Furthermore, existentialists have argued that denial of death has become a necessity today because we, in our modern secularized society, have lost a meaningful interpretation of life and death (Baum and Baum, 1980, p. 185).

Others argue against the idea that the denial of death is a prevailing American characteristic. While acknowledging that our patterns of dealing with death may be problematic, Baum and Baum contend that they do not represent denial. Instead, they believe that because death happens primarily to old people and typically takes place in hospitals, most people rarely directly encounter it and are therefore "being unprepared" for it (Baum and Baum, 1980, pp. 184, 192). Kubler-Ross similarly indicates that we are simply "unfamiliar" with death, because we seldom actually see it (Kubler-Ross, 1975). Backer, Hannon, and Russell conclude that "it is probably more accurate to say that instead of denial, we are ambivalent in our feeling toward death and dying" (Backer, Hannon, and Russell, 1994, p. 1). Kalish submits that analysts have overemphasized the problem of denial because they have not carefully defined and distinguished between what they mean by such concepts as denial, fear, anxiety, and awareness of death (Kalish, 1985).

Even if the denial of death is not a problem, that does not mean that there is no anxiety or fear about dying and death. In order to avoid confusion about how these attitudes apply today, we must be clear about their meanings. In essence, anxieties and fears differ in that fears have quite specific objects while anxieties do not. We can identify what it is that we are afraid of, but we tend to be anxious about the unknown. In that sense, to the extent that we experience either (and as already discussed, these are probably universal realities), fear tends to apply to dying and anxiety tends to apply to death.

There is probably no clear idea of the extent to which anxiety about death affects people today, but there can be little doubt that it bothers people of all ages to some degree, and more so today than even before. Kastenbaum and Aisenberg contend that what bothers us most about death, for example, are thoughts of "annihilation, obliteration, and ceasing to be" (Kastenbaum and Aisenberg, 1972, p. 44). In a day when mass death is not uncommon and the danger of atomic destruction is very real, this kind of anxiety is particularly prevalent. Indeed, Bermann and Richardson found that between 1957 and 1976, there was a substantial growth in awareness of death, especially among young people (Bermann and Richardson, 1986–87).

Fear of dying, however, is something else. That is something that is relatively easy for younger people to avoid since it is largely an experience of older people and typically takes place in isolation. It tends to become increasingly prevalent as people become older. Anxiety about death is apparently less troublesome to elderly people than the fear of dying. The processes of dying typically require having to face probable isolation from families and friends, possible pain, personal humiliation, and the loss of control over everyday life (Backer, Hannon, and Russell, 1994, pp. 25–28).

Attitudes about the deaths of older people tend to be quite different from those about the deaths of younger people. Gadow argues that this is a form of discrimination. Although it is obviously inevitable for everyone, death is no more acceptable to older people than to younger people. Neither the time it happens nor how it takes place should ever be taken for granted (Gadow, 1987).

EXPERIENCES OF DYING AMONG THE AGED

As people grow older, they inevitably gain a growing awareness of their eventual impending death, and this awareness invariably has a major influence on their life experiences and their attitudes about death. Kalish has identified at least five factors that tend to feed that awareness among elderly people. He says that as we age, we (1) have a shortened sense of the finiteness of life, (2) have a sense of being unworthy of further societal investments for our well-being, given the lack of a future, (3) experience a loss of roles, (4) have feelings of entitlement when we live beyond our life expectancy, and (5) feel lonely because of the loss of age peers. These feelings, he says, tend to create elements of fear and anxiety about death, especially on the part of elderly men and nonreligious people (Kalish, 1985).

Marshall has accused gerontologists of having basically ignored the importance of this awareness of death in older people, and of making assumptions about it that have not been tested for validity. It is totally ignored among activity theorists, for example, and treated by disengagement theorists as simply a natural part of aging (Marshall, 1984). In a study of "awareness of finitude," he found, in fact, that it was related to age only indirectly. More importantly, subjects tended to calculate the times of their expected deaths on the basis of (1) the ages at which their parents had died, (2) the ages at which siblings might have already died, (3) ages when friends of the same age had died, and (4) their perceived present health conditions (Marshall, 1984).

This kind of awareness is not so much the basis on which elderly people naturally and peacefully adjust to the inevitability of death, as disengagement theorists assume. More to the point, it represents the uneasy and often crisis-oriented anticipation of the dreaded dying process that may be ahead. This prospect would presumably be particularly poignant for those whose parents or siblings had died lingering deaths and for those who perceived their own health as poor.

Viney studied the relationships between illness and feelings of being threatened with "loss of life" and "loss of bodily integrity." Not surprisingly, she found that those of all ages who were ill were much more apt to feel both types of threats than those who were not ill. Somewhat surprisingly perhaps, she also found that these feelings of threat were stronger among those experiencing serious acute health problems, particularly if they were hospitalized or faced surgery, than those with chronic problems. She found, further, that although both types of threats resulted in some expressions of anger and uncertainty, the threat of bodily integrity tended to be more personally devastating, typically leading to feelings of helplessness and hopelessness as well. It is of interest that those who felt the threat of loss of life tended to be more motivated toward socially active versus passive (dependent) social lives than those threatened with loss of bodily integrity (Viney, 1984–85). Apparently, death is not as threatening to people who are reminded of and forced to face their finitude as how dying may affect them in life. Apparently, also, fear of the loss of bodily integrity is more apt than the prospect of the loss of life itself to make people have a sense of social incompetence. That awareness, in fact, seems to prompt people to pursue social interaction with those who matter to them even more actively than before.

Interaction with others may, in fact, help to alleviate some of the anxiety that often accompanies a growing awareness of death. In one study, for example, in which elderly nursing home residents were compared with those in public housing and in regular communities, it was discovered that anxiety about death was lowest among nursing home residents and highest among those living in the community. The researchers speculated that this was probably due in large part to the fact that those in nursing homes and public housing could alleviate their anxieties about death by talking about the meaning of death with their age peers. It is noteworthy, though, that those in nursing homes also expressed the least amount of "life satisfaction" of the three groups. While *death* was not a problem to them, *living* in that situation and in their conditions was (Nehrke, Bellucci, and Gabriel, 1977–78).

It is one thing for elderly people to become increasingly aware of death and dying and probably quite another to become a "dying person." In one sense, of course, everyone has a limited life span and can, therefore, be thought of as dying. That is not the way we normally view our lives, however. There is a special category of people that are defined in that way, and it is their lives that we want to examine here. Marshall and Levy stress the importance of this point by saying that "Dying here becomes a socially defined status that may override all other statuses and personal concerns" (Marshall and Levy, 1990).

People become thought of, treated as, and live their lives as dying persons when they are diagnosed as being terminally ill with only a limited time to live. Glaser and Strauss analyzed this "dying trajectory" as having two outstanding properties: "duration" and "shape." The duration, of course, depends upon the type of illness and varies greatly from one dying person to another. Dying may take any of a number of different shapes. It may (1) move straight down quickly, (2) move slowly but steadily down, (3) vacillate slowly, or (4) move down, hit a plateau, and then suddenly plunge downward (Glaser and Strauss, 1968, pp. 5–6). These analysts characterize the dying trajectory as a "status passage." It is not only a personal experience beset with extremely difficult emotional adjustments that individuals must make; it has also become part of the social structure and something of a unique way of life for those who experience it (Glaser and Strauss, 1968, pp. 242–47). There are somewhat typical attitudes, behavioral patterns, and types of relationships that are expected of those who are dying.

An important issue related to the way of life of dying persons is whether or not they have a right, and ought to be told about the terminal diagnosis. On the one hand, many physicians have been unwilling to tell them, or even to have someone else tell them, because of concern about how an awareness of their true condition might negatively effect them physically as well as mentally. On the other hand, not telling them may well deprive them of the opportunity to put various aspects of their lives in order (Glaser and Strauss, 1965, pp. 5–11). In the past, many people believed that those who were dying did not need to be told since they would quickly figure it out anyway. The problems with that assumption are (1) it may simply not be true for many people, and (2) it does not facilitate open communication between the individuals who are dying and the significant other people in their lives.

Although, as previously discussed, there seems to be a growing sense among physicians and others that people have a right and ought to be told, the issue has by no means been settled. A personal experience of this author seems appropriate to make the point that what is right in one case may not be in another. A number of years ago, while on a business trip, I stopped off in Spokane, Washington, to visit a family of close friends and learned that the husband/father had terminal cancer and had only two months to live. No one had informed him of his terminal condition, but he obviously knew not only that he was dying but also that his time was very limited. He and I visited for more than two hours and talked openly about his religious convictions and how they helped him to face death. He also requested that I, as a trusted friend, help him put some of his personal records in order so that his wife and family would be well cared for.

As a person who has always favored open communications in all situations between people who love each other, I was bothered that he and his family were denying each other the opportunity to share the meaning of this important life-and-death matter. I asked myself, if he could talk to me about such matters, why not to his family? I considered getting them together and trying to facilitate an open communication between them, but I didn't, hoping that they would eventually come to it themselves. I learned later that they never did, however, and for some time I regretted not having intervened.

In recent years, while studying more about the dynamics of the processes of dying and facing death, I have analyzed that situation again and again. Even though it is even now not completely settled in my mind, I now believe that it would not have been right to intervene. I drew this conclusion from my recollections of the kind of relationship that this man had had with his wife throughout their married life. He was a strong person who had always taken care of his wife, who to him was a loving but dependent person. The fact is that she proved to be a strong and decisive person through the process of his death, but he was better able to endure his time of dying by perpetuating the myth that he had to remain in charge. I believe that she intuitively understood that and was unwilling to destroy that myth in his mind. The kind of relationship that had made them a loving and satisfied couple throughout their married years was thus maintained until he died.

How individuals personally adjust to the fact that they are dying, once they become aware of it, is another issue related to death and dying. A combination of emotional and rational processes is involved. As a way of analyzing these processes in some kind of order and attributing to them some predictability, Kubler-Ross described individuals' responses to the reality that they are dying as moving through a number of developmental stages. A dying person's first response is characterized by denial and isolation, followed by anger, bargaining, depression, and finally acceptance (Kubler-Ross, 1969, pp. 34–121). In essence, this progression describes an active interplay between a one's emotional reactions, a personal crisis, and one's attempts to rationalize and give meaning to that personal crisis. These reactions are not purely subjective. They inevitably have social dimensions as well. Denial and isolation, for example, might be as much a product of others' fear of death and dying as one's own.

Kubler-Ross's stage analysis of dying has been criticized because observations reveal that dying patients do not always experience all of the stages. Neither do they necessarily experience them in the order that she presented them (Backer, Hannon, and Russell, 1994, p. 31). Most analysts are willing to concede that the clinical use of stage descriptions may be helpful to some patients, but even that overlooks a major conceptual fallacy in this kind of typology. There is a very real danger, especially in clinical situations, that the stages will become reified as objective realities apart from the lives of individuals involved. Individuals could be led to believe, on the one hand, that they are pathologically avoiding inevitable elements of normal adjustments if they have not experienced one of the stages in the right order. On the other hand, they may assume that all they have to do is passively wait out the stages and acceptance will finally come. What is actually required is active, not passive, involvement of one's rational capabilities, in the context of one's social environment.

Probably one of the most disturbing parts of living as a dying person is the social stigma that is often associated with it. According to Goffman, a stigmatized person is thought of as in some way "not quite human" (Goffman, 1963, p. 5). When people fail to interact with someone who is dying, their interaction is of course not to imply that the dying person is not quite human. Nevertheless, that is often the effect of such actions.

The observation has been made that, even though far more people die of heart disease than cancer, stigma is hardly ever attached to heart disease but almost always attached to cancer. Some conjecture that it has to do with the difference in our perceptions of the two diseases. Cancer is seen as intractable and is therefore feared (Sontag, 1979, p. 5). It is difficult to understand, though, how cancer is seen as any more intractable than heart disease. It would seem to be even more predictable than heart disease. Physicians seldom determine that heart patients will die within certain time frames but readily do so with cancer patients.

It is undoubtedly the diagnostic designation of the time of death that is the source of the stigma. That designation cogently labels individuals as dying, and that sets them apart from the rest of us. To be treated as different at a time when they are vulnerable and in need of social support can be devastating to those who are dying. The aged are often saddled with a double stigma—old age as well as dying.

HOSPICE MOVEMENT AND THE RIGHT TO DIE

As we have seen, the dying trajectory has increasingly become an almost inevitable part of the death experience in recent years. At the same time, dying as a somewhat unique social process has come under critical scrutiny, and our awareness of the social-psychological problems related to dying has grown.

Out of that awareness, two interrelated movements, have taken hold in the modern world. One has basically taken the form of a rather intensive philosophical discussion of the right of individuals to "die with dignity." The other has been an equally intensive promotion of the hospice program. While there are some differences between these two movements in terms of their philosophical and practical emphases, both represent powerful challenges to the institutionalized, cure-oriented medical model of dying that has become an entrenched part of modern culture.

The hospice movement began in London, England, with an organization called St. Christopher's Hospice. In this program, a caring environment was provided, totally unrelated to any hospital or traditional healthcare facility, in which the needs, desires, and values of dying patients and their families were respected and emphasized.

In 1972, a similar program was developed in New Haven, Connecticut, as the first hospice program in the United States. In the years that have followed, programs have been developed in many American communities, based on the same philosophy but with a variety of structural forms. An international task force, the International Work Group on Death and Dying (IWG), has been formed to study hospice and make policy recommendations. Their most important task has been to recommend standards of care for dying people that would correct what they see as inadequate, unrealistic, and humiliating traditional approaches. Their recommendations stress two major points: (1) Patients, family, and staff all have legitimate needs and interests; and (2) the terminally ill person's own preferences and lifestyle must be taken into account in all decision making (Kastenbaum, 1986, pp. 117–33).

The National Hospice Organization, created in 1978, emphasized that hospice programs (1) should provide psychological, social, and spiritual, as well as physical services to dying people and their families; (2) may provide these services in the homes of the dying clients as well as in institutions; (3) should offer bereavement services to families following the death of the dying persons; and (4) ought to utilize interdisciplinary teams to provide services (Kastenbaum, 1986, pp. 120). In the United States, Hospice became officially approved for elderly people who are terminally ill when Congress made them eligible for it under Medicare in 1982. Marshall and Levy report that "hospice care for the dying currently is available in most communities through hospitals, service agencies, and nursing homes" (Marshall and Levy, 1990).

It should not be supposed that medical care is ignored by hospices. It is a vital part of the care that is provided. However, the purpose is not to attempt cures or postpone death, but to control pain and keep patients as functional as possible as long as possible. Hospice teams are made up of both professionals and volunteers. They typically include physicians, nurses, social workers, clergy members, and community volunteers. Teams are expected to give the dying patients a sense of emotional and social security, to respect and honor their wishes as much as possible, and provide opportunities for them to act as living, rather than dying, persons.

The passage of the National Hospice Reimbursement Act, which became effective in 1983, is an indication of the amount of public support this movement has had in the United States. Under this act, the costs of professional services that elderly people receive in certified hospice programs may be covered by Medicare.

The federal government has also sponsored a comprehensive evaluation of hospice programs in the United States. The study, which was conducted by the Center for Health Care Research at Brown University, included 26 hospice programs across the country. A sizable majority (65 percent) of the recipients in the hospice programs studied were elderly. As many as 17.4 percent were over 75 years of age. Half of the elderly participants were women, and most were married (Mor, 1987). These statistics reveal what might well be something of a serious failure of hospice to reach elderly people with the greatest need for social support: those who live alone in relative isolation. Labus and Dambrot conclude that this kind of discrimination is due to the admission requirements of most home-based hospice programs, which assume that the dying patients have family members in the home who will serve as primary caregivers (Labus and Dambrot, 1985–86).

The elderly participants in the Brown University study were found to be as mentally alert and received as much social support as those who were younger. However, their primary caregivers tended to be their daughters, spouses, or siblings, many of whom were elderly and physically at risk themselves. Investigators also found that elderly patients tended to get less intensive medical care than those who were younger. Mor concludes that, with this kind of statistic, "the possibility has been raised that the all-too-familiar pattern of age discrimination may have intruded itself into the terminal illness phase, even under hospice control" (Mor, 1987).

As a whole, though, hospice has been an enormous success. Even though, as Kastenbaum indicates, it is not the solution to every dying person's needs (Kastenbaum, 1986, p. 130), public support for the programs that have been started is outstanding both in terms of finances and voluntary participation. Opposition to and even criticism of the program are minimal.

The movement for the right to die with dignity shares most of the philosophical assumptions on which hospice is based. Both stress the right of dying individuals to control their own destinies. Advocates of the right to die, however, tend to focus on somewhat different aspects of the claim of individual rights than those emphasized in hospice.

One goal of this movement is to influence state and national policy on how dying people are treated. It is important to clarify what is meant by the right to die with dignity. At issue here is whether dignity can be ensured by stipulating that certain actions are taken, such as refusing specific life-sustaining technology, or if it simply means adherence to the principle of self-determination. The President's Commission for the Study of Ethical Problems in Medicine and Biomedical and Behavioral Research considered this important issue. They reported that many advocates of the movement tend to have the vision that peaceful and aesthetically appealing death can be guaranteed by simply taking certain actions. Commission members cautioned that the major thrust of the movement must be to ensure "that the wishes of dying patients are solicited and respected" (Abram, 1983, p. 24).

The point is made in the commission's report that decisions about taking certain actions can never absolutely settle life-and-death considerations for anyone. Instead, they are made in the context of an inevitable tension between wanting to live as long as possible and fearing what the consequences of continued life might be. According to the authors of the commission's report, the crux of the matter is that individuals are "protected against decisions that make death too easy and quick as well as from those that make it too agonizing and prolonged" (Abram, 1983, p. 23).

Two specific types of actions are stressed in this movement as options that dying people should have the right to exercise. One is the right to reject having their lives continued by the use of artificial life-sustaining equipment or treatments. The thrust of the argument in support of this claimed right is not that medical treatment as such is a bad thing. The point is, rather, that when the best medical knowledge available has already diagnosed someone's condition as terminal, then such treatment will not only be useless but will also rob that person of what meaningful life he or she may have left. To become temporarily dependent upon such technology may indeed be tolerable when there is the possibility of being cured and restored to normal life, but it has become defined as intolerable for increasing numbers of dying people for whom that possibility no longer exists. Medical treatments at that time make sense if they keep a person functional, but not if they hinder what functional capacities he or she may still have.

Some have argued that this is actually a passive form of euthanasia and is therefore morally unacceptable or that euthanasia itself deserves to be supported (Hill and Shirley, 1992). Those arguments miss one important point, however. The reason for rejecting life-sustaining treatments is not to choose death, but to live life out to the fullest extent possible. As Hill and Shirley explain, the facts are that "for the past twenty years, lawmakers, judges, and institutional policymakers have consistently refused to treat suicide and withholding or withdrawing treatment as if they were the same" on the basic assumption that withholding treatments, but not suicide, is a matter of "'putting matters into God's hands' or 'letting nature take its course'" (Hill and Shirley, 1992, pp. 101–102).

The other action that the right-to-die movement has stressed is for individual dying persons to be allowed to die when and where they choose with the aid of members of their families. The argument is that when individuals can no longer function, when death is imminent, and/or when suffering can no longer be controlled or avoided, the continuation of life serves no good purpose. The advocacy of this type of euthanasia is quite controversial. It is vehemently opposed by most religious people and organizations, as well as by most of those in the medical community. The religious perspective is that we humans have no right to "play God" with matters of life and death. Fallible humans, even the most skilled physicians, can never stipulate that someone cannot be cured and has a specific time to live. The omniscient God is the only one who can determine when anyone's life no longer has purpose and it is time to die. While most religions teach that God relieves human suffering, they also teach that only He has the wisdom to determine when the mercy that death represents is appropriate. What is often overlooked by religious opponents, though, is that even they readily rely on many forms of human intervention to relieve suffering, some of which pose clear risks to people's lives (major surgery is an example). Medical practitioners tend to oppose euthanasia from the ethical perspective of their professions. They practice medicine to save and preserve life, not to deliberately promote or contribute to death.

Even though euthanasia has been promoted by many and sometimes even practiced in one form or another in the United States and increasingly supported among the elderly (Leinbach, 1993), it was never legalized in this country until the passage of the Death with Dignity Act, passed in the State of Oregon in November 1994 by 52 percent of the voters. It gives physicians in that state the legal right to give terminally ill adults, who meet a set of eligibility requirements, prescriptions of lethal drugs, upon their request (Dority, 1995). One place in the world where it has been widely practiced by physicians is in Holland. It has been approved by the Royal Dutch Medical Association for those who are terminally ill and request it, provided they are mentally competent and a physician is willing to perform it ("The Netherlands Debates...," 1987). The practice is permitted by the courts and supported by more than two-thirds of the public, even among the Catholic laity ("The Netherlands Debates...," 1987). Some in Holland, though, even among those who practice it, are fearful about where a euthanasia policy might lead. With a growing elderly population, the concern has been expressed that demented elderly patients might well be euthanized in the future for purely economic reasons.

BEREAVEMENT, MOURNING, AND GRIEF

Concerns about death and dying by no means end at the point of the death. As important as what happens to people during the processes of dying is what happens to the survivors of those who have died. Interest in this aspect of death and dying has focused primarily on bereavement, mourning, and especially on grief. These concepts are very much related but have different meanings. A review of the definitions of each of these concepts will help us to understand not only the personal experiences survivors tend to have but something about their social significance as well.

To be *bereaved* means to experience some kind of loss. There are many kinds of losses that we humans normally experience that could be referred to as bereavement. The loss of someone through death is what is usually implied by that term, however. Kastenbaum explains that this kind of bereavement is difficult for survivors, not only because they personally miss the one who has died, but also because the survivor's social status has suddenly and drastically changed (Kastenbaum, 1986, p. 135). This is particularly true for those who experience the loss of their spouses through death. They are not only deprived of the intimacy they typically enjoyed with their spouses, but they are also suddenly thrust into the widowed status—a position in society for which most married people are not prepared.

This aspect of bereavement is largely ignored in the literature on death and dying. That is a regrettable omission because it could help to explain why some people continue to grieve the loss of spouse over a longer time than is normal—a phenomenon that psychological analysis alone has not been able to adequately explain. The point is that the loss of spouse, particularly among elderly people, is a major, socially disruptive event. For example, as reported in Chapter 7, it was discovered in one study that focused on elderly widowed people, that becoming widowed caused the most abrupt and emotionally damaging disengagement patterns of any type of loss that they had experienced, largely because of the social disruption that it engendered (Brown, 1974).

Mourning is another important part of the experiences of those who have lost someone close to them. Kastenbaum defines mourning as "the culturally patterned expression of the bereaved person's thoughts and feelings" (Kastenbaum, 1986, p. 138). We often feel sorry for those who mourn, and yet, to a large degree, mourning is a positive experience for most survivors. It involves them in rituals and ceremonies in which they tend to be surrounded with sympathetic supporters. This helps the survivors to celebrate the lives of those whom they have lost in death.

Funerals are a central component of the process of mourning. Contrary to the rather common notion that funerals are morbid experiences that people must endure in order to comply with social custom, evidence indicates that they are meaningful and helpful to most who are in grief. Kalish describes the funeral idealistically as "simultaneously a rite of passage for the dead person and a show of support for the survivors" and as having "a therapeutic value for survivors by permitting them to grieve openly and to advance their acceptance of the reality of death" (Kalish, 1985). In one study on grief, newly widowed men and women reported having positive feelings about both planning and participating in the funerals of their spouses. They indicated that by planning and then moving through the ceremonies, they were able to publicly express their love, devotion, and attachment to their deceased husbands or wives in meaningful ways. Most of them also said that funeral directors had been supportive to them, as were officiating clergy for those with religious orientations (Kastenbaum, 1986, pp. 142–43).

The extent and severity of *grief* among people who have lost loved ones in death has been a subject of particular interest to students of death and dying. Studies have focused on such questions as why some people grieve more intensely than others, how excessive grief may affect people functionally and in terms of their health status, and why some people continue to grieve beyond what would be considered a normal period of time. Grief is defined as the typical personal response that people make to the losses they experience. We humans feel grief about many types of losses in our lives, but it is most often associated with losses due to death. Depending upon its severity, it not only affects individuals' mental state but also how they think, eat, and sleep. Severe grief clearly places people at physical risk (Kastenbaum, 1986, pp. 136–37).

Studies indicate that the kinds of grief people have depend, at least in part, on three important factors. First, it may be at least somewhat related to whether or not the death of the person being grieved was expected or unexpected. As previously discussed, many people, especially among the aged, die after a period of dying. Some of those who grieve these people's deaths have been with them during the dying period and may have learned to anticipate the death. Although their grief can still be difficult, Tokunaga found it to be less severe than that on the part of those for whom death was unexpected (Tokunaga, 1985–86). More recently, though, Lund has reported evidence that there are few differences in the grief patterns between those experiencing expected loss of spouse and those experiencing sudden loss of spouse unless individuals deliberately do something to prepare for their expected widowhood (Lund, 1989). This assessment of the difference in severity between these types of bereaved persons is made after death has taken place, however. Grief related to expected deaths has been termed "anticipatory grief" (Lindemann, 1944), implying that some grieving is experienced before as well as following death. The anticipatory grief of spouses who have served as primary caregivers is undoubtedly often just as severe as that experienced by those who grieve an unexpected death.

Another factor related to how survivors grieve is what has caused the death of those being grieved. One study, for example, compared the bereavement patterns of elderly survivors of spousal suicides with those who survive natural deaths. Findings showed that while they were no more depressed and suffered no greater mental or physical pathology, survivors of spousal suicide deaths had significantly higher levels of anxiety. The investigators speculated that the differences would probably have been even greater if the death victims had been younger, and that over longer periods of bereavement, the grief of spousal suicide survivors might well be more severe than the other group, even among their elderly sample (Farberow and others, 1987). The primary differences in grief between those whose loved ones have died from different causes may be most dependent on the extent to which survivors can logically blame themselves and are therefore plagued with a sense of guilt. That is certainly true of many others besides survivors of those who have committed suicide.

The third and vital factor affecting the severity of grief is the level of social support that survivors enjoy. Wambach makes the point that grief is not simply an individualized response to loss but is also, to a large extent, a "social construct" that "encompasses public expectations that can influence the grief experience of bereavement." That, she believes, helps to explain to individuals what they may not understand about their own grief (Wambach, 1985–86). Thus, by defining and explaining the process of grief, professional researchers and writers provide widows and others in grief with timetables and guides to follow. While these guides may turn out to be too rigid, they nevertheless provide a form of social support.

More important, though, are affective types of social support. This was illustrated in a study of the extent to which newly widowed elderly people in the Salt Lake City area were helped by supportive social networks during the first two years of widowhood. It was found that the qualitative, more than the structural, aspects of their social networks helped them to avoid depression, to cope, and to maintain satisfaction with life especially among women and older respondents but only modestly (Dimond, Lund, and Caserta, 1987).

Religious organizations are one source of social support for bereaved and grief-stricken people that might be expected to be readily available. Churches, probably more than any other social institution, have historically been concerned about death and bereavement. However, a survey of Christian churches in northern California revealed that, although most pastors were supportive of survivors at the time of the funeral, very little was being done to provide sustained support over time. Typically, the ministers had not even received bereavement training in preparation for the ministry (Sklar and Huneke, 1987–88).

The lack of sustained social support seems to typify our modern culture. It was found in the study of newly widowed people referred to above that those in the sample felt that they were left to reorganize their lives on their own without the help of those in their social networks. Indications from the study were that "community, colleagues, neighbors, and relatives are all inclined to turn back quickly to their ordinary concerns" (Kastenbaum, 1986, p. 143). In addition to the lack of sustained attention by the social network, newly widowed people report that those in their couple-oriented networks simply do not understand and are impatient with the problems involved in adjusting to life as widows (Brown, 1974). It has also been discovered, though, that regardless of the amount and quality of social support, some have severe problems coping with the loss of spouse.

Part of the focus of the Salt Lake City study of elderly widows, just cited, was on those who had been widowed more than two years. Part of that group (18 percent) were found to be "poor copers." They were still unable to accept the death of their spouses, even though they reported having as much and as qualitative social support as the other respondents. What particularly separated them from the rest was that early in their bereavement they tended to cry more, failed to keep as busy, took sleeping pills or tranquilizers more readily, more often wished they were dead, and had lower self-esteem. The investigators did not find that the bereavement caused the lower self-esteem. As they explain, "it is more likely that self-esteem influences bereavement copings difficulties rather than the reverse." Their data revealed that, of all the variables affecting the lack of ability to cope, wishing they were dead was "the best predictor of future difficulties" (Lund and others, 1985–86).

Clearly, elderly widowed people are at special risk in coping with grief (Kalish, 1987). They not only face the grief related to the loss of a spouse, but they are also typically plagued with what Kastenbaum describes as "bereavement overload." As he so aptly points out, "Elderly men and women are more likely to develop a condition in which sorrow has been heaped upon sorrow, loss upon loss" (Kastenbaum, 1986, p. 153).

As a result of the discovery in the Salt Lake City study that a sizable percentage of widowed elderly have elongated coping problems, Lund and Caserta wanted to learn the extent to which participation in self-help groups

provide a kind of help that traditional social networks are not able to. Therefore, they conducted an experimental study of newly widowed elderly men
and women participating in different self-help group approaches—short term
(eight weekly meetings), long term (ten monthly meetings), those led by
professional people, and those led by selected widowed peers (Lund and
Caserta, 1992). Participants completed questionnaires at four different times
during the two-year duration of the experiment, two months after becoming
widowed, after the completion of the eight weekly self-help meetings, following the completion of the long-term groups, and two years following the
death of the spouse. They were asked to indicate what they perceived as their
greatest need, how helpful the group meetings were to them, and how well
their main need was being fulfilled by their participation.

They found that "emotional support" was the main need that the
majority of participants identified. With regard to how helpful the meetings
were and the extent their main needs were being fulfilled, no significant
differences were found between any of the different groups. In general,
participants agreed that the sessions were helpful and that their needs had
been fulfilled, although the mean scores of those in the long-term groups
tended to be somewhat larger than those in the short-term groups. The type
of leader (see Table 16-2) apparently made little difference, but those who
attended more of the sessions reported that the program was more valuable
to them than those who attended fewer. Part of the value to those attending
more sessions was that they tended to participate more actively than the
others. As a result of this experiment, the investigators strongly recommend
that "bereaved older adults be given the opportunity to participate in self-
help groups," and that they should "last longer than eight weekly meetings"
(Lund and Caserta, 1992).

TABLE 16–2   Extent to Which Perceived Need Was Filled by Self-Help Group Format

HOW WELL WAS MAJOR NEED FILLED BY PARTICIPANT*		LONG-TERM		SHORT-TERM	
		WIDOW LED	PROFESSIONAL LED	WIDOW LED	PROFESSIONAL LED
Time 2**	M	3.97	4.25	3.69	3.79
(end of 8 weeks)	(SD)	(1.00)	(0.94)	(1.02)	(1.04)
	N	30	21	35	38
Time 3***	M	4.14	4.26	—	—
(end of long–term)	(SD)	(0.88)	(1.05)	(not asked)	(not asked)
	N	29	19		
Time 4****	M	4.00	4.11	3.57	3.6
(2 yrs. post–death	(SD)	(0.83)	(0.94)	(0.92)	(1.24)
event)	N	27	19	28	35

*1 = Not at all; 5 = Very well
**$F_{(3,120)}$ = 1.48, N.S.
***$F_{(3,146)}$ = 0.20, N.S.
****$F_{(3,105)}$ = 1.82, N.S.
SOURCE: Dale A. Lund and Michael S. Caserta, "Older Bereaved Spouses' Participation in
Self–Help Groups," *Omega*, 25, no. 1 (1992), 47–61, Table 2.

It would be misleading, however, to overemphasize the difficulties experienced by those elderly who become widowed. Studies show, for example, that about 80 percent of elderly widows do not have major problems coping with life in widowhood (in the Salt Lake City study it was even more than that) (Lund and others, 1985–86). Yet, the opposite perception tends to prevail. To discover how perception on this issue coincides with or differs from actual experience, Caserta and Lund compared how well non-widowed (married and "nonbereaved") elderly would expect to cope with the loss of their spouses, with how well those who were recently widowed ("bereaved") said they were actually coping over a two-year period. The two groups were also compared on the amount of stress they either anticipated or experienced. Somewhat surprisingly, those who were widowed consistently reported less stress and higher levels of coping than the other group expected would be true if/when they experienced the loss of their spouses. These authors offer the following explanation for these differences, "Part of the appraisal process in the face of a stressor involved an assessment of resources that are available to aid in one's coping. It may be that the utility of these resources may not be apparent until one is confronted with a threat" (Caserta and Lund, 1992).

CONCLUSION

The two themes that tend to dominate the study of death and dying today are (1) the right of individuals to control their own destinies in death as well as life, and (2) the importance of being relieved of the pain and suffering that so often accompanies the dying experience. Except for what may be found in the religious literature on the subject, discussions on the meaning of death seem to be largely missing from today's literature on death and dying. That may well represent an omission of the most vital aspect of this important subject.

Even with all of the rights we may have of self-determination and all the analgesic technology available today, death is still very much dreaded as a morbid event that raises the clear possibility in people's minds that life itself is futile. With some sense that death as well as life has meaning, however, even death with great pain and suffering seems to become not just tolerable but accepted, and sometimes even deliberately chosen. In that sense dying becomes "the final stage of life" and actually "contributes to personal growth" (Marshall and Levy, 1990). For example, Leviton reported that his father died an "appropriate death." By that he means that his father was allowed to die in a way that he himself deemed appropriate to his personal life. In contrast to many who claim the right of self-determination today, however, he deliberately chose not to take the pain-killing drugs that were readily available to him, and that his family urged him to take, during his final hours of life. Leviton reports that there were at least two possible reasons for his father to suffer the pain of death. He may have wanted either to symbolize his solidarity with his mother and sister, both of whom had had to suffer painful deaths, or similarly, to symbolize his identity with the suffering of Jews and other oppressed people everywhere (Leviton, 1986–87).

Perhaps, then, an appropriate conclusion to this chapter would be to review some of the most salient meanings of death we can find among individual and cultural interpretations. Probably the most obvious meanings assigned to death are those that are provided by religions that emphasize a belief in an afterlife. Some religions believe in the immortality of the human soul and see death as the release of the soul from the body in which it is confined in this earthly life. Other religions such as Hinduism and Buddhism believe that death is not final but is followed by some form of rebirth (Firth, 1993). Still other religions, such as Christianity, see death as the ultimate punishment for human sin but also as a peaceful transition from this life to eternity for believers whom God has forgiven.

The Inuit Eskimo tribe in Northern Canada have a religiously unique interpretation of the meaning of death. The elderly Inuits have been known for their fearless resignation and acceptance of being abandoned by their families and left to die. The harshness of their cold environment has been given as the reason for this phenomenon. Guemple, an anthropologist, discovered, however, that instead it is because of their religious beliefs. They believe that the essence of life is not one's physical body but one's name which gives one an immortal identity with all others who have had the same name. Death simply means returning to the eternal community of those who share a particular name (Guemple, 1983).

Religious beliefs such as these may seem primitive and naive to many people today, compared to the scientific body of knowledge about death and dying that we now have. After conducting a broad-based survey of the explanation of the origin of death in many primitive cultures, for instance, anthropologists Corcos and Krupka expressed dismay about how death was defined. They make the observation that primitive people observe people dying much more than "civilized man" does, and yet "from the many observations primitive people could make, in general, they failed to deduce that all humans eventually die from natural, rather than supernatural, causes" (Corcos and Krupka, 1983–84).

One cannot help but wonder about the logic of such a conclusion. How can scientists draw a distinction between the natural and the supernatural without making nature something of an object of awe and devotion? They make the same logical error as religious literalists who separate religion from nature. If death is a product of nature, which it is, there is nothing about that idea which contradicts that it may also be the product of the supernatural, that is, a matter of what we believe, not of scientific proof. Indeed, the point being made here is that religious belief is one very important definition of the meaning of death that provides people with assurances and the courage to face death.

Another prevalent theme about the meaning of death makes sense to both secularly oriented and religiously oriented people. It is the notion that death in some way or another makes, or ought to make, a contribution to the continuation of life. This general theme is found in a number of cultural settings. The traditional "good death" of the Irish is one example of this theme. They made a point of dying what Scheper-Hughes labeled "head-on"—fully awake and alert, slowly enduring whatever pain they have to, as a symbol of the way they had lived and the way they believe life ought to be lived. Following their death, wakes are held that are elaborate celebrations of their lives in their homes with open caskets (Scheper-Hughes, 1983; Power, 1993).

Suicide has traditionally been a common pathway to death for elderly people as well as for others in Japan. It is important to understand, though, that this is done not out of personal despair, but from altruistic motives, as a sacrifice in behalf of the nation or family well-being. Plath found that even today, a sizable percentage of Japanese elderly would be willing to sacrifice their own lives for the sake of the welfare of their families (Plath, 1983).

Imara has probably best articulated the meaning of death as sacrifice for the sake of life in an analysis of "Dying as the Final Stage of Growth" (Imara, 1975). He points out that change is a necessary part of life, because living without change is not living at all. But changing entails abandoning old ways and breaking old patterns, and that, in essence, is a form of dying in order to grow and continue to live. Painful and agonizing as the physical dying process can be, he insists that it can nevertheless be packed with meaning if one conceives of it as the ultimate time of growth. To do that, he says, we must simply invest the remainder of our lives in creative and appreciative relationships with others, or in dying as a contribution to life. Similarly, Marshall and Levy suggest that, "Dying, in both objective and subjective elements, can be seen as the final career in life, one which is typically, and increasingly, experienced by people when they become old" (Marshall and Levy, 1990).

Kastenbaum has recognized the importance of death having meaning for those who experience it. He suggests that how we die will never "really answer the existential 'why' of life," and that one important meaning that can be attached to death is that it happens in a way that preserves the values by which we have lived our lives (Kastenbaum, 1987). Whatever the meaning that death has for any of us, it ought to be evident that the search for meaning is worth the effort if life and death are to have purpose.

REFERENCES

Abram, Morris B., President's Commission for the Study of Ethical Problems in Medicine and Biomedical and Behavioral Research, *Deciding to Forego Life-Sustaining Treatment: A Report on the Ethical, Medical, and Legal Issues in Treatment Decisions* (Washington. D.C.: U.S. Government Printing Office, March 1983).

Backer, Barbara B., Natalie Hannon, and Noreen A. Russell, *Death and Dying: Understanding and Care* (Albany, N.Y.: Delmar, 1994).

Baum, Martha, and Rainer C. Baum, *Growing Old: A Societal Perspective* (Englewood Cliffs, N.J.: Prentice Hall, 1980).

Becker, Ernest, *The Denial of Death* (New York: The Free Press, 1973).

Bermann, Sandra, and Virginia Richardson, "Social Change in the Salience of Death Among Adults in America: A Projective Assessment," *Omega*, 17, no. 3 (1986–87), 195–207.

Brant, Barbara A., and Nancy J. Osgood, "The Suicidal Patient in Long-Term Care Institutions," *Journal of Gerontological Nursing*, 16, no. 2 (February 1990), 15–18.

Brown, Arnold S., "Socially Disruptive Events and Morale Among the Elderly," unpublished paper presented at the Gerontological Society 27th Annual Meeting in Portland, Oregon, October, 1974. Abstract printed in *The Gerontologist*, 14, no. 5, pt. 2 (October 1974), p. 72.

Carney, Susanne S., Patricia A. Burke, and Richard C. Fowler, "Suicide Over 60: The San Diego Study," *Journal of the American Geriatrics Society*, 42 (1994), 174–80.

Caserta, Michael S., and Dale A. Lund, "Bereavement Stress and Coping among Older Adults: Expectations Versus the Actual Experience," *Omega*, 25, no. 1 (1992), 33–45.

Corcos, Alain, and Lawrence Krupka, "How Death Came to Mankind: Myths and Legends," *Omega*, 14, no. 2 (1983–84), 187–98.

Dimond, Margaret, Dale A. Lund, and Michael S. Caserta, "The Role of Social Support in the First Two Years of Bereavement in an Elderly Sample," *The Gerontologist*, 27, no. 5 (October 1987), 599–604.

Dority, Barbara, "A Quantum Leap for the Right to Die," *The Humanist*, 55, no. 1 (January/ February 1995), 32–33.

Eggerman, Sinda, and Dick Dustin, "Death Orientation and Communication With the Terminally Ill," *Omega*, 16, no. 3 (1985–86), 255–65.

Farberow, Norman L., Delores E. Gallagher, Michael J. Gilewsiki, and Larry W. Thompson, "An Examination of the Early Impact of Bereavement on Psychological Distress in Survivors of Suicide," *The Gerontologist*, 27, no. 5 (October 1987), 592–98.

Firth, Shirley, "Cross-Cultural Perspectives on Bereavement," in *Death, Dying and Bereavement*, eds. Donna Dickenson and Malcolm Johnson (Newbury Park, Calif.: Sage, 1993), pp. 254–61.

Gadow, Sally A., "A Natural Connection?" *Generations*, 11, no. 3 (Spring 1987), 15–18.

Gee, Ellen M., "Living Longer, Dying Differently," *Generations*, 11, no. 3 (Spring 1987), 5–8.

Glaser, Barney G., and Anselm L. Strauss, *A Time for Dying* (Chicago: Aldine, 1968).

Glaser, Barney G., and Anselm L. Strauss, *Awareness of Dying* (Chicago: Aldine, 1965).

Goffman, Erving, *Stigma* (Englewood Cliffs, N.J.: Prentice Hall, 1963).

Guemple, Lee, "Growing Old in Inuit Society," in *Growing Old in Different Societies: Cross-Cultural Perspectives*, ed. Jay Sokolovsky (Belmont, Calif.: Wadsworth, 1983), pp. 24–28.

Hill, T. Patrick, and David Shirley, *A Good Death: Taking More Control at the End of Your Life* (New York: Addison-Wesley, 1992).

Imara, Mwalimu, "Dying as the Last Stage of Growth," in *Death: The Final Stage of Growth*, ed. Elisabeth Kubler-Ross (Englewood Cliffs, N.J.: Prentice Hall, 1975), pp. 147–63.

Kalish, Richard A., "Older People and Grief," *Generations*, 11, no. 3 (Spring 1987), 33–38.

Kalish, Richard A., "The Social Context of Death and Dying," in *Handbook of Aging and the Social Sciences*, eds. Robert H. Binstock and Ethel Shanas (New York: Van Nostrand Reinhold, 1985), pp. 149–70.

Kastenbaum, Robert, *Death, Society, and Human Experience* (Columbus, Ohio: Charles E. Merrill, 1986).

Kastenbaum, Robert, "The Search for Meaning," *Generations*, 11, no. 3 (Spring 1987), 9–13.

Kastenbaum, Robert, and Ruth Aisenberg, *The Psychology of Death* (New York: Springer, 1972).

Kubler-Ross, Elisabeth, *On Death and Dying* (New York: Macmillan, 1969).

Kubler-Ross, Elisabeth, "On the Fear of Death," in *Death: The Final Stage of Growth*, ed. Elisabeth Kubler-Ross (Englewood Cliffs, N.J.: Prentice Hall, 1975), p. 5.

Labus, Janet G., and Faye H. Dambrot, "A Comparative Study of Terminally Ill Hospice and Hospital Patients," *Omega*, 16, no. 3 (1985–86), 225–32.

Leinbach, Raymond M., "Euthanasia Attitudes of Older Persons," *Research on Aging*, 15, no. 4 (December 1993), 433–48.

Leviton, Dan, "Thanatology Theory and My Dying Father," *Omega*, 17, no. 2 (1986–87), 127–43.

Lindemann, Erick, "The Symptomatology and Management of Acute Grief," *American Journal of Psychiatry*, 101, no. 2 (September 1944), 141–48.

Lund, Dale A., "Conclusions about Bereavement in Later Life and Implications for Intervention and Future Research," in *Older Bereaved Spouses: Research with Practical Applications*, ed. Dale A. Lund (New York: Hemisphere Publishing Corporation, 1989),pp. 217–31.

Lund, Dale A., "Identifying Elderly With Coping Difficulties After Two Years of Bereavement," *Omega*, 16, no. 3 (1985–86), 213–24.

Lund, Dale A., and Michael S. Caserta, "Older Bereaved Spouses' Participation in Self-Help Groups," *Omega*, 25, no. 1 (1992), 47–61.

Lund, Dale A., Margaret F. Dimond, Michael S. Caserta, Robert J. Johnson, James L. Poulton, and J. Richard Connelly, "Identifying Elderly with Coping Difficulties after Two Years of Bereavement," *Omega*, 16, no. 3 (1985–86), pp. 213–223.

Marshall, Victor W., "Age and Awareness of Finitude in Developmental Gerontology," in *Understanding Death and Dying*, eds. Sandra Galdier-Wilcox and Marilyn Sutton (Palo Alto, Calif.: Mayfield, 1984), pp. 150–51.

Marshall, Victor W., and Judith A. Levy, "Aging and Dying," in *Handbook of Aging and the Social Sciences*, eds. Robert H. Binstock and Linda K. George (San Diego, Calif.: Academic Press, 1990), pp. 245–60.

Mauksch, Hans O., "The Organizational Context of Dying," in *Death: The Final Stage of Growth*, ed. Elisabeth Kubler-Ross (Englewood Cliffs, N.J.: Prentice-Hall, 1975), pp. 9–10.

Momeyer, Richard W., "Fearing Death and Caring for the Dying," *Omega*, 16, no. 1 (1985–86), 1–9.

Mor, Vincent, "Hospice," *Generations*, 11, no. 3 (Spring 1987), 19–21.

Mumma, Christina M., and Jeanne Q. Benoliel, "Care, Cure, and Hospital Dying Trajectory," *Omega*, 15, no. 3 (1984–85), 275–88.

Nehrke, Milton F., Georgette Bellucci, and Sally Jo Gabriel, "Death Anxiety, Locus of Control and Life Satisfaction in the Elderly: Toward a Definition of Ego-Integrity," *Omega*, 8, no. 4 (1977-78), 359–68.

"The Netherlands Debates the Legal Limits of Euthanasia," *Los Angeles Times*, July 5, 1987, pt. 6, pp. 1, 8–9.

Plath, David, "'Ecstasy Years': Old Age in Japan," in *Growing Old in Different Societies: Cross-Cultural Perspectives*, ed. Jay Sokolovsky (Belmont, Calif.: Wadsworth, 1983), pp. 147–53.

Power, Rosemary, "Death in Ireland: Deaths, Wakes and Funerals in Contemporary Irish Society," in *Death, Dying and Bereavement*, eds. Donna Dickenson and Malcolm Johnson (Newbury Park, Calif.: Sage, 1993), pp. 21–25.

Rabin, David L., and Patricia Stockton, *Long-Term Care for the Elderly: A Factbook* (New York: Oxford University Press, 1987).

Rosowsky, Erlene, "Suicidal Behavior in the Nursing Home and a Postsuicide Intervention," *American Journal of Psychotherapy*, 47, no. 1 (Winter 1993), 127–42.

Scheper-Hughes, Nancy, "Deposed Kings: The Demise of the Rural Irish Gerontology," in *Growing Old in Different Societies: Cross-Cultural Perspectives*, ed. Jay Sokolovsky (Belmont, Calif.: Wadsworth, 1983), pp. 130–46.

Shneidman, Edwin S., "Rational Suicide and Psychiatric Disorders: To the Editor," *The New England Journal of Medicine*, 326 (March 1992), 889–90.

Sklar, Fred, and Kathleen D. Huneke, "Bereavement, Ministerial Attitudes and the Future of Church-Sponsored Bereavement Support Groups," *Omega*, 18, no. 2 (1987–88), 89–102.

Sontag, Susan, *Illness as Metaphor* (New York: Random House, 1979).

Sugisawa, Hidehito, Jersey Liang, and Xian Liu, "Social Network, Social Support, and Mortality Among Older People in Japan," *Journal of Gerontology*, 49, no. 1 (January 1994), S3–13.

Thompson, Edward H., "Palliative and Curative Care Nurses' Attitudes Toward Dying the Death in the Hospital Setting," *Omega*, 16, no. 3 (1985–86), 233–42.

Tokunaga, Howard T., "Death Anxiety and Bereavement," *Omega*, 16, no. 3 (1985–86), 267–80.

Valente, Sharon M., "Suicide and Elderly People: Assessment and Intervention," *Omega*, 28, no. 4 (1993–94), 317–31.

Viney, Linda L., "Loss of Life and Loss of Bodily Integrity: Two Different Sources of Threat for People Who Are Ill," *Omega*, 15, no. 3 (1984–85), 207–22.

Wambach, Julie Ann, "The Grief Process as a Social Construct," *Omega*, 16, no. 3 (1985–86), 201–11.

Wolfson, Michael, Geoff Rowe, Jane F. Gentleman, and Monica Tomiak, "Career Earnings and Death: A Longitudinal Analysis of Older Canadian Men," *Journal of Gerontology*, 48, no. 4 (July 1993), S167–79.

Wolinsky, Frederic D., Christopher M. Callahan, John F. Fitzgerald, and Robert J. Johnson, "Changes in Functional Status and the Risks of Subsequent Nursing Home Placement and Death," *Journal of Gerontology*, 48, no. 3 (May 1993), S94–101.

Zweig, Richard A., and Gregory A. Hinrichsen, "Factors Associated with Suicide Attempts by Depressed Older Adults: A Prospective Study," *American Journal of Psychiatry*, 150, no. 11 (November 1993), 1687–91.

17

Possible Future Trends in Aging

INTRODUCTION

By treating aging from the perspective of social processes, we become keenly aware that what it means to age and become an old person has drastically changed throughout history. Patterns of change have been identified by looking across the broad span of centuries as societies have progressed from nomadic groups on the edge of survival, to settled agrarian communities, to complex industrialized nations. Changes related to aging and old age have been particularly numerous and striking since the 1930s. Cross-cultural comparisons also show us that aging and old age differ in significant ways from one culture to another, but that changes have also taken place within other cultures as well.

If the meanings connected to aging and old age have changed in the past, we can be sure that change will continue in the future. The problem is to predict what those changes will be. Exact predictions of the ways in which the social lives of elderly people will change are, of course, impossible. To try to offer such predictions would be an exercise in futility. However, we can gain some insights about possible future trends by summarizing what seem to be some of the key social processes that we have examined here. By looking at past trends, present conditions, and cultural differences, potential future trends should become apparent.

One particular issue will orient this summary effort—whether and to what extent aging is viewed as merely a combination of losses or more as a transition to another potentially vital stage of life. This issue has been at the heart of the changes that have taken place in the past. It is also central to the meaning attached to old age at present, and will almost certainly continue to influence our assessment of aging in the future.

PAST TRENDS IN AGING AND OLD AGE

An analysis of aging from the broad perspective of history reveals a mixed emphasis on aging as loss versus development. It has recently been discovered that not all past societies honored, respected, or provided care for their older people, as has often been supposed. Instead, a curvilinear relationship characterizes the relationship between the social status of the aged and types of societies over time, moving from low status for those in the most primitive and ancient societies, to relatively high status in more advanced and recent societies, and back again to low status for those in modern contemporary societies.

Indications are, for example, that many nomadic tribes of ancient times depended upon hunting and gathering activities in places where resources were scarce. Their lives were a never-ending struggle for survival. Having to support elderly members who could no longer do their share of the work was a threat to their abilities to survive. Thus, many such tribes abandoned their older members, leaving them behind to die. These were hard times, and relatively few people lived to be old. Abandonment and imminent death of those who did become old may seem cruel by present-day standards, but to them, young and old alike, it was a necessary part of their way of life. Abandonment of the elderly is still practiced among those who live in such harsh environments as the arctic regions of the far North.

With the development of agriculture, societies were able to settle into permanent communities. Division of labor became possible, and land ownership emerged. This was the kind of situation that favored the status and power of elderly people. They became the primary land owners and were thus able to control work and production processes as well as family life. These were times in history when old age was honorable and respected. The amount of control held by old people over the economic and social institutions would be considered unnecessarily excessive to us today. There are also indications that their positions were associated with such high status that they were often denied the affectionate aspects of family life.

Two forces for change over the past 300 years have served to challenge the right of older people to control the economic and social lives of the rest of the population. The first was a movement for individual freedoms that began in the seventeenth century. It was a theme that was stressed in philosophical and religious literature of that era, and has been applied to the political and family structures in Europe and the United States ever since. Young adults could thus declare independence from their elders by marrying, raising their families, and pursuing work careers.

Industrialization was the other major force that challenged the status and power held by the elderly. This movement revolutionized both economic and social institutions. Production moved from the family setting into factories, and families moved to the cities to find work. Ownership of businesses was transferred from patriarchal family heads to corporate structures. Workers were hired, not on the basis of their social standings, but because of their productive skills. In order for elderly people to become and remain employed at any level of production, they had to compete with all other available workers. As we have seen, assumptions about old age incompetencies have placed older workers at a distinct competitive disadvantage. The establishment of the institution of retirement has served to remove them from the work place and to perpetuate assumptions that they are incompetent and, thus, dependent. It has also fed the growing public perception, in recent years, that older people represent a privileged class and an unfair burden on the rest of society.

The notions that aging means loss and old age is a time of dependency have also been nurtured by biological and neurological science in recent history. They have distinguished between diseases and physical and mental aging and have theorized that aging, apart from the effects of diseases, is a gradual process and hardly ever results in death. Nevertheless, they have characterized it as a process of irreversible loss of the capacity to function mentally and physically. A further assumption is that the human organism becomes increasingly susceptible to ever more crippling chronic diseases of the body and the brain. The focus of the scientific research and analysis to the present has been on the extent of loss, with very little attempt to discover possible progressive developments in the aging processes. Some attempts along this line have been made but the concept of aging as merely decline and loss still prevails. Physically and mentally, then, as well as economically and socially, old age has come to be portrayed as a time of increasing dependency. Ironically, the more that life expectancy has increased, the more old age has become characterized in that way.

These powerfully persuasive arguments have left us with the impression that elderly people have decreasing capacities to learn. They have also virtually destroyed the perception of earlier times that the aged possess special forms of knowledge or wisdom.

As a result of these kinds of analyses, a perception of old age as a time of dependency has grown in the recent past. That, in turn, has led to two deeply felt and paradoxical concerns that have permeated entire societies and developed into political issues. On the one hand, concern for the physical, mental, social, and economic welfare of the elderly themselves has produced vast networks of services to take care of their monetary, social, and health needs. On the other hand, concern has also developed about the burden that their care places on society. It is as though our own perceptions of aging and old age have not only robbed older people of a basis of the meaning or purpose of life, but have also come to threaten the quality of life for the entire population. Added to that is the growing tendency to blame the elderly for many of the serious social problems—a kind of process of blaming the victims.

In contrast to this scientific and secular perspective on aging is the religious perspective. A cross-cultural review of a variety of religons reveals that aging can legitimately be perceived as a process of social, mental, and spiritual development and not merely decline. Specifically a lifetime of experiences about the meaning of life's many struggles, and ultimately of death, can produce a kind of wisdom that uniquely belongs to older people, even though, of course, by no means do all older people acquire that kind of wisdom. The possession of wisdom on the part of elderly people gives them a set of societal roles that are badly needed, but are seldom recognized or exercised, in today's modernized secular societies.

PRESENT CONDITIONS OF AGING AND OLD AGE

An understanding of the present conditions in which today's elderly people find themselves gives us reason to be both pessimistic and optimistic about the future. We can best understand the possibilities for the future by analyzing present conditions from the perspective of a struggle between those who view aging as loss and old age as dependency, and those who are beginning to define those entities much more positively. This very real struggle is complicated by both economics and politics. It is a struggle that is not well understood today, probably even by those who are involved. Yet the perceptions of old age and of the future position of the elderly in society are very much dependent upon its outcomes.

On one side of this struggle are well-established and enormously powerful institutions that design and control the services being provided to elderly people. Particularly prominent among these institutions are those that are represented in what has been labeled as the medical-industrial complex (discussed in Chapter 12). It also includes the aging network (discussed in Chapter 14).

It is not being suggested here that the motives of those involved are less than honorable. Neither is there any evidence of conspiracies on their part. There have, in fact, been major differences between some of the parties involved. Nevertheless, all of these institutions clearly have vested interests in continuing to define old age as a time of dependency. They were structured to serve a dependent population. Their continued existence and the profits they make depend upon the perpetuation of that definition. The relatively effective lobbying efforts of such groups as medical and hospital associations clearly demonstrate that, in addition to being motivated to serve, they are indeed deeply involved in a struggle for their own vested interests. A recent illustration of this is the blitz of advertising by the health insurance industry in 1994 to defeat health care reform.

It is true, of course, that elderly people receive valuable services from these institutions. The social lives of many are restored and enhanced, and some are the recipients of the latest in lifesaving technology. The importance of these services is not the issue. At the heart of the present struggle are their costs to elderly recipients as well as to the society as a whole. Large economic entities exist for the sole purpose of making profits by providing medical services to elderly persons. Thus, the high costs of health care for the aged today are due in large part to profits realized by those private entities. Obviously, the more dependent older people become on those providers, the greater the potential profits to the provider. The major "cost" to the older recipients is the loss of independence they experience in order to receive the services. Then there is the political struggle to control the costs of so-called entitlements at the same time that the government is actually creating and supporting the profit-making entities involved in driving up the costs. The effect of that has been to shift the blame and the costs to the elderly and their families since politically the private companies involved cannot be allowed to fail.

There are forces on the other side of the struggle, however. A number of somewhat unrelated efforts are under way primarily on the part of older people themselves to maintain their independence and restore the respect they feel they deserve. Some of these are basically passive but quite effective means of resisting the dependency label. Others are active efforts to declare their independence from the dependency-building forces.

One viable and attractive option that older people today have is to passively choose a lifestyle that simply separates them from the institutions and people who may treat them as dependents. Low-income housing for the aged, retirement centers, retirement communities, and senior citizens' centers make it possible for both poor and wealthy elderly people to live retreatist lifestyles. There they can confine their interactions to age peers, who share their concerns about maintaining their independence. In that kind of lifestyle, leisure provides enjoyable and meaningful activities. A retreatist subculture emerges, out of which they gain a renewed sense of belonging and self-worth. Consequently, they are able to escape the daily insistence, on the part of family members and service providers, that they are dependent. Passive retreat is the lifestyle for which many of the aged have opted today. It tends to be quite satisfying, at least for a time. It does not, however, diminish or even challenge the basic societal assumptions that the elderly are dependent. In times of economic or physical crisis, the elderly retreatists finally become dependent upon those who tend to define them that way. It is also becoming somewhat defeatist in another sense. The elderly in these situations are also being viewed as an elitist group, living off others. Ironically, though, they are not being invited back into the world of work.

Many today are also engaged in active challenges to the dependency-creating forces. One form of active involvement is the formation of and participation in self-advocacy groups on the part of elderly people. The combined efforts of these groups have the potential to greatly influence public perceptions of the elderly and also to have a strong and definitive voice about how they will be served. These advocates are found serving on advisory councils that help to set policy on aging at all levels of government. They are also at work at the grass-roots level. Others are active lobbyists attempting to influence policies related to aging as legislation is being passed. Still others are actively challenging the images of old age that are being presented by the media and are attempting to educate the public about the actual capabilities of older people.

Another form of active resistance to the perception of old age as a time of dependency is practiced by groups that promote whole new definitions of aging, wellness, and dying. They see aging as characterized by potential growth, development, and wisdom, as well as loss. They emphasize the importance of research that focuses on the unique qualities, as well as the losses, of old age. They strongly advocate for the rights of elderly people, as well as others, to refuse services and treatments that they define as stripping them of their dignity. They are claiming the right to live as they choose until they die.

The combination of all of these emphases represents a potentially powerful force to change the perception of aging and old age as a set of losses. Each of these emphases is gaining popularity today. They do not as yet represent one identifiable overall organized effort however. As a result, their political clout thus far remains limited.

CROSS-CULTURAL INFLUENCES

When we look at aging cross-culturally, we find a mixture of beliefs about whether or not aging means loss and old age represents a time of dependency. As noted earlier, in many primitive societies, aging is perceived as the loss of physical abilities, and older people are treated as dependents for whom the society cannot afford to provide care. At least it can be said that those societies do not attempt to keep their older members indefinitely alive and then decry the burden they represent. Instead, they tend to define death with some form of spiritual and sacrificial meaning to which those who are old can associate with dignity.

Throughout this analysis of aging, we have looked beyond primitive societies at a number of developing and developed countries that are vastly different from each other, both culturally and politically. It has been noted that most of them are at one or another stage of the modernization process, and some theorists have argued that this has negatively affected the status of older people, regardless of cultural background. Indeed, some of the available data indicates that to be true to some degree.

Nevertheless, there are situations in some societies that still promote, rather than diminish, the social status of the aged. Oriental societies are particularly helpful to look at in this regard. Even in such an economically developed nation as Japan, for example, a large majority of the aged are still integrated into the extended family. They are still honored, respected, and cared for by family members, even though family members do experience a sense of burden as a result of the day-to-day responsibilities of providing the care.

From another perspective, it is noteworthy that, despite the very competitive, capitalistic atmosphere in which they live, quite a large percentage of Japanese elders seem ready and willing to literally sacrifice their own lives for the sake of their children and grandchildren. A sense of commitment to the family as a group is obviously still strong with elderly people as both participants and recipients. Consequently, their status remains pretty much intact.

The situation in the People's Republic of China provides us with further insights about the social status of older people in today's world. The Chinese elderly have until very recently been very much a part of their extended families, but in a rather unique type of intergenerational interdependency. They shared family roles and responsibilities with the adult children with whom they lived, and they enjoyed an equal amount of authority. An approximately equal commitment of resources by both generations for the maintenance of their homes was also part of their interdependency. Within the family, elders were as vital to family life as any other family members. That is now in the process of changing, however, as a direct consequence of the revolutionary economic reforms that are taking place. One change that will almost certainly alter the place of the elderly in the family is that 50 percent of the elderly people no longer live with their children in three-generational households. They and their children are rapidly declaring their independence from each other, at least in their daily lives.   *China ?*

The community roles that many elderly Chinese have been called on to perform as volunteers still constitute a source of social status. As they retire, at relatively young ages, they rarely if ever retreat to segregated lifestyles. Few opportunities exist for that possibility, nor are they motivated in that direction. Instead, they are actively recruited by the members of their local communities and by government entities to serve in community roles, many of which they are able to perform better than others could. A number of these roles are vital to the organized communities in which they live and represent positions of substantial authority even though those roles are not as authoritative as they once were. It is evident that more of the authoritative roles are filled by retired women than men. In a real sense, the elderly in the People's Republic of China are respected not so much because they are able to compete with younger adults for the same social positions, but because they are expected to hold positions that are unique to them. They are seen as having something to offer society precisely because they are older. The extent to which they are able to maintain those status-maintaining roles, in the midst of such rapid change, remains to be seen, however.

Health and health care constitutes another important source of the positive emphasis on old age that prevails in the People's Republic of China today. Part of the agenda of Communism in that country has been to promote good health for the total population. With limited health care resources available, a major emphasis was placed on prevention. The level of remedial health care that could be offered was made available to the total population as a right. Few, if any, sophisticated, lifesaving technologies have even been available to the Chinese. Thus, long-term care as a social problem does not exist there. The relatively few with crippling, chronic problems are cared for at home until they die. Consequently, while the life expectancy is lower in the People's Republic of China than in the United States, the elderly Chinese are generally healthy. Not as many live to ripe old ages, but those who do tend to be exceptionally healthy. That fact is quickly apparent to Westerners who visit that country today. Old people there give the clear impression of being physically vital. Part of the reason for that is the fact that they place a major emphasis on preventative health care. Health care policy in that country has changed, however, also as a result of economic reforms. Specifically, whether or not many individuals and families have access to health care now depends upon their being able to pay for it.

IMPLICATIONS FOR THE FUTURE

Just as they have changed in the past, the processes of aging and old age will continue to change in the coming years. Some of those changes may well be relatively drastic. Progress in the scientific aspects of aging will surely continue to be made, but dramatic changes in that area do not seem to be on the horizon in the near future. The greatest changes, instead, are apt to be in our perceptions of aging and old age and, consequently, in the formation of public policy related to aging. In that regard, as previously noted, forces for change are already in place.

The direction and intensity of forthcoming changes are by no means certain, however. That depends mostly upon which sides of the political struggle prevail. On the one hand, those who have vested interests in aging continuing to define aging as a time of irreversible loss and old age as a time of dependency are extremely influential. They are highly respected professionally, and are politically well organized and powerful. On the other hand, those who advocate for more positive perceptions of aging and old age lack coordination. Their voices are intense and they are gaining popular support, but their influences on public policy are thus far quite limited. Such groups as the American Association of Retired Persons have developed a somewhat effective lobbying effort, however.

Federal government officials, with their growing concerns about the costs of government, are likely to encourage a redefinition of old age as a time of necessary dependency. Many of them already claim that the majority of older people in the United States no longer live in poverty and have no greater needs than other age cohorts and are calling for cuts in Social Security, Medicare, and Older Americans Act programs. With the pressure of rising federal budgets and competitive demands, the notion that old age is no longer necessarily a time of deprivation will likely become increasingly attractive to government officials involved in setting and implementing policy.

The kind of influence they are apt to have on the redefinitional process may well be more divisive than helpful, however. Their basic assumption seems to be that elderly people as a whole are in reality no different than others in terms of needs and capabilities and that they therefore have no more right to special entitlements than others. The consequence of this kind of position will almost certainly be to inflame the perception of unfairness among younger adults. It suggests that the old represent either an unfair burden or unfair competition. If they choose to remain in the work force, they are unfairly competitive and if they retire they are an unfair burden. Furthermore, that characterization of old age does nothing to establish old age itself as a time of life with its own set of special qualities, or to recognize the real contributions the elderly make to economic development, social stability, and spiritual well-being.

If more positive perceptions and policies on aging materialize, two fundamental things will be necessary: (1) Better comprehensive and definitive information about the special qualities of the aged have to be provided; (2) well-organized, coordinated advocacy efforts will have to be made by a coalition of those who are concerned, particularly elderly people themselves; and (3) their success will be partly dependent upon the extent older people demonstrate concern for intergenerational equity and social stability. In essence it will take the development of a social movement. The emerging emphasis on intergenerational, mutual-supporting relationships is a hopeful sign in that regard.

If there are, indeed, special qualities about aging, they will have to be supported by strong gerontological theories and research in order to challenge those that have in the past been oriented almost exclusively to the concept of loss. As we have seen, gerontologists have had a direct and substantial influ-

ence on policy through their theories and research. They have also helped to
create the perception of aging as loss and old age as dependency. There is the
same kind of potential for them to contribute to more positive perceptions of
aging and old age. With an increasing volume of literature from such sources
as other cultures, the holistic medicine movement, the field of thanatology, and
religion and aging, there is ample information for gerontologists to use in
developing new theories and in continuing research from a less negative
approach.

The issue of retirement will no doubt be important in any reassessment
of the meaning of aging that might be made in the future. Despite the many
optimistic accounts about it from most of those people who are retired today,
it is a concept that has negative connotations for most other people. Thus, it is
at the heart of the perception that elderly people represent an unfair burden
to the younger population. The tendency in the future may well be to develop
public policy that will discourage, if not do away with, retirement, with the
idea that such policy will be in the best interests of older people. Once again,
however, deemphasis on retirement will do nothing to demonstrate that old
age has its own special qualities. It would only serve to thrust them into a
competition for jobs, presumably as equals with younger workers.

Gerontologists will be called upon to treat retirement as the social institution that it has already in large part become. It is already seen as an institution that makes major contributions to society in the People's Republic of
China. Much data exist to enable us to make the same point in the United
States. Specific attention could be given to the economic contributions that
retired people are making through their pension funds, and to the societally
meaningful roles they are beginning to and potentially could play as volunteers. An important point to be made about volunteerism is that it provides
opportunities for older people to perform roles for which they are uniquely
capable. That is an emphasis that deserves to be made in the future as a way
of testing the extent to which old age does indeed have unique qualities.

In order to be successful, the major impetus for coordination of efforts to
advocate for more positive perceptions of aging will almost certainly have to
come from the aged themselves. The recent history of advocacy by others in
behalf of elderly people clearly indicates that it does not work. Not only do
others often misunderstand and misrepresent their needs, but the process itself also implies that older people are incapable of advocating for themselves.

A number of political scientists have questioned how successful older
people have been as their own advocates in the past and whether they can
and will be successful in the future. The bases for this kind of pessimism are
that older people are too diverse a group, that they do not tend to organize
well enough for these kinds of efforts, and that, consequently, they lack the
necessary political power. Only time will tell whether older people can and
will provide the necessary leadership in advocating for more positive public
perceptions of themselves. Some existing trends give us reason to be at least
partially optimistic, however. Increasing numbers of them are already active
advocates, as individuals and as groups. They are advocating at all levels—
grass-roots, city, county, state, and national. They have also usually been
successful. This is important not just because of what they are able to accomplish with these efforts; even more important, their ability to be active and

successful advocates serves as a clear demonstration of the positive potentials of old age.

A further reason to be optimistic about the future potential for older people to lead their own advocacy efforts has to do with their education. The educational level of the aged population is rising and will continue to rise dramatically in the years ahead. This is important in three ways. First, the more education they have the more apt they will be to have acquired the skills necessary to act as advocates. Second, education will tend to increase their knowledge about and sensitivity to the issues involved in aging. Third, education tends to create the desire to acquire more knowledge and learn new skills.

The potential for effective advocacy among the aged of the future is clearly in the works. Predictions of what will come of that potential are not easy to make with any promise of accuracy, however. Gerontology is a truly dynamic area of study. We can be assured that changes will occur, but we certainly cannot know the precise nature of these changes.

Index